101 PROJECTS FOR YOUR PORSCHE 911 1998–2008 996 and 997

By Wayne R. Dempsey

motorbooks

First published in 2013 by Motorbooks, an imprint of MBI Publishing Company, 400 First Avenue North, Suite 400, Minneapolis, MN 55401 USA

ISBN-13: 978-0-7603-4403-3

Library of Congress Cataloging-in-Publication Data

Dempsey, Wayne R., 1972-
101 projects for your Porsche 911, 996, and 997, 1998-2008 / by Wayne Dempsey.
pages cm
Includes index.
ISBN 978-0-7603-4403-3 (softcover)
1. Porsche automobiles--Customizing. 2. Porsche automobiles--Maintenance and repair. I. Title. II. Title: One hundred and one projects for your Porsche 911, 996, and 997, 1998-2008.
TL215.P75D4623 2013
629.28'722--dc23

2013029091

Editor: Jordan Wiklund
Design Manager: Brad Springer
Layout: Danielle Smith

Printed in China

10 9 8 7 6 5 4 3 2 1

101 Projects Website
Please visit the official website for this book: www.101projects.com. This website contains book updates, exclusive photos not published in the book, a Porsche Boxster forum, links to additional sites for more information, and locations where you can purchase the parts and tools mentioned in this book.

About the Author
Wayne R. Dempsey is the author of several highly successful books, including *101 Projects for Your Porsche Boxster* and *How to Rebuild and Modify Porsche 911 Engines*. He has been working and playing with mechanical machines all his life. In college, Wayne earned both BS and MS degrees in mechanical engineering from the Massachusetts Institute of Technology, specializing in flexible manufacturing technology. His introduction to automobiles began when he raced with the MIT Solar Electric Vehicle Racing Team. After a few years building communications satellites for Hughes Space and Communications, Wayne left to pursue an entrepreneurial calling. Literally starting in his garage, Wayne cofounded Pelican Parts, an Internet-based European automotive parts company. Today, Pelican Parts is thriving with the growth in Internet technology. Wayne currently maintains the site and has written most of the technical articles that are featured on the Pelican Parts website, www.pelicanparts.com. Wayne currently owns the 2000 3.4 Boxster conversion profiled in the book "101 Projects for Your Porsche Boxster," a 2001 Aerokit 996 Carrera, a 1999 996 Carrera convertible, a 1974 914-6 conversion, a 1972 RS clone, a 1973 RSR clone, a 1987 959, and a small collection of Porsche 962s.

Other titles by Wayne R. Dempsey
101 Projects for Your Porsche 911 (1965-89)
How to Rebuild and Modify Porsche 911 Engines
101 Projects for Your BMW 3-Series (E30/E36)
101 Projects for Your Porsche Boxster

Contents

SECTION 5: TRANSMISSION

SECTION 6: EXHAUST

SECTION 7: BRAKES

SECTION 8: SUSPENSION

SECTION 9: BODY/INTERIOR TRIM

Acknowledgments

It's obvious that a book of this magnitude does not simply write itself, but needs a cooperative effort from many people in all walks of life. Many people have helped me with this book over the past five years and have joined in my enthusiastic vision of what I wanted it to be. First on the list is Jared Fenton, who assisted me greatly with both the projects and photos for this book. Next is Steve Vernon, who spearheaded the project to convert our Boxster content to a format suitable for a 911 Carrera book. I would like to thank my very patient wife Nori, whom without her unending support and patience this project would never have gotten finished. Also thanks to my three young children, Sean, Holly, and Patrick, to whom this book is dedicated. Special thanks and consideration are due to Tony Callas, Tom Prine, and Casey Gervig of Callas Rennsport who have volunteered their time and resources on countless occasions in order to make this book great. Boxster guru Todd Holyoak deserves a notable shout-out for assisting with the engine information section and for helping to edit and review the entire book. Scott Slauson of Softronic was very helpful with reprogramming the DME and also in giving hints and tips about the cars that weren't common knowledge. Special thanks to Charles Navarro of LN Engineering for all of his help with the engine projects. For their help on both the Boxster and this book in the *101 Projects* series, special thanks are due to Peter Schletty, Chris Fayers, Jim Michaels, Becky Pagel, Carol Droutman, Brad Springer, and Jordan Wiklund for packaging my wordy content into a concise and useable format. Special thanks to Zack Miller for giving me more space to add more content and for putting up with my occasional irascible temper. Of course, no good acknowledgments section would be complete without a note of thanks to my parents, Meg and Ed Dempsey. In the beginning, I'm certain they thought I was headed for trouble, but somehow they managed to turn the tide, and this book is one of many accomplishments that they have been proud of over the years. Also very helpful were Jim Michaels, Ken Fund, Jorge Martinez, Trinidad Winters, John Nutt, Tim Suddard, Jim Schrager, Joe Fabiani, Art Chavez, Lennie Yee, Paul Guard, Bruce Anderson, Gary Hand, Peter Bodensteiner, Pedro Bonilla, Jake Raby, Ray Crawford, Owen Stutton, Michael C. Harley, Stefan Wilhelmy, Joel Reiser, Scott Shores, Loren Cook, Stephen Kaspar, Hans Kopecky, Fletcher Benton, Richard Grauman, Frank Hernandez, Jim Scott, the folks at GMG and VF Engineering, Jay Horak, Randy Leffingwell, and a whole host of others who have given me help and encouragement with this great book.

Introduction

Over its 50-year lifespan, the Porsche 911 has earned itself a reputation as one of the world's greatest sports cars. Not only has the 911 been improved and refined over the years to a near state of perfection, but it has also garnered a huge, loyal following of people who love to restore them. Porsche 911 owners tend to adore their cars with a passion and also enjoy restoring, modifying, and maintaining them to the finest level of perfection. If you're one of these people, then this book was written especially for you.

Information is the key to success in any project or endeavor. Without the proper knowledge, you can make costly mistakes and waste your time as you trudge through the learning process. The projects in this book aim to eliminate any guesswork that you may have while working on your Carrera. My slogan has always been, "Let me make the mistakes and warn you about them, so you won't do the same." Believe me, I've made many mistakes and learned the hard way the best and worst way to repair, restore, and modify these cars. My lessons, as well as the lessons learned by the expert mechanics I've consulted with, are compiled here for you.

Who am I? I am the owner of one of the largest European online parts retailers, PelicanParts.com. I designed and built Pelican Parts especially for the do-it-yourself (DIY) mechanics who love to work on their own cars—people just like me. Our website has hundreds of Porsche technical articles that are the foundation for most of the projects in this book. If you like what you see in this book, you will definitely enjoy more of the same at our website, www.PelicanParts.com.

Let's talk for a moment about the cars themselves. This book covers the first water-cooled Porsche 911, which is also called the 996 internally by Porsche and many other people in the enthusiast community. The first model was produced for the 1998 model year in Europe; in the United States, the first 996 available was the 1999 model year. The Porsche Carrera 996 was produced through 2005. In 2005, Porsche introduced the successor to the 996, called the 997. The first series of the 997 was produced from 2005 through 2008, and the second series was produced from 2009 through 2012. So there is an overlap in the year 2005, which could cause confusion if you don't know which car you have. In general, the 997 has round headlamps, while the 996 has what are known as teardrop headlamps. This book was written only to cover the first series of the 997 (2005–2008); however, a lot of systems on the 2009 and later cars are nearly identical to the earlier cars. So the book is quite applicable to those cars as well, with the exception of the engine, which changed to a completely new direct fuel injection (DFI) engine in 2009.

For the purpose of this book, I call the first series of cars the Carrera 996, and the second series the Carrera 997. Although there were some significant differences between the models over the total production run of these cars, the bottom line is that they have a tremendous amount of similarities between them. This can also be said for the Porsche Boxster, which was built alongside them and shares many of the same parts. In this book, I have included photos from the 996, the 997, and the Boxster. Like most manufacturers, Porsche made relatively small cosmetic changes from year to year, but the overall systems and the procedures for working on them largely remained the same over the entire production run.

The projects in this book are written in a format and style that should empower anyone to work on his or her car. One of the principal drawbacks to owning a Porsche is the high cost of maintaining it. You can literally save thousands of dollars in mechanic's costs simply by performing the work yourself. It is the goal of this book to get more people out working on their 911 Carrera—it's too much fun not to! Plus, when you personally complete a job on your Carrera, you get the added satisfaction of having done it yourself. Working on your own car can give you that emotional attachment to your 911 that is common with Porsche owners.

This book is divided into 11 sections, each focusing on a particular system of the 1998–2012 Porsche 911. The "backyard" mechanic can perform almost all of the projects contained within these pages over a weekend or two. In an attempt to appeal to everyone, some of the projects are basic and some are more advanced. Some of the projects are simply overviews of systems found on the Carrera. For example, Project 18, which covers superchargers and turbochargers, is simply meant to give you an inside look into what happens when you take your engine's performance to the next level.

Most projects follow a distinct how-to format. Step-by-step instructions tell you how to perform the job, what tools to use, and what costly mistakes to avoid. The photos that accompany the projects tell a story of their own. I've spread hints and tips throughout each project, so make sure that you read all the text and captions in the photos before you start.

In addition to this book, I've also created a bonus website that contains additional information and photos that I didn't have room to publish here in print. This bonus content is available for free at the main website for this book, www.101projects.com. In addition, I've added a discussion forum to the site so you can ask questions and get feedback regarding any of the projects in the book. You can often find me and many other Porsche experts there, ready to share knowledge and exchange ideas.

Please don't be afraid to get this book dirty-take it with you underneath the car. Get it greasy. Compare the pictures in the book to your own car. Follow along step by step as you tear into each project. If this book gets dirty, then I will sleep well at night knowing that it's being put to good use.

While this book is a great guide for determining which upgrades and maintenance you need to perform on your 911, it's not meant to be the only book for your car. Limited by a fixed page count, I can't provide the detailed diagrams, torque settings, and factory procedures that are documented in the original factory workshop manuals. If you are planning to work on your own car, I recommend that you invest as much as you can in books and information that will help you along the way. Make sure that you review the Information Resources section in the next section of this book for my recommendations of the best places to find additional technical information for the 911.

This book is not meant to be read from cover to cover but is designed to be flipped through so that you can get an idea of what projects interest you for your Carrera. I've structured the projects so that you can simply open up the book and start working on your car. I do recommend, however, that you read the Tools of the Trade section in the first part of the book, and also Project 1, Jacking Up Your Car, before you start working on any of the projects.

One of the features in this book that I have taken special care with is the index. I find it especially frustrating when a good book has a lousy index, where you can't find anything useful. For that reason, I've personally indexed the book according to the unique words found within each project and also listed each index item under multiple names. This way, if there are different names for a part or procedure, it will still be easy to locate it within the body of the text. For example, brake discs are listed as both "brake discs" and "brake rotors," as they are sometimes called. Please feel free to use the index as one of your primary guides to the book.

Finally, remember that safety should be your number one concern. It's easy to get so intimately involved with working on your Porsche that you forget how fragile and vulnerable the human body can be. Have patience, and think about every action you make. Think ahead as to what might happen if you slip or if something breaks. Using your head a little will go a long way toward protecting yourself.

I hope you enjoy the book, as I have spent a long time compiling this information and filtering it so that it's easy to understand and follow. If you have any feedback or questions for me, you can contact me at this book's dedicated website, www.101projects.com. Enjoy!

911 Carrera Information Resources

I've always said that you can't ever have too much information. This is definitely true when working on just about any automobile. For the Porsche 911 Carrera, I refer regularly to a few really great technical resources when working on my own personal cars. Here's a brief breakdown of what I recommend.

PelicanParts.com. This website has a treasure-trove of technical articles, diagrams, hints, and a neat forum/BBS tied into this book. If you like the material that's presented in this book, then you'll love the increased detail and depth that the PelicanParts.com website has to offer. In addition, Pelican Parts has the Internet's largest parts catalog, complete with just about everything you could want or need for your Carrera. You can even order "dealer-only" parts directly on the site simply by typing the part number into the Pelican Parts search engine.

Bentley Manuals. I wrote this 101 Projects book specifically to complement and to be used in conjunction with the Bentley workshop manual. This manual is a reference bible for working on the 911 Carrera, and I do not recommend that you pick up your wrench until you have one of these in hand. It contains all of the torque specs, parts information, electrical diagrams, and repair procedures that you would find in a typical factory workshop manual. I have purposely tried not to duplicate information that is already published in the Bentley manual, instead saving room for material that is not specifically covered within it. The Bentley manual is currently only available for the 1998–2005 996 Carrera, but much of the information inside is still applicable to the 2005 and later 997 Carreras.

996 Maintenance and OBD II Manual. This two-volume manual set has a small front section dedicated to basic maintenance, but the real content of the book is dedicated to diagnosing problems with the engine management system. The book contains a comprehensive list of all of the trouble codes, what they mean, and what you can do to try to solve the problem. It's a very useful manual that contains information not duplicated in the other aftermarket manuals.

Porsche Service Information Manuals. These manuals are one of the best kept secrets in the Porsche world. Each time Porsche releases a new model of car, they create a really high-quality book for their dealers that explains how the car differs from the previous model year. The book is designed to be read by the service shop mechanics and reviews each system on the car, documenting any new features or updates that may have been introduced with the new model. These are a bit difficult to find at times, but you can sometimes find them on eBay, automotive literature sites, or by ordering them from Porsche if they still have stock on hand.

Porsche Factory Workshop Manuals. Nothing beats having the same information that the techs at the dealership have. The electrical diagrams, factory procedures, torque values, and detailed information overview really make the set indispensable for hardcore do-it-yourselfers. The factory manuals for the 996 are huge—they ship in three massive boxes and weigh almost 80 pounds. While you probably will use this 101 Projects book and the Bentley manual for 99 percent of what you need to know, the factory manuals offer the final word when you need more clarity. The electrical diagrams are essential for difficult electrical troubleshooting.

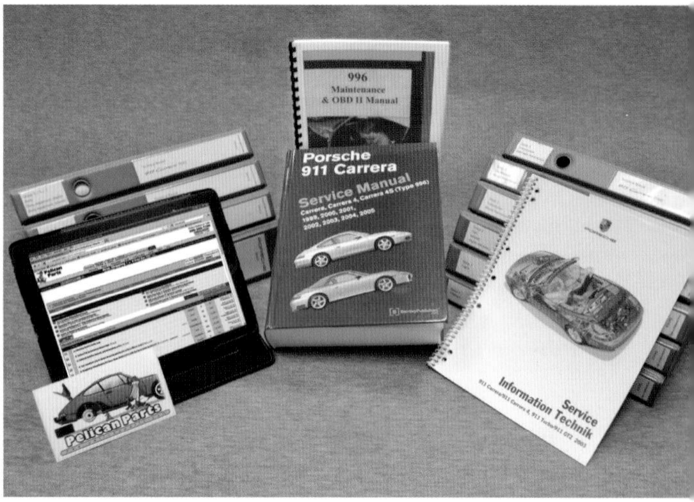

Tools of the Trade

We've all heard the clichés about having the right to tool for the job. Most of us have heard stories about a botched repair or wasted hours because somebody attempted to save a few dollars by putting off buying the right tool. Here are the nuts and bolts of it: even though all good mechanics will admit that there is no substitute for the correct tool, they will also admit that no matter how many tools you have, you will never have every tool you need. I've learned that having just the right tool for the job can turn a five-hour problem into a five-minute fix. The more you work on your car, and the more you look at tool catalogs (like the one at PelicanParts.com), you'll find that you'll cherish the art of buying and acquiring tools. But, you need a good place to start. Here are some of my suggestions to get you started on your way.

THE BASIC TOOL SET

There are literally tens of thousands of tools available to perform an equal number of tasks. Fortunately, it's not likely you'll need all of them.

Everybody has to start somewhere, and for most people that means a small set or kit (often received as a gift). Sets are an excellent way to buy tools, since the discounts are pretty hefty, compared to buying each tool individually. Aside from the cost, one of your primary considerations when buying tools should be quality. The warranty and ease of replacement are other good considerations, but it does no good if you have to mail your broken tool back to Taiwan for replacement or if your tool truck guy doesn't come around at 2 a.m. on Sunday when you need him the most. Ultimately, the best bet is to buy tools that don't break or to carry the spares you need.

Two of the best and most economical places to purchase tools are Sears and Home Depot. They both offer good-quality tools that are mostly American made and seldom break. In addition, both the Sears Craftsman line and the Home Depot Husky line offer lifetime replacements. No matter how much damage is done to your tool, you can take it back to them and they will give you a replacement free of charge. One thing to look out for, though, is to make sure that you purchase the brand that offers the warranty. For example, Sears sells both Craftsman tools and Sears brand tools—the latter is not covered under the lifetime replacement warranty.

The Craftsman and Husky lines are good-quality tools. It's human nature sometimes to "cheap-out" and attempt to purchase tools that are bargain basement. These will usually follow the rule, "You get what you pay for." I advise that you stay away from tools made in Taiwan or China. The quality is usually very questionable.

One exception to the foreign tool rule can apply to what I call "disposable" tools. A few foreign-made socket sets that are cheaper than the American sets sometimes have socket walls that are much thinner than the American sets. This difference allows these sockets to be fitted onto nuts that the American thick-walled sets might not fit. In cases like these, it is nice to have a set of these sockets around, although after about three to four uses, they are usually worn out enough to be thrown away.

Your tool set should consist of some basic items.

Screwdrivers. You should have at least three flat-tip (3/32, 3/16, and 5/16), and two Phillips tip (Number 1 and Number 2) screwdrivers. Inspect the tips of your screwdrivers to be sure that they are not bent, broken, or otherwise worn. A damaged screwdriver is a quick way to strip the head of a fastener, causing an otherwise simple repair to turn into a nightmare. A ratcheting screwdriver is a useful tool as well. This allows you to unscrew fasteners without removing the tip from the fastener.

Adjustable wrench. Many mechanics won't admit to actually owning an adjustable wrench (sometimes known as an adjustable crescent wrench) but usually will have a couple hidden for lapses of laziness. Quality is of the utmost importance when choosing an adjustable wrench. Less expensive wrenches have jaws that will stretch, mar, and otherwise fall apart when used; this is another very good way to damage a fastener and ruin your day. A good adjustable plumber's wrench can also come in handy when you need to remove large stubborn nuts.

Pliers. No tool set would be complete without a few sets of pliers. The three basic pliers are slip-joint, adjustable (sometimes called channel-lock), and needle-nose. The important consideration when choosing most pliers is the teeth. The teeth should be sharp, and they should stay sharp, as pliers are generally used under less than ideal circumstances. Again, don't cheap-out on the pliers. The Vise-Grip brand is very good, and a set of multiple sizes will service you well over many years.

Sockets and drivers. Aside from a variety of sizes, sockets come in either 12 point or 6 point, regular and deep versions. Twelve-point versions are more versatile, but 6-point sockets are stronger and do less damage to fasteners. Socket drives normally come in ¼-, ⅜-, ½-, ¾-, and 1-inch sizes. If I had a choice of only one drive size it would be ⅜ inch. Not only is ⅜ inch most ideal for torque applications on cars (up to about 60 ft-lb), but it also has the greatest number of available accessories. Your socket set should also include a good ratchet (money well spent), a 2-inch extension, a 6-inch extension, and a universal joint.

The Sears Craftsman line used to offer a great 99-piece socket set for about $100 that was entirely metric, but I have not been able to find it lately. They change their product line often, so if you are starting from scratch, I would look there first. A full, complete metric set is a great starting point, and will likely be the cornerstone of your collection. This set contains three socket ratchet drivers in three different sizes, and the associated short and deep sockets. Also useful are a set of universal or swivel joints that allow you to reach difficult nuts. Start with the basic universal joint set, and then buy the one with the built-in sockets when you need them.

A deep-socket metric set is useful as well. Again, Craftsman has a good-quality set that you will find useful all the time. In general, if you find that you need an individual socket, it's wise to purchase a small set that has that size in it, rather than purchase the individual socket.

A really neat tool that I recently discovered is the Stanley ⅜-Inch Drive Rotator Ratchet (Part Number: 89-962). It's difficult to describe in words, but through a set of complex gears located in the body, this ratchet driver allows you to rotate the handle to turn the socket. But unlike other ratchet drivers, you can turn the handle clockwise and counterclockwise in a quick repeatable manner, and it will only turn the socket in one rotational direction. It's very cool, and I suggest that you pick one up for your collection (they are about $40 or so).

Wrenches. The combination wrench is the backbone of any good automotive tool set. Combination usually implies a wrench that is closed (boxed) at one end (like a socket) and open at the other end. There are also other varieties available, such as the double-open, double-boxed, deep-offset, and socket wrench. Ideally you'll need a range of 7mm to 19mm for starters (and a spare 10mm and 13mm will always come in handy). Recently, there have been a number recent innovations in wrench technology. My favorite of these new tools are the GearWrenches, which are combination wrenches with very fine, reversible ratchets built in. They are very useful in all circumstances, and I use the GearWrenches almost exclusively these days. I recommend the 12-piece, all-metric set with the mini reversible switch (see photo). This set retails for about $125 from the tool catalog of PelicanParts.com.

Hammers. Sounds easy enough, but choosing a hammer is as complex as choosing any other tool. There are hundreds of different types of hammers, each in a variety of different sizes. There are ball-peen hammers, claw hammers, soft blow hammers, nonmarring, welding hammers, and picks, just to name a few. The hammer you need to be concerned with is the 16-ounce ball-peen. This is a great all-purpose hammer, but you may desire a 32-ounce, if you really need to hit something hard. Buying a hammer shouldn't be rocket science, but there are some precautions. Aside from the weight and the quality of the head, the handle is an important consideration. There are now a variety of different handles: wood, fiberglass, steel, and reinforced plastic. I prefer a hardwood, like oak, for ball-peen hammers, but all my hammers have different handles, based on how I want the blow to strike certain objects. Regardless of which handle you choose, make sure it is capable of staying firmly attached to the head. A dislodged head will usually land safely on the hood or windshield of your car—or your face if no cars are close by. One trick with wood handles is to soak them in water, which causes the wood to swell to the shape of the head bore. Also useful is a rubber mallet for removing parts without inflicting damage.

Allen/Hex wrenches. Available as a socket, or hex key, you will undoubtedly need a set. There are many variations of this tool: socket drive, T-handle, and multifunction. If you're only going to have one set, a basic right-angle hex key set will give you the most versatility and serve you best. I have found that having a spare 5mm and 6mm to be a necessity, as they do wear out at the least opportune times. The next step up is the socket set that fits on the end of a ratchet driver. These are very useful for applying more torque when you need it.

Torx sockets/drivers. Modern Porsches contain a tremendous number of Torx fasteners. You will need a set of Torx sockets, a set of Torx screwdrivers, and a set of female Torx sockets to remove bolts like those found on the seat rails. Don't try and get away from purchasing these sets: you will definitely need them to work on your Carrera.

Torque wrenches. No good mechanic or weekend warrior is complete without a torque wrench. The ultimate tool for assembly, the torque wrench is used to measure and restrict the amount of torque that is applied to a fastener. This is of the utmost importance, since too little torque can result in a nut falling off or too much torque can damage a valuable part. Make sure that you get a torque wrench with both English and metric measurements labeled on it. I recommend purchasing two wrenches: one for small increments, 0–25 ft-lb, and one for larger tasks above 25 ft-lb. Both Craftsman and Husky sell good-quality, adjustable torque wrenches for about $65.

Electrical repair. You don't need a degree in physics to perform basic electrical repairs on cars, but you do need the right tools. At a minimum you'll need a test light, wire crimping pliers, wire strippers, an assortment of solder-less terminals, and a good multitester. Most parts stores carry inexpensive kits that are suitable for most jobs. Of course a soldering iron is the correct way to make electrical repairs, but often it is not as convenient as solder-less terminals. The automotive electronics company, SUN, manufactures a great hand-held voltmeter, ammeter, tachometer, and dwell meter unit, and its products are available at most local auto parts stores. Wiring diagrams for your year car are also extremely valuable for the process of troubleshooting electrical problems.

Hydraulic jack. Arguably the most important tool in your collection, it's wise not to cheap-out on this one. Although good-quality jacks are often expensive, they are definitely worth it, and they will last a long, long time. Purchase a large jack with a very large lifting throw. Weight capacity is not as important as how high you can lift with the jack. Purchase a 3- to 5-ton jack with the highest lift that you can find. Typical costs for these are in the $150–$400 range, but they are well worth it. The world's greatest floor jack is the DK13HLQ from AC Hydraulics. I discuss how fantastic this jack is in Photo 5 of Project 1. Also necessary are jack stands. I like to have two different sizes around so that I can adjust the car to different heights (see Project 1).

Shop lamp. Another extremely useful tool is the shop lamp. My favorite type of shop lamp is the 3-foot-long fluorescent hand-held unit on a retractable cord. These allow the spring-loaded cord to be wound back into the main housing. The only disadvantage to these lamps is that you have to replace the entire lamp and cord assembly if you break a part of the assembly or accidentally run it over with your car (as has happened to me many times). A good alternative is the fluorescent hand-held lamps without the retractable cords. Stay away from the shop lamps that use a standard 60-watt incandescent light bulb. These get hot and can burn you under the car or, even worse, start fires if oil or gasoline accidentally drips on them. Stick with the fluorescent lamps.

Another good lamp is the shop halogen lamp. These extremely high-powered lamps come with adjustable stands and metal grille covers. Although these lamps get very hot, they give out a lot of light, and are especially useful for lighting up engine compartments and the underside of the car when you're working in that area.

Safety glasses. Anyone who has worked on cars for any length of time, or worked in a machine shop, knows the importance of wearing safety glasses whenever there is a chance that something might get in your eye. Never get underneath the car without them. Always make sure that you have three or four pairs around. You will undoubtedly misplace them, and you want to make sure that you have plenty of spares so that you don't avoid using them because you can't find them.

Miscellaneous. There are plenty of tools that fit into this category. Here are some that you should not be without: X-Acto or craft knife, small pick, tape measure, scissors, a set of good feeler gauges, a hack saw, a set of files, and an inspection mirror. Throughout this book, I recommend specific tools that are useful or required to perform a specific task. Examples include the Motive Products brake bleeder, the Durametric code reader tool, and many others. In most cases, you will need to purchase these tools (or similar ones) in order to complete the task.

THE ADVANCED COLLECTION

The upgraded tool set is simply an extension of basic set. As you perform more tasks, your skills and needs will be further defined and you'll want to extend your investment to meet your needs. A greater range of sockets, wrenches, screwdrivers, and pliers will become increasingly helpful. You should also begin purchasing diagnostic tools.

Some popular tools you might be quick to add are snap ring pliers; socket drive Allen and Torx sets; stubby wrenches; and swivel sockets.

The Dremel tool and angle grinder are two of the most destructive, yet useful, tools for working on older cars. When bolts are rusted solid and there really isn't any alternative, the grinding tools play an important role. No one should be without a Dremel tool, as it is most useful for cutting off small bolts and other pieces of metal that are difficult to reach. The Dremel tool with a flexible extension is particularly useful for reaching into tight places. Be sure to use the fiberglass reinforced cutting wheels for maximum cutting power.

Everyone who works around the house probably has a good variable-speed electric hand drill. However, what are really important are the drill bits. Make sure that you have a good, clean set of drill bits at all times. Bargain-basement drill bits are fine for drilling through wood, but when it comes to metal, you need the best quality you can get. Make sure that you get a good-quality set; otherwise, you may end up hurting yourself or your car.

One tool that is not commonly used but can save you many hours is the electric impact wrench. This tool is similar to the air compressor impact wrenches that are used in automotive shops everywhere, except that it runs on ordinary 120-volt current. The impact wrench is especially useful for removing nuts that can't be well secured and tend to rotate when you are trying to remove them (like the shock tower nut in Project 64).

When serious engine problems are suspected, the tool most people turn to first is the compression tester. This is for good reason, as the compression tester will provide clues to such problems as bad rings, leaking valves, or even a hole in one of the pistons. Also useful is a leakdown tester, which works by pressurizing the cylinder and measuring how much pressure the cylinder loses over time. Although some people consider the leakdown tester to be a more precise measurement, it should be used in conjunction with the compression tester to gain a more complete picture and better diagnosis of your engine (see Project 7).

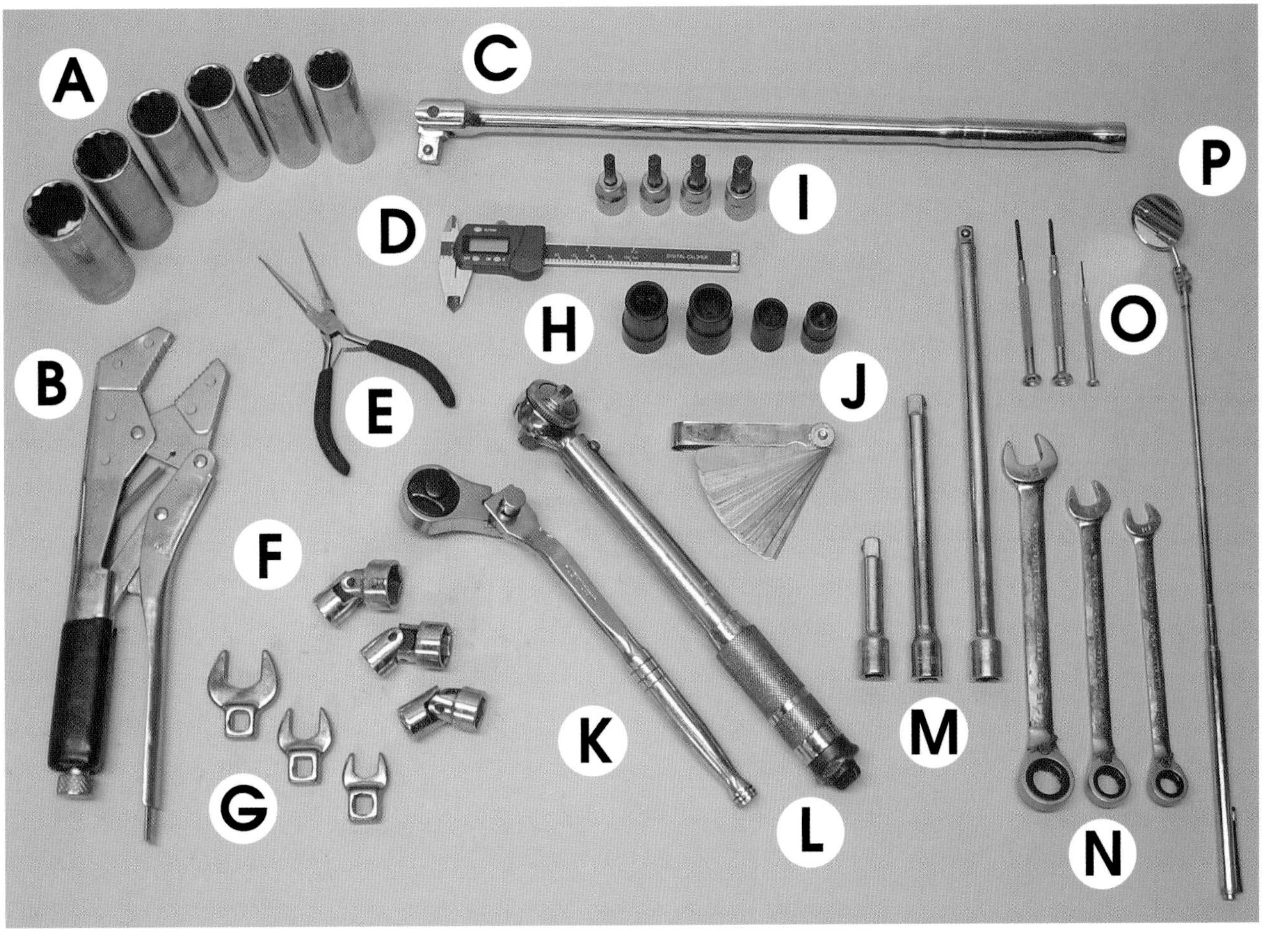

Tools: I've picked out some of the less commonplace tools for this photo. This is a collection of tools that you might not normally think to purchase, but ones that I would consider vital, and use on a daily basis. **A: Deep socket metric set.** This set is most useful for those large fasteners that you really need a socket for. Eventually, you will need one of the sockets in this set—might as well spring for the set all at once. **B: Locking pliers.** These pliers are sometimes called vise-grips and are very good multipurpose tools as long as they are not abused. Don't get lazy and use them instead of the proper tool for the job. **C: Breaker bar.** In conjunction with the deep socket set, you will need a tool that will give you the amount of torque that you need to remove those troublesome fasteners. **D: Digital caliper.** This tool is excellent for making measurements of just about anything. The price on these has dropped in the past few years, so you can pick up a decent-quality unit for not too much money. **E: Needle-nose pliers.** Very handy for grabbing lost screws or nuts or for simply installing small snap rings. Get a good-quality pair that won't bend or break on you. **F: Swivel-foot sockets.** These are great for using your sockets in hard-to-reach places, like the nut on the air conditioning compressor (see Photo 52 of Project 11). You can sometimes get away with a standard universal joint adapter for your socket driver as well. **G: Crowfoot wrenches.** These wrenches are perfect for that one nut that you just can't get to. They are particularly good for removing those hard-to-reach nuts in the engine compartment (see Photo 48 of Project 11). **H: Female Torx sockets.** These sockets are required for working on any modern Porsche. The really strong nuts (like the ones that hold on the seat rails) are typically of this variety and require these sockets for removal. **I: Hex wrench socket set.** Most of us have the standard set of right angle hex wrenches; however, the ability to use a socket driver increases your ability to get into tight places and apply greater torque. **J: Feeler gauges.** You really can't get away without a set of these. They are useful for a variety of measurements in tight places. **K: Flexible ratchet.** I purchased this tool because it looked real cool—not because I could think of a unique purpose for it. However, it has become one of the most valuable tools in my collection. You don't realize the limitations of a standard ratchet until you've tried one of these. I also have an equally useful one that bends forward as well. **L: Torque wrench.** This tool is a must-have in everyone's collection. Purchase a good quality one, and make sure that its range covers the tasks that you need to accomplish. **M: Extension set.** Extensions for your ⅜-inch drive are most useful, but other sizes can also come in handy. Some nuts are just impossible to reach with a standard-length socket and ratchet. **N: GearWrenches.** These ratcheting wrenches are some of my favorite tools. Make sure that you get the metric set with the tiny reversible lever on the end (shown in the photo). **O: Mini-screwdrivers.** You don't know when you will need one, but when you do, they're tremendously useful. **P: Inspection mirror.** Very useful when you just can't see into the rear of your engine compartment or around blind corners.

How to Use This Book

Time: This guide will orient you to the actual time the project takes to complete, including setup, installation, and cleanup. As everyone knows, sometimes the part that the manufacturer claimed could be installed in one hour actually takes three or four. So consider these times a ballpark average.

Tab: Another factor in deciding whether to embark on the project is cost, typically referring to the overall cost of the parts.

Talent: This estimates the mechanical knowledge and skills the project requires. They are numbered as follows:

1 = Beginner; little or no experience
2 = Beginner/Intermediate; some experience, but not a lot
3 = Intermediate; a fair amount of experience and confidence
4 = Advanced; a lot of experience and confidence
5 = Expert; you've seen and done it all

Tools: This component will identify what tools are required. Depending upon your inventory of tools, this may be a deciding factor between performing the job yourself or having your local shop take care of it.

Applicable Years: In some instances, the project may only be applicable to specific Boxster models, configurations, and model years.

More Info: Visit the link to find out more about this project.

Tip: Bits of information to help you with a quicker or better installation.

Performance Gain: Essentially, this will tell you the benefits you should see—in performance, fuel economy, or aesthetics. This measurement touches on your reason for performing the project in the first place.

Comp Modification: Points to other projects that could help you get even more out of the current project.

SECTION 1
BASICS

This section is a good place to start in this book. If you've just purchased your Carrera and it lacks an owner's manual, the Basics section covers what you need to know. No special tools are required, and the projects in this section will give you a good idea of the format and tone of the rest of the book. If you've never worked on your Porsche before—don't worry. These first few projects are very simple and are a good introduction to your car.

PROJECT 1
Jacking Up Your Car

Time / Tab / Talent: 20 minutes / $0 /

Tools: 2-ton jack, jack stands, jack pad tool

Applicable Years: All

Tinware: None

More Info: http://www.101projects.com/Carrera/1.htm

Tip: Stack the wheels under the car as an added safety measure

Performance Gain: Starting point for all work underneath the car

Comp Modification: Check front & rear suspension bushings

About one-third of all tasks that you need to perform on your 911 require it to be raised off of the ground. Simple enough for the experienced mechanic, the procedure of lifting a 3,000-pound car can be a bit unnerving for the amateur. In this project, I'll start out by showing you the best places to jack up your car and how to support it while you're working on it.

First, let's talk a bit about safety. Haphazard use of a floor jack can result in some pretty significant and expensive damage to you or your car. Before you begin raising the car, make sure that you have the wheels of the car blocked so that it can't roll. It's also wise to have your parking brake on as well and the car placed in first gear. You should always use jack stands in pairs to support the car—not simply the floor jack. Even if you are only lifting the car up for a few minutes, make sure that you place an emergency jack stand loosely underneath the transmission, motor, or rear differential just in case the floor jack fails.

Before you begin jacking up the car, make sure that all four wheels are carefully chocked and that the car is on a level surface. Keep in mind that if you raise up the rear of the car, the emergency brake no longer works (it works only on the two rearmost wheels of the car). If you place the car in park (automatic transmissions), it will only lock the rear wheels. Place a few 2 × 4 pieces of wood in front of each of the wheels to make sure that the car will not roll anywhere when you lift it up off the ground.

The ideal place for jack stand supports is right underneath the four standard factory jack supports. Except for the emergency back-up jack stand mentioned previously, I don't recommend that you place the jack stands underneath the engine or transmission, as this can lead to instability.

I typically like to jack up the front of the car first. Use the reinforced area of the chassis shown in Photo 1. If you don't have a soft rubber pad or spare hockey puck for your jack, then fit a rolled up newspaper between the jack and the car to avoid damage to the undercarriage of your car. Lift up the car slowly. It's perfectly okay if the car tilts while the wheels on the opposite side are still on the ground. Depending upon where you placed your jack, both front wheels may come off the ground or both wheels on one side of the car may come off the ground. Lift the car up only enough to get the jack stand underneath while it's set at its minimum height. Place the jack stand securely under the factory jack support area, and slowly lower the car. If your car is spotless, I recommend placing a little bit of newspaper between the jack stand and the car to avoid scratching or scraping the underside of the chassis.

If you are lifting the front of the car, then place a jack stand under the front reinforced plate, lower the car onto the jack stand, and then repeat for the opposite side of the car. Then jack up the rear of the car in a similar fashion using the jack point shown in Photo 2. Jacking the car up from this point will typically raise the entire rear of the car, allowing you to set both rear jack stands in place at the same time. Set the height on the jack stands to be the same as the ones for the front. With the car supported on all four jack stands, you can carefully repeat the whole process to raise the car higher if needed.

Safety is of paramount importance here. Never work under the car with it suspended simply by the jack—always use jack stands. Always use a backup jack stand wherever you place your primary jack stands. One tiny flaw located in the casting process can lead to a jack stand breaking and having the car fall on top of you. If you are going to remove the wheels from the car, be sure that you loosen the lug nuts before you lift the car off the ground, otherwise the wheels will spin and you will have a difficult time getting the lug nuts off. Take the wheels and stack them in pairs

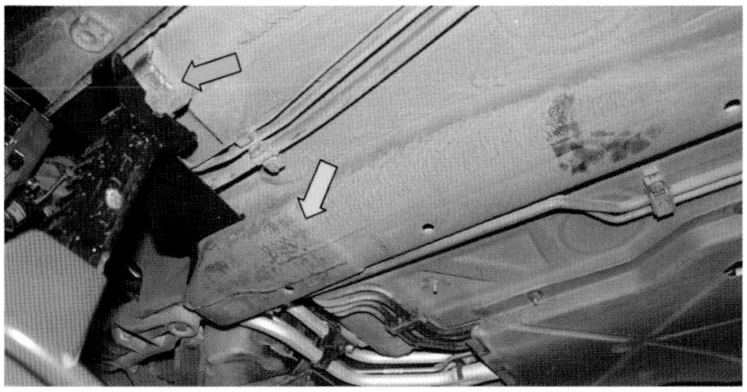

1 There is a reinforced area of the front chassis that makes for an excellent point to jack up the car (yellow arrow). If you place your floor jack under this section, then you will be able to fit your jack stands in the standard factory jack support areas (green arrow). In this photo, the front of the car is on the left.

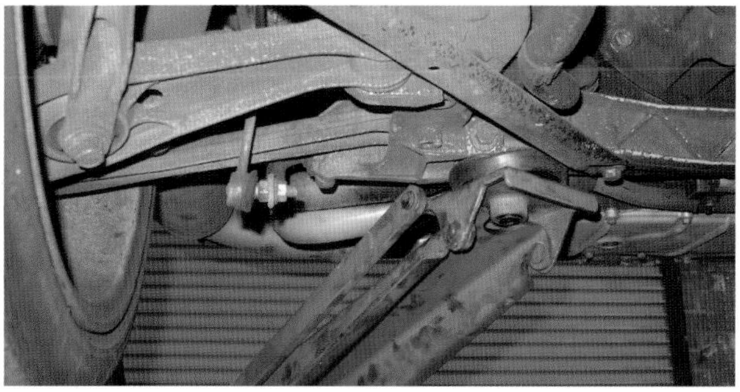

2 Jacking up the rear of the car can be easy—if you have a long-reach jack. My preferred spot is this rear suspension mounting point, which attaches close to the transverse support bar and is very strong. Avoid lifting the car using any part of the engine. Place your jack stands under the standard factory lift points (shown in Photo 3).

3 The best place to support the 911 Carrera with jack stands is under the factory jack support areas. These four spots on each side of the car have metal cup pieces that act as locators for professional-style hydraulic lifts used at repair shops. Placing four jack stands at equal height on both sides of the car like this creates a very stable platform for the car.

4 For better stability and ease of jacking up on the factory jack point, you can use a jack plate tool. This tool attaches to the points under the car and gives you a nice, wide circular surface to use with your floor jack.

underneath the car—this is an added measure of safety in case something fails.

Once you have the car up in the air and supported on the jack stands, position the jack under the engine without lifting it, and push on the car and see if it is unstable on the jack stands. If the car moves at all, you do not have it properly supported. It is far better for the car to fall off the jack stands while you are pushing on it than when you are underneath it. Really try to knock it off the jack stands—you want to make sure that it's perfectly stable. Set the floor jack underneath the engine or transmission while you're working as yet another backup support. Again, it's a wise idea to set up a spare jack stand or two as a precautionary measure against one of them failing.

When you are ready to lower the car, be aware of where you are placing your floor jack. Sometimes you will not be able to easily remove the jack when the car is lowered, or the jack handle may crush or damage part of the chassis or something else on the way down. Proceed very slowly and also be aware that some floor jacks release very quickly. Also be careful to place the car in gear or to engage the parking brake before you lower it. The car may have a tendency to roll away right after it's put back on the ground.

5 Based upon my extensive search for the perfect jack, I must recommend the DK13HLQ from AC Hydraulics. This jack is the best that I have ever seen and is exclusively available at PelicanParts.com. Manufactured with the highest quality in Denmark, this floor jack satisfies all of my requirements and has more than earned its place in my garage. With a minimum height of only 80mm (3.1 inches), the jack will easily fit under any of my lowered Porsches. On the other end, the jack has an unusually high lift of 735mm (29 inches) that enables you to raise your car up onto floor jacks in one swift motion. Combine that with the easy-to-use lift foot pedal, and you have a superior jack that's perfect for any car enthusiast, regardless of which car he or she happens to own.

PROJECT 2
Changing Engine Oil

Time / Tab / Talent: 1 hour / $80 /

Tools: 2-ton jack, jack stands, jack pad tool, filter removal tool

Applicable Years: All

Tinware: Oil filter kit, 7–10 quarts of motor oil

More Info: http://www.101projects.com/Carrera/2.htm

Tip: Make sure that you have a big enough bucket

Performance Gain: Prolonged engine life and reliability

Comp Modification: Install synthetic oil

One of the most common tasks to perform is replacing your engine oil. Frequent oil changes are perhaps the most important procedure you can do to maintain and prolong the life of your engine. However, with the better oils that are available today, the requirement for frequent changes is diminishing. Even though Porsche now recommends oil change intervals that are much farther apart than in the past, I usually recommend that you keep the changes under the 5,000-mile limit. If you don't drive your car too often, you should change the oil at least once a year to keep things fresh.

The first thing you need to do is to make sure that you have everything required for the job. Nothing is more frustrating than emptying your oil only to find out that you don't have a replacement filter or enough oil. You will need an oil filter, the special Porsche oil filter removal tool, a roll of paper towels, a very large oil pan or bucket, and approximately 7–10 quarts of oil. You'll also need an 8mm hex socket tool to remove the drain plug from the bottom of the engine sump. Start by driving the car around, and let it heat up to operating temperature. You'll want to empty your oil when it's hot, because the heat makes the oil flow a lot easier, and more particles of metal and dirt will come out when the oil is emptied.

Once you get the car parked, place the oil pan bucket underneath the oil sump of the car. If your Carrera is too low to the ground to fit your oil change pan bucket underneath, then you will have to raise the car off of the ground (see Project 1). At the bottom of the engine sump there is a plug that is used for draining oil. Remove this plug carefully, and make sure you have a very large oil pan—at least a 10-quart capacity—under it, with a drip pan under the bucket in case you underestimate. The oil will be very hot and will empty out extremely quickly, so be careful not to burn yourself (wear rubber gloves). There will be no time to grab any more buckets or oil pans if you underestimate, so make sure that the one you choose is big enough.

While the oil is draining, it is a good time to remove the oil filter. You want to make sure that you remove the filter with the oil pan still under the car because the oil filter is full of oil, and this oil will have a tendency to drip down out of the filter into the engine and out the drain hole. The 911 Carrera filter is a cartridge-type filter, which is contained within a plastic oil filter housing next to the bottom sump underneath the car. You will typically need the factory oil filter housing removal tool, or a comparable one, in order to remove the housing. Remove the plastic housing, and underneath you will see the cartridge filter. Simply pull on it to remove it from the engine—it will be stuck on a pipe pointing down out of the engine. Have plenty of paper towels on hand, as oil will spill from the filter if you're not careful.

While all of your oil is draining, take the drain plug from the engine and carefully clean it with a paper towel. When the plug is clean, replace it in the car with a new metal gasket. Torque the plug to 50 Nm (37 ft-lb).

Now install the new oil filter. Simply take the filter cartridge and place it on the oil pipe exiting the bottom of the engine. One side of the filter should be slightly beveled to enable you to easily slip the filter onto the pipe. Clean out the inside of the oil filter housing and replace the O-ring with a new one before installing the new oil filter cartridge. Slightly lubricate the O-ring with some fresh motor oil prior to installing it. Now, screw on the filter housing and make it snug tight. Torque it to 25 Nm (19 ft-lb).

Now it's time to fill up your Porsche with motor oil. A lot of people aren't really sure what motor oil to use in their car. Traditionally, the characteristics of motor oil were linked closely to its weight. Heavier-weight oils protect well against heat; lighter-weight oils flow better in cold. In general, if you live in a cold climate, you should use a 10W-40 or similar oil. This oil is a 10-weight oil that behaves and protects against heat like a 40-weight oil. In warmer climates, you should use a 20W-50 oil. This oil doesn't flow as well at the colder climates but gives an extra "edge" on the hotter end. I have put a lot more info on motor oils on the 101Projects.com site—check there for more recommendations.

The question of whether to use synthetic or traditional "dinosaur" oil often comes up among car buffs. *Consumer Reports* (July 1996) ran an extensive test on the two types of oil, altering amongst many different brands. The testers installed freshly rebuilt engines in 75 taxicabs and then ran them through the harshest conditions on the streets of New York City. Placing different brands, weights, and formulations in the cars, they racked up 60,000 miles on the engines, tore them down, measured, and inspected the engine components for wear. The oil was changed at 3,000 miles in half of them, and the rest were changed at 6,000 miles. The results: Regardless of brand, synthetic or traditional non-synthetic, weight, and oil change interval, there were no discernible differences in engine component wear in any of the engines. Their conclusion? Motor oils and the additives blended into them have improved so much over the years that frequent oil changes and expensive synthetics are no longer necessary.

Still, some people swear by synthetic oil. In practice, I don't recommend using synthetic oil if you have an older car with old seals in the engine. There have been many documented cases in which the addition of synthetic oil has caused an otherwise dry car to start leaking. If you own an older Carrera that doesn't have fresh seals in the engine, I would stick to the non-synthetics. However, if synthetic oil was the only type of oil that your engine has seen, I usually recommend sticking with it.

Fill your oil tank from the oil filler hole located in the rear engine compartment. Add about 8 quarts to the engine, and check the dipstick (1998–2005) or the oil level gauge (2005 and later). Continue to add about a half a quart at a time and keep checking the level. Fill it up until it reaches the top mark of the dipstick or gauge—the engine oil level will automatically lower when the oil filter fills up with oil. Make sure that you put the oil filler cap back on the top of the filler hole, otherwise, you will end up with a messy engine compartment when you drive away. While you're at it, also check the seal in the oil filler cap. A vacuum leak in this cap will cause rough running when you go to start the engine.

If you had the car up on jack stands, lower it down to the ground. Now, start up the engine. The oil pressure light should stay on for about a second or two and then go out. Hop out of the car and look at the engine, then take a quick look underneath the car. Verify that there's no volume of oil seeping out of the engine. Take the car out for a drive and bring it up to operating temperature. Shut the car off and then recheck the oil level (careful, the car will be hot). At this point, I like to top the oil off at the top point on the dipstick. Make sure that you dispose of your old oil at a respectable recycling station.

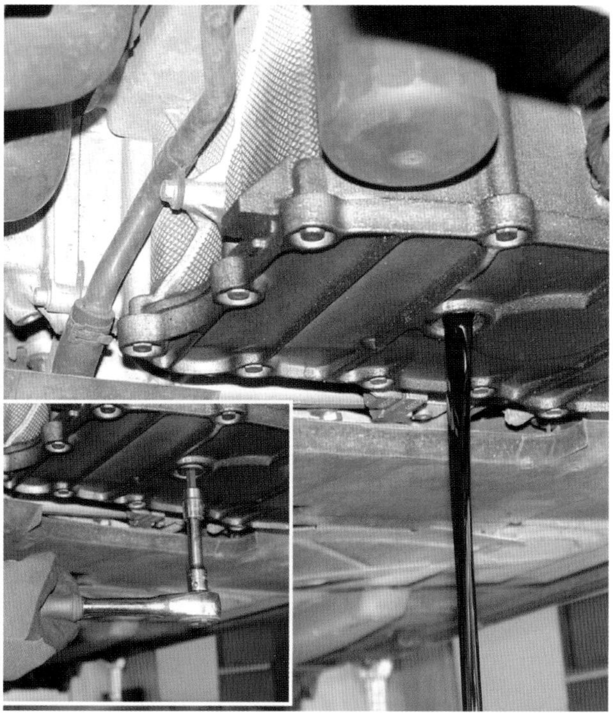

1 Some cars came equipped with a protective pan underneath the engine. You do not have to remove it to change the oil. Begin the oil change process by removing the drain plug underneath the car. The plug should accept an 8mm hex socket tool (inset). I recommend that you replace the small metal gasket underneath the plug each time, as it helps guard against oil leaks.

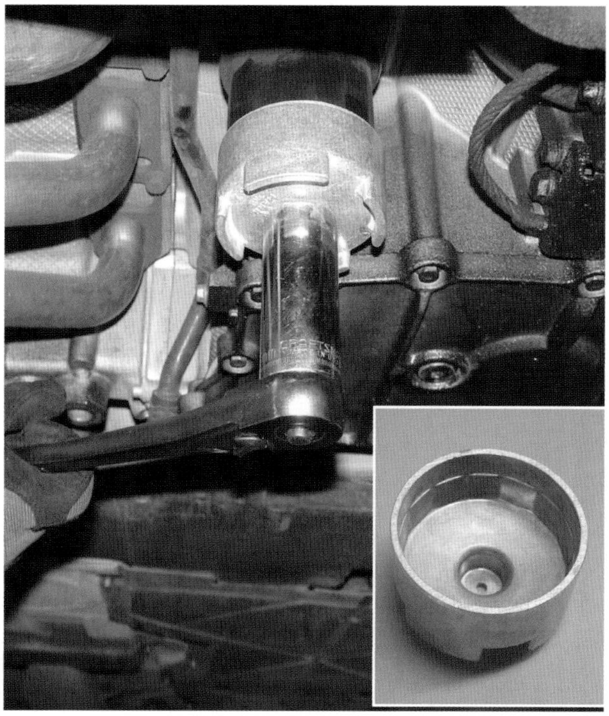

2 The filter housing will probably be stuck and difficult to remove from the engine. The best way to get it off is with the Porsche oil filter housing removal tool. Simply slide the tool on and remove the housing from the engine.

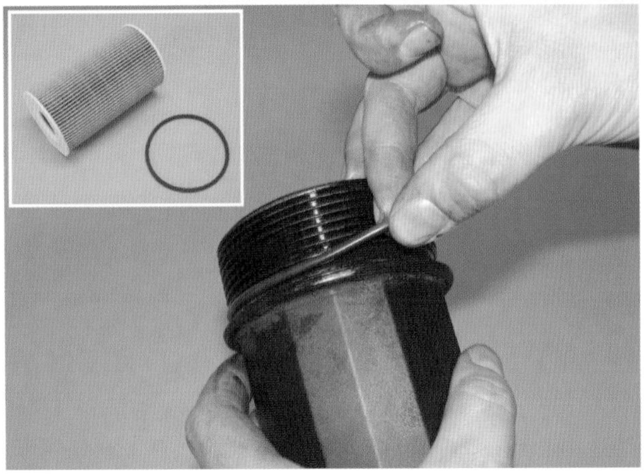

3 Be sure to remember to replace the large O-ring that seals the oil filter housing to the engine. This O-ring should be included in your complete oil filter kit (inset photo).

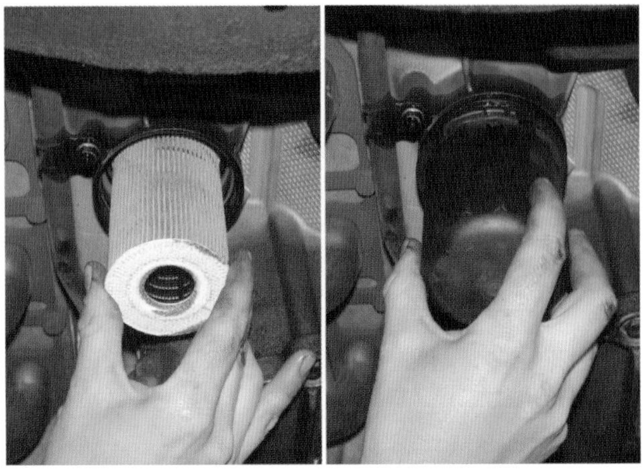

4 Take the filter and push it up onto the oil pipe. There should be one end of the filter that's slightly beveled to ease the installation process. With the filter in place, install the oil filter housing back onto the engine.

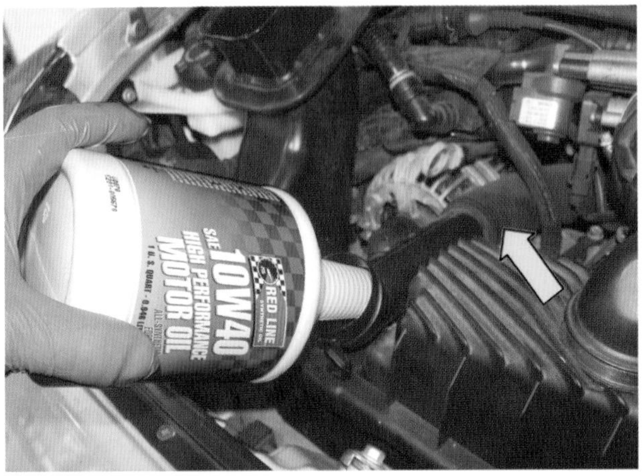

5 Fill your car with oil from the inlet in the rear engine compartment. The oil filler hole is on the left side, attached to the air box housing, and the oil cap is yellow in color. If you're quick and skilled with the bottle, you can pour without spilling. However, most people use a funnel to help prevent a mess. The oil filler tube that connects to the engine is made out of thin plastic and can crack with age (yellow arrow). Keep a close eye out for oil leaking out of the tube, which could make a bit of a mess in the engine compartment.

6 Pull your dipstick and check to make sure you have ample oil in your engine sump (1998–2005 only). Wipe down the end of the dipstick with a paper towel prior to inserting it back into the engine so you can achieve an accurate reading.

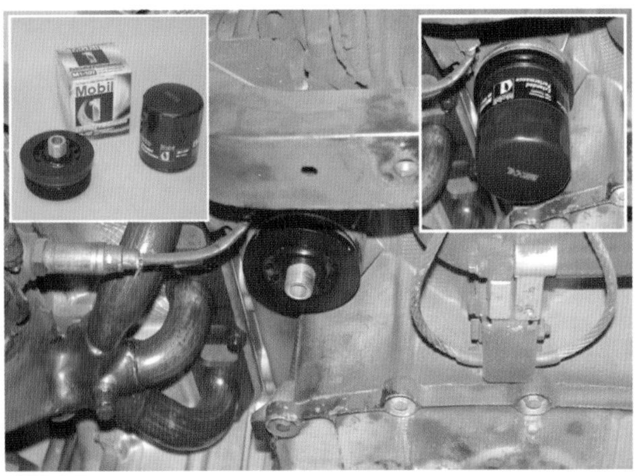

7 Shown here is a full-flow spin-on oil filter adapter, allowing for use of a conventional spin-on oil filter, rather than requiring the use of expensive and inferior replacement cartridge-style filters. Manufactured by LN Engineering, this design makes changing your oil a somewhat simpler task. With the adapter, you no longer have to handle the filter cartridge, worry about contamination of the oil filter housing, or worry about cross-threading the cheap plastic filter housing. The spin-on oil filter adapter also helps improve the longevity of your engine by providing full flow filtration, which means 100 percent of the oil gets filtered without having oil bypass the filter (an improvement over the factory design).

PROJECT 3
Replacing Air Filters

Time / Tab / Talent: 30 minutes / $40 /

Tools: Phillips and flat head screwdriver, 13mm socket, Torx set

Applicable Years: All

Tinware: Air filter, cabin pollen filter

More Info: http://www.101projects.com/Carrera/3.htm

Tip: Replace both air filter and pollen filter together

Performance Gain: Better airflow into your fuel injection system

Comp Modification: Install cone filter or cold air intake

You should change the air filter in your Carrera every 10,000 miles or so. The air filter protects the fuel injection system and the air intake system from dust and debris that can be sucked in under normal operation.

On the Carreras, the filter is just inside the air cleaner sitting in the engine compartment.

To access the 996 Carreras' filter, simply release the seven large Phillips head screws that hold the top of the cleaner to the bottom part of the housing, release the intake boot connection to the throttle body, unplug the mass airflow (MAF) sensor and remove the oil filler tube from the housing. Take a look inside the filter housing—there are usually some leaves or dirt that found their way in there. Clean the housing out before installing the new filter.

To access the 997 Carreras' air filter you must remove the complete airbox housing from the car, as the Torx screws that hold the top of the housing on are secured from the bottom of the housing. Loosen the clamp holding the intake to the throttle body, remove the mass sensor and its harness. If you have a 3.8 you will need to disconnect the wire from the vacuum resonator. Free the oil filler tube from its clip, and gently lift the complete housing from the car. The oil filler tube can break, so be careful when removing the airbox. Once the housing is out of the car remove the retaining screws from the bottom. Make sure to clean the inside of the housing before installing a new filter.

For the Carrera, there are basically two different types of air filters—the stock paper or cloth air filters and

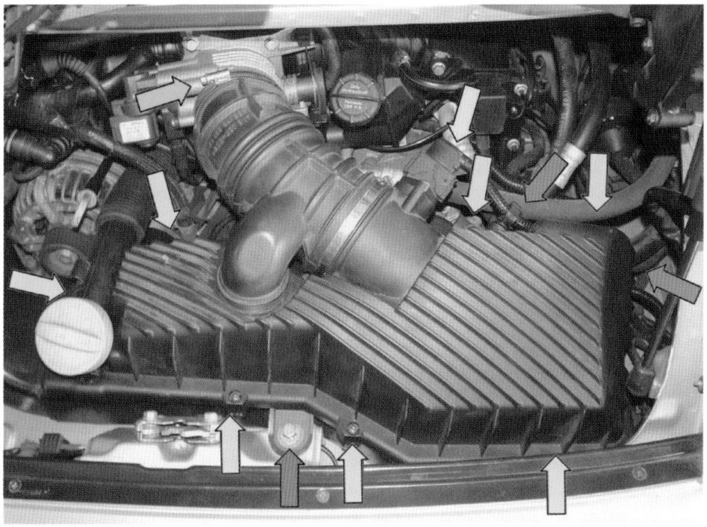

1 The air filter is quite easy to get to on the 996 Carrera. From inside the engine compartment loosen the seven screws that hold the top of the air cleaner housing to the bottom (blue arrows). Then loosen the clamp that holds the intake boot to the throttle body (green arrow). Unplug the mass air flow sensor (yellow arrow) and the clips mounting it to the air box (purple arrows), then unclip the oil filler tube from its home on the left side of the air cleaner housing. With everything disconnected, simply lift up on the housing to expose the air filter. The red arrow points to the bolt that holds the lower section of the air box to the chassis and does not need to be removed to change the air filter.

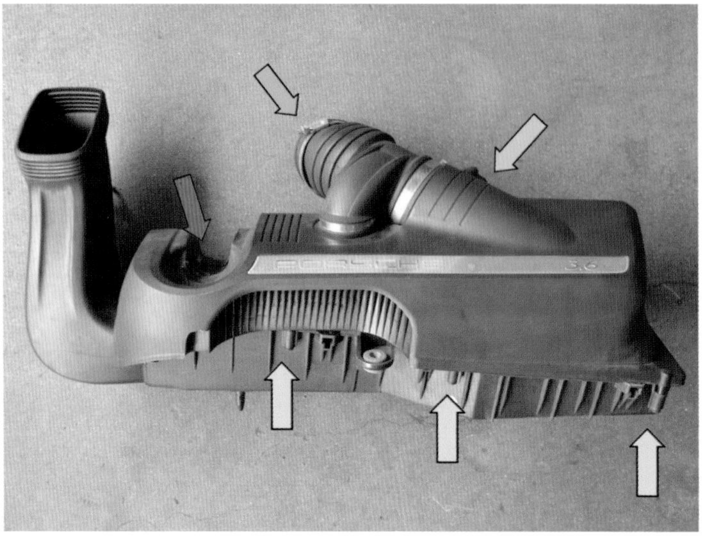

2 On the 997 Carreras, you will need to remove the complete airbox assembly to replace the air filter. On the 3.8-liter engines, the process is similar with the exception that there is a resonator switch installed in the air cleaner housing. In order to remove the air cleaner housing, the cable plug must be disconnected from the electric switch-over valve. This photo shows the airbox housing out of the car. The oil filler tube clip (red arrow), mass flow sensor (yellow arrow), and the throttle body clamp (green arrow) have all been removed or loosened. There are eight Torx screws (blue arrows, three shown) that need to be removed to separate the airbox housing pieces.

aftermarket units. These aftermarket units utilize an oil-soaked fabric to achieve freer airflow. The bottleneck for airflow in the 911 Carrera engine is not necessarily the air filter. The primary advantage of the aftermarket units is that you usually only have to purchase one, and it will last the life of your car.

No matter what your friends tell you, these aftermarket filters will not add any significant horsepower to your engine. Many tests on a dynamometer have revealed that the freer-flow air filters do not suddenly "create" horsepower out of thin air. If you install one of these filters into your car and "swear" there's more horsepower, then have a friend do a blind test for you. Have him switch the filters in and out at random and see if you can tell the difference. This is what is commonly called the placebo effect—perceiving significant gains in performance just because you added a "performance part."

The downside to using these aftermarket filters is that they often do not filter as well as the factory units. In addition, the use of aftermarket filters may cause excess dirt to accumulate in the mass airflow sensor and lead to its premature failure. The bottom line is that you need to carefully research any aftermarket filter before you install it into your car and carefully clean and maintain it thereafter. I personally prefer to use the stock OEM cloth/paper filters to ensure maximum filtering and protection. Whichever one you choose, make sure that it filters as well as or better than the original Porsche specifications.

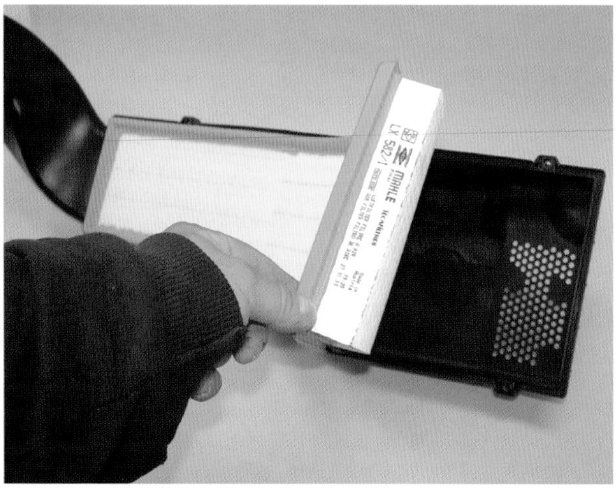

3 Shown here is the upper part of the air cleaner housing with a new filter being inserted. Always wipe out the bottom of the air filter box before putting everything back together.

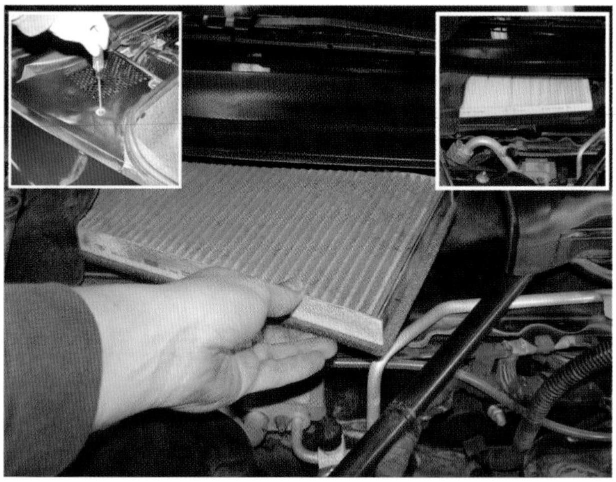

4 While you're replacing the engine air filter, I recommend that you also swap out the cabin air filter as well. Sometimes known as a "pollen filter," the cabin filter is located in the front trunk on the right side of the car. Remove the plastic panel just in front of windshield on the right side (upper left) with a T-25 Torx driver. Then reach in and pull out the filter. Install the new filter in place (upper right) and replace the plastic panel. New cabin filters are available in maintenance kits from PelicanParts.com.

PROJECT 4

Replacing Your Fuel Filter

Time / Tab / Talent: 1 hour / $35 /

Tools: Screwdriver, oil catch pan

Applicable Years: 1997–2001

Tinware: Fuel filter

More Info: http://www.101projects.com/Carrera/4.htm

Tip: Tackle this job only in a well-ventilated area

Performance Gain: Cleaner-running fuel system

Comp Modification: Replace worn-out or cracked rubber fuel lines

One of the basic maintenance projects that you should perform on your Porsche is the replacement of the fuel filter. Starting in 2002, Porsche moved the filter to inside the gas tank and called it a "lifetime" filter that never needs to be changed. For cars with a replaceable filter, I recommend that you replace your fuel filter about once a year or every 10,000 miles. It seems that with today's odd blended fuels, there always seems to be some gas station that has problems with dirt or grime in the gasoline that can clog your tank. I don't think quality control with gasoline stations is really what it used to be. Needless to say, I try to replace the fuel filter at least once a year. If you have a 2002 or later car that needs a new fuel filter, your only option is to replace the entire fuel pump assembly. See Project 22, Replacing the Fuel Pump.

Changing the fuel filter is not a job that I relish. It is almost guaranteed that you will spill at least some fuel on the ground and yourself as you swap out the fuel filter. Be sure to perform the replacement in a well-ventilated area. That means outdoors or in your garage with a few large fans blowing air both in and out. Have a fire extinguisher handy, wear rubber gloves, eye protection, and have a few rolls of paper towels handy—you will need them.

The fuel tank should be as low as possible—drive around until the gas tank is almost empty. This will minimize problems if something should happen to go wrong.

The first step is to jack up the car (Project 1). The Carreras have an intelligent design when it comes to fuel flow. The fuel pump is located in the bottom of the tank and pumps fuel out of the top fuel tank cover. Why is this good? Well, when you go to change the fuel filter, you can pull out the fuel pump relay, crank the car a few times, and be assured that fuel isn't going to flow everywhere if you make a mistake. Some older cars have a gravity-fed system that takes fuel out of the bottom of the tank. With these systems, you have to disconnect the line and clamp it very quickly—otherwise, the entire tank of gas will empty out! Unfortunately, with the Carrera system, you can't get 100 percent of the fuel out, and some will spill when you disconnect the fuel filter. In addition, the filter itself will mostly be full of fuel, too.

With the car up off the ground, crawl underneath the car. The filter is located behind the large plastic panel located in the very center of the car. This panel is held on with some plastic nuts (10mm head)-remove them and the panel should easily drop down. Next, remove the foam fixture piece that wraps around all of the lines in the center tunnel (if applicable), and remove the two bolts that hold the plastic coolant line bracket (see Photo 1). Disconnect the fuel filter ground strap, and loosen up the clamp that holds the filter. Now you want to disconnect the lines to the filter. The Carrera filter has connections that are very easy to attach and remove. Simply push gently on the grey tabs on opposite sides of the plastic connector, and the connection should easily slide off. Take a close look at your new filter for guidance on how this quick-connect connector works. Have a small pail or bucket handy to catch the excess fuel when you release the connection.

When the connections have been released, expect quite a few ounces of gasoline to be coming your way. Be prepared (gloves, eye protection, paper towels, bucket, and a well-ventilated area). Take the filter out by pulling it toward the rear of the car, put it in your bucket, and take it and any leftover or spilled gasoline outside of your garage immediately. Let the garage sit empty for about 15–20 minutes before you re-enter—it will take about that long for the fumes to clear. Then, simply reattach the new filter in place of the old one, observing the direction of the arrows located on the filter—they point in the direction of fuel flow, which is from the gas tank (front) to the engine (rear). Check that the snap-fit connections are properly seated by gently tugging on them. Reattach the ground wire (important!). Tighten the clamp that holds the filter tight. Then reinstall the foam piece (if applicable) and the large center panel.

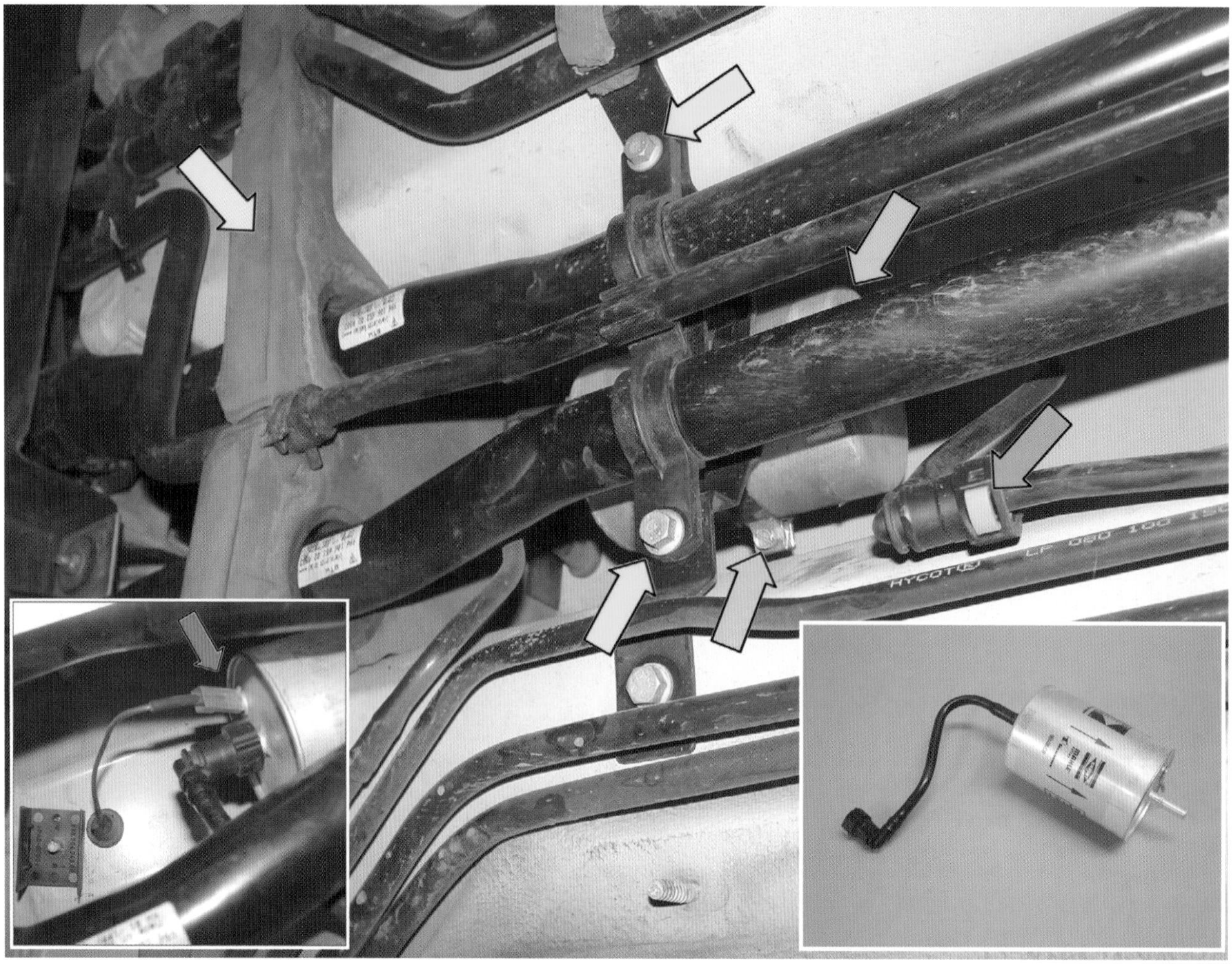

1 The filter (green arrow) is located almost dead center in the middle of the car, hidden somewhat behind the coolant pipes. The blue arrow points to the foam piece that needs to be removed so that you can pull the filter out toward the rear of the car. Removal of the filter is made easier if you remove the two screws that hold on the plastic coolant line bracket (yellow arrows). The orange arrow shows the screw that needs to be loosened in order to release the fuel filter from the clamp. The purple arrow points to one of the two tabs that must be depressed on the quick-disconnect connector. In the lower right, a brand new oil filter is shown. Note the arrows that indicate fuel flow direction printed on the side of the filter. The lower left inset photo shows the small ground strap that needs to be removed from the old filter and reattached to the new one (red arrow). Boxster undercarriage shown here-your Carrera may differ slightly.

PROJECT 5
Replacing Belts

Time / Tab / Talent: 1 hour / $30 /

Tools: Socket set, 24mm wrench for idler pulley

Applicable Years: All

Tinware: Drive belt

More Info: http://www.101projects.com/Carrera/5.htm

Tip: Carry a spare main drive belt with you in case of failure

Performance Gain: No squeaky engine or water pump failure

Comp Modification: Replace water pump and/ or alternator

One of the routine maintenance items that you should perform on your 911 Carrera is the checking and replacement of your accessory drive belt. The belts are driven off of the crankshaft and power accessories such as the water pump, power steering pump, alternator, and air conditioning compressor. There is only one belt on the car that powers it all. It should be checked periodically (every 5,000 miles, or when you change your oil).

The Carrera uses what is known as a poly-ribbed belt (having many channels or ribs on the underside of the belt). The poly-ribbed belt setup utilizes a spring-loaded belt tensioner pulley that provides the proper tension for the belt at all times, making adjustment unnecessary.

When inspecting your belts, the one thing that you want to look for is cracks (see the inset of Photo 1). If you see any cracks at all, you should replace your belts immediately. The cracks will usually occur on the inside of the belt (the surface that typically rides on the surface of the pulley). With the poly-ribbed belts, this is the grooved surface.

With the poly-ribbed belt, replacement is a snap. Begin by gaining access to the rear of the engine. Follow the instructions in Photo 1 to remove the air cleaner and access the rear area of the engine.

The tensioners that hold the belt tight can be easily released using a 24mm wrench. Rotate the tensioner clockwise to release the tension. Simply release the tension on the belt from the tensioner, and then the belt should simply slide off. Release the tension, and then you should be able to unwind the belt from the engine. Tip: If the belt is worn,

1 The drive belt on the Carrera is accessible by removing the air box from the engine bay. Disconnect the wire harness from the mass air flow sensor, upper right (yellow arrow) along with the clips that mount it to the air box (purple arrows). Then pop out the oil filler tube from its holder (blue arrow). On the 996 (1998–2005), disconnect the housing from the chassis by removing the nut that fastens it down (red arrow). Finally, remove the clamp that attaches the intake boot to the throttle body (green arrow), and remove the air cleaner assembly from the car. If you have a 3.8-liter engine, don't forget to disconnect the wire on the back of the airbox for the resonance valve. The lower right inset photo shows a belt that is getting very old and showing numerous cracks in the ribbed surface (red arrow).

simply release the tension on it and snip it with some large tin cutters to pull it out of the car.

Installation of the new belt is easy. Simply slide most of the new belt onto the pulleys, release the tension on the tensioner, and slide the belt onto the tensioner. Check to make sure that the belt is securely seated in all of the pulleys. Verify that the ribbed portion of the belt is set against the crankshaft pulley. Install the belt in the following order:

1. Water pump
2. Alternator
3. Upper idler pulley
4. Power steering pump
5. Air conditioning compressor
6. Crankshaft
7. Flexible idler pulley
8. Lower idler pulley

2 With the air cleaner housing removed you can see all of the various components that are driven by the main belt. On the right are the air conditioning compressor (yellow arrow) and the power steering pump (green arrow). On the left is the alternator (blue arrow). On the bottom is the water pump (purple arrow). The crankshaft (orange arrow) is in the center.

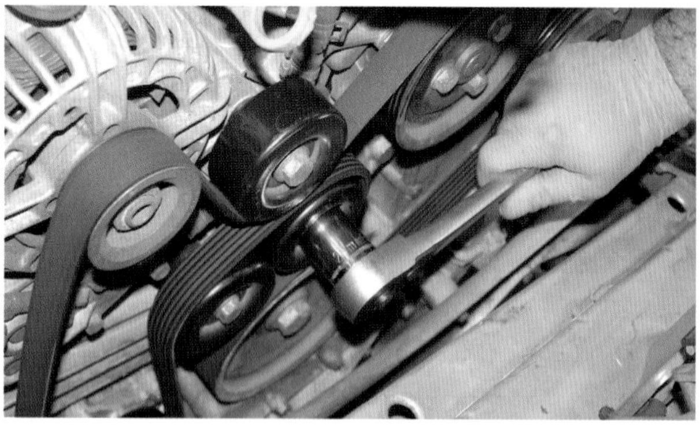

3 To release tension on the belt, simply place a 24mm socket attached to a breaker bar on the idler and turn it clockwise.

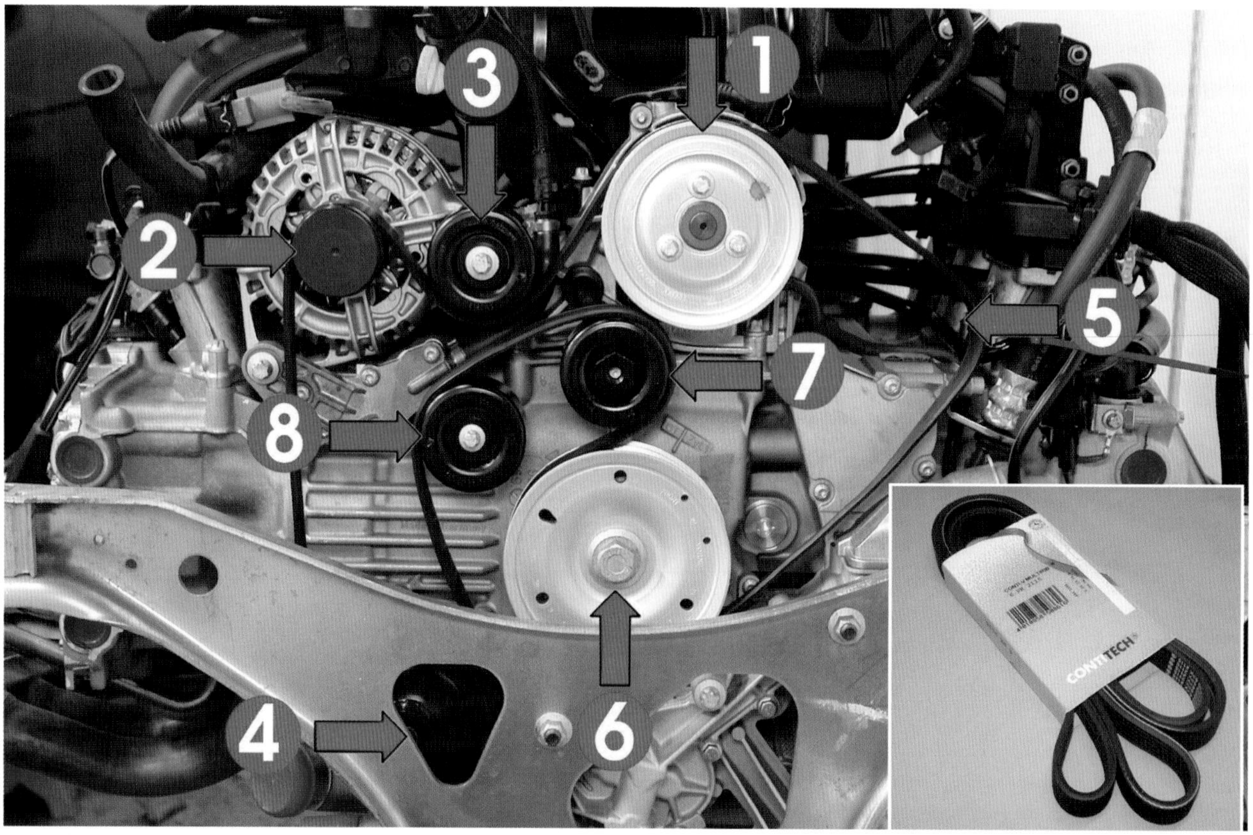

4 Here is a brand new crate 3.4-liter 996 motor direct from Porsche. The various components are 1) power steering pump, 2) alternator, 3) upper idler pulley, 4) water pump, 5) air conditioning compressor (not installed), 6) crankshaft, 7) tensioner pulley, 8) lower idler pulley. On the lower right is a photo of what a brand new belt looks like.

PROJECT 6
Washing Your Car

Time / Tab / Talent: 1 hour / $20 /

Tools: Bucket and hose, flow-through brushes

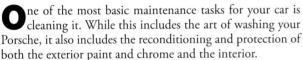

Applicable Years: All

Tinware: Car washing soap, four or five cotton terry towels

More Info: http://www.101projects.com/Carrera/6.htm

Tip: Don't use household detergent, and don't use a chamois

Performance Gain: Slicker-looking Porsche

Comp Modification: Buy a car cover

One of the most basic maintenance tasks for your car is cleaning it. While this includes the art of washing your Porsche, it also includes the reconditioning and protection of both the exterior paint and chrome and the interior.

The first step in washing your car is to determine exactly what it needs. If the car is simply dusty and has been sitting in the garage, then you probably only need to wash it with plain water (no soap). Wet the car down and use a wash mitt to remove any dust that might have settled on the car inside the garage. When washing the car, remember to get the valance panels and the lower rockers. As these panels are closest to the ground, they have a tendency to get the dirtiest.

I don't recommended using a chamois to dry your car. The chamois can trap small particles of dirt in its porous material and can actually cause scratches in the surface of the paint when it's used to dry off the car. A really good alternative is 100 percent cotton terry towels. Make sure the towels have been washed at least once, and don't use a rinse or softener. The softener is an additive that can cause streaks, and it inhibits the towel's absorbency.

If your car suffers from more than simple dust accumulation, then you will need to use a bit of car wash soap. Make sure that you don't use normal household soap or detergent, as this will remove the wax from the surface of the paint. As the wax is oil-based, normal detergents will attack and remove it. The car wash soaps are very mild and shouldn't remove the layer of wax that you have on your car.

Rinse the car completely with water from a hose, taking care not to spray the water in any areas where your seals may be cracking. If your 911 is a few years old, the overall watertight seal of the interior may not be as solid as desired. If your car does leak water, then toss some towels inside the car near the windows or under the sunroof to make sure that you catch any water before it reaches the carpet and seats.

After the car is completely rinsed, start drying it immediately. The new thing for drying cars has become the use of blowing the excess water of the car with a ShopVac on reverse or a leaf blower. While these are both fine, remember, if you use a ShopVac in blower mode, to make sure the filter is clean or you will just end up washing your car again, and if you are using a leaf blower that is gas powered make sure it does not vent its exhaust gases out through the blower nozzle.

It's best to dry the car off out of the reach of sunlight. Pull the car into the garage and dry it off in there. Removing the car from the sun helps keep those ugly water spots from appearing.

The key to keeping the paint free of scratches is to make sure that the towels are clean and free of any debris. Handle the towels as if they were going to be used for surgery. Don't leave them outside, or if you drop them on the ground, don't use them again until they have been washed. Small particles of dirt trapped within the towels can cause nasty scratches in the paint. If you happen to encounter a water spot, use a section of a damp, clean terrycloth towel to gently rub it out.

When you are finished cleaning, it's time to tuck the car away. I recommend that you use a good-quality cotton car cover if your car is spending most of its life in the garage. The cover will protect it from dust accumulation and also might help protect against items falling on the car or cats jumping on it. For cars stored outdoors, covers usually are not a great idea. They have a tendency to trap water, and the wind can make the cloth cover wear against the paint. If your car is not perfectly clean, then dirt particles trapped between the car and the cover will have a tendency to scratch the paint.

One of the most interesting new products to hit the marketplace in recent years is a deionized water washing system. I have used these on several of my cars, and I've been very pleased with the results. Available in small hand-held units or semipermanent installed setups, the systems filter regular tap water through a deionizing filter and provide a quick and easy way to wash your car without having to dry it—the deionized water doesn't leave any ugly water spots. These systems work pretty well, although in practice I was not able to eliminate all of the water spots from the car, so I recommend using them with a set of traditional towels as well to help dry the car.

1 One of the most innovative and time-saving products I've seen in recent years is the flow-through brush from Carrand. These are the perfect car-washing tool for busy people on the go. Simply hook up the brushes to your hose, and water flows through the brush as you're cleaning. Add an automatic soap dispenser, and you can clean an absolutely filthy car in about 10 minutes. My personal favorite is the flow-through wheel cleaning brush. It removes wheel dust and grime within about a minute of use. Used weekly, it's a great way to keep hard-to-remove grit and grime from building up on your wheels.

SECTION 2
ENGINE

The modern Porsche engines are built upon years of experience with the air-cooled 911. Porsche has taken a good, reliable design and continually modified and improved it, making the boxer six-cylinder into a reliable, water-cooled power plant. Still, components wear out and need attention. This section will guide you through engine maintenance tasks and also help you to evaluate what happens when you encounter the rare engine problem.

PROJECT 7
Replacing Spark Plugs/Coils

Time / Tab / Talent: 2 hours / $20 /

Tools: Spark plug wrench

Applicable Years: All

Tinware: Spark plugs, spark plug tubes

More Info: http://www.101projects.com/Carrera/7.htm

Tip: Don't use antiseize on the plugs when installing

Performance Gain: Cleaner, better running engine

Comp Modification: Replace spark plug tubes

The replacement of your spark plugs and spark plug wires (where applicable) is a basic tune-up procedure for just about any car on the road. I recommend replacing your spark plugs every 10,000 miles or about once a year. In reality, you can probably go longer than that; however, you never really quite know how long the plugs are going to last, or you may forget to replace them if you don't set up a yearly schedule.

With the introduction of the M96 engine, Porsche eliminated the use of spark plug wires by integrating six small spark plug coils that sit on top of each spark plug. While this configuration may be a bit more expensive than the typical single coil, single capacitive discharge box configuration, it makes the car's ignition system more reliable by removing a component that constantly wears out and fails (spark plug wires). It's a pretty cool setup not commonly found on older cars. As manufacturing components have become increasingly inexpensive, ignition setups like these have become more common.

Begin by prepping the car. The only thing that you really need to do is make sure that the car is cold. If you try to remove or install spark plugs in a hot car, then you may encounter problems with the spark plugs gumming up or damaging the relatively delicate threads in the aluminum cylinder head. Make sure that the car is cold or, at the bare minimum, only slightly warm to the touch.

Jack up the car (Project 1). While you do not need to remove the wheels to change the plugs, it will give you a little more room to move if you do. The shields protecting the heads will need to be removed on both sides of the engine before you can get access to the coils. On the 996 Carreras, each cover is held on place by two 10mm bolts; on the 997s, they have changed to 8mm Torx bolts. Simply remove them and place them aside.

For each coil, remove the two bolts that attach it to the engine. Unplug the coil wire harness. Then simply remove the coil/plug assembly and place it off to the side. All of the coils are the same, so it doesn't matter which cylinder bank it came from, unless you are specifically trying to troubleshoot a bad coil fault code that was displayed by the main computer.

With the coil assembly removed, you should be able to look down the hole and see the spark plug hiding in there. If the tube has oil in it, it may have cracked or become contaminated. Replace it with a new one (see Photo 3 and also Photo 7 of Project 16).

Spark plug removal is easy. You just need the right spark plug wrench. I have one that I love—it's a spark plug socket with a rubber insert that catches the plug and also has a built-in swivel on the attachment end. These wrenches are readily available from the tools section of PelicanParts.com. This tool is especially useful when trying to remove plugs in hard-to-reach places.

Using a breaker bar, grip the plug and turn it counterclockwise until it is loose. Then pull out your tool and grab the plug. When the plug comes out, you may want to take a close look at it. The spark plug is really the best way to visually "see" what is going on inside your combustion chamber.

Install the new plugs using a torque wrench to measure the amount of torque applied to the plug. This is very important, as it is easy to over- or under-tighten spark plugs. Make sure that the plug is firmly seated in the spark plug socket, as it is very easy to insert the plug into the head and have it cross-thread. This means that the threads of the spark plug don't mesh properly with the ones in the head, instead choosing to "cut their own path." This damages the threads on the head and, in extreme cases, may destroy the threads in the cylinder head entirely. Trust me, you do not want this to happen. Proceed carefully and cautiously here.

Install each spark plug into the cylinder heads without using any anti-seize compound. Torque the spark plugs to 30 Nm (22 ft-lbs). I recently learned that Porsche published a bulletin indicating that it doesn't recommend using anti-seize compound on spark plugs for any of their engines (Porsche Technical Bulletin 9102, Group 2 identifier 2870). The bulletin applies retroactively to all models, and the theory is that the anti-seize tends to act as an electrical insulator between the plug and the cylinder head. This could have detrimental effect on the firing of the spark due to the loss of a good, consistent ground connection.

With the new plugs installed and tightened to the correct torque, you can replace the coils and reattach the coil connectors. When you're done, your engine should look back to normal and run perfectly.

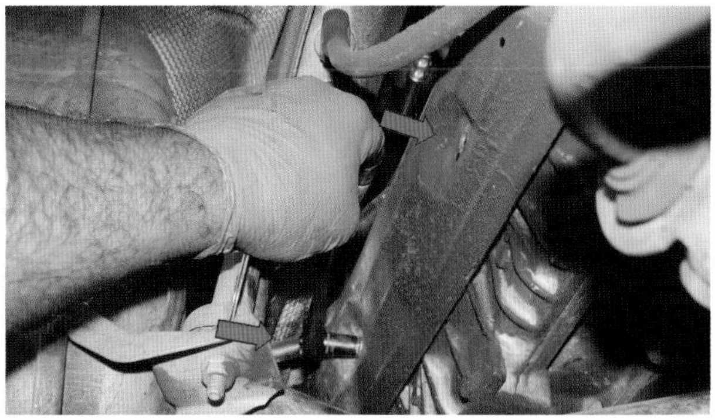

1 The spark plugs are protected by a metal cover. The cover is attached with two 10mm bolts (red arrows). Remove the bolts and cover to access the coils.

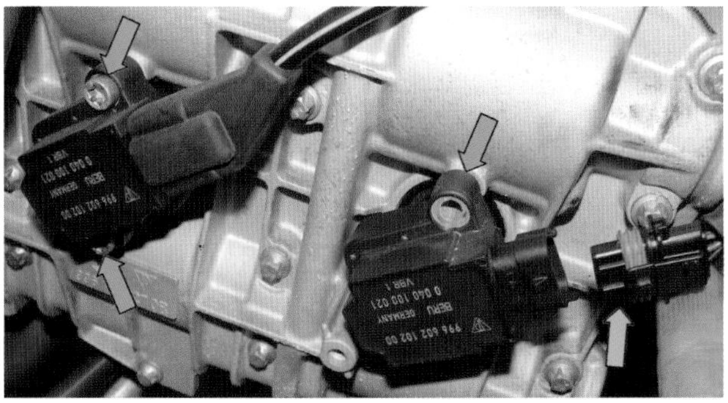

2 Each spark plug has its own individual coil. These are attached to the engine with two bolts (purple arrows). Remove each bolt and then disconnect the coil plug harness (green arrow). The coil should be able to be pulled from the engine once loose.

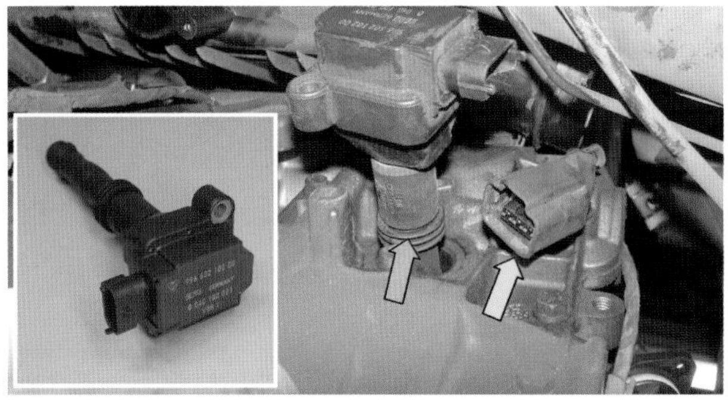

3 This particular photo shows an individual spark plug coil (inset). The blue arrow shows the plug that powers the coil, and the orange arrow shows the mini-bellows that is part of the coil that seals the chamber and keeps dirt and debris out. Be sure that you inspect the coil packs for cracks, particularly if the car has been driven on roads covered with salt. These coil packs can corrode, crack, and then cause misfires.

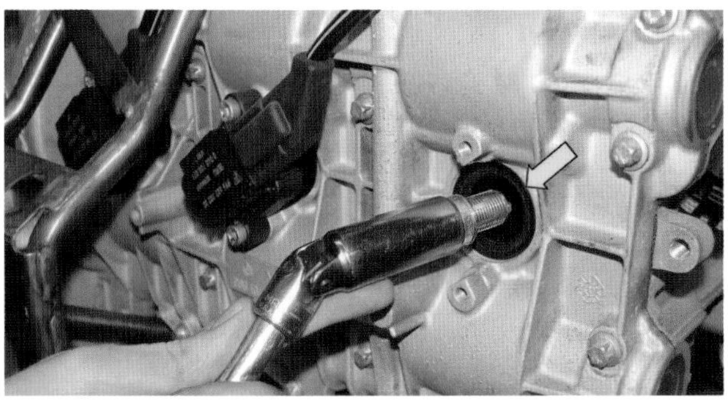

4 I like to use a swivel-socket spark plug removal tool from Craftsman. This tool is great for getting around bends and into hard-to-reach places. If you have a leaky seal on your valve cover, there is the opportunity for the spark plug holes to fill up with oil. When you pull out the spark plug connector/coil combo, you may find that it is contaminated with engine oil. If this is the case, then you should replace the spark plug tubes (yellow arrow, Carrera 996 1999–2004). These are plastic liners that seal the internals of the engine from the spark plug chamber. Use a pair of needle-nose pliers and simply grab the tube and pull it out of the hole. Later 997 Carreras (2005–2008) don't have tubes, but the O-rings in the camshafts housings should be inspected at this time.

5 In the photo inset, you can see an unusual spark plug with all four of its electrodes eaten away (red arrow). I would hazard a guess that this plug was improperly plated from the factory, and as it progressed through its life, the repeated sparking slowly ate away at the electrodes until they were gone. A plug in this condition would misfire often (if at all) and would generate poor performance for this particular cylinder. Surprisingly enough, none of the rest of the spark plugs in this set exhibited this type of damage. This is what leads me to believe it was defective from the manufacturer. On the right is shown a brand new Bosch Platinum spark plug. Spark plugs have varied over the years as engines have been changed slightly due to smog regulations. The important thing to remember is to get the proper ones for your car, otherwise you may encounter odd ignition problems (they are scaled by both electrode type and also by heat range). Spark plugs are cheap—I would go with a brand name like Bosch or NGK and avoid the no-name brands.

PROJECT 8
Carrera Engine Teardown

Time / Tab / Talent: 6 hours / $0 /

Tools: Camshaft holding tool

Applicable Years: All

Tinware: —

More Info: http://www.101projects.com/Carrera/8.htm

Tip: Get two large folding tables to lay all of the parts out

Performance Gain: Figure out what went wrong

Comp Modification: Install a bigger engine

1 This project focuses on a brief overview of the M96 engine and what it looks like inside. The engine featured here suffered a catastrophic failure, likely caused by a lack of oil to the main crankshaft. For the past 10 years, Porsche has offered an engine exchange program where you have to give back your old engine to Porsche when you get your replacement (known as a CORE charge). This means that very few of these engines have been floating around for people to disassemble, as we are doing here. We spent an entire two days at renowned Porsche workshop Callas Rennsport tearing down the engine and inspecting each component. For more detail on the teardown, I have made about 350 more photos of the disassembly process available with detailed captions on the 101Projects.com website. This particular engine was out of a Boxster, but the Carrera engine and Boxster engine are nearly functionally identical with the only discernible differences being changes in the various locations of accessory equipment and plumbing.

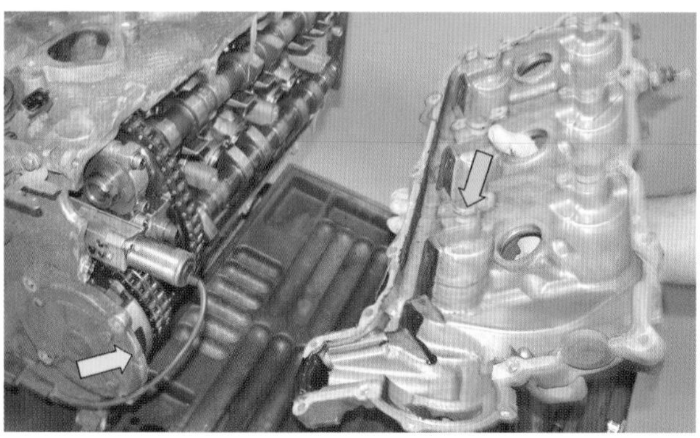

2 Here's the camshaft cover coming off of the engine. It's always a good idea to mark parts so that you know where they go if you try to put them back together again. Here we have marked the camshaft oil scavenge pump so that we know exactly how to mount it again in the future (yellow arrow). It's important to note that the camshaft covers have an integrated camshaft bearing as well. The green arrow points to the section in the cover that holds the camshaft in place.

3 Here's a neat shot of the camshaft cover removed. The top camshaft is the intake camshaft; the lower one is the exhaust. On the earlier cars, they are tied together with a small chain that is attached to a tensioner/advance mechanism that slides back and forth and changes the relationship (in degrees) between both camshafts. This device is controlled by the solenoid in the center (yellow arrow). The green arrow shows the very useful camshaft holding tool that the fellows at Callas Rennsport designed to keep the camshafts in place when removing the side cover. As discussed previously, the camshaft covers contain the "bearing caps" that hold the camshaft to the heads, so when you remove the covers, the cams will pop out if they are not held in place.

4 The two camshafts are removed together. Yes, you can perform the camshaft removal and replacement with the engine in the car (the folks at Callas Rennsport have done that previously on a 911 Carrera), but it's neither fun nor pretty. Lots of careful maneuvering is required. Four bolts hold the top and bottom camshaft end caps. Remove them, but remember which cap goes where. The tensioner/advance mechanism pulls off with both the intake and exhaust camshafts.

5 With the camshafts out of the way, you should be able to pluck the camshaft hydraulic followers out of the cam follower housing. Use your fingers or a suction cup to grab them out of there and be sure to place them in a tray, marking which valve they are matched to. The Porsche factory manuals recommend against using a magnetic tool to pluck out the lifters. Doing so may cause damage, presumably if part of the lifters becomes magnetized. When you reassemble the engine, you want to make sure that you reinstall the followers into the same exact bore that they came out of. This will reduce premature camshaft wear.

6 This photo shows removal of the cam follower housing. Removing this housing exposes the tips of the valves and each corresponding valve spring.

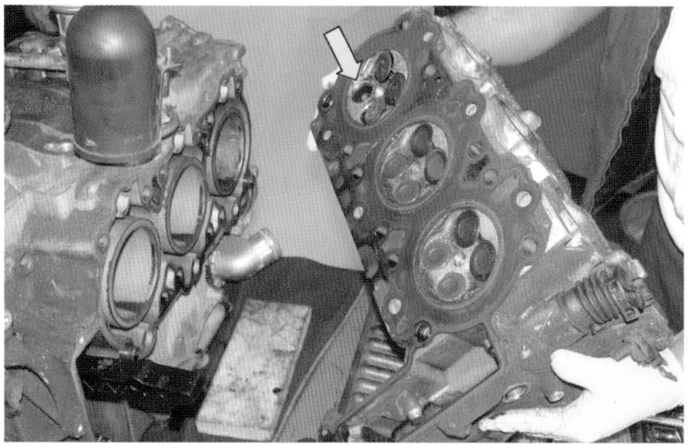

7 Remove the chain ramp bolts and then the chain ramps. Remove the head bolts and then gently tap the head with a hammer to release it from the case. It should slide right off. If it doesn't, you probably forgot a bolt somewhere. Here's a shot of the head coming off. Oops, looks like we're missing a valve (blue arrow)!

8 Yikes, there's that missing valve (blue arrow). It's quite obvious that we dropped a valve here, but it's not clear whether that happened before or after the rest of the damage to the engine. Note the cracks in the cylinder walls of the case (red arrow). This is not what you would call a rebuildable core.

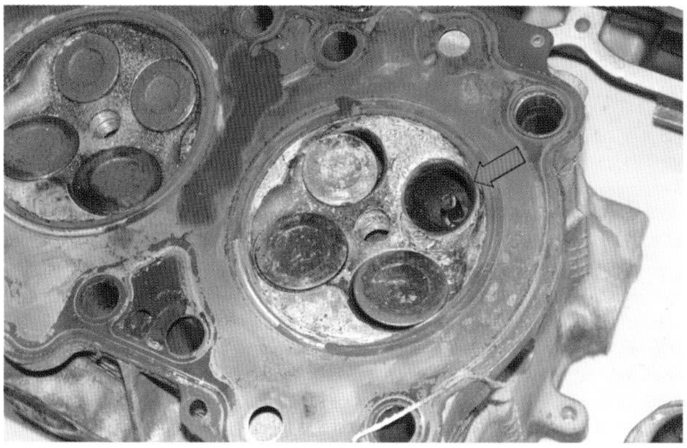

9 This photo shows the damaged cylinder head. The red arrow points to the valve where the head broke off. You can see that the oil from the engine is a light brownish color. This means that coolant and oil mixed together—it's typically a very bad sign if you see this when you change your oil.

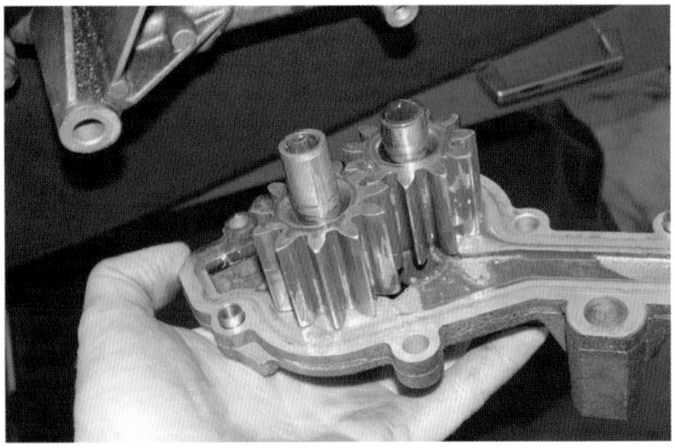

10 Here's the oil pump removed from the engine. A few small bolts hold this in place. Remove them, and it should be simply plucked off.

11 We went to look at the piston, and, oops, it just slid out as there's no more rod attached!

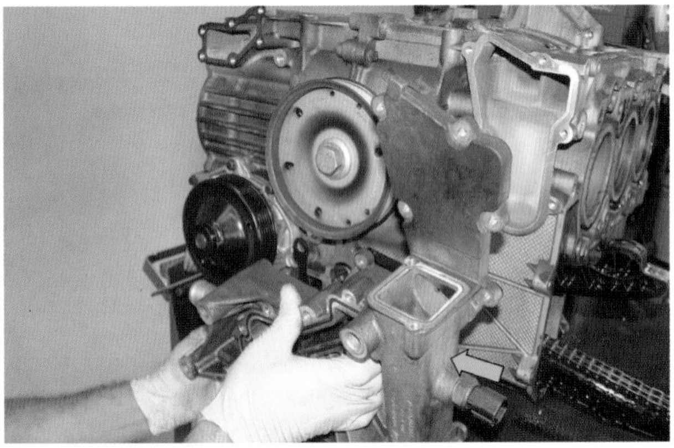

12 Moving on, we now removed the front oil pump housing from the engine.

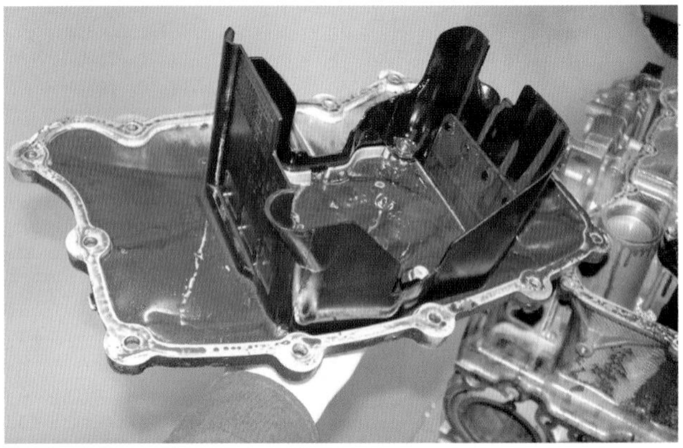

13 The oil pan on the bottom of the motor needs to be removed before splitting the case. These black plastic attachments are oil baffle plates, designed to channel and funnel oil in the sump of the engine.

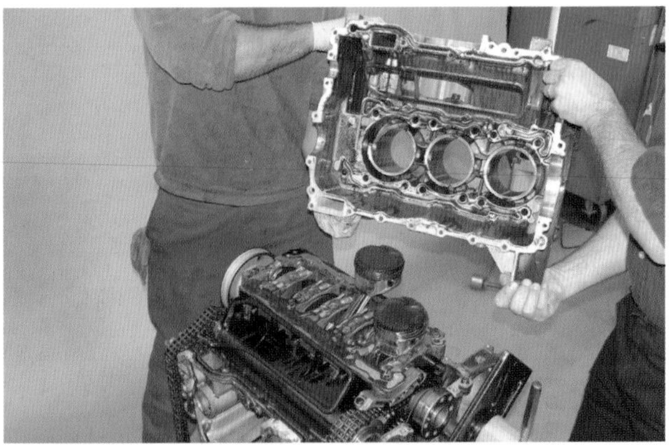

14 Before splitting the case, we moved the arms on the engine stand so that we had three points of support instead of two. This engine stand is a generic one and thus doesn't support the engine as well as a Porsche factory tool. Make sure that you attach the stand to the half of the engine that has the water pump. This will allow you to easily lift the opposite side off of the engine. Rotate the engine so that the water pump side is facing down. With all of the bolts removed (see the 101Projects.com website for more info), you should be able to start prying the case to split the two halves apart. There are a few spots on the case where it's okay to pry them apart. Only use these areas, as you don't want to scratch the case surfaces. There's no seal or O-ring that goes in there—it's just metal-sealant-metal.

15 This appears to be where all the damage began. This bearing (#1) is cooked completely and burned into the crankshaft. This is symptomatic of a drop in oil pressure. The bearing becomes very hot and then basically fuses itself to the shaft. Then the rod seizes and completely breaks. The rod for this cylinder was completely missing. We found it in a half-dozen pieces at the bottom of the engine (more photos on the 101Projects.com website).

16 With a friend nearby, pry up the crankshaft bearing housing, and it should lift off of the engine with the intermediate shaft closely in tow. This is really a two-person job. I would not try to lift this yourself, as the angle is all wrong.

17 Remove the bolts that hold on the oil baffle/separator, and remove the guide for the main chain. You should then be able simply to pick the intermediate shaft up and off of the crankshaft bearing housing.

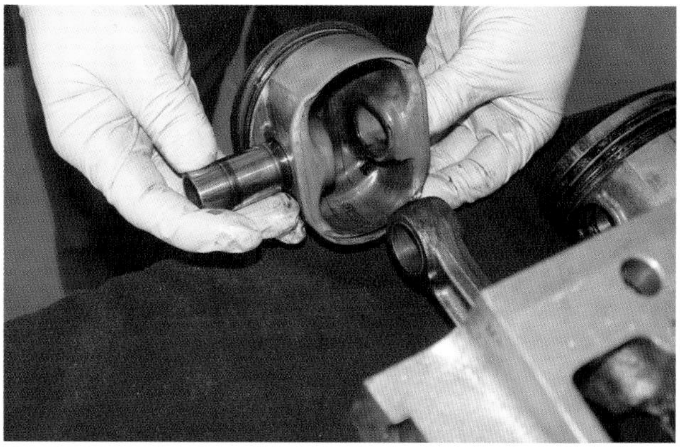

18 Here's one of the pistons with the piston circlip, which is very difficult to install in the engine when it's being rebuilt. You need a special Porsche tool—and lots of patience. I have heard it's like playing that childhood game, Operation: one mistake and you can easily drop the circlip inside the engine.

19 This is something you only really see in modern cars—the bearing housing has a steel insert cast into the aluminum. This type of "insert molding" is presumably for strength around the bearing surfaces. After removing the bolts that hold the assembly together, gently pry it apart.

20 These engines use a cracked-rod design, where the rods are forged and machined and then broken. Then the bearings are installed and they are put back together again. This cracked-rod design is cheaper to manufacture, and the rod bolts don't need to have integrated "guide" pins as part of their design (like the rod bolts used on the older air-cooled engines). Unless you use some type of oversized bearing, you cannot rebuild or remachine these rods.

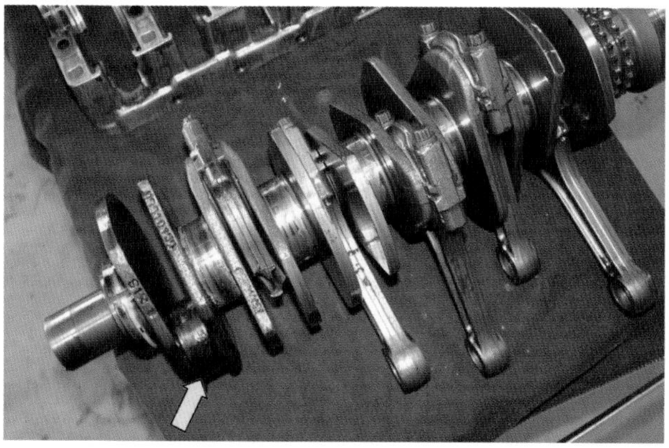

21 Here's another shot of that cooked rod bearing. Definitely caused by a lack of oil. Perhaps the previous owner forgot to check the oil level?

PROJECT 9

Air-Oil Separator Replacement

Time / Tab / Talent: 3 hours / $130–$165 /

Tools: All of them

Applicable Years: All

Tinware: New oil separator

More Info: http://www.101projects.com/Carrera/9.htm

Tip: Take your time and make sure you don't drop anything down into the engine

Performance Gain: No more smoke

Comp Modification: Change the oil

The engine air-oil separator is an emissions device that is responsible for collecting residual gases and vapors contained inside the crankcase and funneling them back into the intake manifold where they can be burned in the combustion chamber. This reduces the overall emissions of the engine.

On the 1998–2006 Carreras, the engine air-oil separator is located at the top left rear corner of the engine. For the 2006–2008 Carreras, Porsche redesigned the system and moved the air-oil separator (sometimes abbreviated as AOS) to the top of the engine under the right side intake. Exactly when Porsche made this switchover between the old and new engines is not well documented—check yours for the location prior to starting the project.

When the separator fails, you will begin to see a large increase in the overall vacuum in the engine crankcase. In the most extreme cases, the air-oil separator fails to separate the oil from the air, and oil is then sucked into the intake manifold. Oil in the intake system is not healthy for the engine, and it can foul spark plugs and destroy catalytic converters at the very least. The failure of the air-oil separator is often but not always accompanied by huge amounts of white smoke exiting the vehicle's exhaust and a generally poor running engine. You may experience a check engine light (CEL) as the oil being drawn into the intake can affect the mixture level. The oil cap may be very difficult to remove when the engine is running due to high vacuum levels. In addition, you may hear a high-pitched squeal from the engine when it's running because air is being sucked in past the crankcase seal due to the extreme vacuum inside the case.

The proper method to test for the failure of the unit is to measure the engine crankcase vacuum with a slack tube manometer. Normal crankcase pressure, measured at the oil filler cap, ranges from about 4–7 inches of water (drill a hole in the top of an old oil filler cap and attach the gauge there). When the air-oil separator fails, the intake manifold vacuum will draw into the crankcase and the levels will reach 9–12 inches or more. If you don't have a slack tube manometer (most of us don't), then you can use a standard vacuum gauge and/or get a rough feel for the level of vacuum pulled by comparing it to a normal running car.

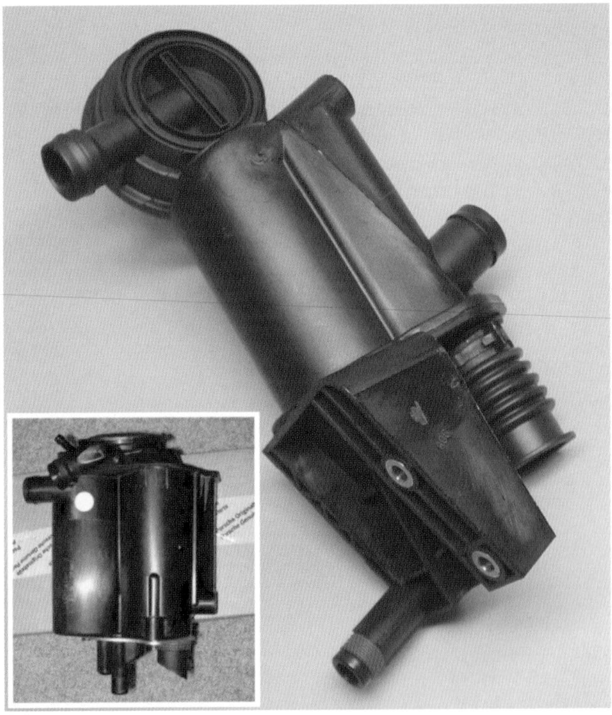

1 Shown here is a new early style air-oil separator for the (1998–2001) 996. The inset photo shows the motorsports air-oil separator, designed for cars that will see higher lateral g-forces than a typical street car.

On the early cars (up through about 2006), there are basically two ways to change the oil separator. The easiest is to drop the engine out of the car. This allows you full access to the lines and connections of the separator. The other method is to remove the separator with the engine in the car. It's a bit daunting, but we have come up with a method for removing it (see photos). On the 2006 and later cars Porsche redesigned the air-oil separator, and while it is still would be easier to do this with the engine out of the car, it is a lot easier than performing the work on an earlier car.

Begin by first disconnecting the battery. You'll be working around the starter motor, and there is always a 12-volt load going to the starter motor. If you accidentally touch it, you can injure yourself or cause a variety of problems with the car's electrical system. Be safe; take the extra time to disconnect it. Another good tip here is to use zipper-top plastic bags to neatly hold all of the various nuts and bolts you will be removing from the engine.

Open the engine lid and begin by removing the airbox. Loosen and remove the 13mm bolt at the very front of the airbox (996) and the hose clamp holding the boot to the throttle body. You'll also have to unplug the connector to the MAF by squeezing the connector. Now pull the boot off the throttle body and remove the airbox from the engine bay (on 3.8L cars and you will have to remove the electrical connection attached to the vacuum line for the resonance valve).

In order to access the oil separator, a lot of stuff has to come off the engine. See the photos for instructions on removal for the 996 Carrera and the 997 Carrera. When you're done with the removal, installation is the reverse of removal. Do not forget to remove any rags from the intakes before reinstalling the plenums!

A motorsports air-oil separator can be used on dedicated track cars. This special separator is designed to work with the higher g-forces that are exhibited with high speed track driving. If your engine has a lot of blue smoke exiting the tailpipe after driving on the track, you may need this upgrade (part number: 996-107-926-00). See the 101Projects.com website for a copy of the Porsche bulletin explaining this upgrade.

2 Open the engine decklid and remove the airbox. Begin by loosening the hose clamp holding the boot to the throttle body (green arrow), then squeeze the tabs on the mass airflow connector to release it (yellow arrows). Now open the harness holder clip (purple arrow). Pull the oil filler tub up and out of its clip on the airbox (blue arrow), and finally unbolt the 13mm bolt holding the airbox inside the engine compartment (red arrow) and carefully lift the airbox out of the car.

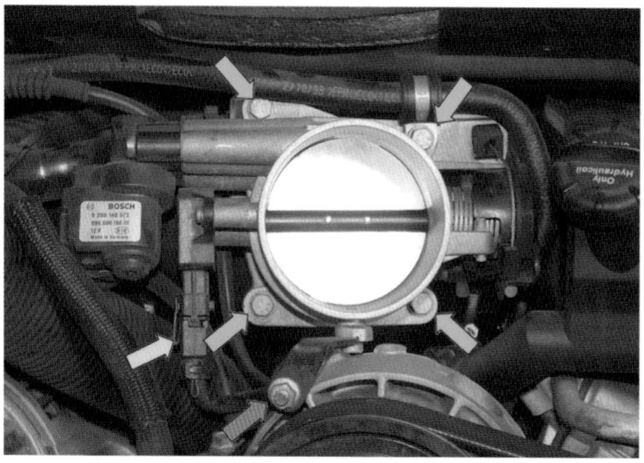

3 Remove the four 10mm bolts (green arrows) and also the 10mm nut (purple arrow) holding the throttle body to the engine. At the same time, also remove the electrical connector going to the throttle position sensor (yellow arrow; photo shows 1999 Carrera manual throttle body).

4 If you have an early car with a throttle cable, rotate the throttle back enough to relieve tension on the throttle cable and slip it out of the plastic cable cam as shown here.

5 **Older cars only**—Rotate the throttle body over to access the hose connection on the backside. On the older cars, use a pair of pliers to loosen and remove the hose clamp holding the hose onto the throttle body. Don't forget to pull the O-ring out of the intake plenum that seals the throttle body to it.

6 **Older cars only**—Follow the hose connection coming off the throttle body back to the control solenoid and press the wire piece in to release the electrical connector. Now place the hose/solenoid assembly off to the side.

7 Once the throttle body is removed, you'll need to remove the first intake plenum. Begin by removing the air hose connection to the air-oil separator. Squeeze the black plastic connector (purple arrow) to disconnect the hose from the plenum. Once free, set the hose connection aside. Now loosen the hose clamps securing the plenum to each manifold. A good idea here is to loosen the inner hose clamps first (red arrows) and then rotate the plenum to help break the seal that may have formed between the rubber and the plenum. Then tighten the inner clamps and loosen the outer clamps (green arrows) and do the same to break the connection between the rubber seals and the intake manifolds.

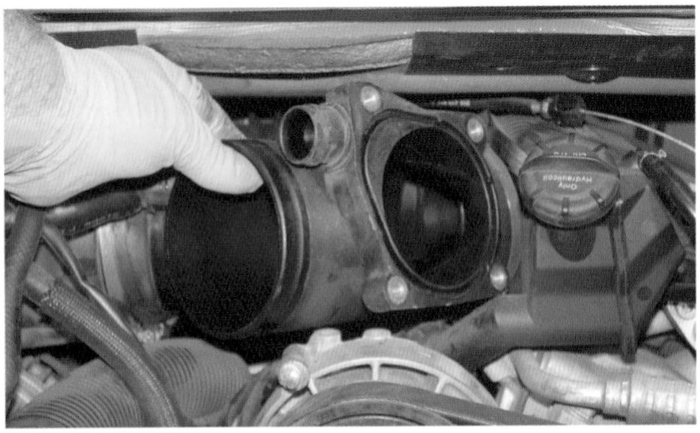

8 Once the hose clamps are loose, you should be able to push the intake seals onto the plenum, then slide the plenum over to one side and pull it free of the manifold as shown here.

9 **1998–2006 Carrera only**—Now remove the rear intake plenum tube. Like the front one, loosen the hose clamps then push the plenum over to one side. Once removed, pull the vacuum hose off the connection to the resonance flap inside the rear plenum. The idea here is to gain as much space as possible inside the engine bay.

10 Remove the two 8 mm screws holding the hose connection to the left intake manifold. These screws also hold the retaining plate for the vacuum solenoid shown here just to the left. Once free, maneuver the hose, plate, and solenoid up and out of the way.

11 Now comes the hardest part of the job: removing the small Torx bolts that hold the left side intake manifold to the cylinder head. A really helpful step is to remove the coolant tank from the car—not absolutely necessary, but it creates a lot more working room. One handy tip is to loosen each bolt to the point where it can be pulled out of the manifold, then use a telescoping magnet to keep from dropping it in the engine bay. Also take note of the accessory bracket on the very front of the intake manifold. Don't forget to reinstall this later. In this picture, we have a 996 engine out of the car to show the location of the six Torx bolts that hold the manifold to the engine (green arrows). The purple arrow points to the air-oil separator that you are trying to reach by removing the manifold on the left side.

12 As you can see here, clearance is the biggest problem with removing the bolts that hold the intake manifold to the engine. In this picture, you can see that the coolant tank has been removed to provide even more access to the manifold bolts (Project 34). The key here is patience. I've found that a combination of ¼-inch drive U-joints and extensions help out quite a bit when removing the bolts. Take your time, and you should be able to get all of them out.

13 Be sure to remember to set aside the bracket at the front of the intake manifold (purple arrow). This is one of those little things that are easy to forget when reassembling the motor. This small bracket supports the radiator hose that is just to the right of it in this photo.

14 With all the bolts removed, carefully maneuver the intake manifold out from under the fuel lines and wiring harness. As soon as you get the manifold out, be sure to stuff some rags or paper towels into the cylinder head ports to prevent any dirt or loose objects from falling in.

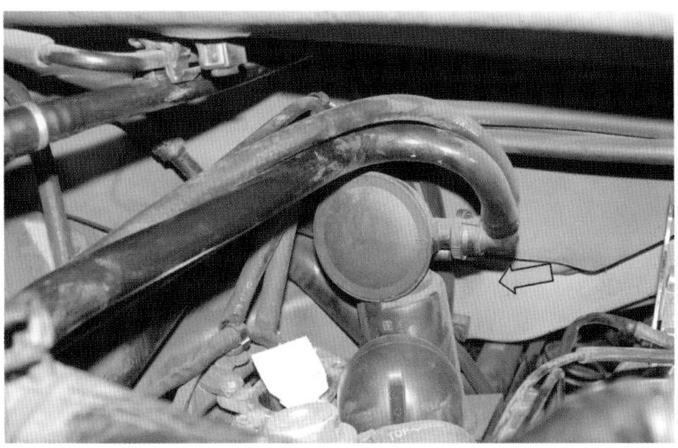

15 With the intake manifold removed you now have access to the oil separator at the very back of the engine (orange arrow).

16 Squeeze the connector on the upper part of the oil separator to release the hose connection as shown here.

17 Now support the car on jack stands and climb underneath the car. In this picture, you can see the oil separator (green arrow) as it bolts to the side of the engine case near the transmission (red arrow). Begin by removing the hose clamp holding the rubber bellows to the bottom of the oil separator and pull it off. Next, squeeze the quick disconnect fitting on the vacuum hose (purple arrow) to remove it from the oil separator. The final step is to remove the two 13mm bolts holding the separator to the engine case (yellow arrows).

19 **2006–2008 997 Carreras only**—Here is the air-oil separator with the power steering reservoir and first intake plenum removed (the AC compressor is still in place). You can see the three vacuum lines (red arrows) and the two water lines (blue arrows) that need to be removed. Just push in on the blue clip and slide the water lines off. There will be a little coolant that spills out when you remove the water lines; keep an eye on approximately how much spills so you will have an idea of how much to replace later. The air-oil separator sits in a tube that connects directly to the crankcase; be sure to clean up all the coolant before removing the air-oil separator so that no coolant leaks into the case. The green arrow shows where the power steering reservoir was connected.

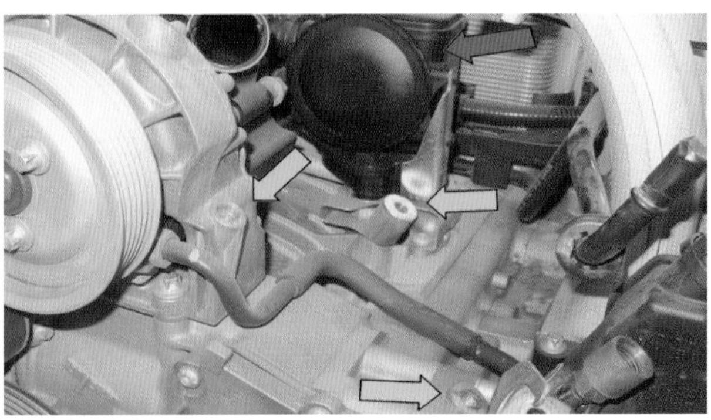

20 **2006–2008 997 Carreras only**—This picture shows the air-oil separator with the AC compressor removed. If you are working on your earlier car and happen to be reading this to see the difference, you might be a little jealous at how much easier it is to remove on the later models. The air-oil separator is shown by the red arrow, while the yellow arrows show where the bolts that hold the AC compressor go.

18 **2006–2008 997 Carreras only**—While the Porsche technical manual recommends that you remove both air intake plenums, for the 2006 and later Carreras I recommend what I have found to be an easier way. You only need to remove both plenums if you are going to remove the air-oil separator from the top of the engine. By removing the two T30 screws on the air-oil separator mount, you can swing it out of the way and remove the separator through where the air conditioning compressor used to be. If you need to remove the second plenum for additional work then you will not need to move the separator mount, but it is a very tight fit on the second plenum, and I have found removing the mount screws easier. This method involves removing both the power steering reservoir and the AC compressor with its lines attached. To do this you will first have to remove the accessories belt. To release the tension on the belt, attach a 24mm socket to a breaker bar, place it on the idler arm, and turn it clockwise (see Project 5). To remove the power steering pump, first use a fluid pump or turkey baster to suck out as much power steering fluid as possible. Once the reservoir is empty, remove the 10mm nut securing the reservoir to the bracket (yellow arrow), then rotate the bayonet lock tab counterclockwise to remove the power steering fluid reservoir from the car. The compressor is held in place by three long 13mm bolts. Remove the two front bolts along the front edge (red arrows). In order to get to the remaining AC compressor mounting bolt, you'll first need to remove the temperature sensor mounted in the right side manifold, in between the first set of runners (blue arrow). The sensor sits in a rubber sleeve that fits into a groove on the intake manifold. It's difficult to see it, but it will slide out. You can now access the remaining compressor bolt from between the intake manifold (purple arrow). You'll need to use a combination of extensions and U joints. This bolt needs to be held in its upward position to remove the compressor. Once the compressor is free, unplug the electrical ground connector (green arrow), lay down a rag or towel to protect the paint of the car, and lay the compressor off to the side of the engine. *This work was performed on a crate engine we had at in the Pelican Parts garage, to better show the location of everything, but can be done easily with the engine in the car.*

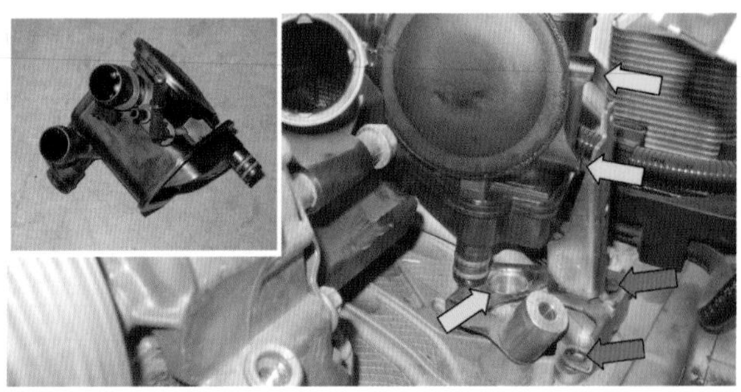

21 **2006–2008 997 Carreras only**—The air-oil separator has been removed from the engine case, but is shown here resting on its mount. The blue arrow shows the opening to the crank where it sits. Make sure to place a clean rag in here so nothing can get into the crankcase while you are working. The two T20 Torx screws that hold the air-oil separator to the mount (yellow arrows) and the two T30 Torx screws (red arrows) that hold the mount to the engine case have been removed. You do not need to remove these screws if you have removed the second plenum as there will be room to remove the air-oil separator from the top of the engine. The upper left inset photo shows the side view of the air-oil separator.

PROJECT 10
Engine Mount Replacement

Time / Tab / Talent: 3 hours / $200 /

Tip: Use long extensions for easier access

Tools: 10mm/13mm/18mm socket, channel locks, floor jack

Performance Gain: Smoother shifting, better handling

Applicable Years: All

Comp Modification: Replace air filter

Tinware: New engine mounts

More Info: http://www.101projects.com/Carrera/10.htm

One of the most common sets of parts to deteriorate on the Carreras are the engine mounts. They are liquid-filled hydraulic mounts, and over time they can develop leaks. They collapse once they leak and can cause a whole bunch of problems and accelerate wear to other critical components. Replacing the mounts isn't an overly difficult job, provided you have a floor jack and some basic tools. In this article, we will go over the steps involved with replacing the engine mounts on your Porsche 996/997.

Begin by opening the rear decklid and removing the airbox from the car. This will provide you with some of the needed access to reach the mounts. Please see our article on engine removal for more info (Project 15). Once the airbox is removed, you'll see the right mount easily. On the 996 Carreras, the left side mount requires the removal of the emissions pump in order to access the mounting bolts. With the 997 there is no pump, and the mount is easily accessible.

Remove the emissions pump by first using a pair of channel locks to remove the hose clamp on the air line. Once free, pull the air hose off. Next, remove the two 10mm bolts and the 10mm nut holding the mounting bracket to the car. Rotate the pump over to access the electrical connection. Disconnect it and remove the pump from the engine compartment.

Now jack up the car and secure it on jack stands (Project 1). Once the car is up in the air, you'll want to place the floor jack in the middle of the engine sump cover. The idea here is to use the floor jack to support the weight of the engine while you unbolt the mounts and replace them. Just jack up the engine until you take the weight off the mount.

From underneath the car, locate the two 18mm nuts on the underside of each mount. This nut holds the engine mount support to each mount. Carefully remove each mount and double-check that the floor jack is supporting the weight of the engine.

Now move back to the engine compartment and remove the two 13mm bolts holding each engine mount in place on the rear engine shelf. Once unbolted, lift the mount up and out of the engine compartment. You may find that it's a bit difficult for the long threaded part of the mount to clear the engine support. Just carefully wriggle the mount out and place the new one in.

1 Open the engine decklid and remove the airbox. Begin by loosening the hose clamp holding the boot to the throttle body (green arrow), then squeeze the tabs on the mass airflow connector to release it (yellow arrow). Now open the two harness holder clips (purple arrows). Finally, unbolt the 13mm bolt (996 only) holding the airbox inside the engine compartment (red arrow). If you have a 3.8 you will need to remove the wire connected to the vacuum resonance valve and carefully lift the airbox out of the car.

2 Here is a 997 engine compartment with the airbox removed. You can easily access both engine mounts (red arrows).

4 From underneath the engine, use an 18mm socket with a long extension to loosen and remove the nut holding the engine mount to the engine support bar. Shown here is the nut on the left (driver) side of the engine (green arrow).

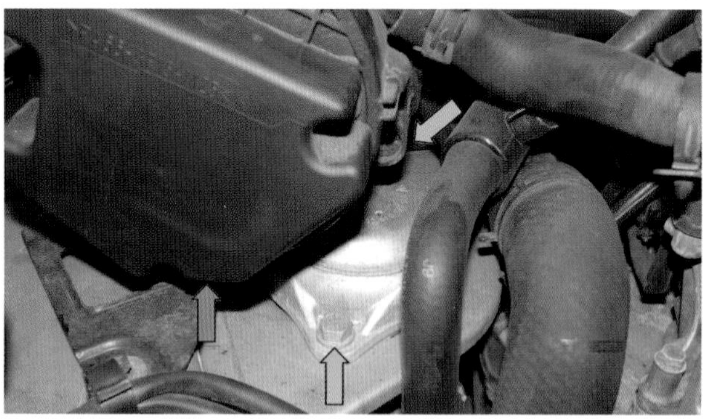

6 Shown here is the left side engine mount on a 996. In order to access the two 13mm bolts holding it in place (green arrows), you'll need to remove the emissions pump (purple arrow). This is not necessary on the 997.

8 Rotate the emissions pump over to reach the electrical connector (green arrow). Unplug it and pull the pump out of the car.

3 Place a floor jack under the engine to support the weight once the mounts are removed. Be sure to use a piece of wood, rubber, or newspaper between the engine case and the jack. In our case, there is a rubber pad on the top of the jack foot. Jack the engine up only enough to take up the weight of the engine. Do not try to support the entire weight of the car; otherwise, you may damage your engine sump plate.

5 Shown here is the nut on the right (passenger) side of the engine (green arrow).

7 Remove the hose going to the emissions pump at the left of the engine compartment. Use a pair of channel locks to loosen and slide the hose clamp back (purple arrow). Twist the hose back and forth to free it from the pump. Then remove the two 10mm bolts at the front edge of the pump (green arrows) and the 10mm nut at the top of the air pump (yellow arrow). This nut also secures the front of the coolant tank to the car.

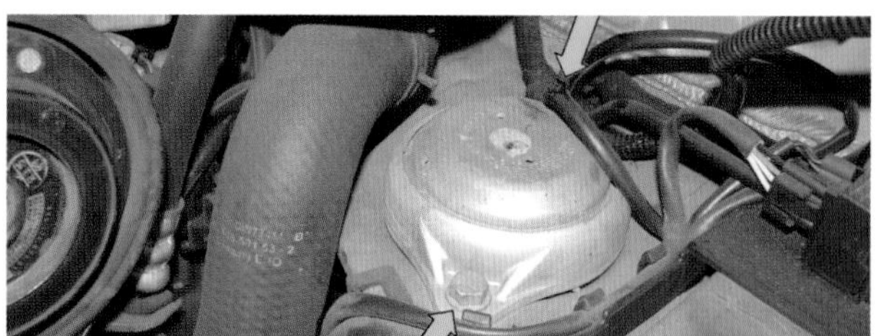

9 The right side engine mount is much more accessible. Simply remove the two 13mm bolts. Once unbolted, lift the old mount out and place the new one in.

PROJECT 11
Installing the IMS Guardian

Time / Tab / Talent: 5 hours / $390 /

Tools: 8mm hex, small flat head screwdriver, crescent wrench

Applicable Years: 1997–2004

Tinware: IMS Guardian kit, oil filter, 7–10 quarts oil, Loctite 5900

More Info: http://www.101projects.com/Carrera/11.htm

Tip: Don't over torque the sump

Performance Gain: Peace of mind

Comp Modification: Replace your IMS bearing

If you are worried about the health of the intermediate shaft bearing (IMS) in your engine but do not want to go through all the work to replace the bearing (see Project 14), there is now another option. The IMS Guardian allows constant engine monitoring through its dash interface. The IMS Guardian couples technology originally created for military aircraft to a specially designed sensor and wiring package. This system was originated with the sole purpose of detecting imminent IMS bearing failures prior to their occurrence. Available for about $400 from PelicanParts.com, it's cheap insurance against expensive engine failures.

The system relies on magnetic chip detection (MCD) technology for monitoring the metal content in engine oil. The sensor consists of two strong, opposing-poles, permanent magnets with an insulated gap of air in between. Each magnet is connected, by a wire, to the wiring harness, comprising an open electrical circuit. The wired magnet unit itself is mounted in a modified oil drain plug replacing the stock drain plug.

As oil circulates throughout the engine, the magnets will attract the small metal debris that is caused by deterioration within the engine and is circulated throughout the engine oil. As the ferrous metal debris is captured in the center of the magnets, it will quickly build up to the point that it will bridge the gap in between the magnets allowing the conduction of electricity and it will close the electrical circuit. Closure of the electrical circuit causes a warning light, installed in your dashboard, to illuminate along with an audible buzzing alert. When the IMS Guardian alert goes off, the driver of the vehicle should turn off the engine as quickly as possible to avoid any engine damage.

Installation is relatively straightforward. Begin by disconnecting the battery. Then drain the oil by removing the 8mm hex bolt in the sump plate. Once the sump has drained, you will want to remove the sump plate itself (see Project 12). It is held in place by thirteen 10mm bolts. When removing it, it is a good idea to leave two of the bolts partially threaded so the cover will not fall on you when it lets loose.

With the sump plate off of the car you will need to clean it very well. You must get all of the metal out and off of the plate. I was able to just use some rags, but if you are going to use a solvent make sure you do not get it on the rubber oil control baffles.

It is important to note that a small amount of ferrous metal floating inside the engine oil is somewhat common to most engines. However, if you find a large amount of metal or any larger metallic pieces, there is a very good chance your engine is on its way to destructing. It would be best not to drive the car and either remove and inspect the IMS bearing yourself or have a professional look at it.

Follow along with the photos for step-by-step instructions on the installation of the sensor and the in-dash switch and indicator.

With everything done, you should now check the system for operation. Turn the key on, but do not start the engine. The IMS Alert Warning Indicator Switch should be illuminated in an amber color. This indicates the system is armed. Press the IMS Alert Switch (lighted portion) to test for operation. The light should illuminate to a red color and an audible alarm should be heard. This indicates a fully functional system.

Congratulations. You have installed the IMS Guardian. Now, just button everything back up, and you are done.

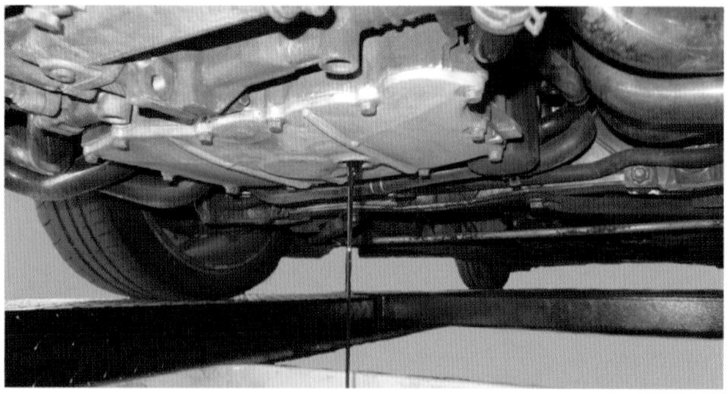

1 The following photos document the installation of the IMS Guardian. After disconnecting the battery, drain the oil from your sump. Remove the sump plug with an 8mm hex.

2 After the oil has drained, remove the sump cover. There are thirteen 10mm bolts holding the plate to the engine. I recommend leaving two bolts slightly threaded (red arrows) so when you remove the cover it does not fall on you. In most cases, you will probably need to pry the cover off. Use the pry area (yellow arrow) by the oil filter. Never pry by trying to jam a screwdriver between the cover and engine case; this can damage the mounting surfaces and cause future leaks.

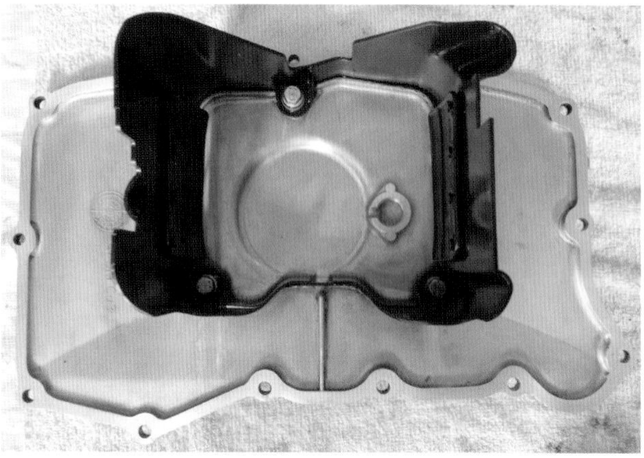

3 Completely clean your sump cover. There should be no old oil or metal on the plate whatsoever. If you need to use a solvent, remove the rubber baffles before applying the solvent.

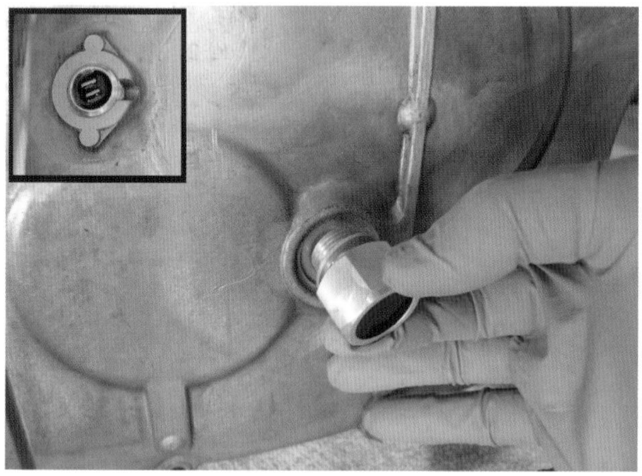

4 Install the Magnetic Chip Detector (MCD) into the sump plate through the drain plug hole. Make sure you use the crush washer provided. Fully hand tighten the MCD. It does not matter which way the magnets are oriented (inset upper left).

5 Inspect and clean the lower engine case area. Pay special attention to the screen on the sump (red arrow) and make sure it is clean and free of any grime or debris.

6 After thoroughly cleaning both surfaces of the engine and cover, apply a very thin bead of sealant (I like to use Loctite 5900). Install the cover and torque the 13 bolts (red arrows) down in a crisscross pattern. Do not overtighten these bolts. Once the sump is tightened down you should see a small bead of Loctite between the case and cover (green arrow). Now move to the MCD. You should have already hand tightened the plug; if not, double-check it now. The MCD is designed to be hand tightened and then tightened another ¼ turn with a wrench (yellow arrow).

ENGINE

7 You will need to pull power from one of the dash switches. I pulled power from the traction control switch, but if you do not have any powered switches on the driver side of the dash, you can pull power from a switch on the passenger side by running the harness through the hole behind the vents. Remove the dash switch plate with your trim removal tool (red arrows).

8 Here you can see the blank area where the intermediate shaft (IMS) switch is installed (red arrow) along with the harness connector (green arrow) for the traction control switch that power will be pulled from.

9 Pop the switch blank from the panel using a small screwdriver (red arrow) and pull out the harness connector from the back of traction control switch (green arrow).

10 Tape the red wire to the main wiring harness and pass them together through the dash. If you put a shop light under the dash it will help "illuminate" the best path for passing the wires (red arrow).

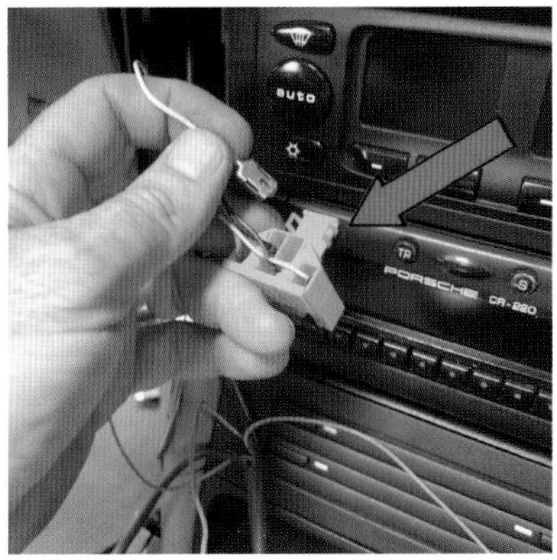

11 Open the connector for the traction control using a small screwdriver and remove the number 3 connector (red arrow). You will need use a small screwdriver to unlock the spade connection inside the connector.

12 Plug the wire you removed from the number 3 connector into the white connector (red arrow). Make sure you insert it in the right direction and it locks into place.

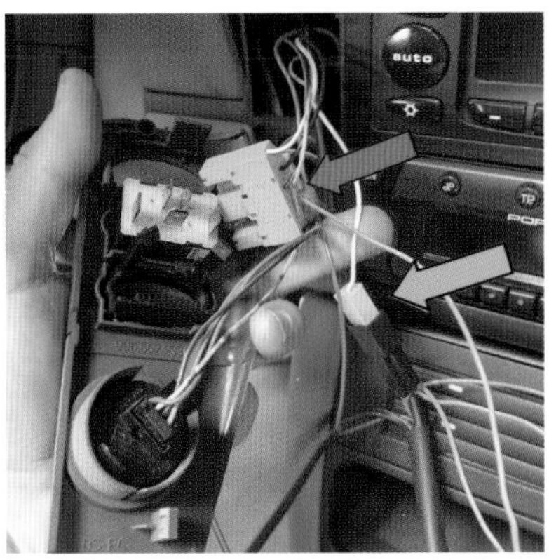

13 Plug the white connector into the black harness (green arrow), take the orange wire from the IMS harness and plug it into the number 3 connector on the traction control harness (red arrow).

14 Install the IMS switch into the blank space and install the IMS harness into the switch (green arrow). Plug the traction control connector back into the switch (red arrow). Now pass all of the wires and the control box into the dash through the opening and reinstall the dash plate.

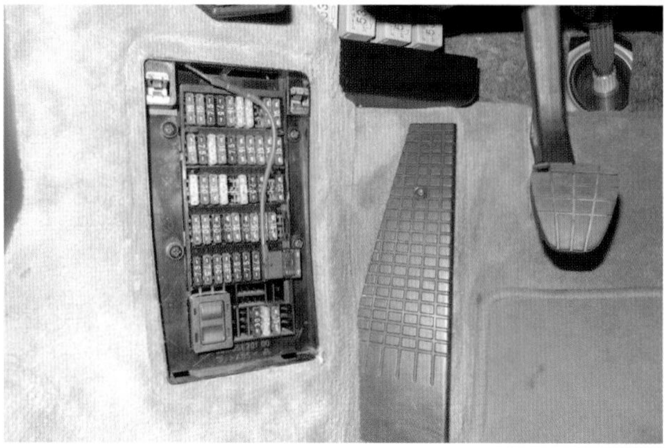

15 Run the red wire down to the fuse panel. You can remove the carpet around the panel and pass the wire behind it in order to give a cleaner look (see Photo 1 of Project 92). Remove a 7.5 amp fuse from the panel and plug it into the fuse adaptor. Plug the fuse adapter into the space on the panel for the fuse you just removed. Make sure you pick a fuse that is for the accessories and is only powered when the key is in the "on" position. In this photo, you can see that we used fuse E8, which is typically reserved for the Telephone Info System, which I don't think many people have installed in their car.

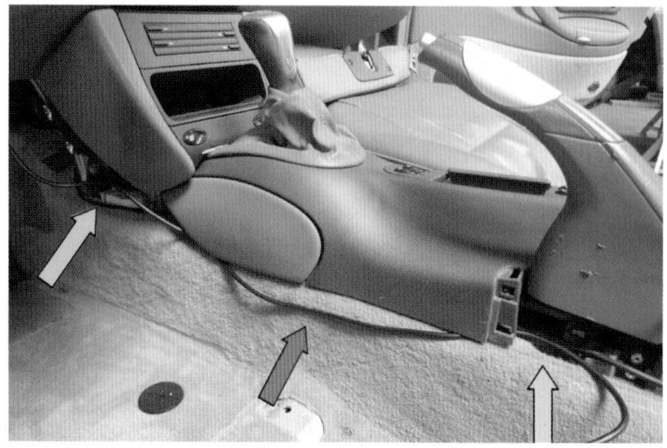

16 Run the main harness back toward the rear of the car, to the area where it is going to pass into the engine compartment. Remove the center console panel (green arrow), and tuck the wire up under the center console (red arrow) and inside the parking brake area (yellow arrow). The seat has been removed in this photo for additional clarity. Both the parking brake handle and center console panel simply pull straight off.

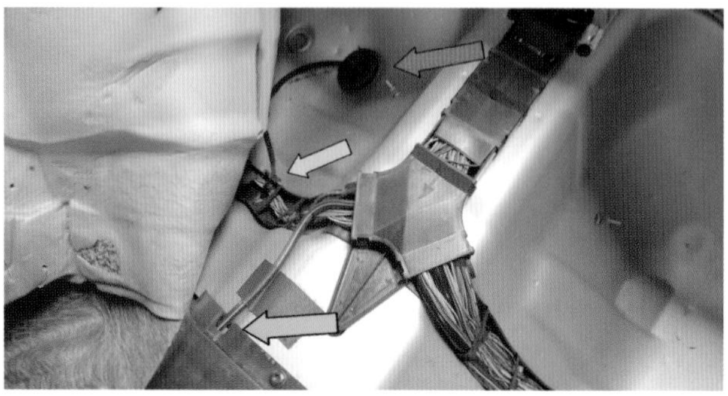

17 On our cabriolet, I ran the wires up and under the rear passenger seat. The harness enters from the center tunnel area (green arrow), runs along the existing wiring loom (yellow arrow), and out through the body plug under the seat (red arrow). Make sure to seal up the plug with some silicone sealant after passing the wire through.

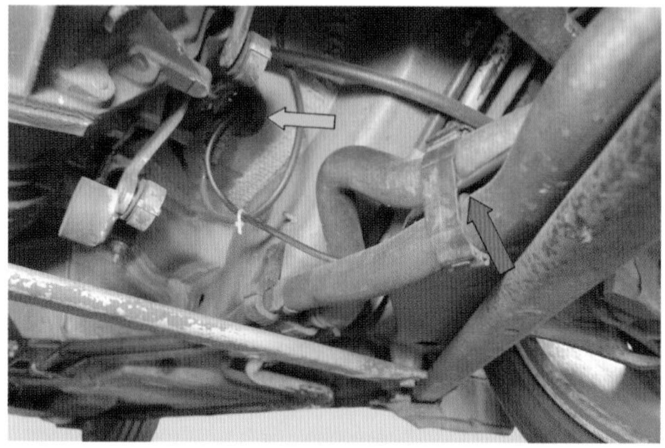

18 Run the wire out of the transmission tunnel (green arrow) and down between the heater hoses (red arrow).

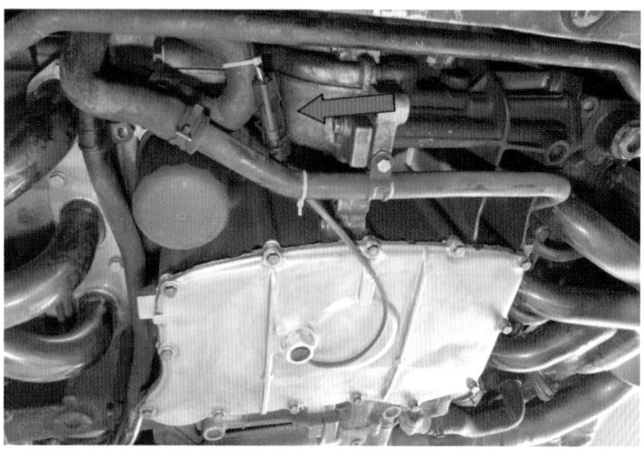

19 Route the MCD wire safely back to the connector to the harness (red arrow) and connect the two pieces. Make sure they click together, which ensures protection against water and road grime. Also be sure you route it in a manner that will keep it away from any moving parts and so it does not hang down below the engine. Take care to use enough cable ties to securely fasten the wiring harness along its path.

20 Here is the IMS Switch installed in the dash. Don't forget to refill your engine with oil before testing out the IMS Guardian!

PROJECT 12
Installing a Deep-Sump Kit

Time / Tab / Talent: 3 hours / $300 /

Tools: Dremel tool

Applicable Years: All

Tinware: Deep-sump kit, pickup tube extension

Tip: Add the pickup tube extension for maximum protection

Performance Gain: Better engine protection in high g-force cornering

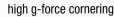

Comp Modification: Change oil

More Info: http://www.101projects.com/Carrera/12.htm

The older Porsche 911 cars had what is known as a dry-sump oiling system. This meant that excess oil from the engine was removed (scavenged) from the bottom of the sump and stored in a separate oil tank. With a dry-sump system, a significant quantity of oil (approximately 12 quarts) is available to be supplied to the engine at all times. With a wet-sump system, the oil is stored in an area below the engine. A traditional wet sump, similar to the one used on the Boxster engine, doesn't hold as much oil as a dry sump and also may suffer from scavenging issues when the car corners and oil is sloshed from one side of the sump to the other.

As a result of the lower oil capacity of the wet-sump design, it's possible that the 911 Carrera engine may exhibit oil scavenge problems under high-performance track driving. The engine is not likely to see these types of forces when driving on the street. One solution to help the problem is to lower the sump and increase its capacity. A deep-sump kit extends the bottom of the engine and adds about a half a quart to the total capacity. That half quart may be just what you need in order to save your engine if your 911 is experiencing high g-forces on the racetrack. Installation is fairly easy and can be performed on the engine with it still installed in the car. Follow the instructions shown in the photos as well as the ones included with the kit.

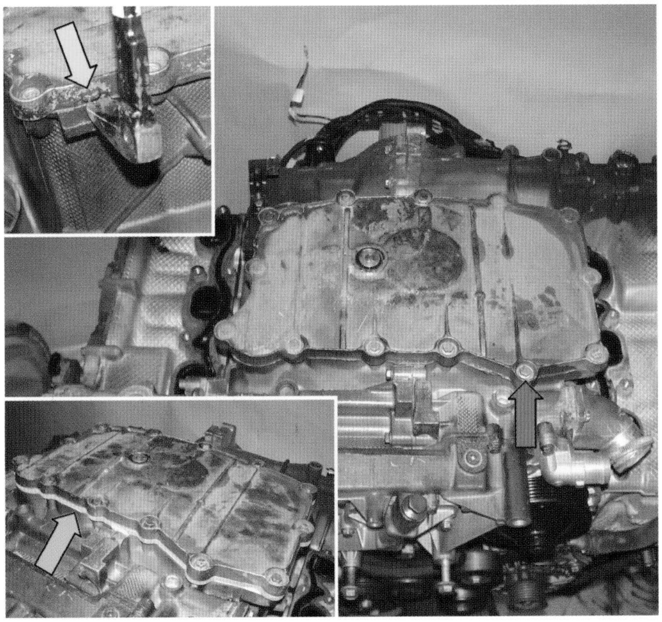

1 After emptying the engine of oil, the first step is to remove the lower engine sump cover. A total of 13 bolts hold the sump cover to the engine (red arrow shows one). Remove all but two of these. Loosen the last two bolts but don't remove them. They will keep the sump plate from falling on you when you pry it free. Have a large drip tray handy when you remove the sump cover, as there will some excess oil that will drip out of the engine. To remove the sump cover, use a pry bar between the two bosses located near the oil filter (yellow arrow). Some light tapping with a rubber mallet might help as well. Do not place any tools on the mounting surfaces of the sump plate or the engine. The engine sump plate sandwiches itself between the case and the stock lower sump as shown by the green arrow.

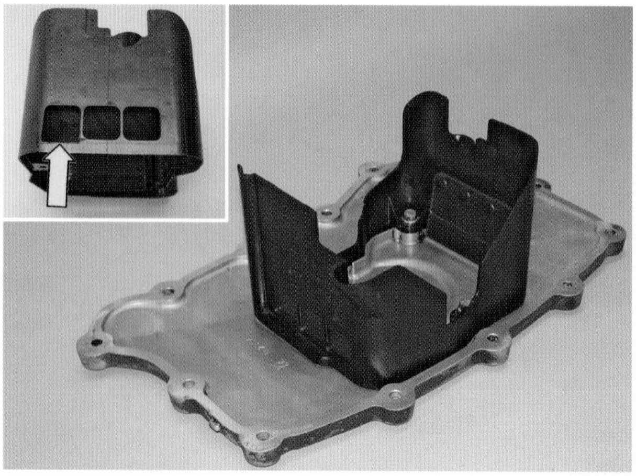

2 Remove the black plastic baffle from the bottom sump plate. The six "windows" on the baffle should be enlarged slightly in order to gain the maximum performance from your additional sump. Using a Dremel tool, carefully modify the baffle, removing about ⅛ inch from the bottom of each window. The inset photo shows the first window modified (yellow arrow). Only take off a small amount of material here—you must leave enough material on the bottom so that the flaps will still seat on the raised bottom lip.

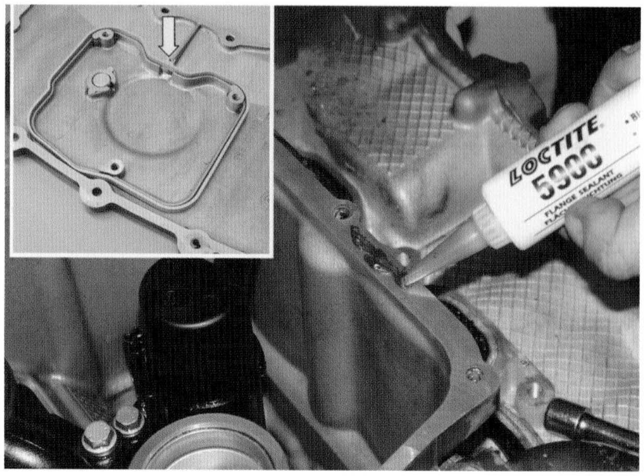

3 Install the baffle spacer onto the bottom of the sump plate. Make sure that the two small tabs line up with the fin that is cast into the bottom of the sump plate (yellow arrow). Install the plastic baffle onto the spacer using the bolts supplied with the kit. Use some Loctite Threadlocker on the screws as you install them. Do not use any gasket sealant on the baffle extension. When you remove the old sump, be sure to carefully clean both the engine side and the sump plate so that you can reseal the sandwich plate upon installation. After meticulously cleaning the two mounting surfaces, I used Loctite 5900 to seal the flange surfaces.

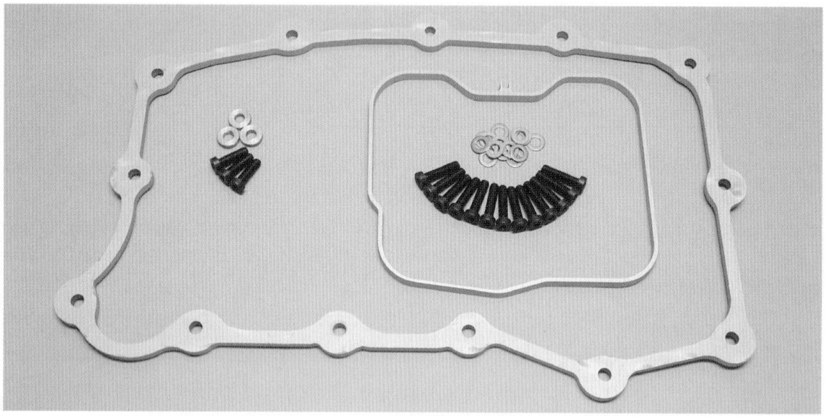

4 Shown here is the Brey-Krause deep-sump kit that we used for this project. This high-quality kit is available from PelicanParts.com and comes complete with the sump spacer, the baffle spacer, and the appropriate mounting hardware.

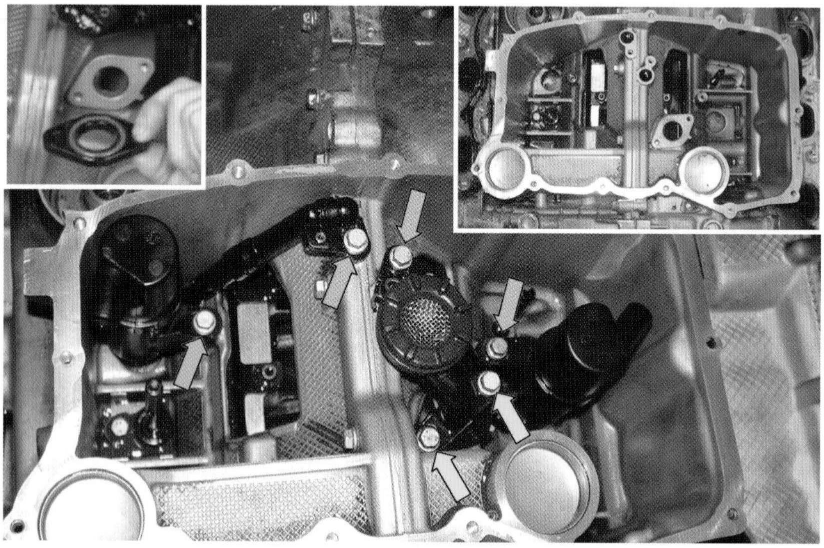

5 Shown here are the lower sump air-oil separators, which help to de-foam the oil in the bottom of the sump. They are held on with two bolts each (green arrows), but seldom need to be replaced. I would recommend that you replace them if you had some type of major engine failure at one time that might have contaminated them (inset photo shows them removed). For the installation of this kit, I chose to add the oil pickup tube spacer, manufactured by LN Engineering (inset photo). This spacer lowers the oil pickup tube all the way down to the bottom of the sump when the deep-sump kit is installed. This allows the maximum amount of oil to be sucked up by the oil pumps (cost is approximately $30). The yellow arrows point to the attachment points for the oil pickup tube.

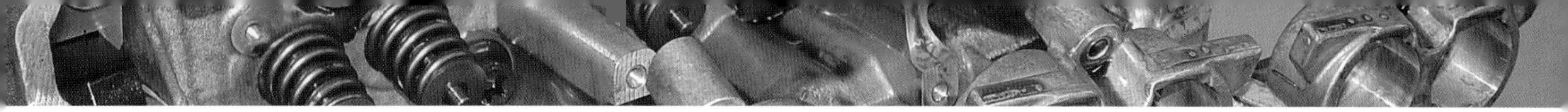

PROJECT 13

Common 911 Carrera Engine Problems

Time / Tab / Talent: As long as it takes / $0–$10,000 /

Tip: Don't wait until your engine blows up to make some necessary upgrades

Tools: Varies

Performance Gain: Long, reliable engine life

Applicable Years: All

Comp Modification: Clutch replacement

Tinware: Replacement upgrades

More Info: http://www.101projects.com/Carrera/13.htm

Using the expertise gained from years of designing and building engines, Porsche developed what is known as the M96 engine for the introduction of the Boxster in 1996. The horizontally opposed engine was developed with a throwback to the traditionally air-cooled motors, having kept the opposing cylinder or boxer layout. The engine was designed from the outset with the goal of providing a common platform for both the Boxster and the upcoming Porsche Carrera. The motor was indeed scalable, encompassing a displacement that ranged from the 2.5-liter Boxster motor all the way up to 3.8 liters at the end of its production run.

The M96 (and subsequent similar M97) water-cooled engine is definitely a strong-performing engine; however, along the stages of its development, it has suffered from some design deficiencies that have been identified and corrected by Porsche over the 11-year lifespan of the engine. It's not uncommon to find a car listed for sale with "new factory engine recently installed" in the advertisement. No one but Porsche knows exactly how many engines were replaced under its recently discontinued engine exchange program. However, simply swapping out a broken engine for another one does not address known weaknesses in the engine due to design deficiencies. The purpose of this project is to identify some of the problem areas of the engine and offer up solutions on how to fix and/or prevent any damage from happening to your engine.

Rear main seal leaks. When the M96 engine first came out, it was perhaps most known for its rear main seal (RMS) leaks. While some of the RMS problems were probably actually intermediate shaft cover leaks (see next section), there were definitely some problems with the seals on the early cars. For the most part this was a "cosmetic" issue, as the leaks did not tend to affect performance, unless they became so severe that they began to affect the proper operation of the clutch. But many engines were torn apart and/or replaced by Porsche under warranty due to this problem, because when you pay $75,000 for a high-performance sports car, you expect it not to leak.

It's not really 100 percent clear what the causes the leaky RMSs. One cause may be the fact that the crankshaft has insufficient support on the rear end. It also may be caused by the fact that the crankshaft carrier support is only pinned minimally in one plane to the outer case. This can lead to shuffling of the carrier—shuffle pinning the crankshaft carrier as is commonly done when prepping an early 911 engine for the track can help the problem.

The seal has been updated to a 997 "Cayenne-style" part number since the engine was originally introduced, and for the most part, the engines no longer leak from this area when this new and improved seal is installed. If you find that your engine is leaking from the RMS (also known as the flywheel seal), then simply install a new one while adding a little bit of Curil-T sealant to help keep it dry (see Photo 10 of Project 45).

Intermediate shaft bearing failures. The intermediate shaft (IMS) bearing is probably the most troublesome of all of the M96/M97 engine problems. The IMS bearing supports the intermediate shaft on the flywheel end of the motor. Porsche designed these motors using a sealed ball bearing that is pressed into the intermediate shaft. These types of bearings are typically used in devices like copy machines and other machinery used in dry conditions. In theory, the area where Porsche designed the bearing to sit is supposed to be dry. However, after years of use within the engine, it would appear that oil and contaminants from the engine seep past the bearing seal, wash out the original lubricant, and become trapped inside. The result is that the bearing now operates in a less-than-ideal environment and begins to wear prematurely. When the bearing wears out, the timing chains on the engine may disengage, and the engine will quickly self-destruct. When the bearing does fail, foreign object debris from the bearing circulates throughout the engine, causing further damage to other areas in the engine.

On the early cars, Porsche also used a center bolt to secure the IMS bearing that was too weak and sometimes snapped. If this bolt breaks, then the intermediate shaft begins to float around in the bottom of the engine, and you can soon experience catastrophic engine failure.

This area is also highly prone to leaks. The seal around the intermediate shaft cover can leak, and it has since been updated and redesigned to prevent leakage. In addition, the three bolts that hold the intermediate shaft cover are through holes that exit into the cavity of the engine case. You must coat these bolts when reinstalling them in order to prevent oil from leaking out through the bolt holes. In general, if this area is leaking, it may indeed be a sign that your intermediate shaft is failing and you should inspect it immediately.

The good news is that the IMS bearing problems are fixable on many cars, thanks in part to a retrofit kit that can be installed with the engine still in the car. See Project 14 for full instructions on how to update your engine.

Cylinder liner cracks. In an effort to reduce costs during production, Porsche utilized a type of insert-mold casting process to directly incorporate Lokasil cylinder liners into the case. While this is a neat way to reduce the total number of parts used in the engine, this design basically casts a wearable part into the engine case. There is no factory replacement for the liners; when they wear, the factory expects you to buy a new engine case. In addition, the design of the cylinder liners allows them to "float" within an area filled with coolant.

Excess vibration and twisting from the normal operation of the engine appears to be causing some cracking in these liners, resulting in a small chunk of the liner breaking off. This "D-chunk" problem ironically seems to occur mostly in gently driven cars. 911 Carreras that are driven hard at the track or on the street do not tend to see this type of damage. At least with respect to the track cars, one theory is that these cars tend to have their oil changed much more often. The problem affects mostly the 2.5 Boxster and Carrera 3.4 engines. When this failure happens, you will see oil and coolant begin to mix together or a slight unexplained coolant loss.

If your engine experiences this failure, it can be rebuilt by installing LN Engineering's Nikasil liners. They take your old case, machine out the cracked or damaged Lokasil liners, and install an aluminum Nickies insert, which is stronger and more reliable than the factory cast-in liner. In addition, with the installation of the liners it's fairly easy to increase the bore of the cylinders, which translates into increased displacement and more horsepower. If you go this route, you will also need to use some aftermarket pistons and perhaps update the software in your digital motor electronics (DME) to accommodate the larger displacement.

Engine casting porosity. As mentioned in the previous section, Porsche used a new cost-effective method to cast most of the oil and water cooling passages directly into the engine case. This reduced the total part count for the engine and also helped reduce assembly time and production cost. Unfortunately, the advanced casting technique seems to have led to a number of engine cases experiencing what has been called "engine porosity." There is not a lot of information available on this problem, but it seems to be related to problems with the initial casting process.

In some cases, there appeared to have been a leak through the internal crankcase walls. The process of pouring the molten aluminum must be tightly controlled, otherwise pockets of air forming in the aluminum may result. Most of the time, postcasting inspections will reveal these flaws, but apparently some were still manufactured into running engines. The result is that oil and water became mixed within these engines. This resulted in coolant being found within the oil (turning it a milky brown color) or oil being found inside the coolant tank.

The expansion and contraction of the engine due to the heat of normal operation can expose this problem as well. I have also heard of engines that simply wept a slow bead of oil right through the walls of the engine case when running. Unfortunately, there's nothing that can be done to fix this problem, short of scrapping the engine. The good news is that most of these problems were discovered on the cars when they were new, and the engines were since replaced under warranty.

Chain tensioner failures. There's been some chatter lately about chain tensioners failing on some of the M96 motors. If your car is noisy on startup and then suddenly quiets down, it may indicate a problem with your chain tensioners. Porsche updated the design of the tensioners in 2000 (TSB Group 1 NR 8/00) and replaced them with an improved design. I recommend that you update and replace your chain tensioners if they are the older style. (See Project 16 for more information on how to identify and replace them.)

Cylinder head cracks. In general, the cylinder heads are pretty well designed on the M96 engine. However, on some 3.2, 3.4, and 3.6 engines, small cracks can sometimes develop around the seats of exhaust valves and extend to the spark plug hole. The mounting point for the cam follower housing is also a weak point. Often these cracks can lead to coolant and oil mixing together. This is not an uncommon problem with automotive cylinder heads in general and can often be repaired by a skilled machine shop that can weld aluminum heads.

Oil system inadequacy. The air-cooled predecessor to the M96 engine incorporated a dry-sump system that was designed to keep a significant amount of oil in reserve for extended performance driving. With the introduction of the M96 engine, Porsche moved away from that design, primarily due to the high cost of implementing a separate dry-sump system. The M96/M97 motors instead were designed with a compromise system, which has an oil sump built into the bottom of the engine—a kind of hybrid between a dedicated dry-sump system and a typical wet sump. As a result of the lower oil-holding capacity and other factors, the M96/M97 engines tend to suffer more from oil starvation problems, particularly during high performance driving.

There are a few things you can do to protect against oil starvation problems. First, be sure that your oil level is always at the high-level mark of your dipstick. The M96/M97 engine doesn't have a vast extra supply of oil, so if you're a quart low, it's a significant amount. Second, you can also add in a deep-sump kit (see Project 12), which will expand the oil capacity of the sump by about a half a quart. Finally, you can install an Accusump oil accumulator system that will protect against unexpected oil pressure drops (see Photo 4 of Project 98).

In addition to the standard issues associated with the nontraditional sump system, the flapper windows on the bottom of the engine are manufactured out of plastic and can break off inside the sump and clog the oil pickup tube. This leads to oil starvation and complete engine failure. The solution is to remove the bottom sump and inspect the oil control windows (see Project 12) and replace them if they are missing or damaged. You can also add aftermarket stainless steel windows for added protection.

As mentioned previously in Project 2, I do not care for Porsche's standard recommended oil change interval of 15,000 miles. The oil in engines tends to become contaminated with fuel and coolant, particularly as the cars age and seals and piston rings begin to wear. I generally like to run a thicker oil and change it every 3,000 to 5,000 miles. Keeping the oil fresh may help prevent some IMS bearing issues and generally prolong the life of your engine.

1 This photo shows the flywheel end of an M96 motor. This particular motor is a 3.4-liter crate motor from Porsche that has been updated with the latest and greatest improvements from the factory. The intermediate shaft (IMS) has the updated bolt (yellow arrow), but the issue of the intermediate shaft failures has still not been completely addressed in this redesign. Although these updated engines tend to suffer from fewer problems than do the early ones, there is still a risk of IMS bearing failure. The rear main seal shown here is the updated and improved one that should not leak.

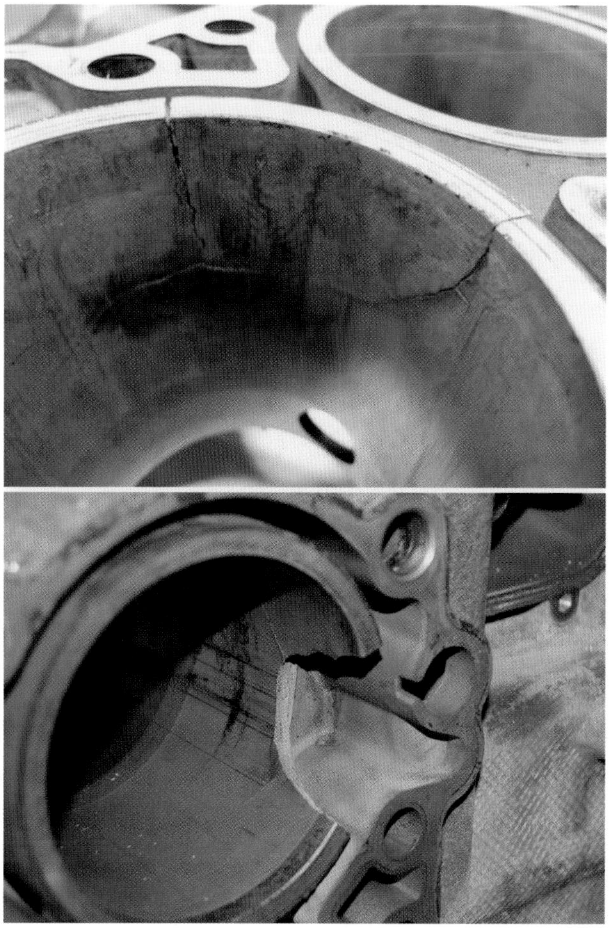

2 This is the infamous "D-Chunk" problem that happens sometimes on these motors. Occurring almost exclusively with the two cylinders in the middle, it is theorized that excess twisting and vibration causes cracks to occur in the cylinder walls. Found mostly on the Boxster 2.5 and the Carrera 3.4 engines, this problem is less pronounced on the later engine because they have thicker cylinder walls. The solution is to machine the case to accept cylinder liners (next photo).

Connecting rod bolt failures. The connecting rods that are used on the 911 Carrera are forged out of steel and utilize what is known as a cracked-rod design. This means that the rods are forged and machined, and then broken along preset stress points. Then the bearings are installed and the rods are put back together again. This cracked-rod design is cheaper to manufacture, and the rod bolts don't need to have integrated "guide" pins as part of their design (like the rod bolts used on the older air-cooled engines).

Unfortunately, it would appear that the rod bolt diameter may be too small for the large loads that these engines place on the rods. A number of recent failures in some early high-mileage engines have hinted that the rod bolts are too small and may be a failure point for the connecting rod.

The failure occurs when the engine is consistently revved at the high end of its rpm range. The stock rod bolts are designed to stretch and permanently deform when tightened down to their final torque values. At rpm's of 6,700 or higher, the rotating mass on the end of each rod (namely the piston and the mass of the rod itself) has a tendency to stretch the

rod bolt further. Repeated stretching of the rod bolts causes them to deform and loosen up, which can result in rod separation and complete engine failure.

Unfortunately, due to the cracked-rod design, the connecting rods cannot easily be rebuilt. The solution is to install aftermarket connecting rods that can accommodate larger, race-proven fasteners like the ones available from Automotive Racing Products.

Variocam solenoids. It's not uncommon for the variocam solenoids to fail on one side, which will result in an uneven or loopy idle. Moisture can get into the mechanism causing it to corrode and eventually fail. The DME computer should easily be able to detect this failure and trigger a check engine light (CEL).

Paper oil filters. The oil filter system on the 911 Carrera is a bit lame in my opinion. Using the stock paper filter can lead to a disintegration of the filter, which can then clog the oil passages of the engine. Although this is a relatively rare problem, I have heard of it happening with cheaper-brand oil filters. Stick to the good-quality brands and also consider upgrading to the LN Engineering screw-on oil filter upgrade (see Project 2).

Air-oil separator failures. The air-oil separator is an emissions device that draws vapors from the engine crankcase and then sends them back into the intake manifold. When this unit fails, the result is oil sucked out of the engine and into the intake. While the air-oil separator will not cause immediate mechanical damage to your engine, it may make it smoke tremendously and/or run roughly (see Project 9).

Oil change intervals. The best recommendation I can make to any modern Porsche owner is to change the oil more often, say every 5,000 miles, as well as use a minimum 5w40 viscosity oil. On cars not equipped with Variocam Plus (up through 2005), use of a 15w50 or 20w50 provides a much higher film strength, which will improve internal bearing life considerably.

Low-temperature thermostat. Also useful is the LN Engineering low-temperature thermostat (see Project 35). This specially designed thermostat starts to open at 160 degrees Fahrenheit instead of 187 degrees Fahrenheit for the factory unit. Keeping the oil cool is key to keeping it fresh, and the lower operating temperatures also help give you a bit more horsepower, too.

3 Here is a fully repaired M96 engine with the LN Engineering Nickies liners installed. The case is prepared by machining out the old liner and completely removing the section that floats in the water jackets. Then, a Nikasil cylinder is press-fit into the case in its place. It's a clever solution to the irreplaceable case problem. The case itself must be a good, rebuildable core and have no major issues (no major damage, no case porosity issues). In addition to replacing the liners with new and improved ones, the process allows you to increase the displacement of the engine at the same time.

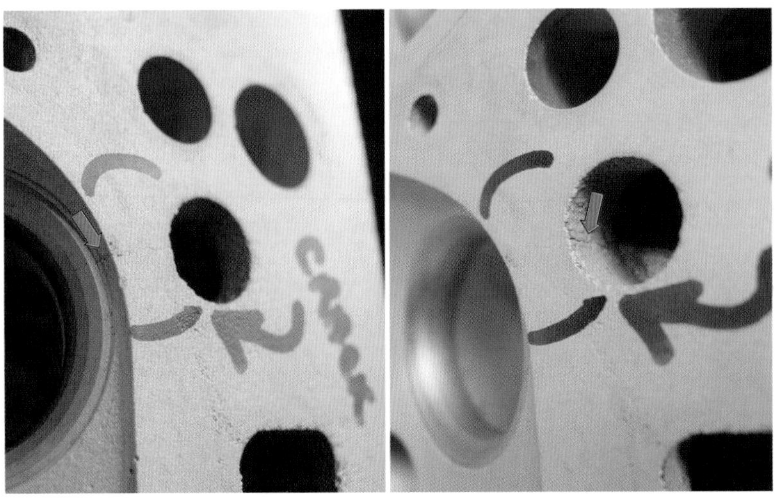

4 Although it may not look like much, this crack is enough to cause a lot of problems. Cracks like these can cause oil/coolant to mix, resulting in contamination of the coolant and/or oil. Cylinder head cracks are common among water-cooled cars and can sometimes be repaired by grinding down the head and then rewelding it.

PROJECT 14
Intermediate Shaft Bearing Upgrade

Time / Tab / Talent: 5 hours / $150–$600 /

Tools: Removal, installation, and camshaft timing tools

Applicable Years: 1998–2005

Tinware: IMS bearing upgrade kit

More Info: http://www.101projects.com/Carrera/14.htm

Tip: Perform this upgrade when doing a clutch job

Performance Gain: Years of reliable running

Comp Modification: Clutch replacement

The M96/M97 Carrera engine has had a checkered past when it comes to reliability (see Project 13). One of the weaknesses identified in recent years by Porsche has been the intermediate shaft (IMS) bearing, which supports the intermediate shaft on the flywheel end of the motor (see Photo 6). Porsche designed these motors using a sealed ball bearing that is pressed into the intermediate shaft (Photo 12). These types of bearings are typically used in devices like copy machines and other machinery used in dry conditions. In theory, the area where Porsche designed the bearing to sit is supposed to be dry. However, after years of use within the engine, it would appear that oil and contaminants from the engine seep past the bearing seal, wash out the original lubricant, and become trapped inside. The result is that the bearing now operates in a less-than-ideal environment and begins to wear prematurely. When the bearing wears out, the timing chains on the engine may disengage, and the engine will quickly self-destruct. When the bearing does begin to deteriorate, foreign object debris from the bearing circulates throughout the engine, causing damage to other areas in the engine. This appears to be one of the most common failure mechanisms present with both the Boxster and 911 Carrera engine.

The center bolt that holds the entire assembly can also fail. If this bolt breaks, it will immediately allow the intermediate shaft to float, and the engine will skip timing. This will result in the complete destruction of the engine in a very short period of time (seconds). Typically, a deteriorating IMS bearing will also cause the center stud to weaken and break. The stud has a groove cut into it axially to allow for a sealing O-ring to seal to the outer cover. This groove causes a stress concentration to occur and promotes the failure of the stud. The solution is to pull out the bearing and replace the stud with a new one that is stronger and manufactured without any grooves (see a comparison of the old and new studs in Photo 5).

So how do you know if you have a problem? There are several warning signs. When you first start your car, you may hear a loud rattling noise that goes away after about 10 seconds or so. When you accelerate, you may also hear this noise, too. This noise is the sound of the chains or the bearing rattling around in the engine because the bearing has deteriorated—the engine is soon on its way to skipping a tooth on the sprocket and costing you thousands of dollars. To detect the early stages of a failure, listen for a sound that is similar to what a throw-out bearing, water pump, or a belt idler pulley sounds like when the ball bearings begin to fail. If you have the car up in the air and running, you can listen carefully and you should be able to isolate the noise to the area of the IMS bearing (bottom rear of the engine, near where it mounts to the transmission), especially if you use a diagnostic stethoscope.

Signs of a failing IMS bearing can also be found by inspecting the oil filter. Shiny metallic debris from the balls used within the bearing itself may travel through the oil system and become trapped in the oil filter as well as small bits of black plastic from the seal on the bearing (see Photo 1). During a routine clutch job, you can also simply remove the IMS cover and take a closer look at the bearing itself (lock and check the camshafts prior to removing the cover though—see instructions below). If the center shaft is wobbly, or the center of the bearing doesn't spin freely, then it's probably on its way to failure.

Another way to check the engine is with the factory PST2 tool, or the Durametric tool (see Project 20). You can compare the deviations in the timing between the two camshafts to see if they vary widely, particularly when revving the engine (see Photo 2). Sometimes a failing IMS bearing will also trigger a check engine light (CEL) warning on your dash, as the car's computer realizes that there is a significant deviation between the two camshaft readings.

WHAT DOES A BEARING FAILURE LOOK LIKE?

If you take a look at Photo 1, you will see the remains of an IMS bearing from an engine with only 31,000 miles on it. Pulling off the IMS bearing cover revealed that the bearing had completely disintegrated and there wasn't much left. This engine was running and the car was driving, but every few seconds it would make a horrible screeching noise. Sometimes it would run for quite a few minutes with no sound at all. Hard to believe, considering that the bearing was completely destroyed.

So what can you do with an engine that has had this much bearing damage? The engine was still running when I took the bearing out, so I know there didn't appear to be any damage to the cylinder heads from the timing chains being out of sync. The oil filter appeared to do its job of blocking most of the bearing debris in the oil. The only thing that you can do when you have a situation like this is to clean everything out very carefully, replace the bearing, and button the engine back up.

WHAT CAN BE DONE TO FIX OR PREVENT A FAILURE?

Luckily, a few solutions are available. First, I recommend that you change your oil every 5,000 miles or sooner and use a higher viscosity motor oil that has additional anti-wear additives. Use Porsche approved 5w40 viscosity motor oils, preferably one that carries an API SJ-SL rating. Use of a 0w40 viscosity should be limited to colder climates in winter months, where cold starts are regularly below freezing, for added start-up protection. Also consider using an oil with more anti-wear additives (like Zn, P, or moly extreme). Recent regulatory changes in the United States have caused oil companies to revise their formulations of oil and reduce the amount of anti-wear components in them. The reasoning behind this is the belief that these components contribute to premature deterioration of the catalytic converters. I'm not so sure I agree with that premise however. The solution to this problem is to make sure that you run motor oil with the proper anti-wear formulations and change your oil often.

Also curious is the fact that cars that are driven tamely seem to have more problems than cars that are driven aggressively. 911 Carrera engines that are used at the track are known to have very few problems relating to the bearing, whereas 911s driven by "little old ladies" tend to show the most damage. The track-day Carrera bearing longevity may be explained by the fact that these cars often have their oil changed after every trip to the track.

The best solution to the problem is to replace the bearing prior to its failure. Porsche Club of America tech advisor, Scott Slauson from Softronic (see Project 25), pioneered a procedure that allows you to replace the bearing with the engine still in the car. Building upon that procedure, LN Engineering and Pelican Parts have both developed bearing replacement kits to swap out the troublesome original bearing.

WHICH BEARING IS INSIDE YOUR ENGINE?

The first step in replacing the bearing is to figure out which one you have in your engine. Three variations were installed over the years. Early cars typically have a large double-row bearing that has a snap clip inside the bearing. Porsche later went to a single-row bearing design when the timing chain design was modified (see Photo 7 for a comparison of the two). Then, around model year 2006, Porsche installed

1 Here are the remains of a destroyed intermediate shaft (IMS) bearing after we removed it from our M96 engine. It fell apart in my hand while I was taking it out of the removal tool. We still didn't find the remains of one of the bearing rubber seals anywhere. Sometimes you can see the signs of an IMS bearing failure. The upper left inset shows what the oil filter looked like when we removed it from our engine. You can clearly see small flakes of metal in the filter. It looks like the filter did a pretty good job of blocking the particles; since this was caught in time, we anticipate that the engine should be fine. Lots of debris ended up getting caught in the oil sump and pickup screen, which is a good thing. If your bearing is trashed when you remove it, be sure to pull the sump off the bottom of the engine, clean it out thoroughly, and replace the two air-oil separators located in the sump area (see Project 12).

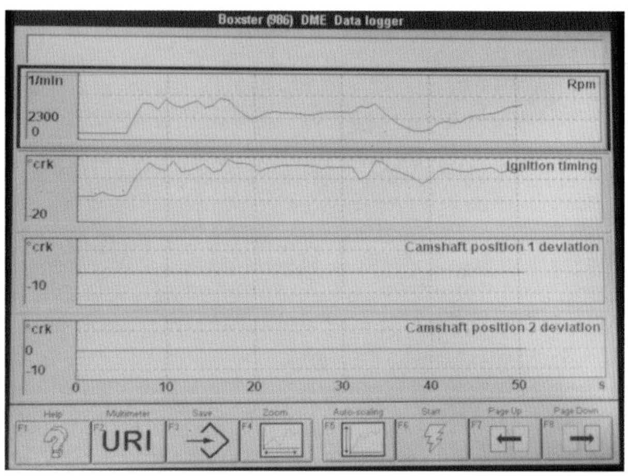

2 Sometimes you can detect a failing IMS bearing by running a test showing camshaft deviations. Using the Durametric tool, or a PST-2, you can set up the screen to log camshaft deviation as a function of ignition timing and rpm. Significant variations between the left and right camshaft banks can be an indicator of trouble with the bearing. In this graph, the deviation is almost zero, which is perfect and does not indicate a problem.

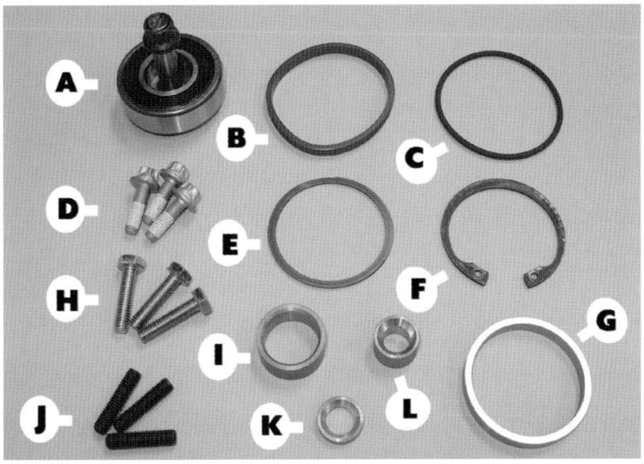

3 This photo shows the parts contained in the Pelican Parts Intermediate Shaft Bearing Replacement Kit. **A:** Improved center bearing bolt, replacement intermediate shaft bearing, center bolt O-ring, center bolt nut. **B:** Updated 3-groove flange seal. **C:** O-ring for older style flange seal. **D:** Three new micro-encapsulated cover bolts. **E:** Spiroloc snap ring (for engine with double-row bearings). **F:** Snap ring (for engine with single-row bearings. **G:** Outer race spacer (for engine with double-row bearings). **H:** Three M6 × 25mm installation helper bolts. **I:** Inner race spacer (for engine with double row bearings. **J:** Three M6 × 1 × 25mm set screws. **K:** Short center bolt spacer (for engine with double-row bearings). **L:** Long center bolt spacer (for engine with single-row bearing).

a third version that is not replaceable. The supposed cut-off on engine numbers is listed in the Porsche factory technical bulletins, but unfortunately, these numbers are not 100 percent accurate, so you need to look at the bearing housing on your engine in order to be 100 percent sure as to which bearing you have installed.

Porsche's electronic parts catalog lists the following engine numbers as the cutoffs for the various engines:

Up to and including engine # M 661 14164, Carrera 996 3.4-liter

From engine # M 661 14165, Carrera 996 3.4-liter

However, as mentioned previously, practical experience has determined that these numbers are not 100 percent correct. Porsche replaced and/or repaired a lot of engines over the years, and as a result there are a lot of engines out there where parts are mixed and matched. For example, the 3.4 Porsche factory motor that I installed in my 3.4-liter conversion has the very-late-style IMS bearing with the 22mm center nut (see Photo 15) but is missing some other upgrades that had been implemented over the years.

The only way to know certainly is to remove your transmission and look. The double-row version of the intermediate shaft was the first version used on these engines and will almost always be found on the early cars. The intermediate shaft cover for the double-row bearing is characterized by a shallow dish; the single-row bearings have a much deeper dish, as shown in Photo 7.

PELICAN PARTS REPLACEMENT KIT

The Pelican Parts IMS bearing replacement kit is shown in Photo 3 and contains everything that you need to perform the replacement in either a single- or dual-row bearing engine. The Pelican kit uses the same bearing that Porsche used when

4 Here are two side views of the Pelican replacement kit: double-row configuration on the left with the spacers in place, single-row on the right. These covers have the updated brown seal (see Photo 8).

originally building the engines, but the kit incorporates a stronger seal on the outside of the bearing. The kit is designed so that the bearing replacement can be performed during a routine clutch replacement (see Project 45). Changing out the bearing during each clutch job will ensure that the bearing is fresh and not wearing prematurely. As stated in the previous section, the failure mode of this bearing is not well known; if it's swapped out and replaced every 30,000–45,000 miles when the clutch is renewed, it should protect your engine from problems.

The kit uses a single-row bearing, just like the later-style Porsche design. For engines that originally had a double-row bearing installed, two spacers are included with the kit (Photo 4). These spacers fill the space that was normally occupied by the double-row bearing. In addition to the bearing replacement, the kit also includes a stronger center stud. Instead of having the O-ring integrated into the stud, the O-ring is placed in a V-shaped sandwich on the outside surface of the bearing housing cover. The Pelican kit is available online at Pelican Parts.com.

LN ENGINEERING RETROFIT KIT

The LN Engineering IMS Retrofit Kit is also an easy-to-install upgrade kit that can be installed with the engine still in the car and provides almost bulletproof reliability to this critical component. This kit costs about $600 and is available online from PelicanParts.com. The upgrade kit incorporates a custom ceramic hybrid bearing (see Photo 5) featuring precision Japanese-made tool steel races and genuine USA-made Timken sintered silicon nitride ultra-low friction roller balls. This bearing, combined with a beefier center stud and a custom-machined housing, ensures that the intermediate shaft problems inherent in the stock design are mitigated. The engine can be upgraded during a routine clutch job and is fairly easy to install thanks to the installation tools designed by LN Engineering specifically for this task.

WHICH KIT TO USE?

I designed the Pelican Parts replacement bearing kit in order to fill a gap within the do-it-yourself (DIY) market. This kit is designed to replace the factory bearing with a very similarly manufactured bearing (with an improved seal and updated center bolt). I recommend that the bearing be swapped out each time a clutch replacement is performed (30,000–45,000 miles). The outer seal is not removed on the kit, instead an improved seal is installed, which should offer longer life than the factory original. Replacement bearings, O-rings,

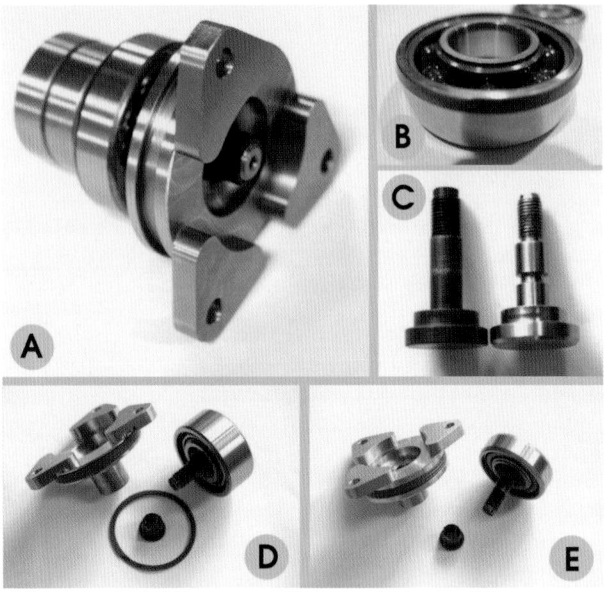

5 This photo array shows the various elements that comprise the LN Engineering upgrade kit for the IMS bearing. **A:** This version of the retrofit kit is installed during the rebuild process and requires the engine be apart. **B:** The improved ceramic coated ball bearing. **C:** Stronger center bolt (left) when compared to the thinner and weaker OEM shoulder bolt (right). **D:** Upgrade kit for early engines with the double-row bearing. **E:** Upgrade kit for the later engines with the single-row bearing.

6 Here's a neat side/cutaway view of the IMS and the LN Engineering IMS retrofit kit installed. This photo shows the IMS upgrade kit installed into a display engine with one half of the engine case missing. Shown here are the IMS timing chain (blue arrow), the IMS gear (yellow arrow), the IMS bearing cover/housing (red arrow), the housing-to-crankcase seal (orange arrow), one of the three bolts that attach the housing to the case (purple arrow), and the engine case (white arrow). The bearing stud and nut are also shown installed in the center of the housing.

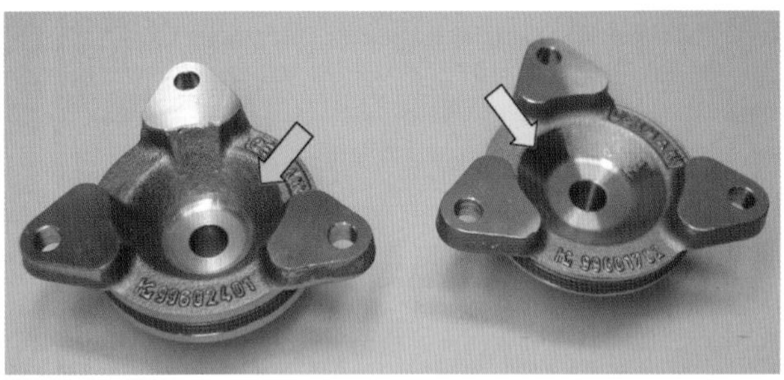

7 Shown here are two late-style IMS covers. The cover on the left has a deep dish and is used in engines that originally had a single-row bearing. The cover on the right is shallower and is used with engines that originally had a double-row bearing. Unfortunately, the records on which engine used which style of bearing is very spotty, so the only real way you can tell is by removing the transmission and seeing what you have installed in there.

8 The top portion of this photo shows the troublesome O-ring that was found on the early IMS bearing covers. The bottom shows a close-up photograph of the improved three-ridge seal. If you pull off the IMS cover and find that you have the early style, then I highly recommend that you upgrade to this later-style cover.

and parts will be available for customers who have already performed the swap at least once and already have the tools, spacers, and the improved center bolt. The Pelican Parts kit uses the stock intermediate shaft bearing cover as a way to reduce the total cost of the kit, though I recommend if you have the older-style single round gasket cover that you replace this with the newer version from Porsche, which is less likely to leak. While Pelican Parts includes both styles of gaskets in the kit, including a replacement gasket for the older style covers, Porsche no longer supports this part.

The LN Engineering retrofit kit contains a stronger-than-stock center stud, a custom machined intermediate shaft end cover, and a special, custom-manufactured ceramic bearing, which is very expensive but has much longer life under harsh conditions. The LN Engineering kit is considered to be the more robust kit and is designed primarily for shops that are installing the retrofit and need that extra guarantee for their customers. The extended-life ceramic bearing (see Photo 5) is only available at this time with the LN Engineering kit, and its inclusion is responsible for a large portion of the cost difference between the two kits.

BEARING REMOVAL

The bearing is located behind the flywheel of the engine, so the first step you need to do is jack up the car (see Project 1) and remove the transmission (see Project 38). Then, remove the clutch and flywheel from the engine (see Project 45). With the car elevated in the air, drain the oil and remove and inspect the oil filter (see Project 1).

Before doing anything else, you want to remove the camshaft end plugs from your engine (see Photo 2 of Project 16). While it is a very tight fit doing this with the engine in the car, it is doable if you take your time. These plugs cover the camshaft timing marks—you will need to check the timing on the camshafts when you are done with the bearing replacement. If you have a pre-2002 engine, then you only need to remove the plugs on the exhaust camshafts (two plugs total). The exhaust camshafts are located on the bottom of the engine. If you have a 2002 or later engine, then you need to remove all four plugs (intake and exhaust), because you will need to check all four camshafts when you are done. For the 911 Carrera, the plugs for the camshafts that drive cylinders 4–6 should be easily accessible at the front of the engine to the right of the flywheel area. The plugs for cylinders 1–3 need can be accessed from the back of the engine by the exhaust.

With the plugs removed, now remove the three bolts that hold the IMS bearing cover (Photo 9). With the bolts removed, you should be able to shine a flashlight down the

9 It all starts here with the IMS cover, located right under the rear main seal (located behind the clutch and flywheel). Using a 10mm socket, remove the three bolts that secure the IMS cover. There's quite a bit of oil residue on the lower half of the cover, which seems to indicate some leakage from the seal. The inset photo shows a completely destroyed IMS bearing. The outer seal and race are missing. The balls have fallen down in the bearing and are basically just sitting there. This engine was very close to self-destructing: it was wise for the owner to turn it off and not drive it any more. As a result, he may have saved the engine from complete destruction. However, the remains of the bearing have circulated out of this area and down to the engine sump: if any metallic particles got past the filter, then they would have caused damage to the rest of the engine (bearings, etc.).

10 The holes that are used to help secure the IMS cover are through-holes, which means they exit out into the engine case. With the cover bolts removed, rotate the crankshaft until you see metal appear behind each of these holes. The IMS has some large relief holes cut in the big sprocket (see Photo 6). You want to rotate the engine until all of the small little holes here are blocked by metal on the sprocket. This way, none of the set screws will go into one of the larger holes on the sprocket. When you install the set screws, they should firm up just below the surface of the case. If they don't, then make sure you don't keep turning them: you may end up dropping them into your engine case, which will make them very difficult to retrieve later on.

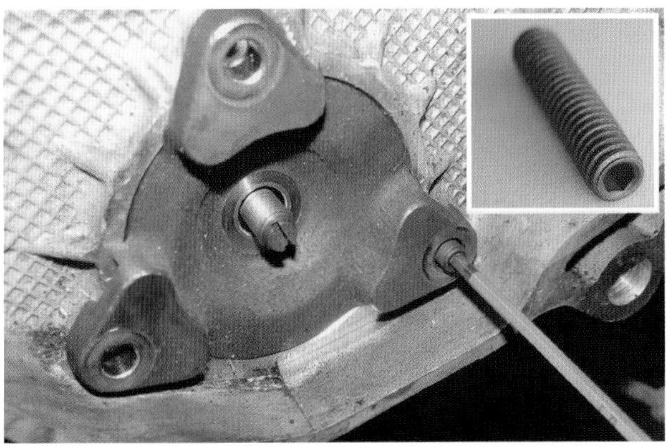

11 After you've lined up the gear behind the cover, insert the set screws into the holes and tighten them down. Don't use the iron-grip-of-death; they only need to be hand-tight. With the set screws in place, you should be able to tap the cover and rotate it back and forth in its bore a bit. The inset photo shows a close-up of the DIN916 M6 1.00 × 25 length set screws included in the Pelican Parts kit that fit perfectly for this task.

12 The yellow arrow shows how the set screw pushes against the sprocket surface and holds it in place. When you're rotating the engine, you want all three set screws to be pushing on the surface of the sprocket, not pushing through one of the open holes (green arrow). Here's another photo of the right side showing how the set screws secure the shaft in place. The screws act just as a friction fit to keep the shaft from moving or rotating while you're working on it.

holes and see the intermediate shaft sprocket inside the engine (Photo 10). What you are looking at is the big sprocket for the intermediate shaft, as shown in Photo 5. What you want to do is rotate the engine clockwise until you can find three spots behind these through holes where the metal surface of sprocket is blocking the holes. You may find it easier to rotate the engine if you remove the spark plugs (Project 7). You will then insert set screws into these holes and push the screw into the sprocket in order to hold it in place while you're performing the bearing replacement (see Photo 12). Rotate the engine until you have found a spot where all three holes are blocked, then install the set screws. Tighten the screws down only hand-tight, but very snug, using a small tool or ratchet. Don't use an iron grip of death, as you don't want to strip out the small M6 bolts. Just make them very snug and tight with your hand.

13 With the set screws in place, mark the camshafts with some marking ink or paint. Mark the two intake camshafts for pre-2003 engines, and mark all four for 2003 and later engines. The pre-2003 engines had the intake and exhaust camshafts tied together with a separate chain, so if one camshaft is properly timed, then the other one should be as well. You want to mark the camshafts to make sure that they do not move or rotate while you're doing the installation and alter the timing of the engine. When you're done with the installation, you will rotate the engine 360 degrees and double-check to make sure these marks all line up again perfectly.

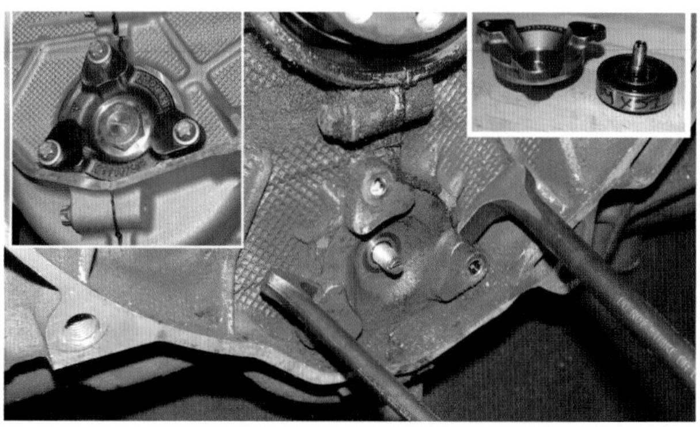

15 This photo shows the IMS cover/housing with the three bolts removed and the center nut disconnected. Use two small pry bars to remove the cover from the engine. The cover shown installed in this engine is a shallow one, meaning that this engine has a double-row bearing inside. The inset photo in the upper right shows a stock cover for a single-row bearing—notice how the inside cone of the cover is deeper. The inset in the upper left shows the 2006-later-style IMS cover with the larger nut. The bearings behind this cover are nonreplaceable because the bearing is physically constrained by the engine case.

With the intermediate shaft sprocket locked in place by the set screws, now is the time that you want to mark the locations of your camshafts. Again, you only need to mark the two exhaust camshafts on the pre-2002 engines. This is because the intake and exhaust camshafts are tied together with a chain of their own, and if one is properly set, then the other is properly set as well (see Photo 22 for more clarification). If you have a 2002 and later Carrera engine, this particular

14 You need to release a bit of the tension on the camshaft chains by unscrewing the tensioners out of their bore. Use a wrench to release the primary chain tensioner located inside the engine block, next to the flywheel (shown on the left). This chain tensioner tightens the chain that connects the intermediate shaft to the crankshaft. In a similar manner, loosen up the chain tensioner for cylinders 1-3, which is located inside the bottom of the cylinder heads (shown on the right, and located on the left side of the car). The yellow arrow points to the aluminum sealing ring, which should be replaced when you reinstall the tensioner.

16 Install the bearing removal tool onto the center stud by threading the center rod piece onto the center bolt that holds the bearing and the cover plate together (inset photo). Make sure that you thread the hexagon-shaped piece down as far as it can go onto the bolt. Slide on the outer cylinder and spin the nut onto the threaded rod. I found it most useful to lubricate the back surface of the cylinder and the nut, too, in order to facilitate easier turning of the nut. With a 24mm wrench and a breaker bar/13mm socket combo, hold the center shaft in place (green arrow) while turning the wrench clockwise (yellow arrow). This will slowly pull the IMS bearing out of the bore of the IMS. For the double-row bearings, you will need to apply quite a lot of force. You will also hear a loud *pop* as the retaining ring snaps out of place. After this pop, the amount of force to remove and pull out the bearing should be moderate.

design uses what are known as vane-cell adjusters and a single chain to link both the exhaust and intake camshafts together (see Photo 22). This design has a tendency to have the camshafts slip when performing the replacement, so you need to be vigilant in checking all four camshafts (see the section on checking camshafts at the end of this project).

Use some marking paint or a scribe to mark the locations of the camshaft with respect to the cylinder head (see Photo 13). Make sure that the marks are clear and visible; you will be rotating the engine 360 degrees when you are done to verify that all of the camshafts line up again with the marks that you created.

With the camshaft timing properly marked and the intermediate shaft secured, it's time to remove the two tensioners that pull on the flywheel-end sprockets of the intermediate shaft. The first one to remove is the tensioner located to the right of the flywheel area. Next, remove the tensioner that tightens the chain that connects the intermediate shaft to the crankshaft, located to the right of the flywheel area (Photo 14). Be sure to have an oil catch pan ready when you remove these two tensioners, as oil will spill out.

Next, remove the center nut from the bearing. I have found that these typically just come off with a 13mm socket, but you may have to use an open 13mm wrench and a screwdriver to hold the center of the bolt as you remove the nut. With the center nut removed, you should be able to slightly tap the cover counterclockwise so that you can get some pry bars underneath (Photo 15). You will need at least two of them to get the cover off (one just won't work), applying pressure in two places at the same time. There is a special tool available from Porsche to assist in removing the cover, but it's quite expensive and not really necessary.

With the cover removed, you should be able to see the bearing underneath. The inset of Photo 9 shows an example of a completely destroyed IMS bearing, and Photo 12 shows more of what a normal bearing should look like. If you accidentally drop the center bolt into the recesses of the intermediate shaft, then simply pluck it out with a magnetic tool. If you have a single-row bearing engine, at this point you will want to remove the large circlip that holds the bearing in place (see Photo 19). If you have a double-row bearing engine, then the internal snap ring will simply snap out automatically when you go to pull the bearing.

A specialized bearing removal tool was developed by the folks at LN Engineering for this task (Photo 16). Thread the center bar of the tool onto the bearing stud and turn it so it threads all the way down to the base of the bearing (see the inset of Photo 16). Slide the removal tool canister over the threaded rod and then screw on the large nut that fits on the threaded rod. Apply some motor oil to the nut and the back surface of the tool to ease the removal process. With the tool in place, hold the threaded rod and turn the nut clockwise to remove the bearing. Be sure to wear safety glasses, as the tool applies a lot of force to pull the bearing out of the engine. Turn the wrench on the nut until the bearing slides out of the engine. For engines with a dual-row bearing, you will hear a loud pop when the internal snap ring pops out of its groove. Be sure to have an oil catch pan or a bucket handy, as a significant amount of oil will most likely exit out of the intermediate shaft bore when you remove the bearing.

Inside the intermediate shaft you will most likely find some oil and debris. Get some paper towels and tape them to the end of a stick and clean out the inside of the intermediate shaft. You can also attach a small rubber hose to the end of your shop vacuum and suck out any debris that might remain in there.

There's a small possibility that your bearing center stud may break when attempting to pull the bearing out of the engine. If this happens, then you need to remove the bearing using an internal bearing puller tool (like the Stahlwille puller shown on www.101projects.com).

BEARING INSTALLATION

If the bearing and center stud did not come pressed together, begin by taking the bearing over to a table vice to press in the center stud. Press in the center stud, taking care only to apply pressing force to the inside bearing race. You can use a regular socket from your toolbox to accomplish this. It does not matter which side of the bearing faces the center stud. (See the inset of Photo 17 for more details.)

Prior to installing the new bearing, verify that your intermediate shaft bore is completely clean and free of debris. Using the bearing installation tool, place the new bearing/stud assembly into the end of the tool. The tool is designed to hold and constrain the bearing while you install it—you need to push the 12mm nut down the shaft of the tool and spin it onto the center stud's threads.

Prepare for the installation of the new bearing by placing it along with the installation tool in your freezer overnight. The cold temperatures will help shrink the bearing races and make it easier to install. This old trick is commonly used when installing wheel bearings.

With the bearing and tool assembly combined tightly together, place the bearing into the bore on the intermediate shaft (Photo 17). Verify that the placement of the bearing is completely centered and square to the plane of the engine case (make sure it's not cocked off in any direction, even slightly). With a plastic hammer, carefully tap the bearing into place. It should go in relatively smoothly and without too much effort.

If you are performing the installation on an engine that uses a double-row bearing, install the outer spacer into the bore as is shown in Photo 18. Then, proceed to install the Spiroloc clip into the groove in the intermediate shaft (see the inset of Photo 19). When the clip is completely installed into the engine, you can then install the IMS bearing cover in place. Take the smaller spacer and place it on the backside cover. Then place the cover on the engine and tap it into place using a small rubber hammer (Photo 20).

If you are performing the installation on an engine that uses a single-row bearing, then you don't need to install any spacers—just simply install the big circlip as shown in Photo 19, and then install the intermediate shaft cover as is shown in Photo 20. With both single- and double-row installations, you will want to use a new seal on the cover. If your cover is the older-style one with the small black O-ring, you will want to upgrade to the newer-style cover and improved seal to

17 If the center bolt is not preinstalled into the bearing, you need to gently press it in. Place an appropriately sized socket against the inner race of the bearing and then press the bolt in using a vice (upper right inset photo). Be sure that the socket only presses on the inner race of the bearing. This will ensure that any force used when you press in the bearing is applied only to the inner race of the bearing. Applying force to the outside race of the bearing when pressing can damage the bearing and shorten its life. You can press in the center stud and then place the entire assembly into your freezer (inset upper left). This trick is commonly used with wheel bearings and shrinks the outer race just slightly when you install it, allowing you to use much less force during the installation. You want to place as little force as possible on the IMS because you don't want to knock it loose from where it's being held in place by the set screws. Using a hammer with a plastic head, carefully tap the end of the installation tool. With the bearing cold from the freezer, it should not require a tremendous amount of force to install. Tap the bearing in using the tool until it's seated against the back of its bore in the IMS.

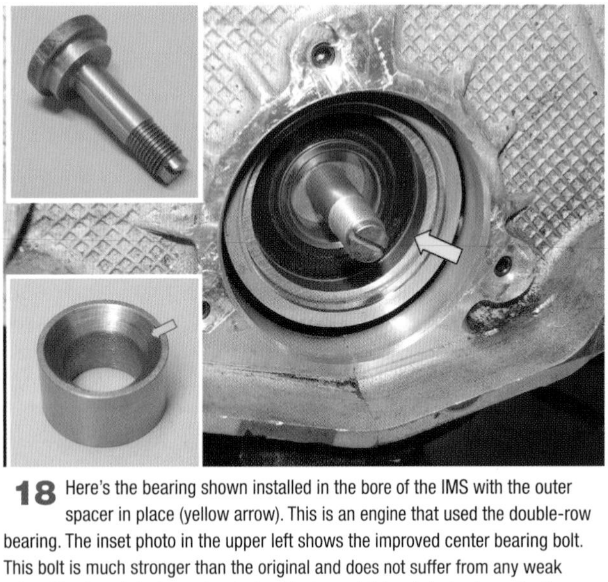

18 Here's the bearing shown installed in the bore of the IMS with the outer spacer in place (yellow arrow). This is an engine that used the double-row bearing. The inset photo in the upper left shows the improved center bearing bolt. This bolt is much stronger than the original and does not suffer from any weak points like the original Porsche design. The lower left inset photo shows the long center bolt spacer for engines with single-row bearings. The secret to keeping oil from leaking out of the bearing assembly lies with the V groove precision-machined into the spacer. This design squeezes the O-ring tightly against the IMS cover plate and the bolt, creating a leak-resistant seal. This design element is very similar to the V-groove washers used on the case through-bolts that are installed in the 1965–1989 Porsche 911 air-cooled engines.

guard against leaks. I also like to place a small bit of Curil-T sealant on this seal when I'm installing it, just as an added measure of oil-leak protection. The cover can only go on in one orientation; typically the numbers/writing on the later-style covers goes at the bottom. When installing the cover, be careful not to pinch or damage the seal, as it has a tendency to get caught sometimes during the installation process.

If for some reason you are having difficulty driving the intermediate shaft cover into place, then you can use the following procedure to assist you. Use three M6 × 25 bolts (included in the Pelican Parts kit) to help guide the cover into place. Place the cover into the bore and tap it down as far as it will go. Then, remove the set screws that you placed earlier (Photo 11). Install the bolts, and then crank each one down in an alternating pattern until the cover is flush with the engine case. When the cover is installed in place, then remove the three M6 × 25 bolts.

With the cover fully in place, you can now remove the set screws. Replace them with new micro-encapsulated bolts included in the Pelican Parts kit (see the inset of Photo 21). The phrase "micro-encapsulated" is a fancy word for bolts that have some sealant on them. It's okay to reuse your old bolts, but be sure that you coat the threads in a sealant like Curil-T or Loctite prior to installation or they will leak. Tighten the bolts down to 8 ft-lbs (11 Nm).

With the cover installed and the cover bolts tightened down and sealed, install the O-ring on the center shaft (Photo 20). I recommend putting a thin layer of Curil-T sealant around this O-ring in order to help seal against leaks. With the O-ring in place, now install the spacer. Finally, install the 12-point nut on the top, tightening it to a maximum of 24 ft-lbs. I also recommend placing a bit of Curil-T sealant underneath this nut.

If you are installing the LN Engineering retrofit kit, then the procedure is almost identical, if not simpler. Install the new IMS bearing cover in the same manner as described

19 For engines with the single-row bearing, the bearing is held in place against the IMS by a big circlip. Using a set of circlip pliers, remove this clip before pulling the bearing, and place it back into its groove after the new bearing is installed. For engines that use the double-row bearing, install the new bearing, the spacer, and then the Spiroloc circlip (inset photo). Thread the clip into the groove and then rotate it to install it in place.

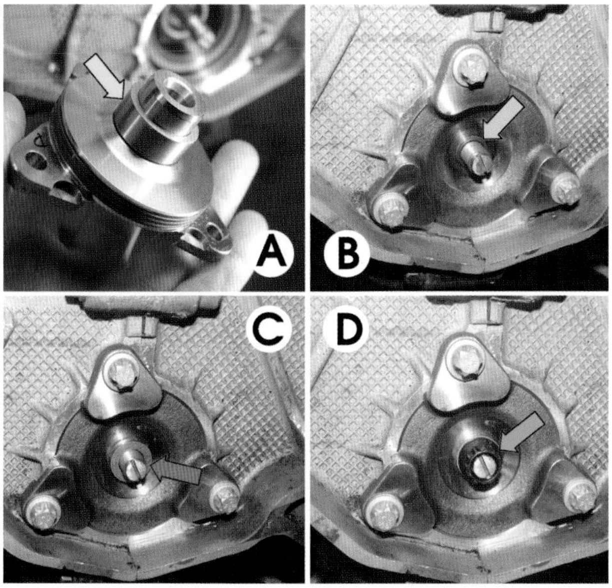

20 **A:** With the bearing, the large outer spacer, and the Spiroloc installed, it's time to install the bearing cover along with the smaller spacer (double-row only). Place the small spacer on the bearing cover as shown by the yellow arrow. If you are reinstalling the bearing cover with the later-style improved seal, I recommend using a new one. **B:** Use the longer M6 × 25 helper bolts contained in the Pelican Parts kit to help seat the cover. Then remove the helper bolts and use the new bolts to tighten down the cover. Torque to a maximum of 8 ft-lbs (11 Nm). If you're not using new bolts, then be sure to coat the threads with a liberal amount of sealant so they won't leak. With the cover in place, slide on the O-ring as shown. I recommend coating the O-ring with a thin layer of Curil-T to guard against leaks (double-row shown). **C:** Install the spacer onto the bearing flange (double-row shown). **D:** Using a screwdriver to hold the center bolt in place, tighten down the 12-point nut to 24 ft-lbs maximum. I also like to add just a touch of Curil-T sealant between the spacer and the nut, just to make sure there is no oil leakage (double-row shown).

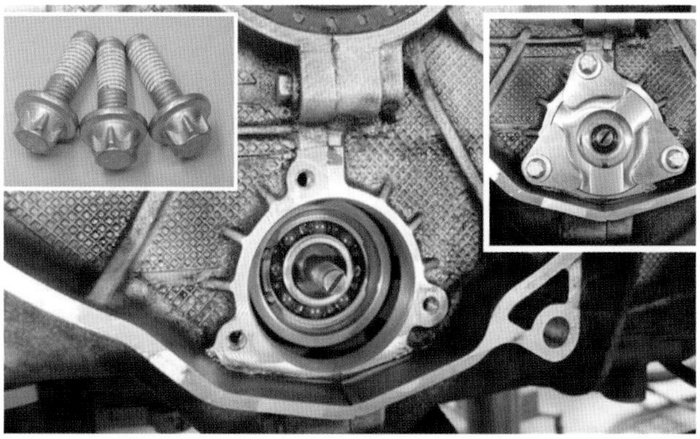

21 This photo shows the LN Engineering ceramic bearing installed into the case. The engineers at LN Engineering have theorized that the removal of the seal will allow fresh motor oil to lubricate the ceramic bearing, thus they have removed the seal from the rear-facing side of the bearing. The upper left inset photo shows three brand new Torx bolts from Porsche for the IMS cover. The bolts are micro-encapsulated, which is a fancy word meaning that they simply have some sealant on the threads. I like to use new bolts to guard against leaks, but you can also reuse your old bolts if you liberally coat the threads with sealant prior to installation. The upper right inset photo shows the LN Engineering IMS retrofit kit installed. Use a small amount of Curil-T or similar flange sealant around the edge of the nut to prevent small leaks.

above. Prior to installation, verify that the O-ring that fits in the center of the shaft is in place and undamaged. Install the 12-point nut on the end using some green Loctite flange sealant as an added protection against leaks. Photo 21 shows the LN Engineering ceramic bearing installed in the case with the open no-seal side facing outwards, and the inset shows the retrofit kit intermediate shaft end cover installed in place.

At this time I also recommend that you replace the rear main seal (RMS) with the new, updated version. See Project 45 for more details.

CHECKING CAMSHAFT TIMING

With the new bearing installed in place, you are basically done with the installation. However, it's very important that you check your camshaft timing prior to reinstalling the transmission and starting the engine. Photo 22 shows how the timing chains are oriented and set up on the five-chain (996 Carrera thru 2001) and three-chain motors (996/997 Carrera 2002 and later). Particularly with the three-chain motors, you need to make sure that you check the exhaust camshaft for cylinders 1–3 (located to the right of the flywheel). This particular camshaft has the least amount of chain wrap, and

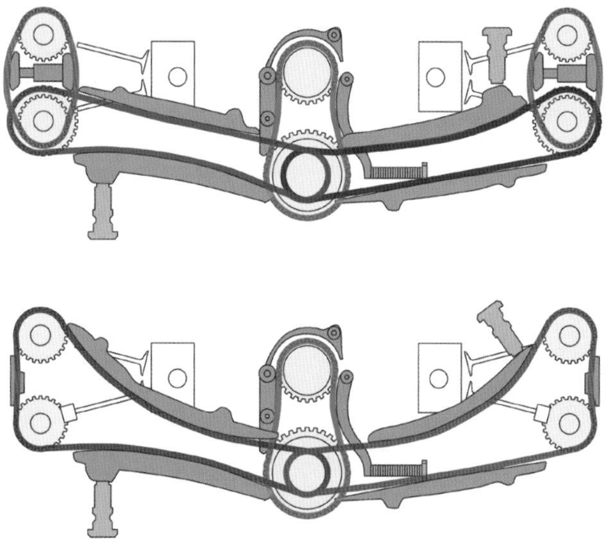

22 On pre-2003 Carrera 996s, the engines all had five chains: two linking each pair of camshafts to the intermediate shaft, one linking the intermediate shaft to the crankshaft, and two linking each camshaft together (top photo). I'm not sure why Porsche designed it this way: most modern cars don't have this many chains. The good news is that on these early five-chain cars, the timing chains almost never skip a tooth when performing the IMS bearing replacement. The chains are very tightly wrapped around each gear and as a result, when you loosen the tension from them, they tend to stay in place. Starting in 2003, Porsche went to a three-chain design, eliminating the chain that tied the two camshafts together (bottom photo). I can only speculate that this was done in order to simplify the construction of the motor (reduce cost and weight). This design works fine, except that there is more opportunity now for the chain to slip off the camshaft sprockets when replacing the IMS bearing. Specifically, the chain has a tendency to slip on the 1–3 exhaust camshaft when the chain is loosened. For this reason, it's very important to check the engine's static timing marks on all four camshafts to make sure that the chains did not skip a tooth. If you start up the motor and the chains are off by one tooth, then the valves can impact the pistons and the engine will self-destruct. It's not very difficult to check the timing; you just need to remember to do it.

removing the chain tensioner to perform the replacement has the potential to loosen the chain and allow the timing to skip a tooth on the sprocket.

To check the timing, simply take the crankshaft and rotate it 360 degrees from where you originally placed it when you installed the set screws. Then check the marks that you made on the camshafts (four marks on all four camshafts for the three-chain motors, two marks on the exhaust camshafts for the five-chain motors). If all of the marks line up perfectly, then you're golden, and you can continue on with finishing up the installation. If any of the marks are off, then there is the potential that the timing chain slipped off of the camshaft sprocket during the installation process. (See Project 16 for more information on retiming the camshafts if this happens.)

If you happen to have the P253 camshaft timing tool, you can use that to check the timing on the five-chain engines. Simply place the engine at top dead center (see Photo 1 of Project 16), remove all four green caps on the camshafts, and install the tool on each side to check each pair of camshafts (see Photo 3 of Project 16). If the tool fits, then the timing is perfect. If it doesn't fit, then you will have to retime the cams (see Project 16). It's very good practice to check the timing on the five-chain motors, but in reality, very few of these have problems, unless the instructions were not followed correctly. Still, I recommend checking the timing prior to reinstalling the transmission—it's cheap insurance.

After you're done checking the camshafts, install new camshaft end caps as shown in Photo 38 of Project 16. Although I like to use a bit of sealant everywhere, these end caps don't tend to leak.

Also important to note, if you have the camshaft tools handy, you might want to check your camshaft timing *prior* to beginning the installation of the bearing. If the timing is slightly off and the bearing appears fine, then you might have some additional problems in your camshaft timing chain mechanism (slipping sprockets on the intermediate shafts, worn pads on the camshaft solenoid mechanisms, etc.). I would advise investigating these problems prior to pulling out the bearing.

Don't forget to change the filter and add oil! See Project 2 for more details. If you pulled the bearing and found some major wear or damage, then you probably want to pull the bottom sump off and clean it out (see Project 12). Also think seriously about replacing the sump air-oil separators, as they tend to get contaminated, too, if you have bearing debris in the sump.

If you check the official website for the book, you will find more reference photos for this project along with a complete list of part numbers of all of the parts used in this project (see http://www.101projects.com/Carrera/14.htm).

IMS GUARDIAN

If you are worried about the health of the IMS in your engine, but do not want to go through all the work to replace the bearing, there is now another option. The IMS Guardian allows constant engine monitoring through its dash interface. The IMS Guardian couples technology originally created for military aircraft to a specially designed sensor and wiring package. This system was originated with the sole purpose of detecting imminent IMS Bearing failures prior to their occurrence. (See Project 11 for the full installation instructions.)

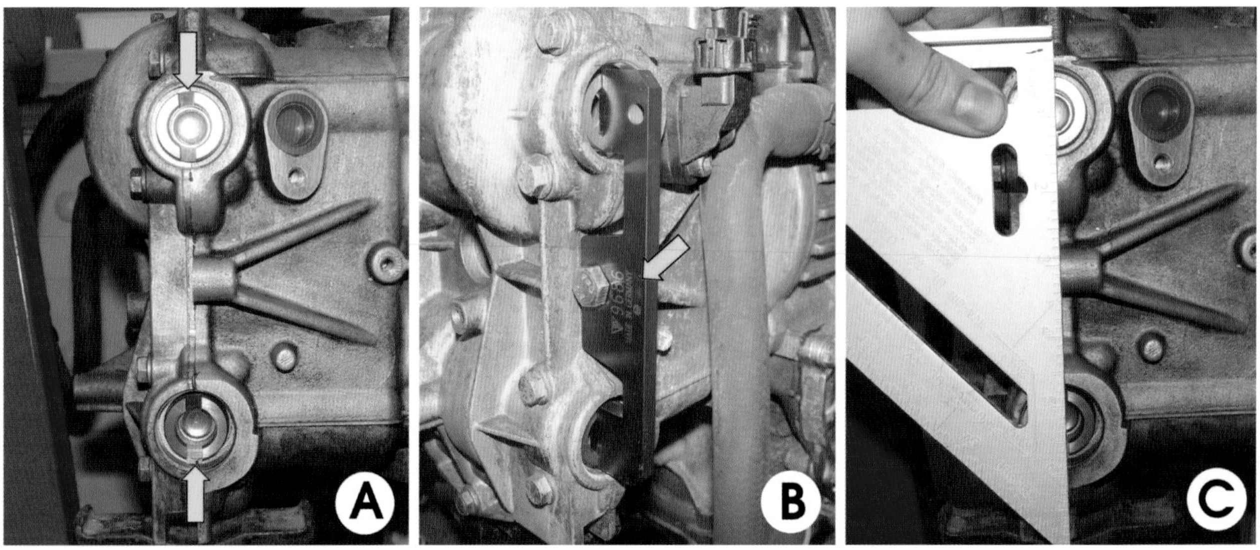

23 **A:** This photo shows the end of the intake and exhaust camshafts for cylinders 1–3 on the three-chain motor. Prior to removing the IMS bearing cover, you should have marked these camshafts. If you didn't mark them, you can set the motor to top dead center (TDC) and then visually inspect them to make sure that they are set to the proper timing. **B:** With the later-style three-chain motors, the camshafts share a long chain that wraps around the outer edge of the camshaft gear. With these motors, you must check all four camshafts to make sure they are properly timed after installing the new bearing. The 9686 camshaft locking tool is shown here locking camshafts 1–3 on this three-chain engine. The engine must be at top dead center for the tool to fit into the pair of camshafts. If it doesn't fit, then try rotating the engine 180 degrees. With the locking tool in place, you can rest assured that your camshaft timing is set properly. I recommend that you check both sides, cylinders 1–3 and cylinders 4–6, although the 1–3 bank is the one most likely to skip a tooth. **C:** If you don't have the camshaft timing tool, you can use a straight edge to line it up against the edge of the camshaft and confirm that the timing is correct (as shown in the photo).

PROJECT 15
Engine Removal

Time / Tab / Talent: 8 hours / $50-100 / 5 wrenches

Tools: All of them

Applicable Years: All

Tinware: Engine, Transmission

Tip: Take your time and double-check everything

Performance Gain: Self-confidence in knowing that you can do the job yourself

Comp Modification: Replace everything that you can with the engine out of the car

More Info: http://www.101projects.com/Carrera/15.htm

The method of engine removal in this project will cover removing the engine and transmission as one unit. It's much easier to perform the work this way than separating the engine and transmission. You don't have a lot of space to work with the engine up in place, so lowering the engine straight down with the transmission makes the process much safer and easier. Another good tip here is to get a bunch of Ziploc bags to hold all of the various nuts and bolts you will be removing from the engine. I like to mark each bag with a Sharpie (i.e., "Intake Manifold Bolts," etc.).

PREPARATION

- Open front and rear decklids.
- Disconnect battery in front trunk (Project 83).
- Jack up car and secure it on jack stands (Project 1).

ENGINE COMPARTMENT

- Remove airbox (Project 3).
- Remove accelerator cable from throttle body or disconnect electronic throttle body (Photo 1 of Project 29).
- Disconnect fuel tank vapor hose (Photo 1).
- Disconnect brake booster fitting to intake manifold (Photo 10 of Project 9).
- Remove serpentine belt (Project 5).
- Disconnect electrical connectors for the oxygen sensors (Photo 4 of Project 48).
- Suction out the power steering fluid from reservoir and remove reservoir (Photo 2 and Photo 3).
- Disconnect harness going to engine bay temperature sender (Photo 5).
- Unbolt A/C compressor from engine, disconnect ground wire, and secure the compressor off to the side. Do not remove the refrigerant lines unless you want to recharge the system (Photos 4, 6, and 7).
- Disconnect both engine wiring loom connectors going to the engine (Photo 8).
- Disconnect fuel lines from driver side fuel rail (Photo 4 of Project 26).
- Disconnect upper coolant hose on passenger side of engine bay (Photo 9).
- On the 996 Carrera, remove hose going to secondary air pump in engine compartment (Photo 7 of Project 10).
- Disconnect power steering hoses in engine compartment (Photo 10).

BUMPER REMOVAL

- Remove upper screws along bumper in engine bay and remove threshold strip (Photo 1 of Project 47).
- Using a 6mm hex, remove rear bumperettes (Photo 3 of Project 47).
- Remove screws along bottom edge of bumper cover.
- Remove the two screws on the lower edge of the bumper cover behind each wheel, along with the fender support bracket (Carrera 997s only; Photo 2 of Project 47).
- Remove rear bumper cover by pulling it at the edges and pulling it off. If you encounter any resistance, double-check that you have removed all fasteners.
- Remove aluminum bumper (Photo 5 of Project 47).
- Remove exhaust heat shields (Photo 6 of Project 47).

UNDER THE CAR

- Remove plastic under trays along front of transmission and center tunnel of the underside of the car (Photo 11).
- Remove crossmember under transmission (Photo 12).
- Drain coolant (Photo 4 of Project 30).
- Disconnect constant velocity (CV) joints from transmission (Photo 2 of Project 42).

- Unbolt clutch slave cylinder from engine (Photo 3 of Project 46).
- Disconnect shift cables from transmission (Photo 13).
- Remove electrical connection to reverse light switch (Photo 7 of Project 45).
- Remove brace between suspension uprights (Photo 14).
- Remove cover pieces and diagonal brace supports on suspension uprights (Photo 15 and Photo 16).
- Secure transmission with jack and remove transmission mount (Photo 17).
- Remove engine ground strap from right (passenger) side of engine bay (Photo 18).
- Disconnect water hoses leading to thermostat and water pump on lower left side of the engine (Photo 3 of Project 35).
- Secure engine underneath with floor jack and remove the engine mount nuts on either side (Photos 3, 4, and 5 of Project 10).
- Slowly lower engine and transmission from car (Photo 19 and Photo 20).

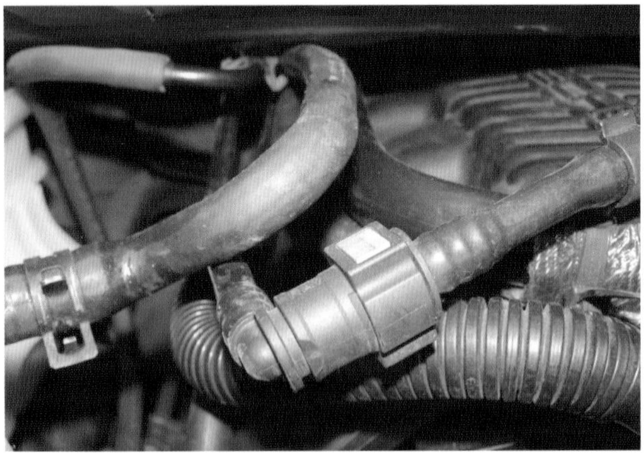

1 Unplug the fuel tank vent vapor hose connection on the upper left side of the engine by squeezing the wire clip on the connector and pulling it out.

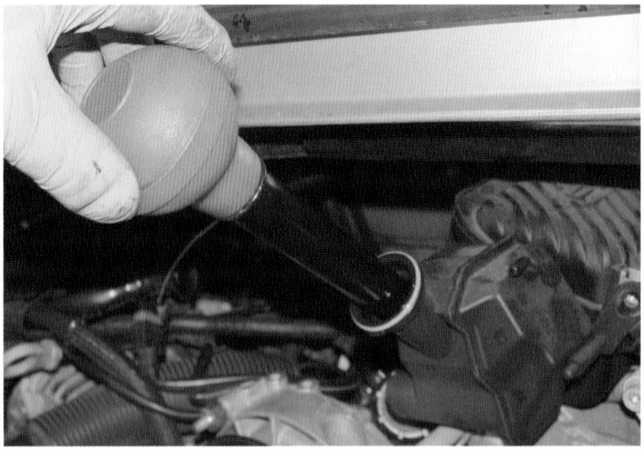

2 Open the power steering fluid reservoir and use either a syringe or turkey baster to suction out as much of the power steering fluid as you can.

3 Once the reservoir is empty, remove the 10mm nut that secures the reservoir to the bracket (green arrow) then rotate the bayonet lock tab (purple arrow) counterclockwise to remove the power steering fluid reservoir from the car.

4 The next step is to remove the AC compressor from the engine with the lines still attached. The compressor is held in place by three long 13mm bolts. Remove the two front bolts as shown here (green arrows).

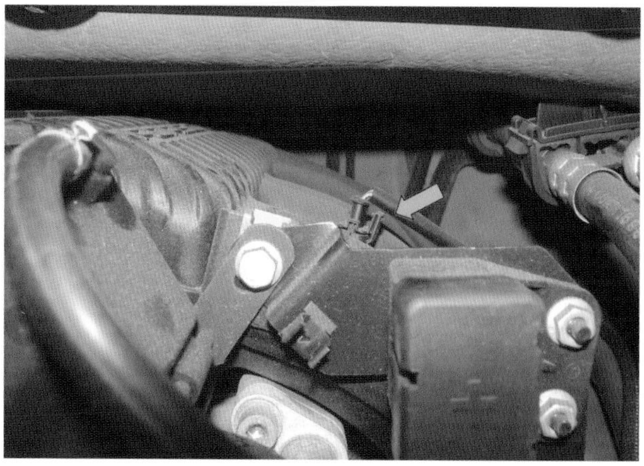

5 In order to get to the remaining AC compressor mounting bolt, you'll first need to remove the temperature sensor shown here (green arrow). The sensor sits in a rubber sleeve that fits into a groove on the intake manifold. It's difficult to see it here, but it will slide out to the right.

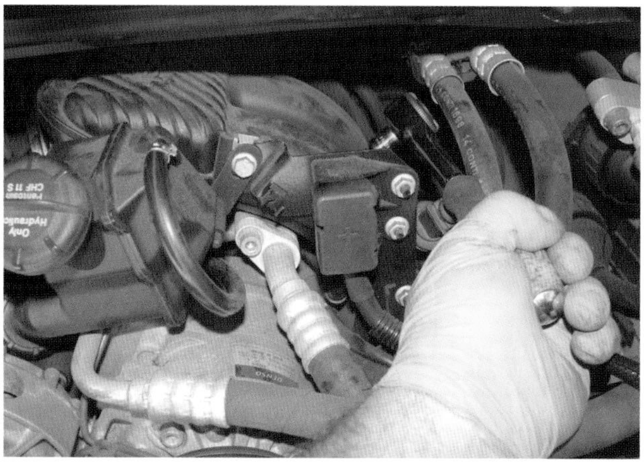

6 You can now access the remaining compressor bolt from between the intake manifold. You'll need a combination of extensions and U-joints. Once the compressor is free, unplug the electrical connector. The bolt needs to be held in its up position to remove the compressor.

7 Once the compressor is removed, lay down a rag or towel to protect the car's paint and lay the compressor off to the side of the engine.

8 Disconnect the two circular connectors for the engine wiring harness on the right (passenger) side of the engine by turning them counterclockwise. As you turn them, they will release themselves from the harness (green arrows).

9 Loosen the hose clamp on the radiator hose on the right side of the engine and remove the hose (green arrow).

10 Disconnect the lines that connect to the power steering pump inside the engine bay along the upper passenger side. You may find it easier to disconnect these lines once the engine is lowered slightly.

11 Underneath the car, remove the two screws and 10mm plastic nuts that hold the plastic undertray in place underneath the front of the transmission and remove the undertray.

12 Remove the two 15mm bolts (green arrows) holding the aluminum crossmember piece between the suspension uprights and remove the crossmember.

13 Remove the ball ends of the shift cables from the transmission by popping them off with a large screwdriver (green arrows). Then remove the shift cable retaining clips by prying them off (purple arrows). Note that on our car, one of the clips was missing and someone had used a cable tie to hold the cable in the retainer bracket.

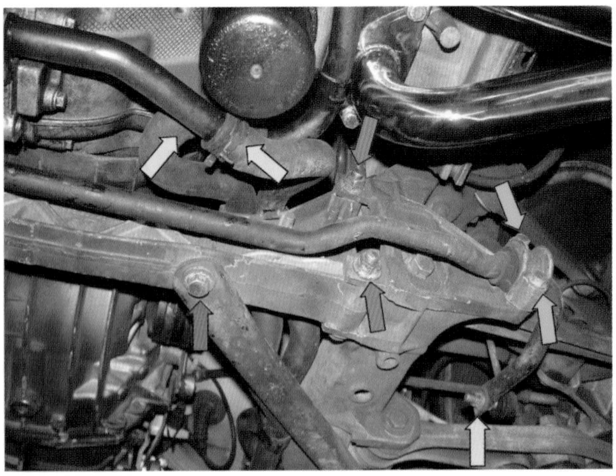

14 To lower the engine and transmission as one unit, you will need to remove the center brace, rear sway bar and also the diagonal braces on the rear suspension of the car. This picture shows only one side, but the other side is similar. Begin by removing the two 13mm bolts (green arrows) that attach the sway bar to the suspension upright. Next, remove the 15mm nut holding the sway bar to the drop link (yellow arrow). Repeat on the opposite side. Set the sway bar aside then remove the 16mm bolt holding the front of the diagonal brace to the center brace (red arrow). Lastly, remove the four 17mm nuts and bolts holding the center brace to the upright (purple arrows). The top bolts of the brace are meant to stay in place so don't try to remove them—just loosening them will do. We need to remove the diagonals to allow the center brace to be removed. Also, loosen and remove the rubber coolant hoses from the metal lines (blue arrows).

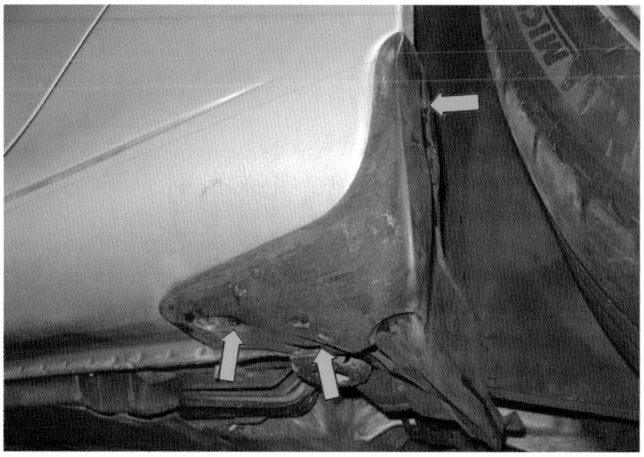

15 At this point, move to the front of the wheelwell. Remove the three screws (green arrows) that hold the lower rear quarter panel trim piece to the body. This piece covers the front mounting bolt for the diagonal braces.

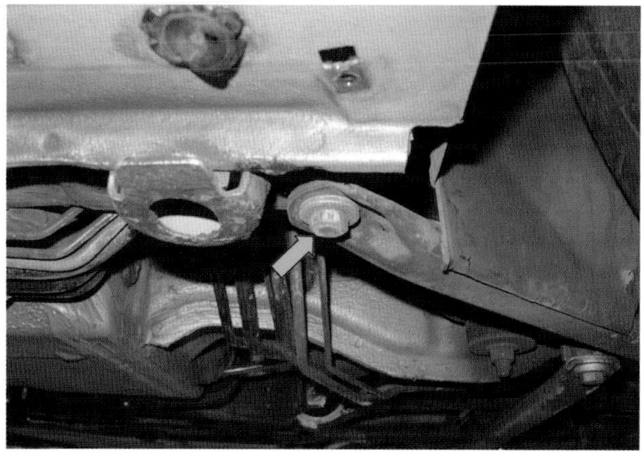

16 Now move inside the wheelwell to access the inner bolt that holds the brace to the chassis (green arrow). Loosen this bolt until you can pull the diagonal down and rotate it around out of the way of the center brace.

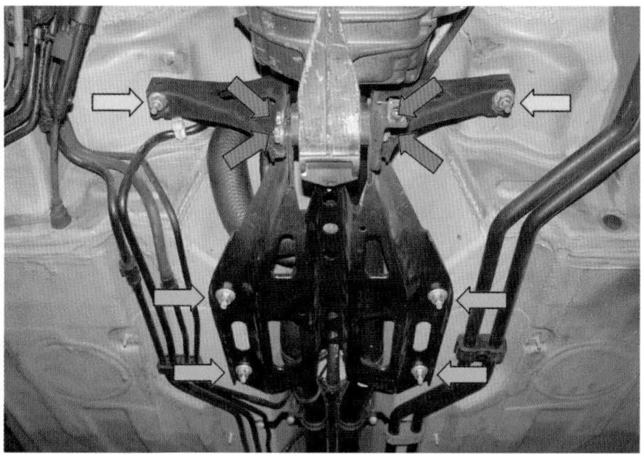

17 With the engine and transmission firmly supported, remove the four 16mm nuts that hold the front part of the transmission mounting bracket to the chassis (green arrows). Also remove the 16mm thru bolts and nuts that hold the bracket to the transmission mount (purple arrows). Remove the lower mounting bracket. Also remove the two 16mm nuts holding the upper mounting bracket to the chassis (yellow arrows).

18 Don't forget to unbolt the ground strap from the chassis on the right (passenger) side of the engine (green arrow). This photo shows where the fender support bracket attaches to the frame (blue arrow, 997 only).

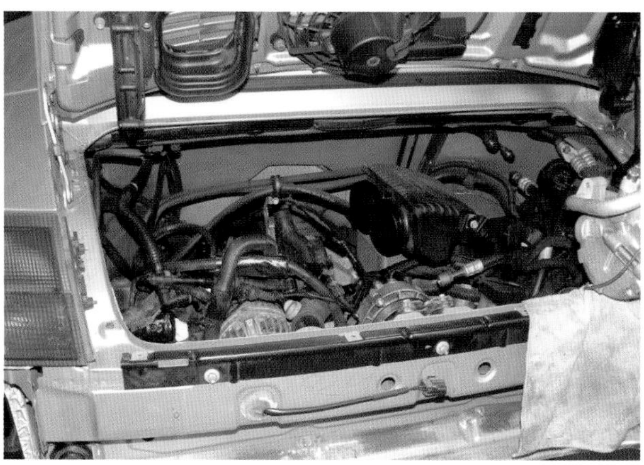

19 Once you're sure nothing is still hanging up on the engine, lower it fully down and out of the car. **Note:** In this picture, the right side intake manifold and plenums have been removed.

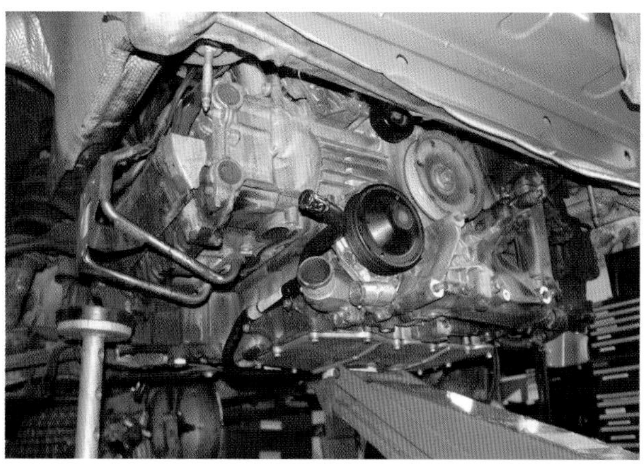

20 Shown here is the engine being lowered out of the car without the transmission attached as well as the exhaust removed. Be sure to orient the floor jack toward the balance point of the engine.

PROJECT 16
Camshaft Swap and Valvetrain Repair

Time / Tab / Talent: 10 hours / $100–$2,500 /

Tools: Camshaft timing tool, crankshaft locking tool

Applicable Years: All

Tinware: New camshafts, lifters, solenoid, etc.

More Info: http://www.101projects.com/Carrera/16.htm

Tip: All of these tasks should be able to be done with the engine in the car, but are far easier with the engine removed

Performance Gain: More horsepower

Comp Modification: Replace intermediate shaft bearing

This project started out as a simple addendum to checking the camshaft timing when performing the intermediate shaft (IMS) bearing replacement (see Project 14). However, after further consideration, I decided to expand it to include all of the items in your valvetrain that you might have problems with in the future. Specifically, this project covers the following tasks or potential problem areas you might encounter on your Carrera engine:

- Fixing camshaft cover leaks
- Replacing the VarioCam and solenoid hydraulic valve
- Swapping out your camshafts
- Checking the camshaft timing
- Replacing noisy lifters (tappets)
- Replacing the external chain tensioners
- Replacing the internal cam-to-cam chain tensioner
- Replacing chain ramps

For the purpose of illustration, we used separate two motors: the five chain motor and a three chain motor. The five chain motor used in this project was out of the car on an engine stand. It's an old Boxster core motor that I purchased for demonstration purposes—it had been involved in a bad fire. The core motor is fine, but all of the injection and sensors were destroyed in the fire, which made it perfect for rebuilding or for photos! I also performed the work on a three chain motor, which is significantly different than the earlier five chain engines. See Project 14 for a description of the two types and how to tell the difference between the two.

All of the tasks illustrated here should be able to be performed on the engine while it is still installed in the car, although clearance is tight and it's somewhat difficult to work under the car. I've broken the tasks into photo captions; read along for the procedures detailing the tasks listed above.

1 **Disassembly of Three-Chain and Five-Chain Engines:** The first step in this whole process is to set the crankshaft to top dead center (TDC) and lock it there. Turn the engine clockwise until the teardrop-shaped hole lines up with the hole in the case. Insert the way-overpriced factory knob in place, or simply use a punch or an appropriately sized drill bit (5/16 size worked well for me). Set the crankshaft at TDC right now; the camshafts rotate at one-half the speed of the crankshaft, so the crankshaft is located either at TDC for Cylinder 1 or TDC for Cylinder 4. If need be in the next few steps, you might have to rotate it another 360 degrees if it's not at TDC for the cylinder bank you're working on. If you're performing these tasks with the engine in the car, then you need to access the rear of the engine. You will need to remove the airbox (see Project 5) to gain access. Since you will be removing the plugs anyways, go ahead and pull them first, as this will make attempting to rotate the engine by hand easier.

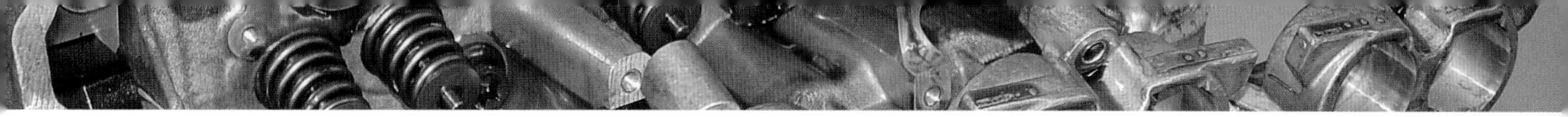

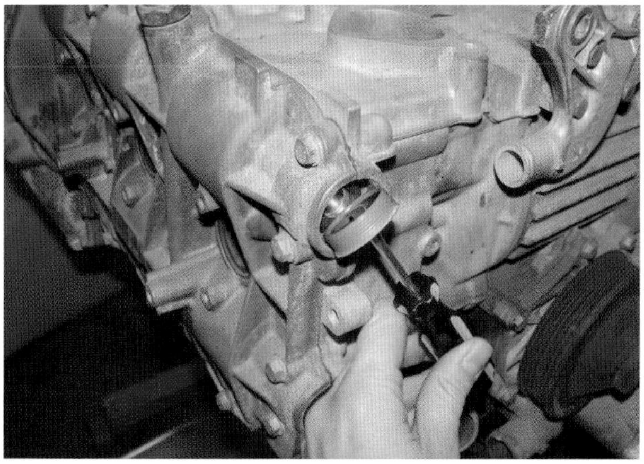

2 Three-Chain and Five-Chain Engines: Now remove the two cam plugs that sit on the end of the two camshafts. You need to remove these green plugs to inspect/check the timing when performing the intermediate shaft upgrade. You basically poke a hole in the center of the shaft and then pull it out. Toss the old ones away, as you will not be reusing them. The engine uses a total of three per head, and the part number is 996-104-215-54.

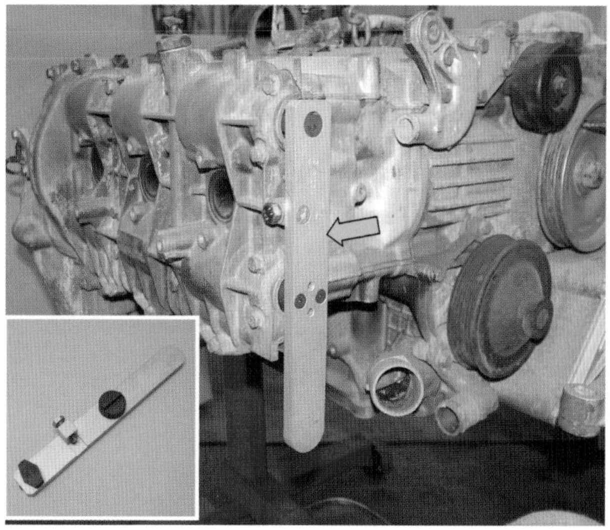

3 Five-Chain Engine Shown: With the plugs removed, now install the camshaft timing tool, P253, onto the end of the camshaft. Normally, you would use Porsche tool 9624 to hold the camshafts onto the end of the motor (see Photo 3 of Project 8), but I found that the camshaft timing tool also pretty much did an adequate job of holding them in place as well. While I personally have most of the tools listed as required in the Porsche factory manuals, I like to try to recommend places where they may not be 100 percent absolutely necessary. This is one of those cases—use the P253 tool instead.

4 Three-Chain Engine Shown: With the plugs removed you will be able to determine which cylinder bank is on compression and which is on overlap. When looking at the ends of the camshafts the cams with the smaller portion of the circle facing the valve cover is on overlap. Now install the camshaft timing tool, P9686 (yellow arrow), onto the end of the camshaft. The smaller circular cut outs (red arrows) in the end of the cams must be pointing toward the valve cover for the tool to fit correctly.

5 Three-Chain and Five-Chain Engines: Remove the oil pump from the cylinder head. It's a wise idea to get a marking pen and mark the pump where it lines up with the engine case; it can be installed backward by mistake. Remove the four bolts that hold the pump to the case (orange arrows)—not the four Allen screws that are internal to the pump. Use two pry bars to simply pull the pump out of the end of the engine.

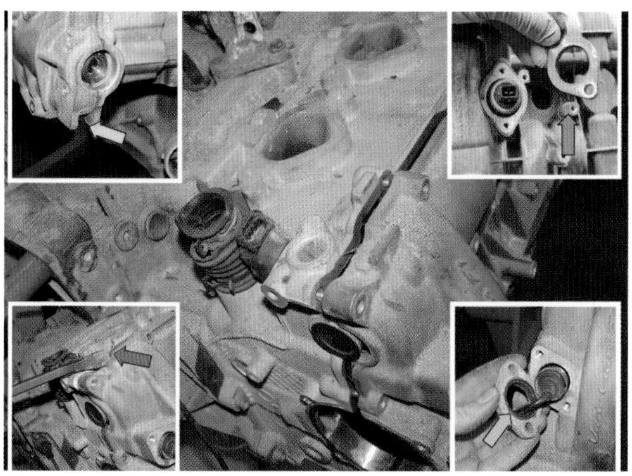

6 Three-Chain and Five-Chain Engines: With the oil pump removed, remove all of the perimeter bolts from the camshaft cover. Also remove the two bolts that secure the cover for the VarioCam solenoid (five-chain motor, green arrow, lower right) and the cover for the solenoid hydraulic valve (three-chain motor, purple arrow, upper right). With everything disconnected, use a few pry bars on the separation areas of the case and the cylinder head (yellow and red arrows) to pry the camshaft cover off of the head.

7 **Five-Chain Engines:** When you remove the camshaft cover, you should see the camshafts and the chains underneath. The top camshaft will want to move outward when you remove the cover, as the bearing caps are designed into the valve cover itself, but the force of the camshaft timing tool against its end should keep it relatively secured. It's okay if it pushes out by a few millimeters. I have heard from various sources that the camshaft can snap if there is enough force placed on it from the valve springs, so make sure that it doesn't move significantly out of its bore. The yellow arrow points to the spark plug tubes (found on early engines). Now would be a good time to replace them and the o-rings that seal them to the cylinder head and camshaft cover.

8 **Three-Chain Engines:** The later three-chain motors do not have the spark plug tubes, but it is still a really good idea to replace the o-rings that bridge the gap between the valve covers and head (red arrows). This head also has internal bearing caps which keep the cams in position.

9 **Five-Chain Engines:** Shown here is the solenoid that activates the valve that turns on the hydraulic oil pressure supply that advances the camshafts for the VarioCam operation. This solenoid has a habit of failing and needing replacement. Once you have the camshaft covers off, replacement is a snap. Simply unscrew the old one and install the new one in its place. At about $200 apiece, they are probably the world's most expensive solenoids.

10 **Three-Chain Engines:** With the valve cover removed you will need to loosen and remove the central bolt on the camshaft adjustment device on the intake cam. You can use the Porsche factory tool P9685 or you can do as I did and use a medium size adjustable wrench. You will be using the head casing for support so make sure you use an adjustable wrench that fits completely over the large backing nut and is snug to the cam housing. With this in place, use a 16mm socket and breaker bar to loosen the central bolt (yellow arrow). This bolt is unusually long with lots of threads (inset, upper right).

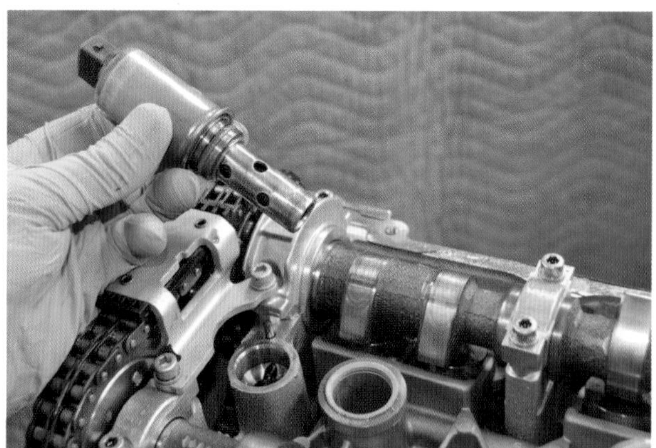

11 **Three-Chain Engines:** You should be able to lift the solenoid hydraulic valve from its place between the cams. It can have a little vacuum from the oil, so if you cannot remove it by hand use a relay puller tool.

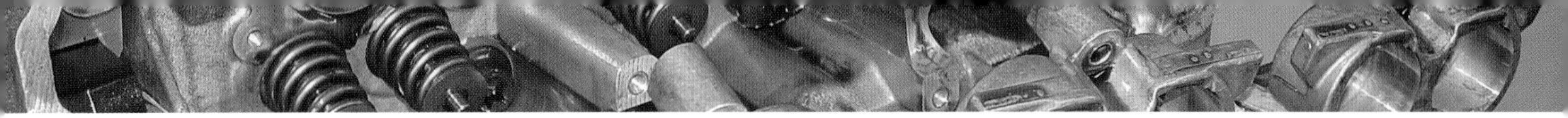

12 **Three-Chain and Five-Chain Engines:** Now, loosen and detach the camshaft sprocket from the exhaust camshaft. Four small bolts hold it on to the camshaft (five-chain main picture, three-chain lower inset).

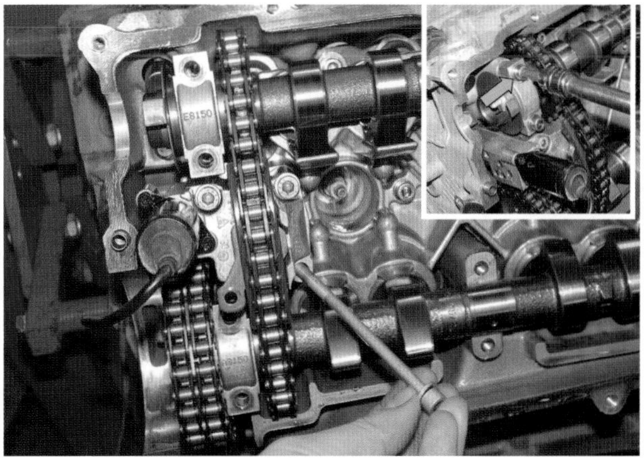

13 **Five-Chain Engines:** Carefully remove the leftmost camshaft-bearing caps on both of the camshafts (green arrow, inset photo). Then remove the three very long bolts that secure the VarioCam chain tensioner to the cylinder head.

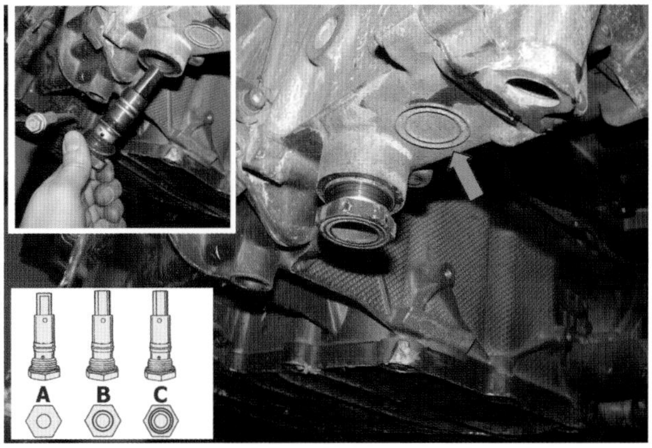

14 **Three-Chain and Five-Chain Engines:** Now, loosen up all the chain tensioners on the motor. This photo shows the chain tensioner for Cylinders 1–3, which is located inside the bottom of the cylinder head. The three tensioners are all different but look remarkably similar. Porsche marked the top of each tensioner with different rings in order to help distinguish among them. **A:** The chain tensioner for Cylinders 4–6 located under the air conditioning compressor. **B:** The main intermediate shaft tensioner, which fits inside the crankcase near the flywheel. **C:** The chain tensioner for Cylinders 1–3, which fits into the bottom of the cylinder head. Note the handy marking on the head itself (purple arrow).

15 **Five-Chain Engines:** With the chain tensioner loosened, the bearing caps removed, and the VarioCam tensioner disconnected from the head, you should be able to slide the gear off the camshaft with your hand. A few gentle taps with a small rubber hammer can also help your cause if it's stuck. Let it sit next to the camshaft in the case. If you are performing this procedure with the engine in the car, be aware that once you remove the cam gear, the camshafts may slide out of the head—be ready to catch them. If you are performing this task on an engine stand, then simply rotate the engine at an angle, so that the camshafts won't fall out.

16 **Five-Chain Engines:** With everything disconnected, remove the camshaft timing tool from the engine. Remove the camshafts and move them over to your workbench.

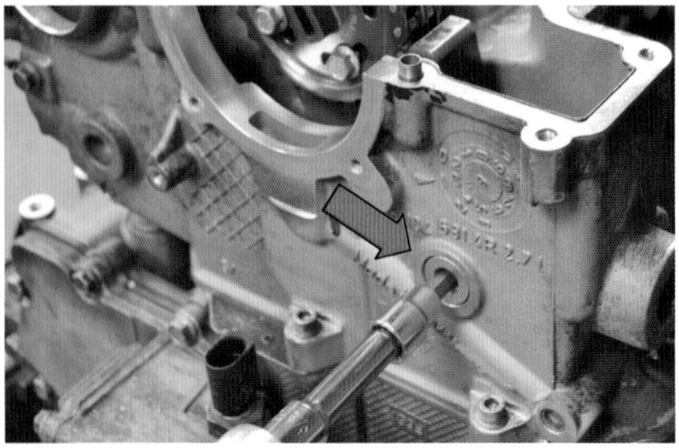

17 **Three-Chain Engines:** On Cylinder Bank 4–6 you will need to use a 6mm Allen tool and remove the chain guide retaining bolt (red arrow).

18 **Three-Chain Engines:** Using a 5mm Allen tool remove the two bolts holding the guide rail between the two cams (red arrows). Remove the guide rail from the head (green arrow, inset upper right). Next use your 5mm Allen tool and remove the remaining six bearing cap bolts (yellow arrows). These caps are cam specific; make sure you note that the intake cap is etched with an "E" and the exhaust is etched with an A1 and A2. Make sure you label them for proper reinstallation later. Remove the alignment tool from the end of the camshafts. Note: "E" stands for einlass, which is the German word for intake/inlet.

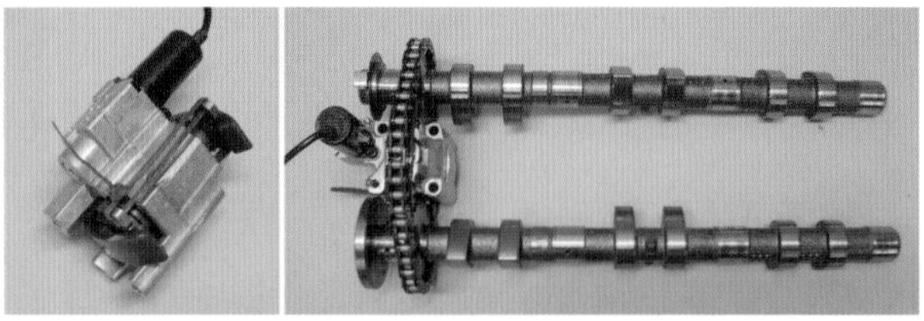

19 **Five-Chain Engines:** Shown here are the two camshafts, the small timing chain, and the VarioCam tensioner that ties them together. A special tool can be used to compress the tensioner to make it easy to remove, but I just opted to use a cable tie instead. It works great, and when you're ready to expand it again, you just clip the cable tie.

20 **Three-Chain Engines:** Slide the sprocket off the exhaust cam and set it aside. Lift the exhaust cam from its seats in the head. With the exhaust cam removed, you can simply lift the intake cam up and back from the variable intake sprocket. The intake sprocket will remain in the head.

21 **Three-Chain and Five-Chain Engines:** With the camshafts removed, you can simply pluck out the lifters (tappets). Check both the lifters and the lifter guides for damage (pockets of wear greater than 1mm, fractures at the edges, irregular contact patterns on the running surfaces, grooves in the oil pockets for the cam lobes). Clean each lifter carefully with a lint-free cloth. I recommend using KimWipes, which I used all the time in the past when I was working in clean rooms building satellites. You can find these at PelicanParts.com—they are perfect for cleaning intricate engine parts where you don't want paper fibers or debris contaminating tiny oil passages. With the lifter clean, dip it in some fresh motor oil. Use whatever motor oil you're planning on using when you refill the car. Press down on the inside of the lifter while it's submerged so that you can clean out the internal passages as best as possible. It's particularly important to clean everything if your engine's oil was contaminated with coolant. Failure to clean and lubricate thoroughly may result in what is known as a noisy lifter—one that doesn't completely engage. This can lead to degradation in engine performance. The Porsche factory manuals recommend not using a magnet to pluck the lifters from their bores (use your fingers or a mini–suction cup device instead).

22 **Three-Chain and Five-Chain Engines:** This is one of the reasons why I don't care for Porsche's recommendation of going 15,000 miles between oil changes. This example shows a camshaft bearing that is scratched and becoming worn. If this were on a 1965–1989 Porsche 911 engine, I would recommend replacing the bearing. However, the camshaft cover and cylinder head are matched pieces, and to replace this bearing, you basically need to replace the entire cylinder head! It's not worth the risk. Change your oil every 3,000 to 5,000 miles with an oil that has a high level of anti-wear additives and keeps bearing wear to a minimum.

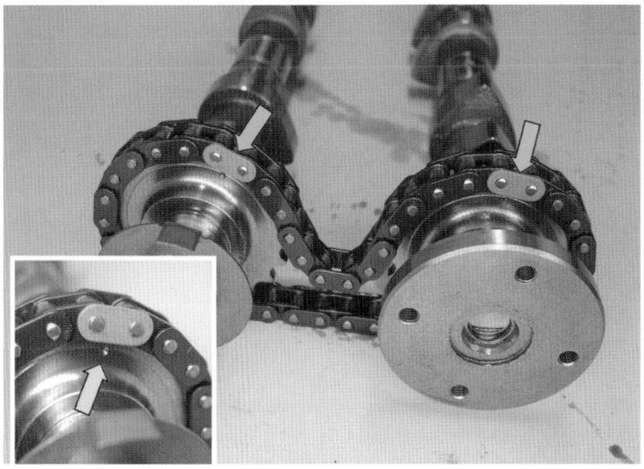

23 **Reassembly of Five-Chain Engines:** Begin the process of reassembly by taking the two camshafts and lining them up on your bench. The cam-to-cam chain has two special links that are colored differently (green arrows). Align these links up with the divots that are located on each camshaft (yellow arrow). Keeping these two links lined up with the divots will keep the two camshafts timed with respect to each other.

24 **Five-Chain Engines:** Using care not to let the chain slip on the camshaft gears, install the tensioner in between the two sprockets. It's also a good time to replace your chain ramps if they appear worn (inset photo, lower right; they simply snap off). You will have to maneuver the tensioner and the camshafts back and forth to get the tensioner in there. Once installed, clip the cable tie and expand the tensioner; this should secure the chain, and the camshafts should be securely timed with respect to each other. Before going on to the next step, you should meticulously clean all of the mating surfaces of both the cylinder head and the camshaft cover (red arrows, inset photo) with gasket remover and a sharp razorblade. Remove all traces of sealant from both surfaces.

25 **Five-Chain Engines:** With all of the sealant material cleaned from the cylinder head, lay the camshaft assembly down into the cylinder head. Double-check that the light-colored chain links and the divots in the camshafts are still lined up properly. On the opposite side of the cylinder head, the lower camshaft should line up with the cylinder head/cover parting line, as shown in the inset photo.

26 **Five-Chain Engines:** Using your left hand, push the camshaft into place while affixing the camshaft bearing cap into place. Tighten down the bearing caps and also tighten down the tensioner housing. It's important to keep in mind that the German word for "intake" is *einlass*, which starts with the letter E, and the word for "exhaust" is *auspuff*, which starts with the letter A: E = intake, A = exhaust. The cylinder head, the camshaft cover, and these two little caps are all machined together and are labeled with the same number so that they won't be mixed up during the assembly process. Since the camshaft cover is machined and matched with the cylinder head, the cover is not available from Porsche as a separate, orderable part number. You must order a complete new cylinder head, which will include the head, the cover, and the caps all matched together. This makes rebuilding and repairing any damage due to camshaft bearing wear very difficult.

27 **Five-Chain Engines:** With the camshaft caps in place and the tensioner tightened down, affix the camshaft timing tool to the opposite end. A set of Porsche tools can be used to hold the camshaft in place while working on the engine at this stage. I found them unnecessary as the camshafts are held in place if you install the timing tool as shown.

28 **Five-Chain Engines:** With the tensioners removed, you should have enough slack to push on the chain sprocket (purple arrow) with your hand. Gently tap the sprocket on the rest of the way using a rubber mallet (inset photo). If you have the Porsche factory chain tensioner tool 9599, then install it into the bottom of the case. Tighten the tension screw until the small rod in the center is flush with the adjustment screw. If you do not have this extremely expensive tool (upper right inset of Photo 29), you can tighten up the tension on the chain using the regular chain tensioner. Reinstall the tensioner completely into the bottom of the case. The green arrow shows the tensioner for cylinder bank 1–3.

29 **Five-Chain Engines:** With the camshafts installed, the timing tool in place, the two bearing caps tightened down, the camshaft solenoid tensioner tightened down, and the primary tensioner reinstalled in the case, tighten down the four bolts that hold the camshaft sprocket to the camshaft. Double-check once again that the special colored links (green arrow) in the cam-to-cam chain are properly lined up with the divot mark in the camshaft (yellow arrow). Temporarily reinstall the camshaft cover using only a handful of bolts, lightly tightened down, and then remove the camshaft timing tool. At this point, spin the engine two full turns to recheck the camshaft timing by reinstalling the tool again. The upper right inset photo shows the very expensive Porsche chain tensioner tool in place (not required).

30 **Reassembly of Three-Chain Engines:** Turn the crankshaft pulley clockwise until the hole marked "U6" lines up with the hole in the case and insert your locking pin. This is the installation position only, you will be turning the crank again during the procedure to time the camshafts.

31 **Three-Chain Engines:** Place the intake cam into its seats on the head taking care to make sure the lobes for Cylinder 4 (yellow arrows) are facing in towards the exhaust cam and that the single hole in the bearing sleeve (red arrow) is pointing directly up. There is a hole in the other side of the bearing sleeve that needs to fit into a dowel in the seat. The only way to make sure it is seated correctly is to have the single hole on the top of the bearing sleeve pointing directly up. The bearing sleeve should sit flush in the seat.

32 **Three-Chain Engines:** Lubricate the exhaust camshaft with clean motor oil and install it so that the lobes for Cylinder 4 are facing in toward the intake camshaft. Reattach the exhaust cam sprocket with the chain installed on it onto the end of the camshaft but do not insert the bolts yet. **Note:** It is import to note that when positioning the cams, the cam lobes need to point towards each other on Cylinder 4 of Bank 4–6 and away from each other on Cylinder 1 of Bank 1–3.

33 **Three-Chain Engines:** When installing the exhaust sprocket on the exhaust camshaft for Cylinders 4–6, make sure holes are oriented toward the most clockwise position (red arrow). Do not install the bolts yet.

34 **Three-Chain Engines:** Lubricate the bearing caps and reinstall them, making sure that you have the correct cap on the corresponding journal (yellow arrows) and tighten them finger tight. Install the upper chain guide rail (inset upper right, green arrow) and install the guide rail bolts finger tight (red arrows). Install the camshaft positioning tool (inset lower right, blue arrow). Reinsert the guide rail screw (see Photo 16) and then rotate engine crank clockwise until top dead center (see Photo 1).

35 **Three-Chain Engines:** The exhaust cam is now in position to install and tighten the cam sprocket bolts. The four M6 bolts on the sprocket shown on the right should now be located in the center of the slots. Install and tighten the bolt on the intake cam (insert upper right). For this fastener, do not reuse the old one off of the engine—this bolt is designed to only be tightened once, as it stretches when tightened to its final torque value. Rotate the engine until the pulley lines up with marking "U6". Follow the same procedures for bank 1-3 with the exception of the cam orientation and the exhaust cam sprocket—it will line up with the holes to the further-most counter-clockwise position. Reinstall and torque all the chain tensioners.

36 **Three-Chain and Five-Chain Engines:** Next, reinstall the oil pump onto the exhaust camshaft using two of the four bolts to affix it to the cylinder head. Carefully line up the tab of the oil pump with the slot on the camshaft and make sure that it's inserted correctly. The two scavenge oil pumps are the same for either side, but they must be installed with the proper side facing up. There are markings for Cylinders 4–6 (green arrow) and Cylinders 1–3 (yellow arrow). The pump must be installed with the markings for the current cylinder bank closest to the crankcase. Standing behind the 911, looking at the engine and the crankshaft pulley, Cylinders 1–3 are on the left and Cylinders 4–6 are on the right. If you get confused, the basic rule is that the two pumps are installed opposite to each other. The oil pump for 1–3 is located on the flywheel side of the engine, and the oil pump for 4–6 is located on the drive belt side of the engine.

37 **Three-Chain and Five-Chain Engines:** Perform a final cleansing of the surfaces with some isopropyl alcohol and let it evaporate fully before applying the sealant. Porsche recommends the use of Drei Bond silicone, type 1209, or Loctite 5900 flange sealant to seal the surface area of the head to the camshaft covers. Don't forget to apply a thin bead of sealant to the bearing saddle areas in the inner part of the head as well (five-chain only). With the sealant applied, tighten down all of the bolts on the camshaft cover in the order shown on this diagram. Carefully tighten each bolt to 10 ft-lbs (12 Nm), which is not a lot of force.

38 **Three-Chain and Five-Chain Engines:** As a final step, insert the camshaft plugs into the end of the camshafts. Lightly tap them into place with a rubber mallet. Tighten down the two remaining bolts on the oil pump and also the two bolts that secure the cover for the solenoid. With one side of the engine complete, move onto the other side and repeat the process, if necessary.

PROJECT 17
Replacing Belt Tensioners

Time / Tab / Talent: 1 hour / $150 /

Tools: 24mm wrench

Applicable Years: All

Tinware: Three tensioner pulleys

More Info: http://www.101projects.com/Carrera/17.htm

Tip: The top and bottom pulleys are different, despite them looking the same

Performance Gain: Quiet running engine

Comp Modification: Replace drive belt

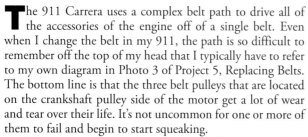

The 911 Carrera uses a complex belt path to drive all of the accessories of the engine off of a single belt. Even when I change the belt in my 911, the path is so difficult to remember off the top of my head that I typically have to refer to my own diagram in Photo 3 of Project 5, Replacing Belts. The bottom line is that the three belt pulleys that are located on the crankshaft pulley side of the motor get a lot of wear and tear over their life. It's not uncommon for one or more of them to fail and begin to start squeaking.

When you get a high-pitched squeaking noise from your engine compartment, it's typically very difficult to diagnose where it's coming from. I like to run the engine and open the engine access lid while I'm carefully listening for the origin of the squeak. Be very careful of your hands and any items that might get stuck or caught in the engine if you're running it with the rear panel off. I often use a can of WD-40 with the spray nozzle extender attached to try to isolate which pulley or piece of equipment is making the noise. With the engine running, I typically soak the bearing shaft of each belt pulley, listening carefully for changes in the squeaking noise. Check every one, including the water pump, power steering pump, alternator, and the air conditioning compressor. Often, the noise will go away when the lubricant finds its way to the bearing. This works about 50 percent of the time to isolate the noise.

Another way to check the pulleys is to remove the drive belt and actually turn them with your hand. Sometimes you can feel significant resistance or hear a grinding noise as you turn each shaft by hand. Again, check each one, including the shafts of all of the accessories. All three of the idler pulleys should feel about the same. The accessories (alternator, water pump, etc.) will each feel different, so it's difficult to tell if there's anything wrong with the bearing unless you spin these on multiple cars every day.

Sometimes a squeaking noise may be caused by a belt that is deteriorating. As belts age they sometimes get worn out and smooth, and that may cause them to slip, which can result in a squeaking noise. If you suspect the belt may be the problem, then I recommend you replace it first. Or, you can try some of the spray-on belt dressing that is available at your local auto parts store. The belt dressing is a temporary fix that makes the belt a little stickier and less prone to slipping.

Fortunately, the tensioners are very easy to replace. Simply remove air cleaner and open up access to the back of the engine (see Project 5). Then remove the drive belt from the engine. Removal of the two idler pulleys is as simple as unbolting them and replacing them with a new one. Be careful not to drop the large washer that is on the front of the two idlers or the spacers in back either. Although they look almost identical; the top and bottom idler pulleys have two different part numbers, so be careful not to mix them up if you are replacing them both at the same time. Reinstallation is a snap; simply install the bolts and tighten to 34 ft-lb (46 Nm) for the upper bolt if it's an M10 × 145 (8.8) bolt or 48 ft-lb (65 Nm) if it's an M10 × 145 (10.9). The lower pulley is tightened to 17 ft-lb (23 Nm). The bolts that are used on the pulleys originally had self-locking compound on them when they were new, so if you are reusing them again, simply add a little bit of blue Loctite 242 to the threads prior to installing them.

The tensioner pulley is a little bit different. It is attached to a spring-loaded arm via a single bolt that is backwards in orientation from the other two idler pulleys. You need to get a 15mm wrench on the head of the bolt behind the pulley and then loosen the pulley with a 24mm wrench on the front. Be careful not to drop the spacer located behind the pulley when you pull it off. Reinstall the new pulley in the same manner, using a small bed of blue Loctite 242. Tighten the assembly to 44 ft-lb (60 Nm).

1 This photo shows the back of the engine and the three pulleys discussed in the text. The yellow arrow points to the top idler pulley, and the green arrow points to the lower idler pulley. Although they look the same visually, these rollers have two different part numbers, two different bolts, and two different tightening specs. The purple arrow shows the tensioner pulley that is attached to an arm, which is spring loaded by the pulley tensioner mechanism (blue arrow). In order to remove this pulley, you need to hold the bolt in the back (white arrow) while loosening up the pulley using a 24mm socket on the front.

PROJECT 18
Turbochargers and Superchargers

Time / Tab / Talent: 30 hours / $3,000–$10,000 / 5 wrenches

Tools: All of them

Applicable Years: All

Tinware: Supercharger kit

Tip: Plan ahead and purchase a kit that fits your personal desires

Performance Gain: Gobs of horsepower and huge bragging rights

Comp Modification: Replace the head gasket, install new pistons

More Info: http://www.101projects.com/Carrera/18.htm

Many people think that turbo and supercharging are the holy grail of power increases. While indeed you can extract a large amount of power from them, people incorrectly assume that any aftermarket supercharger tossed on an engine will instantly generate gobs of horsepower. As with any good, reliable means of generating horsepower, the addition of a turbo or supercharger needs to be carefully coordinated with your engine's design, all the while keeping in mind your desired performance characteristics.

It's important to take a few moments here to talk about turbo and supercharging, or "forced induction" as it is known. A forced induction engine has some assistance when filling the combustion chamber with air/fuel mixture. On a normally aspirated engine, the maximum manifold pressure is atmospheric pressure (14.7 psi). On a forced induction engine, manifold pressure is increased by the supercharger (or turbocharger) to a level above 14.7 psi. The result is that a greater mass of air and fuel is injected into the combustion chamber, resulting in more power.

Both a turbocharger and supercharger are very similar in principle. Both use a compressor/blower to increase the overall pressure of gasses inserted into the combustion chamber (cold side). This increase in pressure results in an air/fuel mixture that is compressed greater than normal. The result is that the denser mixture generates a more powerful stroke. Because of the higher density of the mixture, with forced induction you can create an engine with a smaller displacement that has same energy output as you would have with a larger displacement engine (more power).

What about reliability? Factory-designed forced induction engines (like the Porsche 911 Turbo) are specially designed to accommodate the additional stresses placed on them by the added boost. Engines like these are designed from the ground up and usually have very low compression ratios to compensate for the added pressures when the car is operating under full boost. Bolting a turbocharger or supercharger to a stock engine will result in more wear and tear on the engine. If you are planning on installing a forced induction system on your stock engine, you must plan on purchasing only high-octane fuel. The increased compression in the cylinders will increase the likelihood of detonation, which can destroy your engine very quickly.

HOW THEY WORK

The supercharger is powered by a pulley that attaches to the crankshaft. As the engine's rpm increases, outside air is compressed and mixed with fuel and discharged into the intake system. There are three common types of superchargers: impeller (centrifugal), twin rotating screws (screw-type), and counter-rotating rotors (roots-type). As the engine spins faster, the boost from the supercharger will increase. Typical boost levels for a street Carrera range from 4 to 6 psi. Boost is the measurement of the increase of pressure in the intake charge over normal outside atmospheric levels.

The turbocharger unit drives its compressor from the excess exhaust given off by the engine. Although the backpressure on the exhaust may rob a small amount of power from the engine, the boost from the turbo is generally thought of as free boost. The turbocharger unit is very similar in operation to the centrifugal supercharger, with the exception that it is driven off of the exhaust gases versus a pulley attached to the crankshaft. Typical peak revolutions of turbos can range anywhere from 75,000 all the way up to 150,000.

HEAD-TO-HEAD COMPARISON

Power and efficiency. Whereas the turbo runs off of the exhaust system, a supercharger takes power from the engine crankshaft to run the blower. All things being equal, superchargers sap more power overhead (40–50 horsepower to spin the blower at full boost) from the engine to run the compressor than turbochargers. Turbos are not without horsepower cost—the backpressure from the turbo and restrictions due to the convoluted exhaust piping act to reduce horsepower. However, these losses are minimal when compared to the horsepower cost of driving a supercharger off of the crankshaft. The bottom line is if you're looking to squeeze the maximum amount of power out of a specific displacement (as you would if you were running in certain club racer classes), then the turbocharger systems win hands down over the supercharger.

Power lag. Reduction of lag is a top reason why superchargers are preferred over turbochargers for street cars. Since the turbocharger is spooled up by the exhaust gases from the engine, it doesn't achieve significant boost levels until the engine's rpm reaches a certain level. This results in little or no boost in the lower rpm range. When the boost finally kicks in, it can be an unsettling experience, as the car rockets off as soon as you reach an rpm level that produces boost. This power surge can also place additional stresses on stock drivetrain and suspension components. There are several things you can do to reduce turbo lag (described more in this project), but these "fixes" sacrifice top-end power. A supercharger on the other hand is connected directly to the crankshaft and is spinning and creating boost at all times. Superchargers are able to create significant boost levels at low rpm, so there's typically not much lag. Whereas a turbocharger has power that instantly comes online at about 3,000–4,000 rpm, the supercharger has a nice, even boost curve that generates excellent power off of the line.

Reliability. Turbocharger systems are somewhat complex and thus are considered less reliable than superchargers. In addition, all of the turbo system components work with exhaust gases, which further create additional heat stress and wear on the system. When you first shut off your car with a turbo system, the temperatures can spike inside the turbo and you can experience problems with the impeller bearings being cooked by this high heat (some people install what are known as turbo timers that let the engine run at idle and cool down for a minute or so before shutting off). Turbochargers spin at a much higher rpm than superchargers and thus the bearings inside have a tendency to wear out much faster. Many turbo system exhaust components are handmade, and welds in the seams crack with age.

Heat. The turbocharger system is powered by hot exhaust gases that have a tendency to inadvertently heat up the intake mixture charge. Hot air expands and becomes less dense, so this heating effect works against the compressing action of the turbocharger. Cooler air means a higher density air/fuel mixture, which is the whole point of the installation of a forced induction system. To solve this problem, most turbo systems require an intercooler, which increases the complexity and cost of the system. This hot air is cycled through a large intercooler that cools the air before it is injected into the intake manifold. The cooler air helps to reduce detonation and also increases the density of the air/fuel mixture. In addition to the heat gathered from the exhaust gases, the intake air temperature increases as well when the air is compressed. All turbochargers should be run with an intercooler, and most superchargers can also see benefits from the use of an intercooler.

Installation and tuning. Superchargers in general are pretty easy to install. Many bolt-on kits exist and can be installed over a long weekend. The supercharger kits require only a few modifications to the fuel system, mostly provided in the form of a new software map for the digital motor electronics (DME) to get the engine up and running well. On the other hand, most turbo installations involve complex routing of exhaust pipes, oil lines, and other components—many of which must be modified to fit. Intercoolers are typically a difficult item to fit into the tight space available with the Carrera engine compartment, without the addition of a large rear wing. Although turbo systems can be made to run with the stock fuel and ignition systems (DME), in order to extract the most power out of a turbocharger system, you should probably run the engine using a dedicated and custom engine management system like Tec-3 or Motec.

Cost. In general, both types of systems can be expensive, costing anywhere from $8,000 for a basic kit, up to $15,000 for a complete setup installed and tested on the dyno. In general, since the turbo systems are more complicated, they tend to be slightly more expensive, particularly when you add in the modification costs associated with an intercooler. Another consideration is the cost of installation. Most supercharger setups are relatively straightforward installations, as you only need to modify one side of the engine bay and the intake system. Installation of a turbo setup is much trickier (and a bit more expensive) due to all of the effort involved with the routing and installation of the exhaust pipes. Despite what many manufacturers may say, turbo kits are almost never a straight bolt-on installation. The pipes and brackets are almost always handmade and often require some tweaking to fit.

Power output and streetability. Both turbochargers and superchargers can produce significant power gains, although turbochargers can squeeze more total power out of the system due to the fact that they are run off of the "free energy" from the exhaust system. Because the turbocharger units operate at very high rpm, they can produce very high levels of boost in the upper rpm range and deliver much more peak horsepower at these levels. However, most people don't drive their car at peak rpm all the time on the street. Most of the driving is done in the lower rpm bands, where superchargers have their power advantage. If you want to drive around town with more power off of the line, then a supercharger kit is probably the best choice. If you are going to be racing the car on a track or you want maximum top-end power on the highway, then a turbocharger will allow you to squeeze the most power out of your engine.

SUPERCHARGERS

In general, the most common type of supercharger installed into the Carrera is the centrifugal type. The centrifugal supercharger is most similar to a turbocharger, with the exception that it is driven off of a belt that is connected to the engine's crankshaft. The centrifugal superchargers compress air using a spun impeller. The advantage to these units is that you can often swap out impeller sizes and change the drive pulley to customize the boost curve for your particular needs. Centrifugal superchargers are typically set to generate their peak boost at or near the redline of the engine. In general, they develop more of their boost at higher rpm and offer less boost on the low end of the rpm range. Paxton, Powerdyne, ProCharger, and Vortech are all good quality manufacturers of centrifugal superchargers.

TURBOCHARGER SYSTEMS

Many people incorrectly think that a larger turbocharger will generate more boost and horsepower. In reality, this is not necessarily true. Installation of a larger forced induction unit must also accompany other important changes in the engine. Maximum boost pressure is limited by a pressure relief valve called the wastegate. The wastegate acts to release exhaust gas pressure, slowing the turbine so the engine doesn't suffer from too much boost being applied. Installing a larger turbocharger without making adjustments to the wastegate will result in no increase in maximum boost levels.

How does the size of the turbocharger affect performance? The numeric digits used to describe the turbocharger (K24, K26, K27, etc.) usually correspond to the actual size of the turbo exhaust fan wheel inside the turbocharger (called the hot side). In addition, the wheel on the intake (cold side) compresses the air to create the actual boost. Changing the sizes of the two wheels can alter the overall personality of the turbocharger and can be used to tailor the turbo response to your specific application.

For example, a small turbine wheel in the exhaust combined with a small impeller wheel on the compressor side will spin the turbo up quickly and generate a quick throttle response, but it will also tend to drop off power on the top end. A small turbine in the exhaust with a large blower will generate a good compromise between throttle response and top-end power. To obtain the best top-end performance, a large turbo wheel combined with a large blower wheel can be used together. The downside is that throttle-response will suffer in the lower rpm range.

Installing a smaller turbine wheel in the exhaust means that it will spin up much faster than a larger one. The ideal turbo configuration for everyday street driving is to have a smaller turbine on the hot side, and a larger blower turbine on the cold side. This particular configuration is a good compromise between low-end throttle response and high-end power. The downside to this configuration is that it takes a certain level of exhaust pressure at a minimum rpm to spin up the exhaust (hot side) turbine to the point where it can begin to have an effect on the intake pressures. This is commonly known as turbo lag. In a race engine, turbo lag is typically not a major issue, since the transmission gearing and overall setup of the engine is usually designed to operate within a narrow power band in the high rpm range.

How do you improve performance? Swapping the turbocharger with one that has a different ratio between the wheels can change your turbo engine's characteristics. There are numerous options for turbochargers—each one changes the performance characteristics slightly different from the next. Perform some research and ask others who have installed various units on their Carreras before you spend a large amount of money on a new turbocharger. Adding an intercooler or upgrading your existing one will also increase your overall performance. Simply dialing in more boost from the turbocharger (by changing the wastegate relief valve setting) can give you an immediate performance improvement. Also, increasing the compression in your engine will give you more low-end power. However, these approaches can be extremely hazardous to your engine. Severe detonation from poor quality gas can cause pistons to overheat, and the engine can literally blow itself apart. For more information on turbocharging, see the book *Turbochargers* by Hugh MacInnes or *Maximum Boost* by Corky Bell.

HOW MUCH BOOST?

This is an age-old question that is answered with the old saying, "There's no such thing as a free lunch." How much boost you run on your forced induction system depends upon a wide variety of factors.

What type of induction is it? As mentioned previously, turbo systems come to full boost capability and then bleed off excess with a wastegate. While this arrangement creates great power in the upper rpm range, it also means that you're running at highly boosted levels for extended periods of time. With a centrifugal supercharger, it only reaches maximum boost at the highest rpm, and then only for a few seconds. So, you can run much higher peak boost levels on a centrifugal supercharger than you can with a turbo setup.

Which fuel octane? Running a boosted engine puts a lot of stress on the internals of the engine, as you are pushing more and more power through the drivetrain. However, the real killer for these engines is detonation. If the octane is too low and the compression of the engine too high, then the fuel will explode prematurely, in what is commonly known as engine knocking, or detonation. When the mixture in the combustion chamber explodes, it increases the pressure in the cylinder and pushes down on the piston. When detonation occurs, the piston is still rising and still compressing the mixture. Thus, when ignition occurs, the pressure builds and has no release. The pressure is pushing down on the piston as it's rising, creating a tremendous amount of pressure that has nowhere to go. Unchecked, detonation will destroy pistons and blow out head gaskets. It's the number one killer of forced induction engines. The solution is to reduce your boost levels so that the engine no longer detonates. The engine management system (DME) normally adjusts timing and ignition in response to signals received from the knock sensor to reduce detonation in the cylinders. However, running really high amounts of boost with lower octane fuel can overwhelm the stock system and confuse it. The bottom line is that the higher boost you wish to run, the higher the octane fuel you will have to buy. If you want to head to the drag strip and run all out with as much boost as you possibly can, be prepared to buy some race fuel with octane ratings in the 105–110 range.

What is the air/fuel mixture? When you install a forced induction system onto an engine, you are increasing the amount of air that is injected into the combustion chamber. Most of the time, this will cause the air/fuel mixture to become lean. You must compensate for this occurrence by increasing the amount of fuel that is combined with the air mixture, since that mixture is now compressed and thus more dense. According to modern fuel injection theory, fuel and air combustion achieves its maximum efficiency at a ratio of 14.67:1. Although this ratio may be optimum for good fuel economy, it's not best for maximizing power. On a normally aspirated engine at full throttle, maximum power is achieved with an air/fuel ratio set at about 14.2:1 to 14.3:1. On boosted engines this maximum power ratio is more in the range of 12.2 to 12.4. If your boosted engine is running too lean, the likelihood of detonation will increase as will the operating temperature of the cylinder head. It's very important to make sure that your engine is running on the rich side. I recommend running an aftermarket air/fuel mixture gauge to monitor and protect against the engine running lean.

What modifications have been done to the DME? The DME (digital motor electronics) controls the ignition and air/fuel ratio injected into the engine. Installing a forced induction system is such a major change to the engine that it's difficult to adapt the computer to correctly compensate for the compressed intake charge without performing a complete remapping of the air-fuel mixture program (see Project 25).

What is the compression ratio? Engines that start out with a high compression ratio (like the 2000 Carrera at 11.3:1) cannot be boosted as much as engines with lower ratios. To properly integrate forced induction into any engine, it should be designed from the ground up with forced induction in mind. The higher compression ratios of the 996/997 Carrera engines, don't naturally lend themselves to forced induction kits. In general, forced induction engines are blueprinted to have a very low compression ratio (like the venerable Porsche 911 Turbo with 7.0:1). The bottom line is that you can generate more horsepower from maximizing the boost from the turbo than you can with higher compression. If you run higher compression, then you will be forced to run with less boost at the higher end to avoid destroying your engine. You want to design your engine to have low compression so that you can run higher boost at higher rpms and generate more horsepower. You can lower the compression ratio by a variety of methods: adding a thicker head gasket, installing lower compression custom-made pistons, etc.

How old is the engine? Bearings and clearances wear over years of use. Most companies that sell superchargers don't recommend installing them on a tired engine. The chances that you will blow out your head gasket are quite high as the engine gets older. Increasing the overall compression inside the combustion chamber increases the wear and tear on all the parts in the drivetrain.

Boost Level	Compression Ratio
8 psi*	10.5:1
9–10 psi*	10.0:1
11–12 psi*	9.5:1
13–14 psi*	9.0:1
15–18 psi*	8.5:1

*running on 91 octane

1 Here's a shot of the supercharger kit developed by VF Engineering. These compact cars are very light and very nimble and create quite a performance machine when you bump up the horsepower with one of these kits. Because of the lack of room in the engine compartment, this supercharger kit requires the use of a lot of custom parts, including a whole set of new intake plenums. It's a tough squeeze, but the centrifugal supercharger fits quite nicely tucked in front of the alternator. The kit is professionally designed, and as a result, the engine compartment retains its "stock look." A new airbox is required of course, as well as a complete remapping of the digital motor electronics (ECU).

2 Here are the main contents of the supercharger kit described in the previous photo. Although it takes thousands of hours and testing to successfully design and implement a good bolt-on kit, the actual installation and assembly process can be completed typically over a long weekend by a semi-experienced do-it-yourselfer. One key to success with this particular kit is the fact that the clever designers at VF were able to incorporate a water-cooled intercooler into the tight space inside the engine bay. This helps to reduce the temperature of the boosted/compressed air and significantly increases power output.

The bottom line? Follow a few rules of thumbs when it comes to running forced induction engines. The following table gives you a broad outline of what boost levels you can run for a variety of compression ratios.

CONCLUSIONS

Which forced induction unit to install really depends upon your overall goals, which include ease of installation and budget limitations. If you ask 10 different enthusiasts out there what their preferences are, you will get 10 completely different answers. There are people who are turbo fans, and there are people who are die-hard supercharger recruits. Obviously, this project can only scratch the surface of what's involved in designing and implementing a turbocharger or supercharger system.

You can make some generalizations though regarding the relative performance of these two systems. If you want a drag car with lots of power off of the line, then you should probably go with a supercharger system. This will give you a boost at low rpms and a predictable power curve. If you're looking for top speed on the Autobahn where you want to squeeze out all the power you can, then I recommend a turbocharger system. It will give you maximum power at the higher end of your rpm range. With most supercharger systems, you will achieve maximum boost when you're at redline. With a turbocharger, you will have nearly full boost all the way from about 3,000–4,000 rpm to redline. If you like the feel of a rush of power and the ability to create gobs of peak horsepower, go with a turbocharger. Turbo systems are also considered to be more flexible in that they can often be designed to fit most owners' requirements; superchargers can be a bit more limited. If you want your car to feel somewhat stock with a big push on the high end, then go with a centrifugal supercharger. Of course, if you want more overall power without the hassle of forced induction, you can put a higher displacement engine in your Carrera.

In terms of installation ease, the supercharger systems win overwhelmingly. Turbocharger systems can be made to be better performers, but they generally require more time, money, and installation effort to achieve this.

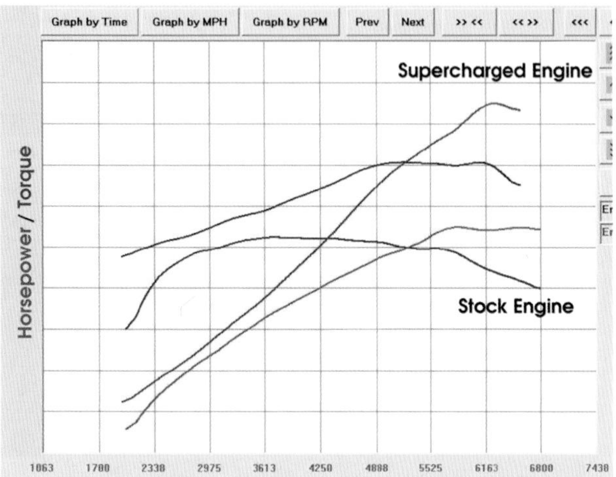

3 This graph shows clearly why supercharger kits are so popular. They take the already aggressive Carrera engines and turn them into monsters. When combined with a lightweight chassis like the Carrera, the combination makes for a powerful and nimble track car with performance exceeding that of a Carrera RS.

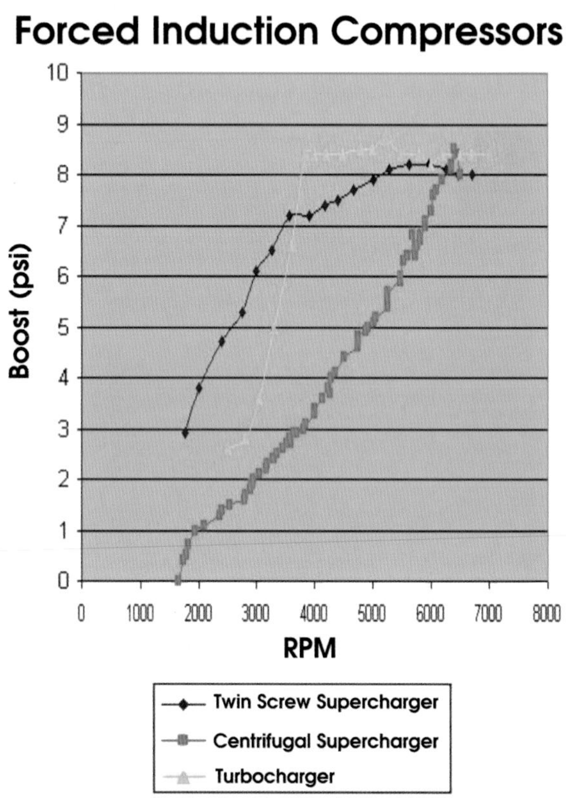

4 This chart shows the different boost levels between a centrifugal supercharger, a twin-screw supercharger, and a turbocharger system. As you can see, the twin-screw generates more boost per rpm than the centrifugal unit. The turbocharger graph shows low boost levels until about 3500 where it rockets up to full boost in a hurry. *Steve Anderson*

5 Shown here is a boost gauge mounted on the driver side A-pillar. I recommend installing one of these in your car if you're running a forced induction system. A boost gauge will give you a snapshot of the health of your induction system and will also alert you to boost levels that may be too high.

SECTION 3
FUEL

Without a doubt, the fuel injection system on your Carrera can be one of the most finicky systems to diagnose and troubleshoot. While volumes could be written simply on fuel injection systems, this section focuses both on introducing the Motronic engine management system and also on identifying common problems and potential pitfalls. Reading through these projects will help you identify and solve problems with your own fuel injection system.

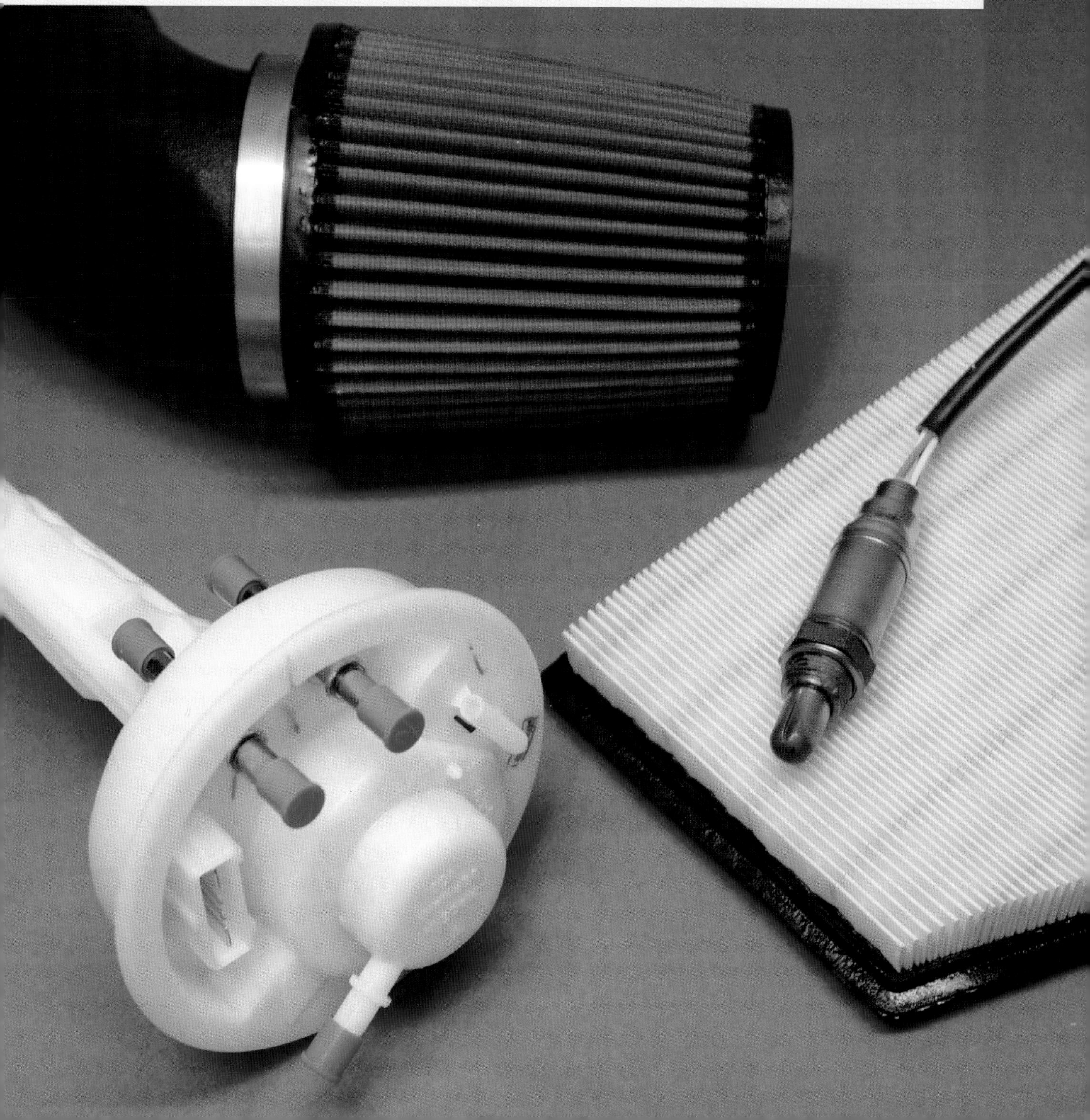

PROJECT 19
Replacing Your Oxygen Sensor

Time / Tab / Talent: 1 hour / $100–$400 /

Tools: Floor jack and jack stands, 22mm wrench

Applicable Years: All

Tinware: New oxygen sensor

More Info: http://www.101projects.com/Carrera/19.htm

Tip: Use anti-seize compound on the threads of the sensor to make it easier to replace it next time

Performance Gain: More accurate air/fuel mixture and better-running engine

Comp Modification: Install an aftermarket exhaust system or replace old exhaust gaskets

The oxygen sensor (also called an O_2 sensor) is one of the most important elements of modern fuel injection systems. A finely tuned fuel injection system with an oxygen sensor can maintain an air/fuel ratio within a close tolerance of .02 percent. Keeping the engine at the stoichiometric level (14.6:1 air/fuel ratio) helps the engine generate the most power with the least amount of emissions.

The oxygen sensors are located in the exhaust system of the engine, and they sense the oxygen content of the exhaust gases. There are a total of four on the Carrera—two for each catalytic converter on the car. The sensor located just in front of the catalytic converter measures the mixture of the exhaust gases exiting the engine. The sensor located after the catalytic converter is used to measure the performance of the converter by comparing the O_2 levels before and after. The amount of oxygen in the exhaust varies according to the air/fuel ratio of the fuel injection system. The oxygen sensor produces a small voltage signal that is interpreted by the electronic control unit (ECU) of the fuel injection system. The ECU makes constant adjustments in fuel delivery according to the signal generated by the oxygen sensor in order to maintain the optimum air/fuel ratio.

You may notice a few signs that your oxygen sensor may be failing. In general, it is difficult to diagnose problems with the sensor unless all of the other components in the fuel injection system have been checked and determined to be operating correctly. Some of the symptoms of a failed oxygen sensor system include the following:

- Irregular idle during warm-up
- Irregular idle with warm engine
- Engine will not accelerate and backfires
- Poor engine performance
- Fuel consumption is high
- Driving performance is weak
- CO concentration at idle is too high or too low
- Check engine light is illuminated

In general, if the oxygen sensor is not working, the car will be running very poorly and will also be outputting a lot of harmful emissions. If the signal received by the computer is out of its normal range, the 911 Carrera's computer will almost always give a warning signal that lights up the check engine lamp. Sometimes the computer may output an error code stating that the oxygen sensor is reading out of range, when in reality the values are out of range because there is something else wrong with the fuel injection system. Prior to replacing the oxygen sensors, make sure there are no other codes being recorded that may affect the O_2 sensor readings. For more info on reading these fuel injection codes, see Project 20.

If you disconnect the oxygen sensor and ground it to the chassis, the ECU will think that the car is running lean (not enough fuel) and will try to make the mixture richer. At the other extreme, if you disconnect the oxygen sensor and replace it with a small AA battery that supplies 1.5 volts, the ECU will think that the car is running really rich and attempt to adjust the mixture to be leaner.

Needless to say, troubleshooting the complete fuel injection system is beyond this project's scope. If you think that the oxygen sensors may be causing some of your fuel injection problems, they should be replaced. In general, I recommend that you do this every 30,000 miles. You have to jack up the car to gain access to the sensor (see Project 1).

Using a 22mm wrench, simply remove the sensor from the exhaust pipe. On the Carrera, the sensors are very easy to reach. On many other cars, you would need a special deep socket with a slit cut in the side to remove it. The electrical plug for the O_2 sensor simply unplugs from the chassis harness. New O_2 sensors should have the same exact plug—

ready to attach to your car. When you remove the O_2 sensor, you will probably find that it is coated with black soot. This is normal for an old, worn-out O_2 sensor. On our project car here, the O_2 sensor was covered in motor oil and coolant. This is a bad sign that corresponds with the seized engine in my project car—I bought it that way. (See Project 13 for more details on the problems sometimes found with these late-model Porsche engines.)

Install your new sensor snug-tight, or if you have the proper slit-tool and a handy torque wrench, then tighten it to 40 ft-lbs (55 N-m). It's also a smart idea to add some anti-seize compound to the threads of the plug before you install it, but make sure the anti-seize doesn't get into any of the slits on the head of the sensor. Check the sensor first though, as new ones sometimes come with anti-seize already on the threads.

You can purchase two different types of sensors: generic ones that allow you to snip the connector off of the old sensor and put it on the new one, and original equipment manufacturer (OEM) sensors with the correct connector. On older cars, I used the generic sensors, but I've had problems with using them on these newer cars. Researching further, I discovered that the wires and connectors are very important on these O_2 sensors. The Porsche factory workshop manuals state the following:

"911 Carrera 4 has a new, water-proof oxygen sensor. Water-proof means that the upper sensor section and housing are connected leak-proof with a later welded seam and previous reference air openings are omitted. Reference air is now taken via the connecting lead and plug connection. For this reason it is important to keep contact solutions, lubricants, liquids or similar products out of the 3-pin plug, since they would lead to sensor failure."

Soldering wires together can interrupt the reference air signal and lead to problems with the sensor. I've also had problems with the Bosch factory Posi-Lock connectors that are supposed to work with these newer sensors. Because the relationship between the connector and the O_2 sensor is so vital to the proper reference signal, I recommend that you only use the correct sensors with the proper plug.

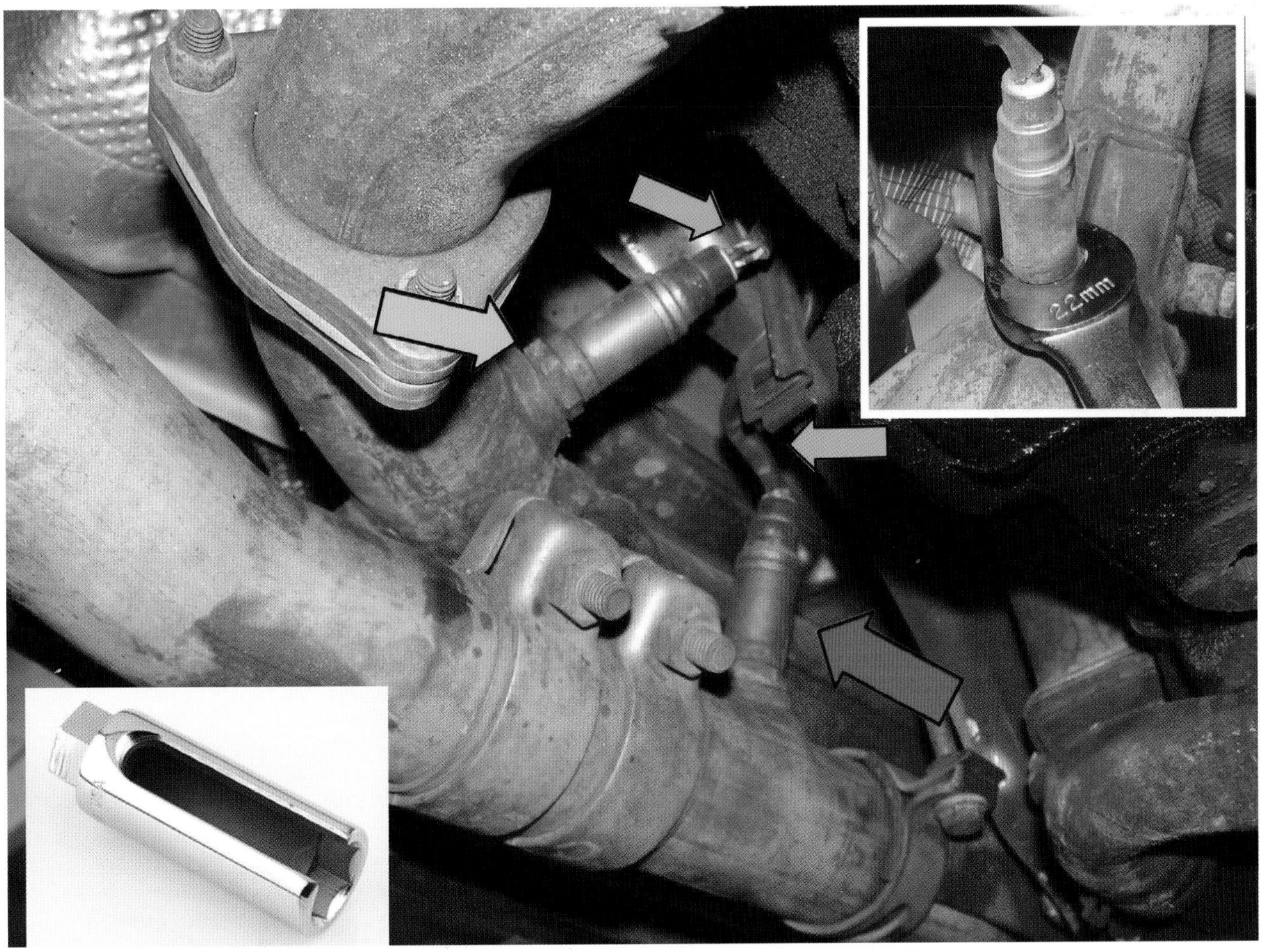

1 Shown here are the two oxygen sensors for the left side of the car (red arrow shows the pre-catalytic, yellow shows the post catalytic converter). On the 997 Carreras, one of the sensors is located on the catalytic converter, but the removal and replacement procedure is the same. The green arrows show the wires that go to the engine shelf where the connectors are located. I have often found that the new O_2 sensors come with the correct plug, but sometimes the cable is way too long. If this is the case, then secure the cable with a nylon cable tie. Make sure that the cable is not located anywhere near any exhaust components—you don't want the heat melting the cable to the O_2 sensor. The photo inset shows the special tool that is sometimes required to remove O_2 sensors in hard-to-reach places (available from PelicanParts.com).

PROJECT 20
Reading Fuel Injection Fault Codes

Time / Tab / Talent: 30 minutes / $300 /

Tools: Durametric Software

Applicable Years: All

Tinware:

More Info: http://www.101projects.com/Carrera/20.htm

Tip: The Durametric software is essential to diagnosing problems

Performance Gain: Better-running engine when the problems are fixed

Comp Modification: Replace O_2 sensor—the computer often shows this error code

Almost all Porsches from about 1984 use a sophisticated Bosch engine management system called Motronic. The Motronic system (also called the Digital Motor Electronics [DME] is hands down the best overall fuel injection system that you can use when you consider price and performance. Ignition timing and fuel delivery are all controlled by a digital map that is recorded in a removable chip within the main fuel injection (DME) computer. The computer takes input from a variety of sensors that are located on the engine—engine coolant temperature, crank angle, throttle position, exhaust gas oxygen (mixture), ambient air temperature, and mass airflow. The DME flash memory chip is programmed from the factory with certain performance characteristics (mostly conservative) so that the engine will react well under a host of varying conditions.

As with any electronic device, components can fail, triggering problems with the system. The Porsche Motronic system is designed to react to these failures and indicate them to the driver, so that they can be fixed. If one of the computer's sensors is not working properly, then the computer may not be able to successfully identify the current state of the engine and choose the appropriate fuel mixture or timing advance level. When this happens, the fuel mileage drops, engine performance suffers, emissions increase, and the car typically illuminates the check engine light.

Pre-1995 Porsches were equipped with what is known as OBD I (On-Board Diagnostics Level I). Starting in 1996, they were equipped with a more advanced version called OBD II, which was mandated by the U.S. government in order to standardize automotive repair and diagnostics. The OBD system is responsible for monitoring and checking all of the fuel injection sensors and systems in the vehicle and turns on the check engine lamp if it finds a problem or irregularity with one of them. If there is a problem with a sensor or component, the computer lodges a diagnostic trouble code (DTC) in the main computer until it is read and reset.

In order to accurately find the sensor and fix the problem, you will need to find out which error code is being triggered by the computer. There is no method to pull these codes out of your Porsche without the use of a computer tool. The factory has produced a version of this tool for use by Porsche dealers called the Porsche System Tester 2 (PST2). Unfortunately, finding one of these is next to impossible, and they cost about $4,000 used anyway. There's a newer version of the PST2 called the PIWIS, but getting your hands on one of those costs about $20,000 and a $1,000 maintenance contract from Porsche. You can indeed use a standard off-the-shelf OBD II reader available at any auto parts store, but it will only give you the standard read-out codes for the fuel injection system—you will not be able to do any extra diagnostics on any other area of the car.

Thankfully though, there is aftermarket software available produced by Durametric that performs almost all of important reading functions that the PST2 does. It runs on a Windows laptop computer, and the cost is about $300 for the home-based version that will allow you to read codes on up to three cars. If you're planning on working on your 911 Carrera at all, I suggest that you pick up this essential tool.

With a standard ODB II code reader, you can access and reset the codes on the car that are related only to the fuel injection system. The PST2 and Durametric software allow you to dig deep into the various systems of the car and read their values (air bag, ABS, Tiptronic transmission, alarm, seat memory, heating and air conditioning). The Durametric tool does not program the computer though; you are still at the mercy of the dealer when it comes to making changes to any of the non–fuel injection settings on your car.

When you obtain the trouble codes output by the PST2, you can look them up in the Porsche ODB II factory diagnostic book (expensive) or refer to the Bentley Workshop Manual for additional details. Both manuals have extensive sections describing the various faults and what is needed to fix them.

Tip: Wire harnesses are a major cause of fault code problems. As the cars get older, the wiring harnesses have a habit of becoming what is commonly known as "work-hardened." This causes the wiring to become brittle and often break inside of its plastic sheath. Only by testing the continuity of the wires end-for-end will you be able to determine whether the wire is broken or not.

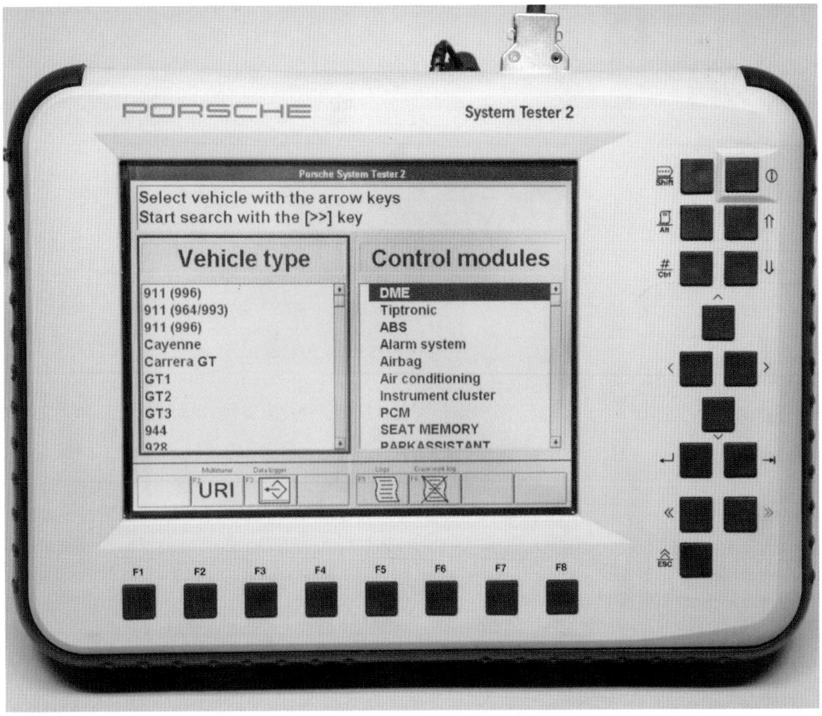

1 Here it is, the holy grail of Porsche code reading. The Porsche System Tester 2 (PST2) is a rare and expensive tool that can be used to diagnose multiple car systems on a variety of Porsches. Every dealer has one of these, or the later-model PIWIS tester, so that the dealer can quickly diagnose problems and change settings on the various computer systems within the car.

2 Both the PST2 and the Durametric software interface with the car through the On Board Diagnostic Level II (OBD II) port located beneath the steering wheel on the lower left-hand side of the car. Make sure that the plug is firmly seated, as it has a tendency to occasionally fall out.

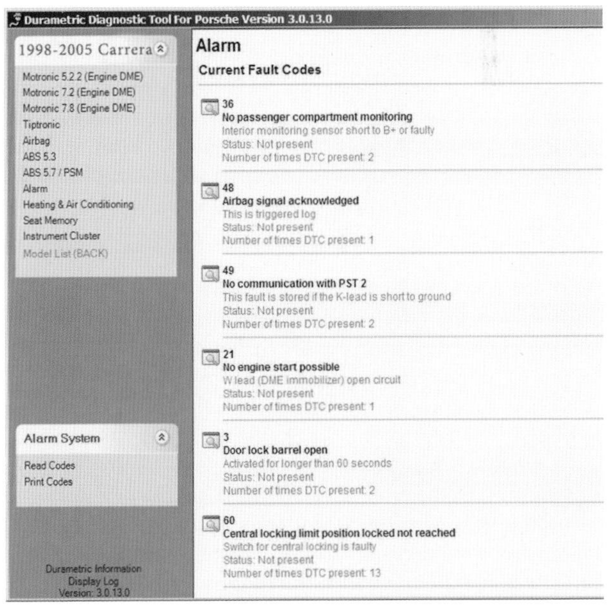

3 Shown here is a screenshot of the Durametric software available for diagnosing various system problems. The software is nearly as powerful as the reading functions on the original Porsche PST2 and is a required diagnostic tool for the do-it-yourself enthusiast.

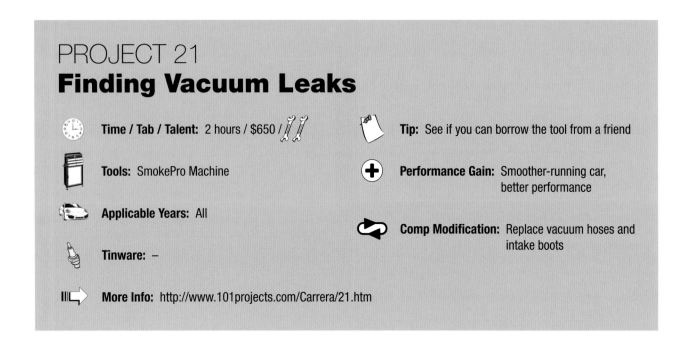

PROJECT 21
Finding Vacuum Leaks

Time / Tab / Talent: 2 hours / $650 /

Tools: SmokePro Machine

Applicable Years: All

Tinware: –

More Info: http://www.101projects.com/Carrera/21.htm

Tip: See if you can borrow the tool from a friend

Performance Gain: Smoother-running car, better performance

Comp Modification: Replace vacuum hoses and intake boots

Today's modern cars have a tremendous amount of vacuum hoses and boots contained with the engine compartment. To the uneducated eye, the engine compartment can easily look like the insides of an oil refinery with all the hoses running in and out. As these hoses and boots age and are constantly exposed to hot and cold temperatures, they tend to break down and develop cracks, which can then cause vacuum leaks. Unfortunately, when the fuel injection system develops a vacuum leak it will tend to confuse the fuel injection computer's sensors, and the car will cease to run properly. You may get decreased gas mileage, rough idling, misfires, and sometimes a check engine light on the dashboard.

Whenever someone contacts me and indicates that their car is running rough, I almost always tell them to check the entire system carefully for vacuum leaks. Without the proper tools, this can sometimes be very difficult. Old rubber boots have a tendency to crack and leak in spots that are not visible to the naked eye. Sometimes squeezing them will show a crack that you can't normally see when the boot is in its initial resting position.

One poor man's way to check for vacuum leaks is to artificially create a leak and see how the engine reacts. The Carrera engine has two primary vacuum systems: crankcase vacuum and intake manifold vacuum. You can test for proper crankcase vacuum by removing the oil cap while the car is idling. The engine should change idle and begin to run a bit rougher with the oil cap off. If there is no change in the running of the engine, then you might have a crankcase vacuum leak somewhere (sometimes caused by a failing air-oil separator—see Project 9). To induce a vacuum leak into the intake manifold, you can disconnect one or more of the hoses that connect to the intake. One example would be the hose that connects to the air-oil separator. If you crack one of these hoses open just a bit and the engine rpm doesn't change, then you might have an intake vacuum leak somewhere.

By far, the best way to test for vacuum leaks is with a smoke machine. Although these are somewhat expensive at about $650, you can rent and/or borrow them from some shops. The machine generates smoke and then blows it through your engine's intake and crankcase. All you need to do is sit back and watch for little puffs of smoke where there is a leak in the system. This can save many, many hours of random troubleshooting and guesswork. For one of my project cars, I wanted to make sure all of my custom-made hoses that were required for the installation of the larger engine were leak-free. I ran the car through the smoke machine and confirmed that everything was airtight and there were no troublesome leaks.

The smoke machine runs on standard household baby oil and generates smoke by heating the oil. The smoke generated is very similar to the type created in model railroad steam engines. The machine also needs to be connected to a shop air compressor. The compressed air is mixed with the smoke and then funneled through the intake system of the engine. In the case of the Boxster, I removed the intake air filter and used a cone adapter that comes with the machine to seal the smoke hose to the intake pipe. The car should be completely cold when you are testing it for leaks, as the rubber hoses and boots are most likely to leak when they are cold and contracted. You should also remove the mass airflow sensor from the system so that the smoke doesn't build up on the sensor and affect its operation. Plug the hole for the sensor with some masking tape.

If you are run a smoke test, make sure your car is cold. As the car warms up, things can expand and seal small leaks. Testing with a cold engine will give you your best chance of finding all the leaks.

After you power up the smoke machine, it will take a minute or two to fully smoke out the car. If your car is completely airtight (a good thing), then you might not see any smoke. You can check to see if the smoke machine is operating correctly by removing the oil cap in the rear trunk. You should see a steady plume of smoke exiting out of the oil filler (this is normal). On the Carrera, you may also see some very tiny plumes of smoke exiting out of the resonance flapper bearings—this is also normal and doesn't affect the operation of the car or indicate a major vacuum leak. If you do see steady plumes of smoke exiting out of the engine compartment, then investigate further. On the 3.4 engine we were testing, there weren't any major leaks, but there were a few minor ones (one of the breather hoses that connected to the radiator tank needed to be tightened).

Although you might think a smoke machine is a limited-use tool, it's highly versatile for solving other problems as well. Basically, any system that contains air can be tested. You can use the system to check climate control systems, leaky headlamp housings, exhaust systems, and A/C lines and compressors (although most A/C leaks are very small and difficult to detect with just a smoke machine). You can also bench test components, such as radiators, prior to installation to make sure that they are factory perfect.

You can even use the smoke machine to detect leaks from door and window seals. First, roll up all windows and seal the car. Then turn on the fresh-air fan motor at its maximum setting (do not set the system to recirculate). Using the smoke machine with a diffuser (a wider nozzle that will slow down the flow of smoke), move around the outside of the car and blow the smoke onto the area you think might have a leak. The fresh-air fans inside the car will create a positive pressure environment that will push air out through any leaks. By slowly blowing smoke on these suspected areas, you can see the smoke pattern become disturbed by the leaking air. This test, of course, requires that you do it inside your garage in an environment where the air is very still.

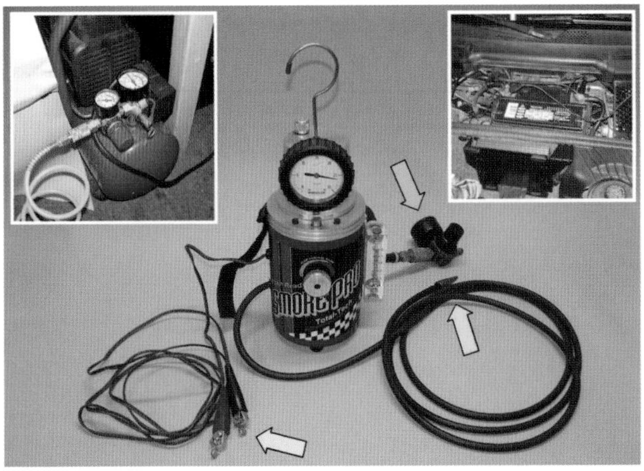

1 Shown here is the Redline Smoke Pro machine. This extremely useful tool is invaluable for finding vacuum leaks within your fuel injection system. The machine's air supply is provided by an air compressor (upper left) that is plugged into a pressure regulator (green arrow). The heater is powered by your car battery (upper right and blue arrow). The compressed air is combined with smoke and then pushed out through the nozzle (yellow arrow).

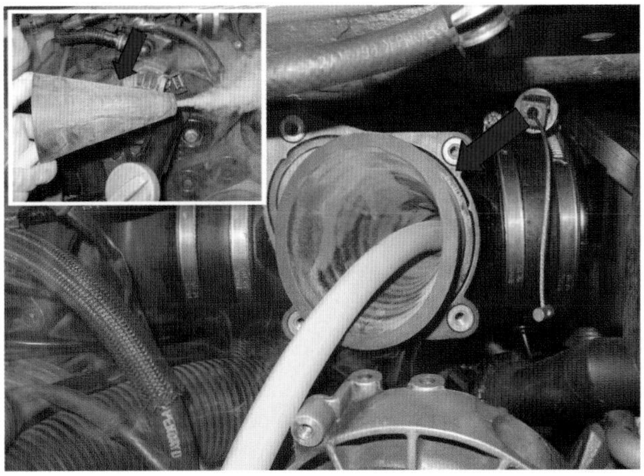

2 With the smoke machine turned on, you can see the trail of smoke that exits out of the nozzle (insert, upper left). You don't want to "smoke out" your mass airflow sensor, so if you are checking the system with the airbox on, make sure be sure that you remove it and tape off or plug the hole prior to pressurizing the system. The sensor is located inside the air filter housing, which you will most likely be removing prior to the test anyway. The Smoke Pro comes with a whole set of adapters that you can use to plug into the intake system. On the Carrera here, we removed the upper airbox and filter and plugged the intake with the rubber cone adapter that comes with the Smoke Pro (blue arrows).

3 With the system pressurized, you can check to see if your engine is "fully smoked out" by removing the oil filler cap. A steady stream of smoke should exit the filler hole. This means that smoke is going from the intake, through the air-oil separator, and into the crankcase. At this point, replace the cap and carefully examine your intake for smoke trails that will indicate vacuum leaks.

PROJECT 22
Replacing the Fuel Pump

Time / Tab / Talent: 2 hours / $300 /

Tools: Oil filter wrench, battery charger

Applicable Years: All

Tinware: Fuel pump, O-ring, sending unit

More Info: http://www.101projects.com/Carrera/22.htm

Tip: Jumper the relay to empty the tank

Performance Gain: More reliable fuel system

Comp Modification: Replace the battery

Some common fuel injection problems can be traced back to a faulty or nonoperational fuel pump. If your pump is noisy and loud or the fuel pressure in the engine compartment is below what is needed for proper fuel injection operation, then it's probably time to replace it. The fuel pump is a not as simple a device as one might think. The fuel actually runs through the pump and acts as a coolant and lubricant for the entire assembly. Therefore, if you let your car run out of gas, make sure that you turn off the pump immediately or you might damage the internal components of the pump. Trust me—not much is worse than a broken or faulty pump leaving you stranded on the side of the road.

Typical fuel pump problems can sometimes be headed off in advance. If the pump is noisy and making loud clicking noises, then chances are that the bearings inside are worn and should be replaced. If the pump continues to make noise even after the ignition is shut off, internal check-valves in the pump may be showing signs of failure. The pump could seize up at some time, or the pressure to the fuel injection system could drop. Either way, the car will not be performing at its peak. Another symptom of failure is the pump getting stuck and then finally kicking in after turning the ignition on and off a couple of times. This could be a clear sign that you are living on borrowed time and that you should replace the pump immediately. Check the electrical connections to the pump before you replace it to make sure that it's not an electrical problem.

The first step in replacement is to prep the car. Remove as much gasoline out of the car as possible (see photos). Here are some other tips:

- Always have a fire extinguisher handy in case an emergency arises.
- Gasoline is highly flammable. When working around fuel and fuel line connections, don't disconnect any wires or electrical connections that may cause electrical sparks.
- Always remove the gas cap to relieve any pressure in the tank prior to working on the fuel system.
- Do not use a work lamp when working near fuel or fuel tanks. If you need some light, use a cool fluorescent lamp and keep it far away from the pump.
- Gasoline vapors are strong and harmful, and they can cause you to become drowsy and not think straight. Always perform work in a well-ventilated area with plenty of fresh air blowing through.
- Always disconnect the battery when working on the fuel system. Leave it disconnected for at least 30 minutes to allow any residual electrical charge in components to dissipate.
- Keep plenty of paper towels on hand, and wear rubber gloves to prevent spilling gasoline on your hands.
- Be well grounded—don't do anything that will create static electricity. Keep all cell phones and pagers a safe distance away.
- Run the car so that the gas tank is near empty, and then remove the remaining fuel as detailed in Photo 1.

The first step is to remove the battery from the car (see Project 83). The lower battery tray acts as both a retaining platform for the battery and a cover for the fuel pump area. Underneath this tray, you will see the top of the fuel tank sending unit. Disconnect the connector that mates with the sender. Now, squeeze and disconnect the fuel lines and breather hose that feed into the top of the unit. There might be some small gas spillage here; have a roll of absorbent paper towels on hand. You might want to find an old pen to carefully plug the lines to prevent further leaks. If there is any fuel in your tank, now would be an excellent time to empty it (see Photo 1 and Photo 2).

The sender is held in place by the big circular disc with the risers on it. A special tool is used to remove and tighten this black plastic ring; however, with a large flathead screwdriver or chisel and a small hammer, you can easily tap the plastic ring loose. Carefully remove the ring from the top of the sender.

Now comes the fun part. Make sure that you are prepared at this stage—and in a heavily ventilated garage and with rubber gloves and plenty of paper towels. Pull up on the top of the sender, and the entire assembly should come right out of the tank (Photo 3). There is a big, thick O-ring that seals the pump to the tank—grab it and put it off to the side. See Photo 4 and Photo 5 for instructions on removal of the pump.

When reinstalling the pump into the car, make sure that the fuel hoses inside the tank don't interfere with the proper operation of the fuel tank sender. I found that my sender was getting stuck and the problem was the hoses. The solution was to open the tank up again and zip-tie the hoses out of the way. I suggest that you verify that they don't interfere with the movement of the sender before you button everything back up.

I recommend that you replace the large sealing ring with a new one. If you do opt to reuse the old one and it doesn't seal well, you might be plagued with a fuel smell in the car from that point on. Make sure that the big O-ring is properly sealed around the outside of the pump and will seal with the opening of the tank. Spin on the large circular ring and use the hammer/screwdriver tapping procedure to tighten it. I tighten mine about as tight as I can get it without feeling that I would break the ring. Reconnect the fuel hoses and the electrical connector.

Reinstall and connect the battery after all fumes have subsided. Then crank the car over and see if it starts. If the car starts and runs for any length of time, then the pump is working fine.

1 This photo shows a safe method for emptying the gas out of the tank in your Carrera. Disconnect the pressure side hose from the top of the pump and connect some clear plastic tubing to the barb (yellow arrow). Carefully connect the car's battery terminals up to a 12-volt supply, making sure that you wrap and insulate both terminals carefully. Jumper the relay in the driver side footwell (see Photo 2) and turn on the ignition; the pump should turn on and begin to pump fuel into your gas can. Watch the level carefully, and shut the pump off when the external tank fills up or when the Carreras fuel tank runs dry.

2 This photo shows the relay panel under the driver side footwell. The fuel pump is not normally turned on unless the engine is running, but you can remove the relay and bypass it using a simple jumper wire as shown here. Remove the fuel pump relay (shown in the inset) and then Jumper Pins 30 and 87 (typically labeled 3 and 5 on the relay panel). This will cause the fuel pump to turn on automatically when you turn the key in the ignition.

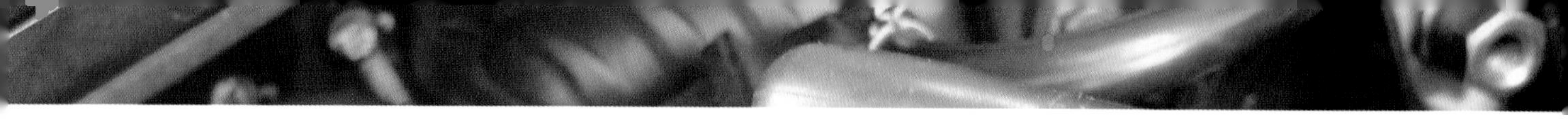

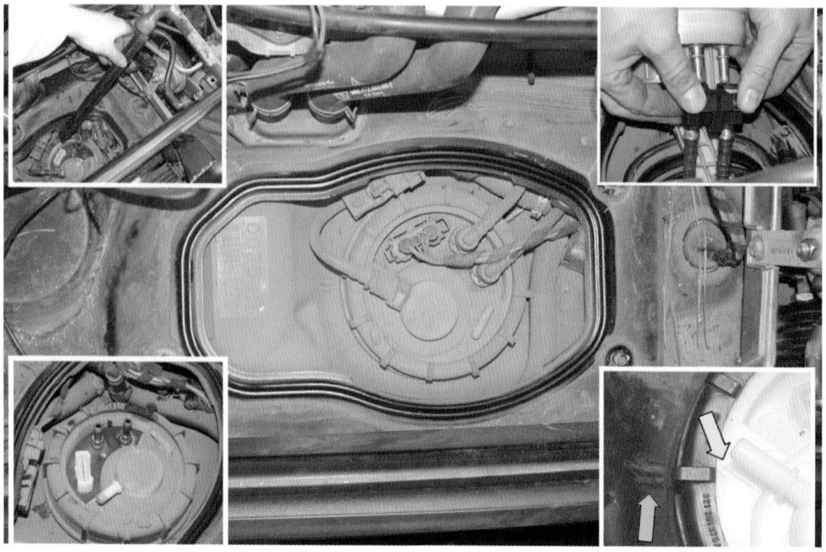

3 Once you remove the battery and the lower tray/cover, you will see the top of the tank and the fuel sender. Squeeze the fuel line connectors and remove them along with the vent hose and the electrical connections (lower left). Use a large chisel and a medium-sized hammer to carefully tap on the outer ring that holds the fuel pump in place (upper left). It should turn and loosen up with a few taps. With the ring loose, pull out the fuel tank sending unit, and you should be able to carefully squeeze and remove the fuel supply hoses that attach to the bottom. When you reinstall the sending unit, be sure to line up the big arrow (blue arrow) with the three lines on the tank (green arrow).

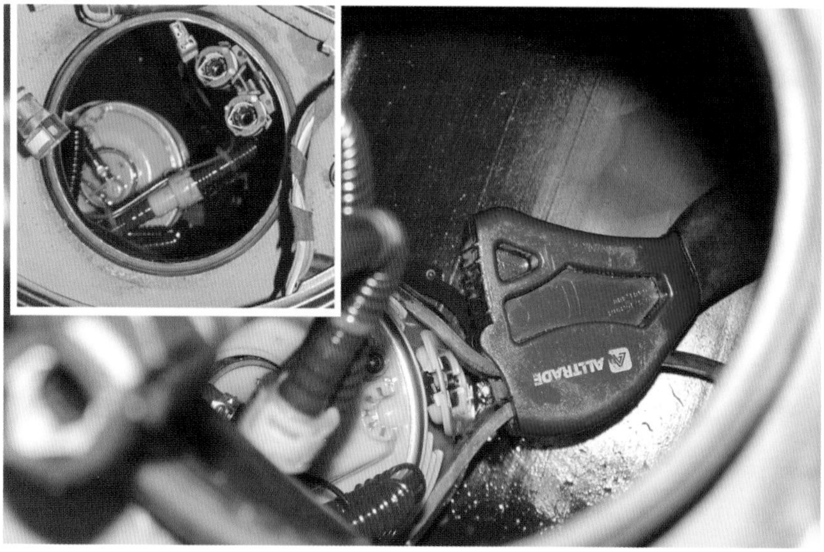

4 The upper left inset shows the fuel pump sitting inside the empty fuel tank. I had a really difficult time removing the pump from the bottom of the tank. Supposedly, you should be able to simply turn it with your hands and unlock it from the bottom, but my grip wasn't strong enough. Instead, I used a rubber oil-filter wrench to carefully wrap the circumference of the pump. One solid twist of the tool, and the pump came free of its locking site on the bottom of the tank.

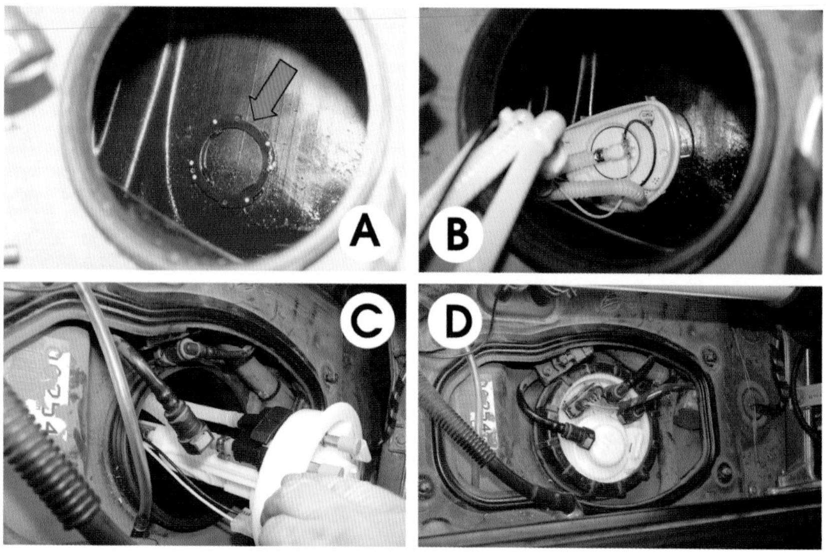

5 Installation is pretty straightforward. **A:** The red arrow shows the circular locking ring that the bottom of the fuel pump snaps into with a twist. This secures the pump to the bottom of the fuel tank. **B:** Shown here is the new pump installed. It looks slightly different than the original, but it's functionally equivalent. **C:** With the new pump in place, install the fuel tank sending unit into the top of the tank. Be sure to connect the hoses from the pump to the bottom of the unit. **D:** Shown here is the new pump installed with the new sending unit all buttoned up and ready for testing. Be sure to put some fuel back into the tank prior to starting the fuel pump up.

PROJECT 23

Replacing Your Fuel Line Vent Valve

Time / Tab / Talent: 2 hrs / $95 /

Tools: 10mm wrench or 10mm socket with socket wrench

Applicable Years: 1998–2005

Tinware: New vent valve

More Info: http://www.101projects.com/Carrera/23.htm

Tip: No smoking while performing this project, remove the fender liner, and take your time

Performance Gain: Being able to put gas in your car

Comp Modification: Replace fuel door actuator

While Porsche produces some of the cleanest running vehicles in the world, the system they designed to get these results can be difficult to understand, and when it goes wrong most people just give up trying to fix it. That doesn't need to be the case. With a little patience, you can solve most of the issues that come up.

Like many things on a Porsche, the EVAP (Evaporative Emission Restraint System) works with a series of switches and vacuum pressure. All of this is done to prevent the emission of harmful fumes from getting out into the environment. The EVAP system is designed to capture these gases and recycle them back into the engine to be burnt later.

If you are having trouble filling up your car with gas, your check engine light keeps coming on, your car will not enter a "ready state" for a smog test, or you hear a howling sound like someone is blowing across the top of an old glass cola bottle, you may have a faulty fuel line vent valve.

This project will deal with the replacement of the fuel line vent valve. Before you begin though, take a moment and check your gas cap. Many of the issues described above can be the result of a bad seal in your gas cap, and it is a lot easier and cheaper to replace or fix your gas cap. If your gas cap is good then it is probably the fuel vent valve that is the issue. The valve opens when you put in the filler hose from the pump and allows you to fill the car with gas. It does this by allowing the air in the tank to be diverted to the charcoal canister. If the valve does not open, it will cause a back pressure problem in the tank as there will be no place for the air to escape and make room for the incoming gasoline. Once the fuel line vent valve opens the air/fuel vapors are diverted to the charcoal canister, where they are stored. Once the engine is running and reaches a certain state, the charcoal canister is purged of the collected vapors by sending them back to the intake manifold to be burnt in the engine.

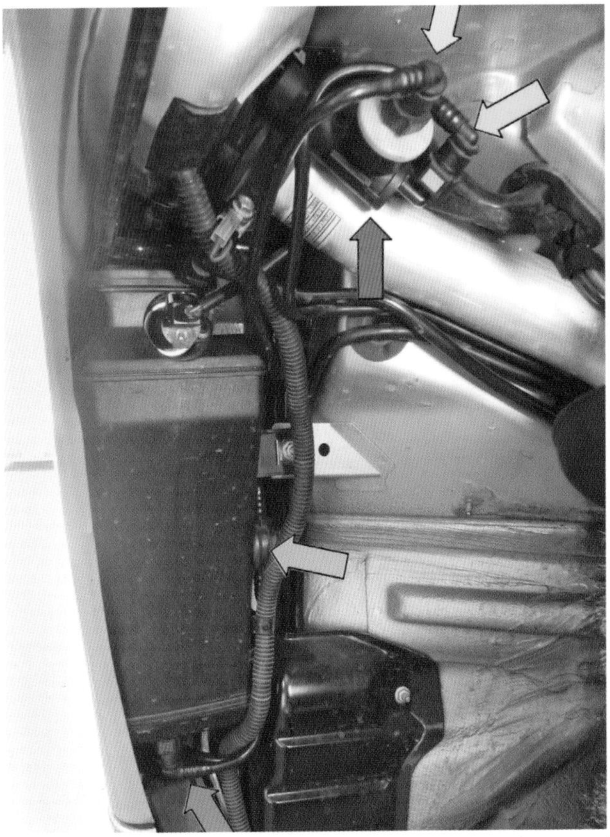

1 This is a picture of the right-side front wheel well with the fender liner removed (see Project 68 for tips on removing the fender lining) – notice the large black EVAP (charcoal) canister. The red arrow shows the actual vent valve. Also shown are: incoming vent line from the gas tank (yellow arrow), line out to charcoal canister (blue arrow), one way check valve (green arrow) and the connection where the fuel vent line enters the charcoal canister (purple arrow). To begin, disconnect the lines (arrows A and arrow C) attached at the top and bottom of the EVAP canister, the electrical connection, which easily unclips (arrow B), and the 10mm nut (arrow D) that holds the canister in place. To remove the canister, gently pull it forward until it comes free.

There is a one way check valve on the air purge line into the canister to stop the emissions from flowing back out to the environment (see Photo 1). If the vent valve does not open, you will have a very difficult time filling the car, and if the valve does not close, the car will think there is a vacuum leak in the system and cause all kinds of problems starting with your check engine lamp lighting up on the dashboard.

If you have a 2005 or later 997 Carrera, Porsche has redesigned the tank ventilation system and eliminated many of the components and lines including the fuel line vent valve.

2 Next, disconnect the top two gas vapor lines (green arrows) on the fuel vent valve by squeezing the tabs on each line.

3 The fuel line vent valve is attached to the fuel neck by a metal bracket. To loosen it, open the gas cap door, remove the gas cap, and remove the 10mm nut holding the bracket to the chassis (yellow arrow). Next, loosen the black plastic piece surrounding the fuel neck by pushing in the four clips (see the red arrows of the inset photo) from behind it inside the fender well.

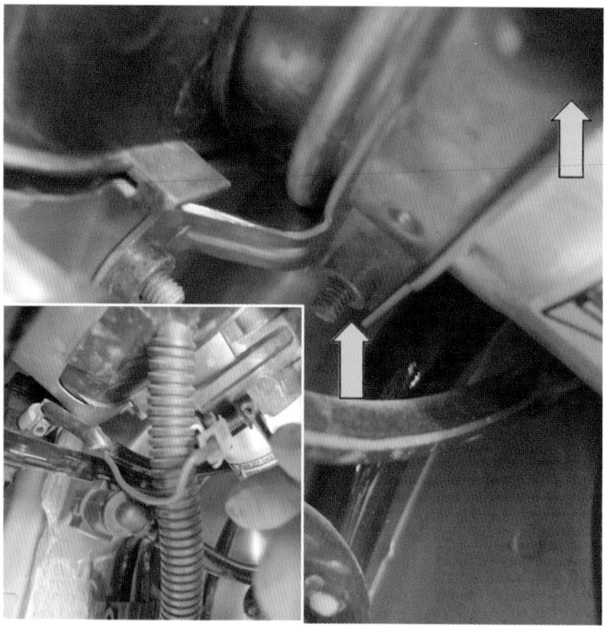

4 Now, from inside the wheelwell, remove the remaining two 10mm nuts and subsequent electrical ground wire (inset photo) holding the vent valve to the fuel filler neck (yellow arrows). You can also rotate the bracket for easier removal.

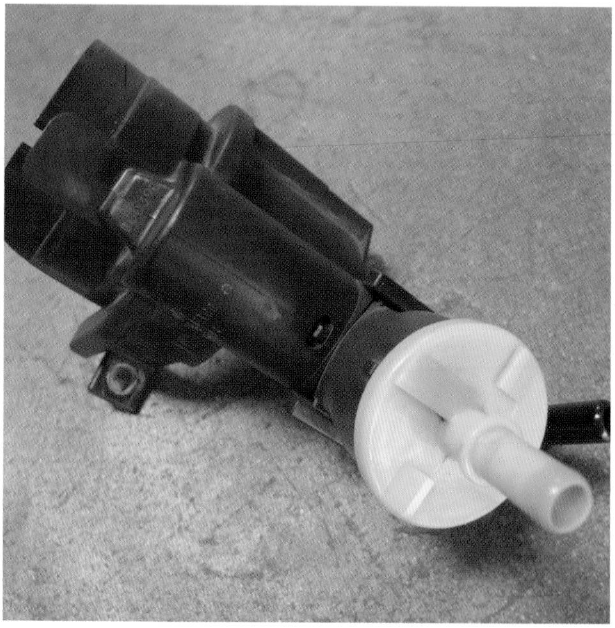

5 This picture shows a brand new fuel line vent valve (available from Pelican Parts.com) removed from the fuel filler neck.

FUEL

PROJECT 24
Installing a High-Performance Air Intake

Time / Tab / Talent: 1 hour / $600 /

Tip: Lay out all of the parts before you begin

Tools: T-20 tamper-proof Torx driver (supplied with kit), flathead screwdriver, 13mm socket, 11mm socket, socket driver, short socket extension

Performance Gain: Greater air intake

Comp Modification: Clean your MAF (mass airflow) sensor

Applicable Years: All

Tinware: EVO Motorsports 996/997 V-Flow Air Intake Kit

More Info: http://www.101projects.com/Carrera/24.htm

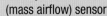

Porsche engineered these cars to the fullest degree, but one of the most common areas Porsche owners can look to for improving their car's original performance (and customize the *feel* of their vehicle) is by installing an aftermarket air intake system.

Fortunately, plenty of companies offer high-performance air intake systems, so take your time, research each kit, and investigate performance gains. For our 996, we decided to go with the 996/997 EVO V-Flow Air Intake Kit manufactured by Evolution Motorsports and sold through PelicanParts.com. The kit comes complete with all the required hardware for installation including the screws, mass airflow (MAF) housing, and air filter.

Installation of this airbox unit is pretty straightforward and will actually complement the engine bay of your Porsche quite well. Follow along with the photos for the exact installation procedure.

1 Open the engine decklid and remove the airbox. Begin by loosening the hose clamp holding the boot to the throttle body (green arrow), then squeeze the tabs on the mass airflow connector to release it (yellow arrows). Now open the harness holder clip (purple arrow). Pull the oil filler tub up and out of its clip on the airbox. (blue arrow) and finally unbolt the 13mm bolt holding the airbox inside the engine compartment (red arrow). Carefully lift the airbox out of the car.

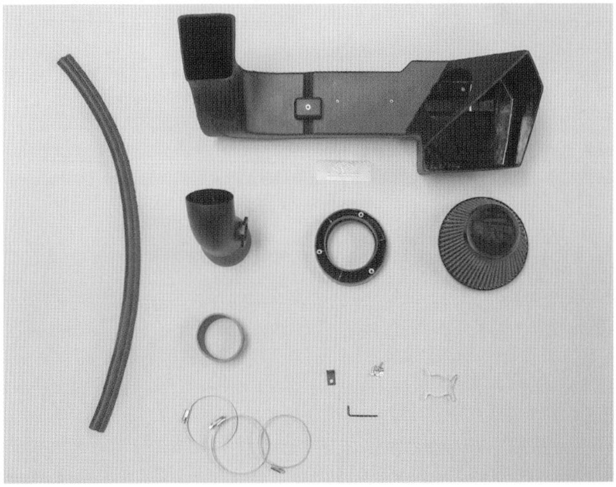

2 Shown here is the EVO Motorsports 996/997 V-Flow Air Intake kit with the airbox, air filter, plastic step-down ring for the air filter, MAF housing, rubber airbox sealing hose, throttle body boot, hose clamps, T-20 tamper-proof Torx driver, oil filler clip, EVO logo plate, an L-bracket, and supplied screws.

Once the system is installed, double-check all connections and fittings and inspect the engine bay for tools left in or around the area. Next, start the car, inspect it for leaks, then take it for a drive. If all is well, enjoy your new high-performance air intake system!

Evolution Motorsports recommends the air filter be replaced every 10,000 miles or so (part number: FILVF997) and only be oiled lightly as excessive oil can cause the MAF sensor to malfunction (which can trigger a check engine light).

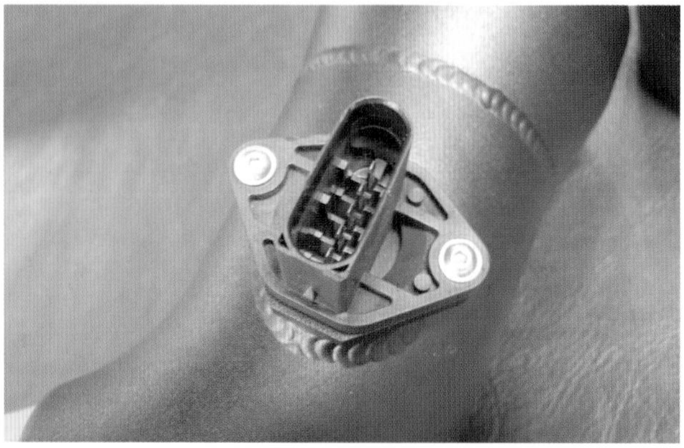

3 Use a T-20 Torx driver and install the MAF sensor into the EVO MAF housing, utilizing the two supplied screws. Before installing the sensor, clean it with some compressed air.

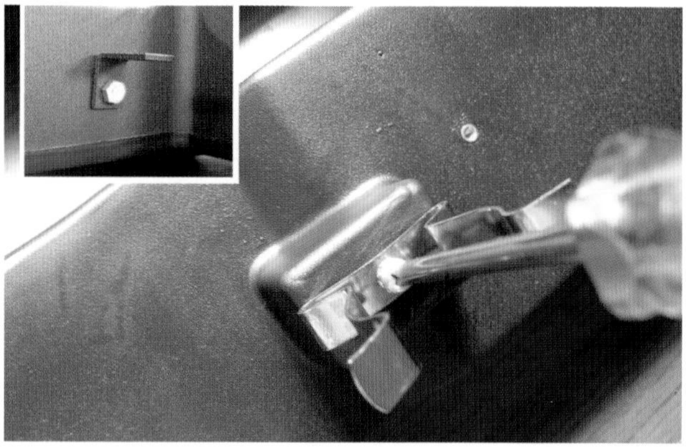

4 Using a Phillips screwdriver, install the oil filler clip to the V-Flow intake unit with the screw provided. Attach the supplied L-bracket to the intake housing with the bolt provided in the kit using a socket wrench with an 11mm socket (inset photo, upper left).

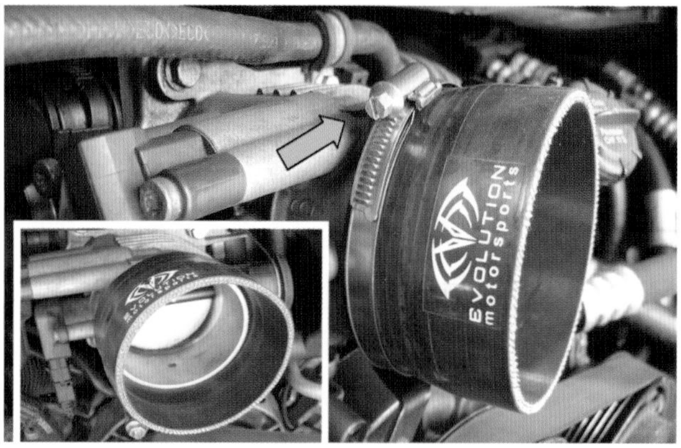

5 Next, fit the supplied EVO Motorsports rubber throttle body boot to the throttle body unit (see inset). Using a flathead screwdriver, fit and tighten a hose clamp to the throttle body boot (see green arrow). Fit and loosely tighten the second supplied hose clamp to the throttle body coupler with a flathead screwdriver.

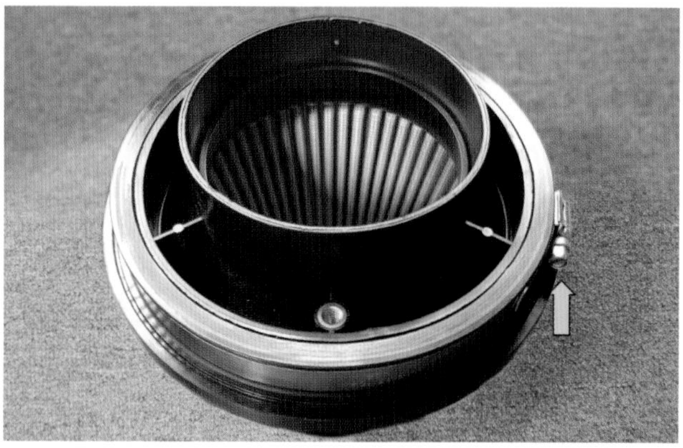

6 Now, take your air filter, loosen the hose clamp with a flathead screwdriver, and fit the plastic step-down ring into the air filter until it sits flush with the air filter opening. Once it's sitting pretty, tighten the hose clamp until the plastic ring sits firmly (yellow arrow).

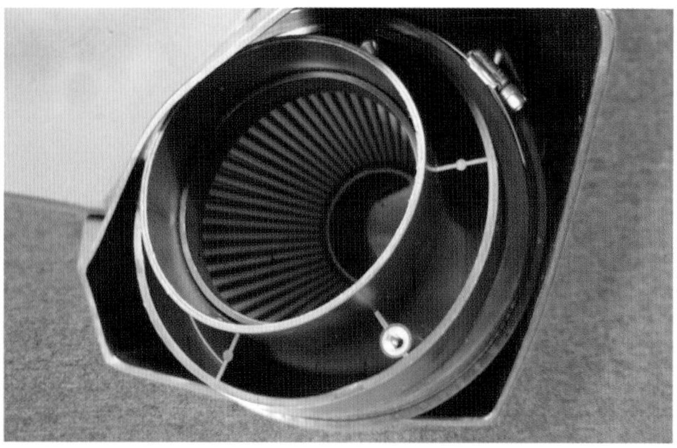

7 Next, install the filter unit into the airbox opening. Do not be afraid to wrestle the air filter into the airbox; the plastic housing is flexible enough to give you a little wiggle room. I found it easy to first fit the smaller section of the filter in first and then rotate the rest of the unit in while expanding the plastic airbox housing lip outward to make room for the step-down ring installed in the filter to fit through the airbox cutout.

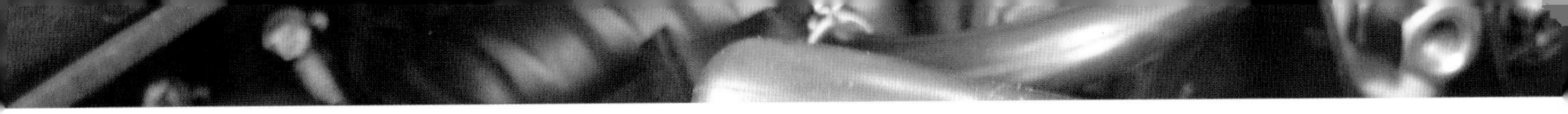

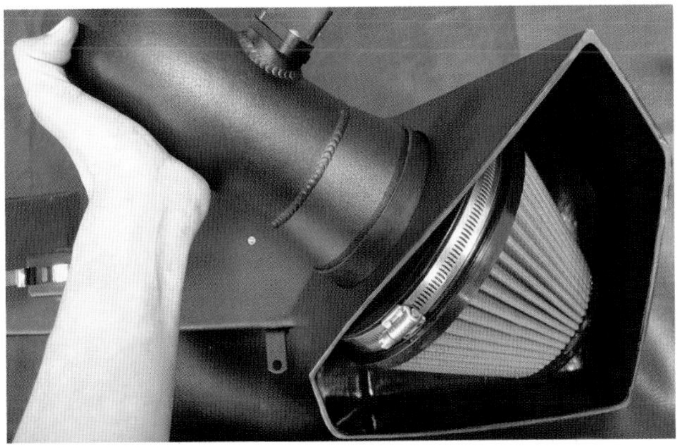

8 Once you have the air filter installed in the airbox (make sure the plastic step-down ring is protruding from the airbox cutout), attach the MAF housing to the plastic filter ring as shown in the picture.

9 Next, fit the rubber hose around the lip of the air filter opening (it just pushes in around the edge). This hose has a cutout that I placed at the tightest corner of the opening, then worked my way around.

10 Once your V-Flow airbox is completely assembled, install the unit the same way you uninstalled the OEM airbox (slide the oil filler tube aside to give you room). Fit the MAF housing opening into the throttle body coupler and align the L-bracket with the airbox bolt hole on the chassis. Now, push the MAF tube into the throttle body boot and, using a flathead screwdriver, tighten the hose clamp. Be sure the MAF tube is completely seated in the coupler before tightening the hose clamp. Take your time with this step to get the best fit.

11 Taking the OEM airbox bolt, fit it through the L-bracket and chassis hole. Using a 13mm socket (and a short extension if necessary), tighten the bolt until the airbox unit sits evenly in place. Again, take your time to get the best fit.

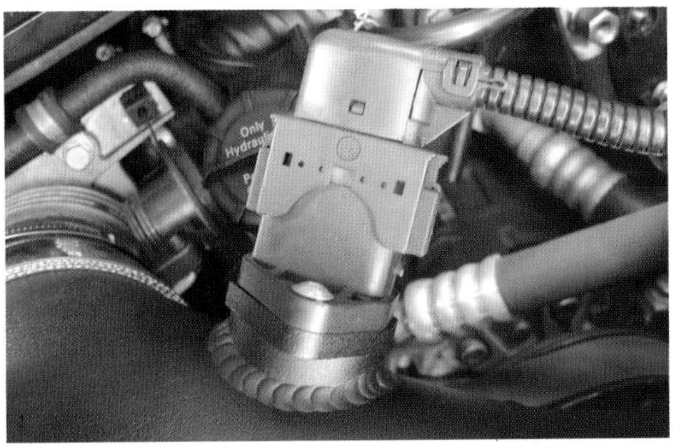

12 Reconnect the MAF wiring harness to the sensor on the MAF housing.

13 Double-check all connections, including the MAF sensor, and ensure all fitments are not loose. Check the tightness of all three hose clamps, including those attached to the throttle body. Once all final checks have been made (and all tools have been removed from in and around the engine), start the car, check for leaks, then take it for a drive and enjoy your new high-performance air intake system.

PROJECT 25
Updating Your DME with Performance Software

Time / Tab / Talent: 1 hour / $700 /

Tools: Windows computer

Applicable Years: All

Tinware: Softronic cable and software

Tip: Required if making any significant changes to the drivetrain

Performance Gain: 10–15 percent more horsepower

Comp Modification: Install a larger engine!

More Info: http://www.101projects.com/Carrera/25.htm

When you consider price and performance, the Motronic system (also called the Digital Motor Electronics [DME]) is hands down the best overall fuel injection system to use. Ignition timing and fuel delivery are all controlled by a digital map that is recorded in a flash memory chip located within the main fuel injection (DME) computer. The computer takes input from a variety of sensors that are located on the engine: cylinder head temperature, crank angle, throttle position, exhaust gas oxygen (mixture), ambient air temperature, and mass airflow. The DME is programmed from the factory with certain performance characteristics (mostly conservative) so that the engine will react well under a host of varying conditions. Major changes to the engine (increased displacement, the addition of different camshafts, etc.) require an updated map to take full advantage of these modifications. Failure to update the Motronic system may actually result in a decrease in performance, as the original system is finely tuned to supply the correct timing and fuel injection values for a stock engine configuration. To gain the maximum benefit from engine modifications, you need to either update the flash software in your DME (easy) or install a programmable aftermarket engine management system (not so easy).

The Motronic system is generally very reliable. Its main failure points are the sensors that send data back to the DME computer. Although I haven't seen it on the modern Carreras just yet, another odd failure point on other older Porsches appears to be the DME relay. Corroded contacts appear to cause this mission-critical part to fail somewhat intermittently. While this is a very rare issue with the Carreras, I do recommend that you carry a spare one, as a failure can potentially leave you stranded on the side of the road. Also vulnerable is the fuel pump relay above the front fuse panel (see Photo 2 of Project 22).

If you are running a stock engine with the Motronic injection, one of the best upgrades you can perform is the installation of aftermarket performance software. As stated previously, the factory programmed the original software to compensate for a wide variety of driving characteristics. These days, you can find software maps that will elevate the rev-limiter, advance your timing, and generally run the engine with less conservatism than the factory programs. The only downside to running a more aggressive map is that sometimes the timing curves are a bit too advanced and may cause detonation on low-octane pump gas (as it is here in California). The 911 Carreras have a knock sensor that will reduce detonation if the timing is too far advanced, and you can also get maps that are specifically tailored to your region if lower octane fuel is the only type available.

One downside to installing a performance software map is that you basically need to run premium fuel with the chip installed. Whereas the stock chip is designed and mapped to provide good performance across a wide variety of operating conditions, the performance chips are typically mapped to assume that you are running high octane gasoline. If you run low octane fuel, the knock sensor will generally prevent detonation, but in general you will not fully utilize the performance improvements of the chip.

Many manufacturers out there sell variations of performance software for the 911. One company that has differentiated itself from the pack is Softronic, founded by former PCA tech guru Scott Slauson. The Softronic software upgrade kit has a few innovative features not found in other DME programming products. The software upgrade is installed using a Softronic cable attached to a typical Windows computer (others often require you to ship them your DME for programming). The DME is updated and reprogrammed using the OBD II port (see Project 20), which allows you the freedom to update your software and then also convert it back to stock when needed. This is particularly useful when you need to bring your car in for emissions testing and the updated software in the computer might make it difficult to pass. The Softronic software makes an exact backup copy of the software on your DME prior to installing the updated maps.

Installation of the software is a snap. Simply install the Softronic software onto your computer and then connect it via the supplied cable to the ODB II port on your Carrera. The software will perform a variety of preprogramming checks, create a full backup on your hard drive, and then install the performance software into your car. Just sit back, drink your coffee, and let the computer do all the work. The total programming time is about five minutes or so.

Performance software is required if you are upgrading your engine to a 3.6 or 3.8 liter. I used the Softronic performance software to install a higher output Porsche 996 program into my stock 3.4-liter engine. The increase in horsepower went from 300 to 322, and torque increased from 258 to 271—quite an improvement. In addition, Softronic was able to custom design our program to fit our particular engine installation profile (engine/intake/exhaust).

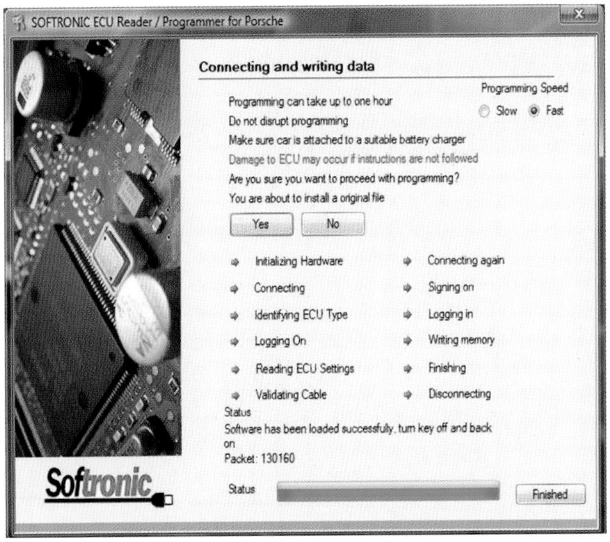

1 It really is as easy as it looks. Here is a screenshot from Softronic's software. Simply plug in the cable into the On-Board Diagnostics Level II (OBD II) port on the Carrera and run the software. It will create a full backup of your existing configuration and install the performance software update in less time than it takes to brew a cup of coffee.

2 This is really as simple as it looks, too. All you need is a laptop or a desktop computer with a long USB extension cable. Plug the connector into the OBD II access port (green arrow), start the software, and in about five minutes your Carrera's software will be upgraded.

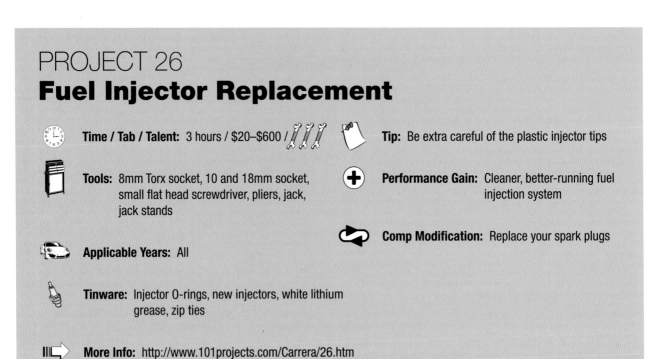

PROJECT 26
Fuel Injector Replacement

Time / Tab / Talent: 3 hours / $20–$600 /

Tools: 8mm Torx socket, 10 and 18mm socket, small flat head screwdriver, pliers, jack, jack stands

Applicable Years: All

Tinware: Injector O-rings, new injectors, white lithium grease, zip ties

More Info: http://www.101projects.com/Carrera/26.htm

Tip: Be extra careful of the plastic injector tips

Performance Gain: Cleaner, better-running fuel injection system

Comp Modification: Replace your spark plugs

In this project, I'll walk you through the process of replacing your fuel injectors. Now, before we begin, a good question to ask would be why would you want to replace them to begin with? There are several myths and misunderstandings regarding fuel injectors. The first one is, "Bigger injectors will give you more power." This statement is completely false. It's the equivalent of saying that adding more lights to your already brightly lit living room will make you see better.

The fuel injectors that are in your Carrera are more than adequate for stock engines and supply more than enough fuel for maximum power and open throttle. For your engine to achieve maximum power, it must have an air/fuel ratio maintained within a certain range. Adding more fuel to the mixture makes it richer and won't necessarily give you any more power. In fact, it is typically the opposite: a richer mixture will foul plugs and won't ignite as easily. The goal of any good fuel injection system (whether it be carburetors or electronic fuel injection) is to maintain the air/fuel ratio (typically about 14.67:1) for ideal combustion and power. Adding higher flow or larger injectors disrupts the balance of the engine, makes the engine's fuel management system run richer, and generally decreases power from ideal levels. It's the same principle as adding more high powered lights to your living room: if the room was adequately lit to begin with, then you won't see better—you'll see worse because it will be too bright for your eyes.

So what are the exceptions to this rule? There are a few. Major changes in the displacement or flow of the engine can cause the engine to run lean. Examples include if you increased the displacement of your engine, changed the camshafts, or if you added a turbo or supercharger. The supercharger or turbocharger compresses the air/fuel mixture and allows more of it to exist within the same size combustion chamber. Therefore, ideally, more fuel should be injected into the combustion chamber when compressed with a super or turbocharger than is normally injected on a normally aspirated engine. Owners who add a supercharger or turbocharger to their car need to be especially concerned about keeping the engine's mixture correct: the tendency is for these cars to run too lean, which can lead to destructive problems like detonation or overheating (see Project 18).

In general, you should not upgrade or replace your injectors with larger ones, unless you have made a significant engine modification that would cause the engine to run lean. If you are replacing injectors, then make sure that you use ones that have stock flow rates for your engine—don't buy ones that have higher flow rates thinking that it will give you more power—it won't.

So why would you want to replace your injectors then? Well, as the engines get old, the injectors tend to fail and leak. If you pull fault codes out of your computer, it may tell you that you have a faulty or leaking fuel injector (see Project 20 for more details on how to do this). You may also find that you can see or smell a particular injector leaking. If this is the case, you may not have to replace the injector itself but may only need to replace the injector O-rings.

While the fuel injection system for the 1998–2005 (996) Carreras is very similar to the 2005–2008 (997) Carreras, Porsche did make a few changes. The 1998–2005 Carreras use a typical pressure regulator on the fuel line that regulates the pressure and returns unneeded fuel back to the gas tank via a return line. With the introduction of the 997 in 2005, Porsche introduced a return-less fuel system. For the 997 Carreras, Porsche has eliminated the return line by incorporating the pressure regulator into the sending unit in the fuel tank. This way only the quantity of fuel needed by the injectors is

pumped to the fuel distributor in the engine compartment. This arrangement has the advantage of not having to return heated fuel back to the tank and also helps to further decrease emissions in the fuel tank, relieving the tank ventilation system of some of its work. The second change is the introduction of the EV-14 fuel injector. Porsche used the EV-6 injector from 2002 to 2005 (996) and the newer style, EV-14 starting in 2005 with the introduction of the 997. The EV-14 allows for better atomization of the fuel, and its narrower diameter places its injection point 5mm deeper in the intake runner. All of these changes help with meeting stricter emission standards.

The first step is to prep the car. I like to tell people to pull out the fuse for the fuel pump (see Project 4) and then try to start the car. The car will turn over and then die. Do this about two or three times; it will help drain excess fuel out of your system. Open the gas cap to help depressurize the system. Then, make sure that the car has cooled down; you don't want to be working with gasoline when the car is hot. Have a fire extinguisher handy—some spillage of fuel will occur—it's nearly impossible to prevent. Also, wear chemical resistant gloves if you don't want to get any gasoline on your hands and make sure that you have plenty of paper towels or rags on hand to help you clean up. Perform the injector removal in a clear, open, and well-ventilated space, and it may not hurt to have an assistant around in case there are any problems.

To change out your injectors, you are going to need to lower your engine. It is not hard to do and will make this job a lot easier. While I have heard of people changing out their injectors with the engine in the car, I do not recommend it.

If you are planning on completely removing the fuel rails from the car, you will need to remove the two intake plenums to access the fuel line mount at the front of the engine; but, if you are just replacing the injectors, you do not. (See Project 9 if you want to remove both plenums.)

Begin by removing the airbox. Loosen and remove the 13mm bolt at the very front of the airbox and the hose clamp holding the boot to the throttle body. You'll also have to unplug the connector to the mass airflow sensor (MAF) by squeezing the connector and unclip the harness from its connectors. Now pull the boot off the throttle body and gently remove the airbox from the engine bay. If you are working on a 3.8, don't forget to remove the wire connection on the back of the airbox for the vacuum resonance valve.

From this point on we will break the article down by models and years.

FOR THE 1998–2005 (996)

On the left side of the engine, clear some room to work. Begin by removing the overflow tube from the coolant reservoir and the air pump hose. I like to zip-tie these together with the other hoses and connection at the back of the engine to keep them out of the way.

Next step is to safely jack up the rear of your car (see Project 1). You do not need to lift the front of the car if you do not want to. Once the car is safely supported in the air, place the floor jack in the middle of the engine. From underneath the car, locate the two 18mm nuts on the underside of each mount and remove them. Then slowly lower the engine no more than 40mm. Depending on the size of your hands and how much room you need in the engine compartment, some people just loosen the 18mm nuts, leaving them on the studs. Either way, make sure you safely support the engine (see Project 10).

Once the engine is lowered and supported, remove the supply and return fuel lines from the rail on the left side of the engine. The supply line is 19mm and the return line is 17mm. Support the fitting with another wrench when loosening, and have some rags on hand as a little fuel may spill out.

After the fuel lines are disconnected, reach in and disconnect the wiring harness to the top of the fuel rail. While doing this you will be able to see the rear 10mm bolt holding the rail on, but you will pretty much have to do the one at the front of the engine by feel.

Remove both bolts holding the rails in place. Once the rails are free, you can simply pull up on the rails to remove the injectors from the manifold. They may stick a little so try wiggling them if they don't come straight out.

Move to the passenger side of the engine. On the right side, remove the electrical connections for the oil pressure sender. Mark both leads and slip the connectors off.

1 **996 Carrera (1998–2005):** Open the engine decklid and remove the airbox. Begin by loosening the hose clamp holding the boot to the throttle body (green arrow), then squeeze the tabs on the mass airflow (MAF) connector to release it (yellow arrows). Now open the harness holder clip (purple arrow). Pull the oil filler tub up and out of its clip on the airbox (blue arrow) and finally unbolt the 13mm bolt holding the airbox inside the engine compartment (red arrow). Carefully lift the airbox out of the car. If you have a 3.8 make sure you unplug the connection on the back of the airbox for the resonance valve.

2 To access the left side fuel distribution rail you will need to remove the coolant tank overflow hose (blue arrow) and the air pump hose (red arrow). I like to gather these hoses and lines and tie them together out of the way with a cable tie.

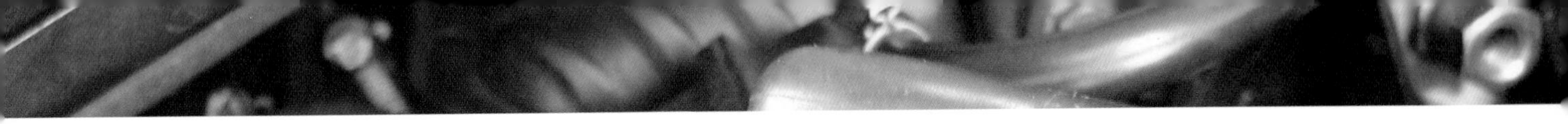

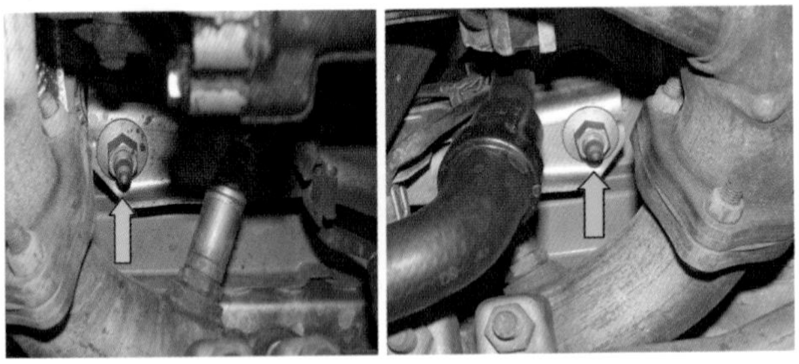

3 Safely jack up and support the car. Place a jack under the engine and support its weight (see Photo 3 of Project 10). Once everything is safely supported you want to remove the 18mm nuts connecting the engine to the mounts (green arrows). Then slowly lower the engine a maximum of 40mm.

4 Once the engine is lowered and supported, you need to remove the supply and return fuel lines from the fuel rail. The supply line is 19mm, and the return line is 17mm. Support the base of the fitting with another wrench when loosening it, and have some rags on hand as a little fuel may spill out.

Next remove the vacuum line coming out of the fuel pressure regulator and disconnect the wiring harness from the fuel rail. Remove the two 10mm bolts and pull the injectors from the manifold.

When you have lifted up your fuel rail, you should be able to push it out of the way enough to pull the metal securing clip from where the injector mates to the fuel rail. Expect some fuel spillage from the rail. Once it is removed, you will be able to pull out the injectors. You may have to tug a little bit to get it out, but don't use excessive force. Sometimes repeated wiggling helps. Take care with the injector tips; they are made of plastic and are not available separately from the $150 injectors. Do not damage them.

With the injectors out of the fuel rail, you can now take them to be cleaned and calibrated. Over the years, the injectors become dirty and may also not distribute flow evenly amongst all six. It costs about $150 for all six to be cleaned, tested, and calibrated. New injectors cost anywhere from $150–$200 apiece, making their replacement a somewhat pricey endeavor.

There are three types of injector leaks: they can leak fuel into the manifold from the nozzle, they can leak fuel into the engine compartment from the fuel rail, and they can leak air (vacuum leak) from the manifold. The first leak cannot be fixed at home; you need to have the injector repaired or replaced (I recommend replacement, as it will be probably be pretty old anyways). The fuel rail leak is easy to contend with; simply replace the old, fat o-ring that seals the injector to the fuel rail (PN: 944-110-901-01). This should be done anytime the injectors are out of the car.

The third leakage area is a bit of a catch-22. On some of the early cars (through 2000), the tip of the injector needs to be removed from the injector. While this seems easy, and indeed it is easy to remove, it is just as easy to damage the tip when you remove it. The method that I use to replace one of the seals in the tip works well, but it also can slightly ding and damage the green plastic fragile tip of the injector. The 2001 and later injector o-rings can be easily removed without damaging the injector.

If you are replacing all your injectors or the O-rings, make sure that you place a very tiny, tiny bit of white lithium grease—or the Porsche recommended Optimol MP3—on the edges that will be pressed into the fuel rail and the manifold. This will aid in the insertion of the injector and the reassembly of the fuel rail. It will also help to prevent the o-ring from pinching and will guard against tiny leaks as well.

Installation is basically the reverse of removal. You may find it easier to insert the injectors into the manifold first if you have enough room (instead of into the fuel rail first). This only works on the 996 Carreras. Double-check to make sure that all of the fat o-rings are securely seated when you reattach the fuel rail. When you are ready to fire up the car, have an assistant on hand, in case there is a fuel leak. Have the assistant watch the injectors and the fuel lines to make sure that there are no leaks.

FOR THE 2005–2008 (997)

Follow all the steps up to and including removing the airbox. On the 3.8 engines, be sure to remove the connection to the resonance valve on the back of the airbox.

On the left side of the engine unclip the two coolant hoses and the brake booster pipe on the crossmember and lay them off to the side. Remove the plastic lines and the cable plug from the switch-over valve.

Loosen the lines for the brake booster. To do this, remove the plastic protection piece, push the holder forward and pull off the line. Put the plastic protector piece back on right away to keep any dirt or debris out.

Disconnect the vent line for the coolant tank. These are rapid action couplings: press the lugs and pull off the line.

The next step is to safely jack up the rear of your car (see Project 1). You do not need to lift the front of the car if you do not want to. Once the car is safely supported in the air, place the floor jack in the middle of the engine. From underneath the car, locate the two 18mm nuts on the underside of each mount and remove them. Then slowly lower the engine no more than 40mm. Depending on the size of your hands and how much room you want to work in the engine bay, some people just loosen the 18mm nuts, leaving them on the studs. Either way make sure you safely support the engine.

Now remove the cable duct from the fuel rail. Simply unplug the camshaft positioning sensor, lift up the duct, and place it off to the side.

Next remove the two 8mm Torx bolts holding the fuel rail down. Be careful not to drop these down into the engine compartment as they can be a pain to find. Once the bolts are off, simply pull the injectors and rail from the manifold as a unit.

Moving to the right side of the engine, you want to remove the cable duct. To do this simply, pull the duct off of the fuel rail, unplug the wiring plugs from the injectors, and move it to the side.

Remove the two 8mm Torx bolts, and pull the rail and injectors from the manifold as a unit.

If you are replacing all your injectors or the O-rings, make sure that you place a very tiny, tiny bit of white lithium grease—or the Porsche recommended Optimol MP3—on the edges that will be pressed into the fuel rail and the manifold. This will aid in the insertion of the injector and the reassembly of the fuel rail. It will also help to prevent the O-ring from pinching and will guard against tiny leaks as well. Two O-rings seal the EV-14 injectors to the fuel rail and manifold. Always replace the O-rings when servicing your injectors.

Installation is basically the reverse of removal. On the 997, you will need to attach the injectors to the fuel distribution rail first then insert it into the manifold as a unit. Double-check to make sure that all of the O-rings are securely seated when you reattach the fuel rail. When you are ready to fire up the car, have an assistant on hand, in case there is a fuel leak. Have them watch the injectors and the fuel lines to make sure that there are no leaks.

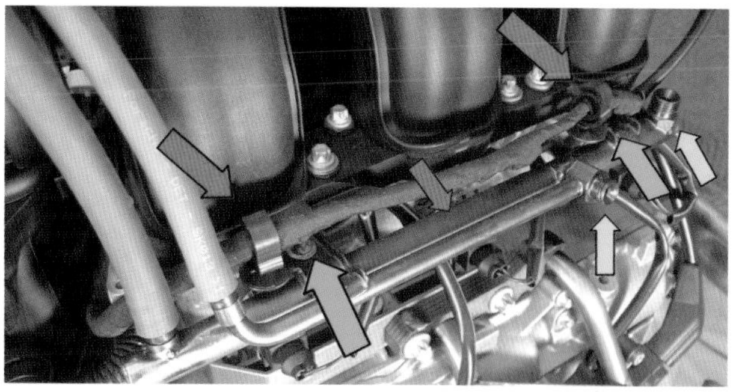

5 Here you can see everything that needs to be removed from the fuel rail (purple arrow) on the left side. The fuel lines have already been removed (blue arrows). The wiring clips (red arrows) and 10mm bolts (green arrows) are next.

6 Unplug the wire harness from each injector (yellow arrow). Unclip the harness from the fuel rail (blue arrows), and place it off to the side. Disconnect the harness from the oil pressure sender (orange arrow). Then unbolt the fuel rail from the manifold (green arrows) and lift the rail upward. You may also want to pull off the rubber U-hose that connects to the pressure regulator. As you pull up on the fuel rail, some fuel may stick in the manifold or some may come out with the fuel rail—it all depends upon a variety of factors.

7 Release the fuel rail from the tops of the injectors by removing the small square retaining clips that fasten and secure the injectors to the fuel rail (blue arrow). Use a pair of needle-nose pliers to pull this clip off. It pulls off from the front (it's C shaped) and should slide off with a reasonable amount of force. This task is performed with the rail still installed on the engine, but is shown out of the car here in this photo for clarity. The inset photo in the upper left shows the fuel pressure regulator removed from its housing (simply slide off the clip holding it in place). The inset photo in the lower right shows the injector once you remove it from the fuel rail. The big fat O-ring will offer quite a bit of resistance (yellow arrow). The same O-ring that holds the injector to the fuel rail (red arrow) is also the same type that is used to hold the injector to the manifold.

8 To remove the nozzle O-ring, first cut it off carefully with a razorblade. Be careful not to damage the green plastic tip when you cut through the O-ring. Then, remove the O-ring with a pic, again taking care with the tip. Finally, to get the new O-ring on, you will need to remove the tip. The best method I figured out for removing the tip was to get a small 8–9mm crescent wrench and apply uniform pressure against the tip. However, this still results in some of the plastic on the tip becoming marred. Pressing up with the wrench using a surprisingly large amount of force will make the tip pop off of the injector. At this point, you can attach the new O-ring and snap the tip back on.

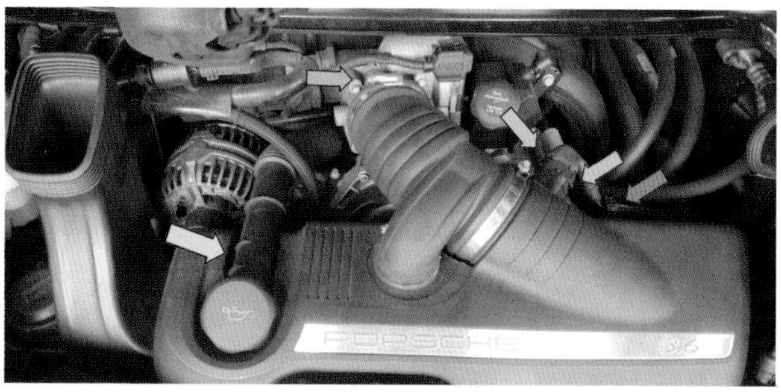

9 **997 Carrera:** Open the engine decklid and remove the airbox. Begin by loosening the hose clamp holding the boot to the throttle body (green arrow), then squeeze the tabs on the MAF connector to release it (yellow arrows). Now open the harness holder clip (purple arrow). Pull the oil filler tub up and out of its clip on the airbox (blue arrow) and carefully lift the airbox out of the car. If you have a 3.8, make sure you unplug the wire connection on the back of the airbox for the resonance valve.

10 On the left side of the engine unclip the two coolant hoses and the brake booster pipe on the crossmember and lay them off to the side (blue arrows). Remove the plastic lines and the cable plug from the switch-over valve between the intake runners (yellow arrow). Loosen the lines for the brake booster (purple arrow). To do this remove the plastic protection piece, push the holder forward and pull off the line. Put the plastic protector piece back on right away to keep any dirt or debris out, and then disconnect the vent line for the coolant tank (red arrows). Check for slack in your wiring going to the O_2 sensors on both sides, and if it looks like it will be tight, disconnect the wiring (green arrow). Now see Photo 11: safely jack up and support the car. Place a jack under the engine and support its weight. Once everything is safely supported, remove the 18mm nuts connecting the engine to the mounts (green arrows). Then slowly lower the engine a maximum of 40mm.

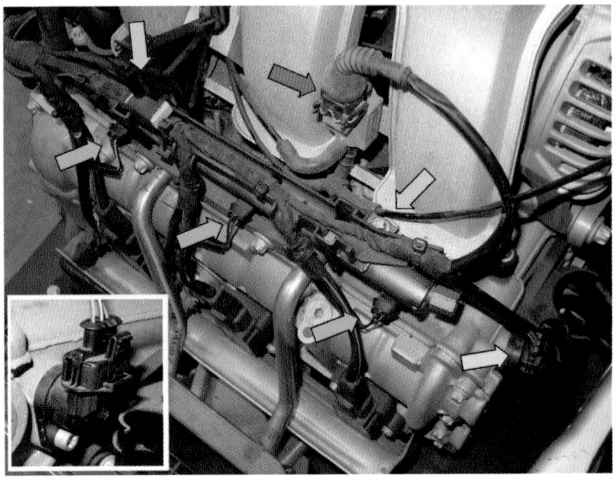

11 To remove the left side fuel distribution rail, you will first need to remove the switch-over valve (red arrow), push in the metal wire and pull the plug out, and then remove the plug from the camshaft positioning sensor (blue arrow and inset, lower left). Now you can slide the wiring harness duct off of the rail. Remove the two 8 mm Torx bolts (yellow arrows) that hold the fuel distribution rail to the manifold and pull the injectors and rail from the manifold as a unit. Remove the plugs from the injectors (green arrows) and set the wiring duct aside.

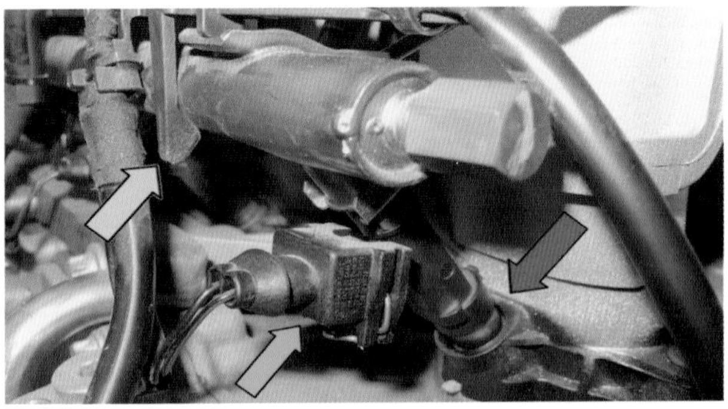

12 This photo shows how the wiring duct is connected to the fuel rail (blue arrow), how the electrical plugs are connected to the injectors (green arrow), and how the injectors sit in the manifold (red arrow).

13 On the right side of the engine remove the wiring harness duct from the fuel rail by simply pulling it up. It is held in place by plastic clips (blue arrow). Unplug the wiring plugs from the injectors (green arrows), push up on the wire clip and pull the plug out, and set the harness and duct aside. Unbolt the two 8mm Torx bolts holding the rail in place and pull the rail and injectors from the manifold as a unit.

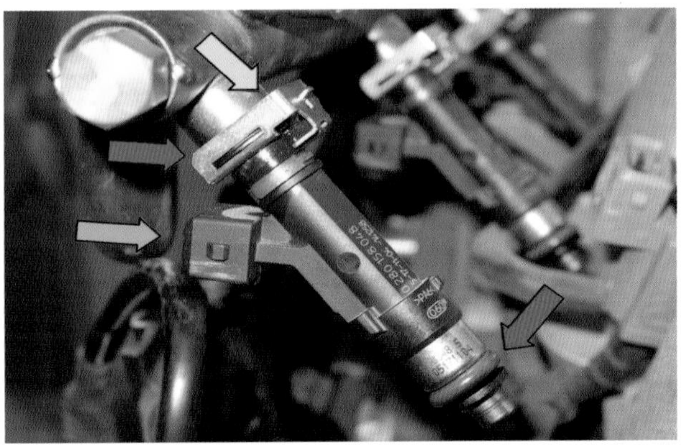

14 The metal clip (blue arrow) can be removed with a small screwdriver or needle-nose pliers. Two O-rings need to be replaced when you remove the injectors: one is shown (red arrows) and the other is hidden by where it sits in the rail. The green arrow shows where the wiring plug goes. After servicing or replacing the injectors, install the injectors onto the rail first, making sure the retaining clips engage correctly. Then reinstall the rail and injectors back into the manifold as a unit. The remainder of the installation is the reverse of removal.

PROJECT 27
Replacing Engine Sensors

Time / Tab / Talent: 1–3 hours / $300–$900 /

Tools: –

Applicable Years: All

Tinware: Engine sensors

More Info: http://www.101projects.com/Carrera/27.htm

Tip: Check the codes first prior to replacing sensors

Performance Gain: Optimal running engine

Comp Modification: Replace oxygen sensors

1 I've split this project up into various photos of the sensors and their locations on the engines so that you can easily find them when you need to replace them. The ambient air temperature sensor measures the air temperature in the engine compartment. This tells the digital motor electronics computer how hot it is inside the engine compartment, so that the engine compartment fan can be turned on or off. This sensor (yellow arrow) is simply held in place by a rubber grommet that is attached to the intake manifold on the right side of the engine near the battery cable junction box (green arrow).

2 The coolant temperature sensor is located on the pulley side of the engine off to the right side of the car near the cylinder head. This sensor measures the temperature of the coolant and is used to adjust mixture levels as the engine begins to heat up to optimum operating temperature.

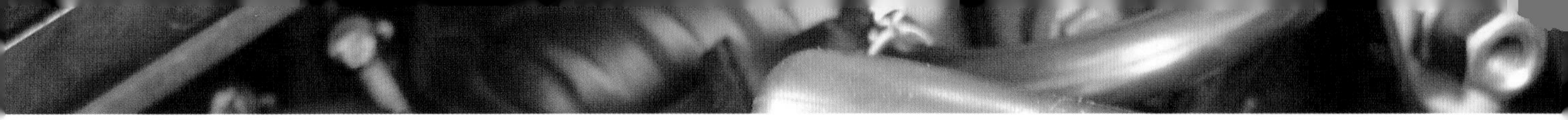

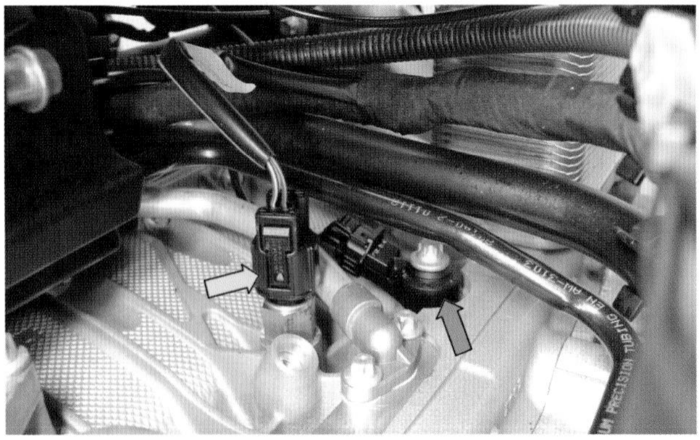

3 The oil level sensor/oil temperature sensor is shown by the blue arrow. This is a somewhat unique sensor in that it contains both level and temperature sensing functions within a single unit. Beginning in 2006 Porsche moved the air-oil separator to this location and moved the oil level/temperature sensor to the opposite side between the starter motor and air pump. The two knock sensors (purple arrow) remained in the same locations. Each one is installed on both the left and right sides of the engine block. Located under the intake manifold, both of these sensors are relatively difficult to get to (you need to remove the intake tubes to access them—see Project 9).

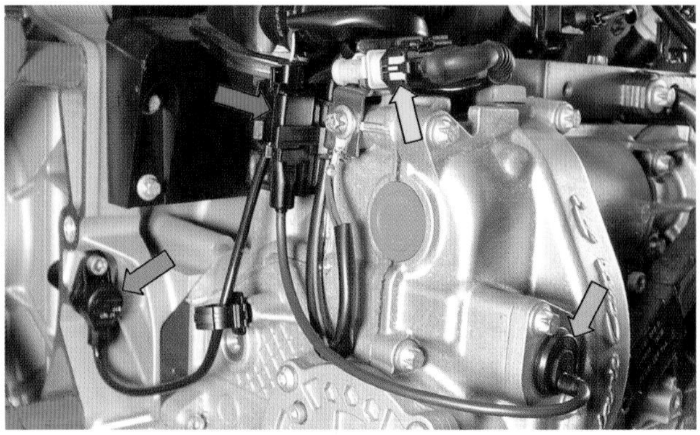

4 This photo shows the group of sensors located on the left front of the engine near the flywheel. The purple arrow shows the crank angle sensor, or flywheel sensor, which reads the toothed flywheel as it rotates past the sensor (harness plug shown by yellow arrow). The orange arrow shows the camshaft timing advance solenoid (red arrow is the connector). You can access the sensor/solenoid from underneath the car and the electrical connections from the engine compartment.

5 Shown here is the camshaft position sensor. One located on the top of the right cylinder head toward the rear, and another is located on the left cylinder head toward the front for the five-chain motors used up to about 2001. For 2002 and later three-chain motors, the sensor is located on the top of the right cylinder head toward the front and on the left cylinder head toward the rear (inset photo, blue arrow).

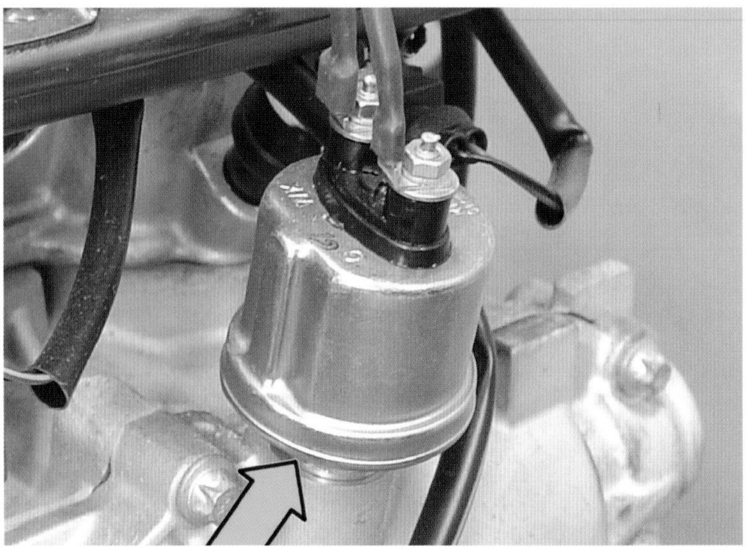

6 This photo shows the oil pressure sender/switch. Located on the left-side cylinder head, this sender is a combination unit that senses pressure and also includes a low-pressure switch as well. Grab the sender by the base using a wrench. Don't grab it by the canister; otherwise, you may damage the unit and cause it to leak. Use new sealing rings to guard against oil leaks.

PROJECT 28
Mass Airflow Sensor Troubleshooting and Replacement

Time / Tab / Talent: 1 hour / $300 /

Tip: Try cleaning the unit first

Tools: Tamper-proof T20 Torx driver

Performance Gain: Smoother-running engine

Applicable Years: All

Comp Modification: Replace air filter

Tinware: Mass airflow sensor (MAF)

More Info: http://www.101projects.com/Carrera/28.htm

The mass airflow sensor (MAF) is located inside the engine compartment and is used to measure the amount and temperature of air that is entering the engine at any one time. Older-style meters used on fuel injection systems in the 1980s measured air volumetric flow, which worked fine, but then you also needed a separate sensor to figure out how cold or dense the air was. The MAF senses the total amount of air passing the sensor and allows the fuel injection system to adjust the fuel mixture to compensate for cold weather and/or high altitude conditions. The MAF also incorporates an internal intake air temperature sensor that measures the temperature of the intake air.

The first indicator that you might have a problem with the MAF is the presence of a check engine light (CEL) on your dashboard. The check engine lamp can be caused by a wide variety of problems with the engine; you need to read the codes from the computer to get a starting clue as to what the problem is (see Project 20 for details on reading the codes). It's perfectly safe to continue to drive the car while the CEL is on, as long as it is not flashing. However, the engine will not be operating at peak efficiency, and you will most likely experience a loss in power and a decrease in gas mileage as a result. It's best to get the problem taken care of relatively quickly, as running the engine in this condition can potentially cause damage to other components, such as the catalytic converters.

The computer will know if something is wrong with the MAF because it will compare the values being output by the sensor to expected values that it should be receiving. This commonsense check by the computer helps diagnose problems with every component in the system. If the MAF becomes dirty and is falsely indicating to the engine that the car is receiving very little air while at full throttle, then the computer will most likely kick back an error code.

To gain more information about the problem, you can try disconnecting the sensor completely and take the car for a drive. If you take short drives (30 minutes or less) with the sensor disconnected, it shouldn't cause any major damage to your car. The engine management system (DME) will enter into a type of "limp mode" that will compensate for the missing MAF. If engine performance improves dramatically when disconnecting the MAF, then the problem quite likely lies with the MAF.

Vacuum leaks and other air leaks in the system can cause MAF sensor errors. If you have a crack or leak in your air intake downstream of the sensor, then the MAF will be sensing less air than the engine is actually receiving. If the clamp on the throttle body happens to come loose and fall off, then the MAF will indicate almost no air being sucked through the intake, yet the engine will be sucking air directly from the engine compartment into the throttle body. The bottom line is that you should carefully inspect all of your hoses, clamps, and intake tubes for air leaks prior to replacing the sensor (see Project 21).

The MAF is located inside the air filter housing (see Project 3 for more detail on access to the sensor). For some reason, Porsche made it unusually difficult to remove the MAF by securing it with a T20 tamper-proof Torx screw. You need the special tamper-proof Torx drivers, which are not typically found in everyone's toolbox but usually can be purchased at a good local auto parts store. Although the holes on the MAF look symmetrical, they are not, and the unit can only be installed in one direction. See Photo 1 for a close-up of the MAF. Removal is easy once you have the tool. Simply remove both screws holding it in place and pull it out.

It's very important to keep the sensor clean. If the air cleaner isn't working too well, it could allow dust and debris to collect on the MAF. If you've had a problem with your air/oil separator, it could have contaminated the sensor as well. Oil sucked into the engine intake from a defective separator can easily find its way back to the intake tube. If you have had major engine problems (like our project car with the blown-up

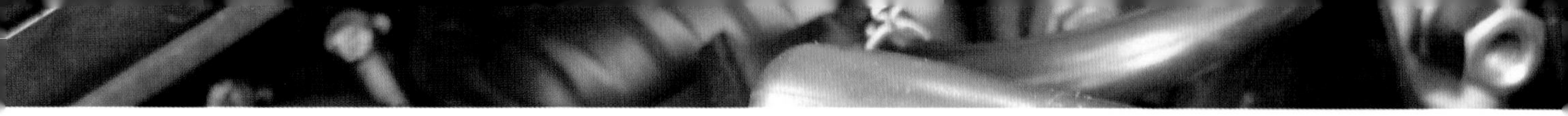

engine), then you may find a ruined MAF. On our donor car, the MAF was soaked in oil and coolant residue that had found its way all over the engine. If you have an aftermarket reusable air filter, beware of how much cleaning and filtering oil you use on it. Excess oil may get sucked into the intake and find its way onto the MAF. To keep your MAF healthy, I recommend changing or cleaning your air filter often (see Project 3).

If you are replacing your sensor, it is extremely important that you get the proper one for your car. There are two basic types: one for the cars that use a traditional throttle cable (1999 only) and one for cars with an E-gas electronic throttle (2000 and later). In addition, the later-style E-gas sensor has been updated at least twice as of this writing. Porsche updated the sensors in the Carrera in 2002 with the introduction of the 3.6 liter engine. Here is a chart that shows the differences between all of the sensors.

In general, if the old sensor you're removing has a 123.00 or 124.00 sensor, then you should replace it with a sensor with the same part number. If the old sensor you're removing ends in 125.01, then replace it with 986.606.125.01 (the latest version available).

After reinstallation, reset the CEL using your code reader (see Project 20). You can also disconnect the battery for a short while to reset the lamp, but I don't really recommend this approach (see Project 20). On 1999–2002 Carreras, you can disconnect the battery for more than 20 seconds but less than 50 seconds to clear the trouble codes without having to enter your code back into your radio. On pre-2003 cars, the computer's CEL memory is cleared after being disconnected for 20 seconds, but the radio code is needed after being disconnected for 50 seconds.

After you have replaced or cleaned the sensor and cleared the code, you need to drive the car to see if the code returns. If the same error code appears, then the problem probably lies elsewhere. Most of the time when you have an error code indicating a problem with the MAF, it is usually solved by the installation of a new sensor. However, the computer can become confused sometimes and give misleading error messages. Wire harness issues, DME problems, and secondary air injection equipment problems may all give false MAF error codes. At this point, it's best to dive into the factory manuals and start going through the laborious test procedures contained in there.

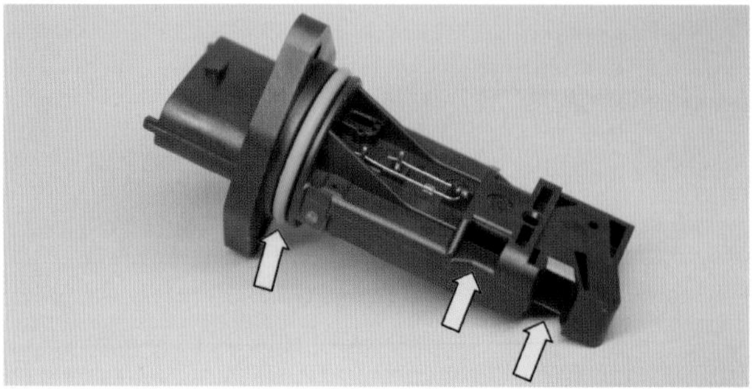

1 Shown here is the mass airflow sensor (MAF). The main sensor fits in a hole in the air intake, downstream of the air filter. The green O-ring seals the sensor to the intake tube (yellow arrow). If you're having trouble with your MAF, you can try to resurrect it by cleaning it. Lightly spray the areas shown with the blue arrow with electrical contact cleaner—the one that I recommend is CRC Mass Air Flow Sensor Cleaner. Spray it and then shake the sensor so that any dirt or debris is washed away. Don't touch any of the sensor elements with anything (like your finger or a brush), as this will damage them almost immediately. Let it dry completely prior to reinstallation.

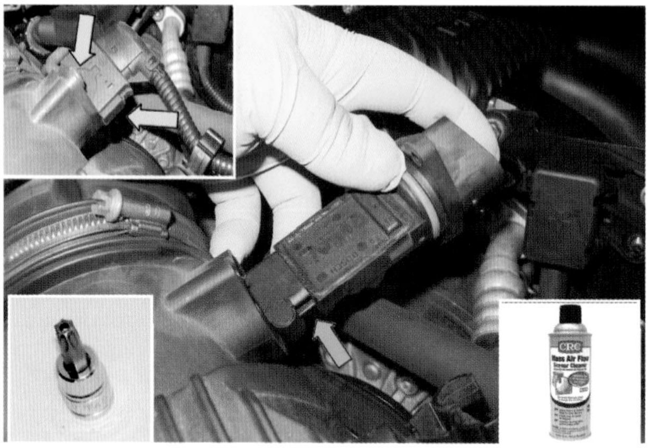

2 You need a T20 tamper-proof Torx bit (inset, lower left) to remove the MAF from its home in the intake pipe (inset, upper left, blue arrows). It's typically easier to pull the sensor out of the intake tube first and then disconnect the electrical harness. Be sure not to touch any of the sensor elements that are exposed. Clean the entire housing area prior to installing your new sensor. Take note of the opening at the bottom of the sensor (green arrow). The new sensor must be oriented so that the opening faces the air incoming into the engine.

Porsche Part #	BOSCH Part #	Application	Notes
996.606.123.00	0-280-217-007	1999 996 Carrera 2 (2 wheel drive)	Sensor for use with cable throttle cars
996.606.124.00	0-280-218-009	1999–2001 996 Carrera 4 (4 wheel drive) 2000–2001 All 996 Carreras 2001–2005 996 Turbo 2002–2005 GT2 2005 996 Turbo S	Original sensor for E-gas cars
986.606.125.01	0-280-218-055	2002–2005 996 Carrera & Carrera 4S 2006 Carreras 2007–2012 997 Carreras 2002–2004 Carrera 4 2007–2012 Carrera 4 and Carrera 4S 2005, 2007–2012 Carrera S 2004–2005 GT3 2007–2012 Targa 4 and Targa 4S	Latest updated sensor
997.606.125.00	0-280-218-192	2007–2009 997 Turbo	Shared with Cayenne

PROJECT 29
Throttle Body Cleaning/Intake Plenum Replacement

Time / Tab / Talent: 3 hours / $15 / 🔧🔧

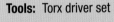

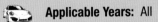

Tools: Torx driver set

Applicable Years: All

Tinware: New O-ring or idle control valve gasket

More Info: http://www.101projects.com/Carrera/29.htm

Tip: Remove the throttle body and let it soak in carburetor cleaner overnight

Performance Gain: Smoother-running engine

Comp Modification: Replace intake plenum boots

1 The Carrera throttle body is a precision piece of equipment that is subject to a rather harsh environment. After years of reliable service, the throttle body may become dirty or clogged, which may result in lowered performance. You may find that there is a lot of built-up dirt, particularly if a previous owner didn't change the air filter too often (inset). Instructions on how to access the throttle body are detailed in Project 9. Remove the throttle body bolts (green and purple arrows) and disconnect the wire harness (yellow arrow) from the intake plenum; then, take it over to your workbench and clean it out using some carburetor cleaner. Run lint-free cloths through all of the passages and make sure all the dirt and debris is removed. Be sure to check your intake plenum boots for cracks while the throttle body is off and replace them if necessary.

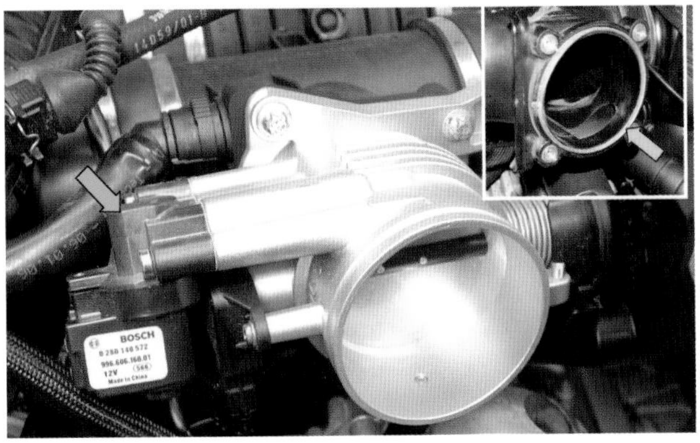

2 This is what your throttle body should look like after you've finished cleaning it. Shown here is the early style cable throttle with the idle control valve (green arrow). This valve controls the air that passes by the throttle. If it's clogged, you will get erratic idle and warm-up problems. Be sure to use a new gasket when you remount the idle control valve to the throttle body. With the throttle body completely clean, remount it to the intake plenum using a new rubber gasket (yellow arrow, inset photo).

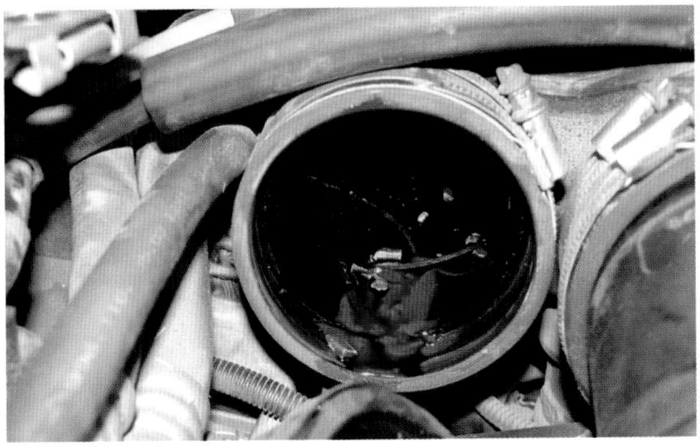

3 Clean out any oil and debris from the inside of your intake plenum, and replace the rubber hoses/boots if they are old or cracking. This photo shows the inside of the intake plenum on one of our project cars, which had a disastrous engine failure. Those small pieces of metal that you see there are leftover piston rings! Normally, you will only find oil and gas residue in the intake plenum. If your air-oil separator has failed, then you will indeed find plenty of excess oil in here—and also coating the throttle body—that needs to be removed.

SECTION 4
WATER

Porsche built some great engines with these Carreras. The rear-engine design, however, made for some tricky routing of water hoses, and some creative solutions were developed. As a result, some issues are unique to these cars, and failures in the water-cooling system can account for a significant portion of overall engine failures and breakdowns. Fortunately, the engine's reliability can be significantly increased through careful attention paid to the maintenance of the cooling system.

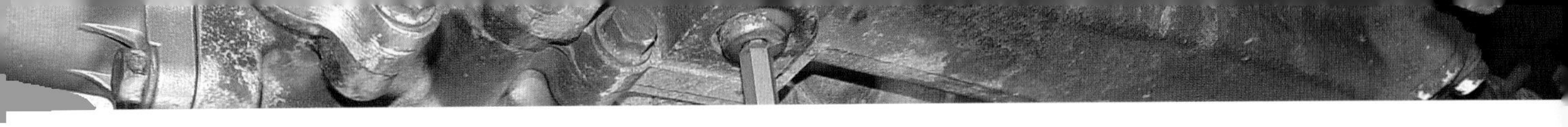

PROJECT 30
Coolant Flush/Replacement

Time / Tab / Talent: 2 hours / $120 /

Tools: Large bucket, socket set

Applicable Years: All

Tinware: 6–12 quarts of coolant

More Info: http://www.101projects.com/Carrera/30.htm

Tip: Make sure your bucket is big and wide to catch the coolant stream

Performance Gain: Prevents electrolysis in your engine

Comp Modification: Water pump and hose replacement

One often neglected task on many cars is the maintenance of the cooling system. In general, Porsche recommends that you flush and clean out your cooling system once every 36 months or approximately every three years. I like to perform this task on my own cars about once a year or, if I let it slip, once every two years. The reason for this time frame is that old, exhausted coolant can actually cause irreversible damage to your engine components—I found this out firsthand when I recently replaced the head gasket on one of my older BMWs. It looked like the previous owner hadn't changed the fluid once in the past 10 years. As a result, there were many parts of the engine that were corroded and showing severe signs of wear.

A properly maintained cooling system must have a few things in order: adequate supply of coolant, a radiator that acts as a heat exchanger with the outside air, a fan or airflow source, a water pump to keep the coolant circulating, and a thermostat to regulate the engine at its optimum operating temperature. The coolant must also have the correct mixture and chemical compounds to promote heat transfer, protect against freezing, and also inhibit corrosion. To keep your 911 operating correctly, it's important to check the level, strength, and overall condition of the coolant on a regular basis. You also need to change the coolant before it degrades to the point where it doesn't perform its job adequately.

A fact that I keep hearing kicked around revolves around the reported findings of the U.S. Department of Transportation, which states that cooling system failures are the leading cause of mechanical breakdowns on the highway—not exactly surprising, since proper cooling maintenance is one of the most neglected areas of most cars.

Electrolysis. One failure mode associated with dirty coolant is known as electrolysis. Electrolysis occurs when stray electrical current routes itself through the engine coolant. The electricity attempts to find the shortest path, and impurities in the coolant often generate a path of least resistance that the electricity travels across. The source of this stray electricity is often from electrical engine accessories that have not been properly grounded. A missing engine or transmission ground strap can also cause the coolant to become electrified. Sometimes the path of least resistance becomes a radiator, a heater hose, or even the heater core. These components are often well grounded and offer a ground path from the engine to the chassis by means of the semi-conductive path of the coolant.

Electrolysis can destroy your engine quickly. Although it's semi-normal to have very small amounts of voltage potential in your coolant system, values greater than about a tenth of a volt can start reactions between the coolant and the metal in your engine. In particular, electrolysis affects primarily aluminum engine components, resulting in pitting and scaring of the aluminum surface. This eating away of the metal can cause coolant system leaks and, in particular, radiator leaks around aluminum welds. Cast-iron components are also vulnerable, but typically the aluminum metal parts fail first. Often, electrolysis can be easily seen attacking aluminum cylinder heads (see Photo 1).

How can you test for electrolysis? Other than actually seeing visible signs of erosion, you can perform a current flow test. Connect the negative terminal of a voltmeter to the chassis ground. Test for adequate continuity by touching another point on the chassis—the resistance should be near to zero. With the engine cold and running, submerge the positive probe into the coolant tank, making sure that the probe does not touch any metal parts. The voltage should be less than .10 volts. If not, methodically turn off or unplug each electrical accessory until the reading reads below .10 volts. Have an assistant switch accessories (like the A/C compressor, heater blower, etc.) while you measure the voltage.

If an accessory doesn't have an on/off switch, test it by temporarily running a ground from the housing of the accessory to the chassis. Ground each component and check the voltmeter. If the wire restores a missing ground connection to the accessory, then you've found a component with a faulty ground.

During this test, be sure to check the starter. Not only will a poorly grounded starter struggle to turn over the engine, it will also zap away tremendous amounts of metal in your cooling system components. Watch the meter carefully when starting the engine. Any voltage spike will indicate a faulty ground connection.

Coolant system additives. Many people are rightly skeptical of coolant system additives—there are a lot of myths in the automotive industry. Luckily, the coolant system additives are in the category of good practice, for reasons I'll explain here. It all begins with chemistry. Like today's modern oils, many of today's modern coolants incorporate some of the chemicals that help cooling and increase heat flow around your cooling system components. As more and more automotive components are made out of aluminum and radiators become smaller, the use of these additives becomes more advantageous.

Aftermarket coolant system additives are known as surfactants. What is a surfactant? A surfactant, or surface active agent, is a molecule that has a water-loving (hydrophilic) end and a water-fearing (hydrophobic) end. Localized boiling of coolant in the cylinder head can create large shock waves that can wreak havoc on your engine, particularly on aluminum components. Without going into too much boring detail, these surfactants also help reduce the amount of air in the cooling system and control the amount of foam within the system.

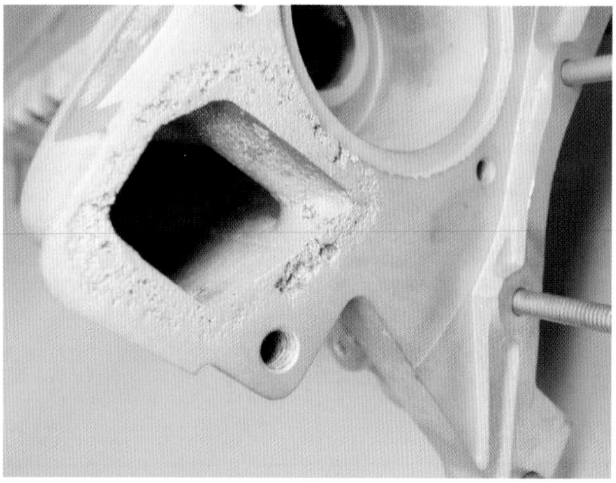

1 This photo shows a picture of the thermostat area of a BMW cylinder head that has been partially damaged by electrolysis. Notice how the aluminum has been eaten away and eroded by the chemical/electrical reactions. The process works somewhat like electrical discharge machines (EDM). These machines work by passing a large electrical current through metal, literally zapping away bits of material until nothing remains. Unfortunately, the electrolysis process works in a similar way, zapping bits of metal in proportion to the amount of electrical current passing through the coolant. A poorly grounded starter can literally destroy a radiator or head within a matter of weeks, depending upon how often the car is started. A smaller current drain, like an electric cooling fan, may slowing erode components over many months.

In general, using these additives is beneficial to your cooling system for three main reasons. First, they reduce harmful cavitations and foaming that may occur when your water pump is kicking out fluid at a rapid pace. This reduced foaming helps to prevent damage to aluminum surfaces. Second, the use of these additives aid in the transmission of heat from the coolant to the radiating surfaces within the radiator. Even if your car runs very cool, these additives add an extra level of protection in case a thermostat or similar component fails. Finally, the additives contain corrosion inhibitors. Most cars on the road have cooling systems that do not contain the ideal 50/50 water/antifreeze ratio that the antifreeze manufacturers design for. The additives help minimize potential corrosion by maintaining adequate pH levels. Even if your antifreeze already contains surfactant additives, the use of these additional additives is typically beneficial because most cars are shortchanged on the 50/50 coolant/water mix.

In general, these are the benefits of additives such as Water Wetter:

- Reduce corrosion due to rust and electrolysis
- Increase the "wetting ability" of water and improve heat transfer, thus reducing cylinder head temperatures
- Clean and lubricate coolant system seals like those found in the water pump
- Reduce the formation of foam and cavitations, which can cause corrosion
- Reduce the effects of "hard water" in the cooling system

In general, the addition of these additives is cheap, and it's a proven benefit too—no snake oil here. Using the additives on a perfectly maintained car can also provide a significant margin of error in case something goes wrong. Porsches are not generally known for cooling system failures, but keeping the odds on your side can prevent a costly head gasket replacement.

It's important to keep your cooling system at the correct pH as well. Water has a pH of 7 and is considered neutral. Battery acid is highly corrosive and has a pH of about 2–3, whereas baking soda is very alkaline and has a pH of about 10–11. In general, you want to make sure that your coolant has a pH greater than 7. Any pH less than that will result in an acidic mixture, which will start to corrode your engine. The corrosion inhibitors in additives and antifreeze are added specifically to keep the pH above 7. A properly mixed 50/50 split between water and antifreeze will yield a pH of about 8–9. Over time, the glycol (one of the main components of antifreeze) will break down and degrade, creating acidic compounds. The alkaline corrosion inhibitors must be adequate enough to neutralize these acidic byproducts over the life of the coolant. Minerals in the water, heat, dissolved oxygen, and other factors gradually deplete the coolant of its corrosion inhibitors. Once gone, the mixture will become acidic and will begin to eat away at your engine.

Cooling system maintenance—Checking the level. It's very important to check your coolant level regularly, as this will help detect leaks that can siphon off coolant and cause overheating in your engine. You should regularly check the coolant level in the coolant reservoir, making sure that

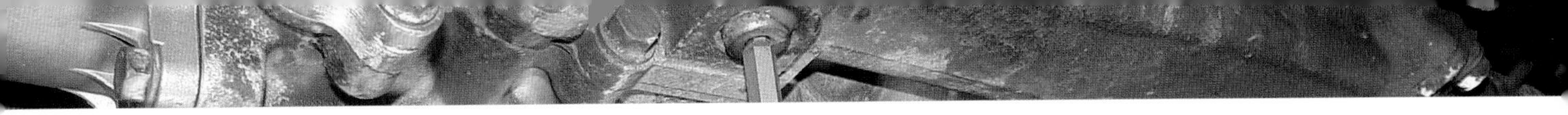

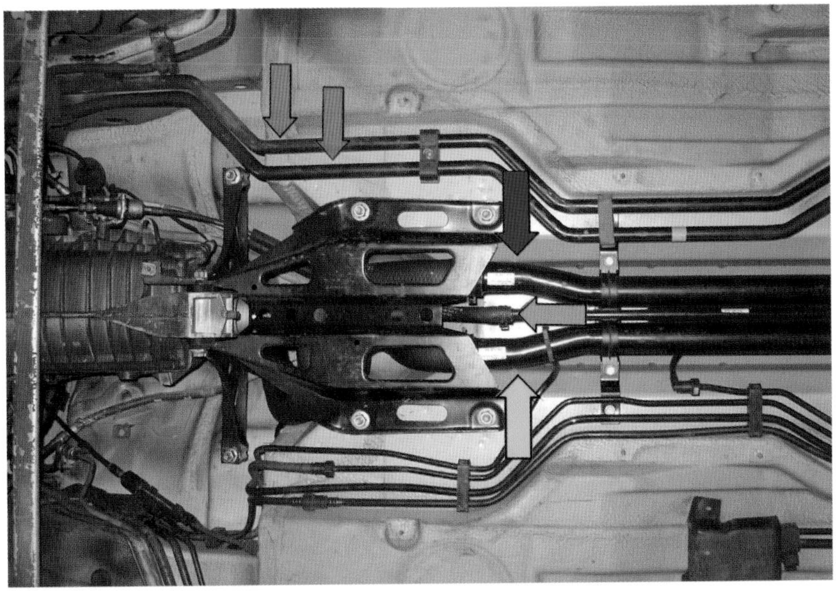

2 This photo shows the various lines under the rear of the 996 Carrera. Blue arrow: Cooling line to upper right side of engine. Green arrow: Coolant line from the water pump on the lower left engine Red arrows: Heater supply/return lines. Purple arrow: Radiator vent line, which should not need to be disconnected.

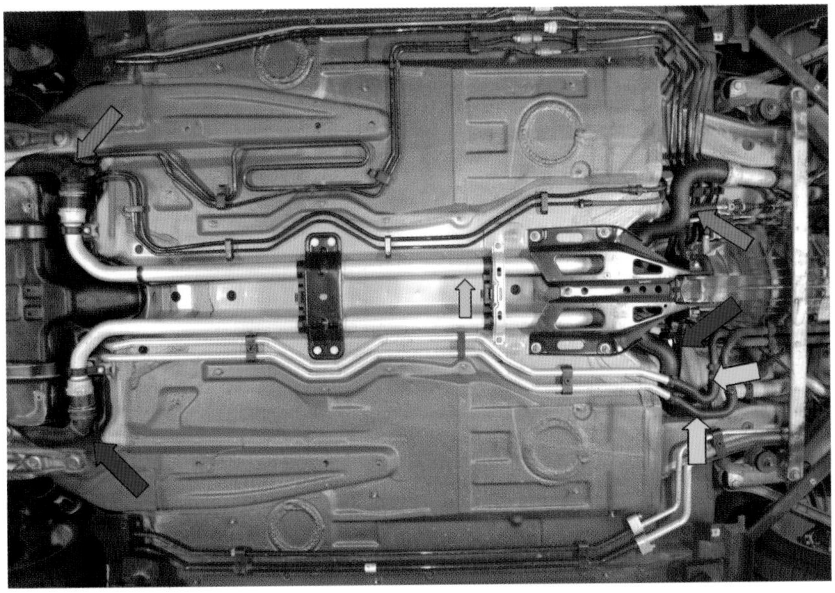

3 Under body hoses for the 997 Carrera (connected to metal pipes). Red arrows: From water pump. Blue arrows: To upper engine block. Yellow arrows: Heater core hoses. Green arrow: Vent lines.

it is within the prescribed high/low marks. These marks are printed on the side of the coolant container, located in the rear trunk. The container is slightly transparent, and you can see the current coolant level within.

Your Carrera will lose a little bit of coolant here and there over time due to evaporation and/or sporadic leakage. However, a significant loss of coolant over a very short period of time almost certainly signifies a leak in the system. Sometimes a leak can be seen when you park the car overnight. Often the coolant leaks out and then evaporates while you're driving, leaving no telltale mark of coolant on the pavement. If you suspect a coolant leak, visually inspect all of the hoses, the water pump, the reservoir, and the radiator for seepage or the "weeping" of coolant out of seams and gaskets. Check the seal on the radiator cap. Check that the radiator cap is fastened securely. If you suspect a leak that you cannot see, a pressure test from a professional mechanic can verify the integrity of your system.

If you can't find any visible leaks and the system appears to hold pressure, then check to make sure that the cap is good and is rated for the proper pressure. Verify that the cap you have for your Carrera is the proper one for your engine. If you look inside the coolant tank and the coolant is muddy or cloudy, then you may have a serious head gasket problem. Oil may be leaking past the gasket and mixing with the coolant. This typically means that the engine needs to come apart and the head gaskets resealed, which is a complex and expensive repair, as you might imagine.

If the system does not hold pressure, and you're still at a loss where coolant might be disappearing to, then you might want to start looking in the oil. A faulty head gasket will often cause coolant to leak into the oil. If you remove the oil

4 This photo shows the removal of the coolant drain plug located on the bottom of the engine.

5 This photo shows the coolant expansion tank (red arrow), the coolant tank cap (blue arrow), and the expansion valve (green arrow). You flip up the metal clip in the bleeder valve to bleed the system. Remember to close it when done.

cap and find a yellow murky substance, then you probably have a faulty head gasket. The oil level may be elevated and you will be able to see droplets of coolant inside the oil filler hole. If coolant is leaking past the gasket into a combustion chamber, you will see steam exiting out of the tailpipe, and the spark plugs will foul easily. In addition, the exhaust will be contaminated with the silicate corrosion inhibitors found in the coolant, and your oxygen sensor will be destroyed—plan on replacing it if you have experienced this problem.

If you can't discover what happened to the coolant, it may be because there was a temporary overheating problem and some of the coolant boiled over. In this case, top off the coolant and keep a very close eye on it. It's not uncommon for overheating issues to suddenly destroy a head gasket.

Checking coolant strength and condition. You should periodically test the strength and condition of your coolant to ensure that you have achieved the optimum balance for your Carrera. This is just as important for protection against heat as it is for protection against freezing. An imbalance between water and antifreeze levels will change the boiling point and/or freezing point of the mixture. A 50/50 mixture of water and ethylene glycol (EG) antifreeze will provide protection against boiling up to approximately 255 degrees Fahrenheit (with a 15 psi radiator cap). This mixture will protect against freezing to a chilly -34 degrees Fahrenheit. On the other hand, a similar 50/50 mixture of propylene glycol (PG) antifreeze and water will give you protection from -26 degrees Fahrenheit to about 257 degrees Fahrenheit.

If you increase the concentration of antifreeze in the coolant, you will raise the effective boiling point and lower the freezing point. While this may seem beneficial on the surface, having an antifreeze content of greater than 65–70 percent will significantly reduce the ability of the coolant to transmit and transfer heat. This increases the chances of overheating. As with most things in life, it's good to maintain a healthy balance.

Beware: You cannot accurately determine the condition of your coolant simply by looking at it. The chemical composition and concentrations in the coolant are very important; if the chemistry is off, then your coolant may be harming your engine.

As mentioned previously, it is important to keep the coolant fresh. The main ingredient in antifreeze, ethylene glycol, typically accounts for 95 percent of antifreeze by weight. It does not typically wear out, but the corrosion inhibitors that comprise the remaining 5 percent typically do degrade and wear out over time. Keeping the coolant fresh is especially important with engines that have both aluminum heads and cast-iron blocks.

I recommend that the coolant be changed at least every two years or every 25,000 miles. I'm not a huge fan of long-life antifreeze—if these longer-life fluids are mixed with conventional antifreeze (a very easy mistake to make), the corrosion inhibitors react and reduce the effective protection of the long-life fluid. If you do have this long-life fluid installed in your car, only add the same type of antifreeze to the car. Don't mix and match regular and long-life fluid.

Unfortunately, it's tough to determine if your long-life coolant has been mixed or topped off with ordinary antifreeze. Although some coolants are dyed a separate color (like Dex-Cool in GM vehicles), when mixed with standard antifreeze, that separate color typically isn't enough to overpower the bright green color of standard antifreeze. In general, unless you know the entire service history of your Carrera, it's a wise idea to err on the side of caution and use a shorter service interval for changing your coolant.

Okay, so how do you check the coolant in your system? I recommend using little chemical strip tests that measure how much reserve alkalinity is left within the coolant. The test strip changes color when immersed in the coolant. You can then compare the final color change to a reference chart in order to determine the condition of the coolant. Obviously, if the coolant tests poorly or is borderline, you should plan on replacing your coolant very soon.

An additional note: EG and PG) antifreeze have differing specific gravities, so make sure that you use the correct type of test strip when testing your coolant. Otherwise, you may end up with false readings. EG antifreeze is very toxic to pets and small animals yet smells and tastes pretty good to them, so make sure that you keep old coolant away from them.

CHANGING THE COOLANT IN YOUR 911 CARRERA

Okay, so I've convinced you that your coolant needs changing. The good news is that it's relatively straightforward on the 911 Carrera. Begin by getting a large drip pan to place underneath your car. My favorite choice is kitty litter boxes, as they are large, are made of plastic, and will hold a lot of coolant. The Carrera six-cylinder engines will hold about 5–6 gallons, so make sure that whatever container you use is capable of holding all of that coolant.

With your Carrera cold, elevate it on jack stands (see Project 1) and remove the plastic protective panels that cover the radiator hoses on the underside of the car. Place the heater temp controls all the way to high, turn the ignition to the on position, and turn on the passenger compartment fan to its lowest setting. Do not start the car. By turning on the heater, you are opening the valves to the heater core, which will allow you to drain the coolant located in the core. Move to the rear trunk and slowly remove the radiator/reservoir cap inside the trunk to allow any coolant system pressure to vent out.

Now it's time to empty the coolant—refer to Photo 2 for the location of the hoses that need to be disconnected. At the bottom of the engine, open the drain plug located in the oil pump housing and let the coolant empty into your large bucket. When the flow has stopped, replace the plug using a new O-ring and torque to 7–11 ft-lbs (10–15 Nm). Next disconnect the two large radiator hoses that feed the supply and return coolant lines to the front of the car. I also like to disconnect the front lower hoses from the radiators as well, but this requires removing the front bumper cover (see Project 68 and Project 32).

When all of the coolant has drained, reconnect the hoses using new hose clamps. I used to only recommend the use of good quality German screw-type clamps, but I'm slowly coming around to the annoying spring-clip type that were used in the initial assembly of the car. These clips have an advantage over the clamp type in that they apply constant pressure when the hose expands or contracts as the car heats and cools.

Next, disconnect and empty the coolant from the two heater hoses. Reattach with new hose clamps. Now it's time to refill the coolant and bleed the system. In the rear trunk, on the left side of the engine bay, is the coolant tank (see the red arrow in Photo 5). Remove the filler cap (see the blue arrow in Photo 5) and fill the tank up to the top of the fill level, then flip up the metal clip that opens the bleeder valve (see the green arrow in Photo 5). Start the car and run it at idle, topping off the coolant to the maximum level, until no more coolant can be added. Rev the engine, let it settle down, and top it off again if the level decreases. Be sure during the whole process that the car does not exceed 176 degrees Fahrenheit (80 degrees Celsius) while bleeding the system. If the car gets too hot, it will interfere with your ability to fill and bleed the system to the proper level.

Now, reinstall the reservoir cap and let the car continue to warm up at about 2,500 rpm for 10 minutes or until the thermostat for the front radiators opens up. When the thermostat opens and coolant starts flowing forward, the electrical radiator fans should turn on. Now allow the car to continue to warm up a bit more, revving the car to about 5,000 rpm every 30 seconds or so. Remove the reservoir cap slowly, letting any built-up pressure dissipate. There should not be any tremendous pressure built up because the bleeder valve is still open at this time. Top off the coolant in the tank to the maximum level, reinstall the cap, and repeat the process of revving the engine to about 5,000 rpm for another five minutes.

Now, allow the engine to idle for a few minutes until you hear the radiator fans cycle on and off at least once. Turn off the engine, and slowly remove the reservoir cap again, relieving any pressure that might have built up there. Top off the coolant until it reaches the maximum level indicated on the coolant tank gauge, located on the side of the tank. Flip down the metal clip to close the bleeder valve. If you have an automatic transmission car, then replace fuse B1 in the driver side door kick panel.

I'm sure one question you're about to ask is, "What type of coolant should I use?" The Porsche factory manuals indicate that the coolant used inside the Carrera engines should be considered a "lifetime" fluid, and mixing regular fluid with this life-time fluid is not recommended. I prefer to use the Porsche factory coolant in my cars. At $35 a gallon, it can be somewhat more expensive than generic coolant, but the Porsche coolant is not premixed. Plan on using about 19 liters (5 gallons) of coolant for cars without a center radiator. The center radiator cars take about 6 gallons of coolant. Add one more liter as well if you have an automatic transmission. If ordering coolant for your flush job, I would be sure to order an extra gallon—you might need them to top off down the road, and the Porsche OEM coolant can be difficult to find in a pinch. The part number for a 1-gallon (3.79-liter) container is 000-043-301-05-M100, and it costs about $35 per gallon from PelicanParts.com.

6 I personally like to use the Porsche factory coolant, which is a bit more expensive, but specially formulated for the cars. However, if you use a standard off-the-shelf coolant that meets or exceeds the factory's specifications, then that should suffice as well.

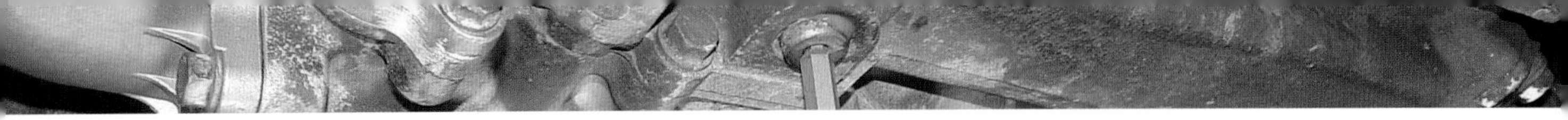

PROJECT 31
Coolant Hose Replacement

Time / Tab / Talent: 1–8 hours / $20–$400 /

Tools: Knife, handheld hex tool set, pliers

Applicable Years: All

Tinware: Water hoses, coolant

More Info: http://www.101projects.com/Carrera/31.htm

Tip: Use the better-quality German squeeze clamps

Performance Gain: Prevents catastrophic hose breakdown

Comp Modification: Replace radiator; bleed coolant system

I've owned a lot of cars over the past several years, and the 911 Carrera by far has the most radiator hoses of all of them. When Porsche designed this car, it really didn't try to reduce the amount of rubber used in the assembly. As a result, the task of replacing all of the radiator hoses on the car is a really big chore. One of the more difficult parts is actually figuring out where they are all located! For that purpose, I've created a table of hoses and general locations to help you check your hoses and replace them if necessary.

Please keep in mind that slight variations in hoses and locations have occurred over the length of production of the Carrera.

I recommend inspecting your rubber hoses every two years or so. As they age, they have a tendency to get hard and brittle. When you gently squeeze a hose, it should be relatively soft and easy to indent with your hand. It shouldn't feel like it is brittle or crunching when you squeeze it. It should spring back to its original shape pretty quickly after

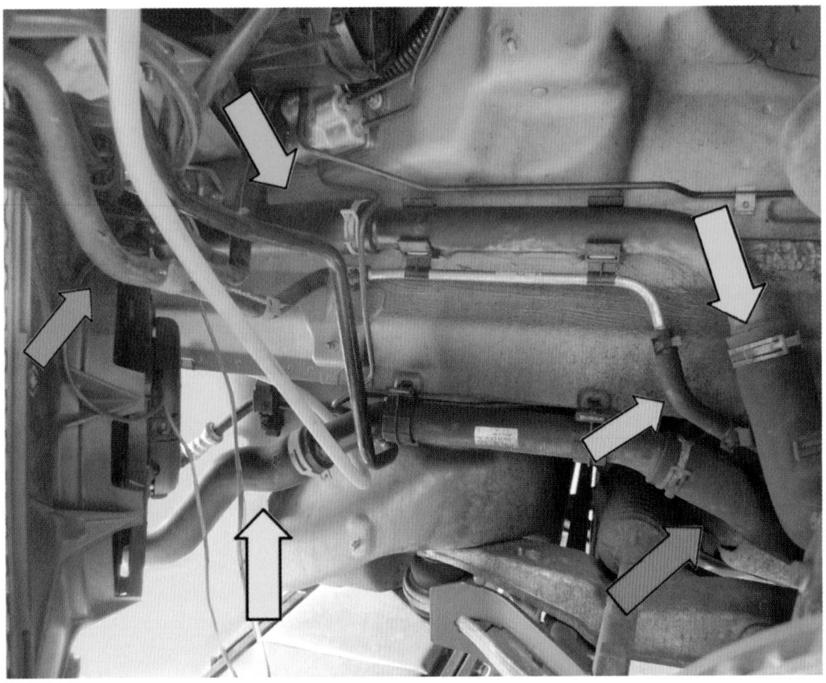

1 996 Carrera (1998–2005) Front Hoses (connected to radiators, left side shown)

- Bottom radiator hoses: left and right (blue arrow)
- Top radiator hoses: left and right (green arrow)
- Radiator vent hoses: left and right (purple arrow)

Intermediate Hoses (connected to metal pipes in front wheelwells, left side shown)

- Upper hoses: left and right (yellow arrow)

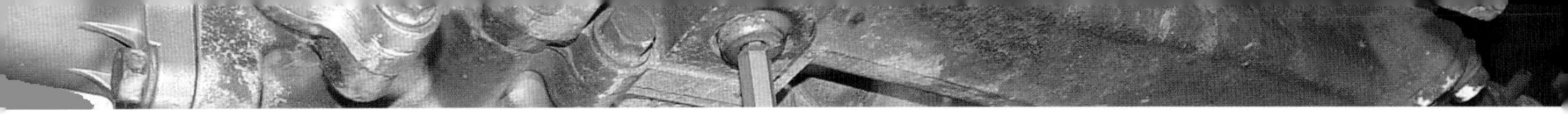

being compressed. If it feels very hard, then it might be time to replace it. If there is a bulge in the hose or any type of crack in the surface of the hose, then you should replace it as well. Also check for wetness or leaks around where the hoses create their connections. That is a sign that the hose should be replaced. Some hoses may be coated with some leftover Cosmoline from the factory; don't mistake these for bad radiator hoses.

Unfortunately, there's no exact milestone on when to replace your radiator hoses. The recommended automotive industry standard is about four years or 60,000–80,000 miles. On some cars, they may last 10 years or longer depending upon how the car is driven or how it's stored during winter or summer months. Since there are so many hoses on the 911 Carrera, I suspect that many of these cars will have many of their original hoses still installed many years down the line.

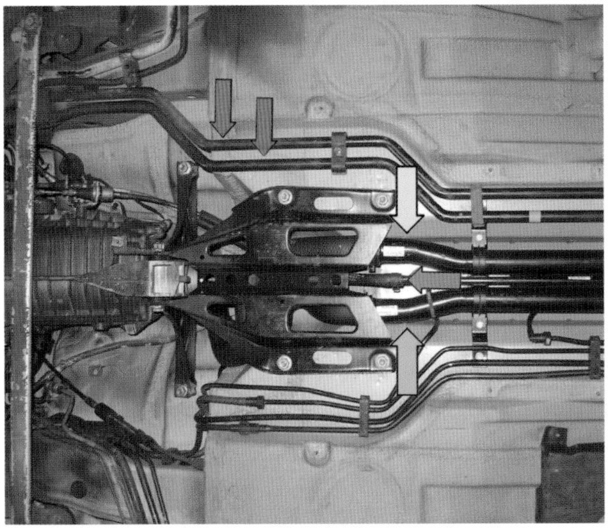

2 **996 Carrera (1998–2005) Rear Hoses**

- Coolant line to upper right side of engine (blue arrow)
- Coolant line from water pump (green arrow)
- Radiator vent hose (purple arrow)
- Heater core hoses (red arrows)

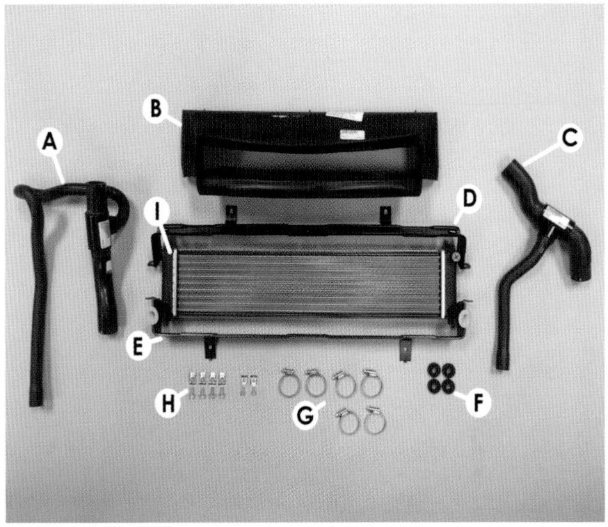

3 **996 Carrera (1998–2005) Center Third Radiator Hoses 996**

- Left side (A)
- Right side (C)

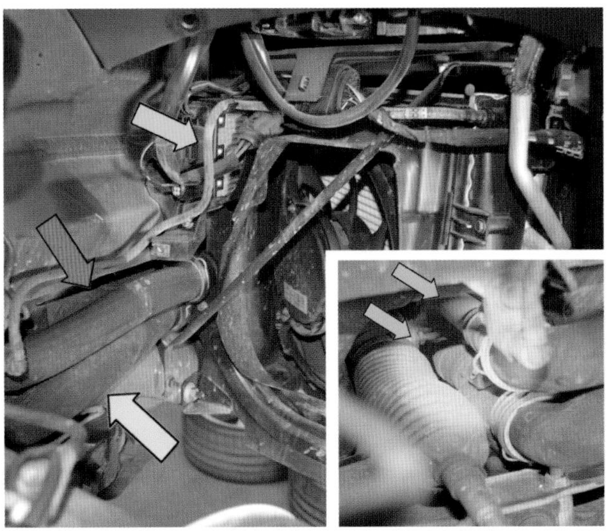

4 **997 Carrera (2005–2008) Front Hoses (connected to radiators)**

- From water pump (red arrow)
- To engine block (blue arrow)
- Vent line (yellow arrow)
- Cross over hoses (inset, green arrows)
- Hoses from front radiators to center radiator (not shown, see Project 32)

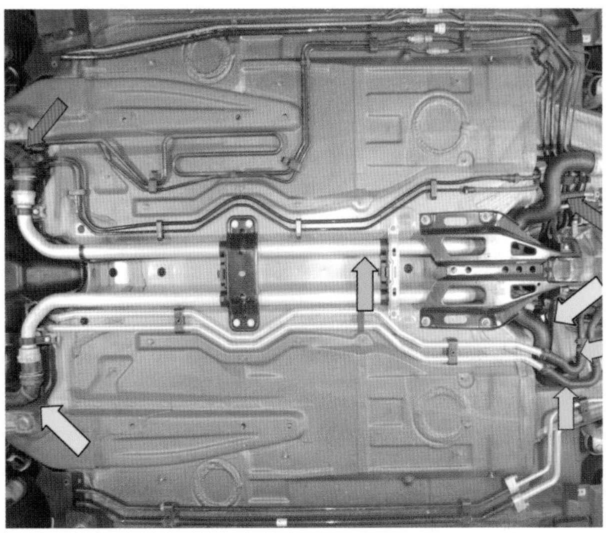

5 **997 Carrera (2005–2008) Under Body Hoses (connected to metal pipes)**

- From water pump (red arrows)
- To upper engine block (blue arrows)
- Heater core hoses (yellow arrows)
- Vent lines (hidden above, green arrow)

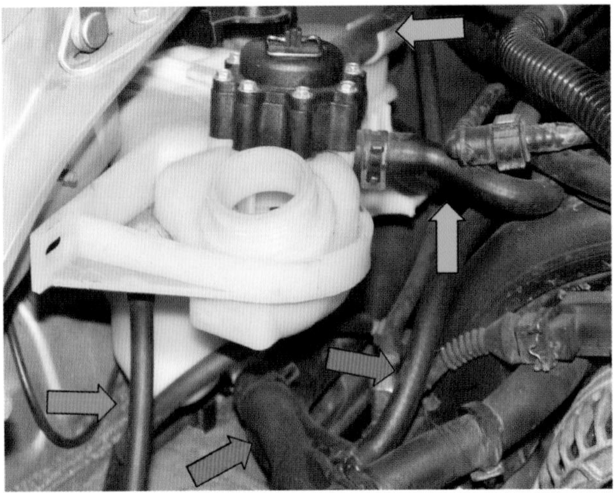

6 Hoses Common to both the 996 and 997 Carrera
Coolant Tank Hoses

- Lower hose connections to coolant tank (red arrow)
- Upper coolant tank hoses (green arrows)
- Coolant tank overflow hose (purple arrow)

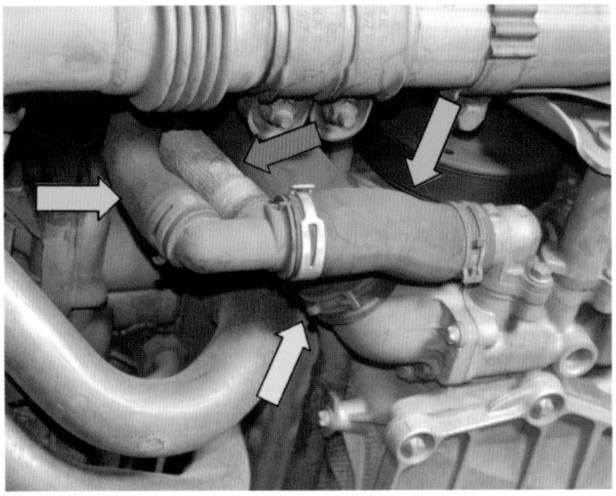

7 Hoses Common to both the 996 and 997 Carrera
Engine Hoses

- Thermostat hose (blue arrow)
- To splitter hose (green arrow)
- Return to engine hose (yellow arrow)
- Heater hose (red arrow)

8 Carrera 996: Use some pliers or channel locks to release the clamp and slide it down the hose (orange arrow). Then, use a razor knife to cut a slit along the length of the hose (green arrow). This will allow you to peel back the hose and easily remove it from the metal pipe.

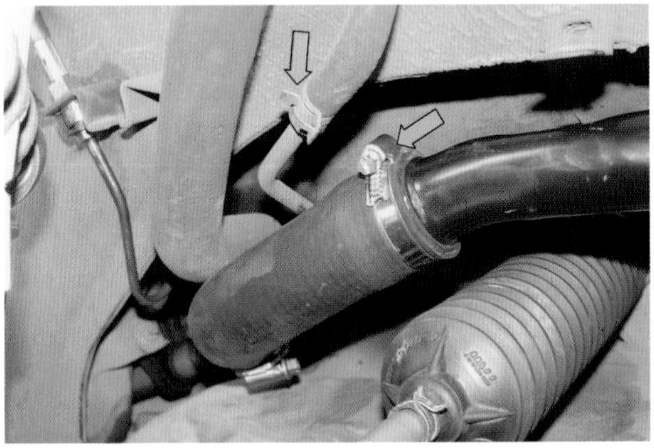

9 The standard hose clamps used on the car when new are difficult to attach properly (orange arrow). The nice advantage to these clamps is that they supply constant pressure around the hose even when it expands or contracts. For ease of installation, I often use German original equipment manufacturer (OEM) screw-type hose clamps that will not loosen up or fail over time (green arrow).

10 Porsche redesigned some of the hose connections for the 997 and changed them to the quick-disconnect type. With these connections you simply pull out (but not completely off) the metal clip on the joiner (blue arrows) then pull the old hose off. Clean out the connection, push the wire clip back in, insert the new hose with the quick connector, and push until you hear it snap in place.

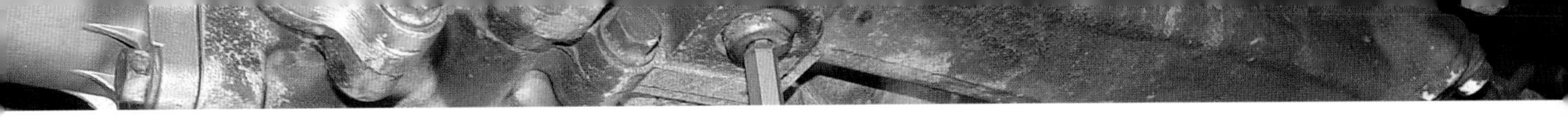

PROJECT 32
Installing a Center Radiator

Time / Tab / Talent: 8 hours / $550 /

Tools: 8mm socket, socket wrench, flathead screwdriver, marker, Phillips screwdriver, pliers or a crowbar, jack stands, floor jack

Applicable Years: All cars without center radiator

Tinware: Center radiator, brackets, hoses, clamps, nuts, bolts

More Info: http://www.101projects.com/Carrera/32.htm

Tip: Cut your front bumper instead of buying a new one

Performance Gain: Cooler-running engine

Comp Modification: Clean out side radiators and replace hoses

The venerable GT3 design includes a center-mounted radiator that was also sometimes installed on various Carrera models as well (mostly Tiptronic transmission equipped cars). The larger, more powerful engine dictated the use of the front-mounted radiator in addition to the two standard side radiators. Adding the front-mounted radiator is a good upgrade for cars that will be driven in hot weather or have undergone some performance modifications. In particular, if you're going to be taking your Carrera out to the track someday, I indeed recommend the installation of the additional radiator. It will provide some significant added protection against overheating, as it typically reduces the highest operating temperatures by about 10–20 degrees Fahrenheit (7–12 degrees Celsius) after installation.

The first step is to gather all your needed parts and preassemble the radiator assembly on your bench (see Photos 1 and 2). Pay careful attention to the radiator inlets and outlets as well as the frame tab locations as it's very easy to assemble this backward the first time. Lay out all your parts and make sure that you have everything that you need prior

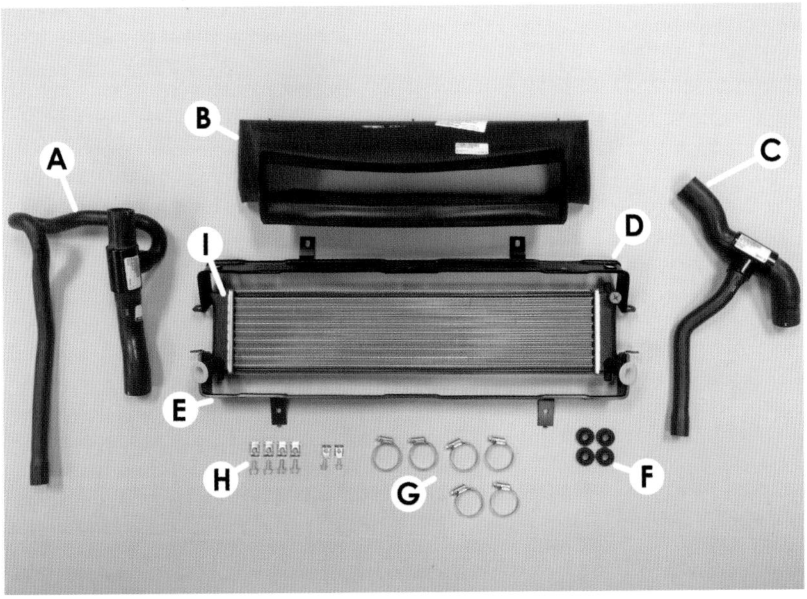

1 Here are the parts that you will need for your 996 center radiator installation. The parts are available from PelicanParts.com as complete kits for either the 996 (1998–2005) or the 997 (2005-2008) Carreras: **996 Shown (1998–2005) A:** Driver side radiator hose (996-106-665-58). **B:** Front rubber air guide (996-575-141-02). **C:** Passenger side radiator hose (996-106-666-55). **D:** Upper radiator bracket (996-504-487-02). **E:** Lower radiator bracket (996-504-485-02). **F:** 4 Radiator spacers (930-113-430-00). **G:** Hose clamps (Qty 2: 999-512-499-00 and Qty 4: 999-512-551-00). **H:** Mounting hardware (Qty 4: Hex Bolt M6 × 12 - 900-378-036-09, Qty 4: Speed Nut M6 - 999-507-550-02, Qty 2: Hex Bolt M8x16 - 900-378-074-09, Qty 2: Speed Nut M8 - 999-591-869-02). **I:** Center radiator (996-106-037-51). **997 Not Shown (2005–2008)** Center Radiator (997-106-037-02). Upper Retaining Frame (997-504-487-00). Lower Retaining Frame (997-504-485-00). Rubber Moldings Qty 4 (997-106-437-00). Hexagon Head Bolts M6X16 Qty 2 (900-378-035001). Speed Nut M6 Qty 2 (999-591-882-02). Hexagon Head Bolts Qty 4: (900-378-074-09). Speed Nuts M8 Qty 4 (999-591-869-02). Air Duct Radiator Center (997-575-141-00). Water Hose Return Line (997-106-639-03). Water Hose Supply Line (997-106-638-03)

2 This photo shows the new center radiator with the upper and lower mounting brackets installed. This side of the radiator faces the rear of the car. Pay close attention to the tabs on the radiator brackets: the top tab attaches near the front, the bottom tab attaches near the rear of the bracket. When installed, the radiator will be facing slightly upward at an angle.

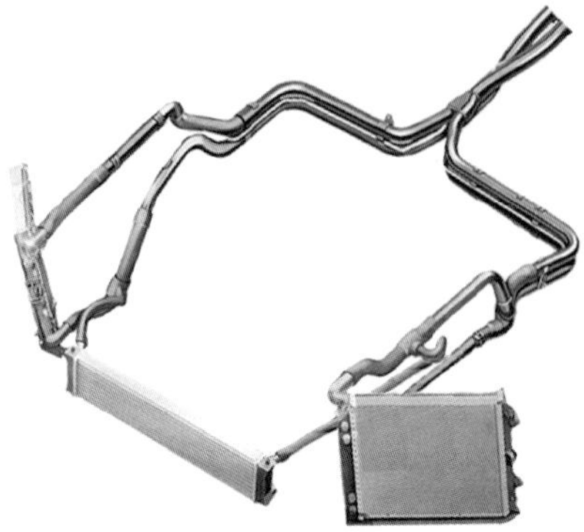

3 Here's a useful diagram showing the routing of the hoses for the three radiator setup. As shown in the photo, you need to replace the lower radiator hose on the right side of the car and the upper radiator hose on the left side of the car. The center radiator "taps" into the hoses for the left and right radiators and provides additional cooling. In the 997, the supply and return hoses for the center radiator are much simpler. They attach directly to the supply side on one radiator and the return side on the other via a short hose.

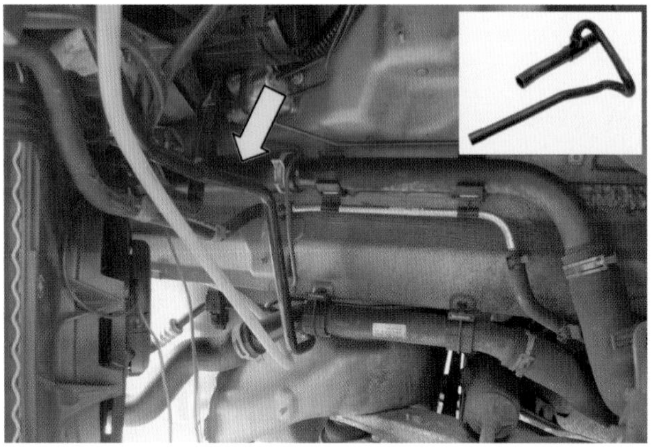

4 This photo shows the upper radiator hose that needs to be replaced on the left side of the car.

to tearing apart the car. This project details the installation on an early 996-type car, but the upgrade kit for the 2005 and later 997 cars is very similar (different part numbers though).

Next, jack up the car, remove the two front wheels and remove the front bumper cover and the lower part of the inner wheelwell liners (see Project 68). Next, remove the air scoops, detach the air conditioning condensers, empty the engine coolant, and loosen the radiator assembly so that you can drop down the whole assembly (see Project 33 for instructions on these tasks).

Replace the lower hose on the passenger side with the new three-way hose that will feed the radiator. Use new adjustable hose clamps, as shown in the bottom of Photo 1. Rotate the hose so that the small section of the hose is properly oriented to mate with the top of the center radiator port. Now, replace the hose on the upper left side, again positioning the small portion of the hose so that it will mate with the top of the center radiator when installed. This left-side hose twists and bends in a crazy pattern—use Photos 3 and 4 as a guide on how to properly route it.

I also realized that the center radiator bracket may cut into the air conditioning lines that run near the upper bracket of the center radiator. I solved this issue by adding extra protection with zip ties and pieces from a rubber hose to wrap the air conditioning lines (see Photo 7).

Now attach the center radiator to its position in the center of the car. Loosely attach the radiator using the top two M8 bolts and the corresponding speed nuts that clip into place on the chassis (see Photo 7). Attach and clamp the left and right hoses to the radiator—loosen and remove one of the M8 bolts if you need to gain enough room to secure the hose. When the hoses are secure, attach the remaining M8 bolts and speed nuts and secure the radiator to the chassis.

To finish, reattach the radiators and air conditioning condensers and tighten up all of the hardware that holds them in place. Refill the car with the coolant you removed, or use a new quantity of coolant equal to what came out when you disconnected the radiator hoses. Start the car up and let it run for a few minutes to check for leaks.

After confirming that the car is leak-free, attach the rubber surround onto the center radiator, install the left and right rubber air ducts, and reinstall the wheelwells and the bumper cover. When modifying your bumper cover to accommodate the center radiator, you can cut your own insert out as per the instructions I provide with Photos 8 and 9. Cutting is not necessary on the 997 as the center section just unclips and can be removed.

When everything is buttoned up properly, bleed the entire cooling system as described in Project 30. Over the next few days, check the coolant level regularly, and also check for coolant leaks when you park the car.

The factory thermostat starts to open at about 187 degrees Fahrenheit (86 degrees Celsius) and only fully opens at almost 210 degrees Fahrenheit (99 degrees Celsius). This means that the effects of the front-mounted radiators are limited until the engine gets very hot. For this reason, I recommend installing a low-temp thermostat in conjunction with the center-mounted radiator upgrade. See Project 35 for more details.

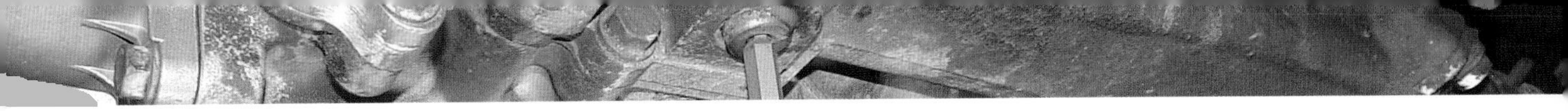

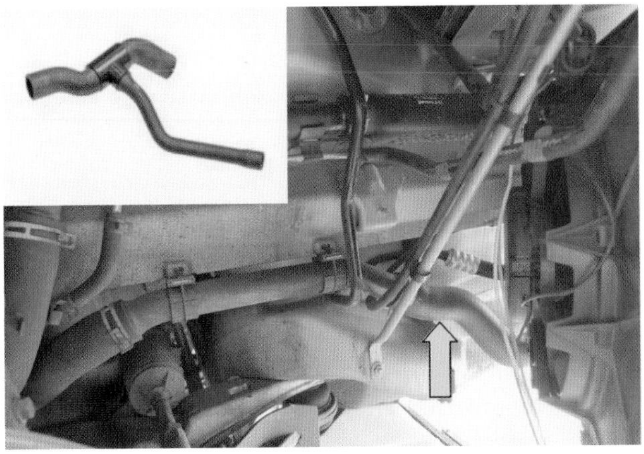

5 This photo shows the lower radiator hose on the right side of the 996 that needs to be replaced as part of the upgrade.

6 This photo shows a 997 with the front bumper and right side air diverter removed. Porsche redesigned the radiators for the 997, which makes the installation of a center radiator very easy. The new radiators have a built in quick disconnect for the hoses to the center radiator. Pull the quick disconnect wire on the left radiator (lower part of the radiator, yellow arrows) and insert the new hose. On the right side remove the quick disconnect wire on the radiator (upper part of the radiator, green arrows) and insert the new hose. Attach both hoses to the center radiator. The AC lines have also been rerouted and are no longer an issue with interference. The inset photo shows the supply hose (purple arrow) and the return hose (red arrow) to the left-side radiator.

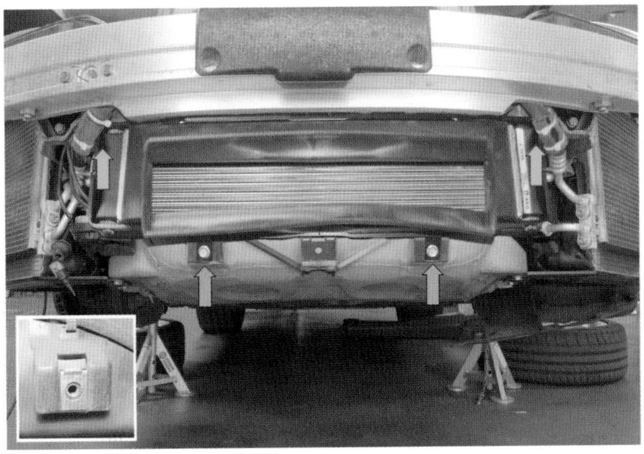

7 Shown here is the center radiator installed on a 996 just prior to putting the front bumper cover back on. Note how the air conditioning hoses have been wrapped with protective rubber (old radiator hoses) since the upper center radiator bracket tends to wear into them (green arrows). The lower left inset photo shows the proper orientation of the speed nut fasteners—the chassis should already have the mounting brackets built in (inset photo and purple arrows).

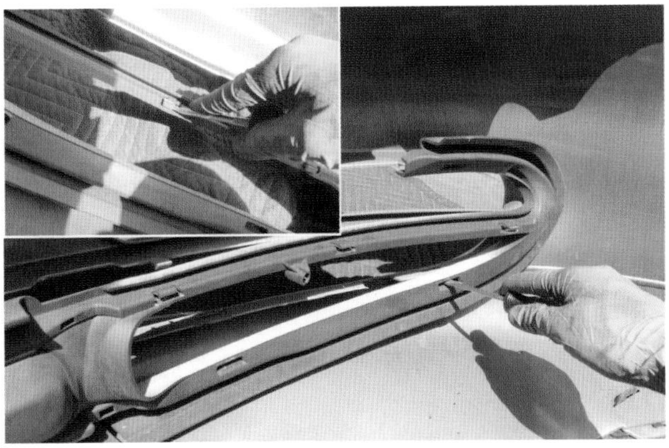

8 On the 996, you can cut out the opening for the front radiator yourself and reuse your old bumper cover. Behind the front bumper, is a plastic air inlet panel that is clipped in along the bumper cover. Using a flathead screwdriver, unclip the 20 clips. Ten clips require one motion: push the screwdriver into the clip and lift up to unhook the clip from the bumper cover. The rest of the clips require you to lift the clip with the screwdriver while pulling the air inlet panel away from the bumper cover. On the 997, you do not have to worry about any modifications, as the center piece just unclips and comes right off.

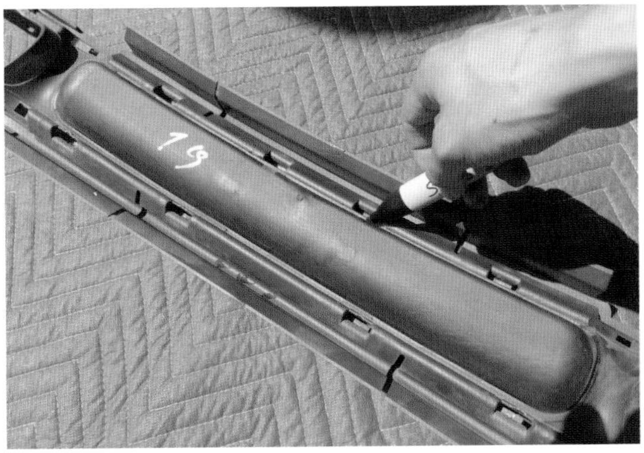

9 Once your air inlet panel is removed, use a marker to trace the outline of the opening for the center radiator. Using a Dremel tool and a milling bit, carefully make your cut in the air inlet panel. Test fit the inside plastic retainer to make sure that they fit together well. If all is well then reinstall the air ducts and the front bumper.

10 Here's a photo showing the center radiator installed. The rubber air guide inside connects to the inner retaining piece and channels air through the center radiator.

PROJECT 33
Radiator and Fan Replacement

Time / Tab / Talent: 4 hours / $180 /

Tools: Torx driver set

Applicable Years: All

Tinware: Radiator, hoses, coolant

Tip: Install the center radiator for improved cooling

Performance Gain: Cooler-running engine

Comp Modification: Replace hoses; repaint front bumper

More Info: http://www.101projects.com/Carrera/33.htm

Proper maintenance of your coolant will go a long way toward extending the life of your radiator. The cooling systems on most cars are often very neglected as most owners don't know much about them (see Project 30 for more information). The most vulnerable components in the entire system are the radiator and the heater core as they tend to be damaged by corrosion and electrolysis. Poor maintenance of the system can result in the buildup of corrosion elements in both the radiator and heater core, creating clogs and leaks that decrease cooling performance. If the engine overheats, the additional heat from the coolant can also damage sensitive plastic attachments and components.

When replacing your radiator, you want to make sure that you replace it with one that meets or exceeds the original equipment manufacturer's (OEM's) cooling standards. Although Porsche cooling systems don't typically fail very often, age and neglect may lead to overheating problems. Therefore, it may be a wise idea to install a center-mounted radiator that performs a better job of cooling than the standard pair (see Project 32). I also recommend replacing your water pump, radiator hoses, thermostat, and any hose clamps too (PelicanParts.com sells complete kits for this replacement). All of these components can be damaged by a cooling system that has overheated. It's also a good time to swap out your old belt.

The first step in replacing your radiator is to remove all of the coolant from the system (see Project 30). Now, you need to gain access to the radiator. Remove the front bumper cover and pull back the front part of the inner wheelwell liners (see Project 68). It is possible to remove the radiators without removing the front bumper cover, but it takes only a few minutes to remove it, and it makes the job a whole lot

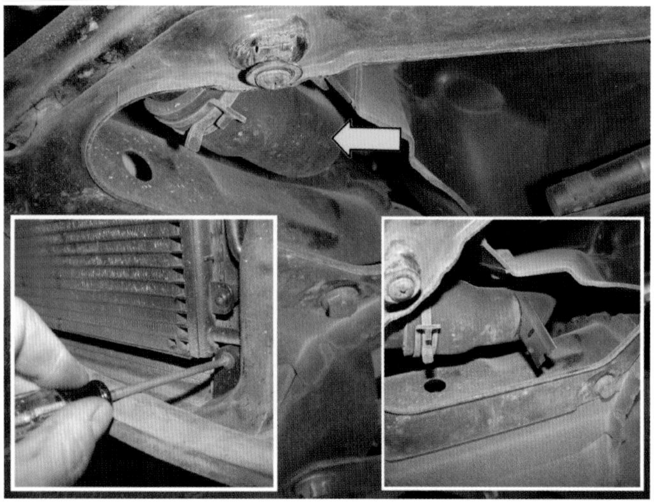

1 With the front bumper removed (Project 68), you should have easy access to both the right and left radiators. Begin by removing the large rubber air funnel that is located in front of each radiator—it is held on with five screws (lower left). Then, cut a slit in the lower radiator hose (996 only) and allow the coolant to empty out of the radiator and hoses (yellow arrow).

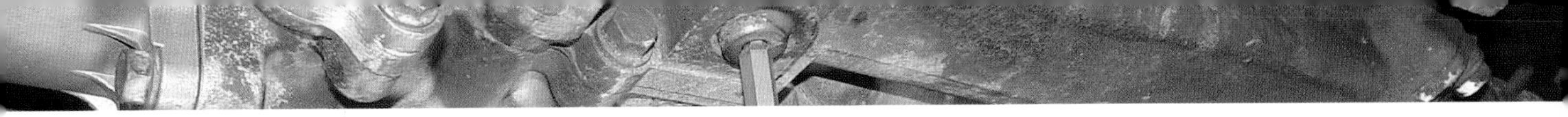

easier in my opinion. Follow the removal procedure detailed in the photos to remove the radiator/fan assembly.

The installation is basically the reverse of removal. Use new clamps on your new radiator hoses. Top off and bleed your coolant system as detailed in Project 30. Keep an eye on the front of your car for coolant leaks for about a week after the installation and tighten up any hoses that show any signs of leakage or weeping.

It's a good idea to use these instructions to clean out the radiators every spring, as they tend to collect a lot of debris, which decreases their cooling efficiency over time. This condition can also lead to moisture collection and premature corrosion of the radiator.

It's also a good idea to check the proper operation of the radiator fans while you have access to them, as the resistor packs that help to power them tend to fail. You can turn on and test the fan speeds using the Porsche PST2 tool, or you can simply turn on the air conditioning system, and either should trigger the high-speed level of the fans. If you start the car and let it warm up, it should start the fans in low speed mode before graduating to the higher speed mode.

2 Detach the air conditioning condenser from the front by removing the two bolts (green arrows) and sliding it out of its mounting tab (red arrow). Using a cable tie, secure the air conditioning condenser to the chassis to keep the condenser pipes from becoming damaged while you're working on the radiator (upper left inset). The lower left inset photo shows the rubber air funnel for the right side of the car. The temperature sensor boot must be carefully threaded out of this boot upon removal.

3 On the 997, the air conditioning condenser is mounted to the front of the radiator using one bolt on the outside (red arrow) and two clips located on the rear (blue arrows and inset upper right). Remove the bolt and slip the condenser from the clips. The yellow arrow shows how debris can build up inside the air ducts. This radiator is from a one-year old Southern California car, which doesn't get exposed to the same type of leaves and debris as other locales. If you live in area that sees four seasons, you should check your ducts at least once a year. The lower left insert shows the Torx bolt that holds the fan shroud on to the back of the radiator (green arrow).

4 **996 Carrera:** This photo shows the backside of the 996 radiator and fan assembly with the inner fender liners removed (see Project 68). In order to remove the radiator and fan assembly, you need to disconnect the small radiator vent hose (red arrow). I recommend replacing this hose during this procedure, so you might save some time and effort by just clipping it off. Unclip the vent hose from the radiator bracket (blue arrows). The green arrow shows the upper radiator hose. In a similar manner, I also recommend just cutting it, since you will be replacing it anyways. Sometimes it can be nearly impossible to remove the hose from the radiator, and you will need to cut it off to remove it (inset photo). If you decide not to remove the front bumper cover, then you will need to remove the fender brace (white arrow), and detach the headlamp vent hose as well.

5 **997 Carrera:** This photo shows the back side of the 997 radiator and fan assembly with the inner fender liners removed (see Project 68). In order to remove the radiator and fan assembly you need to disconnect the radiator vent line (blue arrow). The 997s use quick disconnects on the radiator lines, so even if you are going to be replacing the hoses, you should not need to cut the lines (see Photo 10 of Project 31. The vent line is a simple push-in, pull-out connection, and the water hoses use the quick-disconnect clips (yellow arrow). After disconnecting the hoses remove the Torx bolt (green arrow) that secures the fan shroud and then remove the two smaller bolts that hold the radiator in place (red arrows). Move underneath the radiator and remove the two clips (inset, purple arrows).

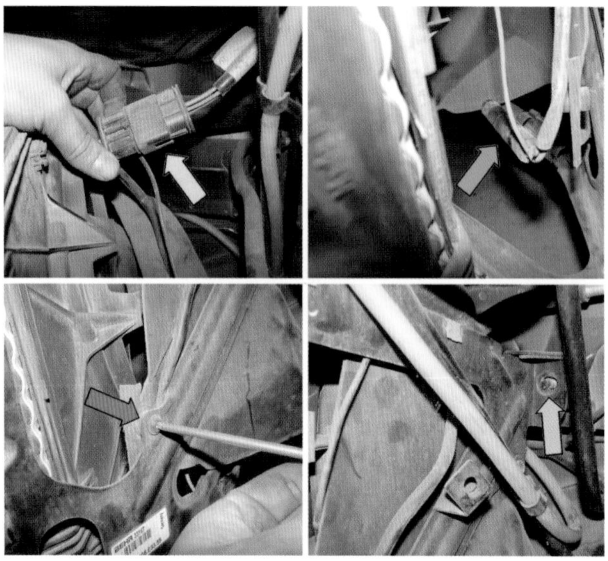

6 The yellow arrow in this photo of the 996 radiator shows the electrical connection to the fan that must be disconnected. Pull out the resistor pack from its bracket and loosen the wire harness (green arrow). Disconnect the rear radiator air guide from the metal radiator bracket (red arrow). Finally, disconnect the bracket from the chassis by removing the nuts that hold it in place (blue arrow).

7 Here is a shot of the 996 radiator area after the radiator has been removed. The radiator-like unit on the left is the air conditioning condenser.

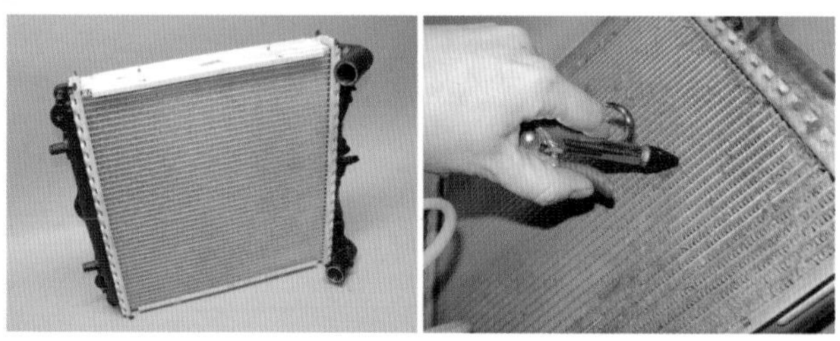

8 On the left is shown a brand new OEM 996 replacement radiator. If you are merely replacing the radiator fan and are reinstalling the old radiator, be sure to blow out the dirt and debris with some compressed air (right).

9 The radiator fan assembly is clipped to the rear of the radiator using metal snap clips (inset photo). Remove these snaps, and the fan assembly should lift right off. The fan is attached to the fan housing via three mounting screws located on the backside. A new fan is shown in the lower right.

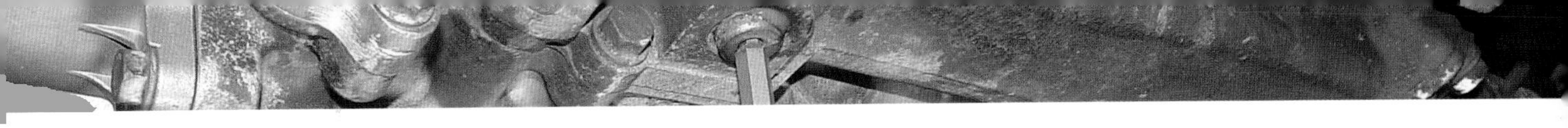

PROJECT 34
Coolant Expansion Tank Replacement

Time / Tab / Talent: 2 hours / $145-$345 /

Tools: Pliers, 10mm wrench and socket, turkey baster

Applicable Years: All

Tinware: Expansion tank, coolant

More Info: http://www.101projects.com/Carrera/34.htm

Tip: Wait overnight so that the coolant is cold

Performance Gain: No more coolant leaks

Comp Modification: Coolant flush

The replacement of the coolant tank is probably one of the top 10 jobs that typically need to be done on an older Carrera. The coolant tank is manufactured out of plastic and is prone to breaking. In addition, the plastic tank itself often cracks with age and leaks coolant on the rear of the bulkhead. Porsche has redesigned this part several times over the past decade, and to this day, there are still problems with the tanks.

When should you replace your tank? If your tank is looking old or yellow, or if you are finding a pool of coolant in the engine compartment, then it's probably time to replace the tank. I also recommend replacing the coolant tank when it's really old, particularly if you have your engine out of the car. The hoses inside the engine compartment can be difficult to reach, and having the engine out of the car makes a very difficult job a lot easier.

If you are losing coolant from your engine and you're not sure where it's going, then you can perform a few relatively simple tests to check. First, get an air pressure adapter that will allow you to hook up a shop compressor to your coolant tank cap. Then, pressurize the system to about 13–15 psi. Let it sit, and see if you can hear or see any coolant escaping. If the coolant is getting past the head gasket into the crankcase, it will mix with the oil and you will be able to see that easily when you empty the oil. If the head gasket is leaking coolant into the cylinders, then they will begin to fill up with coolant and you can see this when you remove the spark plugs.

When the car warms up, both the heat and pressure of the coolant starts to attack the seam along the edge of the tank, eventually causing it to fail, and the car starts leaking coolant. Take a look around the coolant tank. In some instances, you can easily see that it has been leaking. In others, you may only see a faint trace of coolant beginning to emerge from the molding seam. It's important to tackle this problem as soon as possible. Failure to do so could cause a complete loss of coolant and perhaps even engine damage.

The first step is to disconnect the battery. This prevents any possible electrical damage to the system. Please refer to our article on changing the battery for more info.

Now let the car cool down. You might want to wait overnight to make sure that the coolant is not hot. If you open the coolant tank with the car warmed up, it could burn you. There is heat and also pressure in the system. When you are sure that the coolant is not hot, remove the cap and use either a turkey baster or a large syringe to siphon the coolant out of the tank. You'll want to keep siphoning until the level is just at the bottom of the tank. This prevents coolant from spinning all over the ground when you remove the tank. Keep in mind that when you remove the tank from the engine compartment, the level will drain back down through the bottom hose. Another option is to completely drain the coolant from the car. Please refer to our article on coolant flushing for more info.

You'll notice that the coolant tank is wedged pretty tightly into the engine compartment. It may seem that there isn't enough room to maneuver it out. You'll first need to remove the emissions air pump at the front of the tank. Follow along with the photos for the exact replacement procedure.

You'll probably get a bit of coolant leaking out of the bottom of the tank during the removal process. This is normal. Just be sure to clean up any remaining coolant from underneath. It's important to remember that engine coolant tends to attract animals due to its smell and taste. If animals drink the coolant, it could make them very sick or worse.

Once all the coolant hoses going to the tank have been removed, you can start to remove the tank from the engine bay. This is the hardest part of the whole job. In our case, our car is a cabriolet, which reduces the amount of room you have on top of the engine bay. Carrera 4 models are similarly difficult due to the extra components. On regular coupe models, you should be able to simply remove the tank at this point. In our case with our cabriolet, we needed to lower the motor slightly to remove the tank (see Photos 7 and 10).

Before you install the new tank, you'll probably want to take some time and clean the area around the tank. More than likely, you'll have a buildup of corrosion and baked coolant all over the bulkhead. Clean all of this off before you install the new tank. Some of it may be heavily baked on. You may need to use a stiff brush and a good household cleaner to get it off. A special word of caution here: If you use a product like Simple Green to clean in these instances, be sure to rinse it down with water. Sometimes, the chemical properties of Simple Green can attack aluminum if the cleaner is left on the metal for extended periods of time.

Once your new tank is installed, fill the tank with coolant until it registers between the minimum and maximum lines molded into the tank. Start the car and let it warm up. Now recheck the level and add coolant if it has dropped. Follow the instructions on how to bleed the cooling system (Project 30). Pop the cap on the new tank, and that's it!

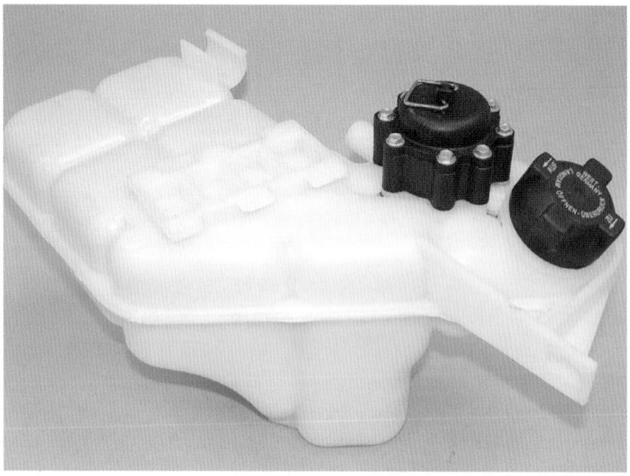

1 Shown here is a new coolant expansion tank with cap for the Carrera as purchased from PelicanParts.com. It has been suggested that the newer tanks have been reworked to prevent the seam from failing; however, I couldn't find any noticeable difference between the two tanks.

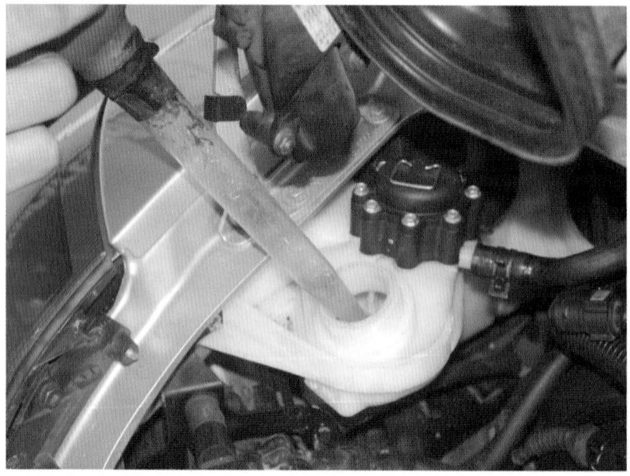

2 Use a turkey baster or large syringe to siphon out the coolant inside the old tank. You don't have to get it perfectly dry, but just enough to where the level is at the bottom of the tank. When you lift the tank up and out of the engine compartment, the remaining coolant will drain back down through the lower hose.

3 Begin by removing the hose going to the emissions pump at the left of the engine compartment (996 only). Use a pair of channel locks to loosen and slide the hose clamp back (purple arrow). Twist the hose back and forth to free it up from off the pump. Then remove the two 10mm bolts at the front edge of the pump (green arrows) and the 10mm nut at the top of the air pump (yellow arrow). This nut also secures the front of the coolant tank to the car. Once free, unplug the electrical connector going to the pump.

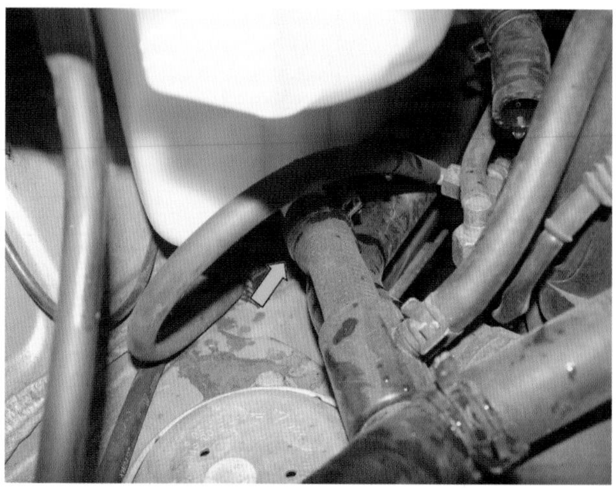

4 Loosen and remove the hose clamps on the lower hose connection to the coolant tank (green arrow).

5 Loosen and remove the hose clamps on the upper hose connections (green arrows). You may want to carefully take a small screwdriver and work it between the hose and the tank connection. Coolant hoses sometimes stick to these connections and have to be "worked" loose. Just carefully work all the way around it and pull it off.

6 On the left side of the engine (997 only) unclip the brake booster pipe on the crossmember and lay them off to the side (blue arrows). Remove the plastic lines and the cable plug from the switch-over valve between the intake runners (yellow arrow). Loosen the lines for the brake booster (purple arrow). To do this, remove the plastic protection piece, push the holder forward, and pull off the line. Put the plastic protector piece back on right away to keep any dirt or debris out, and then disconnect the vent line for the coolant tank (red arrows). Check for slack in your wiring going to the O2 sensors on both sides, and if it looks like it will be tight, disconnect the wiring (green arrow).

7 The engine may need to be lowered slightly to allow the coolant tank to be removed from the engine bay. This was required for our convertible car; on some models, you may get away without having to lower the engine. Place a floor jack with a rubber pad or a few rolled up newspapers under the oil pan. This will protect the aluminum from damage. Do not support the entire weight of the car with the jack—it's only placed there to support the weight of the engine.

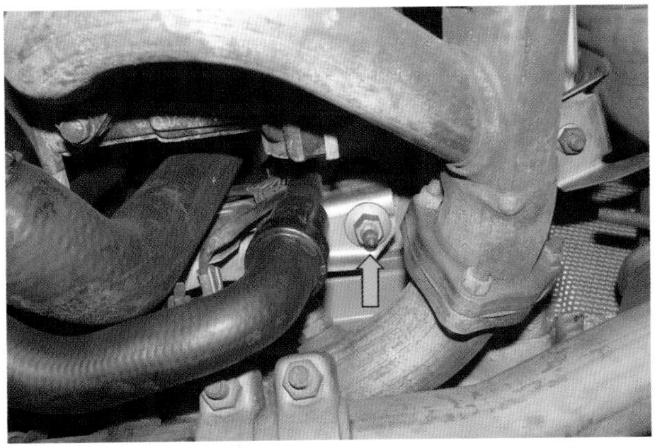

8 Remove the 18mm engine mount nut on the right side of the engine (green arrow).

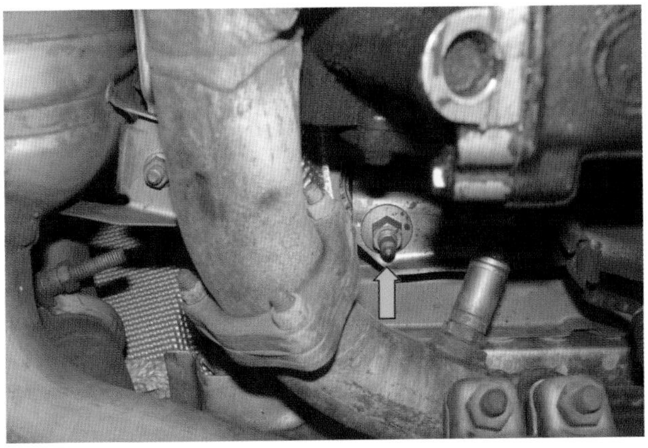

9 Remove the 18mm engine mount nut on the left side of the engine (green arrow).

10 With the engine lowered, pull the coolant tank toward the engine (direction of green arrow). This will disengage the tank from the mounting bracket in the engine compartment.

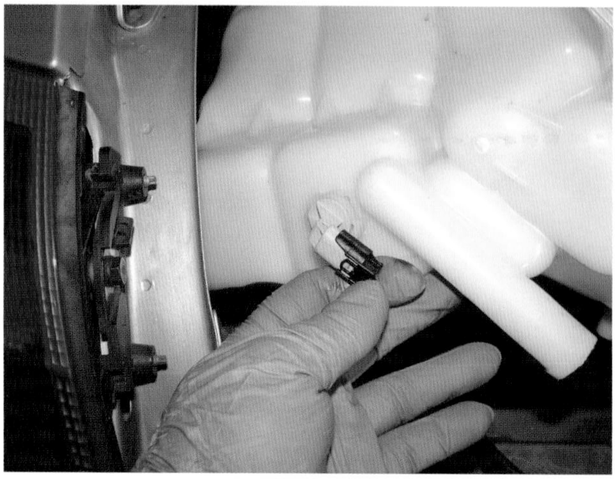

11 Don't forget to remove the electrical connection to the coolant level sender at the bottom of the coolant tank. Once free, pull the old coolant tank out of the engine bay.

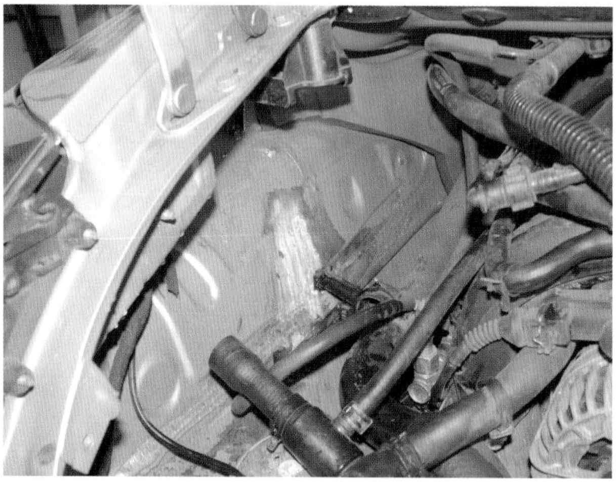

12 Once the coolant tank is removed, your engine bay should resemble this photo. Left behind is a mess of baked coolant on the bulkhead located behind the coolant tank. This is where the tanks often leak from. It's a good idea to spend some time and clean everything up before you continue.

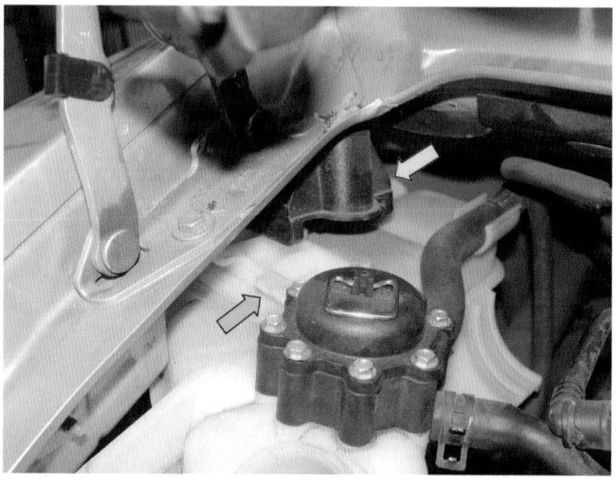

13 Fit the coolant level sender to the new tank and reconnect the electrical connection. Position the new tank in the engine bay. It can be a little tricky to get the "teeth" of the new tank (green arrow) to line up in the bracket (yellow arrow) on the car. Once the tank is positioned, push it back as far back as it will go, making sure that the front edge of the tank fits over the mounting stud. At this point, refit the coolant hoses to the new tank. If any of the hoses look suspect, replace them before continuing. Also be sure to reconnect the electrical connection to the air pump. Reinstall the two 10mm bolts and the 10mm nut that also secures the coolant tank to the bulkhead. Don't forget to raise your engine back up if you had to drop it down.

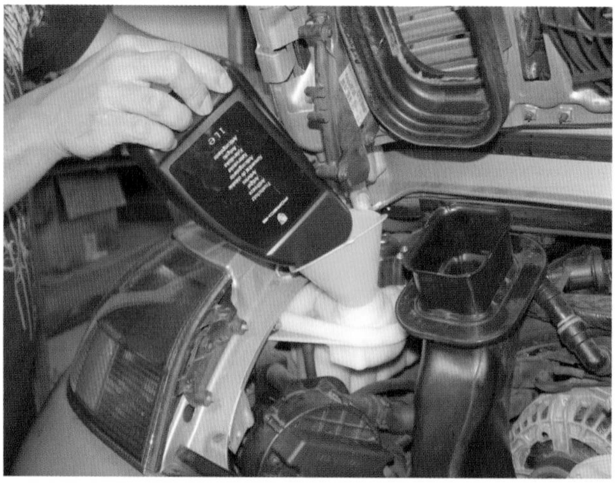

14 The last step is to refill the coolant tank so that the fluid level lies between the MIN and MAX marks. I also recommend that you follow the factory procedure for bleeding air from the system once you've refilled it with coolant (see Project 30).

PROJECT 35
Water Pump and Thermostat Replacement

Time / Tab / Talent: 2 hours / $450 /

Tools: Swivel socket set

Applicable Years: All

Tinware: Water pump, thermostat, and gaskets

More Info: http://www.101projects.com/Carrera/35.htm

Tip: Install the low-temp thermostat for better performance

Performance Gain: Protects your engine against overheating

Comp Modification: Replace radiator hoses

The modern water-cooled Porsches have been known to have troublesome problems with their cooling systems. Two of the principle areas of failure are the thermostat and water pump.

Begin the replacement process by jacking up the car (Project 1) and removing the lower plastic tray that covers the front part of the engine and the coolant hoses. Disconnect the lower hose that is attached to the water pump (see Photo 3), and let the coolant empty into a five-gallon or larger bucket. If you are replacing the thermostat, too, then now would be a good time to disconnect the hose attached to it as well.

The next step is to gain access to the water pump. This requires the removal of the main belt (see Project 5). With the belt removed, the back of your engine should be relatively accessible. Unfortunately, the engine mount bar is still in the way and needs to be removed. Place a floor jack underneath the engine and gently raise it to support the weight of the engine. Don't actually lift the car or the engine; simply place the jack under the lower engine cover until it lightly makes contact. In general, you should never lift the engine from the bottom sump. But for the purposes of simply supporting the weight of the engine while replacing the engine mounts, the cover should suffice (see Photo 3 of Project 10). Begin by removing the brackets that hold the catalytic converters to the engine mount bar (see Photo 2). Next, loosen the bracket from the engine by removing the nuts shown in Photo 1.

Seven bolts attach the water pump to the engine, and access to some of them may only be achieved from underneath the car. I recommend using a flex 10mm socket to get into the tight spots.

When the engine was assembled, Porsche installed the coolant manifold and the water pump together. Therefore, they use a shared gasket, which you must cut apart in order to remove it from the engine. Photo 4 shows the gasket removed from the water pump housing on the engine, and Photo 5 shows where you must clip it in order to remove it. The new gasket must also be modified prior to installation (see Photo 5). With the pump removed, check the inside bore where the water pump fits for debris or corrosion. With a wire brush, remove any corrosion or debris that may have built up there. Clean off the water pump mounting surface on the engine and install the water pump with the new gasket. Tighten down the bolts to 10 Nm (7 ft-lbs).

At this time, I also recommend that you remove the thermostat housing (located below the water pump) and replace the thermostat as well. The thermostat is a relatively cheap part that can fail quite easily, which leads to your engine overheating. Simply disconnect the thermostat hose if you haven't already, and unbolt the thermostat from the engine. The thermostat used to be sold separately from the thermostat housing, but now Porsche and the aftermarket suppliers simple sell the whole assembly as one integrated unit.

The factory thermostat starts to open at about 187 degrees Fahrenheit (86 degrees Celsius) and only fully opens at almost 210 degrees Fahrenheit (99 degrees Celsius). This means that the engine needs to get very hot before it starts sending its coolant to the front radiators. For this reason, I recommend installing a low-temperature thermostat in place of the factory one. LN Engineering has developed a thermostat that starts opening at 160 degrees Fahrenheit (71 degrees Celsius) and is fully open at about 180 degrees Fahrenheit (82 degrees Celsius). Lower coolant temperatures translate into lower oil temperatures, and the dyno tests that LN Engineering has performed on the cars with the low-temp thermostat installed have revealed a small increase in horsepower (typically about 5 horsepower). It is my guess that Porsche designed the thermostat to open a bit later in order to help the cars run a bit hotter, which typically helps with emissions testing and the burning off of water in the oil, which can then lead to longer oil change intervals. Installing the low-temp thermostat is a smart idea for engine longevity—it's available for about $175 from PelicanParts.com.

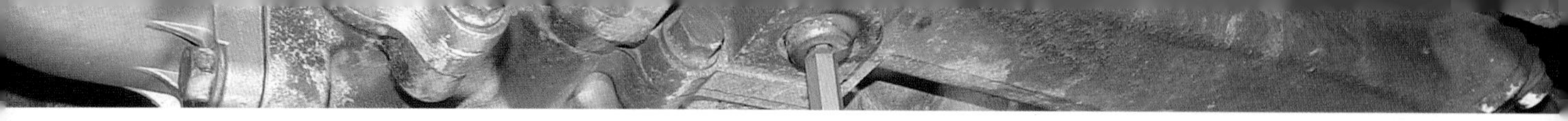

1 In order to gain the necessary access to remove the water pump, first loosen the brackets that connect the catalytic converters (green arrows). Next remove the two bolts that connect the bracket to the engine mount (red arrows). Now loosen but do not completely remove the 15mm bolts on the engine carrier bracket (blue arrow; not all are shown). Finally remove the small M6 centering bolt (yellow arrow). You should now be able to wiggle/push the bracket out of the way, giving you clearance to remove the water pump.

2 The water pump (red arrow) is located next to the crankshaft on the left side of the car. In order to remove the pump from the engine, you need to remove the engine mount bar (yellow arrows) from the back of the engine photo.

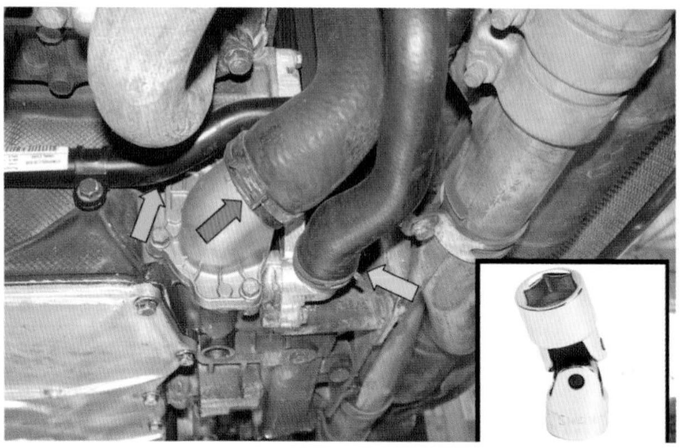

3 Disconnect the main hose to the thermostat, as indicated by the red arrow. In order to gain enough clearance to remove the thermostat, you may find it easier to disconnect the water pump hose shown by the yellow arrow. For the tight spaces near the thermostat, I recommend using a swivel-foot socket (green arrow and lower right inset photo).

4 Here's what the engine looks like with the water pump removed. For the 1998–2005 Carreras, you need to cut the old metal seal in order to get it off, as part of it is still trapped in the engine off to the right (it's a dual-purpose gasket). With the new gasket properly trimmed, it should fit into place (lower left).

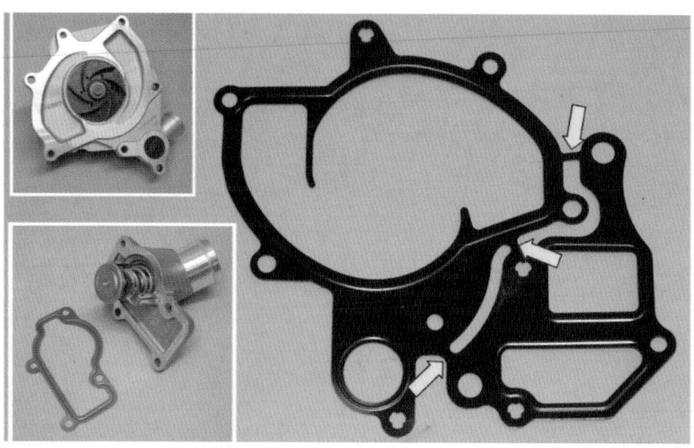

5 The water pump seal needs to be trimmed prior to installation (1998–2005 only). The part off to the right is separate from the water pump and is typically only used when rebuilding an engine. Trim the seal at the yellow marks and use the part on the left. The upper left photo shows a brand new water pump. The lower left shows a new thermostat and seal. The newer-style Carrera thermostat is integrated into its aluminum housing.

6 Install the new thermostat using a new gasket (lower left).

SECTION 5
TRANSMISSION

These three areas—the transmission, clutch, and rear axle assemblies—have been combined into one section because they are all interrelated and linked together. The transmission and clutch can be a mysterious setup, leading many owners to ignore and neglect maintenance until it's too late. This section aims to demystify the transmission, clutch, and rear axle assemblies, and it also provides some upgrades and improvements for performance.

PROJECT 36
Replacing Your Automatic Transmission Fluid

Time / Tab / Talent: 3 hours / $150 /

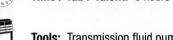

Tools: Transmission fluid pump, 17mm hex tool, 6mm, 8mm hex tool, T-30 male Torx driver, infrared thermometer

Applicable Years: All

Tinware: Automatic transmission filter, gasket kit

More Info: http://www.101projects.com/Carrera/36.htm

Tip: Don't neglect this maintenance—transmissions are expensive to replace

Performance Gain: Long-life transmission

Comp Modification: Oil change

Replacing your oil is easy. Porsche knows that this needs to be performed once about every 3,000–5,000 miles and designed the car that way. On the other hand, changing the tranny fluid is not an easy task, and you can probably bet that the previous owner of your car did not perform this task as often as he or she should have.

What are the symptoms of low automatic transmission fluid? I experienced this when I purchased a car with a known transmission problem. When the car was stopped suddenly via the brakes and then the accelerator was immediately pressed, the transmission would slip, and then slam into gear, lurching the car forward. I had a strong suspicion that the transmission was low on fluid. A thorough inspection of the car showed the remnants of significant leakage of transmission fluid.

What causes this symptom with the transmission? Well, when you slam on the brakes, all of the fluid in the transmission flows to the front of the car and away from the fluid pickup, which is located toward the rear of the transmission. With the fluid at the front of the car, the transmission loses fluid for a very short while. Automatic transmissions use the fluid both as a hydraulic fluid and a coolant; they won't work if there isn't any fluid running through them. After the car has stopped and the fluid has moved back toward the pickup, the transmission begins to work normally. If the transmission had the proper levels of fluid, then this condition would not occur. Needless to say, after I replaced the transmission fluid and checked the levels, the problem disappeared. The previous owner had let it run down about 2 quarts low (the Carrera transmission takes about 10 quarts, with about 4 quarts replaceable during a fluid change). Driving for any more time with the transmission in this state would have led to substantial damage and could have resulted in a wrecked tranny (replacement cost: $2,500 or so).

Okay, enough background on the automatic transmission. The first step in replacing your fluid is to jack up your car so that you can reach the underside of the transmission (see Project 1). It is very important that the car be level—don't jack up just the front or rear of the car. Make sure that it is as level in the air as it is on the ground. The reason for this is that you will be checking the transmission fluid by removing a drain plug and checking the fluid level. If the car is not level, then you will not achieve an accurate reading. Also elevate the car with the rear tailpipe sticking way outside the entrance of your garage—you will be running the car while it's on the jack stands in order to top off the fluid.

With the car elevated in the air, the first step is to remove the plastic underbody trays. These are held in place by three Phillips screws and a series of plastic 10mm nuts (see Project 37). Set the trays aside and locate the two 15mm bolts holding the aluminum crossmember piece between the suspension uprights (see Photo1). Wear safety glasses when you're under the car, as you never know what small piece of dirt may fall into your eye.

The next step is to remove all of the existing fluid from the main transmission sump. There is a drain plug on the bottom of the sump that can be used to empty most of the fluid contained inside. Remove the drain plug and let the

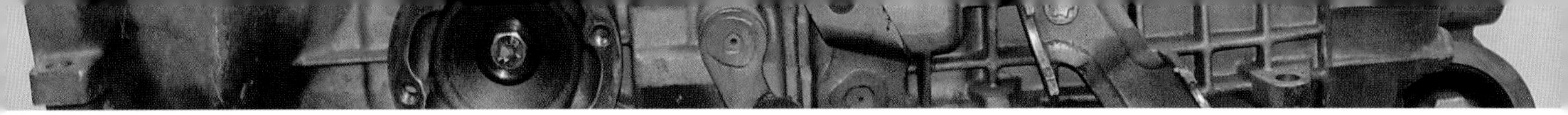

fluid flow out into a container. Your container should be able to hold at least three gallons (about 12 liters) of fluid. Once the fluid is empty, replace the drain plug. This plug should be tightened to 40 Nm (29 ft-lb).

Now you will proceed to remove the sump from the bottom of the transmission. You need to remove the sump so that you can replace the transmission filter, clean the sump magnet, and also remove the extra fluid that may be trapped inside. You remove the sump by removing each of the small Torx bolts that attach it to the bottom of the transmission. Once those are out, you should be able simply to pull on the sump cover and it should fall off. Be aware that there will still be some transmission fluid in the sump that can spill out if you're not careful.

Plastic cat litter boxes make excellent containers for catching fluid in these types of situations. They are wide and large enough to prevent you from making quite a mess on your garage floor. Turn your attention now to the sumps and clean them out. Then, remove the transmission filter from the bottom of the transmission.

What type of fluid do you use in your automatic transmission? The Carrera requires a special type of fluid that you cannot easily find in most auto parts stores: the part number for the 1998-2005 is 000-43-207-00 and the 2005-2008 is 000-043-204-90. The Carrera also can use off-the-shelf Esso LT 71141 for the 1998–2001, and ATF 3353 Plus for the 2002–2005 or Pentosin ATF-1 all are available along with gasket/filter kits from PelicanParts.com. The 2005 and newer Carreras use newer "light-running oil," that has extended the service life. Be sure to check your owner's manual for the transmission oil specific to your car. I would avoid using any other type of fluid in your transmission. Also, use the same fluid for the entire replacement process—mixing and matching different types of transmission fluid can cause your transmission to fail.

With the new filter in place, you will now reinstall the lower sump. No need to fill it with fluid—simply bolt it up into place. Torque each bolt to 11 Nm (8 ft-lb), and use a crisscross pattern as shown in Photo 7. Now it's time to fill the sump with fluid. Using a hand pump attached to the bottle of transmission fluid, thread the hose up into the filler hole and through one of the access holes in the side of the filler baffle (see Photo 6). Fill up the transmission sump until fluid starts to significantly run out of the filler hole. A few drips can be expected when the fluid runs down the side of the hose; when the fluid level is at the top of the filler, it will start to exit the filler hole rapidly. Replace the filler plug and tighten it hand-tight.

At this point, you are ready to start the car. Keep in mind that the transmission fluid can only be checked when the transmission temperature is within a semi-narrow range. This temperature range is 85–100 degrees Fahrenheit (30–40 degrees Celsius). You will need to start the car and let it warm up before you can check the levels. Depending upon the outside temperature, it may take up to 45 minutes for it to reach this temperature. Check the temperature of the fluid by using one of those handy infrared laser thermometers. Years ago, these used to cost thousands of dollars, but nowadays, you can pick one up for about $50.

You will be running the car while it is up and on jack stands. This can be dangerous if the car is not secure on the jack stands—check them again before you continue. You will also be running the car for an extended length of time while it warms up and you will need to make sure that you perform this outside (on level ground) or funnel the exhaust gases out of the tailpipe and out of your garage. At a hardware store, I found a long, flexible aluminum tube that is typically used for venting gas dryers out to the atmosphere (see Photo 9). If you clamp this tightly to the end of your tailpipe and run the other end out of your garage with the garage door open, you should be able to safely have the car idle inside the garage. Also make sure that you use an electronic carbon monoxide monitor inside your garage (also available from most hardware stores) as an added measure for safety.

Climb into the car, place your foot on the brake, and start it. If you hear anything amiss, or encounter any unusual problems, then shut off the car immediately. It should start and idle normally. You will need to let the transmission warm up until it is in the operating range indicated above. Note that this will make the bottom of the sump feel warm to the touch, not hot. Use your infrared thermometer to periodically check the temperature. Again, it should take 10–45 minutes depending upon the outside temperature to heat the transmission to this level, if the car is simply idling.

With the car at the proper temperature, remove the filler plug and begin filling the transmission again. It's okay to use your finger to gently stick the hose attached to your pump up inside the transmission. At this time, the fluid should be warm to the touch. But be careful not to burn yourself on the catalytic converters, headers, or the mufflers while under the car. When the fluid begins to empty out of the filler hole, replace the filler plug again, and tighten it hand-tight.

Now, sit inside the car, apply the brake pedal, and slowly shift the transmission through reverse, and first and second gear, using the manual shift lever. Leave the car in each gear for about 10 seconds. Repeat this twice, move underneath the car again, and remove the fill plug from the bottom of the transmission. With the engine still running, top off the transmission once more until fluid comes out of the fill hole. Replace the fill plug, using a new sealing O-ring. This plug should be torqued to 80 Nm (59 ft-lb).

That's about all there is to it. When you've topped off the fluid, lower the car down off of the jack stands and take it for a short drive. If all is well, you shouldn't notice any difference in performance or operation. If you were having problems with the transmission slamming into gear, then these issues should be gone by now. One last thing to note: The automatic transmission also has a built-in differential that requires standard gear oil. Check and fill your gear oil as per the instructions in Project 39.

1 In order to gain access to the bottom transmission sump, you will need to remove the rear plastic under body trays and the aluminum cross bar. The under body trays are held in place by three Phillips screws and a series of plastic 10mm nuts. The cross bar is held in place by two 15mm bolts (green arrow).

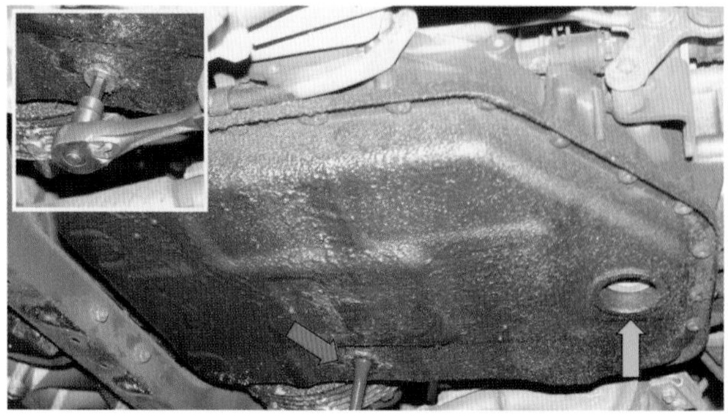

2 I recommend that you start the draining process only when the car is cold (red arrow). When the car is warm, a lot of the transmission fluid will be trapped within the transmission itself. When the car is cold, almost all of the transmission fluid will have seeped out and be trapped in the lower sump. Note that this is opposite from the procedure for changing the oil—where you should empty it when the engine is hot. That is because the engine oil is thinnest and flows best when it's hot. The transmission fluid has a totally different viscosity. Working on the car when it is cold also assures that you will not be burned by hot exhaust, transmission, or engine parts. The green arrow shows the transmission filler plug, and the inset photo shows the 17mm hex socket required to remove the transmission drain plug.

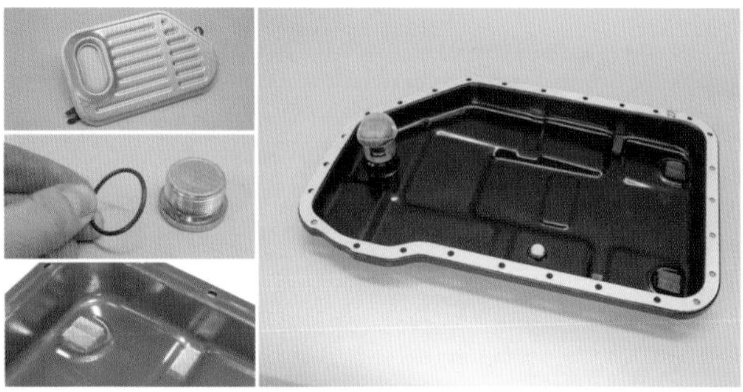

3 Using a lint-free cloth, carefully wipe down the inside of the sump (I use KimWipes, available from PelicanParts.com). You want to use a lint-free cloth, because tiny cloth fibers left in your transmission sump can clog the transmission and filter. The sump needs to be clean, spotless, and look brand new, as shown on the right. Make sure that you remove any remaining gasket material from the edge of the sump cover. A new transmission sump gasket has been lined up with the holes, and the assembly is ready for installation back onto the transmission. In the upper left, the new transmission filter is displayed. You should always use a new O-ring on the transmission filler plug, as shown in the middle left photo. Pay close attention to the magnet in the bottom of the sump (shown on the lower left). You should be able simply to pluck this magnet from the bottom of the sump and clean it.

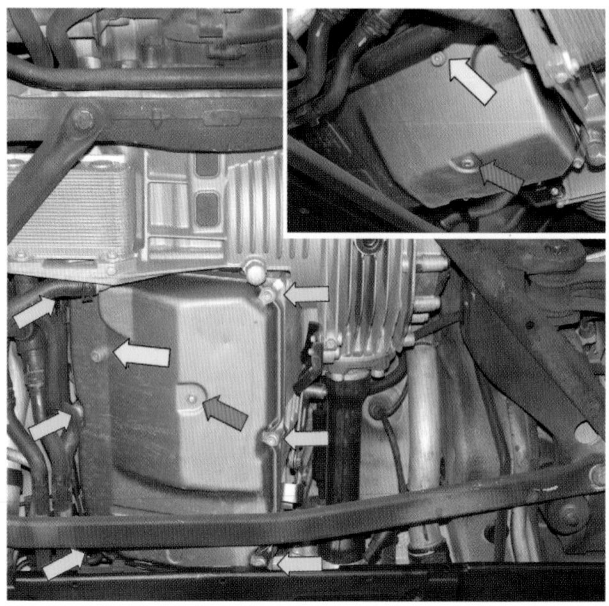

4 The 2002 and later Carreras use a different style of oil pan, gasket, and retaining bolts (shown here on a C4). The pan is held on by six bolts and clamping sleeves (yellow arrows). Both the drain and fill plugs are now 6mm. The drain plug is located on the bottom of the pan (red arrow) while the fill plug is located further up and to one side of the pan (blue arrow). When reinstalling the pan, make sure you tighten the bolts in a crisscross pattern.

5 The transmission fluid filter is a large canister that is attached to the bottom of the transmission that needs to be removed and replaced. Remove the bolts that attach it to the bottom of the transmission and carefully pull off the filter. Discard it in the trash. Check the mounting surfaces where the sumps attach to the transmission, and remove any excess gasket material that may have been left there. When you reinstall the filter into the transmission, use the same bolts that you just removed. These bolts should be torqued to a very light 6 Nm (4.5 ft-lb). The inset photo shows the new filter installed.

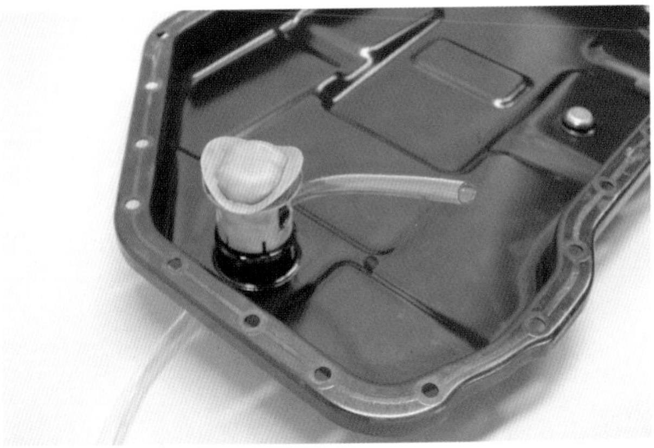

6 Getting the hose into the sump area so that you can fill the transmission can be a bit tricky if you're not aware of where the hose is supposed to go. This photo shows the hose threaded up the bottom of the filler hole and sticking out into the transmission sump. When the sump is installed back onto the transmission, you will need to feed the hose up the filler hole and through the openings in this baffle attachment.

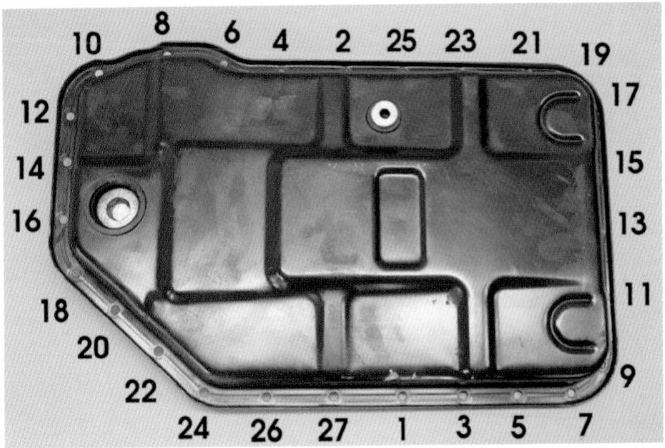

7 With the sump installed, tighten the bolts according to the following pattern. These bolts require very little torque—only 11 Nm (8 ft-lbs). Be sure to clean off any dirt or debris that may be on the screws prior to reinstalling them.

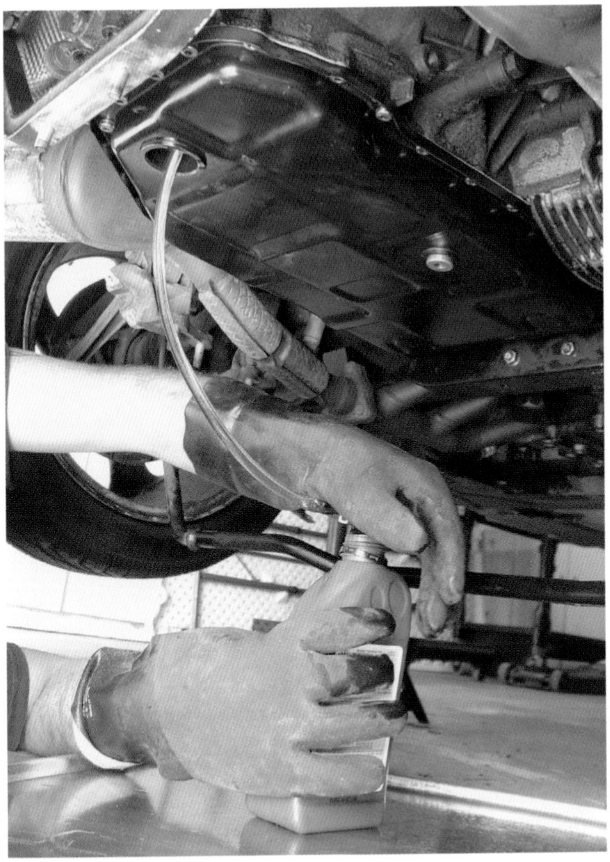

8 You will need to use a transmission fluid pump, which you can find at almost any local auto parts store, in order to fill the sump. The pump works just like a liquid soap pump in your bathroom. The transmission fluid should be pumped into the bottom of the sump through the transmission fill hole. Remove the plug, place one end of the pump into a bottle of transmission fluid, and start pumping. Pump fluid into the filler hole until fluid begins to run out rapidly. Clean up the small spill (be sure to use a large oil drip tray during this process), then replace the fill plug only slightly tighter than hand-tight (you will be removing it again shortly when you recheck the levels). *Very similar-style Boxster transmission shown in this photo.*

9 Carbon monoxide is dangerous, and although today's modern cars don't emit too much of it, you can still kill off some brain cells by breathing it in. Play it safe and route the exhaust from your tailpipe out of your garage area or perform the job outdoors on level ground. Use a standard dryer vent hose attached to both exhaust ports (left and right) and plug the sides of all tailpipes if you happen to feel exhaust escaping.

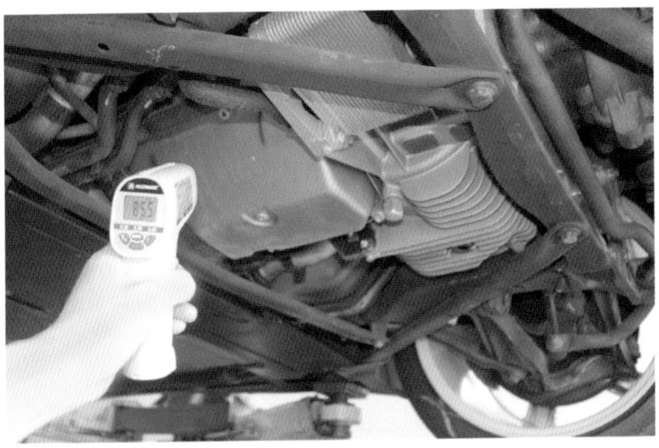

10 The infrared thermometer is one of those whiz-bang devices that never ceases to amaze me. Years ago, these used to cost thousands of dollars, but nowadays, you can pick one up for a mere $50. Monitor the temperature of the transmission sump by pointing the thermometer at the bottom of the metal sump in the center.

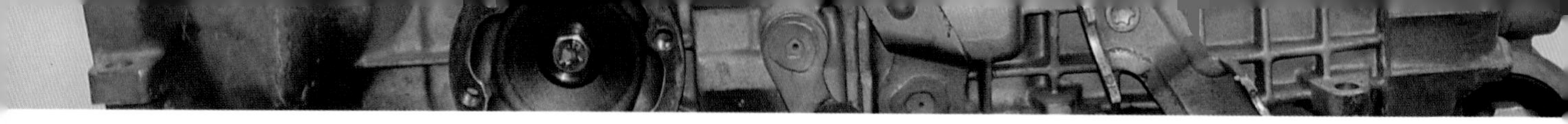

PROJECT 37
Transmission Mount Replacement

Time / Tab / Talent: 8 hours / $130 /

Tip: Be safe

Tools: All of them, in addition to a Sawzall (shop press)

Performance Gain: Car works again

Comp Modification: Replace clutch

Applicable Years: All

Tinware: Transmission Mount

More Info: http://www.101projects.com/Carrera/37.htm

As a car ages, it's often very common for the engine and transmission mounts to deteriorate. The rubber that is contained within the mounts becomes old and brittle, and doesn't perform a good job of isolating the drivetrain from the rest of the chassis. Old, worn out transmission mounts can cause shifting problems because the drivetrain is no longer firmly held in its position. One sign of this failure is a knocking noise under hard acceleration and braking. A visible sign that the mounts need replacing is the appearance of cracks in the rubber of the mount or if the ears of the rubber mount ripped in half. The rubber will deteriorate over the years and need to be replaced, even if the car has relatively few miles on it. An easy way to check if the mount is bad is to place a floor jack under the transmission mount and jack up the transmission. If you can easily raise the transmission without also raising up the car, it's a good sign that the mount is shot. Keep in mind that even good mounts will have a certain amount of free play in the rubber.

The design of the transmission mount on the 996 seems to be a bit underengineered, relying on only one central mount to secure the entire engine/transmission assembly to the car. It also seems that there is no clear or easy method to replace the mount if the center rubber portion fails. The part doesn't even show up in the factory parts diagrams, just an obscure part number for the replacement of the entire forward half of the transmission. The mount itself is pressed into the end of the transmission with no apparent way of removing it. We here at Pelican considered several ways of performing the job with the transmission still installed in the car, using everything from floor jacks to vices to ratchet straps. Eventually, we came to the conclusion that the only way of really doing the job right is to remove the transmission and use a large shop press.

A press is usually nothing more than a steel frame with a bottle jack or hydraulic cylinder, used to press together or separate parts using large amounts of mechanical force. It's one of those tools that every good shop should have. It's also one of the tools that you may not find in every home garage due the space they take up and also the cost of a high-quality unit. Because of this, it might make more sense to take the transmission to a shop willing to let you use one for the 10 minutes it takes to press the new mount into the transmission housing.

Inexpensive shop presses are usually available at your local discount tool house for under $100. In instances like this, it sometimes makes sense to buy a cheaper one and have it around for those once in a while jobs. If you are moving on to more serious jobs, like pressing out wheel bearings on a regular basis, it's a no-brainer to invest in a high-quality press.

Begin by putting the new transmission mount in the freezer to help shrink the bearing down in size for easier installation. Now you need to remove the transmission from the car (see Project 38). Make a note of the two nubs molded into the old mount. These nubs indicate the up and down orientation of the mount once installed. It's a good idea to make a small mark on the transmission with a permanent marker or a scribe to help you line up the new mount.

If you're lucky, the rubber ears inside the mount will have torn enough to allow you to place the blade of a reciprocating saw inside to start cutting the center section of the mount out. If it has not torn all the way through, you'll need to use something like a hacksaw to cut the rubber enough to get the saw blade in. Trust me, the reciprocating saw is your friend for this particular task; you'll be at it a long time if

you intend on using a hand saw to get through the rubber. Proceed cautiously: make sure that the transmission is well supported and can't move. I used a ratchet strap to hold the transmission down on to the workbench. Even then, you'll need an extremely firm grip on the saw, and be very careful not to cut into the aluminum outer housing of the transmission. Once you have cut out the rubber ears, push the center section of the mount out.

One thing we found particularly interesting is that the outer casing of the stock transmission mount was made of plastic rather than steel as on the replacement mounts. Our project car had less than 30,000 original miles on it, so it's reasonable to assume that it this was original transmission mount. The procedure we used to remove the outer retaining ring left behind was to make two cuts on the ring and then pop the two pieces out. Take a hacksaw and position the blade inside the mount. Now cut a slit in the mount outer ring just deep enough to free the ring of the transmission. Take care not to cut into the inner bore of the transmission housing. You may need to make another cut 180 degrees across from your original cut in order to release it from the transmission casting. With the cuts made, simply pop the halves out and you are ready to press the new mount in.

Now you'll have to set up the transmission in the press sideways. Typically a good press will also come with an assortment of blocks so that you can align whatever item you are pressing into whatever work piece. You'll need to support the transmission so that the mounting flange sits as level to the face of the press. Getting exactly the right angle involves placing shims and blocks under various points of the transmission. It will probably take a bit of time to get everything lined up just right. You will also want to make sure that you are supporting the underside of the transmission mounting "ear" on all sides. Ideally, a circular piece, 4" in diameter would be ideal; you can get a piece like this from the plumbing department of most hardware stores. Once you have it all lined up, use a level to ensure that the mounting ear is perfectly level. It also helps to strap the bellhousing side of the transmission down to the workbench to prevent it from lifting up as you press in the mount.

Grab your now-cold mount from the freezer. Take the new mount and line up the nubs in the new mount with the alignment marks you made earlier. Now set the mount in the top of the mounting ear. Ideally, you'll want to press the mount in only by the outer mounting ring. You need to find a 4"-diameter ring (plumbing store) and place a steel plate on top to clear the protruding inner portion of the mount. In a pinch you can also just press on the inner portion of the mount, but that is not ideal and may weaken the rubber as you install it.

Once everything is lined up, start pressing the mount in. Take care when you do this not to cock the mount in the hole. You risk breaking the ear off the transmission. Take your time and verify that the mount goes in perfectly straight. Keep pressing until the outer mounting ring is flush with the transmission ear. Once it's flush, you're all set and ready to put the tranny back in the car.

1 Begin by making a visual mark of the orientation of the mount. The flat metal portion of the mount faces up as shown here (blue arrow).

2 The first step is to cut out the center metal section of the old mount. In some cases, the center section can simply be pushed out if the rubber "ears" have ripped away from the outer ring. In other cases, you'll need to cut these ears. If most of the rubber is already torn, you can use a hacksaw to cut away the remaining rubber and push the center out.

3 You'll probably want to use a reciprocating saw to cut away the ears if there's a good amount of the rubber left. If you can't get the saw inside the mount, you'll first need to cut away enough of the rubber to allow the saw blade inside. Use extreme caution, use safety goggles, and make sure you have the transmission firmly supported when doing this. Also, make sure that you don't start cutting through the outer ring of the mount and into the transmission.

4 This picture shows the center section of the mount cut out.

6 Now pry the old ring out of the transmission. If the ring is plastic like on our project car, it should simply snap in two. If it is made out of metal (like our replacement mount), you may need to do a bit of bending before it will come out of the transmission.

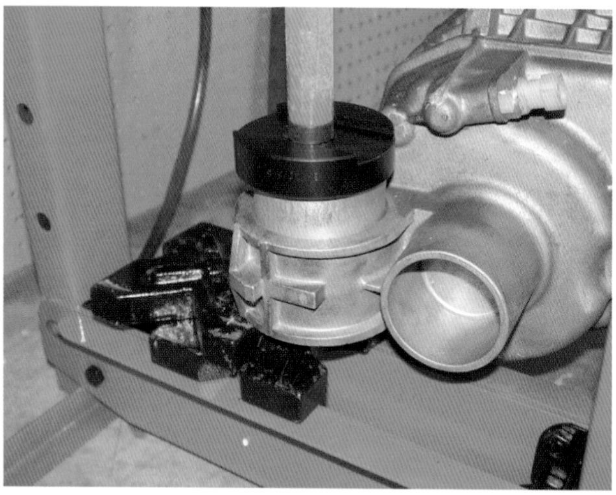

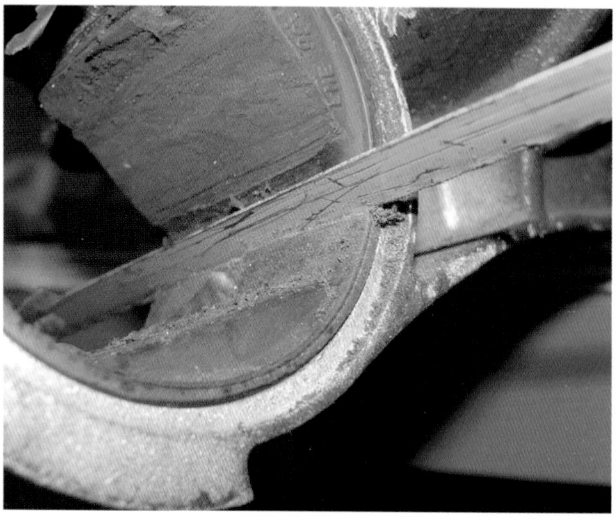

5 You'll now have to remove the outer ring. I did this by making a cut along the edge of the mount, cutting just deep enough to break through the outer ring but not enough to cut into the transmission casting. Originally, I had planned to make another cut 180 degrees on the other side in order to release the tension on the inner ring, but as soon as I made the first cut, I realized that the ring was made of plastic rather than metal and it slipped right out. If you have a metal ring, you probably will have to cut another groove in order to release the old mount from the transmission case.

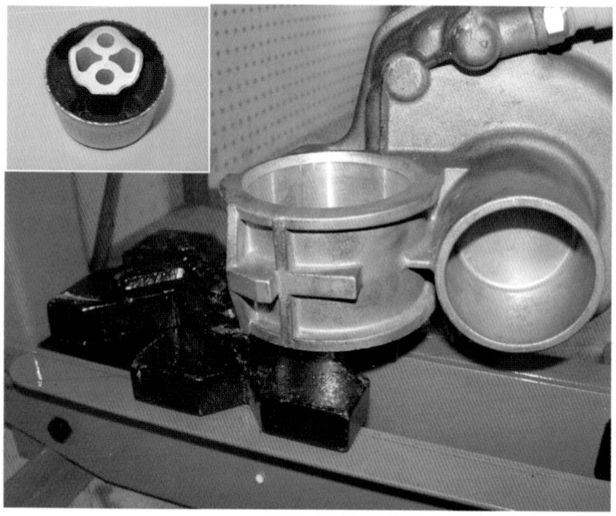

7 Place the transmission sideways in the press and use wood or metal to support it. You'll want to get the transmission ear as close to 90 degrees straight up as you can. At the same time, you'll need to support the bellhousing end of the tranny to keep it from pivoting up as you press the mount in. This is the most time-consuming part of the job—making sure everything is aligned correctly. You'll also want to make sure that the edges of the ear are well supported or you could end up breaking a chunk off it. The new mount is shown in the inset photo.

8 Now grab the new mount out of the freezer and orient it in the ear so that the flat section points up relative to the transmission. Try to get the mount as straight as possible. You'll notice that the center section sits higher than the edge of the mount, so ideally you'll need a tool with the center section removed for clearance. In a pinch, the rubber itself has enough flex in it to allow you to press on the center section until you hit the outer wedge of the new mount. Work quickly and press the mount in until the two edges of the new mount are flush with the outer surfaces of the transmission casting.

PROJECT 38
Transmission Removal

Time / Tab / Talent: 8 hours / $0 /

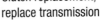

Tools: All of them

Applicable Years: All

Tinware: Transmission

Tip: Have a buddy help you when you're ready to drop the unit

Performance Gain: Ability to access engine

Comp Modification: Clutch replacement, replace transmission mounts

More Info: http://www.101projects.com/Carrera/38.htm

Some jobs on the Carrera require removal of the transmission, such as replacing the intermediate shaft (IMS) bearing (Project 14) or the clutch (Project 45). To the beginner, this may seem a bit daunting, but it really isn't that difficult. The key is to make sure you are well organized, have a good set of tools, and set aside plenty of time to do the job.

The first step is to disconnect the negative lead from the battery (see Project 83). You'll be working around electrical connections while you're under the car, so it just makes sense to be safe and prevent any possible damage to both you and the car. Second, jack up the car and support all four corners on jack stands (Project 1). You'll want to have the car as high up in the air as possible here to help with clearance. A quick note here on jack stands: it makes sense to invest in a good quality set. Here at Pelican Parts, we use steel flat-top adjustable jack stands. These are about the best you can get, with a very high individual weight capacity.

Now crawl under the car and remove the plastic underbody trays. These are held in place by three Phillips screws and a series of plastic 10mm nuts. Set the trays aside and locate the two 15mm bolts holding the aluminum crossmember piece between the suspension uprights. You might want to drain all the fluid from the transmission at this point. It isn't required that you drain the fluid to drop the transmission, although it is a good idea if the fluid has not been changed in a long time (see Project 39).

Now begin to remove the six 8mm hex bolts holding each constant velocity (CV) joint to the transmission (see Photo 2 of Project 42). You'll find that it's kind of difficult to access all of them. The best success comes from finding a spot under the car where you can reach the bolt, then lock the car in gear and put the emergency brake on. Once the bolt is lose, put the car in neutral, release the emergency brake and rotate the axle until you can reach the other bolts. Once all of the bolts have been removed, the CV joint should just pop off the side of the transmission. As you take them off, set them to the side and crawl over to the left (driver) side of the car.

Just behind the bellhousing of the transmission, you'll find the slave cylinder for the clutch. Disconnected the cylinder to remove the transmission (see Photo 3 of Project 46). There are basically two ways to do it. You can either leave the slave cylinder bolted to the transmission and disconnect the hydraulic feed line or unbolt the slave cylinder from the transmission and leave the hose connected. It's easier to unbolt the slave from the transmission. If you unbolt the slave, you won't have to bleed the circuit of air later on. Unfortunately, it's a bit difficult to access. There are two 13mm bolts that hold the cylinder on that aren't visible with the transmission in place. You'll find that the bolts are a bit easier to reach with a socket and 4" extension once the left CV axle has been disconnected. Once both bolts are removed, carefully pull the slave cylinder out of the mounting boss on the transmission and set it aside.

Move over to the right (passenger) side of the transmission and locate the two shift cables connected to the transmission (see Photo 13 of Project 15). Both will need to be removed. The ends of the cables simply pop off the ball joints on the shift levers - you can use a large standard screwdriver to pop these off. You'll also see a metal clip holding each shift cable to its mounting bracket. Pry the clips off and slide the cables out of the brackets. At this point, also disconnect the electrical connection going to the reverse lamp switch right behind the cables (see Photo 7 of Project 45).

Now you'll want to remove the bolts that hold the transmission. You won't have to worry about the transmission falling off the engine at this point because the input shaft of the transmission as well as the rear mount will hold it in place. This is probably the most difficult part of the job because of the odd angles you will have to contort yourself into to reach the bolts. All of the bolts are 16mm except for the lower two. On the right side of the engine, there is a 13mm nut and bolt.

On the left side of the engine there is an odd triple square bolt at the bottom of the case. You'll need the correct tool to remove this bolt. Don't try to do it with an Allen wrench or a Torx. You'll just end up stripping out the inside of the bolt and making things even harder for yourself.

One of the tools you'll want to consider getting for this job is a transmission jack. These specialized, scissors-style jacks are essential for this type of work. You can usually find one for under $100, and most come with a cradle already formed to fit on the underside of most transmissions. They also usually come with a strap to prevent the tranny from falling off the jack. Place the jack directly under the transmission and jack it up until you just take up the weight of the transmission. At the same time, you'll want to support the rear of the engine with a floor jack. Like the transmission, just take up the weight of the engine.

At the front (toward the front of the car) of the transmission, there are two brackets that make up the mounting system (see Photo 17 of Project 15). Both of them overlap right at the rubber transmission mount and are held together with two long 16mm nuts and bolts. The brackets themselves are held to the car with 16mm nuts. Now, before you remove anything, make sure the transmission jack is securely holding the weight of the tranny. Once you are sure that the transmission is secure, remove the two 16mm nuts and bolts on the rubber centered mount, then remove all of the remaining 16mm nuts. Now remove the lower mount bracket and begin to lower the transmission jack. As the transmission lowers, you'll be able to remove the upper piece.

Once you remove that upper piece of the transmission mount, you'll want to jack the transmission back up level with the engine. It's a good idea to firmly support the engine at this point. You'll have a bit of wiggle room to work with the jack stands to get the engine secured. Don't rely on a floor jack to hold the engine for extended periods of time. Always use jack stands.

Now you'll have to separate the transmission from the engine. Typically, you should be able to just pull back on the transmission, which will then slowly begin to slide the input shaft off of the engine, revealing the clutch. Take your time, and make sure that the transmission isn't hanging up on the input shaft. The key here is to keep the bottom edges of both the engine and transmission level as you pull. Once the input shaft slides out of the clutch, you'll be able to lower the transmission down and out from under the car. At this point, you'll be able to access the clutch, the IMS bearing and real main seal (once the flywheel is removed). You can replace the rear transmission mount if needed.

Reinstalling the transmission is essentially the reverse of removal, although a couple little tricks will make it a bit easier. The most difficult part of reinstalling is getting the grooves of input shaft to slide properly into the center splined bore clutch disc. What you want to do is to first lightly grease the splines of the input shaft. This will help the splines slide into the clutch disc. Don't overdo it here. You don't want to get any grease on the clutch lining. As the clutch spins, the grease can get thrown out onto the lining, which can cause the clutch to slip.

You'll want to line the transmission up to the engine as close as possible, making sure that all of the mounting holes are in the same plane. Also, it helps to rotate the engine's crankshaft slightly as you push on the transmission, in order to allow the input shaft splines to mate up with the clutch disc. It's likely going to take some time to get the angles just right enough to where you can get a couple of bolts through the mounting holes for both the engine and transmission. Eventually, you'll get it just right, and the transmission will just slide right on in one fell swoop.

1 Shown here is the 996 transmission removed from the car. Some jobs on the 996 require the transmission to be removed, such as a bad intermediate shaft bearing (Project 14) or a worn out clutch (Project 45). In any case, removing the tranny isn't that difficult. In this project, I will go over all the steps involved.

2 Begin the engine drop by removing the two Phillips head screws and 10mm plastic nuts that hold the plastic undertray in place underneath the front of the transmission.

3 Remove the two 15mm bolts (green arrow) holding the aluminum crossmember piece between the suspension uprights and remove the crossmember.

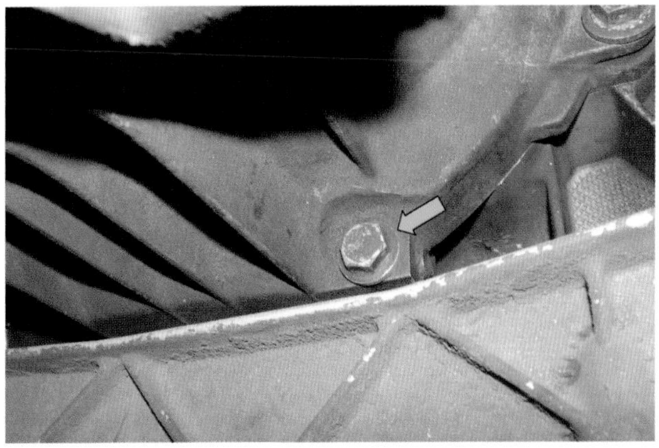

4 You'll now want to remove all of the bolts that hold the transmission to the engine. All of these bolts are 16mm except for the bottom two. The one on the left (driver) side is a 13mm thru bolt with a 13mm nut.

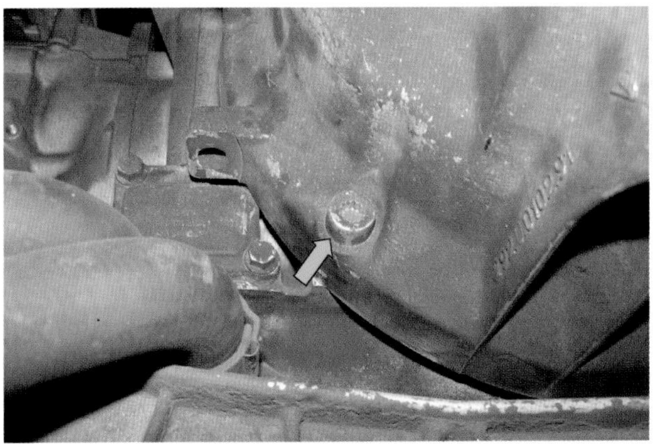

5 On the right (passenger) side of the transmission is a female 10mm tri-square bolt. Don't try to remove this bolt without the proper tool. You'll just end up stripping out the inside and giving yourself even more headaches. The proper tool is available from the PelicanParts.com tool catalog.

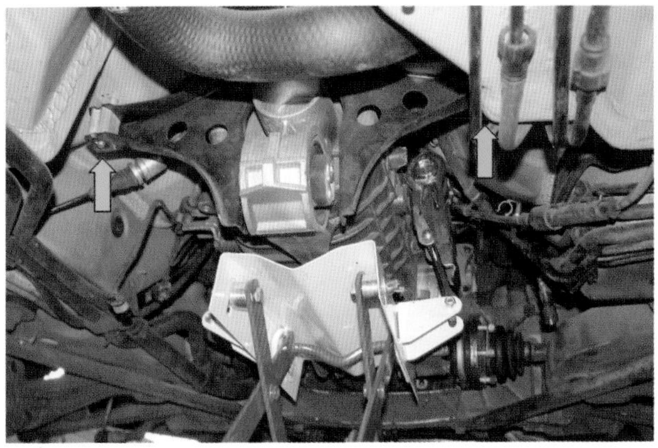

6 Now remove the two 16mm nuts holding the upper mounting bracket to the chassis (green arrows). Once the transmission has been lowered, you will be able to slide the upper mounting plate over the transmission.

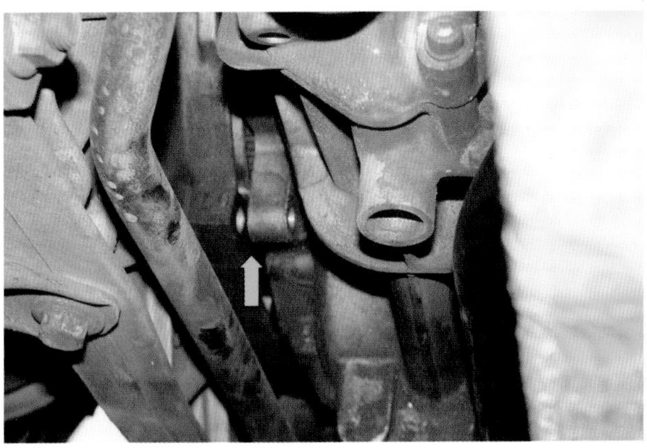

7 This photo shows a small sliver of the bottom of the transmission as we are pulling it away from the engine. The engine weight is supported by a jack stand. As you pull away the transmission from the engine, you will see a small gap begin to appear (green arrow). This indicates that you are proceeding correctly and the transmission is beginning to come out.

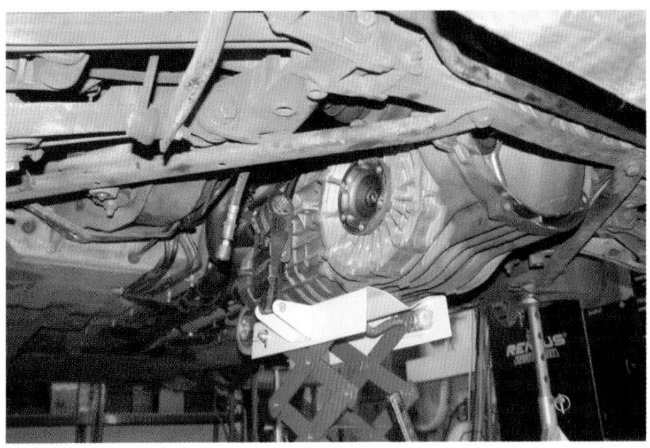

8 Although you can do it by yourself, I recommend having a transmission-drop buddy around to help you. Using your jack, carefully line up the bottom of the jack with the bottom of the transmission as shown. If you position it just right, you will be able to balance the transmission perfectly on the jack. Don't put your arms, legs, or face underneath the transmission as you are pulling it out: once the input shaft slides out from the center of the clutch it will become really wobbly on your jack. Lower it to the floor carefully and pull it out from under the car.

PROJECT 39
Replacing Transmission Fluid

Time / Tab / Talent: 1 hour / $25 /

Tools: 16mm triple-square tool, 17mm hex socket (five-speed), 10mm hex socket (six-speed)

Applicable Years: All

Tinware: Transmission fluid

Tip: Make sure that you have a 4-quart drip pan and plenty of paper towels

Performance Gain: Longer life for your transmission

Comp Modification: Use high performance transmission fluid for better shifting

More Info: http://www.101projects.com/Carrera/39.htm

One of the easiest tasks to perform on your manual transmission Carrera is to change the transmission oil. The Carrera transmission is known as a transaxle. It includes all the standard components of a normal transmission, plus an integrated differential. This design is possible because of the rear-engine design of the Carrera. The transaxle design is more compact and theoretically lighter in weight since you don't need a dedicated differential.

The differential and the transmission both share the same lubricating fluid. It's very important to make sure that the fluid in your transmission is at the proper level, otherwise your transmission will experience significant wear. The synchro rings and sliders all depend on a slick surface in order to match speeds when shifting. If your transmission is low on oil, the wear on these components will accelerate significantly. In addition, shifting the car will be more difficult. One of the first things that you should check on a 911 Carrera that is having problems shifting is the level of the transmission oil. Keeping the differential and all the associated gears well lubricated should also help increase your fuel mileage.

The transmission oil also helps to keep temperatures down inside your transmission. The engine is one of the primary sources of heat for the transmission as it conducts and radiates through and around the points where the engine and transmission are mounted. The transmission also creates heat itself as the gears and synchros turn within its case. Keeping the transmission fluid at its proper level helps to mitigate heat problems. Having a large reservoir of oil to spread the heat throughout the transmission helps to keep temperatures down. On some of the higher-performance Porsche transmissions, there is even an external transmission cooler that operates similar to the engine cooler.

I recommend that your transmission fluid be changed every 30,000 miles or about once every two years. This number is a rough estimate and may vary depending upon your use of your 911 (track versus street). There are many moving parts in the transmission, and they have a tendency to drop small microscopic metal particles into the oil. Specifically, the synchro rings wear down slowly over time, actually with every shift. While the transmission bearings are not as sensitive to oil contaminants as the engine bearings, they can still exhibit wear from these particles in the oil.

The Carrera transmissions have two plugs for filling and emptying the transmission oil, located on the side and the bottom of the case. A 10mm hex socket is all that is required to remove both the drain plug and the filler plug.

The first step in checking or filling your transmission is to gain access to the plugs. Jack up all four corners of the car (Project 1), making sure that the car is perfectly level with respect to the ground. Then remove the rear plastic underbody trays.

If you are simply checking the level of oil in your transmission, start by removing the filler plug on the side of the transmission. This is the plug that you add fluid to. Simply stick your finger in the hole and see if you can feel fluid at the bottom level of the hole. If you can feel the fluid level with your finger, then your fluid level is about right or perhaps will need only a little topping off.

If you cannot feel the fluid level, then you will need to add transmission oil to the case. If you are planning on changing the oil, then remove the plug on the bottom of the transmission case. It's a wise idea to try to empty the transmission oil when the car is warm, as this will make the oil more viscous and it will flow out easier. Make sure that you have a drain pan capable of handling at least 4 quarts of transmission oil. Check the fluid in

the pan to see if you see any unusual metal pieces, or grit in the oil. The transmission holds about 2.8 liters (3.0 quarts).

While the fluid is emptying out, you can use this time to clean out the drain and filler plugs. The bottom drain plug should have an integrated magnet in it that traps metal debris. Using a cotton swab or a paper towel, carefully clean out all of the black debris and particles that may have found their way in there.

Replace the bottom plug on the transmission, but don't tighten it too tightly (18 ft-lbs, or 25 Nm, maximum). These plugs do not have a tendency to leak (transmission oil is thicker than engine oil). If it does leak later on, you can always tighten it a little more. Now, add transmission oil to the case. The best method for this is with a hand-operated oil pump. These are available from most auto parts stores and attach to the top of the plastic transmission oil bottle. They work similarly to the liquid soap dispensers you find in most bathrooms. Pump the transmission case full of fluid until it just starts to run out the filler hole. Replace the filler plug and clean up the few drips that might have run out of the hole. Tighten down the filler plug in a similar manner to the drain plug.

The automatic transmission cars also have a differential built-in to the transaxle. This differential uses the same type of fluid as the manual transmission and must be checked and filled in addition to the automatic transmission fluid. On the automatic cars, there is no drain plug, however, so the gear oil must be drained by loosening the outer differential cover (see Photo 2). Or, you can possibly get around this by inserting a fluid vacuum pump into the fluid fill hole and sucking out all of the old fluid. You top off the fluid and fill the differential in a similar manner to the six-speed manual transmission. Simply unscrew the plug and fill until the fluid starts flowing out of the hole. The automatic transmission differential uses the same fluid as the manual transmissions and takes about 0.8 liter (0.85 quart). Tighten up the plug to 22 ft-lb (30 Nm).

In many cases, generic transmission gear oil that meets or exceeds SAE 75W90 will suffice perfectly fine. Also very effective are the Porsche factory lubricants (typically manufactured by Shell Oil) or Mobil Delvac Synthetic Gear Oil 75W-90. In addition, if you have a limited slip differential (LSD), be sure that you get transmission fluid that is appropriate—using a fluid that is too slippery can reduce the torque bias effects of the differential and make it less effective at distributing torque.

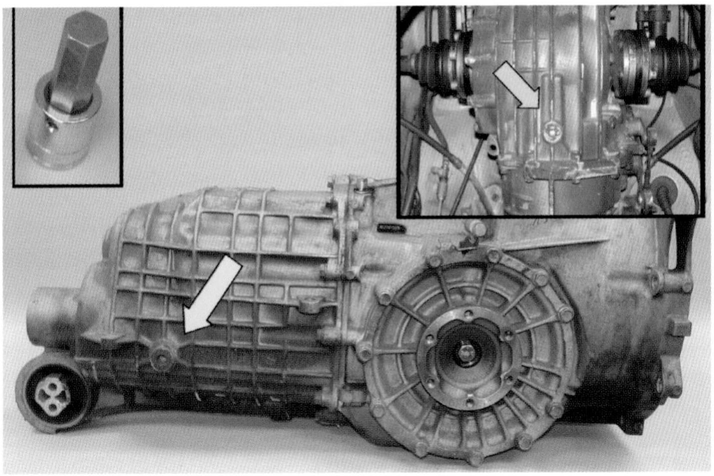

1 This photo shows a typical six-speed Carrera transmission with both the drain plug (inset upper right, yellow arrow) and fill plug visible (blue arrow). You need a 10mm hex socket in order to remove either plug (inset upper left).

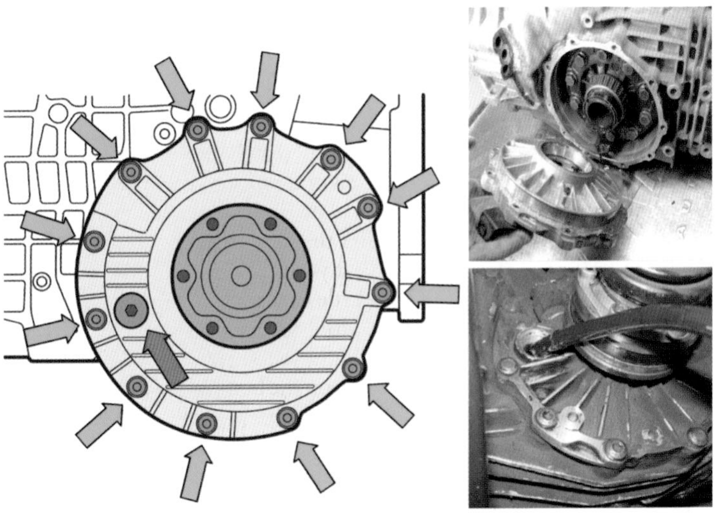

2 Shown here is the side of an automatic transmission from a Carrera. The green arrows point to the differential cover bolts that need to be loosened to drain the differential gear oil. If you can't loosen the cover bolts then you need to remove the center bolt and pull out the stub axle. The red arrow points to the bottom of the fill plug. Top off the fluid to the edge of the bottom of the fill plug, just like on the six-speed transmission (inset lower right).

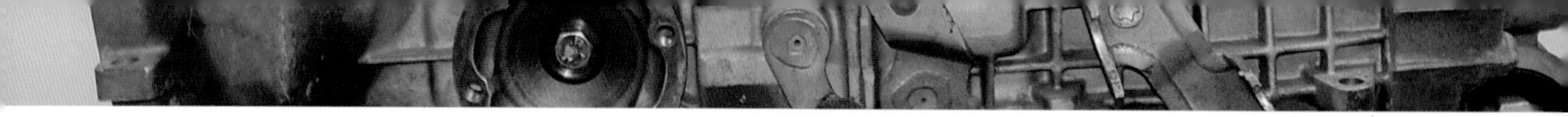

PROJECT 40

Limited Slip Differential (LSD)/ Carrier Bearings and Seals

Time / Tab / Talent: 8 hours / $2500 /

Tools: Torx set, slide hammer, gear puller

Applicable Years: All

Tinware: LSD, differential carrier bearings, seals

More Info: http://www.101projects.com/Carrera/40.htm

Tip: It's best to perform this installation with the transmission out of the car, during a clutch job

Performance Gain: Better traction and performance

Comp Modification: Clutch replacement

While there certainly isn't enough space in this book to cover a complete transmission rebuild, there are a few tasks that can be performed to upgrade and restore the differential portion of the transmission. I didn't have a spare Carrera transmission to disassemble for this project, so I used a Boxster five-speed transmission. The process is very similar, with the only major exception being the fact that it's a mirror image of the Carrera six-speed transmission (the differential is on the opposite side).

Transmission internals. If your transmission is leaking from the driveshaft area, your differential seals are probably shot. The photo array in this project shows you how to pull your axles and replace these seals. At the same time, you can replace your differential carrier bearings. These are the bearings that support the output flanges in the transmission. Sometimes when you have a grinding noise or high-pitched whine that you cannot locate, it can be your differential carrier bearings. Often when you've replaced your wheel bearings (Project 41) and your constant velocity (CV) joints (Project 42) and you still have a whining noise, it's the carrier bearings that are worn.

The best time to perform this work on your transmission is when you have it out of the car for a clutch job or engine work. You can perform these tasks with the transmission still installed in the car, but it makes life much more difficult if you do so.

When you install a new differential into your transmission, you need to make sure that you have the proper shims for the differential carrier bearings. When you install your new differential, you will need to provide a measurement to the shop that provided the differential so that they can find you an appropriate shim set.

Limited slip differentials (LSD). Gears in the differential allow the gears to rotate at different speeds but supply torque (rotational force) to each axle equally. If one wheel is on ice and another wheel is mounted firmly on pavement, the wheel on ice will spin at twice the speed of the ring gear, while the wheel on the ground will not spin at all. Each wheel gets the same amount of torque, and since the wheel on the ice requires very little torque to spin, the wheel on the ground also receives very little torque. Likewise, in performance driving, when turning around a corner, the weight shift due to cornering forces may increase or reduce the effective weight placed on each drive wheel. If, for example, during cornering, the inside drive wheel comes completely off the ground (unlikely, but let's assume it for demonstration purposes), then the situation becomes very similar to the case where one wheel was on ice and the other was on the ground. The differential will supply less torque (power) to the outside wheel as the inside wheel begins to slip. This is the primary argument for using an LSD. It's important to note that under normal, everyday street driving, you will almost never encounter this situation. Thus, the installation of an LSD is often overkill for street-only cars.

An LSD contains small plates inside called clutches that limit and constrain the movement of the side gears. Springs or spring plates inside the LSD force the gears outward against the clutch plates, which in turn forces them outward against the differential housing. The friction between the plates causes the side gears and housing to rotate at the same speed. However, the springs and clutch plates are not strong enough to prevent normal differential rotation of the wheels on curves. When one wheel loses traction, however, the clutches will limit the "slip" and provide some additional torque to the nonspinning wheel. The amount of torque provided is

determined by the clutch plates and the springs and is called the torque bias.

Torque bias indicates the ratio of the torque that can be transmitted to the high-torque (high-grip or ground) axle divided by the low-torque (low-grip or ice) axle. A standard open differential often has a built-in torque bias ratio of about 1 to 1.3. An LSD can provide almost any torque bias level depending upon the arrangement of the clutch discs and strength of the springs inside. Stronger springs means a higher torque bias.

A torque bias of about 1.4 (40 percent) is best suited for mid-performance street cars that will inhabit the occasional autocross or cars that will be driven on the track with stock engines and suspension. A more aggressive bias of 1.6 (60 percent) is best for modified street/track cars that have stiffer suspension and perhaps an upgraded or larger engine. Track-only cars that are not going to see any street time often run LSDs with torque bias levels of 1.8 (80 percent).

Clutch-type LSDs provide excellent lock-up on both acceleration and deceleration, and the units can be customized by changing the sequence of the internal clutch plates and springs. Differential lock-up on deceleration allows for late braking and very aggressive driving into high-speed turns.

You also need to make sure that you fill your transmission with fluid that is compatible with your differential. Typically a manufacturer will have some recommendations for transmission gear oil that works well with their particular differential. If you use oil that is too slippery, you may reduce your torque bias and render the LSD less effective. If you use oil that is not slippery enough, you may increase the bias and encourage premature wear of the clutch discs inside the LSD.

As stated previously, LSDs are not necessarily ideal for street driving. The clutch-pack limited slip can have a nasty habit of locking up the rear differential at inopportune times, like when you are cornering a road in the rain or on slick surfaces like ice. The reason for this is that sometimes these surfaces don't provide enough friction to provide for the normal differential action that allows slip between the two wheels. The LSDs also have other drawbacks. They tend to be noisier than open differentials, the clutch discs wear out because they are friction components, you need to use special transmission lubricants, tire wear is increased, and overall fuel economy is reduced. They also exhibit a slight time lag between when the clutch springs compress and when the torque is transferred. For these reasons, I primarily recommend that people avoid traditional LSDs in street cars.

If you're looking for an alternative to an LSD for your street car, then I recommend looking at what is known as a torque biasing differential (TSB). These differentials are similar to conventional open differentials but can lock up if a torque imbalance occurs. Through a complex arrangement of gears, the TSB units provide some biasing of torque toward an unloaded axle, but only if that particular axle remains planted firmly on the ground. The TSB differentials are a good choice for street cars because they act mostly like an open differential, except when cornering begins to skew the traction between both wheels. TSB units, such as the differentials manufactured by Quaife, only provide lock-up on acceleration though, which makes these units better suited for slower-speed turns like those you would find during an autocross. Using a high-bias clutch-type LSD in an autocross would likely cause a significant amount of unwanted understeer.

Transmission gear ratios. Another thought to consider is your choice of transmission gears. A poorly matched transmission can make the most powerful engine seem sluggish. Nearly all of the 996 and 997 Carrera engines have a somewhat high rpm powerband (like the early 911 S). Because of this, you will probably want a transmission with very close ratio gears, which will allow you to maintain your optimum powerband and maximize the power output to the wheels. The six-speed Carrera transmission is ideal for this purpose. It's not uncommon to find Porsche race cars specifically designed for long tracks and rolling starts that have a "tall" first gear. This basically allows the racers to use first gear for actual track use, which effectively creates a true six-speed transmission for racing. Such a car would be very difficult to drive on the street because "off-the-line" performance would be quite sluggish. However, on the track in the narrow powerband is where the drivetrain would shine, delivering peak power in a powerband closely matched to the transmission and the type of racetrack. For more information on choosing gear ratios, see Chapter 9 in the book *Gearing and Differentials in Race Car Engineering & Mechanics* by Paul Van Valkenburgh.

1 The first step is to remove the half shafts from the transmission. Begin by removing the center bolt that fastens the half shaft to the transmission. To pull out the half shaft, I used a slide hammer, combined with an old constant velocity (CV) joint, as shown. Place the end of the slide hammer shaft against the half-shaft flange and then fasten it down with two CV bolts. Tap the hammer along the shaft and the half shaft should slide out of the transmission. Another method you can use involves placing two bolts into the half-shaft flange and then using them to wedge the half shaft out of the transmission (inset photo). This is the method documented in the Porsche factory manuals. The photos for this particular project are from a Boxster transmission, which is extremely similar to the Carrera transmission. Some of the photos have been flipped around and modified to display similarity to the Carrera transmission housing.

2 Here's a photo of the half shaft after it has been pulled out of the transmission. Although it's more difficult in the tight space, you can remove the half shaft while the transmission is still in the car. For clarity in the photos, these tasks were performed on a transmission that was out of the car and on my bench.

3 After you have the half shafts removed, you can replace the differential shaft seals. There is one on each side of the transmission, and these seal the driveshaft flanges to the transmission case. If they are old and leaking, then you will see transmission fluid leaking around your axles. Pull out the old seal, and then gently tap in the new one.

4 With the half shafts removed, you can then pull off the differential cover. Remove the screws on the outside of the cover (inset photo). Removing the cover will expose the differential inside the transmission. Be sure that you have emptied all of the transmission fluid out of the unit before you remove the cover—otherwise you will have a big mess on your hands. Be prepared for some residual fluid to leak out when you remove the cover. The six-speed Carrera transmissions have a large O-ring on the differential cover (not shown on this transmission) that I recommend replacing when you reseal it.

5 With the cover removed, you should be able simply to pull out the differential. This is what an open differential looks like. It has planetary gears that distribute and provide equal torque to each wheel. This type of differential allows for both wheels to rotate and spin at different rates of speed, such as when the car is going around a corner or turn.

6 Here's the view inside the transmission case. The curved gear on the right (yellow arrow) is attached to the pinion shaft and mates with the ring gear that is attached to the differential. On some transmissions there is a magnet in the case that attracts debris and metallic parts that have worn in the transmission (blue arrow). Take a paper towel and thoroughly clean this magnet, removing any grit or grime attached to it.

7 If you are replacing the differential carrier bearings, then use a bearing puller to remove the old ones off of the transmission. If they are difficult to pull off, then you might try lightly heating the bearing with a propane torch to loosen it up.

8 New bearings need to be pressed on in a similar manner. If you heat them in an oven or on a hot plate beforehand, it can make their installation much easier (obviously don't pick them up with your bare hands as shown in this photo if they are hot). The open differential is shown here with new carrier bearings installed. Don't forget the spacer and any shims that you may have taken off when you disassembled the unit. If you are installing a new differential, then you will need to obtain new shims that are matched to your transmission.

9 Shown here is a limited slip differential (LSD) from Guard Transmission. GT is one of the leading providers of LSDs to the Porsche market, having earned its stripes designing race transmission components for the cars that competed in the GT class of the American Le Mans series. In addition, GT is an original equipment manufacturer supplier to Porsche AG with components used in the factory race cars on a regular basis. The unit I chose here is a street/track version with 60/40 biasing, which is ideal for a 911 Carrera with a stiffer suspension.

10 Here is the GT LSD installed onto the ring gear and fitted with new bearings. As mentioned previously, be sure to confirm that you install the correctly sized shims with the new differential, as there have been some changes over the years.

11 Here's a side shot of the GT LSD installed back into the transmission. The inset photo shows how the half shafts sit inside the differential (shown without the differential cover installed).

12 When reinstalling your half shafts, be sure to use a new circlip on the end as mentioned in the Porsche factory manuals. The part number for all 1998–2005 Carreras is 996-332-249-00 and for 2005–2008 is 997-332-249-01.

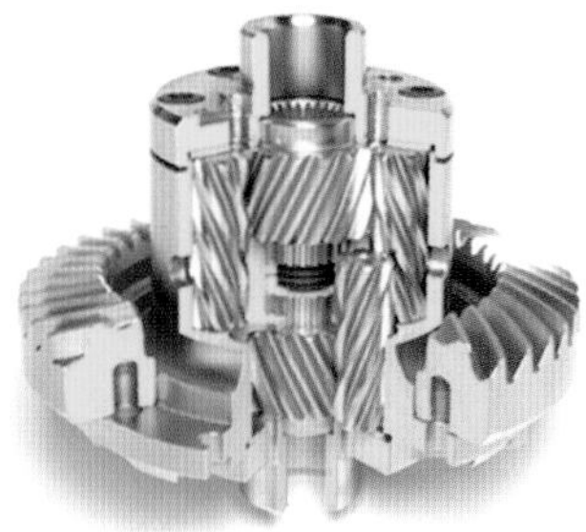

13 Shown here is a Quaife Automatic Torque Biasing Differential. This is a slightly different type of LSD that is often a good compromise between street and track use for everyday drivers. Geared LSDs, such as the Quaife units, provide friction through the gears and their supports rather than the clutch plates found in typical LSDs. However, both output shafts must be loaded in order to maintain the proper torque distribution within the unit. If one shaft of the differential becomes free, then no torque is transmitted to that shaft, and the differential behaves very much like an open differential at that point.

PROJECT 41
Replacing Wheel Bearings

Time / Tab / Talent: 4 hours / $120 /

Tools: Wheel bearing puller, breaker bar, or torque wrench

Applicable Years: All

Tinware: Wheel bearing

More Info: http://www.101projects.com/Carrera/41.htm

Tip: Put the bearing in the freeze prior to installation

Performance Gain: Smooth driving, no wheel noise

Comp Modification: Replace constant velocity (CV) joints and boots

1 Wheel bearing replacement has always been one of those tasks that I have found very difficult to explain in text. So, for this project, I have simply arranged them in order with captions. This first photo shows the wheel hub after the car has been raised (Project 1), the caliper removed, and the brake disc removed (Project 56). Also, before you raise the car off the ground, remove the center wheel hubcap (see Photo 3 of Project 100) and loosen the axle nut (blue arrow) with a very long breaker bar while the tire is still on the ground and car is in gear with the parking brake on. The photos for this project are of a front wheel bearing for a four wheel drive 996 Turbo, but the whole assembly is very similar to the 2WD versions.

2 We're going to be removing the whole wheel bearing carrier here, so we need to disconnect everything that is connected to it. Disconnect the tie rod from the wheel bearing carrier (inset photo; see also Project 60) and also loosen the clamp nut (green arrow) that holds the shock (see Project 64). Disconnect the sway bar drop link (Project 60). Disconnect the wheel speed sensor at its connector.

3 If you didn't loosen up the axle nut while the car was still on the ground, you can use an impact tool to remove the nut (inset photo). This nut is on very tight, and you might have to work at it with the impact wrench in order to get the nut off.

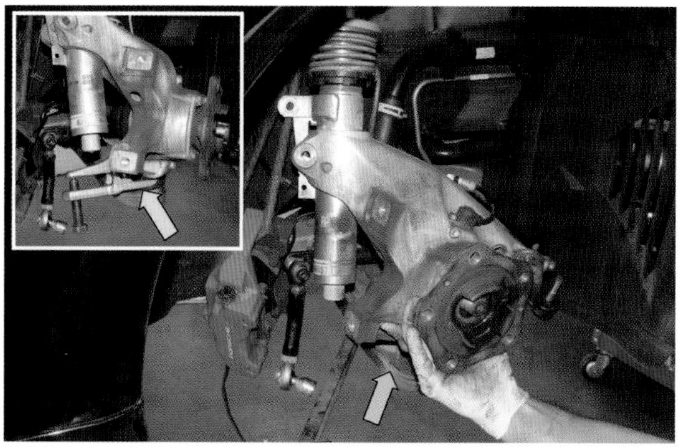

4 Use a high-quality ball joint removal tool (yellow arrow) to separate the ball joint from the wheel bearing carrier. When the joint is loose, use a pry bar (blue arrow) to push the control arm (green arrow) down while you lift up the carrier. Push the control arm out of the way and then you should be able to slide the carrier off of the shock. If you can't deflect the control arm enough, then loosen the bolt at the other end of the control arm and you should be able to drop it down further. Don't retighten this bolt until the car is back on the ground in its fully weighted position. Remove the wheel speed sensor from the carrier when you have it on your bench.

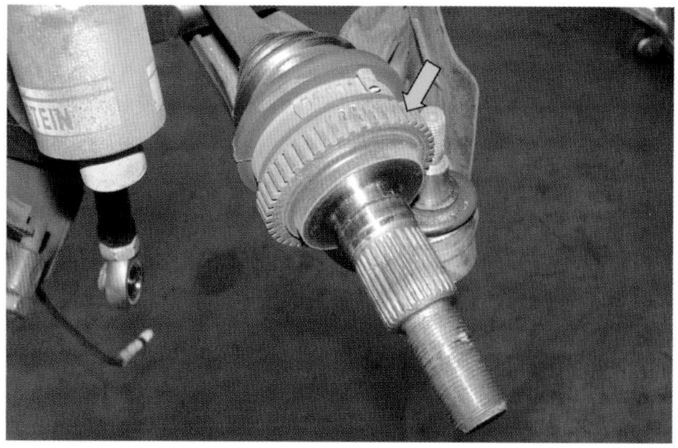

5 Here's the axle with the carrier removed. Again, this is from a 4WD 996 Turbo, so there's a drive axle attached to this particular carrier. This design is very similar to the front and rear 2WD Carrera wheel carrier though. The toothed section of the axle generates a signal that is read by the wheel speed sensor that is mounted inside the carrier. If your constant velocity (CV) joints need attention or your rubber boot is ripped or damaged, now would be the ideal time to replace it (see Project 42).

6 The problem with this car was suspected to lie within the wheel bearing, but I wasn't 100 percent sure. With the carrier out and on the bench, a simple spin of the bearing gave the answer—the bearing was toast. It felt like there was sand or something in the bearing and its rotation was rough, not smooth.

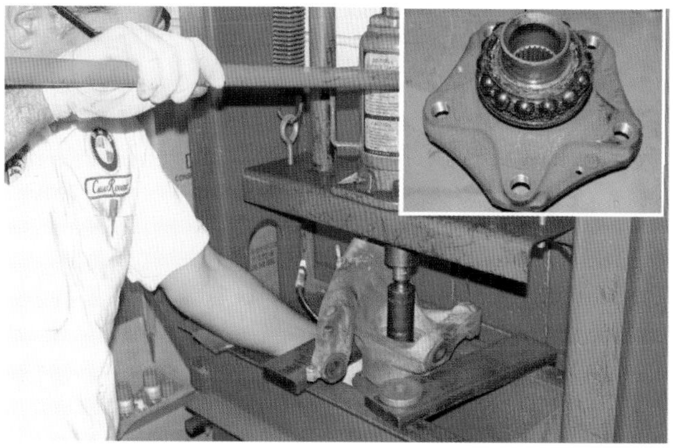

7 Positioning the wheel bearing carrier in Callas Rennsport's hydraulic press, I pushed out the inner hub (the part that the brake disc and wheel attaches to). As is common with wheel bearing replacements, the bearing itself fell apart and half of it remained attached to the hub (inset).

8 To clean up the hub, we used a standard bearing puller to remove the remains of the wheel bearing off of the hub. The inset photo shows the hub cleaned up with all remnants of the old bearing removed.

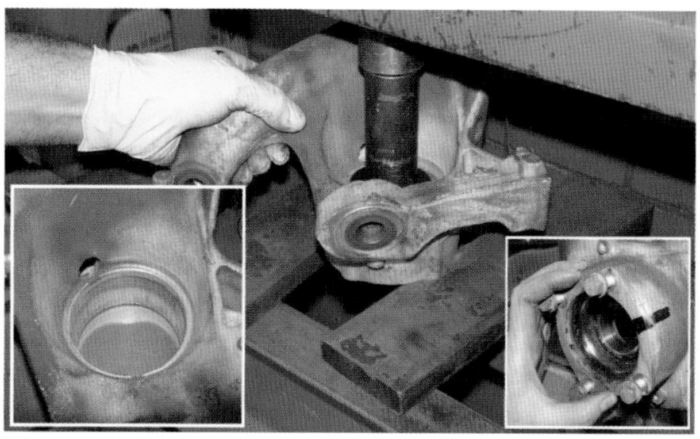

9 When the hub was removed from the wheel bearing carrier, the bearing split into two parts: one was stuck on the hub and the remainder was stuck inside the carrier. We went back to the press to remove the remains of the bearing. Remove the bearing retainer plate first (inset, lower right). With the bearing completely pressed out of the carrier, it should look like the inset photo in the lower left.

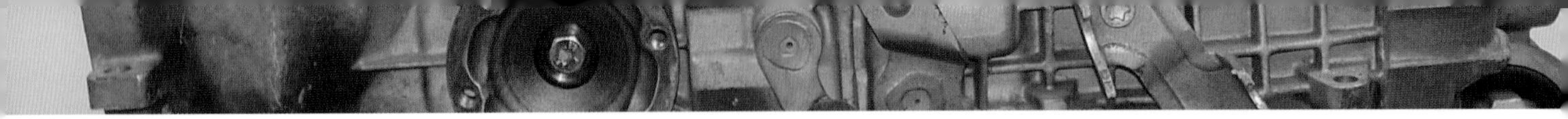

10 Here's a neat photo showing the physical damage on the worn-out wheel bearing. The blue arrow shows pitting of the bearing surface—once this starts in a section of the bearing, it tends to continue and get worse. The bearing should be smooth like the section indicated by the purple arrow. The other half of the bearing is also showing the same deterioration and pitting. Although the seal on the bearing looked intact, this amount of damage leads me to believe there had been some type of contamination issue at play here.

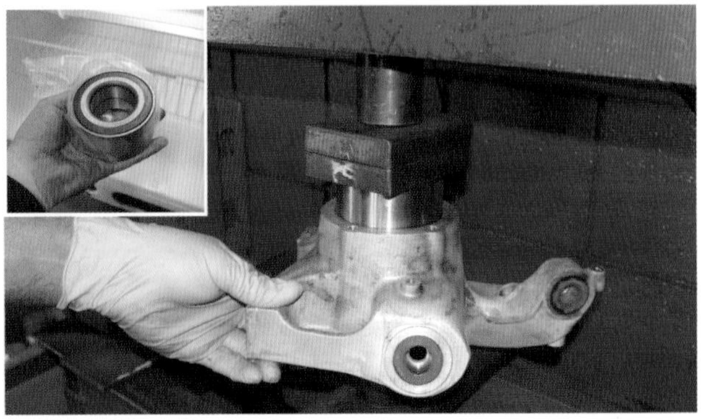

11 Using the hydraulic press, you can easily install the new bearing. New bearings should be kept in the freezer right up until they are installed in the car (inset). If they are very cold, it will make pressing them into the wheel carrier much easier. During installation, press on the outer race of the bearing only—don't place any force on the inner race, as this can damage the bearing. When researching this article for the 101 Projects book, I performed the replacement at Callas Rennsport and came across this question. In the old days, it used to matter which way the bearing was installed (the lighter orange seal used to go to the inside of the bearing). But these days, if you have the older-style toothed-ring ABS sensor, it doesn't matter, and some of the bearings don't even come with different colored seals on them. I contacted the manufacturer just to confirm that the orientation no longer matters. This is what Tony Callas of Callas Rennsport has been teaching for the past several years in his master mechanic classes.

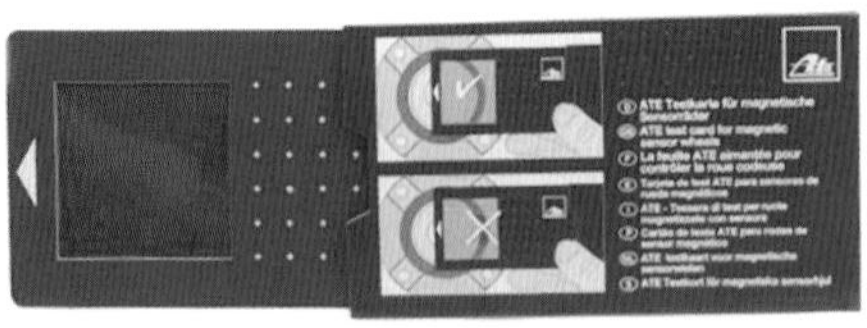

12 On the newer cars that have integrated ABS sensor wheels into the bearing, you need to make sure that the sensor side goes next to the sensor itself. You need a special $15 magnetic tool to "see" through the seal and figure out that the sensor "wheel" is there. The new active wheel speed sensors work with magnetic sensor wheels, which are integrated in the rubber sealing ring of the wheel bearing. For this, the rubber is enriched with iron dust and then given magnetic fields, which are highly sensitive. It is not possible to simply check the magnetic sensor wheels visually. Therefore, before a new wheel bearing is installed, it is absolutely necessary that the wheels be checked as the direction of installation must be determined. In addition, when checking errors in the ABS it may also be necessary in the case of sensor errors to check the magnetic sensor wheels. Simply hold the card next to the bearing and the magnetic fields of the sensor wheel will be shown visually in the display window of the ATE test card. This test card tool is available from Pelican Parts (PN: 760130-M4).

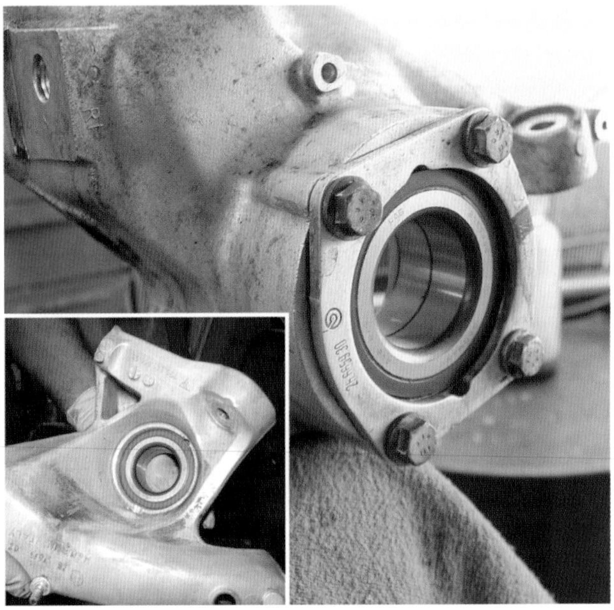

13 Shown here is the wheel bearing carrier from both sides with the new bearing installed and the bearing retainer plate in place.

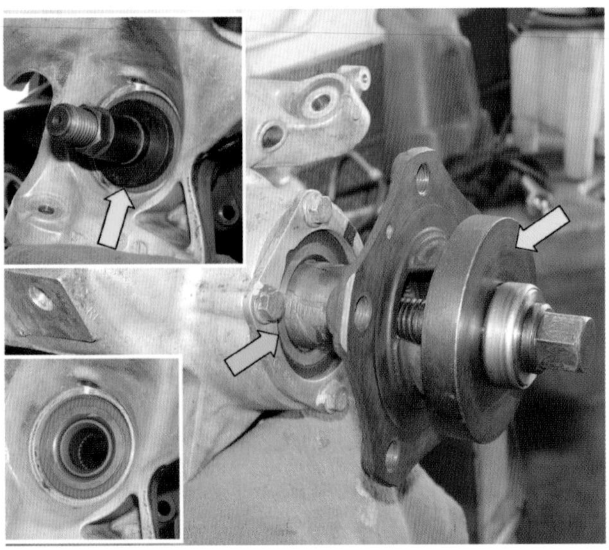

14 With the new bearing installed in the wheel bearing carrier, it's time now to install the hub back into the inside race of the bearing. This is performed using a wheel bearing installation tool (blue arrow). Using a circular backing plate that is the same size as the inner race (yellow arrow), the tool pushes the hub inward while compressing on the inner race. Crank down the bearing installation tool until the inside surface of the hub rests against the surface of the inner race of the bearing (green arrow). The inset photo in the lower left shows what the back side of the installed bearing/hub assembly should look like when the hub is fully installed. Test the hub on the bearing with a few test spins. Don't be alarmed if it doesn't spin too freely—new bearings are generally pretty stiff at first.

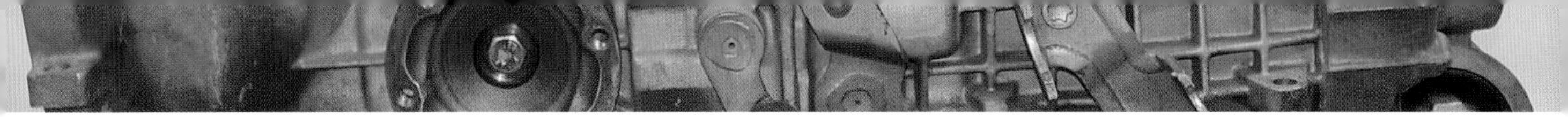

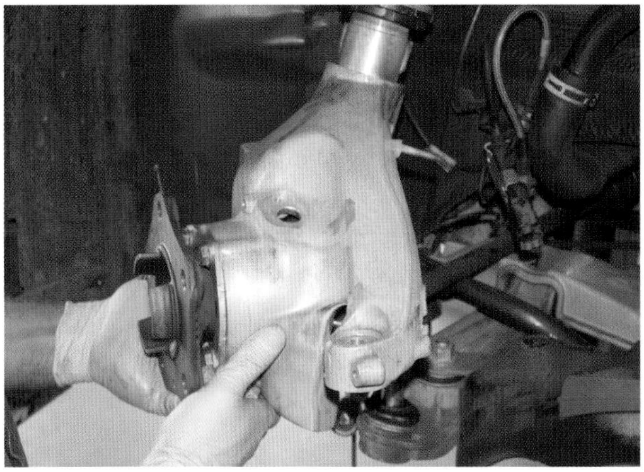

15 Reinstall the wheel bearing carrier onto the car, securing the ball join, shock tower, sway bar, tie rod, speed sensor connection, brake disc, brake caliper, and anything else you disconnected in the process. Tighten up the axle using a brand new nut.

16 With the car back on the ground, use a really big torque wrench to tighten up the axle nut. If you don't have a really big torque wrench, you can use a long breaker bar and your bodyweight to apply the torque. The torque value for this nut is 340 ft-lbs, so if you divide 340 by your weight (for example 200 pounds), you will need to stand on your breaker bar with your full weight, 1.7 feet (1 foot 8 inches) away from the center of the wheel. Do this with the breaker bar perfectly parallel with the floor.

17 It's important to note that you do not always need to remove the wheel bearing carrier from the car in order to remove the wheel bearings. In the case of the 4WD Turbo, it was necessary because the axle was inserted in the inside of the carrier, and it was not possible to remove it without removing the carrier. In some cases, you can replace the wheel bearing with the carrier still installed in the car and avoid using the hydraulic press altogether. In this photo (and Photos 18 and 19 as well), you can see part one of a bench demonstration of the process of pulling out the wheel hub using the tool. Put a backing plate on the inner race and use the tool to pull the hub out of the bearing (the bearing will break apart at this point).

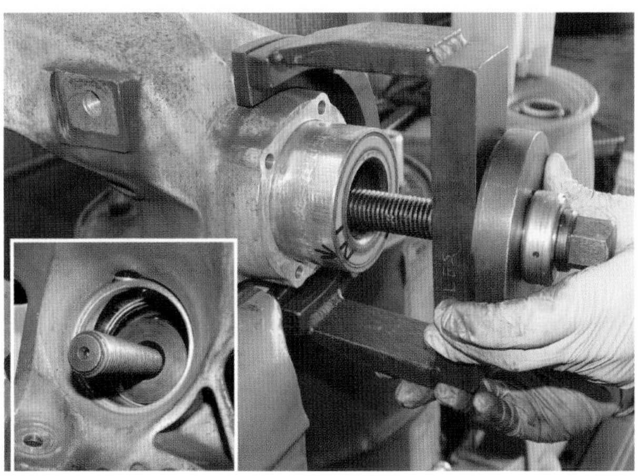

18 Here's part two of the process of pulling the bearing using the tool. With a backing place the diameter of the outer race on the back side, the tool can simply pull the rest of the bearing out of the bore using the long center screw.

19 Part three of the process involves using the tool to press in the new bearing. Using a really big backing plate that compresses against the back of the aluminum wheel bearing carrier, the front part of the tool compresses the wheel bearing into place. Finally, the installation of the hub into the carrier is performed in the exact same manner as shown in Photo 13.

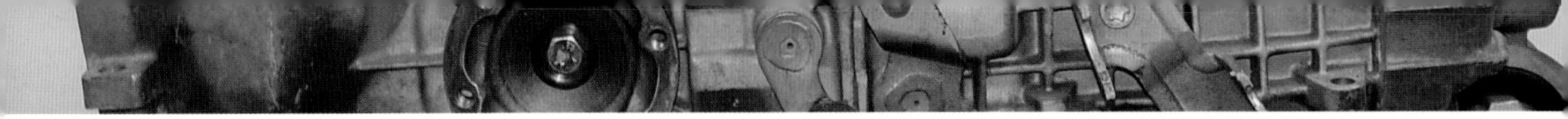

PROJECT 42
Replacing CV Joints, Boots, and Axles

Time / Tab / Talent: 4 hours / $350 / 🔧🔧🔧

Tools: Hex socket tool set

Applicable Years: All

Tinware: CV joints or complete axles, CV joint grease, gaskets, CV boots

Tip: Use the weight of the car to hold the axle while you loosen the axle nut

Performance Gain: Smoother drivetrain

Comp Modification: Replace your rear wheel bearings

More Info: http://www.101projects.com/Carrera/42.htm

One of the most common suspension items to replace or service on the Carrera is the constant velocity (CV) joints that connect the wheels to the transmission. These bearings, packed in grease, experience a tremendous amount of use throughout the years and thus have a tendency to wear out after about 100,000 miles or so. One of the clear signs that the joints need to be replaced is the distinct sound of a *clunk, clunk, clunk* coming from the rear axle when the car is in motion.

In some cases, the boots that cover and protect the CV joints will be torn and will need replacing. The procedure for replacing the boots is very similar to the procedure for replacing the entire joint. New boots should be installed each time a CV joint is replaced.

For the Carrera, Porsche sells only the inner CV joints or a complete replaceable axle. The new axle contains both the inner and outer CV joints, as well as the boots that cover and protect them. Although the inner Carrera CV joints are available separately, I typically recommend installing the complete axle. All you need to do is bolt it up to the car, and you don't have to mess with disassembly or CV joint grease.

If you are going to be replacing the entire axle, then you first need to loosen up the big axle nut. With the car on the ground, in gear, and the emergency brake on, remove the center hubcap (see Photo 3 of Project 100) and use a long breaker bar to loosen up the drive shaft flange axle nut. This nut is tightened to more than 460 Nm (340 ft-lbs); it will take quite a bit of force to loosen it up. Lift the car up again and remove the wheel once more. If you are going to be replacing the inner CV joint only, then you can leave this nut alone.

The next step in replacement of boots, joints, or axle is to jack up and raise the car off of the ground and remove the road wheels (see Project 1). Then, remove the bolts from the inner CV joint using a hex socket (see Photo 2). In order to gain access to the CV bolts, rotate the wheel of the car until you can clearly get your hex socket on the bolts. Then, pull the emergency brake and place the transmission into first gear. Now you can loosen the bolts without having the axle spin. When you have removed all the bolts that you can from this angle, release the brake, take the car out of gear, and rotate the wheel until you can reach the next set of bolts. When all of the bolts are removed, suspend the end of the drive axle with some rope or wire.

With the CV joint disconnected from the transmission, you can work on replacing either one of the CV boots or the inner CV joint. If you're replacing the entire axle, then you can skip these steps, as the axles come complete with new joints and boots. Remove the six bolts and the half-moon washers from the joint and pry off the dust cap (see the blue arrow in Photo 2). Then remove the circlip that holds the CV joint onto the axle (Photo 3). Cut or disconnect the clamp that holds the boot to the shaft, and the old CV and boot should simply slide off of the shaft. In general, it's a really bad sign if large balls from the bearing start falling out. That's a clear indicator that you need to replace the joint. If you are reusing the joint again, make sure that you carefully place it in a plastic bag and avoid getting any dirt or grime in it. Even a crystal of sand or two accidentally placed in the CV joint can help it wear out prematurely. Inspect both CV joints for any wear prior to installing them back into the car. If you are simply replacing the boots, then carefully pry the old boot off of the joint. It is pressed onto to the end of the joint in a similar manner as the dust boot.

With the inner CV joint and boot completely removed, your axle should resemble the inset of Photo 4. If you are replacing the boot on the outer joint, undo the clamp, and remove the boot and cover. Replacement boots aren't typically sold with the metal mounting plate attached, so you'll have to pull the old boot off of the plate and transfer the new one to it. Reinstall it using a new pinch clamp, but don't tighten it quite yet. Reassemble your old CV or a new one onto the axle. With the new boot attached, rotate the joint through its entire motion before tightening the small, inner boot clamp—you don't want it to be too tight.

Whether you're reinstalling your old CV or using a new one, I recommend repacking the joint with grease. Also make sure that you place plenty of grease in and around the boot. Move the joint in and out as you insert the grease to make sure that you get it well lubricated, as the new CV joints do not come pregreased. My preferred choice of lube is Swepco 101; a $12 tube should be good for about four joints total. When reinstalling the bolts into the transmission flange, make sure that the bolt threads are free of grease. Any grease on the threads can cause the bolts to come loose and create a dangerous situation. Also, all your CV bolts should be checked after about 500 miles of driving.

If you are replacing the entire axle, you can use two different methods: you can remove the entire wheel bearing carrier (detailed in Project 41), or you can slide the axle out of the hub if you have enough clearance. Unfortunately, you have to remove a bunch of suspension components and lift the rear wheel carrier up high in order to get the axle out from underneath the transmission (see Photo 6). In addition, the axle will often get stuck in the wheel hub due to corrosion or rust—it may need some encouragement with a big hammer to be removed.

Once you have the entire assembly back together, take the car out for a drive and check the rear for noises. All should be smooth and quiet, and the boots should no longer leak.

1 Shown here is an inner constant velocity (CV) joint replacement kit. The kit comes complete with the joint, the boot, a new boot clamp, new bolts, a new circlip, a new axle nut, and enough CV joint grease to lubricate the joint. On the 911 Carrera, the outer CV joint is not available separately, but must be purchased as part of a complete axle. This is because the joint is integrated into the stub axle and cannot be separated. If the boots are damaged and leaking, then you should replace them, because dirt and debris can find their way inside.

2 This photo shows the process of disconnecting the inner CV joint from the transmission. Use a hex socket tool to easily remove each of the six bolts that secure the joint to the transmission. With the joint disconnected, remove the bolts and the half-moon washers. There is a dust cap (blue arrow) that protects the CV joint. Carefully pry this dust cap off to access the circlip underneath.

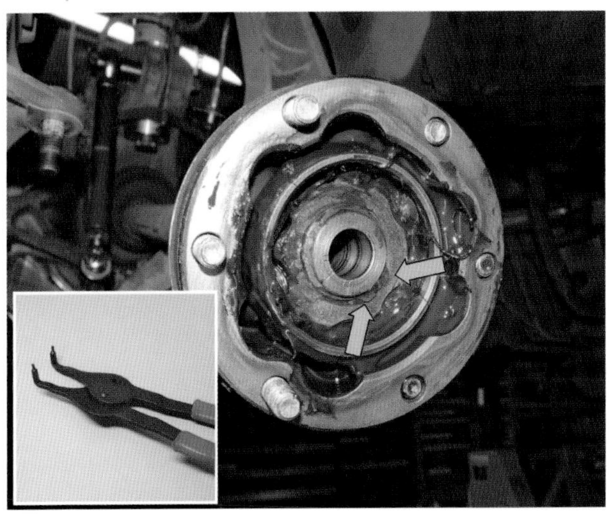

3 The CV joint is held onto the axle by a circlip, which is very difficult to see in this photo. The two orange arrows point to the ends of the circlip that must be removed by using a set of special circlip pliers designed specifically for the task (inset).

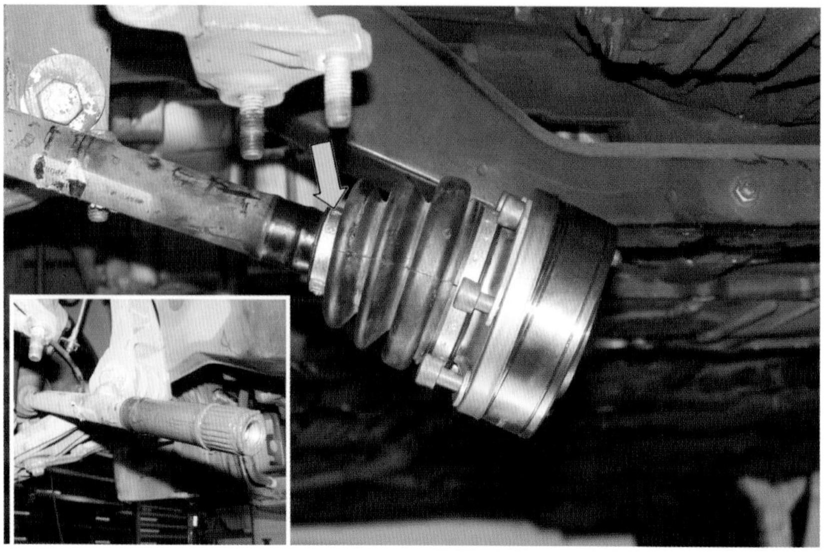

4 The four CV joints are located in the rear of the car, attached to both the transmission flanges and the stub axles on the trailing arms. I recommend that you replace the joints in pairs—either both of the inside ones or both of the axles. Chances are if one of the joints is showing signs of wear and deterioration, then the other three will not be far behind. This photo shows the new CV joint installed with a new boot and boot clamp (purple arrow). The inset photo shows the axle with the boot and CV removed. You need to remove everything off of the inside end of the axle as shown, in order to slide on new boots for both the inner and outer joints.

5 If you are replacing the entire axle, then you need to remove the outer axle nut (yellow arrow). This is best done with the car on the ground by placing a long breaker bar on the nut while the wheel holds it steady. Pry off the small inner hubcap to gain access to this nut while the wheel is still on the car (see inset photo here and Photo 3 of Project 100).

6 You can use two methods to remove the axle from the car. You can remove the wheel bearing carrier as detailed in Project 40, or depending upon which transmission and drive train you have (manual/Tiptronic/C4), you may have to lift the wheel carrier and remove a few different rear suspension pieces to gain enough clearance to be able to pull the axle assembly out of the car. As you can see in this photo, clearance is tight no matter what you do. There is no "easiest" approach to gaining clearance; it really depends entirely upon what else you are working on/replacing on the car.

PROJECT 43
Installing a Short Shift Kit/ Shifting Improvements

Time / Tab / Talent: 3 hours / $150–$350 /

Tools: Screwdrivers, hex drivers

Applicable Years: All

Tinware: Short shift kit (SSK)

Tip: If you wish to renew your shifter without installing the short shift, just use the improved bushings

Performance Gain: Shorter shift throws

Comp Modification: Replace your shifter cables

More Info: http://www.101projects.com/Carrera/43.htm

One of the most popular additions to the 911 Carrera is the installation of a short shift kit (SSK). The kit shortens the length of throw on the stock shifter, theoretically giving you the ability to shift faster. Installation is a moderate task and should only take the better part of an afternoon.

For the purpose of this project, I chose the Porsche factory SSK, which is nearly identical to other SSK kits on the market (B&M manufactures the kit for Porsche). Both types available from PelicanParts.com.

The factory kit is shown in Photo 2. It comes complete with everything that you need to replace your shift lever and replace many of the shift bushings that have a tendency to wear out. Specifically, this kit contains Delrin bushings for the shifter arm and shift lever. The kit is very well constructed, and all of the parts fit together with very tight tolerances.

The process of installing the SSK involves basically swapping out the shift lever with the old one and installing the new bushings. Follow the steps shown in Photos 1 through 11 to remove the shifter and install the kit. When you have reinstalled the kit into the car and reattached the cables, be sure to test the shifter through all gears. Only when you have confirmed the shifter is working properly should you reinstall the center console.

It might take a while for you to get used to the short shift kit in your car. At first, I didn't really care for it, but after driving the car with it installed, I didn't want to go back to the standard shifter. If you're not sure about whether you'll like the short feel, I suggest that you drive someone else's car that has a short shifter installed. The procedure to remove the kit takes as long as the steps to install it, so if you're not sure, try it out beforehand.

On a side note, many people install SSKs in their cars thinking that it will fix problems that they are having with their transmission. The SSK will not solve any problems and will in most cases make a poorly shifting car shift even worse. The reason for this is that with the SSK, the torque arm on the shift lever is much shorter, giving you much less "resolution" on your shifter. It's similar to having a gas pedal that only travels 1 inch over its range instead of 2–3 inches (see Project 94). You have less precision in how much throttle you want to give the car. In a similar manner, with the SSK you will have less precision on where the shift rod is placed. It's a wise idea to tackle the core problems with your transmission (synchros, shift bushings) prior to the installation of the SSK (see the other transmission projects in this book).

There may come a time in the ownership of your 911 when you feel that the shifting performance of the car is not quite what it's supposed to be. Renewing the shifter bushings and the cable ends as detailed in this project are a good first step in ensuring crisp shifting. The other end of the shifter cable can wear too (see Photo 13 of Project 15). Unfortunately, at this time the only way to renew the transmission-end bushings is to replace the entire cable. Replacement is pretty straightforward; it involves disconnecting the cable from the shifter and then feeding it through the engine compartment to the transmission. On some cars, excessive deterioration of the engine or transmission mounts can cause erratic shifting. This is less of an issue with a cable-driven shifter like the 911 Carrera, but crisp, firm mounts do help overall performance. See Projects 10 and 37 for complete instructions on replacing the engine and transmission mounts.

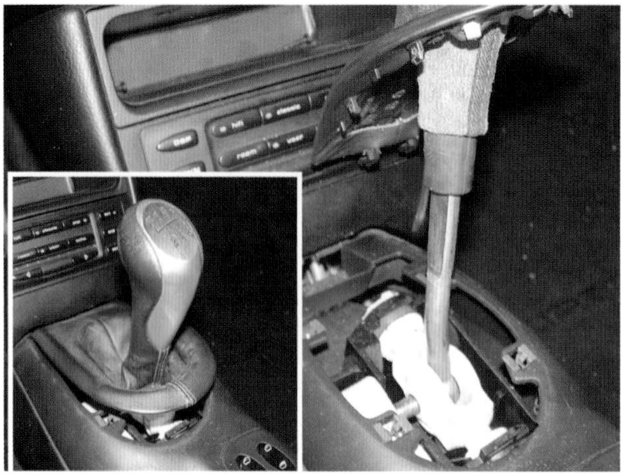

1 Begin by unclipping the shifter boot from the rear and lift it up (inset). To remove the shifter knob, some cars use a set screw and some require you to twist the lower collar 90 degrees and then lift to remove. Remove your old knob by simply pulling upward on it—be careful not to smack yourself in the face accidentally!

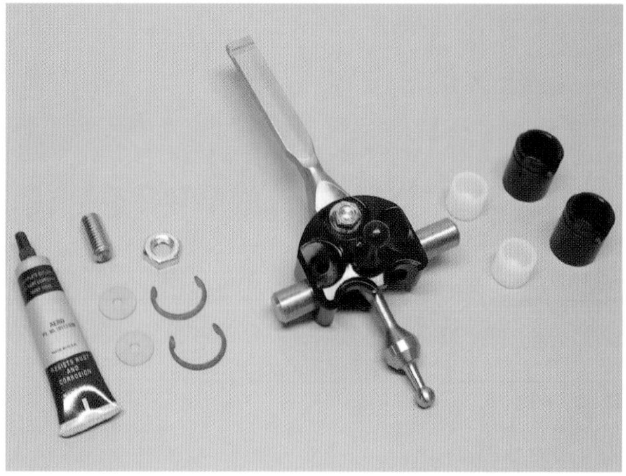

2 Shown here is the Porsche factory short shift kit. The kit consists of a metal shifter, a set of improved bushings and aluminum bushing carriers, and associated mounting hardware.

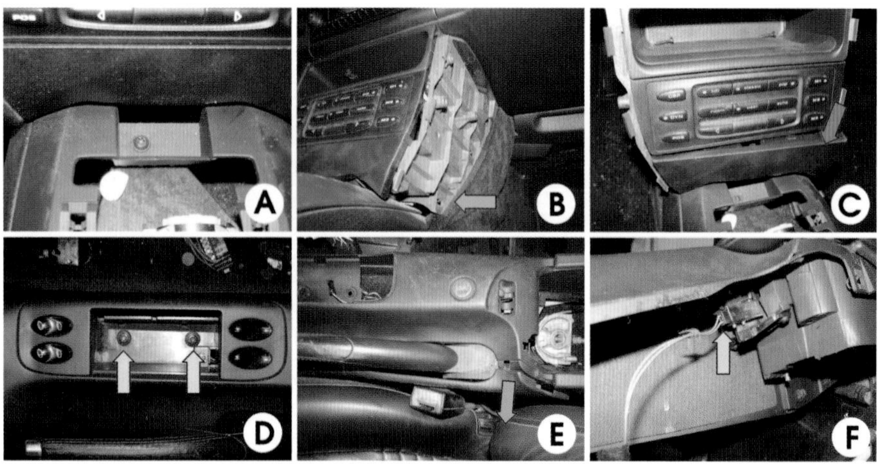

3 Shown here are the various steps required to remove the center console. **A:** Remove front retaining screw, located under the shifter boot. **B:** Pull off side cover (it snaps off) and remove lower screw (green arrow). **C:** Pull off the front lower console cover (red arrow). **D:** Remove the coin tray insert, remove the two screws (yellow arrows), unplug and remove window switch assembly, and remove the additional screw found underneath. **E:** Pull back the e-brake side cover and remove it (pull in the direction of the purple arrow). Also remove the rear storage compartment; there is a screw hidden underneath the small rubber mat inside the compartment, and another screw is hidden under the small coin holder (three total in the rear). **F:** Unplug any remaining harnesses still attached to the console.

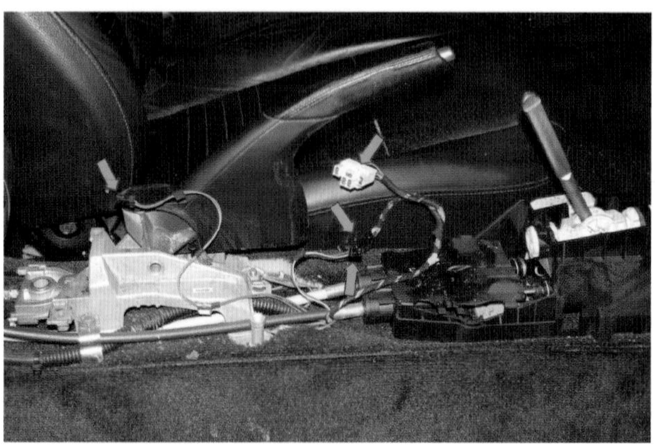

4 This photo shows the center console removed. The purple arrows point to wire harnesses that need to be removed prior to pulling the console from the car.

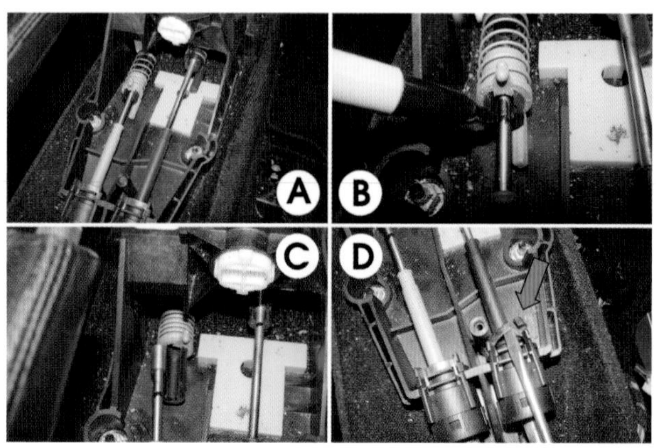

5 With the center console removed, you can now work on disconnecting the cables from the shifter. **A:** Remove the plastic shifter cover and you will see the cables underneath. **B:** Mark the existing position of the cables with a permanent marker so that you can reassemble them in the same position as when they came apart. **C:** Slide the spring-loaded retainers toward the front of the car and release the cable from its holder. **D:** Unclip the shift cables from the rear of the shifter housing and place them off to the side. Finally, unscrew the shifter housing from the floor and remove from the car.

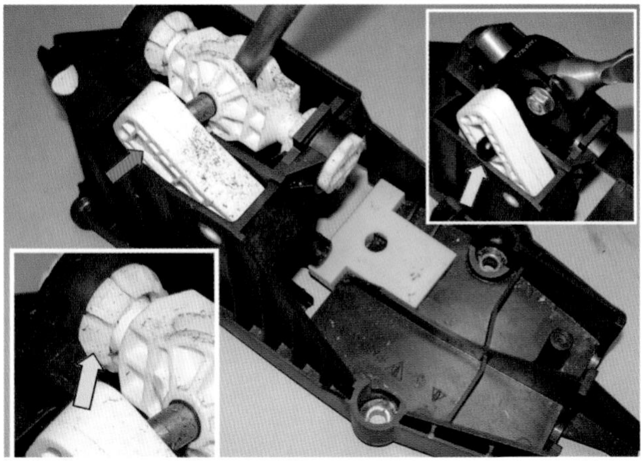

6 The stock shifter uses a square bushing that rides in the side cam piece (red arrow). The new short shifter uses a metal ball instead; lubricate this ball prior to assembling it into the shifter. To remove the old stock bushings, use a razorblade and chip away at the edges of the bushings. When the edges have been removed, slide the bushing out of the bore and remove the stock shifter. If you are reusing the cable end, pop it off of the old shifter and install it onto the new one (see Photo 9).

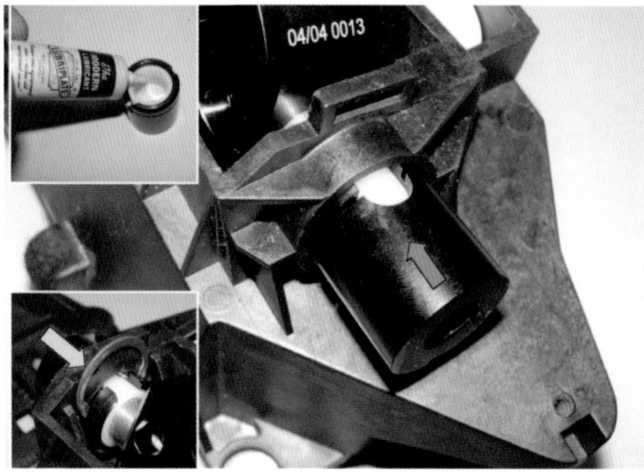

7 The new bushings are installed onto the aluminum cylinders located on either side of the shifter. Place the washer between the bushing and the bottom of the cylinder. Place the bushing on the shifter shaft, push it in toward the shifter (the direction of the purple arrow), and then fasten it in place using the circlip (yellow arrow, lower left). The circlip goes on the inside of the shifter housing to hold the metal housing from falling out in the direction opposite of the purple arrow (see Photo 9). Be sure to prelubricate the bushing prior to assembly (upper left).

8 Reduce the end play in the shifter by turning the set screw with a hex driver. Turn the set screw until it's tight, and then back it off about $\frac{1}{4}$ to $\frac{1}{2}$ turn. Lock it in place with the jam nut to secure the assembly. The set screw and jam nut can be installed on either side of the shifter.

9 I recommend using new cable ends (yellow arrow) when refurbishing your shifter; they will aid in keeping a crisp, reliable feel in your shifter. Lubricate the ball end of the shifter with some white lithium grease prior to installing the cable end. You may have to use some significant force to get the cable end attached. Use a hammer to tap it on if necessary.

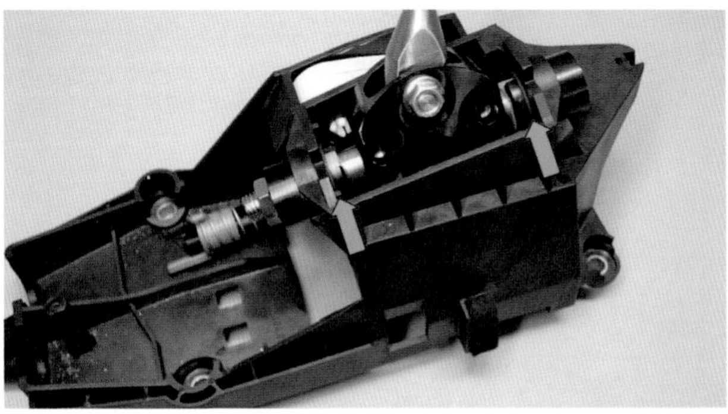

10 Here is the shifter assembly, completely upgraded with the new factory short shift kit and the improved bushings. The two purple arrows point to the location of the two installed circlips. Reinstall the kit into the car, reversing what you had done previously. Use plenty of grease on all the bushings and pivot points.

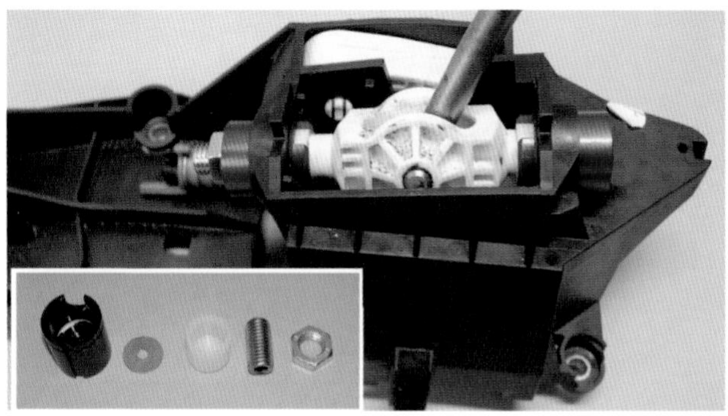

11 At this time, replacement bushings for the stock shifter do not appear to be available separately; you have to purchase a whole new shifter, at a cost of about $200! Fortunately, the short shift kit contains a set of improved bushings that can also be used with the stock shifter. If you wish to keep your stock shifter and renew the feel in your shifter, then I recommend picking up a set of these improved bushings. One bushing kit is shown in the inset (two required).

PROJECT 44
Installing an Aftermarket Shift Knob

Time / Tab / Talent: 2 hours / $50–$200 /

Tools: Bench grinder

Applicable Years: All

Tinware: Shift knob, boot, finishing ring

More Info: http://www.101projects.com/Carrera/44.htm

Tip: Be careful not to smack yourself in the face removing the old knob

Performance Gain: Cooler shifts

Comp Modification: Install short shift kit (SSK)

One of the most popular and easiest upgrades for your car is the addition of an aftermarket shift knob. Let's face it, the steering wheel, gauges, and shift knob are the three main items on the car that you have a personal interaction with. Why not spruce them up a bit? I personally find the Carrera original equipment manufacturer (OEM) shift knob in particular to be quite boring. The shift knob I chose for this article is the MOMO Shadow carbon fiber, available for about $90 from PelicanParts.com. I also used a black MOMO Endurance shift boot and the Endurance finishing knob that attaches to the bottom of the shifter. Installation takes about two hours, as you need to remove the shifter from the car (unless you have the short shift kit installed). Some slight modifications are needed to the shifter handle to make the aftermarket knobs fit, but this is relatively easy to do.

Begin by removing the existing shift knob from your shifter (see Project 43 for instructions). If you have the factory short shift kit (SSK) installed, then all you need to do is unbolt the shifter handle from the inside of the shifter (see the inset of Photo 3). If you have the standard shifter in your car, then you will have to remove it (see instructions in

1 The factory shaft is just a little too wide to accommodate most of the aftermarket shift knobs. Using a common bench grinder, simply grind a bit of the handle down on each side until the width is about 13.75mm. Bevel the edges of the handle so that it will easily fit inside of the shift knob, and test fit the knob on the end of the handle (short shift kit shown in the inset photo). Wear eye protection and gloves while grinding the handle down; it will easily become hot to the touch.

Project 43). With the shifter removed, lightly grind down the edges of the shift handle, as detailed in Photo 1. You only need to remove a very small amount of material. Measure and test fit the knob to make sure it fits on the shaft and then reinstall the shifter and console. You also might be able to use sandpaper and/or files to modify the shifter while it's still installed in the car, but that seems like it would be a lot of work and would create a bit of a mess in your interior.

Attach the boot to the retaining frame as detailed in Photo 2. Install the boot, place the finishing ring on the shaft, and then install and tighten the knob using the three set screws at the bottom of the knob. Finally, screw on the finishing ring and then attach the top of the boot to the finishing ring by stretching the top of the boot over the bottom of the ring. The final result is very professional-looking and looks better than stock!

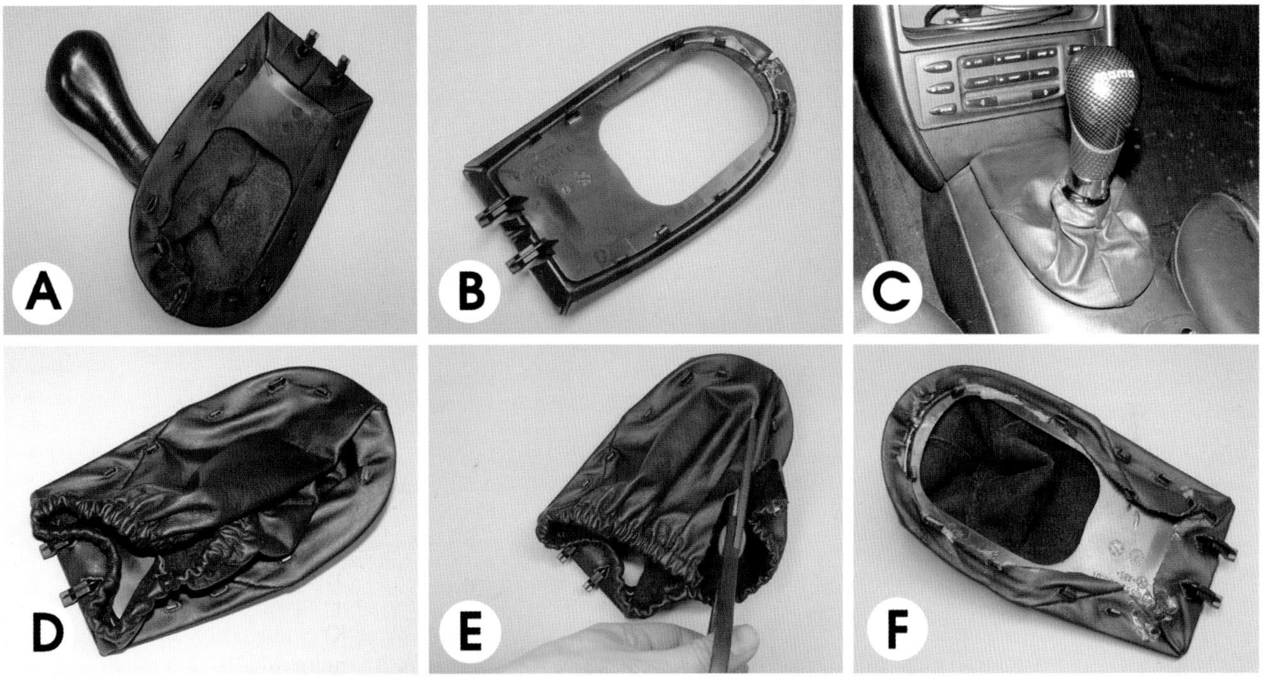

2 Remove the shift boot retaining frame from the existing shifter. **B:** If you don't want to destroy your existing shifter, then you can simply order the retaining frame, PN: 996-552-655-01 (cost about $8). **C:** Wrap the new boot around the frame and test fit it in on top of your shifter. Move the shifter into all of the gear positions 1-2-3-4-5-6-R and make sure you have enough slack in the boot. **D:** Poke holes in the boot for the tabs on the back of the retaining frame. **E:** Carefully cut the excess material on the boot using a pair of scissors. **F:** Finally, using some 3M or Permatex Super Weatherstrip adhesive, glue the edges of the leather to the retaining frame.

3 Here's the finished product. The shift boot finisher shown in the photo is chrome, but it's also available in black and silver as well. The final installation looks very professional—as good, or better, than stock! The inset photo shows a shortcut that you can use if you have the short shift kit installed. Simply unbolt the center shifter from the metal housing and remove it so that you can easily modify it on your workbench.

PROJECT 45
Clutch Replacement

Time / Tab / Talent: 12 hours / $750 /

Tools: Torx socket set, clutch alignment tool, flywheel lock, torque wrench

Applicable Years: All

Tinware: Complete clutch kit

More Info: http://www.101projects.com/Carrera/45.htm

Tip: Purchase a kit with everything in it, not some simple version

Performance Gain: Smoother shifting, no power loss

Comp Modification: Replace intermediate shaft (IMS) bearing; install lightweight flywheel

One of the most common repair procedures for the manual transmission 911 Carrera is the replacement of the clutch assembly. Unfortunately, it is a rather big process involving the removal of the transmission. The good news is that it's really not a super-difficult job if you have some information and a few hints and tips.

How do you know if your clutch is beginning to fail? There are a few ways to tell. First, you should figure out how old your current clutch is. If your car is driven with mostly highway miles, then clutches can last almost forever. However, if you often drive around town somewhat aggressively, then you will probably have to replace your clutch at about 30,000 miles or so. With a hydraulic clutch system like the one on the 911, it can be a bit more difficult to determine the exact problem than with an older-style cable clutch system. Spongy pedals, excessive free play, and grinding noises all indicate problems with the clutch or hydraulic system. Strange noises that change when you push in the clutch pedal can indicate a pilot bearing or throw-out bearing beginning to fail. Finally, if your clutch begins to slip when the pedal is not depressed, then chances are your clutch disc is worn or the spring plates in your pressure plate have worn out.

The first step is to remove your transmission from the car (see Project 38). Once the transmission has been removed, you will want to remove the pressure plate. On this particular car, I found that some of the pressure plate bolts had problems rounding out when I went to remove them. If this happens, then dig out your trusty Dremel tool and cut them off in about one minute. Don't waste your time trying vice grips or other foolish methods; you can cut them off, and you don't need to worry about damaging the pressure plate because you're going to be replacing it anyways. When you're ready to remove the last bolt, grab the pressure plate with one hand—it's easy for it to fall off when the last bolt is removed. The disc should also pop out when you remove the pressure plate.

With the pressure plate removed, you should be able to see the flywheel. The 911 Carrera uses a dual-mass flywheel, which is a two-piece component that is bonded together. This changes the natural frequency of the flywheel and reduces vibrations in the engine. Unfortunately, this flywheel can be expensive to replace. Porsche has released a technical service bulletin on checking the dual-mass flywheel (TSB 911 8/02 1360), which I have placed on the 101Projects.com website for reference. Basically, the test procedure is to twist the pressure plate surface of the flywheel about 15mm to both the left and the right and check to see if it returns to approximately its original position. If the flywheel cannot be twisted at all, or if the flywheel can be twisted beyond the 15mm without a noticeable increase in the spring force, then the flywheel is likely to be faulty. Typically it's a wise idea to replace your dual-mass flywheel every 100,000 miles or every other clutch replacement.

The next step here is to remove the flywheel bolts. You can use a socket and breaker bar along with your flywheel lock. With the bolts removed, your flywheel should be able to be tugged off of the crankshaft.

At this point, you'll want to turn your attention to the transmission and refurbish the throw-out bearing and arm. Start with the throw-out bearing guide tube. This is the small tube that the throw-out bearing rides on when the clutch is disengaged. As the throw-out bearing slides back and forth on the tube, the tube has a tendency to wear out. Remove the bolts that hold the guide tube to the transmission. Remove the guide tube, and inside you will find the main shaft seal. Using a small screwdriver, punch a small hole in one of the indents in the surface of the seal, pick out the

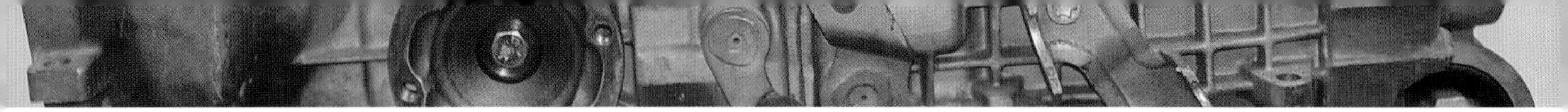

old seal, and remove it (see Photo 5). Clean out the inside of the bore where the seal fits and install the new one. Tap it in lightly with the end of a socket extension, taking care to make sure it doesn't go in half-cocked. Install the seal so that it is flush with the flange. Now install the new throw-out bearing guide tube. Although the factory manuals state to install the guide tube without any grease, I like to apply a light coat of white lithium grease to help things along. Check the small retainer clip, the pivot pins, and the throw-out arm pivot piece (see Photo 6). Lubricate the two pivots with white lithium grease. Take the new throw-out bearing, snap it on the throw-out arm, and attach the arm to the transmission. The throw-out arm is now ready for assembly back into the car.

Now would also be an excellent time to replace your intermediate shaft (IMS) bearing. This bearing has been responsible for more than its share of Carrera engine failures over the years, and access is easy with the clutch removed (see Project 14).

Now, it's time to turn our attention back to the flywheel end of the engine. Porsche Technical Service Bulletin 8/02 1360 says to check the dual-mass flywheel by twisting it approximately 15mm to both the left and the right, checking to make sure that it returns to its approximate starting position. If the flywheel can be twisted beyond about 15mm with no noticeable increase in spring force or if it cannot be twisted at all, then it probably needs to be replaced. If the flywheel checks out okay, then replace the flywheel pilot bearing and the flywheel seal as shown in Photos 9 and 10.

Now you're ready to reinstall the flywheel onto the engine. Always use new flywheel bolts, as they are only meant to be tightened and stretched once. Install your new or reconditioned flywheel onto the engine, then install the new flywheel bolts and torque them down. You must use a torque wrench and a flywheel lock to tighten the flywheel (see Photos 11 and 12).

With the flywheel mounted, now take your clutch alignment tool and place it in the center of the pilot bearing. Install the clutch disc onto the flywheel (see Photo 13). Then install the pressure plate onto the flywheel, compressing the clutch disc. Use new pressure plate bolts to keep everything fresh. When the pressure plate is tightened down to its proper torque, remove the alignment tool. The disc, pilot bearing, and pressure plate should all be aligned (Photo 14).

Reinstall your transmission as per the instructions in Project 38. Reattach your slave cylinder, the backup lamp switch, and the driveshafts. At this time, I also recommend that you bleed your clutch system (see Project 46).

I wish I could say this was an easy job, but it's not. It's not impossible, but there's a lot of stuff to remove and a lot of tricky spots. One of the things that you want to do is purchase a complete kit that contains everything that you need for the job—all of the nuts, bolts, and bushings, as this will be a huge timesaver. The only place that currently sells such a kit is PelicanParts.com.

Lightweight flywheel. While reducing this weight will not buy you any more horsepower, it can increase your engine's response and acceleration. The reasoning behind this replacement is that the rotational mass of the engine takes time to "spin up" when you accelerate. Decreasing the rotational mass of the engine allows for quicker response times when accelerating because more energy from the engine is being used to accelerate the mass of the car, instead of accelerating the mass of the engine components. In addition, reducing the mass of rotating engine components has a two-fold result on performance: you not only make the engine quicker, but you are also reducing the total weight of the car. This is discussed further in this book under Weight Reduction in Project 98. The flywheel and other rotational components serve to raise the rotational or angular momentum of the engine so that the engine will continue to rotate smoothly until the next compression stroke. Adding a lightweight flywheel/

1 Here's what your engine will look like after you have removed your transmission. Shown here is the pressure plate (blue arrow). There is a jack stand underneath the engine supporting the weight that is normally supported by the transmission.

2 Attach your flywheel lock (see Photo 11) and constrain the flywheel in position as you remove the flywheel bolts. With the flywheel off, remove the flywheel seal underneath. Using a screwdriver, puncture and remove the seal. Be careful not to damage any of the side surfaces where the seal mates to the engine case.

components allows you to adjust engine rpms much quicker. However, it will also drop down in rpm much quicker as well when you let off of the throttle. This drop often makes the car difficult to drive on the street in day-to-day traffic conditions. Also be sure to only use a spring-centered clutch disc with a non-dual-mass flywheel (see Photo 4).

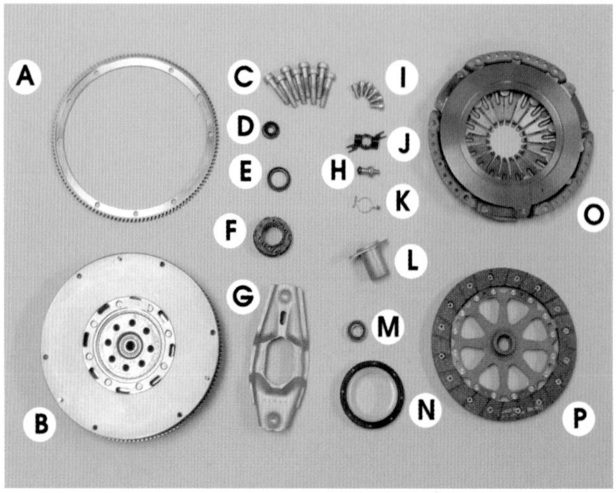

3 The first step is to make sure that you gather all the required parts for the job before you begin. It is very frustrating to get halfway through a replacement job only to find out that you need a part or a tool that you don't have. Here is photo of the PelicanParts.com clutch SuperKit that contains a comprehensive set of clutch replacement parts for a Carrera. **A:** Ring gear (for demonstration purposes, already installed on flywheel) **B:** Dual mass flywheel **C:** Flywheel bolts **D:** Clutch sealing ring **E:** Input shaft seal **F:** Throwout bearing **G:** Clutch release lever **H:** Pivot ball pin **I:** Pressure plate bolts **J:** Throwout arm pivot piece **K:** Retaining spring for pivot piece **L:** Throwout bearing guide tube **M:** Pilot bearing (for demonstration purposes, already installed in flywheel) **N:** Engine flywheel seal **O:** Pressure plate **P:** Clutch disc

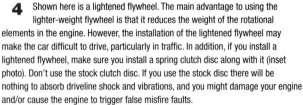

4 Shown here is a lightened flywheel. The main advantage to using the lighter-weight flywheel is that it reduces the weight of the rotational elements in the engine. However, the installation of the lightened flywheel may make the car difficult to drive, particularly in traffic. In addition, if you install a lightened flywheel, make sure you install a spring clutch disc along with it (inset photo). Don't use the stock clutch disc. If you use the stock disc there will be nothing to absorb driveline shock and vibrations, and you might damage your engine and/or cause the engine to trigger false misfire faults.

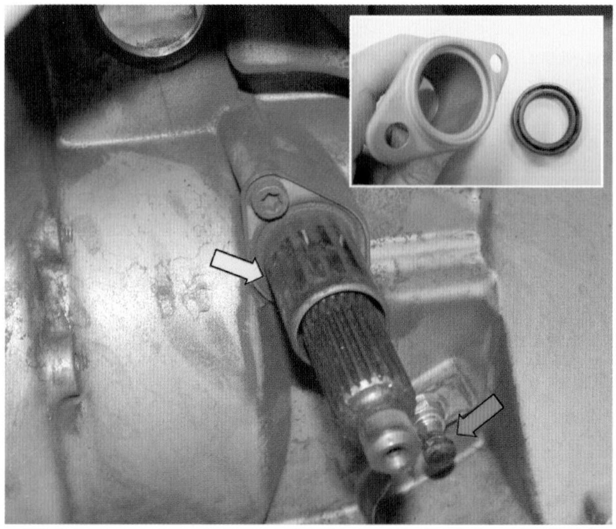

5 This photo shows the transmission mainshaft with the throwout bearing guide attached (blue arrow) and the pivot ball pin (red arrow). Pluck the old seal out of the transmission bore and tap in a new seal.

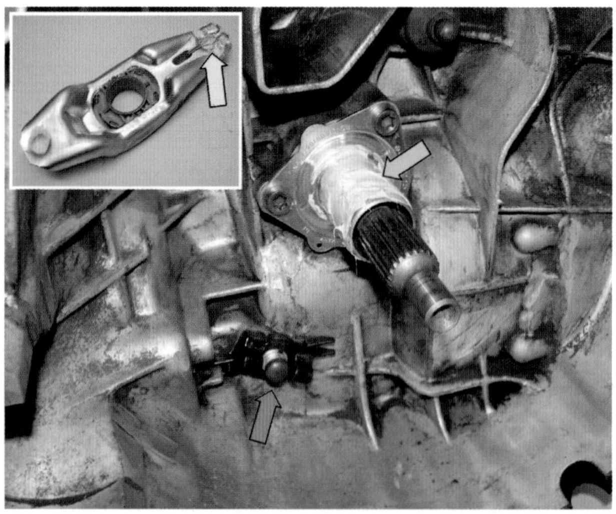

6 The throwout fork (inset) is attached at one end with a small metal clip (yellow arrow). Remove the fork from the transmission by pulling outward on the fork and unhooking the clip from its catch on the bottom. Clean the entire assembly and then lubricate everything with white lithium grease, including the throwout bearing guide tube (green arrow). Make sure that the parts are assembled correctly, as per the photo. The throwout bearing clips onto the throwout arm as shown in the inset photo. Pay special attention to the orientation of the pivot piece and pin (red arrow). *Boxster transmission is shown here. The Carrera transmission is a mirror image.*

7 If your backup lamp switch is giving you trouble, now is the perfect time to replace it. The switch is located on the end of the transmission near the rubber mount. Replacement is as simple as removing it from the top of the transmission case (blue arrow).

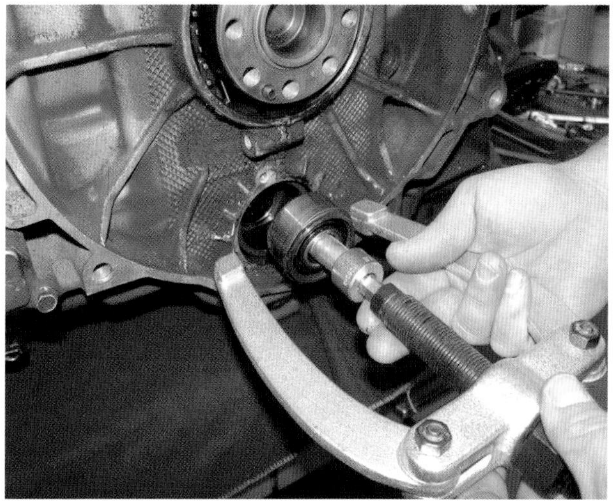

8 Shown here is the infamous intermediate shaft bearing that is responsible for so many engine failures on both the Boxster and the 996. Recent advances from crafty engineers in the aftermarket have developed a solution to remove and repair this bearing while performing a clutch replacement. To ignore this bearing while performing your clutch replacement is somewhat foolhardy—the majority of engines that have blown up in recent years have been attributed to the failure of this bearing. (For more information, see Project 14.)

9 **A:** The pilot bearing holds the transmission input shaft in place and aligns the transmission with the crankshaft. **B:** To remove the flywheel pilot bearing, use an appropriately sized socket and gently tap it with a hammer. **C:** The new bearing should fit easily inside the hole in the crankshaft. **D:** Use a deep socket to evenly tap in the bearing so it's flush with the surface of the flywheel (inset).

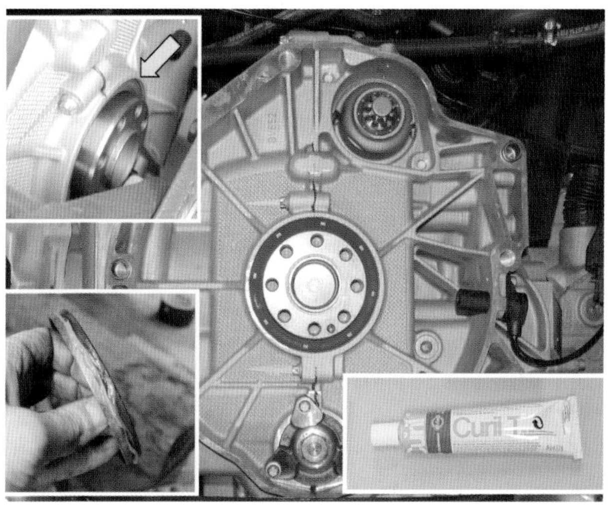

10 Take your new flywheel seal and coat it with a light touch of Curil-T. Then install it onto the engine, taping lightly around the edge. The newer-style seal is supposed to be seated about 14mm or so below the end of the crankshaft. This means that the seal will sit recessed about 3mm or so beyond the edge of the case (yellow arrow). A special Porsche tool is designed for the installation of this seal, but I simply made my own using some plastic pipe from the local hardware store that was the same diameter of the seal. Tap lightly and carefully, making sure that the seal doesn't become cocked in its bore. Clean up any leftover sealant that squeezes out.

11 I use a simple flywheel lock that is basically a strip of metal with two large slots in it (arrow, right). This allows you to attach the lock to a bolt affixed to the engine case and to one affixed to the flywheel, where the pressure plate bolts normally mount. This inexpensive lock works great on almost any car. With the lock in place, torque the bolts, working in a crisscross pattern. Start by tightening all the bolts to 50 percent of their final value, and then go around again and tighten them to the final value. Then crank them another 120 degrees as shown in the next photo.

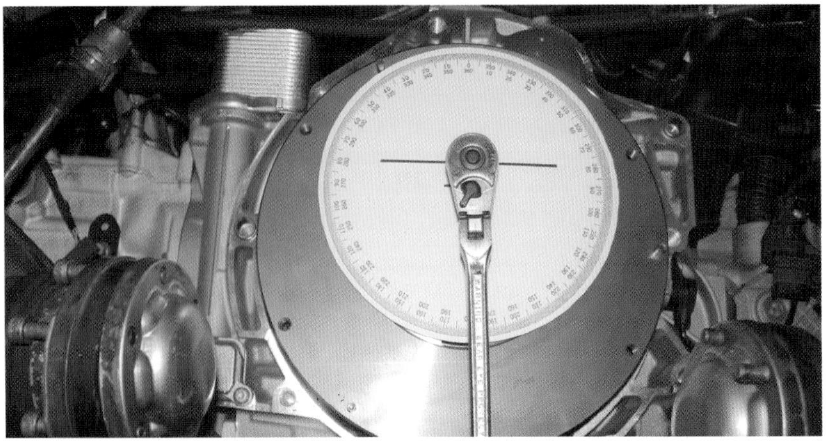

12 Shown here is a simple degree wheel that I made for tightening flywheel bolts. Download and print out the wheel on a thick piece of paper. Then, get some 3M tack adhesive and spray the back, so it sticks to the flywheel like a stick-on note. Then, crank each bolt 120 degrees clockwise to achieve the proper tightness/stretch of the flywheel bolts. You can download and print out the template of the degree wheel from the 101Projects.com website.

13 The clutch alignment tool (green arrow) is used to align the clutch disc (red arrow) with the pilot bearing, pressure plate, and flywheel (blue arrow).

14 Without the alignment tool (blue arrow), it would be nearly impossible to insert the transmission input shaft into the pilot bearing when mating the engine and the transmission back together. When the pressure plate bolts are all tightened down, you should be able to easily pull out the alignment tool, and the pressure plate and clutch disc should be centered with respect to the pilot bearing (inset). I recommend using new pressure plate bolts when performing a clutch replacement project.

PROJECT 46
Replacing Clutch Hydraulics

Time / Tab / Talent: 2 hours / $150 /

Tools: Socket set, flare-nut wrench

Applicable Years: All

Tinware: Clutch slave cylinder

More Info: http://www.101projects.com/Carrera/46.htm

Tip: Replace when performing a clutch job

Performance Gain: Reliable shifting and clutch operation

Comp Modification: Bleed the brake system

The Carreras have a hydraulic clutch engagement system—there are no cables involved with the actuation of the clutch. Although this actually creates a more reliable clutch system over time, there can be a failure or breakdown of the system if the slave or master cylinder gets old and begins to leak or fail. A spongy feel to the clutch pedal, grinding of gears when shifting, long pedal travel, and hydraulic leaks under the car are all signs that one or more components of the system have failed. The first place I like to start is the clutch slave cylinder, as it is easy and inexpensive to replace.

Replacement of the slave cylinder is also pretty easy. Its location is easy to get to from underneath the car. Start by jacking up the car (Project 1). The slave cylinder is located on the left side of the transmission—two bolts fasten it to the transmission. Begin by disconnecting the hydraulic line from the cylinder. Make sure you use a flare-nut wrench to remove the hose. These hydraulic fittings have a tendency to strip if you use a regular wrench. Also, inspect the clutch slave line—you might want to replace it if it's bulging or shows signs of cracking in the rubber. Before you disconnect the line, make sure that you have a drip pan to catch the fluid that will leak out.

Now, remove the two bolts that hold the cylinder to the transmission. The slave cylinder should remove easily. Install the new one and reattach the clutch fluid line. Place a little bit of white lithium grease on the tip of the slave cylinder prior to installation.

Replacement of the clutch master cylinder is fairly straightforward. Begin by removing the plastic cover to the left of the battery in the front trunk. Using a turkey baster, remove enough brake fluid to lower the level in the reservoir below the fill hole for the clutch master cylinder. Then disconnect both the supply line and the slave cylinder line (see Photo 1). Next, from underneath the dash, disconnect the master cylinder from the pedal and unbolt it from the car (see Photo 2). Have a whole bunch of paper towels handy to wipe up any spilled brake fluid—the stuff is very hazardous to your car's paint.

The system now needs to be bled. I like to use the Motive Products Power Bleeder (available from PelicanParts.com) for this task. For more information on using the Power Bleeder, see Project 49 on bleeding brakes. Fill up the fluid reservoir to the maximum level, and attach the power bleeder to the top of the master cylinder reservoir. Press in the clutch pedal. Pump up the pressure in the bleeder to about 22 psi. Move to underneath the car and attach your bleeder hose to the bleed nipple on the slave cylinder. Open the bleeder valve by turning it counterclockwise, and let the system bleed out until no more bubbles appear.

When finished, remove the bleeder system, lower the car, and try the clutch again. The pedal should have a good feel to it, and the clutch should engage normally. If you are still having problems, you should try replacing your clutch master cylinder next.

1 In the front trunk, under the plastic cover, you will find the clutch master cylinder. Empty the fluid reservoir below the clutch fill hole, and then disconnect both the filler hose (red arrow) and the hydraulic line that leads to the slave cylinder (pry out the locking clip—yellow arrow).

2 From underneath the dash, remove the clevis pin (yellow arrow) and the circlip that attaches the clutch master cylinder to the clutch pedal. Unbolt the two attachment bolts (green arrows) and slide the master cylinder out. The inset photo shows a brand new clutch master cylinder.

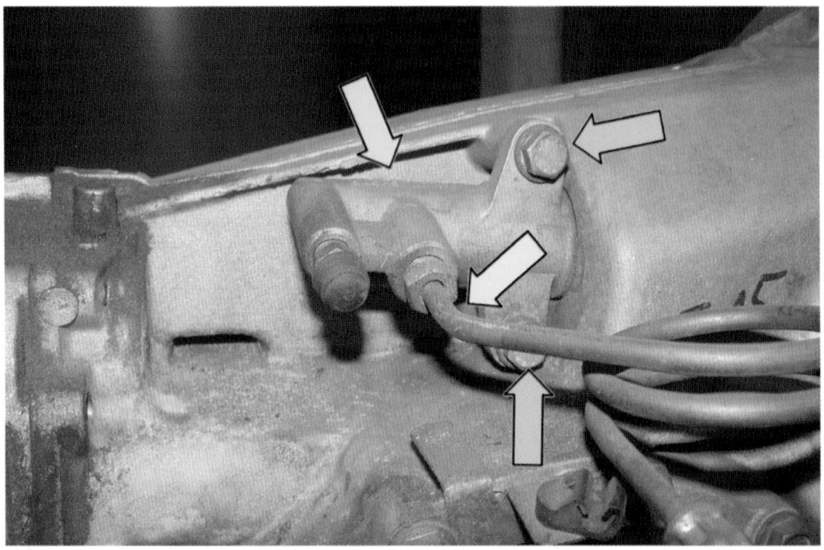

3 Shown here are the various components associated with the slave cylinder. The yellow arrow points to the slave cylinder and the green arrow is pointing to the bolts that attach the slave cylinder to the transmission. The blue arrow shows the slave cylinder hydraulic line.

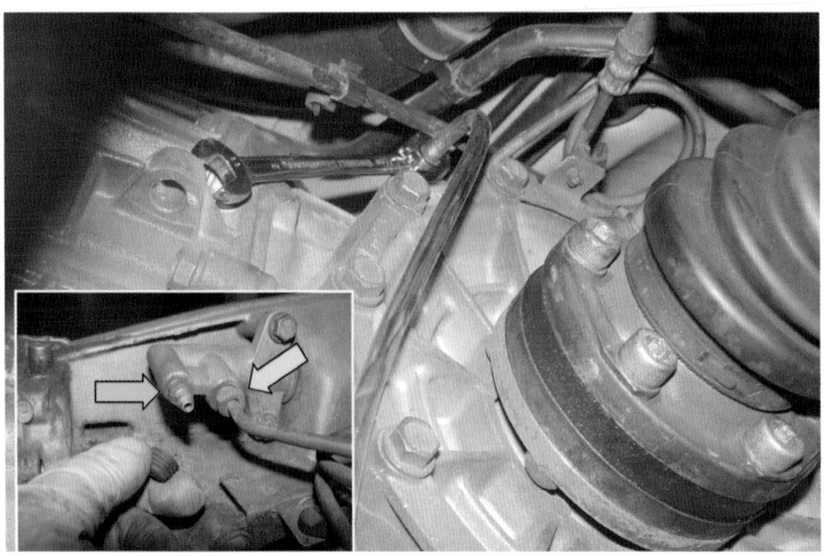

4 This photo demonstrates the process of bleeding the slave cylinder. To disconnect the fluid line, use a flare-nut wrench to loosen the fitting shown by the yellow arrow. The green arrow points to the bleed nipple (with the rubber cover removed), which is required for bleeding air out of the clutch system.

SECTION 6
EXHAUST

Fortunately, Carrera exhaust systems are relatively simple, and upgrading or replacing components is fairly easy. This section shows you how to swap out mufflers and also how to install a performance exhaust system.

PROJECT 47
Muffler Replacement

Time / Tab / Talent: 4 hours / $250–600 / (3 wrenches)

Tools: 10mm/13mm/17mm sockets and wrenches, screwdrivers, penetrant spray, channel locks

Applicable Years: All

Tinware: New mufflers

More Info: http://www.101projects.com/Carrera/47.htm

Tip: Soak any rusty nuts or bolts overnight with penetrant oil

Performance Gain: More power, better sound

Comp Modification: Replace headers and catalytic converters for even more power gains

An easy way to add a small increase in power to almost any car is to add a set of aftermarket mufflers. The reduced backpressure can result in an engine that flows air easier, resulting in an increase in horsepower. However, the amount of power that you can expect to gain depends on a variety of factors. Exhaust design in itself is somewhat of a black art. I recommend that you research the set of mufflers you wish to buy very closely and see if the manufacturer has dyno-proven results.

On a Carrera engine, the exhaust system is already limited due to the space requirements of the rear engine design. However, it is fair to say that gains of up to 15 or more horsepower are attainable by changing out the stock mufflers for a set of aftermarket ones.

Keep in mind that this chapter is also written to illustrate the replacement of the stock muffler. If your muffler has rusted out at the bottom, simply follow the steps to replace your muffler and end any annoying exhaust leaks. While the 997s have a different style of fasteners for the exhaust—and use Torx screws in place of Phillips—the basic geometry of the exhaust is the same as well as the procedures for removal and replacement.

Follow along with the photos for the replacement procedure. Before you start removing the fasteners that hold the muffler to the engine, it's a good idea to inspect them for rust and/or corrosion. Many times, I've had exhaust bolts simply snap the second any torque is applied to them. Spray each fastener with a high quality penetrant oil such as Kroil

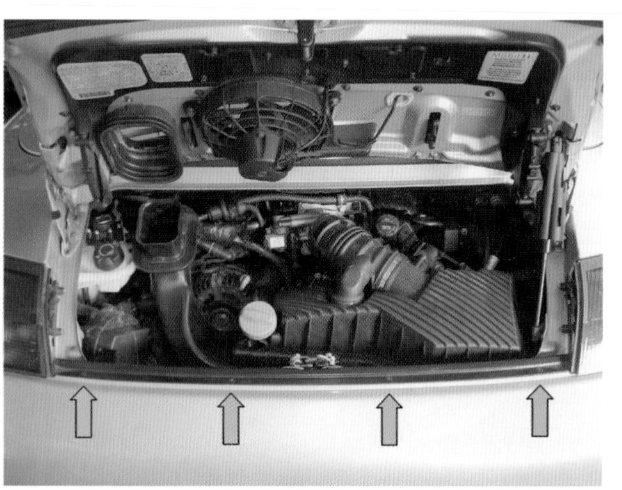

1 Loosen and remove the four screws that hold the bumper threshold strip in place. Remove the strip and set it aside.

2 Remove the screws along the bottom edge of the bumper cover as shown here (green arrows) and also on each side of the bumper cover.

or Liquid Wrench but not WD-40. WD-40 is not actually a lubricant, and it won't work to free up rusted or corroded exhaust fasteners as effectively as a dedicated penetrant oil. The oil will soak into each joint and make things much easier. It's even a good idea to let the oil soak in for a day or two beforehand.

Additionally, if you have access to an acetylene torch, freeing up stuck exhaust bolts becomes incredibly easy. Simply heat each fastener until it glows cherry red and pop it loose with a wrench. Obviously, if you choose to use this method, use extreme caution as you can very easily burn though many things that do not react well to fire. Sometimes a small propane torch can assist too, but I've often found that propane burns too coolly to make too much of a difference when it comes to removing fasteners.

Remove the exhaust tips on each muffler if you plan on transferring them to the new mufflers. They are held on with a compression clamp. Loosen the bolt and remove the clamp along with the tip. You'll also need to remove the mounting bracket on the back of each muffler and transfer it to the new muffler. These brackets are held on with two long 13mm nuts and bolts. Remove the bolts and pry the bracket out of the mounting tabs on the back of the muffler. Don't forget the small mesh gaskets in the ears of each bracket-transfer these over to the new mufflers. Installation of the new mufflers is the opposite of removal.

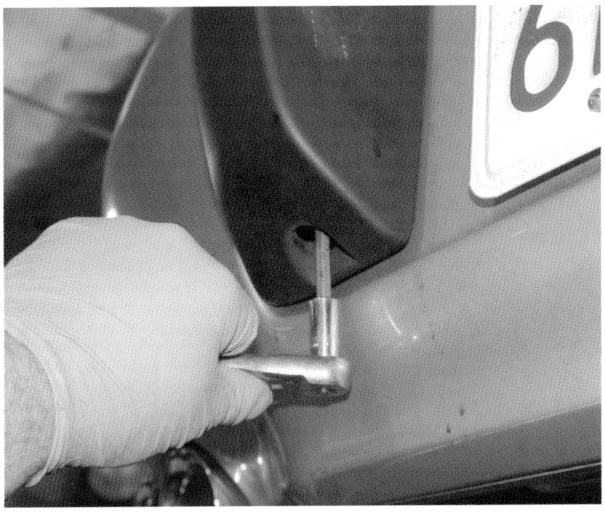

3 Look underneath each black plastic bumperette. You'll see a small access hole with a 6mm hex bolt inside. Loosen the 6mm bolt, and you will be able to swing the bumperette up and off the bumper from the bottom.

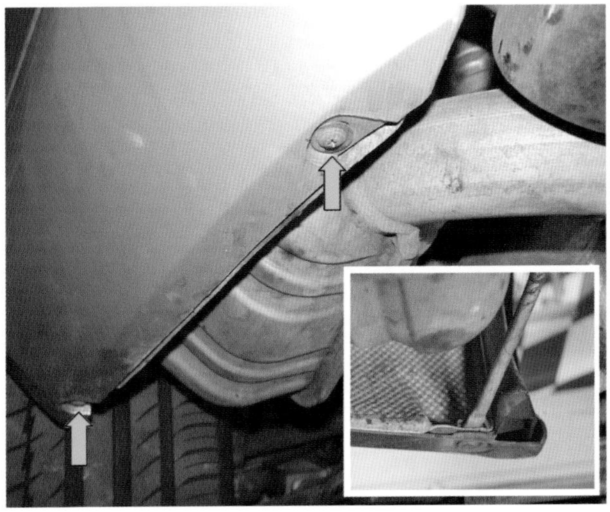

4 Remove the two Phillips head screws along the bottom edge on both sides of the bumper cover (green arrows). On the 997s there is an additional body support piece attached to the leading edge screw (inset, lower right), you will need to remove this as well. At this point, you can give the bumper cover a good tug toward the back of the car and it should slide off.

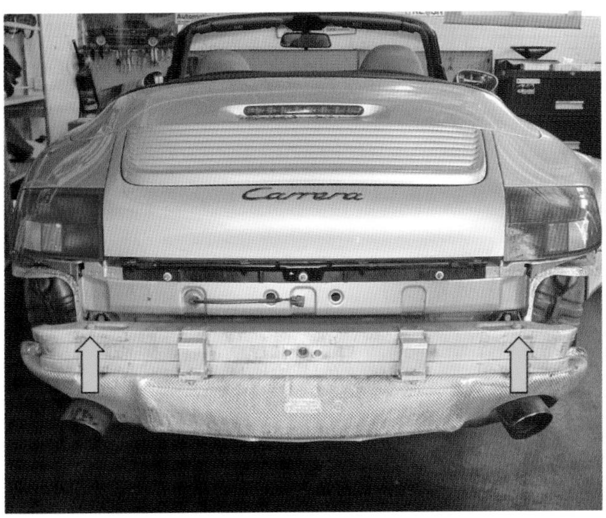

5 Once the bumper cover is removed, you'll need to remove the bumper itself. Loosen and remove the two 19mm bolts shown here (green arrows). Then remove the bumper with the heat shield attached.

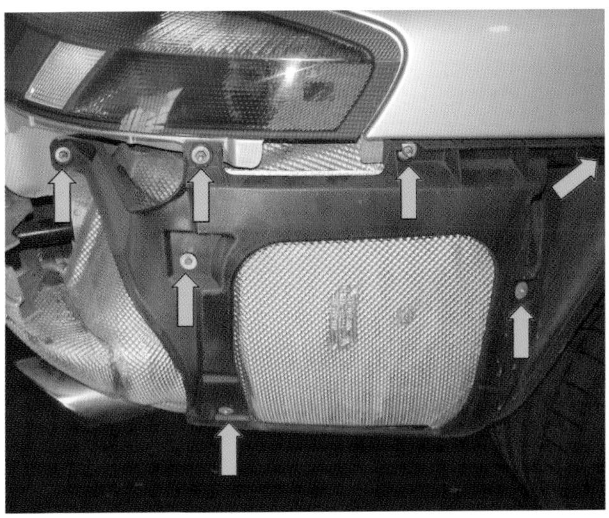

6 Remove the 10mm nuts holding each exhaust shield over the mufflers on each side of the car and take the exhaust shields off.

7 Shown here is the left-side muffler attached to the car with the heat shields removed. Loosen the clamp shown here to allow the exhaust tip to be removed from the muffler (green arrow).

8 Loosen the 17mm nuts on each exhaust clamp holding the muffler to the catalytic converter. Once loose, pull the clamp inboard enough to allow the pipe from the muffler to pull out easily once the muffler is unbolted.

9 Here is the bracket that attaches the muffler to the side of the car. Note the three holes (green arrows). Three studs on the back of the other muffler bracket pass through the holes and are secured with three 13mm nuts. It is possible to remove these three nuts with a ratcheting wrench, although getting a photo of them in place is nearly impossible. I also advise you to have a helper hold the muffler as you remove the nuts. These mufflers are heavy. You don't want it dropping in your lap just as you remove the last nut.

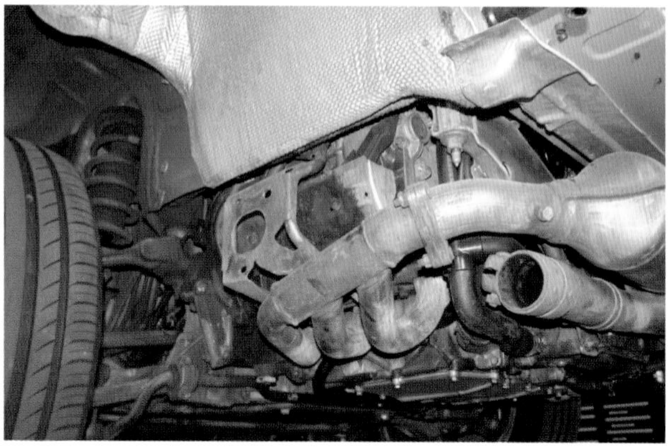

10 Here is the left side of the car with the muffler completely removed.

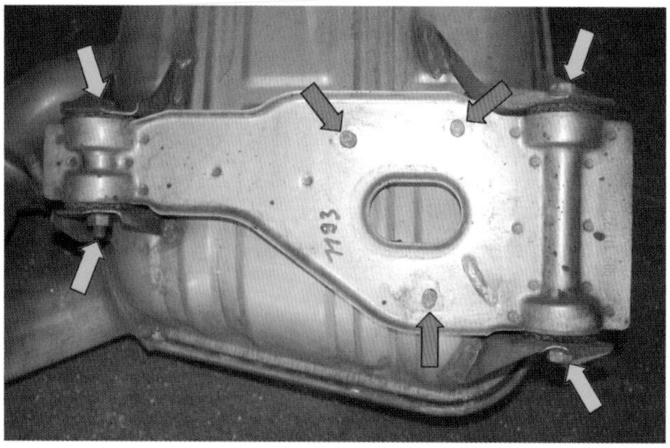

11 Shown here is the bracket that attaches directly to the muffler. You'll need to remove this from the old muffler and transfer it to the new muffler. Loosen the 13mm nuts while counter-holding the long 13mm bolts (green arrows) to remove them. Also note the three studs that attach the muffler assembly to the side of the car (red arrows).

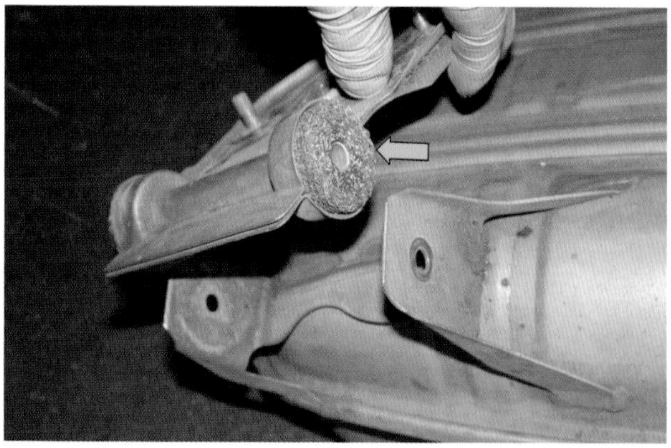

12 Don't forget the small mesh gaskets that sit in the cups of the muffler brackets when transferring them to the new mufflers.

PROJECT 48

Installing a High Performance Exhaust System/Catalytic Converter Replacement

Time / Tab / Talent: 8 hours / $4000 /

Tip: If your CATs are toast, replace your entire system with a sport exhaust system

Tools: All of them

Performance Gain: 20–30HP depending on exhaust design and other factors

Applicable Years: All

Tinware: Exhaust

Comp Modification: Replace oxygen sensors

More Info: http://www.101projects.com/Carrera/48.htm

Replacing the exhaust system on any car is a good way to make a little more horsepower and also enhance the sound of the engine. This upgrade is done by increasing the diameter of the exhaust tubing and/or smoothing out the angles and bends in the exhaust system. The resulting effect is the reduction of exhaust system back pressure, which most of the time creates more power.

In this chapter, I'll go over the steps involved with replacing the stock exhaust on the 996 with a new unit manufactured by Fabspeed and sold through PelicanParts.com. This setup is manufactured out of stainless steel and is computer-numeric controlled (CNC) mandrel bent for optimum flow and fewer restrictions than the Porsche factory exhaust. They feature 50mm header pipes that connect to a dual muffler system The Fabspeed exhaust system is low profile and weighs 30 pounds less than the Porsche factory system. While the 997s have a different style of fasteners for the exhaust—and use Torx screws in place of Phillips—the basic geometry of the exhaust is the same as well as the procedures for removal and replacement.

NOTE: It is very common for the nuts and bolts on older cars to rust and make exhaust components very difficult to remove. This very well may be the case with your exhaust. If so, then you might need to grind off the nuts and/or heads of the bolts to get the headers off of the car. It's not an easy job, and it is complicated by the lack of room underneath the car. If you have extreme difficulty, then take the car to your local mechanic. The header bolts are very prone to breaking and if they are highly rusted, they should be heated up red-hot with an oxy-acetylene torch to assist in their removal.

On our project 996, we had a couple bolts break off as we tried to remove them. At first, we attempted to remove the reminder of the bolt with an easy-out stud removal tool but found that just would not remove the remainder of threads left in the cylinder head. Our only option was to drill the remainder out and install a Heli-Coil in place.

1 Here is a picture of a complete exhaust system. You can tell this exhaust is from a 997 as it has the newer style joiners as well as the rear fender support bracket, but the layout is exactly the same as the 996. For demonstration purposes, follow the path of the exhaust from the left side of the engine. The exhaust leaves the engine via the headers (yellow arrow), enters the catalytic converter (blue arrow), travels to the muffler on the right side of the car (green arrow), and exits the tail pipe on the right side (red arrow). The lower bumper fasteners are shown by the purple arrows.

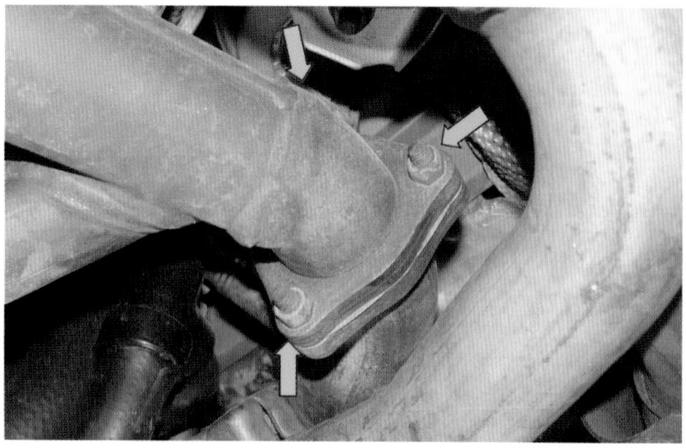

2 Follow along with Project 47 on the removal of your mufflers. In addition to the removal of the mufflers, you need to disconnect the catalytic converters. Remove the three 13mm bolts (green arrows) that mate the exhaust headers to the catalytic converter pipes on each side of the car. You'll need to use a 13mm wrench to hold the nuts as you remove the bolts.

3 Crawl underneath the car to remove the six 13mm bolts on each side of the engine. It's a good idea to soak these bolts in penetrating oil for a few days before trying to loosen them as they have a tendency to snap off.

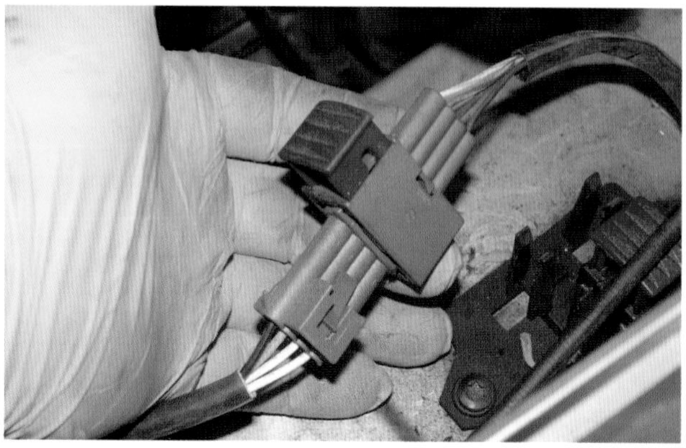

4 Pull up on the red tabs to separate the connectors going to each of the four oxygen sensors on the rear engine shelf. The black connectors attach to the oxygen sensors before the catalytic converters. The gray connectors go to the oxygen sensors after the catalytic converters. If you plan on reusing your oxygen sensors, remove them from the exhaust at this point.

5 Refer to Project 47, Photos 8–12 for the procedure for removing the mufflers. After the mufflers are off, loosen the 19mm clamp that holds each catalytic converter to the car (green arrow). You'll probably have to pry the clamp open slightly to get it over the lip of the mounting plate (purple arrow). At this point, lower the catalytic converters off the car.

6 Remove the muffler brackets, following the procedures documented in Photos 11 and 12 of Project 47. Place the mounting plates in the new mufflers as shown here. In our case, we had pry the ears of the new muffler slightly open in order to fit them.

7 Crawl under the car and fit the new headers up in place. It can be a little tricky to fit the bolts through the holes in the header, through the new gasket, and up to the cylinder head. You may need a helper to hold it in place while you thread the bolts in. At this point, we want to just snug up the bolts. You want the header to be able to move just a little bit so that we can get everything to line up. It's been my experience that no exhaust system ever lines up perfectly.

8 Take the new catalytic converter assembly and thread in the oxygen sensors, making note of which one goes where. There will be a small hex head plug in each sensor port. Remove these plugs and tighten in the sensors snugly. Mount the new catalytic converter on the engine mounting plate and use the supplied clamps to secure it to the plate. You'll probably have to pry the clamps open somewhat to clear the lip on the plate.

9 Now crawl under the car again and tighten down the header bolts fully to 19 ft-lbs. It's a good idea to use new bolts here with just a slight dab of anti-seize compound to prevent them from seizing up in the future. As you tighten, keep an eye on the header-to-cat flanges. Snug the bolts down as you tighten the header bolts to keep everything in line. Once all of the header bolts are torqued, fully snug down the header-to-cat flanges and tighten them to 22 ft-lbs of torque. Route the wiring for the oxygen sensors up through the engine compartment and plug them back into the connectors on the engine shelf. Bolt the header flanges to the catalytic converters using the supplied copper hardware. Tighten these bolts to 22 ft-lbs of torque.

10 Now fit the old exhaust clamps to the ends of the catalytic converter (green arrow). Slide the end of the new muffler into the clamp along with the studs of the mounting plate into the bracket on the engine. Tighten the exhaust clamps down and refit the three 13mm nuts on the back of the muffler bracket.

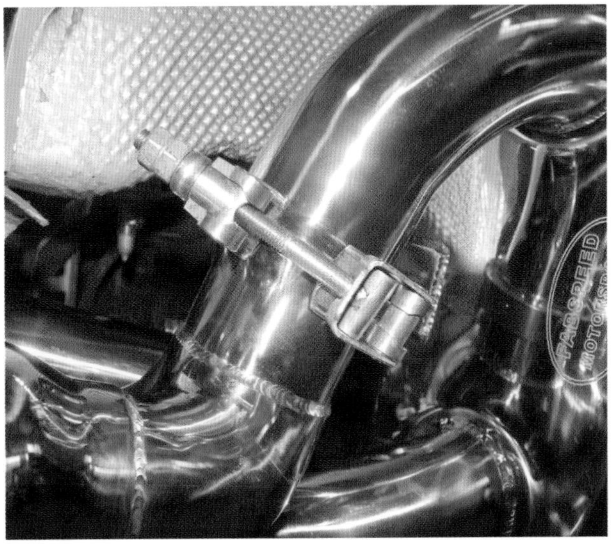

11 Here's where it gets a little tricky. It will be easier to tighten the 11mm nuts on the clamps with the bumper cover removed from the car, however with the bumper cover installed, you have very little room to get a wrench inside. I would recommend marking both the exhaust tip and also the muffler outlet with a permanent marker or use painter's tape to give you a reference line. Put the bumper cover back on, align the tip then mark the position where you want it to sit. Then remove the cover and tighten up the exhaust clamp.

12 Here's a shot of the new catalytic converter assembly with the bumper cover refitted. Be aware of one fact: the new muffler system puts out a lot of heat that will slightly deform the edges of the rear bumper cover.

SECTION 7
BRAKES

Your brakes are probably the most important system on your Porsche. No matter how fast you go, you will always need to stop—and sometimes rather quickly. It's of paramount importance to keep your brakes in top condition. The stock Carrera braking system is a very capable setup if properly maintained. The projects in this section detail the troubleshooting, restoration, upgrades, and maintenance of your all-important brake system.

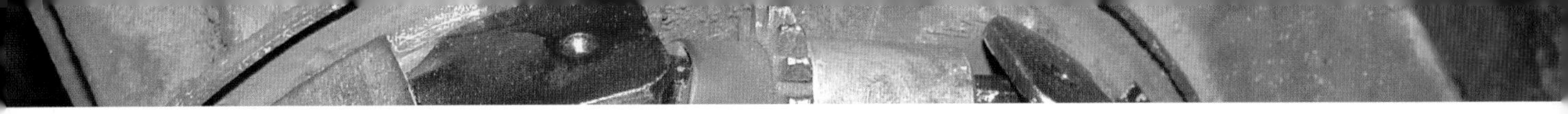

PROJECT 49
Bleeding Brakes

Time / Tab / Talent: 2 hours / $20 /

Tools: Power Bleeder, 11mm wrench, floor jack, jack stands

Applicable Years: All

Tinware: 3-plus quarts of brake fluid

More Info: http://www.101projects.com/Carrera/49.htm

Tip: Use different-colored brake fluid so you know when your system is flushed

Performance Gain: Quicker, firmer stopping

Comp Modification: Rebuild the brake calipers

Bleeding brakes is not one of my personal favorite jobs. There seems to be a bit of black magic involved with the bleeding process. Sometimes it will work perfectly, and then other times it seems like you end up with a lot of air in your system. The best strategy to follow when bleeding brakes is to repeat the procedure several times in order to make sure that you have removed all the trapped air from the system.

The basic 911 Carrera brake system with anti-lock brakes (ABS) 5.3 and 5.7 without Porche Stability Management (PSM) can be bled using traditional methods. For cars with traction control or PSM, you need to use the Porsche System Tester 2 (PST2) in order to activate the valves in the hydraulic unit during the bleeding process. If your car has a PSM off switch on the dashboard, then you should go to a shop that has a PST2 so that the brake system can be bled completely and properly.

There are currently two popular methods of bleeding the brake system: pressure bleeding and vacuum bleeding. Pressure bleeding uses a reservoir of brake fluid that has a positive air pressure force placed on the opposite side of the fluid, which forces it into the brake system. Vacuum bleeding is where you fill the reservoir and then apply a vacuum at the bleeder nipple to pull fluid through the system.

The method that I've come up with combines the first method described above and yet a third finishing method. Basically, I advocate bleeding the system with the pressure bleeder and then using a family member to stomp on the pedal to free up any trapped air in the system. If the family member really owes you big-time, you will be the one stomping on the pedal and they can spill brake fluid all over themselves.

The first step in bleeding your brakes is to jack up the car and remove all four wheels (see Project 1). The next step is to fill the system with brake fluid. I recommend using colored brake fluid, such as ATE SuperBlue, in order to determine when fresh fluid has been flushed through the entire system (although lately it has been difficult to find due to changing US regulations). One of my favorite tools for pressure bleeding is the Motive Products Bleeder. The system has a hand pump that you can use to pressurize the brake fluid to just about any pressure. A small gauge on the front of the brake fluid reservoir indicates the pressure of the brake fluid inside. The very large reservoir can hold about two quarts of brake fluid—more than enough for most brake flushing and bleeding jobs. Retailing for about $50 online from PelicanParts.com, the bleeder kit is a very useful and cost-effective tool to have in your collection.

The system bleeds by pressurizing a bottle filled with brake fluid from air from an internal hand pump. The procedure is to add fluid, attach the bleeder to the top of the reservoir cap, and pump up the bleeder bottle to about 25 psi using the hand pump. This will pressurize the system. Check to make sure that there are no leaks around the bleeder or where it attaches to the top of the master cylinder reservoir.

Now start bleeding the system. Start with the right rear caliper, the one that's located the farthest away from the master cylinder. Bleed the right rear caliper by attaching a hose to the bleed nipple, placing it in a jar, and then opening the valve by turning the bleeder nipple counterclockwise with an 11mm wrench. Let the fluid flow out until there are no more bubbles. If you don't have a pressure bleeder system, you need to find someone to press on the pedal repeatedly to force fluid through the system. Another solution is to get a check valve and place it on the nipple while you stomp on the pedal (see Photo 3). This will work for getting fluid into the system, but you will still need a second person for the final step to make sure you have bled the system completely. The Carrera calipers have two bleed nipples—bleed the outer ones first.

When no more air bubbles come out, then move to the next caliper. Bleed them in this order: right rear caliper, left rear caliper, right front caliper, left front caliper. Bleeding in this order will minimize the amount of air that gets into the system.

Repeat the process until you can no longer see any air bubbles coming out of any of the calipers. Make sure that you don't run out of brake fluid in your reservoir or you will have to start over again. It is wise to start out with about a ½ gallon of brake fluid in the pressure bleeder and another ½ gallon on the shelf in reserve. Depending upon your car, and the mistakes you may make, I recommend having an ample supply. Also, only use new brake fluid from a sealed can. Brake fluid is hydroscopic, meaning that it attracts water and water vapor, which diminishes its performance. Brake fluid containers left exposed to air will have the fluid inside compromised after a short period of time.

If you had to replace the master cylinder, or if the system needs a large amount of fluid, then supplement the bleeding process by opening up the right rear nipple and then pressing down on the brake pedal two or three times. Slowly release the pedal. Repeat for the other three corners of the car.

During the bleeding process, it's very easy to forget to check your master cylinder reservoir. As you are removing fluid from the calipers, it will be emptying the master cylinder reservoir. If the reservoir goes empty, then you will most certainly add some air bubbles in to the system, and you will have to start all over. Keep an eye on the fluid level and don't forget to refill it. Make sure that you always put the cap back on the reservoir. If the cap is off, then brake fluid may splash out and damage your paint when the brake pedal is released. If you are using a pressure bleeder system, make sure that you often check the level of brake fluid in the bleeder reservoir so that it doesn't accidentally run dry.

If you are installing a new master cylinder, it's probably a wise idea to perform what is called a dry bleed on the workbench. This is simply the process of getting the master cylinder full of brake fluid and "wet." Simply add some brake fluid to both chambers of the master cylinder and pump it a few times. This will save you a few moments when bleeding the brakes.

Now, make sure that all the bleeder valves are closed tightly. Disconnect the pressure system from the reservoir. Now, get your family member to press down repeatedly on the brake pedal at least five times, and then hold it down. Then open the bleeder valve on the right rear caliper. The system should lose pressure, and the pedal should sink to the floor. When the fluid stops coming out of the bleeder valve,

1 Here are few little tricks that you can use when changing your brake fluid. The company ATE makes a brake fluid called SuperBlue that comes in two different colors. It's a smart idea to fill your reservoir (green arrow) with a different-colored fluid and then bleed the brakes. When the new-colored fluid exits out of the caliper, you will know that you have fresh fluid in your system. Make sure that you use stock DOT 4-brake fluid in your car. The use of silicone DOT 5 fluid is not recommended for street use, and never mix DOT 4 and DOT 5 fluid together or severe component corrosion can occur. Shown here is the Motive Products Power Bleeder. Available for about $70 from PelicanParts.com, it is a huge timesaver when it comes to bleeding your brakes.

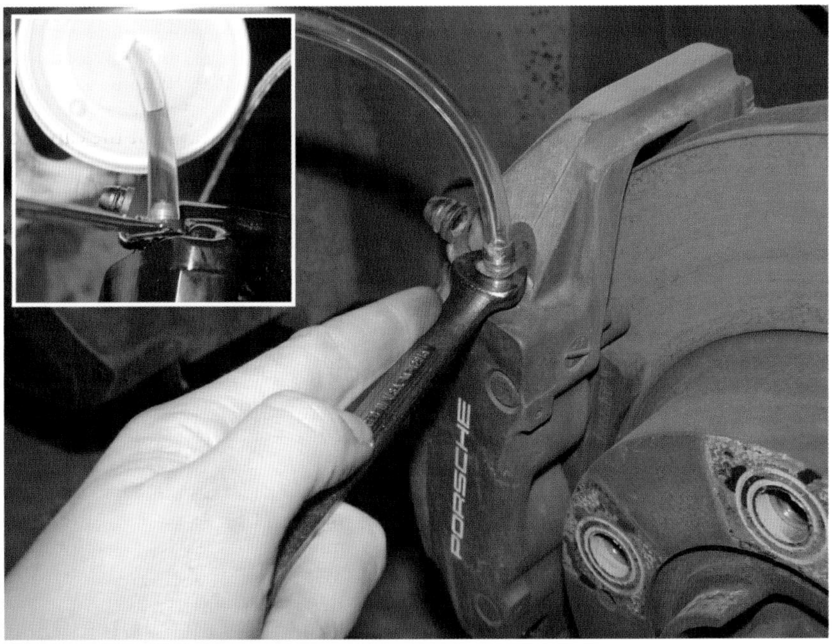

2 Open the bleed nipple by loosening it in the caliper by about a quarter of a turn. If you can fit a flare-nut wrench over the bleed nipple, then I recommend using one to help avoid rounding out the nipple. Let the brake fluid run out of the caliper until no more bubbles appear (inset). You should also routinely flush and replace your brake fluid every two years. Deposits and debris can build up in the lines over time and decrease the efficiency of your brakes. Regular bleeding of your system can also help you spot brake problems that you wouldn't necessarily notice simply by driving the car. Also, never reuse brake fluid—always use new, fresh fluid. In addition, don't use brake fluid that has come from an empty can that has been sitting on the shelf or sitting in your Power Bleeder for a while. The brake fluid has a tendency to absorb moisture when sitting on the shelf. This moisture "boils" out of the brake fluid when you start using the brakes and can result in a spongy pedal.

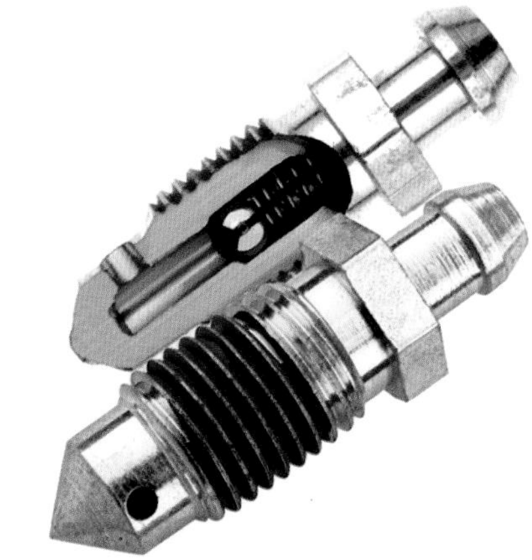

3 There is a relatively new product out called Speed Bleeders. These small caps replace the standard bleeder valves located on your calipers. The Speed Bleeder has a built-in check valve that eliminates the need for a second person when pedal bleeding the brakes. Simply open the bleeder valve for a particular caliper and step on the brake pedal. The Speed Bleeder will allow brake fluid to cleanly bleed out of the system without sucking air back in. When used in conjunction with a pressure bleeder system, you can achieve a pretty firm pedal bleeding the brakes by yourself. I still recommend using the two-person pedal-stepping method as a final procedure, simply because the high pressure from this method can help unclog trapped air bubbles.

close the valve and then tell your family member to let his or her foot off of the pedal. Do not let your helper take his or her foot off until you have completely closed the valve. Repeat this motion for each bleeder valve on each caliper at least three times. Repeat this entire procedure for all the valves in the same order as described previously.

I recommend that you use this procedure as a final step, even if you are vacuum or pressure bleeding. The high force associated with the pressure from the brake pedal can help free air and debris in the lines. If the brake fluid doesn't exit the nipple quickly, then you might have a clog in your lines. Brake fluid that simply oozes out of the lines slowly is a clear indication that rubber lines might be clogged and constricted. Don't ignore these warning signs—check out the brake lines while you are working in this area (see Project 55).

Now, let the car sit for about 10 minutes. Repeat the bleeding process at each corner. The pedal should now feel pretty stiff. If the pedal still feels spongy, make sure that you have the proper adjustment on your rear calipers or drum shoes. Also, you may need a new master cylinder, have a leaky caliper, or have old spongy flexible brake lines.

For cars with the standard ABS 5.3, the bleeding method detailed here works very well. If you find that your ABS-equipped car feels spongy on the brake pedal, take the car to a deserted parking lot and engage the ABS system by stopping short a few times. Then go back and re-bleed the system—it should take care of the spongy pedal.

Another important thing to remember is that brake fluid kills—paint jobs, that is. Brake fluid spilled on paint will permanently mar the surface, so be very careful not to touch the car if you have it on your hands and clothing. This, of course, is easier said than done—don't bleed the system in a tight garage. The probability of spilling on yourself and then leaning against your car is too great. Rubber gloves help protect your hands from the paint. If you do get a spot on your paint, make sure that you blot it with a paper towel—don't wipe or smear it. It's also important not to try to clean it off with any chemical or other cleaning solutions.

PROJECT 50
Replacing Brake Pads

Time / Tab / Talent: 2 hours / $150 /

Tools: Screwdriver, isopropyl alcohol, wooden block

Applicable Years: All

Tinware: Brake pads

More Info: http://www.101projects.com/Carrera/50.htm

Tip: Check your brake discs when replacing your pads in case they have worn too thin

Performance Gain: Better braking

Comp Modification: Caliper rebuild, brake disc replacement, install stainless steel brake lines

Replacing brake pads is one of the easiest jobs to perform on your 911. In general, you should inspect your brake pads about every 10,000 miles and replace them if the material lining of the pad is worn down enough to trigger the pad replacement sensor. In reality, most people don't inspect the pads very often and usually wait until they see the little brake-warning lamp appear on the dashboard. It's a wise idea to replace the pads and inspect the discs as soon as you see that warning lamp go on.

If you ignore the warning lamp, you may indeed get to the point of metal-on-metal contact, where the metal backing of the pads may be contacting the brake discs. Using the brakes during this condition will not only give you inadequate braking, but it will also begin to wear grooves in your brake discs. Once the discs are grooved, they are damaged and there is often no way to repair them. Resurfacing will sometimes work, but often the groove that is cut will be deeper than is allowed by the Porsche specifications. The smart thing to do is to replace your pads right away.

Brake pads should only be replaced in pairs: replace both front pads or both rear pads at a time. The same rule applies to the brake discs that should be checked each time you replace your brake pads.

The procedure for replacing pads on all the wheels is basically the same. There are slight configuration differences between front and rear brakes, but in general the procedure for replacement is similar. The first step is to jack up the car and remove the road wheel (slightly loosen the lug nuts before you lift the car off of the ground). This will expose the brake caliper that presses the pads against the disc. Make sure that the parking brake is off when you start to work on the pads.

Begin by using a pair of needle-nose pliers to remove the brake pad sensor (see Photo 1). The pads are held within the caliper by two retaining pins. There are also small retaining clips that hold these two retaining pins in the caliper. Start by removing the small retaining clips and then tap out the retaining pins using a small screwdriver and a hammer (see Photo 2). When the two retaining pins are removed, the cross spring that holds the pads in place will fall out. Now the pads can be pried out with a screwdriver (Photo 3). Use the small holes on the pads that normally surround the retaining pin as a leverage point for removing them. They may require some wiggling to remove, as it is sometimes a tight fit. It is important to keep in mind that the caliper piston is also probably pressing against the pads slightly and will add to the difficulty in removing them.

Once you have the pads removed, inspect the inside of the caliper. You should clean this area with some compressed air and isopropyl alcohol. Make sure that the dust boots and the clamping rings inside the caliper are not ripped or damaged. If they are, then the caliper may need to be rebuilt (see Project 51).

At this point, you should inspect the brake discs carefully. Using a micrometer, take a measurement of the disc thickness. If the disc is worn beyond its specifications, then it's time to replace it along with the one on the other side. See Project 56 for more information.

The installation of the new brake pads is quite easy. You will need to take a small piece of wood or plastic and push the caliper piston back into the caliper. This is because the new pads are going to be quite a bit thicker than the old ones, and the piston is set in the old pad's position. Pry back the piston using the wood, being careful not to use too much force (see Photo 4). Using a screwdriver here is not recommended as it can accidentally damage the dust boots and seals inside the caliper. Make sure that you push both pistons (inside and outside) back in the caliper.

Be aware that as you push back the pistons in the calipers, you will cause the level of the brake reservoir to rise. Make sure that you don't have too much fluid in your reservoir. If the level is high, you may have to siphon out a bit from the reservoir to prevent it from overflowing. Also make sure that you have the cap securely fastened to the top of reservoir. Failure to do this may result in brake fluid accidentally getting on your paint.

When the piston is pushed all the way back, you should then be able to insert the pad into the caliper. If you encounter resistance, double-check to make sure that the inside of the caliper is clean. You can use a small hammer to tap it in, but don't use too much force. When the pads are in place, insert the retaining pins and spring clip back into place. It's wise to use a new set of pins and clips when replacing your pads. Make sure that you replace the pin retaining clips inside the small holes in the retaining pins.

In general, I recommend removing and replacing the brake pads one side at a time. When the piston is pushed back into the caliper, it will try to push out the piston on the opposite side of the caliper. Leaving the brake pad installed on one side keeps the piston from being pushed out too far.

You also may want to spray the back of the brake pads with some anti-squeal glue. This glue basically keeps the pads and the pistons glued together and prevents noisy vibration. Some brands of pads may come with anti-squeal pads already attached to the rear surface. Anti-squeal pads can also be purchased separately as sheets that are peeled off and stuck on the rear of the pads.

When you are finished with both sides, press on the brake pedal repeatedly to make sure that the pads and the pistons seat properly. Also make sure that you top off the master cylinder brake fluid reservoir, if necessary. Brake pads typically take between 100 and 200 miles to completely break in. It's typical for braking performance to suffer slightly as the pads begin their wear-in period. Make sure that you avoid any heavy braking during this period.

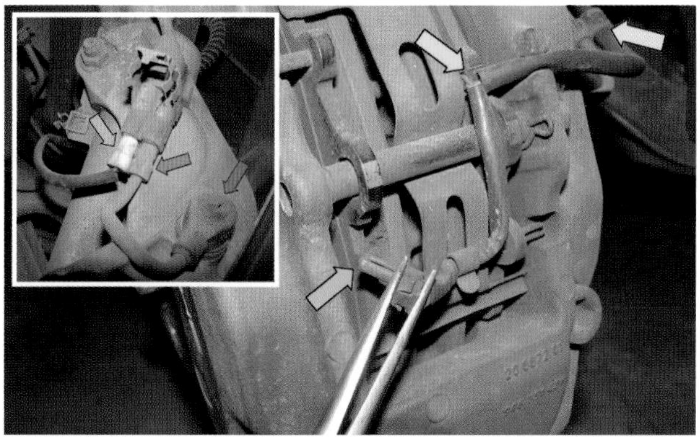

1 Grab the brake pad sensor (yellow and green arrow) with a pair of needle-nose pliers. If your brake sensors activated the lamp on your dashboard, they should be replaced with new ones. Disconnect the sensor, and plug in the new one—the plug for the sensor is located in the top of the wheelwell (orange arrow). This photo also shows the wheel speed sensor and plug (red arrow and purple arrow), which are used with the anti-lock braking system (ABS)

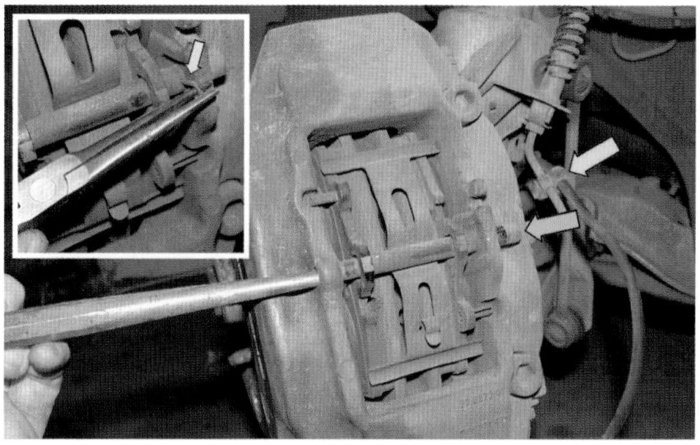

2 To remove the old pads, pull out the small pin retainers (blue arrow, inset), and tap out the retaining pins (green arrow) with a screwdriver and a small hammer. They should slide out pretty easily, as there is usually no load on them. If there is much difficulty encountered during the removal process, then tap on the pads slightly to remove pressure from the pins. The yellow arrow points to the electrical cable clip for the brake pad sensor.

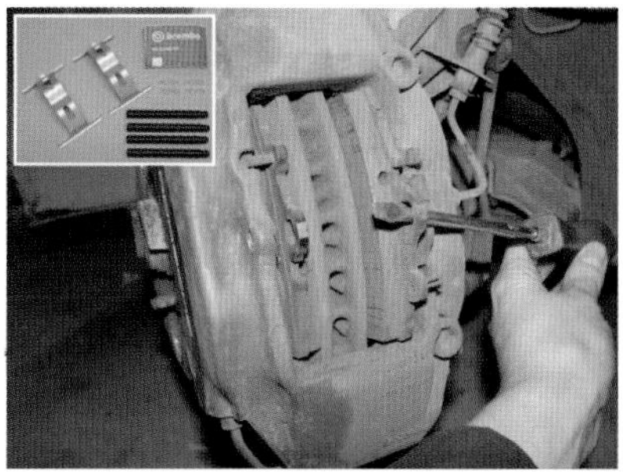

3 Pulling out the pads usually involves the use of a screwdriver for leverage. The pads are loose in the caliper, but it's a pretty tight fit, and there is usually lots of dust and debris in the caliper. Wiggle the pads back and forth in order to pry them free. Although these parts usually can be reused, some people prefer to install new retainer kits. The kits include two new retainer springs, four pin clips, and four pins that are used to hold the pads into the caliper.

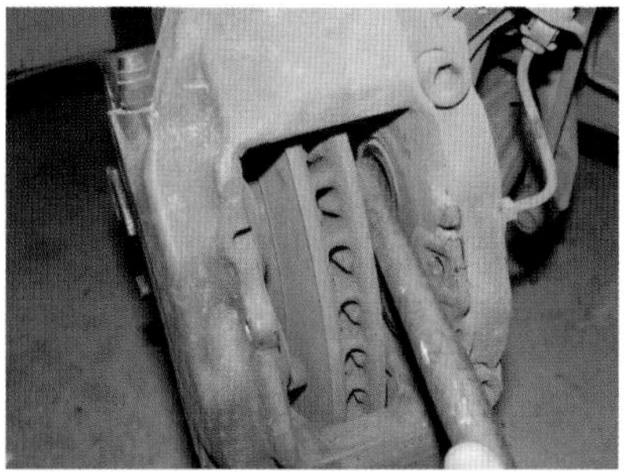

4 When you are ready to install the pads back into the caliper, use a wooden or plastic handle to push back the caliper pistons. Don't use a screwdriver, as you might damage some of the piston seals. Keep your eye on the fluid level in the master cylinder reservoir; it can overflow when you push back on the pistons.

5 Don't forget to reinstall the small retaining clips for the pad retaining pins. The completed assembly should be carefully tested before you do any performance driving. Brake pads can also take several hundred miles to fully break themselves in. Exercise care when driving with brand new brake pads.

PROJECT 51
Rebuilding Brake Calipers

Time / Tab / Talent: 6 hours / $60 /

Tools: Flared-end wrench to remove brake lines

Applicable Years: All

Tinware: Brake caliper rebuild kits, brake fluid, silicone assembly lube

Tip: Soak the caliper in parts cleaner overnight, if possible

Performance Gain: Better braking—no more sticking calipers

Comp Modification: Replace the flexible brake lines; replace brake pads and discs

More Info: http://www.101projects.com/Carrera/51.htm

If your car is pulling to one side when braking, then there is a good chance that you might have a sticky caliper that needs to be rebuilt. The rebuilding process is actually a lot simpler than most people think. It basically involves removing the caliper, cleaning it, and then reinstalling all of the components with new seals. Very often, the most difficult part of the task is the process of actually removing the caliper from the car.

The first step is to jack up the car (see Project 1) and remove the caliper. Refer to Project 56 for details on removing the caliper from around the brake disc. Refer to Project 55 for more details on disconnecting the brake line from the caliper.

Once you have the caliper free and clear from the car, take the piece over to your workbench and begin the disassembly process.

The first step is to remove each of the four pistons from the calipers. One method of removal is to use compressed air to blow out the piston. Using a small screwdriver, remove the dust boot that surrounds the piston. Place a small block of wood in the center of the caliper to prevent the pistons from flying out of the caliper. Blow compressed air through the caliper bleeder hole to force the piston out of its chamber. Start slowly and gradually increase pressure until the piston reaches the block of wood. Make sure that the piston doesn't come all the way out of its chamber. After the piston is far enough out, you should be able to get a grip on it with your fingers. Be careful when working with the compressed air, as it is more powerful than it appears and can make the pistons suddenly fly out of the caliper unexpectedly.

Using a rag to protect the sides of each piston, carefully remove all of them from the caliper using either your hands or a large pair of vise grips. Make sure that you don't touch the sides of the pistons with any metal tools, as you don't want to scratch this surface.

If the piston is frozen, then more radical methods of removal may be necessary. Using a block of wood, you can try pounding the half of the caliper on the block of wood until the piston begins to fall out. If the piston starts to come out and then gets stuck, push it back in all the way and try again. Eventually, the piston should come out of the caliper half. Another method is to use the car's brake system to release the pistons. Reconnect the caliper to the car and have an assistant pump the brakes to force out the piston.

Once the pistons have been removed from the caliper, carefully clean both the inside and outside of the caliper using brake cleaner or another appropriate solvent. All of the passages should be blown out with compressed air, and it's a good idea to let the whole assembly sit in some parts cleaner overnight. If the piston or the inside of the caliper is badly corroded or pitted, then the caliper should be replaced. A little bit of surface rust is okay; it should be polished off using a coarse cloth or other coarse material. Make sure that you thoroughly scrub out the entire inside of the caliper and the piston so that they are perfectly clean.

After the caliper and piston have been cleaned and are dry, coat the caliper and piston with silicone assembly lube. If you don't have this silicone assembly lube handy (it's available from PelicanParts.com), then make sure you coat the entire assembly with clean brake fluid. Do not get any lube or brake fluid on the dust boot.

Insert the new piston seal into the inside of the caliper piston groove. It should fit smoothly in the groove yet stick out only slightly. Make sure that you wet the seal with a little brake fluid prior to installation. Now install the dust boot onto the piston, so that the edge of the boot fits into the inside groove of the piston. Then, insert the piston slightly into the caliper. It should slide in easily. Push the piston all the way into the caliper. As the piston reaches

the internal O-ring, you will encounter some resistance. Make sure that the piston doesn't become cocked as you insert it. If you have trouble inserting the piston into the caliper, you may want to softly tap it with a plastic hammer or use a small piece of wood to compress the piston into its home position in the caliper housing. Finally, make sure the outer rim of the seal mates properly with its groove in the caliper housing.

Install the brake pads (Project 50), and remount the caliper onto the car. Bleed the brake system (Project 49), and you should be good to go. Make sure that you carefully check the brakes on the car before you do any significant driving.

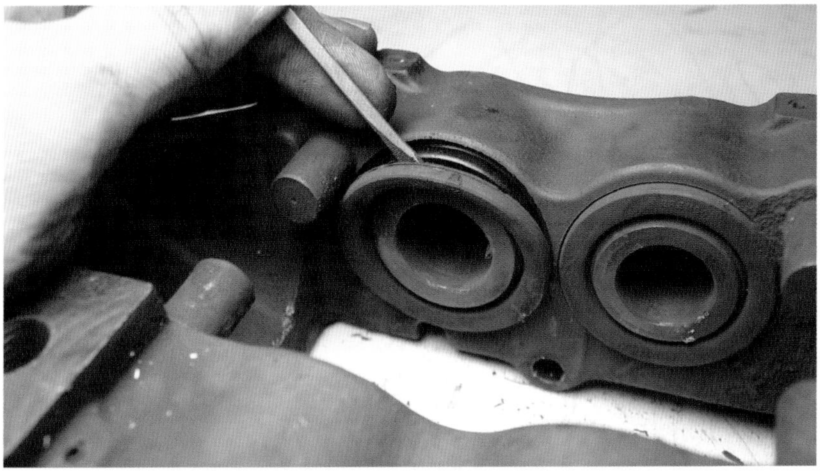

1 Remove the outer seal by simply prying it out of the caliper housing. The new seals are installed in reverse fashion but may require some finesse work to get them properly seated in their grooves.

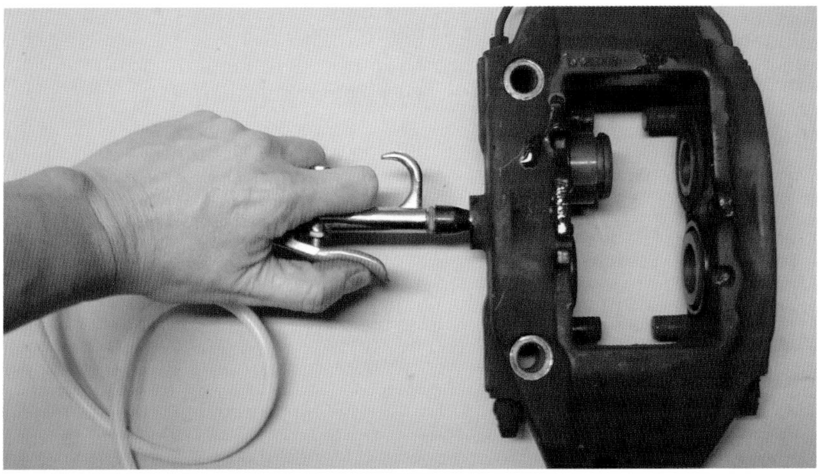

2 The best method I've found for removing the caliper pistons is to use compressed air to blow them out. Beware though: start with low pressure and then increase it if it's not enough. It's easier than you might think to send your pistons flying across the room with 100 psi of air pressure!

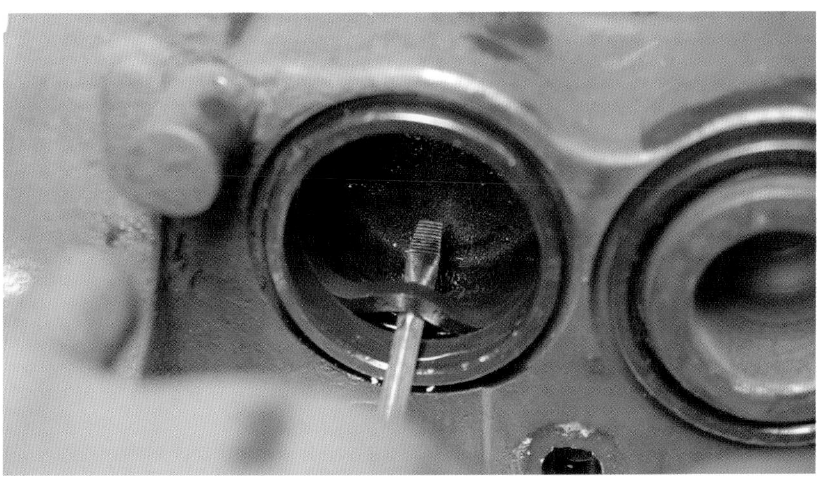

3 Make sure that you replace the inner piston seal. This seal is what keeps brake fluid from leaking out past the cylinder. Also be sure that you clean the entire inner cylinder for dirt, debris, and corrosion. Don't scratch the inside of the caliper cylinder while you are working on it or you may have problems with the caliper leaking when you reassemble it.

PROJECT 52
Parking Brake Adjustment

Time / Tab / Talent: 1 hour / $0 /

Tools: Long screwdriver, 13mm wrench, flashlight

Applicable Years: All

Tinware: NA

More Info: http://www.101projects.com/Carrera/52.htm

Tip: Properly adjusting your parking brake can reduce the amount of drag on your road wheels

Performance Gain: Better parking brake performance

Comp Modification: Replace brake pads or discs

Over the years, the parking brake on your 911 may become unadjusted and fail to perform properly. The adjustment of the brake shoes that control the parking brake is an easy process and shouldn't take you more than an hour to accomplish.

The first step is to raise the rear of the car and remove the two road wheels. This step will allow you access to the rear calipers. Make sure that the parking brake lever is released and the car is in neutral. Using a screwdriver, push back slightly on the brake pads until the brake disc is allowed to turn freely on its spindle. Be careful to check the fluid level in the master cylinder reservoir, as pushing the pads back will make the fluid level rise and may cause it to overflow.

Once the brake disc can be moved easily, move to the cockpit of the car. Underneath the rear cover on the center console, you will see a rubber insert with a plastic panel underneath. Remove the rubber insert and the Torx screw underneath, and pry up the plastic panel. Now loosen the two nuts that attach the handbrake turnbuckle so that the two cables become slack. If there is any tension on these cables, then it will be difficult to adjust the handbrake.

The adjustment of the parking brake shoes is accomplished by turning a small gear or sprocket with a screwdriver. Unfortunately, this sprocket can only be reached through one of the lug nut holes in the brake disc.

Rotate the brake disc until you can see the small adjusting sprocket through the lug nut hole (see Photo 1). You may need a flashlight for this procedure. Reaching in through the hole, use a screwdriver to rotate the cog until the parking brake shoe is tight and the rotor can no longer be rotated. It's probable that the cog assembly got turned around at one point when the shoes were replaced, so you will have to play with the mechanism a little bit to see if you need to turn the cog up or down to tighten. If you are turning the sprocket a lot, and the brake disc isn't tightening up, then you are probably turning it the in the wrong direction. Repeat this procedure for the opposite side of the car. After you have the sprockets adjusted so that the brake shoes just press up against the inside of the disc and you can no longer turn the disc, back them off nine notches, making sure that the disc can spin after the ninth notch.

Now move back to the cockpit of the car, and pull up on the handbrake several times to help seat the cables. Finally, pull up on the handbrake so that the ratchet clicks through two notches. Now, tighten up the cables using the nuts at the bottom of the handbrake lever. Note: This procedure is for the 996 (1998–2005) only; the later-model cars have a self-adjusting system that should be good for the life of the cable. Tighten each of these nuts to the point where there is just a bit of slight resistance on each of the two rear wheels. Now, release the lever and verify that the wheels turn freely. The brake discs should be free to rotate with the handle in the down position but fully locked by the time that the handbrake is pulled up a few notches past the two clicks.

When you are finished, recheck the master cylinder reservoir, and also step on the brake pedal a few times in order to make sure that the pistons have repositioned themselves properly against the brake pads. Also verify that the parking brake lamp on the dashboard illuminates as soon as the handle is pulled up (there's a switch near the base of the handle that triggers this lamp).

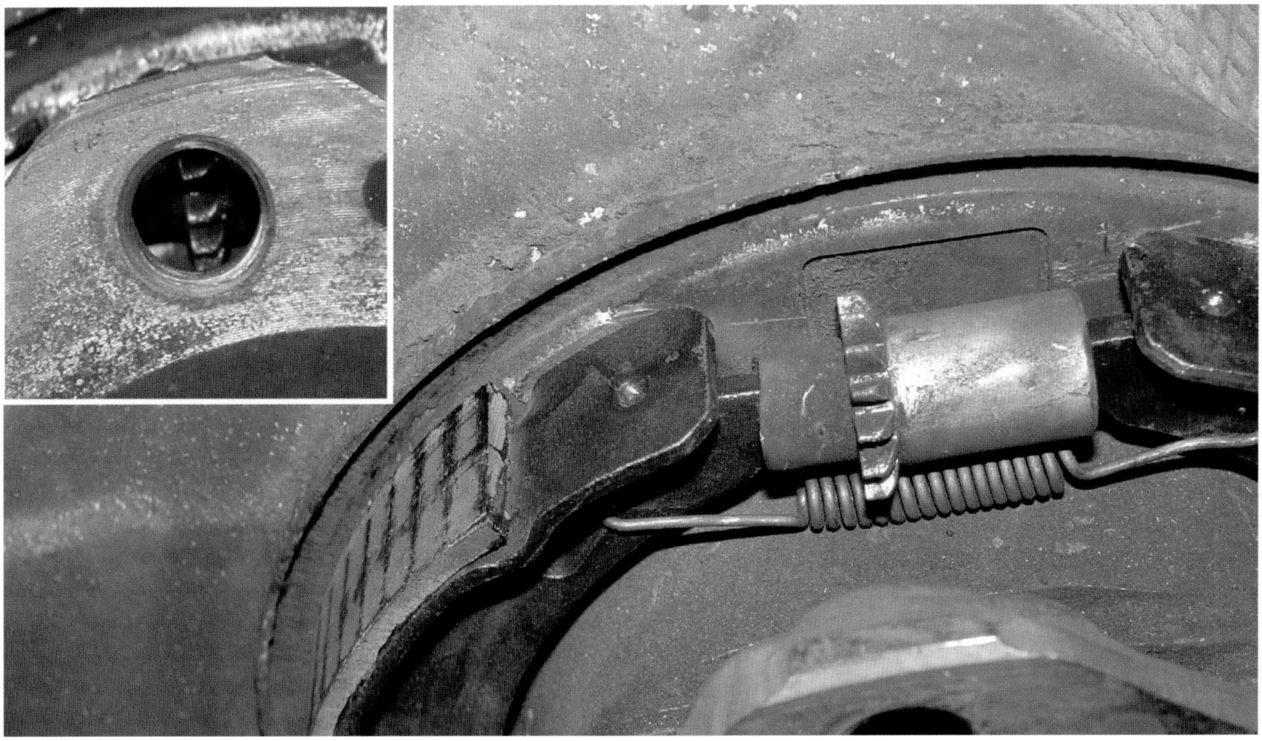

1 Removing the rotor reveals the mechanism for the parking brake adjustment. As the small cog is turned, the parking brake shoes are pushed outward toward the inside of the disc. The proper adjustment of the shoes exists when the shoes are just about to touch the inside of the disc. The photo inset identifies the location of the sprocket when you are trying to look through the access hole in the brake disc. Removal of the brake disc is not necessary for adjustment.

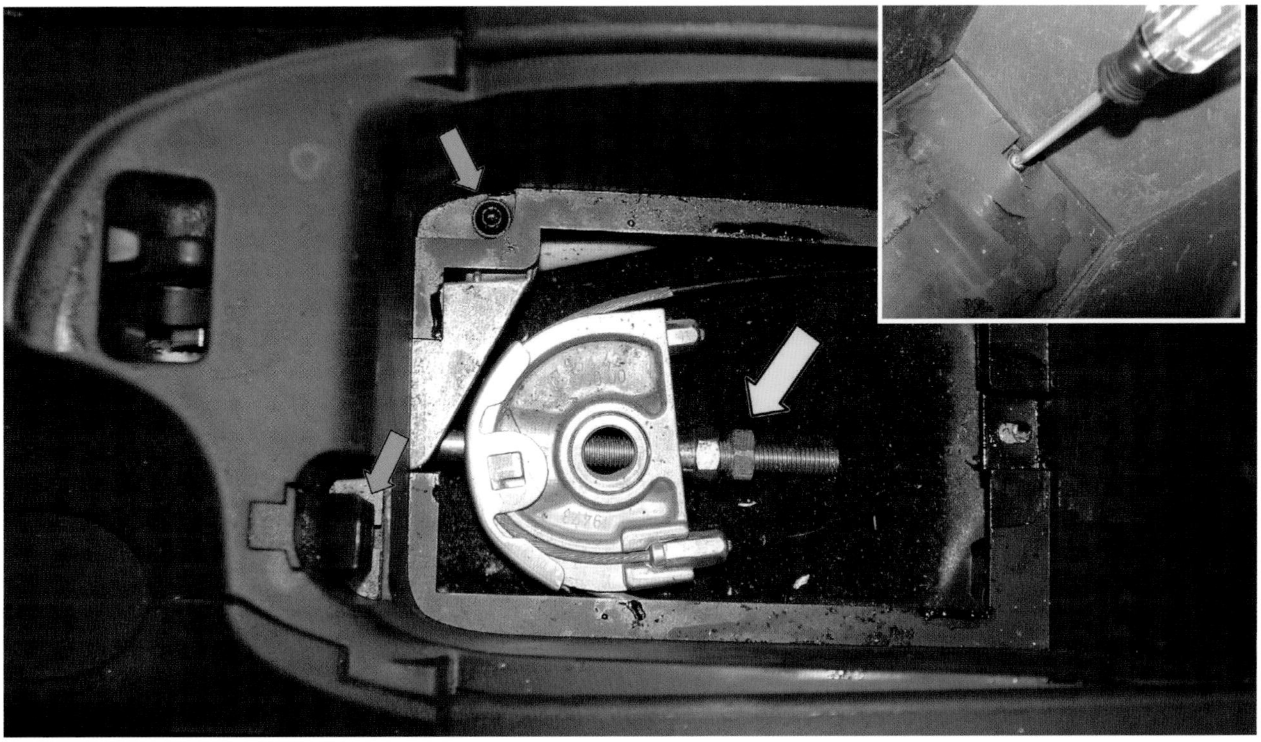

2 Shown here are the ends of the two parking brake cables wrapped around the turnbuckle. The two nuts that lock together need to be loosened (yellow arrow) prior to your adjustment process and then tightened up later on. The two purple arrows show two screws needed to remove the entire console (required for Project 43). The 2005 and later Carreras have a new automatically adjusting control cable on the parking brake. You will still need to adjust the brake shoes (as shown in Photo 1), but the parking brake handle is designed to self-adjust the cable for its entire service life.

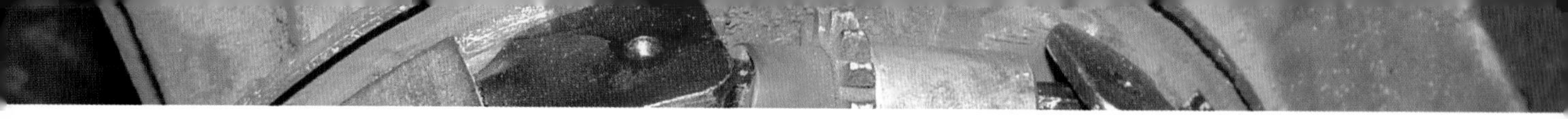

PROJECT 53
Big Brake Upgrade

Time / Tab / Talent: 12 hours / $1500–$3000 / (2 of 5 wrench icons)

Tools: Flare-nut wrench

Applicable Years: All

Tinware: Brembo big brake kit, brake fluid

More Info: http://www.101projects.com/Carrera/53.htm

Tip: Check the fit of your wheels after you mount the caliper

Performance Gain: Shorter stopping distances and reduced brake fade

Comp Modification: Replace rear pads, discs, and emergency brake shoes

The standard 911 Carrera braking systems have always been good, but for really high performance applications, they can always be better. If you're going to be doing any significant performance driving, it's a very wise investment to upgrade your brakes.

High-performance kits aren't cheap: they range in price from about $1,500 to $3,000, with the top end of the dollar range belonging to the premium brand kits from Brembo. Some may find this an expensive price to pay, but when you figure that it includes the cost of a caliper rebuild, new discs, and new brake lines, the cost becomes a bit more reasonable. In addition, you can expect the following improvements from your upgrade:

- **Shorter stopping distances.** Depending upon the application and road conditions, you can experience up to 20–30 percent shorter distances. The faster you are traveling the greater the improvement.
- **Repeatability.** Even the simplest brake systems can stop a car very well once or twice. However, as the brake fluid and pads heat up, performance decreases, and each stop gets longer and longer. Installing a big brake kit will give you remarkably shorter stops consistently.
- **Reduce or eliminate brake fade.** The larger brake discs on the big brake systems are able to dissipate heat that causes brake fade and failure. Each component in the big brake system is designed for performance braking, which includes the proper cooling of the system. Whether you're coming down a steep mountain or blasting from turn to turn on a racetrack, the bigger brake systems are better equipped to prevent overheating than the stock system.
- **Better control and modulation.** With a performance brake setup, you achieve a better pedal feel, brake harder, and still maintain control. The big brake systems work flawlessly with the Carrera's anti-lock braking system (ABS).

The big brake kits typically only come with equipment to replace your front brakes. This is because the front brakes typically perform 80 percent or more of the stopping—sometimes more during panic stops. I don't recommend putting a high-performance big brake system on the rear, because this can cause the rear brakes to lock up prematurely and actually increased stopping distances and a loss of control—exactly what you're trying to avoid! Performance systems already installed on the rear are often coupled with anti-lock controllers or proportioning valves to prevent rear brake lockup.

The big brake setup that we chose for this project is manufactured by Brembo and was supplied by PelicanParts.com. Brembo is one of the leading brake system manufacturers and an original equipment manufacturer (OEM) supplier to world-class sports car manufacturers, such as Porsche and Ferrari. The Brembo Big Red kit we used for this upgrade is widely considered to be one of the best you can buy for the 911 Carrera.

The only real requirement for the kit is that you have 17-inch or larger wheels on your car. The stock Carrera wheels will fit and were installed on this car at the time of the upgrade. Not all 17-inch wheels will allow the huge calipers to fit, so make sure that you plan in advance and verify that your wheel combination will work with the larger brake systems. Some thin spacers may be necessary for some wheels.

The first step is to loosen the lug nuts on your wheels and then raise the front of the car (see Project 1). You might want to raise the rear of the car as well, as I recommend that you inspect and refurbish your rear brakes at the same time so that you have fresh components on all four corners of the car.

For example, on this particular car, I installed new rear rotors, new rear brake pads, and new parking brake shoes to match.

With the car up in the air, remove the two road wheels and disconnect the brake pad sensor. Then unbolt and disconnect the brake caliper from the car (see Project 56 for detailed instructions on removing the caliper and brake disc). Tie the caliper up out of the way and do not disconnect the brake line at this time. Make sure that there is no tension on the brake line; even though we will be replacing it you, don't want to make a habit of hanging the caliper by the brake hose.

Now, remove the small screw that holds the brake disc to the hub. The brake disc should simply lift off. If not, then you may need to tap it with a rubber mallet. If there is any dust or debris in this area, be sure to clean it out thoroughly.

Now place the new rotor on the spindle. Look for a left and a right rotor; they usually have a sticker on them, but you can also tell the difference by the way that the internal fins are cast into the disc (see the inset of Photo 2). Use the brake disc locating and mounting bolt to secure and correctly register the brake disc with respect to the hub. The holes for the wheel studs should be correctly lined up with both the brake disc and the spindle. Use a spare wheel lug nut to help secure the disc to the spindle if needed.

The pads should be preassembled in the caliper, but if they're not, now is the time to insert them into the caliper. Remove the two retaining pins by tapping them out with a small hammer and the end of a punch or small screwdriver. Insert the pads and replace the pins. Take the new Brembo caliper mounting adapter and place it on the strut assembly (see Photo 3). Now, mount the new, huge caliper to the strut with the adapter sandwiched in between. Tighten the bolts to the values detailed in the installation instructions and use a dab of Loctite 271 on the threads to make sure they don't come loose. There should be an embossed arrow on the front of the caliper that indicates the direction of the disc rotation. When mounting the calipers on the spindle, the arrow should always point up (see Photo 4).

At this point (before you disconnect the brake line to your old caliper), I suggest that you perform a test fit of your wheel to your spindle. You want to make sure that there are no interference problems when the wheel is fully mounted. Cover the caliper first with a piece of tape to protect the paint in case the wheel happens to scrape the caliper. Put the wheel on the spindle and tighten it down with two lug nuts. Then give the wheel a spin and make sure that it turns freely without rubbing or scraping on the caliper or any other brake system component. If you discover a clearance problem, you may have to use a spacer and longer wheel bolts (see Photo 6).

When you have verified that the wheel turns freely, remove it and set it aside. Now attach your new braided brake hose to the brake caliper. There should be a small copper washer that will seal the line fitting to the caliper. Route the brake line through the small bracket that secures it to the strut (see Photo 7).

Now, using a flare-nut wrench, quickly disconnect the old rubber hose from the steel hard line that connects the hose to the main brake system (at the top of the inner wheelwell). Don't use a regular wrench on the hard line—only use a flare-nut wrench, as is explained in Project 55. Reconnect the new line quickly, minimizing the amount of brake fluid that leaks out of the system.

With the brake line attached, now clean up any spilled brake fluid (beware—it is very harmful to paint). Now, repeat the process for the opposite side. When you have completed the install, you will need to bleed the brake system (see Project 49). After the brakes have been bled, reattach the road wheels, lower the car, and tighten the lug nuts to 74 ft-lb (100 Nm).

The brake system needs to be broken in before you can really test its performance. First, you should make sure that your emergency brake system is working properly—just in case anything goes wrong and you need to pull that lever to stop the car. Before you drive the car, pump the pedal and make sure that you have firm pressure. Have an assistant push the car while you have your foot on the brake—just to test that the system is working.

Drive the car slowly to a nearby parking lot or deserted area. Now, perform about 15–20 stops from 55 miles per hour to 10 miles per hour using light pressure on the pedal. This will increase the temperature on pads, the caliper, and the rotors and will help mate the pad and the disc's friction surface together. After these repeated stops, drive the car around town for a few miles and try to avoid using the brakes. This will allow the components to cool back down. Now park the car and look at the brake discs. They should be a grayish-blue color consistently across the surface of the disc. If this color is not consistent, then repeat the 15–20 heating stops and the cooling procedure.

An additional easy update is the installation of the GT3 brake duct spoilers. They replace the existing plastic inserts that are attached to the front suspension and funnel more air to help cool the brakes. The left and right part numbers are 996-341-117-91 and 996-341-118-91.

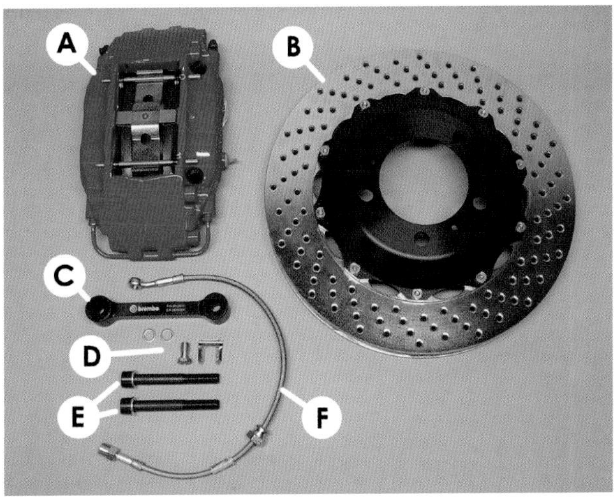

1 Shown here is one half of the Brembo big brake upgrade kit as purchased from PelicanParts.com. The kit includes everything that you need for the installation: two calipers, two rotors, two brake lines, two brackets, and two sets of pads and retaining clips. Truly a sight to be seen, it's unfortunate that all of this braking beauty has to be hidden behind the wheels. **A:** Brembo caliper. **B:** Brembo brake disc. **C:** Caliper adapter. **D:** Brake line hardware. **E:** Caliper mounting bolts and washers. **F:** Stainless steel brake line with metal grommet.

2 Mount the disc to the hub and temporarily fasten it with the brake disc locating screw (red arrow). Verify that the disc turns freely and doesn't hang up on any part of the strut or hub assembly. The discs are specific to each side of the car; verify from the diagram that the proper one is mounted according to how the wheel turns when the car is moving forward.

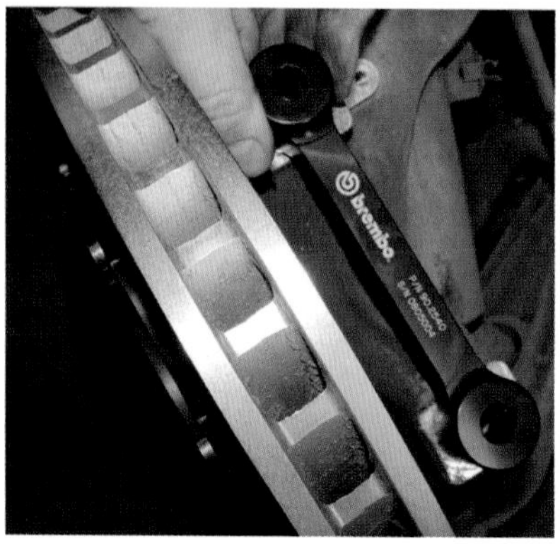

3 The caliper is mounted in a similar position as the factory one, using the same original bolt holes as mounting points. The spacer is sandwiched between the caliper and the mounting surface.

4 Shown here is the caliper mounted to the strut assembly. The embossed arrow on the caliper should always point upward (green arrow). The brake pads should be installed in the caliper from the factory.

5 Perform a test fit of the road wheel to the hub to make sure that there are no interference problems. Place some tape on the painted surface of the caliper, just to make sure that the inside of the wheel doesn't accidentally scratch the surface of the caliper. The Porsche original equipment manufacturer SportDesign wheels shown in the photo work very well with the Brembo kit. Clearance is very tight, but with the addition of a spacer, the wheel fits as if the kit were tailor-made for this

6 After checking the clearance of the caliper with the SportDesign wheels, I discovered that I needed some thin spacers because the caliper was contacting the inside of the wheel. The solution is easy—a set of 4mm spacers and 38mm-long lug bolts from PelicanParts.com. It's very important not to forget to use the longer lug bolts when you add the spacers to your hub.

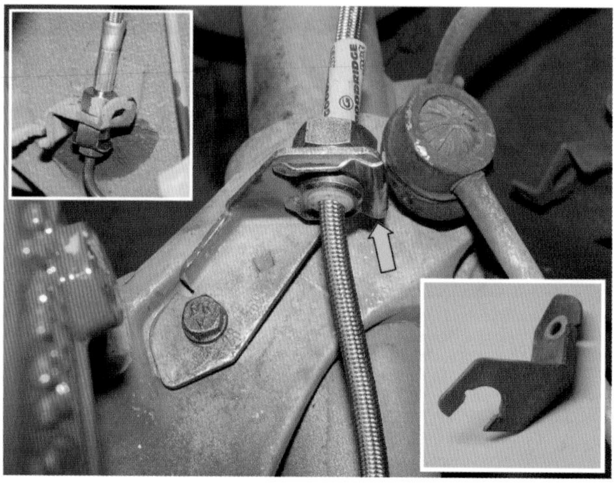

7 This photo shows the attachment of the new stainless steel brake line. The fitting on the chassis side fit well with the new line (inset, upper left), but the small bracket that holds the line and clamp (green arrow) to the strut had to be slightly modified with a Dremel tool. The center hole needed to be opened up to accommodate the larger brake line fitting (inset, lower right).

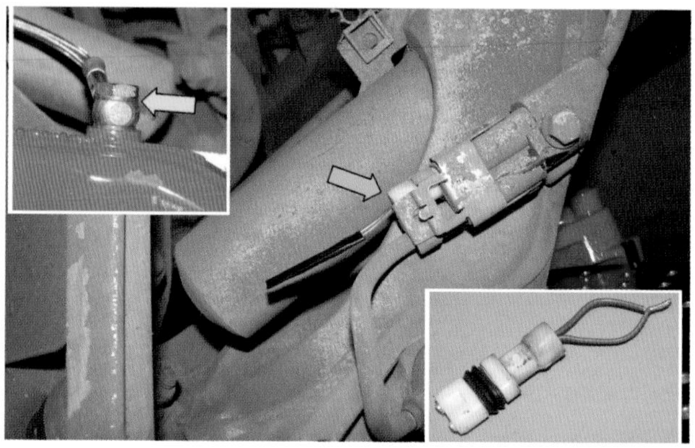

8 The Brembo system does not have an accommodation for the brake pad wear sensors, so you will need to trick the system into thinking the pads are within spec. This is easy: Simply take an old sensor, clip its wires, and connect the two together. Cover the ends with some electrical tape, and insert the connector back into the strut housing. Be sure to inspect your pads for wear periodically since the brake pad wear system is now disabled. In the upper left inset photo, you will see the point where the brake line enters the brake caliper (yellow arrow). This line attaches to the lower part of the caliper, and the bleed nipple should be on top of the caliper.

PROJECT 54
Parking Brake Shoe Replacement

Time / Tab / Talent: 3 hours / $110 /

Tools: Rubber mallet, screwdriver, small pliers

Applicable Years: All

Tinware: New parking brake shoes, springs

More Info: http://www.101projects.com/Carrera/54.htm

Tip: Wear safety glasses when working around the spring-loaded mechanisms

Performance Gain: Better parking brake performance

Comp Modification: Replace the brake pads and brake discs

If your parking brake is not functioning properly, then perhaps it's time that you replaced the parking brake shoes. The first step in the process is to make sure that the parking brake cables and handles are adjusted properly. (Refer to Project 52 for details on this procedure.)

The parking brake shoes can only be inspected after the removal of the rear brake discs. (Refer to Project 56 for the procedure for this removal.) After you have the brake discs off, you can visually inspect the shoes for wear. The shoes should have some brake lining along the top and should not have any heavy grooves cut into them. Compare your brake shoes to the new shoes in the pictures for this project to determine if you need to replace yours.

After the brake disc has been removed from the brake assembly, remove the small parking brake adjuster by prying it out from between the left and right parking brake shoe. Make sure that the parking brake handle is all the way down for this procedure. Be careful while you are performing this removal, as the adjuster is spring-loaded and the springs may fly out when you are prying it out.

When you have removed the adjuster, take a set of needle-nose pliers and remove the long spring that that holds the left and right shoes together near where the adjuster was mounted. Again, be careful of the spring, as it may fly off unexpectedly. Make sure that you wear safety glasses during this entire procedure.

Now remove the conical spring-retaining mechanisms at the far left and right of the assembly. Press in the spring, and then rotate the spring so that you can slide it out of its slot in the back. You made need to stick your head around the backside of the axle carrier in order to see how to remove the hook on the end of the spring. Make sure that you don't lose the parts if they happen to fly out.

Now remove the long spring from the bottom of the two brake shoes. Use the needle-nose pliers again, and be careful not to catch your fingers in the process.

After the springs have been removed from the parking brake assembly, both the top and the bottom shoes should simply lift off of the assembly. The new shoe should be installed in an opposite manner to the removal process. Reassemble the parking brake by attaching the lower spring first, then the two conical springs, and then the spring toward the top. It's important to note that this reassembly involves quite a bit of maneuvering with a pliers and is not an easy task—you'll probably swear at the car a couple dozen times.

When you are finished, test the assembly by operating the emergency brake handle a few times. Carefully check the springs and make sure that they are properly seated in the restraining holes in the brake shoes. Loosen up the parking brake cables before you reinstall the brake disc and make sure that you recheck and adjust the parking brake mechanism (Project 52) before you reinstall the caliper and the brake pads.

1 Remove the small adjusting cog assembly by using a large screwdriver to push it out from between the two parking brake shoes. With some effort, the cog assembly should pop out, leaving a little bit of slack between the two parking brake shoes. Be very careful when installing the new shoe, as the retaining springs have a tendency to snap out of place and fly out. Make sure that you keep your hands out of the way, and use safety glasses when installing or removing the springs. The inset photo shows a brand new parking brake shoe. Compare your old one to this one here in the photo to see if it needs to be replaced.

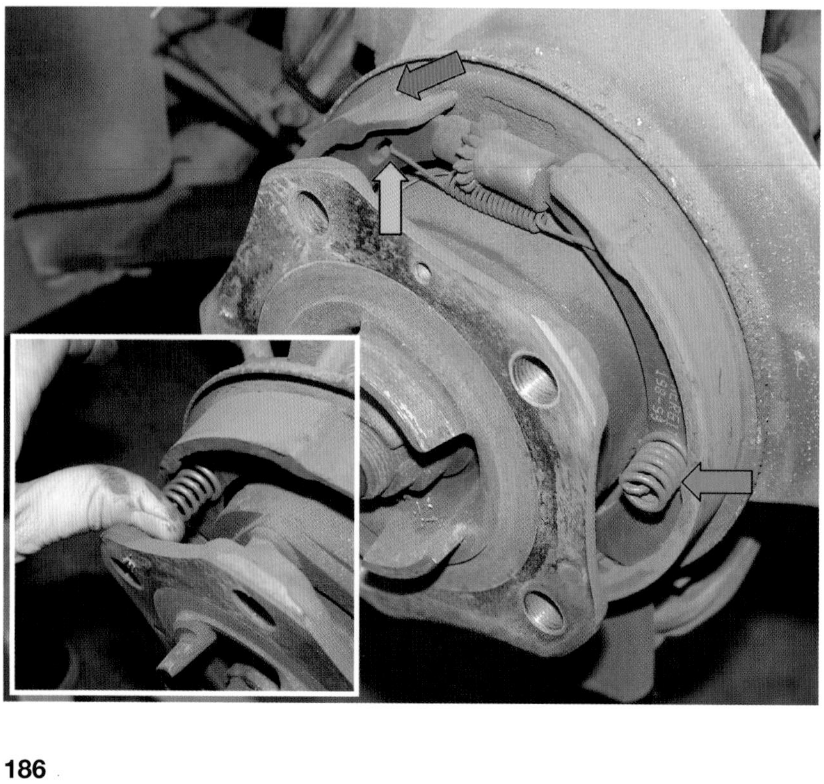

2 Using a pair of pliers, grab and unhook the parking brake spring from the brake shoes (green arrow). Be careful of the spring; it is under a lot of tension at this point. Use a pair of vise grips and a pair of needle-nose pliers to twist the spring and unlatch it from the assembly. Also undo the small spring retainer (inset) that secures the brake shoes to the rear trailing arm. If you're not sure if your parking brake shoes are worn, take a close look at the ones shown here (red arrow). The brake lining on this particular shoe actually looks pretty good and probably wouldn't warrant replacing.

PROJECT 55
Brake Line Replacement

Time / Tab / Talent: 4 hours / $95 / 2 wrenches

Tools: 10mm/11mm crescent flare-nut wrench

Applicable Years: All

Tinware: New brake lines or stainless steel brake lines

Tip: Make sure that corroded rubber from old lines didn't end up in the caliper

Performance Gain: Better braking performance

Comp Modification: Rebuild calipers, replace brake pads, flush brake system, and replace master cylinder

More Info: http://www.101projects.com/Carrera/55.htm

One of the most popular projects for the 911 is the replacement of the flexible brake lines that connect from the main chassis of the car to the brake calipers. These lines are made out of rubber and have a tendency to break down and corrode over many years. The rubber lines should be carefully inspected every 10,000 miles or so. They can exhibit strange characteristics, such as bubbling and expanding prior to actually bursting. Needless to say, failure of these lines is a very bad thing, as you will instantly lose pressure in one half of your brake system.

Faulty brake lines in the front of your Porsche can cause all sorts of steering problems when braking. It is common for bad hoses to cause a car to dart from side to side to when braking. Bad hoses allow pressure to build up in the caliper but sometimes do not release this pressure properly when the pedal is depressed.

The first step in replacing the brake lines is to elevate the car. Remove the wheels from each side of the car, as this will make it much easier to access the brake lines. To prevent a large amount of brake fluid from leaking out, I recommend pushing the brake pedal down just to the point of engagement and block it there. If you do this, you will lose less brake fluid and less air will enter into the system.

Now it's time to disconnect the brake lines. Make sure that you have some paper towels handy, as there will be some brake fluid that will leak out of the lines. Brake fluid is perhaps the most dangerous fluid to your car, as any amount spilled on the paint will permanently mar it. If you do get some on the paint, make sure that you blot it and don't wipe it off. Be aware that your hands may contain some brake fluid; don't even touch anything near the paint on the car with your hands.

The brake lines themselves can be very difficult to remove. The goal of this job is to remove the lines without damaging anything else. In this case, the easiest thing to damage (besides your paint) is the hard steel brake lines that connect to the flexible rubber lines. These lines have relatively soft fittings on each end and often become deformed and stripped when removed. The key to success is to use a flare-nut wrench. This wrench is basically designed for jobs like this one where the fittings are soft and might be heavily corroded. The flared end of the wrench hugs the fitting and prevents it from stripping. It is very important to use only one of these wrenches, as it is very easy to damage the fittings using a regular crescent wrench.

The other disastrous thing that can happen is that the fitting can get stuck to the rest of the hard line. The fitting is supposed to turn and rotate on the end of the line, but sometimes it becomes too corroded to break free. When this happens, the fitting and the line will usually twist together, and it will break the line in half. Be careful when you are removing this fitting to make sure that you are not twisting the line.

If you do damage the hard line or strip the fitting, then the replacement line might be a special order part that will have to be shipped in from Germany. You can usually find the correct length line at your local auto parts store, but then you will have to bend it into shape, and most of the time, this is a very difficult process that requires a few special tools. The moral of this story, and this entire book, is that you should use the right tool for the job (the flare-nut wrench).

After you have disconnected the hard metal line, you can now remove the flexible lines from the car. At both ends, the lines are attached using spring clips. Use a good pair of vise grips to pull them off of the car.

Installation of the new lines is straightforward and the easy part of the job. Before you start attaching the lines, make

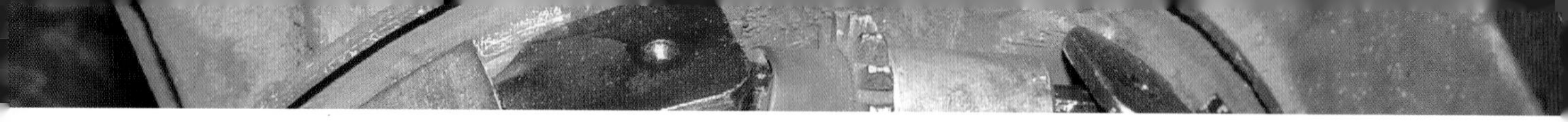

sure that you have the correct ones for your car. There are a few different types and a few different lengths, so make sure that the ones that you are putting on are the same length and have the same fittings as the ones that you are removing. If the line you install is too short, it may stretch and break when your car goes over a bump.

When it comes to replacing brake lines, many people install stainless steel braided lines on their car. Rumor has it that the stainless steel sheath keeps the rubber line from expanding under pressure and actually delivers better performance than do the standard lines. While this reasoning sounds good at first, it's mostly hype. The stainless steel braided lines are often made of the same rubber underneath and are simply protected by the outside sheath. Even if the sheath were tight enough and strong enough to prevent the lines from expanding, it really wouldn't make a difference in braking. Even if the lines expand a little, the resulting pressure that is exerted at the caliper will be almost the same.

Regardless of the rumor mill, I will recommend that you place the stainless steel lines on your car because the outside sheath protects the lines from dirt, grime, rocks, small animals, and other things you might run over with your car. The stock lines already have a metal "spring" that insulates them, so the gain is minimal.

The other thing that might warrant your consideration is the label for the department of transportation (DOT) certification. The original rubber lines were required to be certified under a certain set of specifications dictated by the DOT for use on U.S. highways. Often, the stainless steel lines are aftermarket components that are not DOT certified and are subsequently listed for "off-road use only." In reality, these lines are more than adequate for use on your car, and any concern over the use of them is not really necessary. However, for those who want to be absolutely sure and certified, some manufacturers who make DOT-certified stainless steel lines, but they are usually more expensive than the noncertified ones (DOT lines are available at PelicanParts.com).

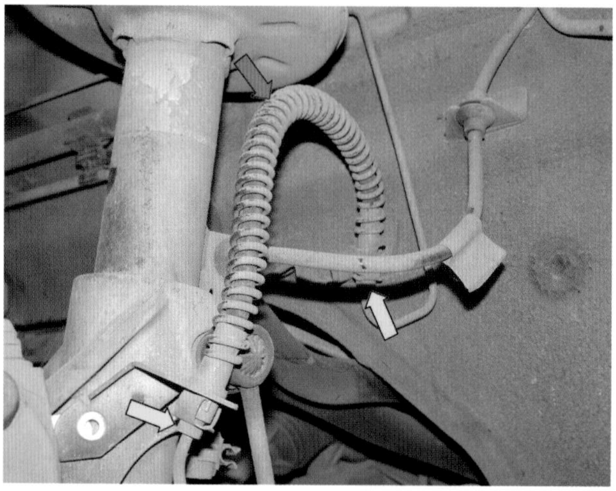

1 Old rubber brake lines are often responsible for poor brake performance. As the car ages, the rubber begins to break down and can clog the lines, leading to very little pressure getting to the calipers. The brake lines should be renewed if they are old or if you are having problems with your brakes. The red arrow points to the flexible brake line on the front of the car that needs to be replaced. The yellow arrows point to the fittings on the hard brake lines that need to be released using a flare-nut wrench.

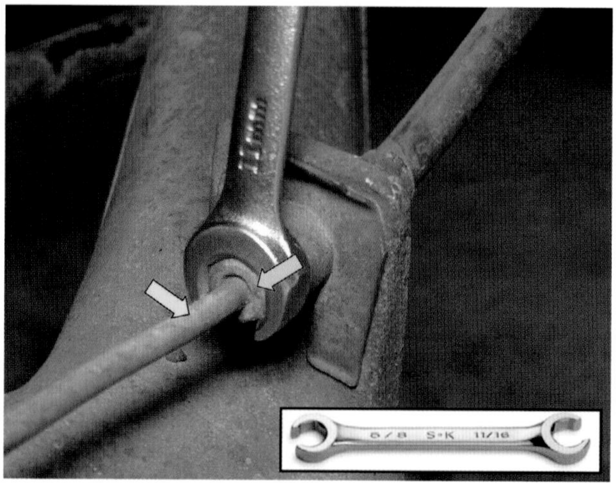

2 A required tool is the flare-nut wrench that fully wraps around the brake line. If you use a standard wrench, then there is a high chance of rounding off the corners and permanently damaging the hard brake lines. These fittings are not very strong and will become stripped if you don't use one of these wrenches. Once the fitting becomes stripped, the line needs to be replaced (usually a special order part from Germany). Also make sure that the fitting is turning (blue arrow), not the line itself (yellow arrow). It is very easy to twist off the ends of the hard lines when the fitting binds.

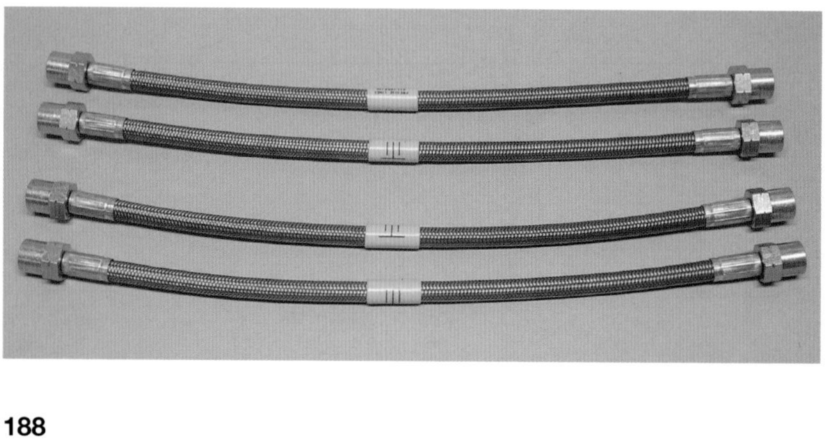

3 New stainless steel lines are identical in size and length to the original ones that shipped with the car. The advantage to the stainless steel lines is that they have a protective coating on the outside that prevents the elements from attacking them as easily. There is a downside though. The stainless steel sheath doesn't allow you to inspect the rubber inside to see if there is any significant deterioration. Some of the aftermarket lines are made out of Teflon or have Teflon components to help increase their durability.

PROJECT 56
Replacing Brake Discs

Time / Tab / Talent: 3 hours / $600 /

Tools: Phillips head socket tool, rubber mallet, socket set, micrometer

Applicable Years: All

Tinware: Brake discs, new pads, new emergency brake shoes (if required)

Tip: Adjust your emergency brake while you have access

Performance Gain: Better, safer braking

Comp Modification: Replace brake pads, emergency brake shoes, install stainless steel brake lines, and install new wheel bearings

More Info: http://www.101projects.com/Carrera/56.htm

Brake discs (or rotors as they are often called) are a very important part of the braking system. The brake pads rub against the discs to create a friction force that is responsible for slowing down the car. If the rotors become too thin or develop grooves in them, then their ability to stop the car decreases.

When replacing brake pads, you should always measure the thickness of the brake discs. If they fall below the specified value for your car, then they should be replaced with new ones. Check for grooves in the rotor, and make sure that you take several measurements of the disc in several different places to guarantee that you get an accurate reading. If the brake disc has a groove in it, then it should most certainly be removed and resurfaced by a machine shop or simply replaced with a new one. Discs with grooves not only brake less efficiently, but they also heat up to higher temperatures and reduce your overall braking ability.

The measurements that you take with your micrometer should be made from the center of the disc. It is common for original equipment manufacturer (OEM) rotors to have the minimum thickness stamped on the rotor hub (as is the case with the Porsche Ceramic Composite Brake (PCCB) option.

Type	New	Min. Thickness
Front Rotor (Carrera)	28mm	26mm
Rear Rotor (Carrera)	24mm	22mm
Front Rotor (C4S)	34mm	32mm
Rear Rotor (C4S)	28mm	26mm

If you can't find this information, use the following chart to determine if your rotors need to be replaced.

If you do find that you need to replace your rotors, the process is a relatively simple one. The procedure for the front or the rear rotors is very similar, but for the sake of this project, we'll look at replacing the rears, which is slightly more complicated due to the addition of the rear parking/emergency brake. With the rear rotors, if the parking brake shoes are very worn, then you may need to back off the adjustment sprocket in order to be able to remove the rear disc (see Project 52).

The first step is to jack up the car (see Project 1) and remove the road wheel. If you haven't already, remove the brake pads from the caliper (see Project 50). The flexible rubber brake hose is attached to the trailing arm of the car via a large clip. This clip retains both the flexible line and the hard line that connects to the rear caliper. Remove this clip so that you will be able to remove the caliper without bending the hard metal brake line.

Now, unbolt the caliper from the trailing arm where it is mounted. There should be two bolts that mount the caliper and hold it in place. After you remove these two bolts, you should be able to slightly move the caliper out of the way of the disc. Exercise caution when moving the caliper around and make sure that you do not let the caliper hang from the rubber brake line as this will most certainly damage the line.

Once you have the caliper out of the way, remove the small screw that holds on the brake disc. You will need a Phillips head socket tool for this task (you can try using a big screwdriver, but odds are the screw will be on too tight and you may end up stripping it). At this point, make sure that the parking brake is off. You should now be able to pull

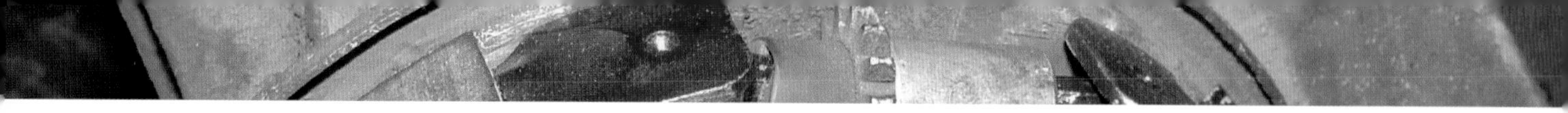

the disc off of the hub. If there is any resistance, use a rubber mallet to tap the brake disc off. Sometimes the disc will require some heavy smacks with a rubber mallet to get it off.

If you are having a difficult time getting the disc off, it's probably because the parking brake shoes are stuck on the back of the disc. You might need to adjust the parking brake so that it's not gripping the disc (see Project 52).

Installation of the new brake disc is a snap; simply push it onto the hub. Before you install the new disc, take a close look at your parking brake shoes and see if they warrant replacing. If you can see metal on the shoes, or if the previous owner had a hard time remembering to remove the emergency brake, then it might be a good time to replace these. After you install the new discs on both sides, you should test your parking brake and adjust it if necessary (see Projects 52 and 54).

After the new disc is installed, replace the retaining screw, reattach the caliper, and install new brake pads. Your new rotors should last a long time, and you should see an improvement in your braking after the wear-in period for your new brake pads.

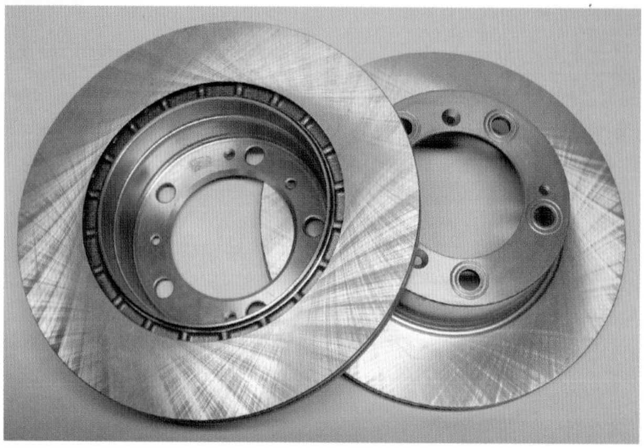

1 The front and rear brake discs look almost identical. The rear brake discs have an inner "drum" area that acts as the surface for the emergency brake to press against. While all the Carreras have disc brakes at all wheels, the rear parking brake mechanism is most similar to a drum brake system. You may want to paint the inner hats and edges of the discs with some high-temp paint. This will keep them from rusting after you install them.

2 Before you remove your brake discs, it is important to first measure them to see if they need to be replaced. Use a micrometer to perform the measurement. If you use a dial caliper, then you might get a false reading because the disc wears on the area where the pads make contact, not on the edges of the disc. Make sure that you take several measurements in a few different places on the disc in order to compensate for potential low or high spots.

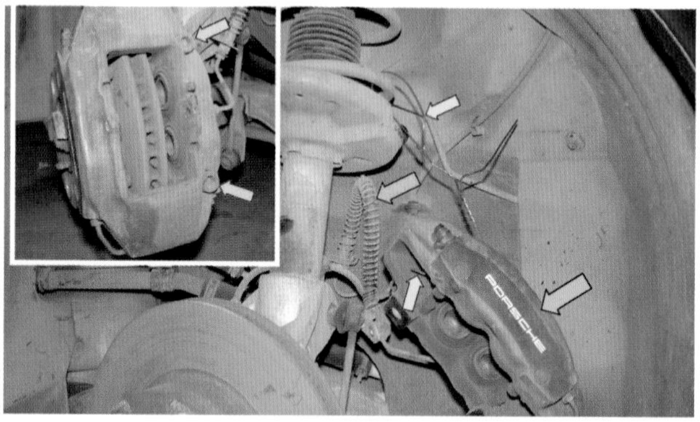

3 Removal of the caliper is accomplished by unbolting the two hex bolts that mount it to the arm (yellow arrow). The caliper (green arrow) can be pushed out of the way and doesn't need to be physically disconnected from the brake line. Hang the caliper from a string or coat hanger (blue arrows) so that you don't put unnecessary tension on the rubber brake line (orange arrow).

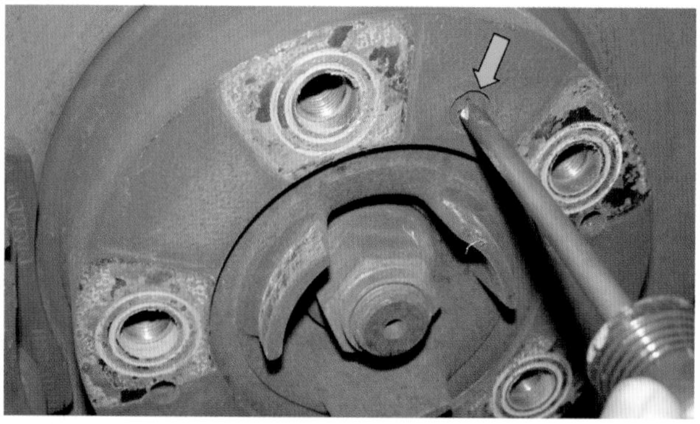

4 Two small locator screws hold the brake disc in place. Use a big screwdriver or a Phillips head socket tool to remove this screw, and the brake disc should slide off of the hub. Keep in mind that the lug nuts that hold on the wheel apply the majority of the force that constrains the disc to the hub—not this screw.

5 The new disc can be tapped on with a rubber mallet. If installing the rear discs, make sure that you have your parking brake shoes adjusted away from the inside drum, or they might interfere with the installation of the disc. New discs may not be perfectly flat and may take a few hundred miles of break-in to achieve their maximum braking efficiency.

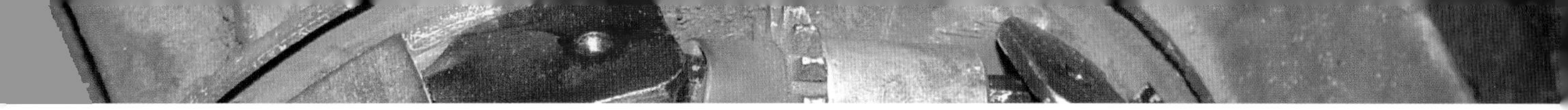

PROJECT 57
Master Cylinder Replacement

Time / Tab / Talent: 3 hours / $100–$300 /

Tools: Brake bleeder, torque wrench

Applicable Years: All

Tinware: Master cylinder, brake fluid

More Info: http://www.101projects.com/Carrera/57.htm

Tip: Make sure that you keep all brake fluid away from your paint

Performance Gain: Better braking; no more leaky master cylinders

Comp Modification: Replace brake booster and install stainless steel brake lines

Without a doubt, your brakes are one of the most important systems on the car. The heart of the brake system is the master cylinder, which controls the hydraulic pressure of the entire system. Unfortunately, over many years, the master cylinder has a tendency to wear out and leak. The leakage can occur internally or externally, resulting in a weakened braking system. If you have any problems with your brakes—and you think that they are related to the master cylinder—you should probably replace it.

The master cylinder is located in the driver side front trunk area under a large plastic panel. To gain access to the master cylinder, you need to remove this panel. Begin by pulling up the hood seal and removing the three Phillips head screws located on the top of the panel. Rotate the slotted plug on the lower front corner of the panel and remove it, disconnecting the trunk lamp harness as you go. Now, remove the strainer from the brake fluid reservoir and then remove brake fluid using a turkey baster or a suction device. Or, you can also bleed the entire system of fluid by emptying the brake fluid out of one of the caliper bleed screws (see Project 49). Be aware that some residual fluid will remain inside the master cylinder and that brake fluid is very damaging to paint. Disconnect the brake fluid level sensor from the reservoir.

Now you need to remove the reservoir. Disconnect the clutch master cylinder supply line; you will need to carefully push in the press-fit connector with a small wrench as you pull on the line. If you are not replacing the reservoir, then

1 The master cylinder is hidden behind a plastic panel located in the front trunk. Remove the large plastic screw that hold the trunk liner down (blue arrow) and the three small Phillips head screws (yellow arrows), and pull the liner out. There is a front trunk lamp (red arrow) embedded in the liner—remember to unplug the harness connected to this lamp.

I recommend just leaving it connected and pushing the reservoir off to the side. Simply pull up on the reservoir to remove it from the O-rings that seal it to the master cylinder.

With the reservoir disconnected, place a towel under the master cylinder and disconnect the two brake line fittings. As with the installation of new flexible brake lines, it is very important not to strip out the fittings on the lines. You should always use a flare-nut wrench to remove the fittings from the master cylinder (see Project 55). It's also a wise idea to spray the area with some WD-40 or other lubricant if the lines seem to be heavily corroded. Cap the open brake lines with plastic covers to prevent brake fluid leakage. Remove the two nuts that attach the master cylinder to the brake booster, and you should be able to remove the master cylinder.

Installation is basically the reverse of removal. If you are replacing the anti-lock brake system (ABS) control unit or the brake booster, then refer to Project 58 for instructions on how to accomplish that task.

When the master cylinder is reinstalled, it's time to bleed your brake system. You may want to dry bleed the master cylinder on the bench in order to prime it before you start the install. (For more information on bleeding your brakes, see Project 49.) Following the bleeding of the brakes, reassemble all the surrounding parts in the trunk that you have disassembled, and make sure that everything is tightened. Reinstall all the carpets and fasteners.

When you are ready to drive the car, make sure that you test the brakes beforehand. Don't drive near other cars, and prepare to use the emergency brake if necessary. It's probably a wise idea to bleed the brakes again a few days after you install the new master cylinder to make sure that you have removed all of the air from the brake system.

2 Here's what you will see when you remove the front trunk liner. The purple arrow shows the vacuum-powered brake booster, which is the muscle behind the power-brake system. The orange arrow shows the brake fluid reservoir, which supplies hydraulic fluid to both the brake and clutch systems. The red arrow shows the anti-lock braking system hydraulic control unit. The white arrow points to the master cylinder. The yellow arrow indicates the connection for the reservoir level sensor, and the green arrow shows the vacuum line that powers the brake booster. Finally, the light blue arrow shows the electrical connector that plugs into the front trunk lamp.

3 Shown here is a close-up of the master cylinder connections. First, empty out the reservoir, and then disconnect the clutch system supply tube (green arrow). Then, disconnect the two brake lines attached to the side of the master cylinder. Only use a flare-nut wrench (blue arrow, inset) as you otherwise may end up damaging the connectors on the lines.

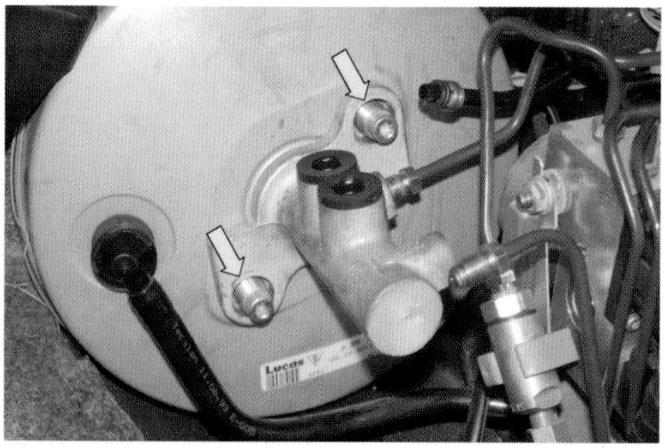

4 With the brake lines disconnected and the reservoir removed from the top of the master cylinder, remove the two nuts that fasten the master cylinder to the brake booster (yellow arrows).

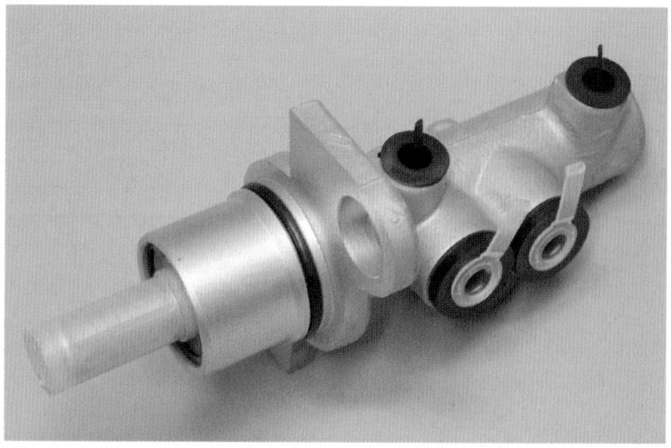

5 Shown here is a brand new master cylinder with five protective caps attached. Carefully remove the caps right before you are ready to install the unit and/or the brake lines.

PROJECT 58
Brake Booster and ABS Control Unit Replacement

Time / Tab / Talent: 3 hours / $250 /

Tools: Brake bleeder, torque wrench

Applicable Years: Brake Booster (1999-2005 996)
ABS Control Unit (All)

Tinware: Master cylinder, brake fluid

More Info: http://www.101projects.com/Carrera/58.htm

Tip: Make sure that you keep all brake fluid away from the paint

Performance Gain: Better braking assist

Comp Modification: Replace master cylinder; install stainless steel brake lines

The 911 Carrera is equipped with power brakes that utilize excess vacuum from the engine in order to assist with the pressure needed to apply the brakes. The vacuum is routed from the engine via a long plastic hose that runs up the side of the car, into the front trunk area, and plugs into a large circular brake boost canister that the master cylinder attaches to. After years of use, the rubber diaphragm inside the booster may leak or fail, causing the power assist function to lose its efficiency. In addition, this may cause an engine vacuum leak, which can affect the proper metering of the fuel injection system. Before you replace your brake booster though, be sure that you check the vacuum hose connections that run to the engine to uncover any leaks there (see Project 21). Beginning with the introduction of the 997, a mechanical vacuum pump was installed on the engine instead of a conventional air pump to provide the brake booster vacuum. This design enables a high and constant level of vacuum supply.

The first step in removing the booster is to remove the master cylinder (see Project 57). With the master cylinder removed, disconnect the three fittings from the top ABS control unit that were not attached to the master cylinder. Remove the ABS controller harness plug—the plastic tab on the side slides outward to allow the plug to pull up and off. Pull the brake line pressure regulator out of its clip. Loosen the two nuts on either side of the ABS controller and lift the controller out of the retaining bracket, maneuvering around the existing brake lines.

1 In order to gain access to the linkage that connects the brake pedal to the booster actuator, you need to remove the alarm horn (purple arrow). The upper right inset photo shows the vacuum hose plug that connects the engine vacuum line to the booster. Tug on this gently to remove it from the booster housing.

Now move to the other side of the booster, near the front firewall. Remove the clip that secures the brake booster actuation rod to the brake pedal rod and separate the two (see Photo 2). New boosters have an updated design that includes an integrated boot and an internal screw. This change was put into place for cars manufactured after September 13, 1999, and to use the newer-style booster with the older cars, you need to update the brake push rod and the hardware associated with it. The process of updating the older cars is a bit of a pain, but instructions are documented in a 16-page Porsche Technical Bulletin Boxster/Carrera 6/01 4770 031 (Brake Booster Seal at the Firewall Changed). See the 101Projects.com website for more information on this update.

With the booster rod disconnected, now disconnect the vacuum line on the front of the booster. Remove the two very long Torx T-45 bolts that secure the brake booster to the firewall. These bolts are the same ones that the master cylinder nuts attach to. With the bolts off, the booster should simply separate from the wall.

Installation of the new booster is basically the reverse of disassembly. With the new brake hardware in place, carefully bleed the brakes according to the instructions found in Project 49.

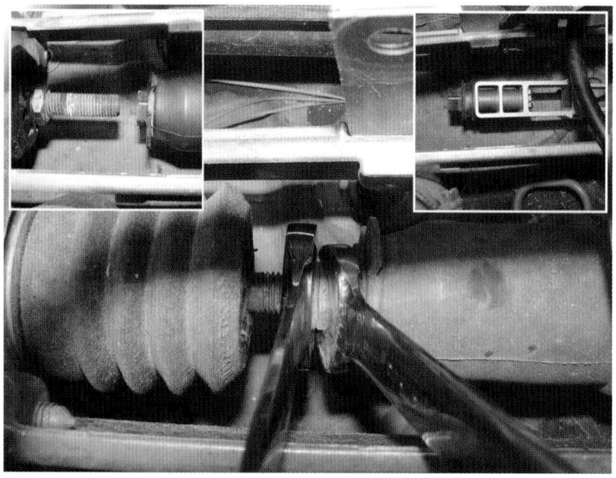

2 Use a set of wrenches to loosen up the connection between the booster actuator and the pedal cluster rod. This photo shows an early 2000 chassis; later cars have a booster with a longer bellows. The photo in the upper right shows the booster and pedal cluster disconnected. The pedal cluster rod (upper left) must be changed if the booster is replaced with a newer-style one.

3 This photo shows what needs to be disconnected in order to remove the anti-lock braking system (ABS) control unit. Using a flare-nut wrench, disconnect the main brake lines (yellow arrow). Then release the ABS electrical connection by pulling the connector release handle in the direction of the red arrows. Finally, unbolt the ABS unit from its bracket (purple arrow shows one of the mounting points).

4 Shown here is the front trunk with the master cylinder and ABS control unit removed. At this point, the bolts that hold the booster to the firewall have been removed, and the unit is ready to be removed from the car. The photo in the lower right shows the ABS control unit mounting bracket, which needs to be removed so that you have enough clearance to pull the booster out (remove nuts—yellow arrows).

5 Here's the new booster and master cylinder installed. At this point, simply remove the protective caps from all of the openings, install the ABS unit, reconnect the vacuum line, and reconnect the brake lines. Don't forget to bleed the entire brake and clutch system (Project 49).

SECTION 8
SUSPENSION

As cars get up there in age, one thing is almost always certain—suspension components will begin to wear out. This creates a sloppy feel to the car, which is exactly the opposite of what the original Porsche designers intended. Fixing and repairing the effects of age is straightforward—in most cases, suspension components need to be disassembled, evaluated, and then possibly replaced. This section details the overhaul of the Carrera suspension and also offers some projects on suspension upgrades that you can perform along the way.

PROJECT 59

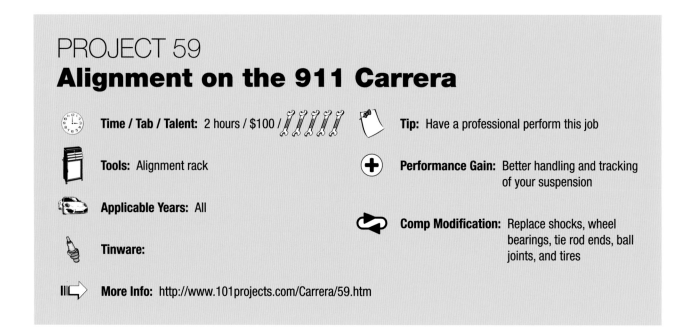

Alignment on the 911 Carrera

Time / Tab / Talent: 2 hours / $100 /

Tools: Alignment rack

Applicable Years: All

Tinware:

More Info: http://www.101projects.com/Carrera/59.htm

Tip: Have a professional perform this job

Performance Gain: Better handling and tracking of your suspension

Comp Modification: Replace shocks, wheel bearings, tie rod ends, ball joints, and tires

The Porsche 911 Carrera is known for its good handling and excellent suspension system. Of course, precise handling and cornering are nonexistent if the car is not aligned properly. Five different specifications must be within spec to properly align the chassis: front-end caster, camber, toe, and rear-end camber and toe. On the stock Carrera, the settings that you can easily change are for camber and toe on the front and rear suspension. Caster is adjustable if you replace the suspension control arms with ones used on some of the GT racing cars. Also, unlike the earlier Porsche 911, the ride height is not adjustable using the factory suspension components. To change the ride height you need to upgrade the front and rear suspension to a fully adjustable coil-over system or install lowering springs (see Project 61).

If the alignment of the suspension is slightly off, then you might get some significant tire wear and a loss of power and fuel economy. The most common sign of a misaligned front suspension is the car pulling to one side of the road when driving straight. Although the home mechanic can perform the basic front-end toe-in setting, I suggest that you allow a trained professional with an alignment rack make the other adjustments. It's nearly impossible to determine the correct angles and settings for your car without the use of an alignment rack.

Camber refers to the tilt of the wheel, as measured in degrees of variation between the tire centerline and the vertical plane of the car. If the top of the wheel tilts inward, the camber is negative. If the top of the wheel tilts outward, the camber is positive. On the Porsche 911 Carrera, the camber should be slightly negative for Euro-spec cars and slightly positive for the U.S.-spec cars. On some older cars, the chassis deformation due to rust and age can sometimes lead to the camber adjustments and measurements being slightly off. If the car has been in an accident, then often times the resulting chassis damage will show up in an alignment that indicates values not within spec.

The front stock Carrera suspension has a limited range to which the camber setting can be adjusted. If you wish to run more negative camber (useful for racing purposes), then you can install aftermarket upper strut mounts that allow you to dial in more than one whole degree of additional negative camber (see Project 61 for more details). Installing aftermarket strut mounts can also be used to correct the chassis camber when it falls out of factory specifications. In addition, you can install the GT3 lower control arms—a two-piece unit that allows you to shim the arm for additional camber adjustments (see Photo 8).

Worn suspension bushings may also add to odd alignment measurements. As the bushings and suspension mounts age, they have a tendency to introduce some slop into the suspension system, which can result in poor alignment readings. Lowering your 911 (through an aftermarket strut swap) will also change your alignment specifications from the factory defaults. If your alignment specialist tells you that your fixed specifications are outside the factory ranges and your car has not been in any accidents, then it's likely that some of your suspension components are worn and need to be replaced (see Project 60). Lowering your 911 beyond about 1 inch or so may result in an inability to set the proper toe on the rear suspension without the use of adjustable rear toe links. The stock adjustment does not have enough flexibility to accommodate the proper toe and correct camber with a ride height change greater than 1 inch or so.

The rear wheels should be set from the factory for a slight negative camber (about -1.0 degrees), as the trailing arms tend to bend slightly outward as the car accelerates under power. Since one half of the wheel is mounted firmly on the ground, the top of the wheel has a tendency to twist outward when power is applied. Setting the rear wheels to have a slight negative camber means that under power they will be mostly neutral.

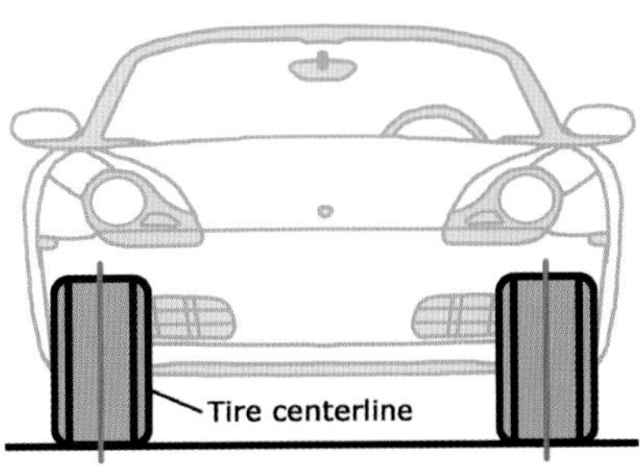

1 Zero Camber. When the car is aligned with zero camber, it means that the wheels are directly perpendicular to the ground. The tires make even contact with the road and exhibit a minimal amount of wear and friction when turning. The weight of the car is distributed evenly across the tire tread, but the steering control can be a bit heavy. Tire sizes are shown smaller than scale and camber angles are exaggerated for ease of illustration in these diagrams.

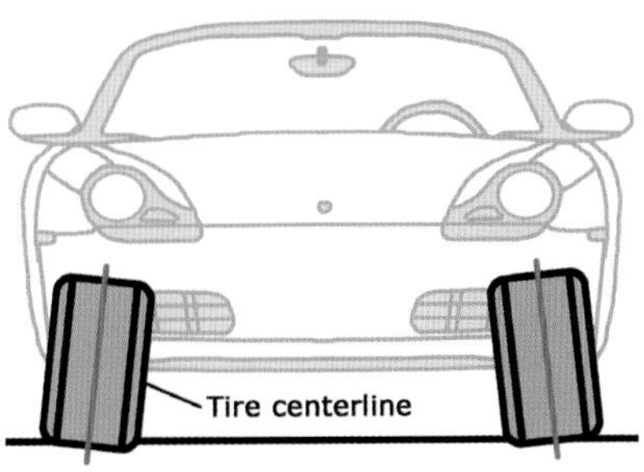

2 Negative Camber. The lower parts of the tires are angled outward, causing tires to wear more on the inside edges. The 996/997 Carrera has an independent front suspension, which creates a slight negative camber when traveling over bumps. As the suspension compresses upward, the wheel tilts in slightly to avoid changing the track (distance between left and right wheels). Although this momentarily changes the camber of the wheel, it prevents the tires from scrubbing and wearing every time the car travels over a bump.

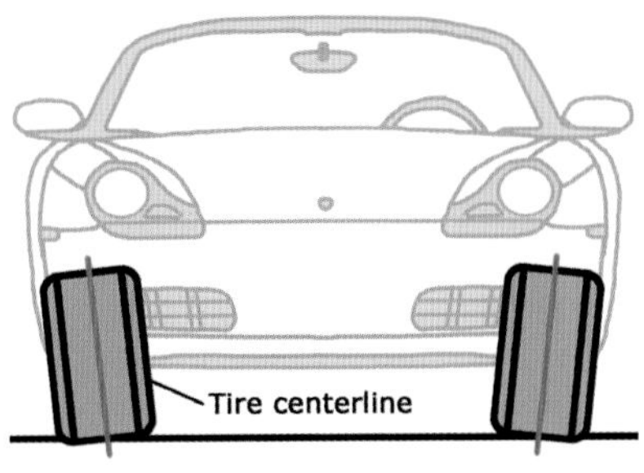

3 Positive Camber. This can cause the outer edges of the tires to wear more quickly than the inside. Positive camber is sometimes designed into the suspension to provide increased stability when traveling over bumpy roads or through turns on the typical high-crowned roads.

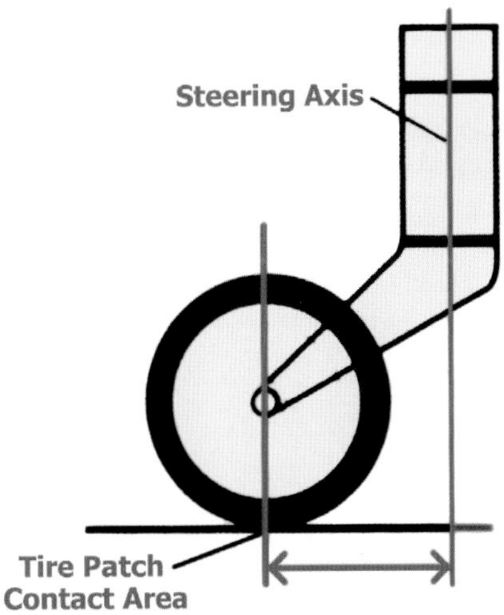

4 Positive Caster. The concept of positive caster is best demonstrated by the wheels of a shopping cart. The steering axis of each wheel is located in front of the point where the wheel touches the ground. The load of the cart is in front of the wheels, and as the cart moves forward, the wheels rotate on their axis to follow the cart's direction. This creates an inherent stability that tends to keep the wheels straight, unless they are forcibly steered in a different direction.

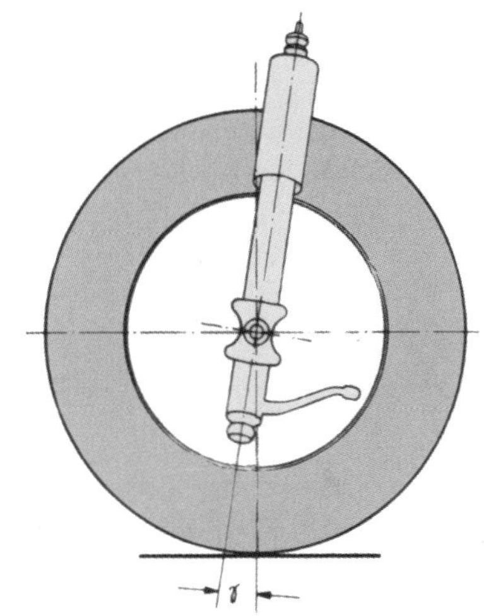

5 All 911 Carreras have slight positive caster, which creates an inherent stability when the car is moving in a straight line. With the angle of the strut tilted back, it places the steering axis and the load in front of the contact patch where the tire meets the pavement. Like the shopping cart example in the previous illustration, the car tends to move forward in a stable, straight line until the wheels are turned in a different direction. The rear trailing arms of the 911, by their design, have extensive positive caster built in.

Caster is the angle that the steering axis is offset from the vertical plane. On the 911 Carrera, the strut points toward the rear of the car, resulting in a positive caster angle. From the factory, the default caster angle should be about 8 degrees. The amount of caster in the suspension directly influences the control and stability of the wheels when traveling in a straight line. Since the Porsche rear suspension utilizes a trailing arm design, which has a tremendous amount of built-in caster, there is no specification for the rear caster. Front suspension caster is very good for high-speed stability—it helps to keep the wheels aligned and straight. If you wish to reduce the amount of front caster, you will need to install the GT3-style front control arms that allow you to vary the caster angle for the car (see Photo 8).

Toe refers to the angle of the two wheels with respect to each other. If a car has toe-in, it means that the front edges of the wheels are closer to each other than the rear edges. Toe-in is adjustable by changing the length of the tie rods (see Project 60). With rear-wheel-drive cars like the 911, sometimes the front wheels try to move toward a toe-out position under power. Setting the wheels to have very slight toe-in can help neutralize this effect. Toe-out occurs when the front edges of the wheels are farther apart than the inner edges. Some toe-out is necessary when turning, since the angle of inclination of the inner wheel must be tighter than the outer wheel. The rear toe should be set as close to neutral as possible.

So how should your Porsche be set up? If you are planning to race your car, then you need nonstock suspension components, and you will probably want as much negative camber as allowed by the racing rules. This setup will counter the car's tendency to straighten out in turns, and you want the maximum tire patch on the road when you are cornering. Setting the camber to a negative value means that when the camber starts to change to slightly positive through turns, the negative setting will help neutralize this effect. There's also a misnomer that a lot of caster is good for racing. While adding more caster to your suspension can indeed make it handle better, the reality is that introducing too much caster into the suspension can reduce your track times. On a perfectly balanced rear-wheel-drive car, adding too much caster can have a tendency to transfer loading from the outside front and inside rear tires to the opposite corners. This can upset the balance and cause a corner entry push. The bottom line here is to seek professional help for alignment specifications and any answers to questions that you might have, and don't accept the common misnomers about suspension upgrades—do your own independent research. Two books that I refer to on these topics are *Race Car Engineering* by Paul Van Valkenburgh and *How to Make Your Car Handle* by Fred Puhn.

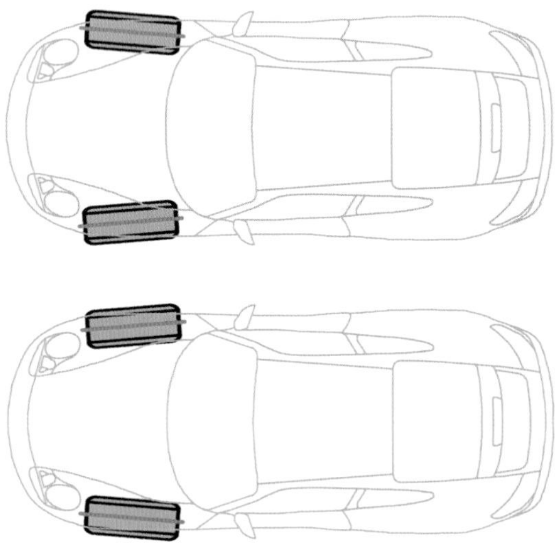

6 **Toe-In and Toe-Out.** The toe of the front suspension refers to the angle of the two wheels with respect to each other. Significant toe-in or toe-out will cause extreme tire wear, as the wheels constantly try to move toward each other (toe-in) or move away from each other (toe-out). The result is that severe friction is created on the tires, and at highway speeds, the tires will wear significantly and power/fuel economy will suffer.

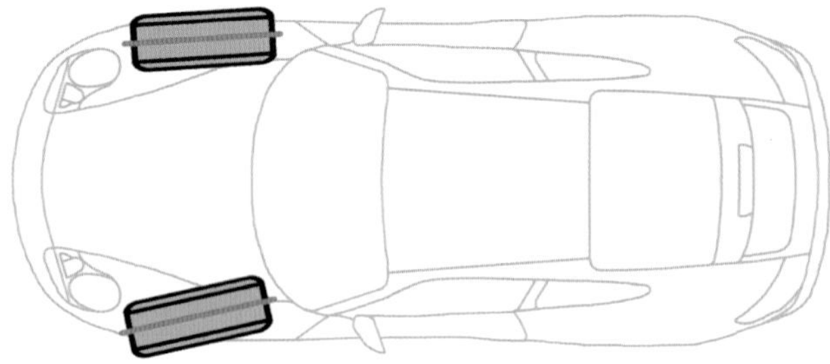

7 **Toe-Out through Turns.** When going around a turn, the inner wheels will turn at a tighter radius than the outer ones. This is so that both wheels will be able to turn around the same point without any tire wear. The outer wheel turns at an angle less sharp than the inner wheel. This minimizes the amount of "scrub" of the tires on the pavement as the car turns.

8 The only way to get the proper measurements for aligning your car is to have it professionally done on an alignment rack. The proper alignment of your Porsche is not something the home mechanic can reliably perform. Don't cheap out either: the 911 Carrera has a lot of adjustment that needs to be set and measured, so be sure you take your car to an expert who has done plenty of them previously. The crew here at Pelican Parts typically uses Johnson's Alignment in Torrance California for all our project and personal cars. This photo shows our project Carrera being corner balanced at Johnson's on top of four scales. Corning balancing is the process of shifting weight from one corner of the car to another in order to achieve an optimum balance. The inset photo shows how the scales determine the weight on each wheel. Changing the value of each corner is typically achieved by raising and/or lowering the suspension spring height by very slight amounts.

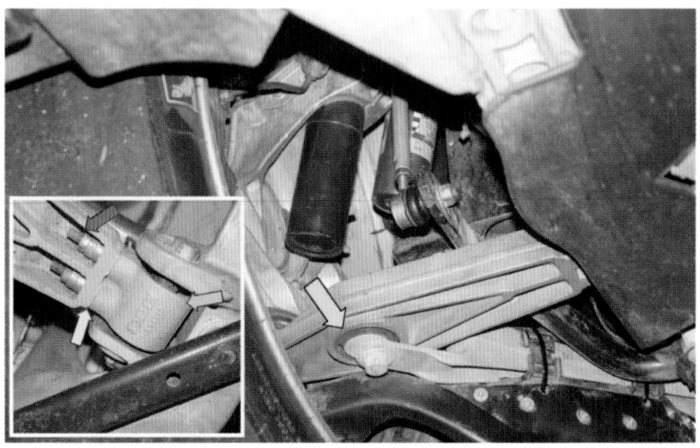

9 This photo shows the underside of a Porsche Cup racing car with fully adjustable suspension. Specifically, this photo shows the GT3 adjustable control arms. The caster can be adjusted using an eccentric bolt that mates with the control arm (yellow arrow). The inset photo shows the opposite side of the control arm, which is a two-piece design that can be shortened or lengthened depending using shims, based upon the amount of additional camber required (blue arrow). The green arrow shows the smaller inside part of the control arm; the red arrow shows the studs that mount into the outer part of the control arm. Add or subtract shims between the two in order to increase or decrease the camber.

PROJECT 60
Suspension Overhaul

Time / Tab / Talent: 20 hours / $200–$3,000 /

Tools: Thin wrench set, pickle forkball joint tool, Torx driver set

Applicable Years: All

Tinware: Control arms, wishbone brackets and bushings, tie rods and boots, sway bar bushings and drop links

More Info: http://www.101projects.com/Carrera/60.htm

Tip: For a complete suspension overhaul, replace everything that can possibly wear out

Performance Gain: Tight, crisp handling

Comp Modification: Replace shocks and springs

Lots of bushings and joints on the 911 Carrera suspension can wear and become loose after many miles of driving. If your car's steering wheel vibrates when traveling on the highway, then components in your front suspension most likely need to be replaced. In general, I recommend replacing every wearable part in the suspension every 80,000–100,000 miles. This preventative measure will ensure you a crisp, firm-handling ride. Four main components need attention when you overhaul the front suspension: control arms, ball joints, sway bar bushings, and tie rods. On the Carrera, the rear suspension is a similar, slightly different version of the front; replacement procedures are almost identical. The PelicanParts.com online catalog has complete replacement kits with everything you need for your overhaul, making the job of acquiring the parts substantially easier.

Tie rods. One of the most common parts to replace are the tie rods. These rods have two universal joints on each end and control the angular position of each front wheel when the car is steered. If the tie rods' joints are worn, then precise steering is impossible and the car will also have wobbly front wheels and a possible alignment problem. Sometimes vibrations in the steering wheel can be caused by worn out tie rods too.

Replacement of the tie rod is relatively simple—if you have the proper tools. Each tie rod is attached to the wheel bearing carrier with a beveled fit. This means that the tie rod is securely pressed into the spindle arm and cannot be removed without a special tool. The best tool for removal is a pickle fork, an angled pitchfork tool designed specifically for this task. Do not attempt to hit the top of the rod end with a large hammer, as this will only serve to bend or damage your strut. Place the pickle fork between the strut and the rod end and then hit the tool repeatedly with a large hammer. The wedge in the pickle fork will drive the rod end out of the arm. You may have to hit the pickle fork quite a few times before the rod end will pop out of its location.

Start by removing the top self-locking nut with a Torx socket wrench (Photo 2). Place the pickle fork between the spindle arm and the rod end and then hit the tool repeatedly with a large hammer (Photo 3). The wedge in the pickle fork will drive the rod end out of the arm. You may have to hit the pickle fork quite a few times before the rod end will pop out of its location.

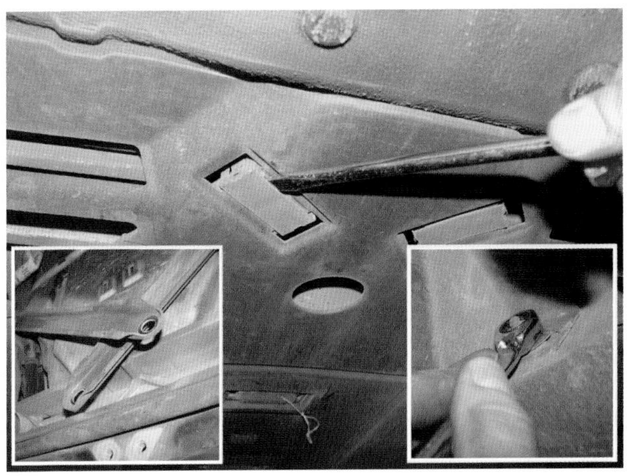

1 A large portion of the front suspension is covered by a large plastic tray. Remove this tray prior to working on the front suspension. The tray is held on with small metal clips that need to be pried off and also a few plastic nuts that need to be removed (lower right). The lower left shows the two crossbraces that need to be loosened and moved out of the way if you are removing the sway bar.

2 Removal/installation of the outer tie rod is started by holding the inner ball joint with a Torx T30 driver and turning the nut. Once the nut is off, then you can use a pickle fork tool to pop the ball joint out of the wheel carrier (see Photo 3).

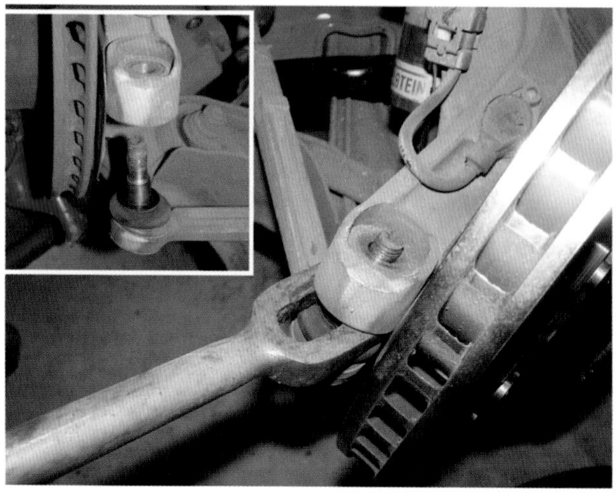

3 The steering tie rods are removed in a similar manner to the ball joints. The pickle fork tool is essential for popping the tie rod ends out of the end of the strut. Proceed cautiously, as the rubber boot can easily be damaged when you remove the tie rod end. However, if you are replacing the tie rod end anyways, then this shouldn't be a concern. You can also use a clamping tool like the one shown in Photo 4 of Project 41.

Once you have the outer rod ends disconnected, remove the boot clamps that attach and secure each end of the rubber boot (bellows) to the tie rod and the steering rack. You will see the exposed metal shaft of the steering rack. Make sure that you don't get any dirt or debris on the rack while you are working on it. Now, it's time to unscrew the old tie rod from the rack. This sounds easier than it really is. The old tie rod may be quite snuggly secured to the rack and could require significant force to remove it. A few specialty wrenches are designed for this purpose, but I've always had good luck with channel locks and/or a plumber's wrench.

Before the final install of the new tie rod, place the new one and the old one side by side on a workbench and adjust the new tie rod so that the length from the rod end to the rack-mating surface is the same. You want to set the two lengths of the tie rods to be equal so that you can minimize the change in alignment of the car (Photo 4). You will have to get the car realigned regardless, but it's a good practice to get the alignment close so that you can safely drive to the alignment shop. Mark the final position of the tie rod end on the new tie rod (white paper correction fluid comes in handy here) and then remove it. Don't install the new rod end yet.

Before you screw the tie rod into the rack, make sure that you spread a few drops of Loctite or Permatex Threadlocker onto the threads. After you insert the tie rod into the rack, use a pair of large vise grips or channel locks to tighten it down. There really isn't too much to grab onto with a regular wrench, and chances are you won't have the special thin wrench that is required to tighten the tie rod. The torque specification for the tie rod to the rack is 59 ft-lbs (80 Nm).

Once the tie rod is tight, place the rubber boot over the tie rod and onto the steering rack. You will have to remove the rod end on the end of the tie rod in order to make the boot fit. Use pliers and screwdrivers to stretch the boot over each

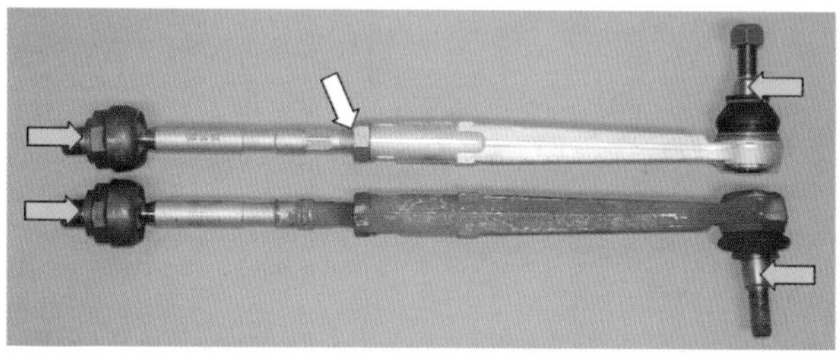

4 Before you install the new tie rods, you should attempt to get each one as close as possible in length to the originals (the distance between the green arrows should be the same). Place them on your bench and compare the lengths, then mark the position of the tie rod end using some white correction fluid (small white arrow). Adjust the new ones as necessary to the lengths of the old ones. This will enable you to get as close as possible to the toe-in alignment adjustment. You will still need to take the car in for an alignment, but you want to get as close as possible to minimize tire wear while you're driving to the alignment shop.

end. Once the boot is in position, install two new clamps over the two ends of the boot to secure it to the rack housing.

After the boot is installed, reattach the tie rod end. Make sure that the length of the tie rod is the same as the measurement of the old one. Adjust the position of the rod end to match up with the mark that you previously made when you compared it to the original tie rod. The torque specifications are as follows:

- Tie rod nut that mates into the wheel carrier and has a lock nut to hold the tie rod ball joint in place: 56 ft-lb (75 Nm)
- Tie rod lock nut that holds the ball joint onto the tie rod itself: 37 ft-lb (50 Nm)

To complete the job, install the new rod end into the front control arm. Perform the same procedure for the opposite

side. The car should be taken straight to an alignment shop, as it is very easy to mess up the toe-in of the front suspension when you are replacing the tie rods. If you are planning on performing any other front suspension work that might affect the alignment, it would be advisable to do it now, since you will have to realign the car anyway.

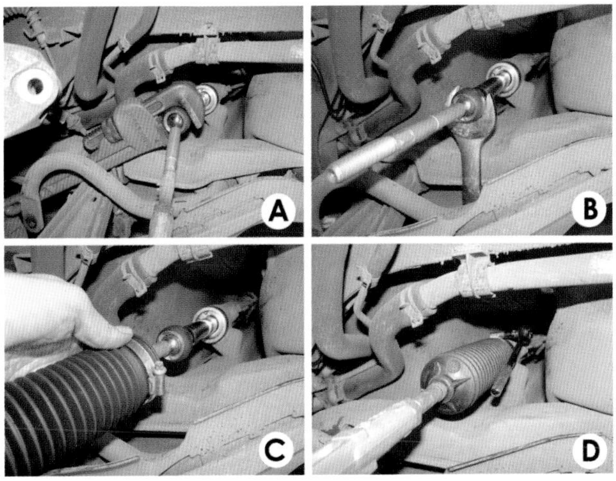

5 Shown here are several steps in the tie rod installation process. **A:** A good tool I've found to remove tie rod ends is a plumber's wrench. I've had good luck removing the tie rod ends with this tool, especially when access to the area is tight, as it is on the 911 Carrera. **B:** The new tie rods are screwed into the ends of the steering rack. Although there is a torque specification for this, it's nearly impossible to measure without the use of a special installation tool. I typically tighten it as tight as I can using the plumber's wrench. Add some Loctite or Permatex Threadlocker to the assembly as well, as shown in Photo 6. **C:** Prefit the boot and clamps, and slide them onto the tie rod. **D:** It's an understatement to say that the original equipment manufacturer clamps are a bit difficult to work with. I believe that they are meant to be used during the car's assembly when good access can be had to all areas. So instead, I typically use standard hose clamps, which I feel are better constructed and easier to install.

Wishbone/control arms. The 911 Carrera uses two separate components to create a virtual A-arm suspension that integrates four joints: two ball joints, one center connection, and one rear rubber bushing. Many suspension problems can be traced back to worn out control arm/wishbone ball joints or bushings. Shaking of the steering wheel at high speeds is a good indicator that the control arm/wishbone bushings are worn, the ball joints are worn, or the control arm itself has become bent.

The ball joints, located at the bottom of the strut and attached to the chassis end of the control arm, help the entire assembly pivot and rotate as the control arm turns and pivots and the suspension rides up and down. Needless to say, these critical components can wear out over time and should be replaced every 100,000 miles or so or if the front suspension is beginning to feel a little wobbly.

Both ball joints are integrated into the two assemblies and are not replaceable (you must replace the entire control arm and/or wishbone). Removal of the control arm involves the following steps: disconnect the inner ball joint and disconnect the attachment point to the wishbone (see photos 10 and 11). The wishbone removal requires that you disconnect the wheel bearing carrier from the wishbone (attached with the outer ball joint) and the control arm. For the outer ball joint, the nut is easily accessible on the lower part of the strut. The ball joint is attached with a beveled fit, similar to the tie rod ends. This means that the ball joint end is securely pressed into the spindle arm and cannot be removed without a special tool. The best tool for removal is the angled pickle fork discussed previously. Installation of the new ball joint, which is integrated on the wishbone, is easy—simply insert it into its hole and tighten down the nut on top. Follow the photo array in this project for guidance on which components need to be disconnected for replacement.

Sway bar bushings. As 911s age, the tendency is to find them with worn-out bushings, particularly the sway

6 On just about every other car I've worked on, there are locking tabs that act as a stopgap measure to prevent the tie rods from backing out of the steering rack. Surprisingly, the 911 Carrera lacks these, so I prefer to apply some Loctite or Permatex Threadlocker compound to ensure that the tie rods stay in place. Carefully clean out the inside of the steering rack prior to screwing on the tie rods with the Threadlocker applied to the threads.

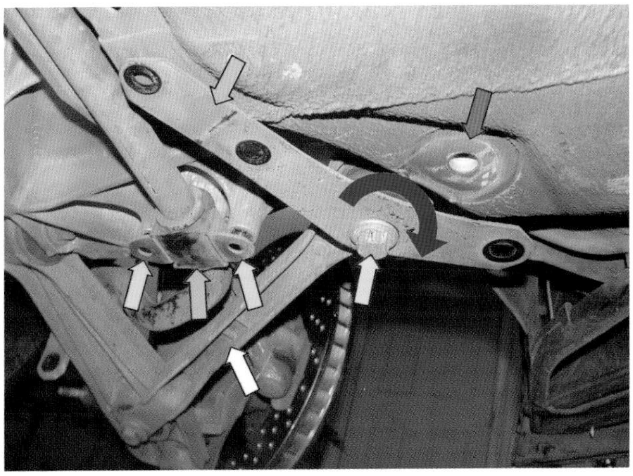

7 The front control arm (white arrow) is attached to a boomerang-shaped plate (orange arrow) that is bolted to the bottom of the chassis. In order to loosen the control arm connection and remove the sway bar bushing (green arrow), remove the two bolts on either side of the sway bar bushing (yellow arrows) and the large bolt at the rear (red arrow). You do not need to remove the bolt indicated by the light blue arrow. Finally, rotate the boomerang out of the way (dark blue arrow).

bar bushings. The first step in replacing the bushings is to figure out if they need to be replaced. Carefully inspect them for cracking, and also check to make sure that their inner diameter hugs the sway bar tightly. If they do not appear to be worn, then simply apply a little bit of lithium grease inside the bushing. If they are worn, then they will need to be replaced.

Replacing the bushings is very easy. With the car elevated (see Project 1) and the front wheels removed, simply disconnect the bracket that holds the sway bar bushing (see Photo 7). The bar and bushing together should drop down slightly if you release both sides at the same time.

The new replacement bushings are split down the middle, so they should easily slide onto the bar and into the bracket (see Photo 9). Remove the old bushings and insert the new ones, making sure that you coat the bushings with some white lithium grease on the inside.

The sway bar drop links are an easy replacement, too. Both the top and bottom parts of the drop link contain small ball joints that attach to the strut tower and the sway bar. Remove the nut from each of the two mini ball joints on each end of the drop link. The small ball joint may present a bit of a challenge; you may need a special thin wrench to remove the retaining nut (see Photo 8). Installation of the new drop links involves simply bolting them into place while holding the ball joint from spinning using the thin wrench. The replacement of the rear sway bar bushings is nearly identical to the front.

It's important to note that you should always use brand new factory hardware when replacing suspension components. Most of the nuts and bolts used in the front suspension have self-locking compounds impregnated into their threads. Reusing old hardware can result in nuts or bolts coming loose and causing a dangerous situation.

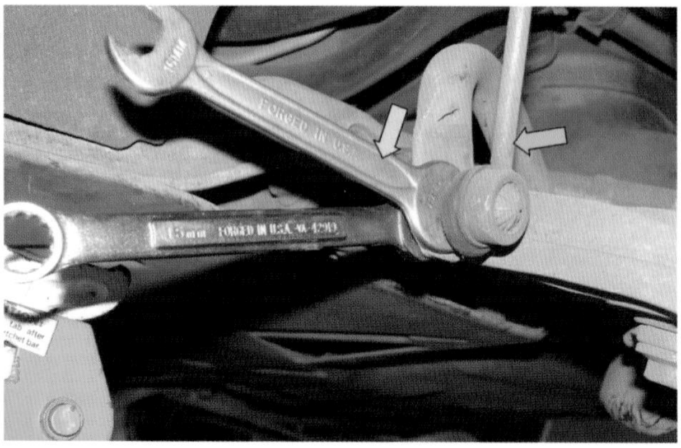

8 The drop links (green arrow) may present a challenge to remove, as the ball joint on the top of the link may spin when you try to remove the outer nut. If this happens, you will need to use a thin wrench (yellow arrow) to hold the ball joint in place while you loosen the nut. You can purchase a set of these wrenches that are specifically designed to fit into places where a normal, thick wrench will not (available in the tools section of the PelicanParts.com online catalog). They are typically about 1/8 inch thick and are a very useful tool to add to your arsenal.

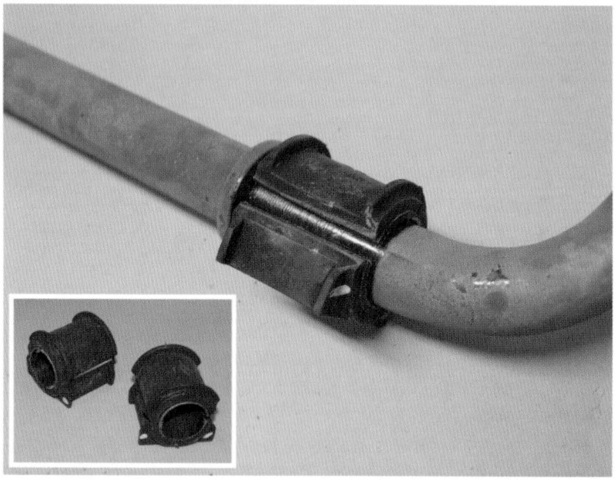

9 Good condition sway bar bushings are essential to good handling. To perform a complete renewal of the front suspension, you should replace the sway bar bushings and drop links as well. The bushings have a slit down the center so that you can easily pry them on and off the sway bar.

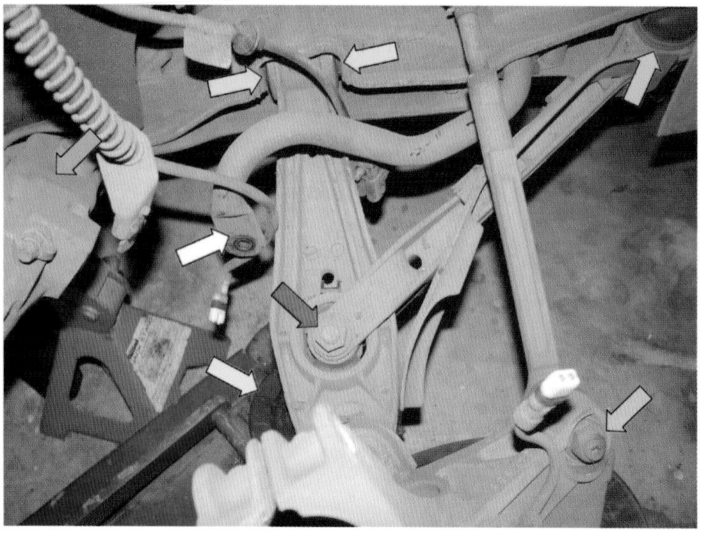

10 Shown here is the top view of the front suspension. Since the front shock has been removed, the assembly must be supported by the floor jack (blue arrow). The brake caliper is tied up and hung from wire on the left (purple arrow). The tie rod is connected to the wheel carrier as shown by the orange arrow. When removing the shocks, you need to loosen the main bolt that attaches the wishbone to the chassis (yellow arrow). Don't remove it; only loosen it, as this will give you enough free play to drop the assembly down and remove the front shocks. The control arm is connected to the center of the wishbone (red arrow), and the boomerang-shaped plate shown in Photo 7 (green arrow). Finally, this photo also shows the sway bar (white), which has been disconnected from its drop links (not shown).

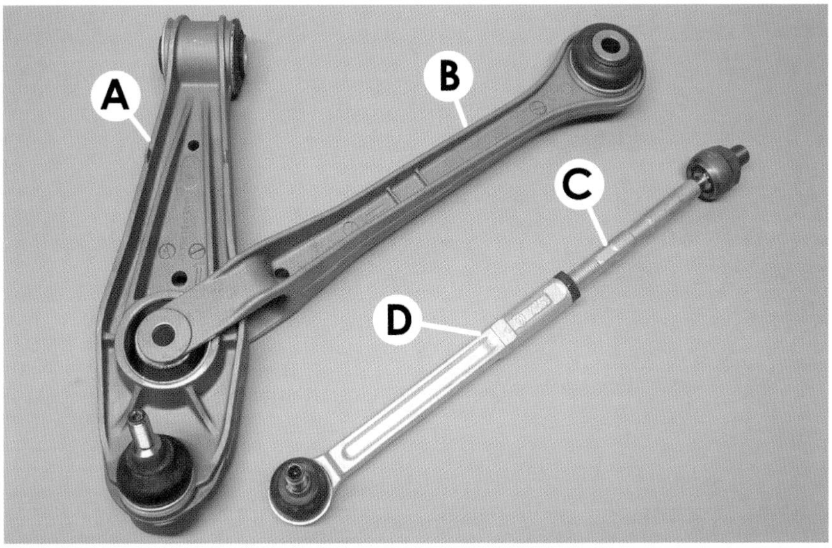

11 This photo shows the main components of the front suspension on the Carrera. **A:** This is the wishbone, and it supports the wheel carrier, which wraps around the shock and contains the wheel bearing. **B:** The control arm constrains the movement of the wishbone so that it travels in a mostly up and down manner. **C:** The inner tie rod attaches to the steering rack and is mated with the outer tie rod (D). Changing the effective length of the tie rod assembly (C and D together) changes the toe-in alignment specification for that side of the car (see Project 59). **D:** The outer tie rod attaches to the wheel carriers and transmits steering input from the rack to the carrier.

12 Although I haven't quite seen it yet on the 911 Carrera, this steering column rubber coupling tends to age and wear out on other cars. At this time (2013), the only way to replace this coupling is to replace the entire steering column. At $1,600 or so, that's a bit cost prohibitive. I suspect that as these cars age, an aftermarket replacement part will become available.

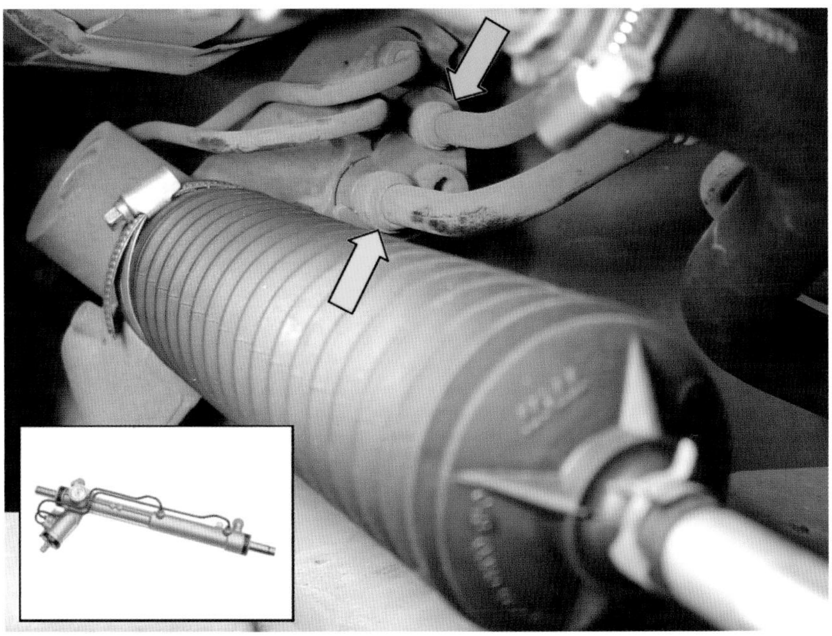

13 There's a night-and-day difference between a new and used rack. The inset photo shows a Genuine Porsche rebuilt power steering rack-and-pinion assembly. If the rack wears out, then you will find that your steering will be sloppy. Also common are leaky racks that deposit power steering fluid on the floor of your garage. Be aware though: sometimes it may only be the power steering lines that are leaking and need to be replaced—not an expensive rack (green arrow = pressure line; yellow arrow = return line). Carefully check the rack and lines first, prior to spending your money on a rebuilt rack. The most common leakage point for the rack is out the ends. If you cut open your tie rod boot and a lot of power steering fluid starts flowing out, then chances are that the seals in the ends of your rack are worn and it needs to be rebuilt or replaced. Unfortunately, there are no individual repair parts available for you to fix the rack yourself; it must be sent back to the manufacturer.

PROJECT 61
Performance Suspension/ Lowering Your Carrera

Time / Tab / Talent: 25 hours / $3500 / 4 wrenches

Tools: Bilstein height adjustment tool

Applicable Years: All

Tinware: PSS10 Performance suspension kit

Tip: The PSS10 kit is a good value if you want a sporty suspension and lower ride height

Performance Gain: Stiffer suspension, firmer ride

Comp Modification: Replace suspension bushings

More Info: http://www.101projects.com/Carrera/61.htm

Shocks and springs. The PSS10 performance suspension kit from Bilstein is one of the top performing kits available for the Carrera. The system includes two front coil-over spring/shock setups and two rear coil-over spring/shock assemblies. Both the front and rear springs are easily adjustable for tweaking the exact ride height that you're looking for. The kit is a bolt-in replacement available for almost all Carreras. The PSS10 kit incorporates adjustable spring perches for both front and rear height adjustment. Installation of the kit is no more difficult than installing stock shock absorbers and new springs (see Project 64). This kit is constantly being updated by Bilstein, so the photos in this article may differ slightly from the actual kit available currently on the market. In general however, the installation procedure should be the same. Also recently made available for the 911 Carrera is the Bilstein Damptronic kit, which has electronically controlled dampening settings.

After you have installed the PSS10 kit, you need to have the car realigned. Due to the design of the front suspension, the alignment specs will change when you lower the car from the stock height. (See Project 59 for more details.) In addition, lowering your 911 can cause issues with clearance of wider wheels and tires. Before you test the suspension to the max, make sure the tire and wheel clearances are okay.

Sway bars. For our project car, I chose to use upgraded sway bars, drop links, and strut mounts manufactured by Tarett Engineering. The sway bars are lightweight, hollow, and 26.8mm in diameter, and they weigh about one-half the weight of the stock solid bar with equivalent stiffness. These sway bars are also fully adjustable with multiple mounting holes located on each end so that you can increase or decrease stiffness by moving the drop links in or out.

Many times owners will want to upgrade their sway bars to larger units with more torsional stiffness. If you install a larger engine, or are planning on creating a dedicated track car, then adding a stiffer bar will give you a flatter ride and help with cornering. As with anything in this world though, there is a tradeoff. Stiffer sway bars may result in a rougher ride around town, particularly on bumpy pavement. Installing a sway bar that is too stiff may actually decrease performance if one of the front wheels begins to lift during hard cornering. It's best to speak with someone who has run a particular sized bar in their car and see how it performed for them on the street and on the track.

Adjustable drop links. The best way to set the drop link preload is with the car on flat ground after it's been aligned and corner balanced. After the car is balanced it will have the correct theoretical weight on each wheel so that handling will be the same going into left or right hand turns. It will also help to minimize the chances of a wheel locking up under hard braking. You want to set the drop links so that there is no sway bar preload that can affect this balance. It may be possible to get the preload close with the car up on jack stands and the suspension hanging, but it is far more accurate to set it with the suspension loaded (car on the ground).

To remove the sway bar preload, you only need to adjust one drop link on each sway bar. With the drop links connected on both ends and the center jamb nuts loose, rotate the center link in either direction to lengthen or shorten the link. If you're rotating it the correct direction (reducing preload) it will begin to feel easier to turn. Conversely, the drop link will become more difficult to rotate if you're turning it in the wrong direction. Once you get to the point where you reach neutral preload, the drop link will be very easy to turn and then will start to become more difficult to turn as you pass

the optimum setting. Rotate the drop link back to the neutral point and lock the center jamb nuts.

With the 911 Carrera, the front preload should be set with the wheels pointing straight—if the wheels are turned it will slightly preload the sway bar. Additionally, the rear drop link preload should be set with the front wheels facing straight; turning the wheels will tip the car slightly, causing the rear sway bar to preload as well. Since the front drop link also connects to the strut, it needs to accommodate the strut turning when the wheels are turned with steering input. Therefore, the drop link rod ends need to be phased relative to each other such that they don't bind when the wheels are turned. The specially machined spacers installed on each side of the drop link rod ends are designed to roll into the rod end housing and provide an appropriate amount of clearance needed to accommodate the wheels turning lock to lock.

Even with these special spacers, proper rod end phasing is still required. To accomplish this, first adjust the preload as described previously. Lock only one jamb nut on each of the drop links. Next, rotate the wheels to full lock in one direction. Working on one side at a time, rotate the upper and lower rod ends in the same direction until they bind and will not rotate farther. Then tighten the loose jamb nut. The rod ends should now be phased properly. If it's set properly, there should be no binding and you should be able to rotate the entire link slightly between bind points. Next rotate the steering to the opposite lock and check the opposite side to see if the link will still rotate slightly. If there is more free rotation of the link with the steering at full lock in one direction, make an adjustment to get it close to being equal for both sides. Then repeat for the other drop link.

Front strut mounts/camber plates. The camber plates are a bolt-in replacement for the factory strut mounts. They eliminate the compliant factory rubber bushings and replace them with precision Teflon-lined spherical bearings for a tighter front suspension and quicker steering response. The increased precision reduces front wheel camber changes during hard cornering, which maintains the optimum tire contact patch for improved traction and better handling. Two sets of mounting holes allow for more than 1.1 degree of extra negative camber.

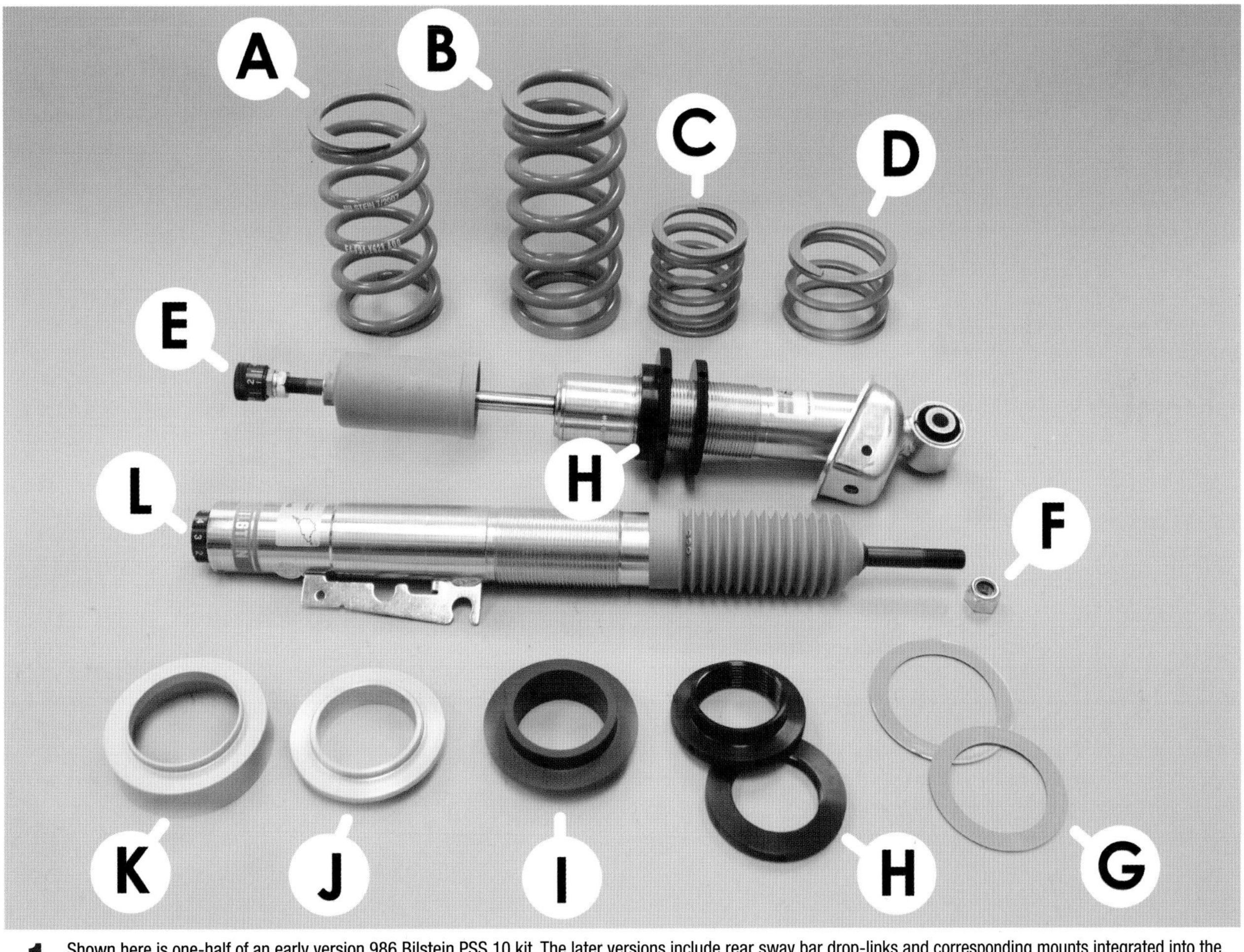

1 Shown here is one-half of an early version 986 Bilstein PSS 10 kit. The later versions include rear sway bar drop-links and corresponding mounts integrated into the bottom of the rear shocks. **A:** Front upper spring **B:** Rear upper spring **C:** Front lower spring **D:** Rear lower spring **E:** Fully adjustable rear shock absorber **F:** Lock nut for front shock absorber **G:** Slip inserts for front spring retainer **H:** Spring perch supports **I:** Upper/lower spring retainer front shock **J:** Upper/lower spring retainer rear shock **K:** Rear spring top plate **L:** Fully adjustable front shock absorber

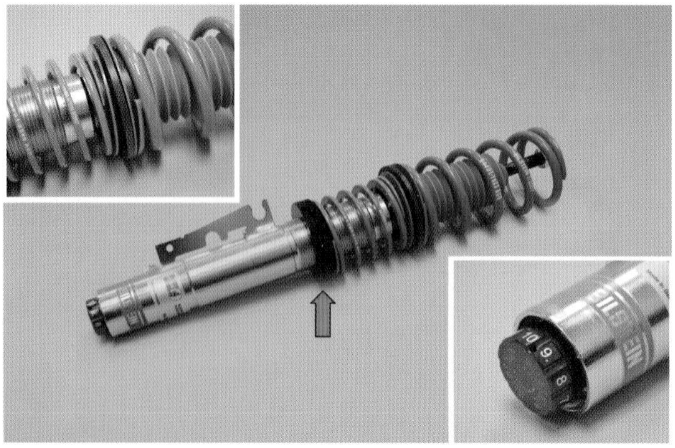

2 Shown here is a close-up of the front PSS10 shock. The upper and lower springs are separated by the spring retainer and two blue plastic slip inserts (inset, upper right). The adjustment knob is located at the bottom of the shock for easy adjustment (inset, lower right). Turn the knob to 10 for a softer ride, or turn it to 1 for a stiffer performance feel. The adjustment of the ride height is accomplished by rotating the spring perch and retainer (red arrow) up or down the length of the shock.

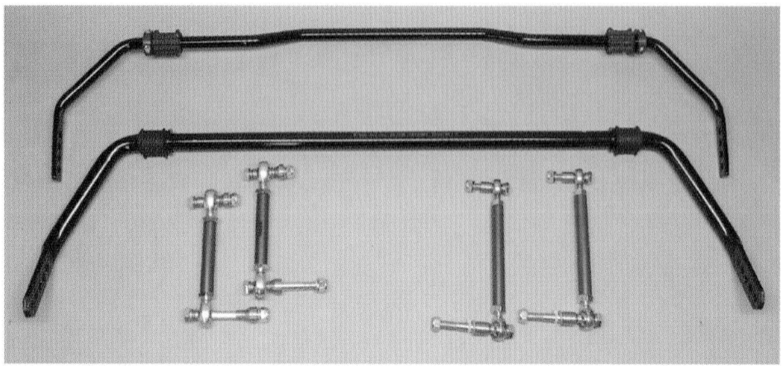

4 Shown here are aftermarket front and rear sway bar kits from Tarett Engineering. This performance kit is specifically designed to work with the 911 Carrera and includes new bushings and drop links. The bar has multiple adjustment settings. Bolting the drop links to the outer holes produces a softer ride, whereas using the inner holes results in a stiffer suspension. Depending upon your model of Carrera, the angles and shape of the bars may differ slightly from the ones in the photo shown here.

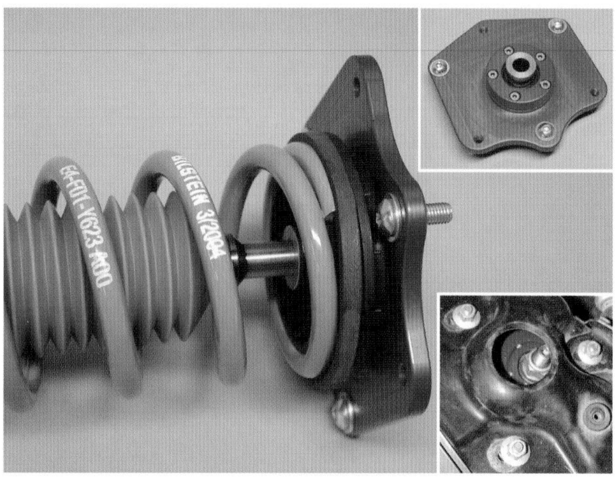

6 This photo shows the Tarett Engineering front upper strut mount attached to the PSS10 kit. The upper right inset photo shows the bottom side of the bearing assembly. The lower right inset photo shows how the strut mount moves the top of the shocks inward to achieve the maximum amount of negative camber.

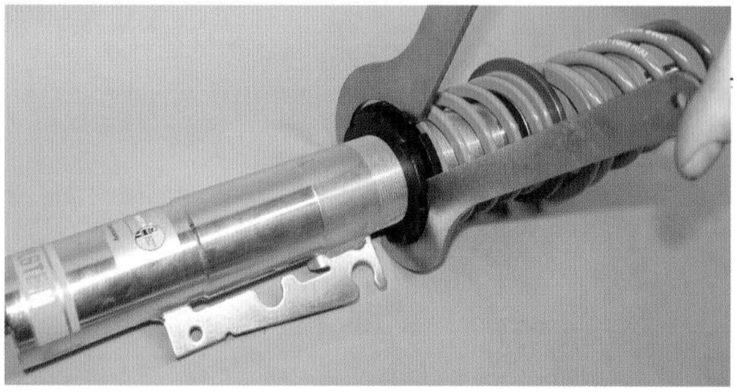

3 The ride height of the suspension is adjusted by changing the location of the lower spring perches on the shock housing. Using the two special Bilstein adjustment tools, you can lower or raise the perches. Lock them together when you've achieved the proper height.

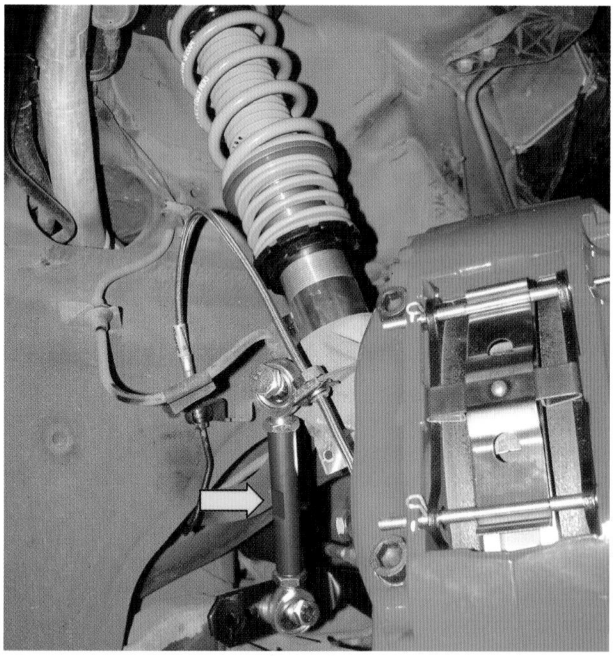

5 This photo is quite possibly my favorite in this entire book. With one shot, it shows the PSS10 system, the Tarett Engineering drop links, adjustable sway bars, upper camber plate strut mount, and the Brembo big brake kit (Project 53). The yellow arrow shows the adjustable drop links, which need to be dialed in along with the rest of your suspension components.

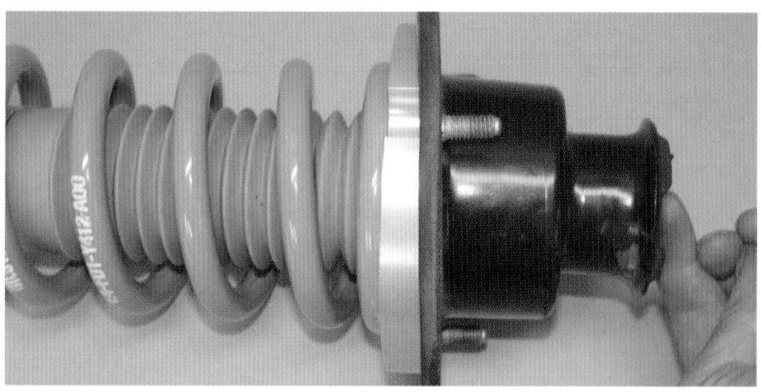

7 The rear shocks are set up very similarly to the front ones, except for the top shock mount, which is attached against an angled upper aluminum plate. This allows the shock to mate at the correct angle to the chassis.

PROJECT 62

Installing a Strut Tower Brace

Time / Tab / Talent: 30 minutes / $50–$500 /

Tip: Spend your money on something else.

Tools: Socket set

Performance Gain: Stiffer chassis

Applicable Years: All

Comp Modification: Replace pollen filter.

Tinware: Strut brace

More Info: http://www.101projects.com/Carrera/62.htm

The Porsche 911 is well known for its agility and superb performance in handling. However, because of the design of the chassis, there exists a weakness in the handling of the cars. The front shock towers are not well supported in the modern Carrera chassis—they are somewhat isolated and unsupported. As a result, the towers can bend and flex under heavy cornering. This flexing can cause detrimental changes in the handling of your car, because in general, the stiffer the chassis, the better the handling of the car. Camber strut braces are designed to maintain the distance between the shocks under heavy cornering. A bar linking the top of the shock towers ensures that the towers do not bend when the chassis is flexing.

Well, that's what the marketers say when selling these bars. The strut bars are yet another controversial product that many people feel the need to install on their cars. On some cars, the early Porsche 911s, for example, the installation of the strut bar is an important chassis stiffening device. Because of their rear engine design, the front chassis can be decidedly weak, particularly when rust has started to affect the chassis stiffness. But the Carrera rear-engined chassis is different; it's supported by a much more rigid frame, which includes a very strong sheet metal structure that runs the width of the car. Included in this structure are two welded strut braces that can be seen in Photo 1.

Which strut bars are most effective? First of all, I have little faith in the strut bars that are manufactured out of aluminum. Aluminum is not a very strong metal—you can often bend aluminum pipes with your hands. Add to that the fact that most of the strut bars must have some type of angle in them in order to fit neatly around the engine and under the hood—there's no straight shot across the engine bay. This combination creates a very weak support when you think of the forces you're trying to counteract. In my opinion, the aluminum strut braces are merely window dressing for the engine compartment.

I'm also not fond of bars with hinges built in to the strut mounts. If they move at all, the shock towers are likely to see movement that would place the strut brace in both compression and tension. This means that a stiff connection between the strut towers is vital to proper operation of any strut bar. Any time you place a fastener in the assembly, you will introduce backlash and slop in at least one direction (compression or tension). This results in the bar becoming ineffective in at least one of those directions.

The best strut tower braces are the one-piece units manufactured out of thick steel pipe welded together. These will offer the best protection against any chassis flex when installed between the two strut towers. Unfortunately, I can't say that I've seen one installed in a late-model 911 Carrera that I actually thought would provide additional stiffness.

I also find it surprising that if you ask die-hard racers who drive their 911s on the track, most of them don't run with a strut brace and can't feel the difference even when pulling some significant side loads (1.4G) out of the corners. For dedicated track cars, the strut towers are often reinforced with steel pipe that is welded diagonally across the front trunk compartment. Another problem I see is that the Carrera already has reinforcement bars bolted from the shock towers to the chassis. These bars already provide a tremendous amount of structural support for the towers.

The bottom line? If you believe that a strut bar will do you some benefit or if you are looking to spruce up your front compartment, then adding one to your car is a relatively simple task—just bolt it on top of the strut towers. If your goal is increased performance, then I would suggest that you spend your money elsewhere.

1 Shown here is a great-looking carbon-fiber strut bar that extends across the rear of the battery. This bar in particular is only really good for show, in my opinion. The aluminum brackets that these bars are manufactured out of are relatively weak, are designed with multiple fasteners, and are weakened further by the angled bracket design. Ironically, the entire strut brace is hidden by the side plastic covers, thus diminishing its visual appeal as well.

2 I included this photo of an E30 BMW M3 to illustrate what I feel a good strut brace should look like. Although not as attractive, the brace shown in this photo is probably one of the most effective I've seen. It's a thick, large diameter steel pipe that directly reinforces the shock towers and requires significant forces to deflect and bend. Despite the fact that there are two rather large angles in the brace, the strength of the steel pipe should more than compensate for the reduced rigidity. These are the types of bars that I recommend if you're going to be installing one in your car. Unfortunately, the lack of room in the Carrera's front trunk make the installation of this style somewhat prohibitive.

PROJECT 63
Steering Wheel Replacement

Time / Tab / Talent: 1 hour / $150–$1000 /

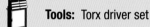

Tools: Torx driver set

Applicable Years: All

Tinware: Steering wheel and hub adapter

Tip: Use a steering lock bar to help loosen the wheel

Performance Gain: Good improvement in driving feel—much improved looks

Comp Modification: Upgrade your dashboard information computer

More Info: http://www.101projects.com/Carrera/63.htm

One of the most exciting and rewarding projects that you can perform on your 911 is the replacement of the standard four-spoke steering wheel. In addition to the gorgeous factory three-spoke wheel, you can choose from a wide variety of aftermarket wheels as well. Let's face it: the stock 911 Carrera wheel is not something that many people can get too excited about. Installing a wheel of your choosing cures all that.

It's important to mention a word about safety here. All the later-model Carreras came from the factory equipped with driver side air bags built into the steering wheel. Air bags are important pieces of safety equipment, and I fully recommend keeping them in place. That said, you cannot install a nonfactory aftermarket steering wheel and also keep your air bag in place, unless you purchase an aftermarket wheel specifically made for the Carrera with an integrated air bag (Aitwe manufactures one such wheel). With that in mind, I recommend that you install an aftermarket wheel only if your car originally didn't come with a driver side air bag or if you are converting your car into a club racer or weekend track car. You can still choose to install the wheel into your street car, but be forewarned: air bags are probably the best protection you will have in a crash. Also, state and local regulations may legally restrict what you can do with your air bag.

That said, I recommend upgrading to the factory three-spoke wheel with the integrated air bag. The wheel is a bolt-on upgrade, and it looks very good too—particularly the gold crest in the center of the air bag.

The first step is to disconnect the battery and wait at least 15 minutes (see Project 83). This is very important, as the air bag itself is a dangerous explosive package and can be accidentally set off by a variety of factors. Also, the air bag control system is designed to remain operational for up to 15 minutes after the battery has been disconnected. The next step is to remove the air bag from the steering wheel by disconnecting the two T27 Torx screws that attach it to the front of the wheel (see the insets in Photo 2). Extend the steering wheel as far toward the rear of the car as you can go to afford yourself the maximum amount of room to get your Torx tool in there. With the screws loosened (they do not come out of the air bag) and the air bag loose from the wheel, disconnect the small harness, remove it, and place it aside.

The next step is to remove the wheel itself. If you don't happen to own an impact wrench, there is another neat trick that I developed for removing the steering wheel. First, take one of those obnoxiously large, red steering wheel locks and clamp it onto the steering wheel. The long handle on the lock will allow you to gain a significant amount of leverage on the wheel. Then insert the deep socket onto the center steering wheel nut. Compressing together the steering wheel lock handle and the long handle attached to the socket will enable you to loosen the steering wheel nut. Under no circumstances should you ever turn the steering wheel all the way to the end of the rack and use the end stop to hold the wheel while you remove the nut. The steering wheel has a lot of leverage, and you can easily damage your rack and pinion if you apply a large amount of torque to the wheel.

Once you have the nut off the wheel, take some white correction fluid or a marker pen and mark the steering wheel and the shaft so you know which spline to place it back on. Then simply pull the wheel off of the steering column. If the wheel is stuck on the splines and doesn't want to come off, take a rubber mallet and gently tap the rear of the wheel until it begins to move. If you are installing an aftermarket wheel, place the new wheel onto the included steering wheel hub and then onto the car. Be sure that you properly hook up the horn and test it before you tighten the wheel down again. For the Porsche three-spoke wheel, the installation of the new wheel is basically the reverse of the removal process.

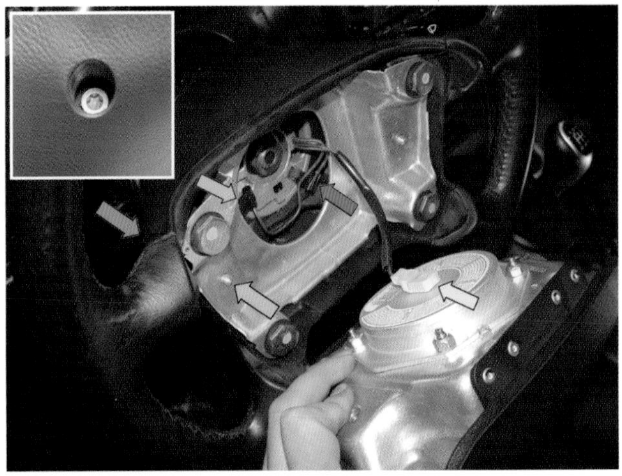

1 Shown here is one of my favorite steering wheels of all time: the Porsche factory three-spoke wheel. Available as an option on the cars when they were new, this upgrade is pretty spendy (about $1,000 for the wheel and the new air bag) but, in my opinion, definitely worth it. Remember, you can recover the cost of your new wheel by selling your old air bag on eBay or the classifieds section of PelicanParts.com. The part number for the wheel in black is 996-347-804-54-A28, and the part number for the air bag with the gold crest is 996-803-089-02-A28.

2 Removal of the air bag itself is pretty easy. Remove the two screws on either side of the back of the steering wheel column by using a T27 Torx driver (upper left photo). These holes are somewhat hidden from view and have tiny access holes in the backside of the steering wheel. The purple arrow shows you where you need to insert the Torx driver, and the orange arrow indicates the tail end of the Torx bolt. With these two screws loosened, the air bag should simply pop out of the center of the wheel. Disconnect the wire harness to the air bag (blue arrow shows where it plugs into the air bag), and place it aside. Also disconnect the horn wires (green and red arrows). Make sure you disconnect the battery and wait at least 15 minutes before attempting to remove the air bag.

3 A trick that I developed for removing steering wheels involves locking the wheel with one of those steering wheel locking devices. Don't allow the steering wheel to lock against the mechanism in the lock cylinder, and don't let it bottom out against the steering rack. Using a breaker bar and the locking device in this fashion, you can easily remove the steering center nut.

4 Before you remove the wheel, mark its position on the shaft with a permanent marker (inset). With the wheel retaining nut removed and the wire harnesses disconnected, you should be able to pull the steering wheel off of the splined hub in the center. Thread the wires through the hole in the wheel as you remove it from the steering shaft.

5 Although you lose the safety of the air bag, the new steering wheel really spices up the interior of the car and gives your Porsche that Motorsport feel. If you are removing the air bag, you need to "trick" the air bag computer into thinking that it's still connected. Placing a 0.3 ohm resistor across the two terminals of the connector will indicate to the computer that the air bag is still in place, and it won't trigger the air bag lamp. This should allow your system to continue to properly control and operate the passenger side air bag. The installation of a MOMO aftermarket wheel requires the use of a ½-inch washer under the steering wheel nut because the shaft is not threaded deep enough for the aftermarket wheels.

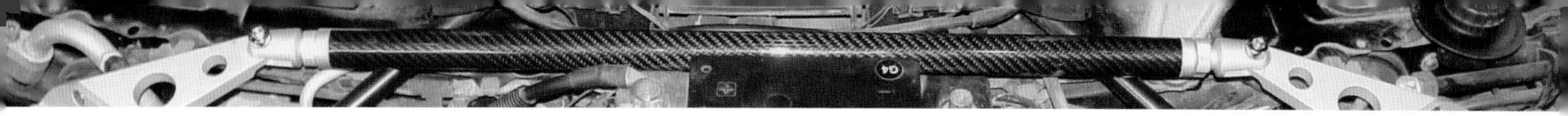

PROJECT 64
Replacing Shocks and Springs

Time / Tab / Talent: 8 hours / $1,200 /

Tools: Spring compressor, floor jack, jack stands

Applicable Years: All

Tinware: Shocks, springs, and hardware

More Info: http://www.101projects.com/Carrera/64.htm

Tip: Purchase an electric or air impact wrench for this task

Performance Gain: Smoother, crisper handling

Comp Modification: Install performance springs and lower the suspension

Another great project for your Carrera is the replacement of the front and rear shocks. I usually recommend that you replace both the front and the rear at the same time, as they take roughly similar abuse over their lifetime, and the fronts or rears are not likely to be more or less worn than the other ones. As a rule, the shocks should always be replaced in pairs (left and right together). The replacement procedures for the front and rear shocks are very similar.

I recommend that you replace shocks every 50,000 miles or so or if they start to show signs of fading or wearing out. If you push down on a corner of the car, it should spring back with almost no oscillation up and down. If the car bounces up and down, then you probably need new shocks. Different driving patterns may also affect the life of shock absorbers. Cars that are raced or often driven on windy roads may need to have their shocks replaced more often than street cars. It is also important to remember to have the car realigned if you install performance springs into your car that lowers it from its stock level. Changing the height of the suspension changes the values of the alignment/suspension settings.

With the car elevated in the air (see Project 1) and the wheels removed, start with one strut and remove the brake caliper (see Project 56). Unplug any brake sensors that may be connected to the caliper and disconnect them from the strut (see Photo 1). Use some rope or wire to tie the brake caliper aside so that it doesn't hang by its rubber hose. Now, disconnect the sway bar drop link from the wheel bearing carrier (see Photo 2). In the front trunk compartment, mark the location of the three nuts that hold the shock to the tower and then remove them (Photo 3). Finally, loosen but do not remove the bolt that attaches the wishbone to the chassis (see Photo 4). This will allow you to drop the strut downward to its lowest point so that you may pull it out from the car after you remove the shock insert and spring.

With the strut assembly and wheel bearing carrier loose, you should be able to push down on the wishbone and maneuver the shock down over the top of the fender. If your car has been lowered or has had some other suspension changes made from the stock configuration, you may need some extra wiggle room. In this case, use spring compressors to compress the spring and remove it while the strut is still under the fender. Then you should be able to compress the shock further and remove it from the bottom of the fender. When working close to the fender here, be careful that you don't scratch your paint—cover it with a moving blanket or something similarly soft to protect the paint finish.

With the strut assembly off and on your workbench, install the spring compressor onto the spring and compress it until it no longer is tight in the strut assembly. While compressing the spring, be sure that you wear safety goggles; these springs are under a lot of pressure, and it is possible that the spring compressor may slip off suddenly. Place the two halves of the compressor on exactly opposite sides of the spring. I have found it very useful to use two ratcheting wrenches (I prefer the ones manufactured by GearWrench and available at PelicanParts.com) on each side of the compressor to assure that I achieve even and equal compression on both sides. Failure to maintain even compression when compressing the springs can make the compressor slip off.

With the spring compression removed from the strut assembly and the springs loose on their perches, remove the center nut that is attached to the top of the shock (see Photo 6). The reassembly process on the Carrera doesn't necessarily require an impact wrench, but it can sometimes make the job easier. So if you don't have one, now is a great time to buy one. I recommend an electric one—no air compressor is required (see Tools of the Trade at the end of this book).

With the upper strut mount removed, you should simply be able to lift the old spring off the bottom spring perch. If you are reusing your old springs, then simply place them back onto the top of the lower spring perches. If you are replacing your springs with new ones, then move the spring to your workbench and slowly release the spring compressor on your old springs. Compress the new springs in a similar manner. You can use stiffer springs like Eibach Performance Springs, which serve to create a stiffer suspension and lower the car a little more than an inch in both the front and the rear.

Install the compressed spring assembly back onto the lower spring perch and reassemble the assembly (see Photo 8). Reinstall the dust boot/rubber bumper assembly over the shock to protect it from road debris and grime. Reinstall the upper spring plate and spring pad, taking care to verify that the plate is nestled correctly against the top of the spring. Inspect your upper strut mount and bearing carefully prior to assembly. The mount is manufactured out of rubber; both the rubber mount and the bearing will wear over time. I recommend replacing both of them if they look old or if they haven't been replaced previously. Reinstall the upper strut mount on top of the spring plate, and tighten up the retaining nut. Always use new hardware when replacing your shocks—all of the nuts are self-locking and will lose some of that self-securing ability if they are reused.

Reinstall the shock assembly into the wheel carrier, and attach the lower sway bar drop link (which also functions as the pinch bolt for squeezing the shock assembly). Install the assembly back into the top of the shock tower. The upper strut mount may have to be rotated a couple of times in order for you to properly line up the studs integrated into the mount with the holes in the chassis tower. Attach the three nuts at the top of the tower, lining them up with the marks you made when you removed them. Reinstall the brake caliper (Project 56) and any other components you may have disconnected. Plug in the sensor connectors that you may have disconnected, and route the wires and hoses back through the tabs in the strut.

As indicated in Photo 4, it is important to point out that the final tightening of the main suspension components/bolts should only be done with the car sitting back down on the ground. Tightening up the bolts on the bushings when the car is up in the air can give them an incorrect preload that will then stress the bushings once the car is lowered back down and the weight of the car causes the rubber bushings to stretch. If this happens, then the bushings will tend to wear prematurely.

Replacing the rear shocks on the Carrera is easier than replacing the front shocks. Begin by jacking up the car, supporting it on jack stands (see Project 1). From inside the

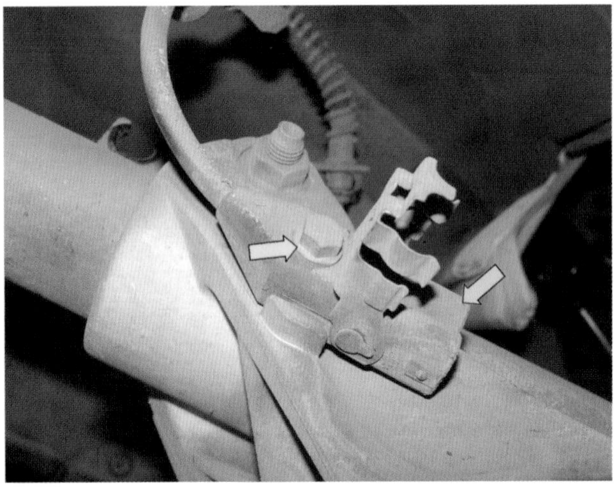

1 With the cable disconnected from its holder, make sure the wheel speed sensor and brake pad sensors are unplugged from their connector (green arrow). Then remove the bracket entirely by unbolting it (yellow arrow).

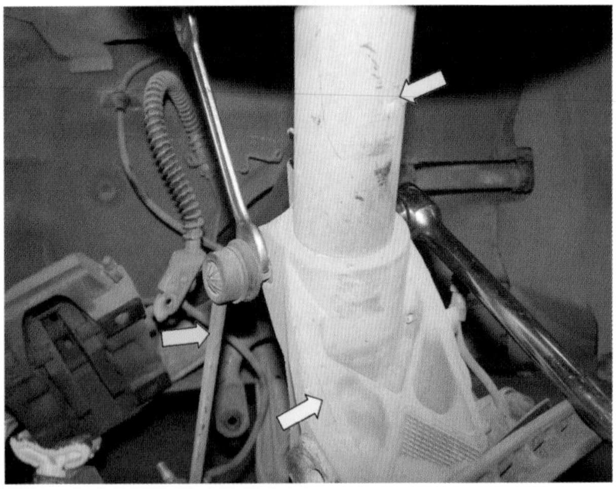

2 The shock (yellow arrow) is held onto the wheel carrier (blue arrow) by a long bolt that is integrated into the sway bar drop link (green arrow). Remove the bolt/sway bar link, and then the shock should be free to be pulled out of the wheel carrier.

3 An electric impact wrench is a very handy tool for both removing and installing new shocks. The tool allows you to tighten nuts without having the shock shaft rotate. The three nuts that hold the front shock to the tower are shown by the yellow arrows. Mark the position of these nuts prior to removal; you want them to be in the same spot when you put them back on.

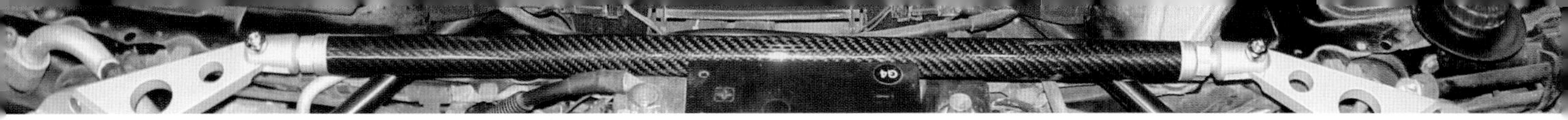

car, remove the panel behind the rear seats. On convertible models, you'll need to remove the carpeting from under the body flap. (See Photo 10 of Project 71) for more information.

Once the upper mount is accessed, mark the location of the three 15mm bolts that hold the strut to the chassis with a permanent marker. Support the underside of the control arm with a floor jack and unbolt the 15mm nuts inside the car that hold the strut in place.

From underneath the car, disconnect both sway bar end links from the sway bar. Hold the 17 mm nut on the inside of the sway bar link while removing the 15mm nut on the outside. Once removed, use an 18mm socket and wrench to remove the bolt holding the rear strut to the control arm. You may have to knock the bolt out of the hole with a long drift. Now use a pry bar to lift the rear strut off its mount of the control arm.

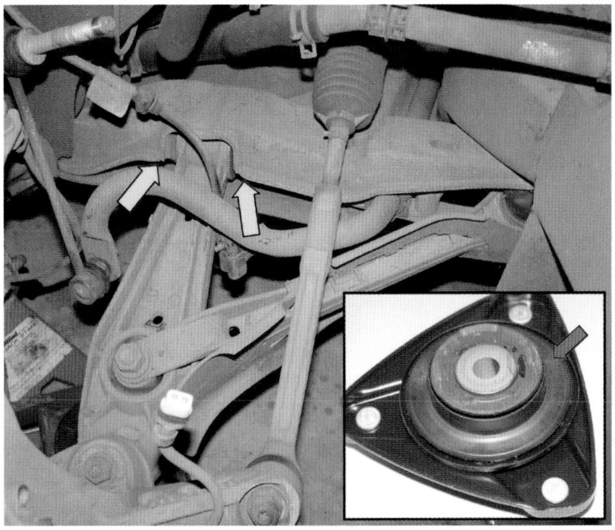

4 The yellow arrows in the photo show the bolt that needs to be loosened in order to gain enough clearance to lower the shock and clear the edge of the fender. You don't need to remove the bolt; simply loosen it so that the arm can rotate a bit more than is possible through the deflection of the rubber bushing. Don't retighten this bolt until the car's tires are back on level ground and the suspension is fully loaded. The lower right shows a new bearing installed in a new front strut mount.

5 With the wheel carrier supported by a jack, lower it down so that you have enough clearance to rotate the assembly out from under the fender. Then, pull on the shock to remove it from the wheel carrier (green arrow). Watch out that you don't accidentally scratch your paint.

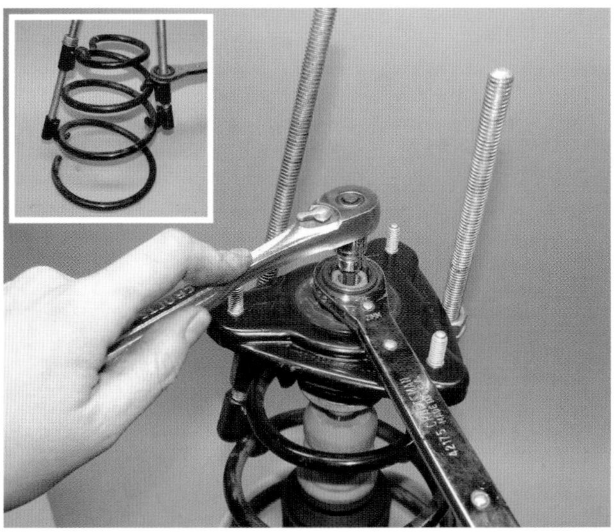

6 Use a hex socket to hold the shaft of the shock as you tighten the nut and clamp down the entire assembly. In order to get the springs compressed enough to be placed on the shock, you will need a spring compressor like the one shown in the upper left. When the assembly is clamped down with the locking nut, then carefully release tension on the spring compressors and remove them.

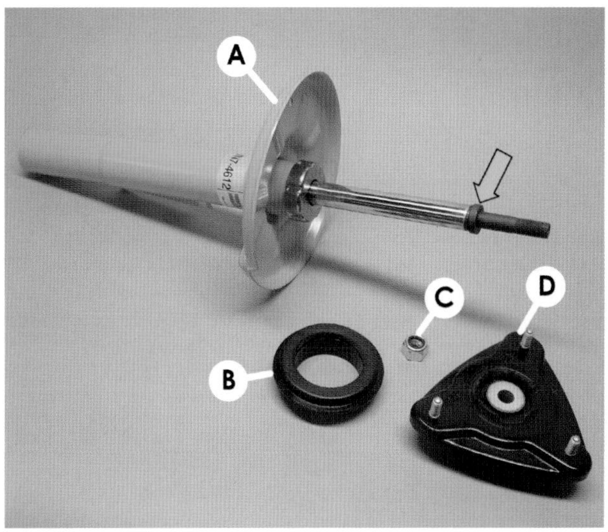

7 When replacing shocks, I recommend installing new parts. Shown here is a new front shock (A), a new strut bearing (B), a new lock-nut (C), and a new front strut mount (D). Your Bilstein shocks should come with a beveled washer on the shaft (green arrow).

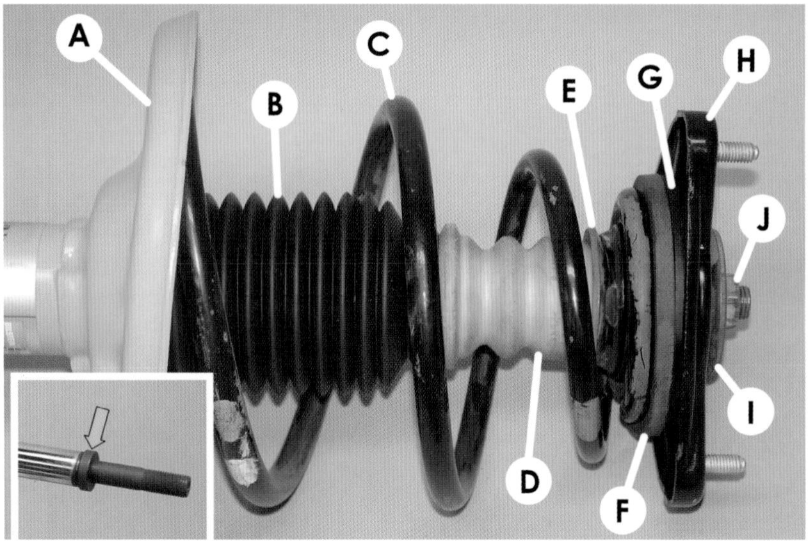

8 This diagram shows the installation of a new front shock and how all the bits and pieces fit together. These new Bilstein shocks came with a tapered washer that needs to be fit to the shaft prior to assembly (see Photo 7). **A:** Shock **B:** Bellows **C:** Spring **D:** Bumper stop **E:** Cup washer **F:** Foam insulator **G:** Upper strut bearing **H:** Upper strut mount **I:** Cup washer **J:** Nut

9 When removing or installing the shock, be sure to remove and replace the wire harness for the brake pad and wheel speed sensors. Don't forget the beveled washer when installing the new shocks (inset).

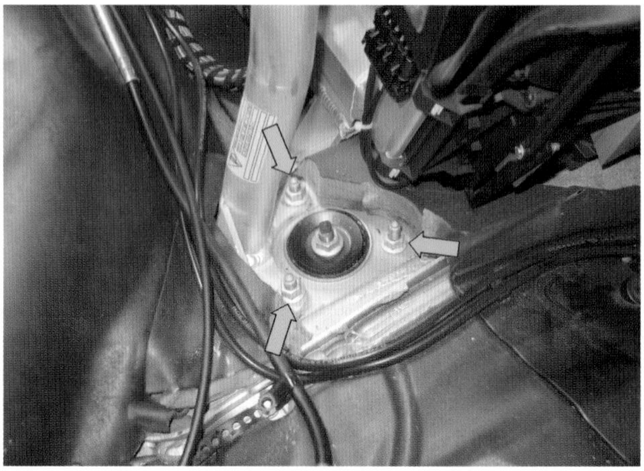

10 Shown here are the 15mm nuts that hold the upper rear strut mount in place on a 996 convertible (green arrows). You may need to remove some of the sound-deadening material in order to access it. On coupe models, the upper strut mount is accessible through a small panel behind the rear seats.

11 Disconnect the sway bar end link from the sway bar. Hold the 17mm nut on the inside of the sway bar link (green arrow) while removing the 15mm nut on the outside (yellow arrow).

12 Counter hold the 18mm shock bolt (purple arrow) while turning the 18mm nut (green arrow). Once removed, you may need to use a drift to drive the bolt out of the mounting hole. Once out, pry the lower strut up and out of the control arm.

SECTION 9
BODY/INTERIOR TRIM

You spend a large amount of time inside the car, so why not make it as pretty on the inside as it is on the outside? A great looking interior improves the overall appearance of your Carrera and also makes it more fun to drive. In a similar manner, a few moments spent on small exterior items can simply wipe away the effects of aging on your car. This particular section is a grab bag of projects that deal with everything from headlamp upgrades to door equipment repair. Whether you're planning on replacing your hood shocks or installing a rear spoiler on your car, the projects in this section will help you improve the overall performance and exterior looks of your Carrera.

PROJECT 65
Replacing Lenses and Bulbs

Time / Tab / Talent: 30 minutes / $15–$250 /

Tools: –

Applicable Years: All

Tinware: New lenses, bulbs

More Info: http://www.101projects.com/Carrera/65.htm

Tip: Don't tug heavily on the lenses when removing them—they may break

Performance Gain: Better-looking exterior, clearer lamps

Comp Modification: Upgrade to clear corners and clear/smoked rear lenses

Few projects are as easy as lens replacement yet improve the look of your car so significantly. Replacing old, faded lenses not only improves your Carrera's overall appearance, it also increases its safety as well. Faded lenses tend to be harder to see and block much more light than brand new ones. On the front of the 911, the side marker lenses are removed by simply pulling on them. A snap-tab holds them in place.

The rear lenses are very easy too—they are simply held on with screws that you can access in the rear trunk. Pull back the trunk lining and you should have easy access to the screws and the bulbs. The third brake light is easily accessible from the exterior of the car.

If you are replacing bulbs, make sure that you replace the old bulbs with the same exact style and wattage as the originals. Swapping in higher wattage bulbs could damage wiring and possibly melt the lens and bulb holder.

The photos show the replacement process on the 1999–2001 Carrera—the 2002–2005 is very similar.

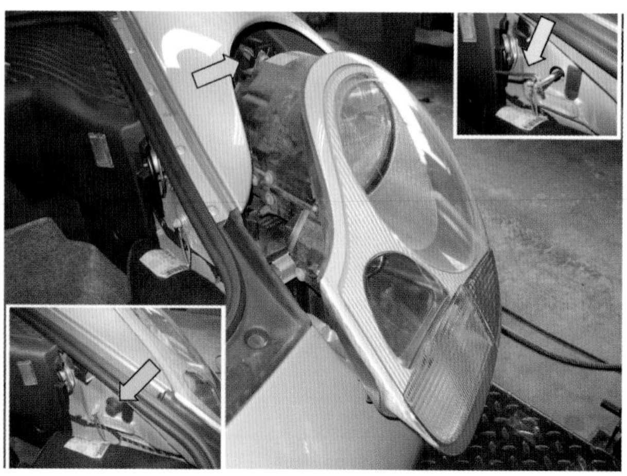

1 The headlamp assemblies are held in the car by a clever latching system incorporating a cam lever and release tool. Pull back the side carpeting on the inside of the trunk and locate the black rubber plug (green arrow). Pull the plug out of the body. With the plug removed, you can see the headlight release cam assembly inside. Insert the tool supplied in the vehicle tool kit (blue arrow). Turning the release cam will eject the headlamp assembly from the car. It is designed so that it will automatically disconnect the electrical connections when you remove the housing. To release the headlight housing, rotate the tool 180 degrees toward the front of the car. You can see the harness connector for the headlamp assembly (yellow arrow).

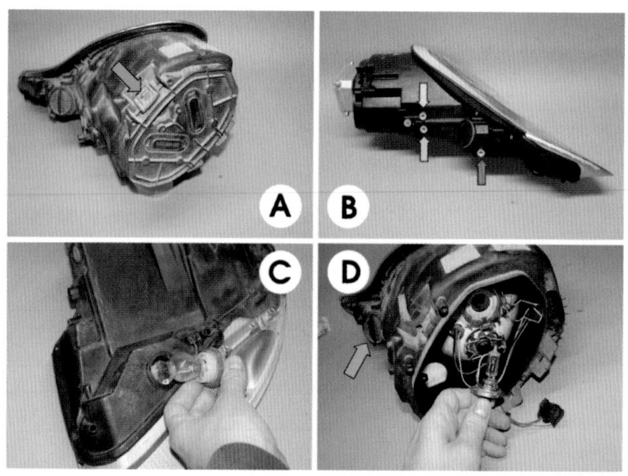

2 The Carrera headlamp is a somewhat complicated piece of equipment. **A:** To replace bulbs inside the assembly, first detach the end cover by squeezing the tabs on both sides (one side shown with green arrow). **B:** These are the adjustment wheels and can be turned by inserting a 5mm hex head tool through access holes located in the chassis. Red = fog lamp adjustment; yellow = left/right adjustment; blue = up/down adjustment. **C:** The turn signal/parking lamp bulb is accessed through the bottom of the assembly. **D:** The two halogen bulbs are clipped into the rear of the lamp and are easily accessible once you remove the end cover. Don't touch the bulb with your fingers, as the oils in your hand will damage it. The purple arrow points to the access hole you use to replace the fog lamp bulb.

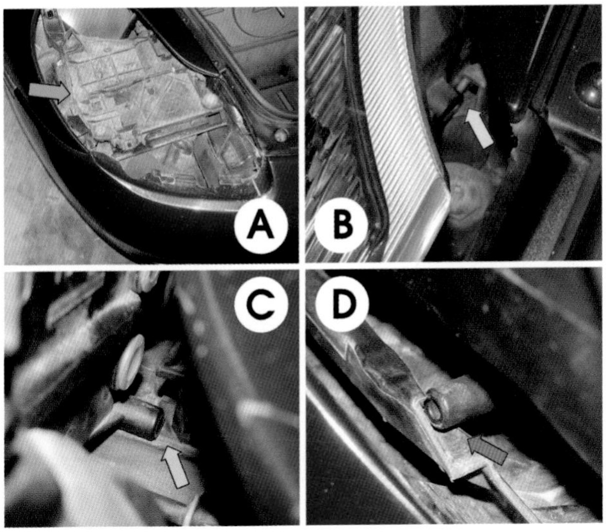

3 Installing the headlamp back into the car can be a bit tricky. **A:** The headlamp mates with the carrier plate (green arrow) and harness connector. A bar integrated within the carrier plate locks the headlamp assembly into place. **B/C/D:** Three circular tabs on the headlamp assembly fit into three channels located on the carrier plate. It's important to look carefully as you install the headlamp to make sure that these tabs are properly aligned in the channels. With the assembly pushed back into the fender, use the headlamp tool from your 911 Carrera tool kit to lock it into place. If you don't have this tool, you can use a 5mm socket. With the tool facing upward, rotate it toward the rear of the car to lock it into place, or rotate it toward the front of the car to unlock.

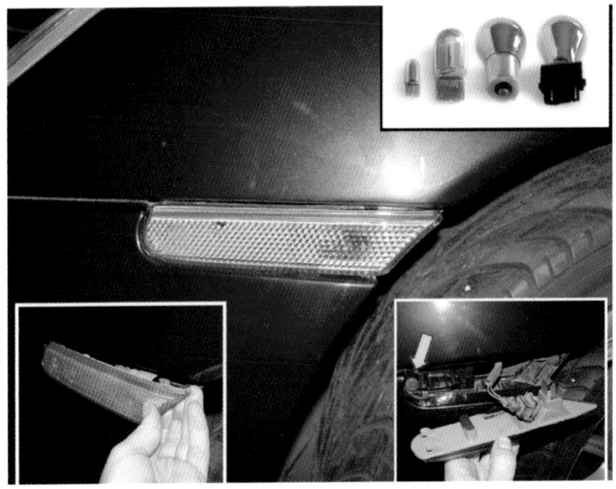

4 New side marker lenses take about one minute to install. I prefer the clear ones with orange bulbs. Simply reach in and pull on them to remove the lenses, and then unclip the harness by pressing on the thin metal clip. For some reason, the amber U.S. lenses that are stock equipment just don't cut it. In order to maintain legal standards, you must run orange bulbs inside the lenses. This can cause the lens to take on an orange hue. There's a product out there that I recommend called Stealth Bulbs (inset) that is available online at PelicanParts.com. These bulbs are silver coated on the outside, but glow bright orange when electricity is applied. They look clear when installed in the clear lenses, but retain the orange illumination required for U.S. roads.

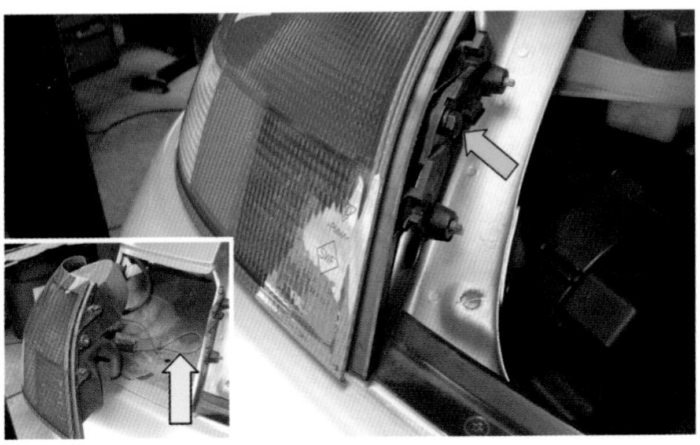

5 Open the engine lid and remove the 10mm bolt shown here to release the taillight housing from the body (green arrow). Once the 10mm bolt is removed, pull the taillight housing back to remove it from the body as shown here. You can also see the emergency pull cable for the engine lid directly underneath (blue arrow).

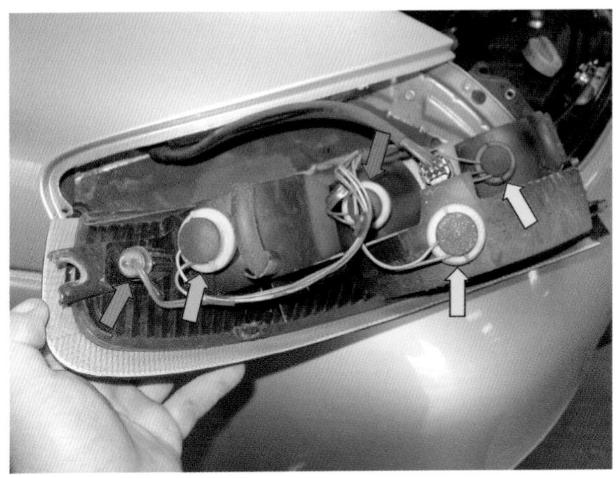

6 This picture shows the rear of the taillight housing. To remove the bulb holders, turn each one counterclockwise and pull the bulb out. This picture shows the locations of the various bulbs in the taillight housing: side marker light (purple arrow), rear fog light (green arrow), reverse light (red arrow), turn signal light (yellow arrow), tail/brake light (blue arrow). **Note:** The taillight housing shown here is flipped upside down for ease of illustration.

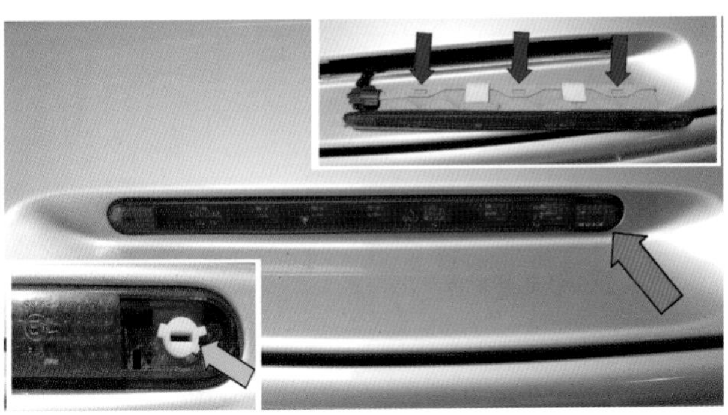

7 Shown here is the third brake light directly above the rear engine lid. Pry out the small insert piece on the third brake light lens (red arrow) with a small screwdriver. Under the insert, you'll see a small locking tab. Rotate the locking tab (green arrow, lower left) 90 degrees counterclockwise and pull the entire third brake light assembly out of the rear of the car. To access the bulbs inside the third brake light, disengage the six locking tabs both on the top and bottom of the housing (blue arrows; inset, upper right). To change the bulbs in the third brake lamp, unplug the harness connector, and then you should be able to unsnap the bulb carrier from the rear of the lamp. Be careful not to break any of the delicate plastic tabs on the bulb carrier.

PROJECT 66
Installing a New Hood Crest and Emblems

Time / Tab / Talent: 30 minutes / $60 /

Tools: Small socket set, dental floss

Applicable Years: All

Tinware: Hood crest, seal, two speed nuts

More Info: http://www.101projects.com/Carrera/66.htm

Tip: Don't tighten the crest too tightly, or you might crack the gels on the front

Performance Gain: Sharper looking hood

Comp Modification: Replace rear emblem

Over many years, the Porsche crest located on the front hood can take a beating. Rocks, gravel, soot, rain, snow, sleet, and other debris can scratch and dull the finish of the crest so that it no longer shines the way it should. The good news is that the replacement of the crest is one of the easiest projects that you can do, and it significantly improves the looks of your car.

It is important to note that you should only use the original Porsche crests manufactured under license from Porsche. In past years, there have been some counterfeit crests available for about half the cost, but the original equipment manufacturer (OEM) ones from Porsche are typically of a much higher quality.

Several different styles of the crest have been produced, so if you are looking for 100 percent originality, you may want to look for a crest that is new old stock (NOS). It is also important to replace the rubber seal that mates the crest flush with the hood.

1 This before (left) and after photo (right) really shows the difference that a new crest can make. As with the lenses on the car, it is difficult to tell how tarnished and old the hood crest has become without looking at a brand new one. With such an easy installation, it is perhaps the quickest method of instantly improving the exterior looks of your 911. The new crest is so shiny, it's hard to take a good picture of it!

Attach the crest using two small self-threading nuts on the inside of the hood that Porsche calls speed nuts. The speed nut is a small aluminum disk with a putty-like insert that allows it to hold the emblem snug without the danger of denting or damaging the hood of the car. The speed nut also stops water from leaking into the inside of the sheet metal.

To remove the old crest, simply open the hood and unscrew the nuts using a small 8mm socket and extension. Be careful that the speed clips don't fall into the recesses of the hood. When installing the new crest, place the rubber gasket around the crest and test fit it against the hood. Sometimes the small prongs on the crest may need to be bent slightly in order to make them fit the holes. Be sure not to bend them too much, or they will break off.

It's also a wise idea to get a small piece of masking tape, and tape the crest and seal to the hood before you install it. The speed nuts are meant to be attached once, and removing and reinstalling them can damage the small studs on the crest. Use a small dental pick to fit the gasket around the crest before it's completely tightened down. Tape the crest to the hood to make sure that the rubber seal doesn't slip out of position while you are tightening the speed nuts. Proceed slowly, and check the seal before you tighten up the nuts. This is a very simple job that can be messed up if you don't keep a watch on the seal.

2 The inside of the hood is manufactured with access holes so that you can remove and replace the crest. Make sure that you don't tighten the two speed nuts too much, or you can crack some of the plastic gels embedded into the front of the crest or damage the hood. The inset shows a complete Genuine Porsche crest with the crest seal and two speed nuts.

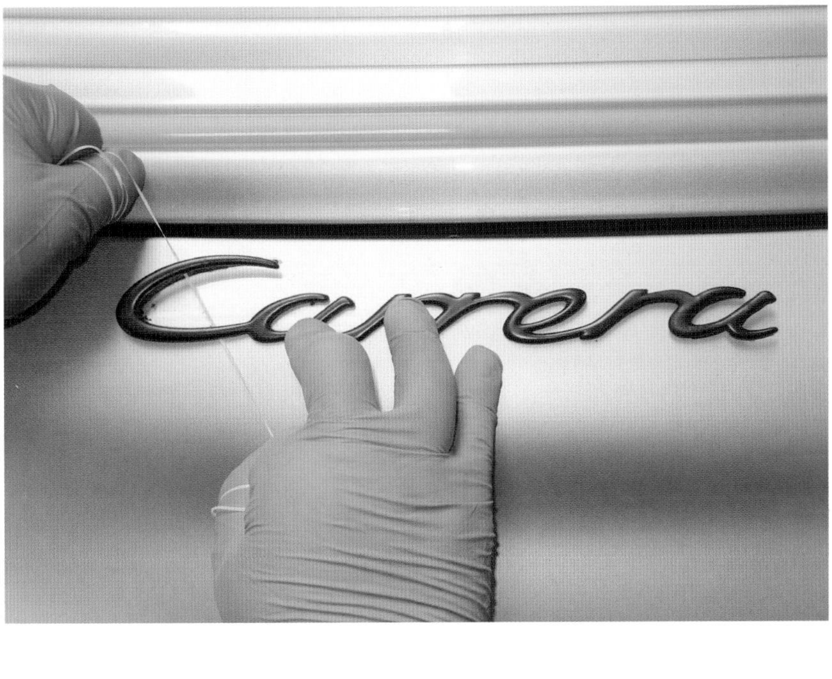

3 Replacement of the rear plastic emblem is relatively easy. New emblems come with a pre-applied adhesive that's similar to double-sided sticky-tape. A trick to removing the old emblem is to use dental floss. If possible let the car sit in the direct sunlight for an hour and then get a few strips and work them under the emblem, cutting away the old adhesive. When the emblem is off, carefully clean the area with some isopropyl alcohol, and then apply the new emblem.

PROJECT 67

Installing the Das Schild Protector

Time / Tab / Talent: 30 minutes / $300 /

Tools: –

Applicable Years: All

Tinware: Das Schild protector set

More Info: http://www.101projects.com/Carrera/67.htm

Tip: Install both the front and rear liners

Performance Gain: Protects your trunk lid

Comp Modification: Replace your hood crest

The Das Schild protector is a neat product designed to protect the front and rear trunk lids from damage due to items floating around in your trunk. At first thought, it may seem like an unlikely scenario, but loose or oversized items stored in your trunk can often leave unsightly dings in your hood or trunk that can be very difficult to repair. The manufacturer of the liner also claims that it assists in preventing dings from outside of the car from ill-placed baseballs or the occasional hail stone.

The liner is manufactured out of thermoformed, lightweight ABS plastic and exudes a very high quality finish. The cost for a front and rear set is about $350 from PelicanParts.com. Installation is very simple: place the liner into the recesses of the front or rear trunk lid and attach it into the factory lid bracing with the included plastic snaps.

1 Shown here is the front hood with the Das Schild protector installed. The liner is manufactured out of lightweight ABS plastic and easily installs in minutes. With the protective lining in place, it looks like it's a Genuine Porsche factory part.

2 Installation is literally a snap. Simply take the liner and place it against the trunk lid. The liner is held in place using small plastic push clips that fit inside the slots that are already in place in the front trunk (inset).

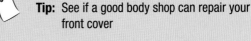

PROJECT 68
Front Bumper and Wheelwell Removal/Replacement

Time / Tab / Talent: 30 min / $850 /

Tools: Flathead screwdriver, Phillips screwdriver, Torx set, pliers or a crowbar, jack stands, floor jack

Applicable Years: All

Tinware: Front bumper cover

More Info: http://www.101projects.com/Carrera/68.htm

Tip: See if a good body shop can repair your front cover

Performance Gain: Cleaner looking car

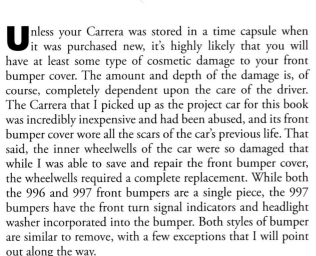

Comp Modification: Modify 996 liners; install center radiator

Unless your Carrera was stored in a time capsule when it was purchased new, it's highly likely that you will have at least some type of cosmetic damage to your front bumper cover. The amount and depth of the damage is, of course, completely dependent upon the care of the driver. The Carrera that I picked up as the project car for this book was incredibly inexpensive and had been abused, and its front bumper cover wore all the scars of the car's previous life. That said, the inner wheelwells of the car were so damaged that while I was able to save and repair the front bumper cover, the wheelwells required a complete replacement. While both the 996 and 997 front bumpers are a single piece, the 997 bumpers have the front turn signal indicators and headlight washer incorporated into the bumper. Both styles of bumper are similar to remove, with a few exceptions that I will point out along the way.

The first step is to jack up the front of the car (see Project 1). Loosen the lug nuts on your wheels prior to jacking if you are planning on removing the wheelwell liners. The next step in removing the front bumper cover is to remove the screws that attach it to the top of the chassis. Remove the front trim panel by turning the plastic screws a half turn (996 only). The 997 trim is simply secured with Velcro from below. The plastic trim panel can then be removed, exposing the screws securing the bumper.

Next, you need to pull out the side marker lamps from the corner; they pull straight out (996 only). After disconnecting the bulb from the unit, look in the area where the side markers were and you will see two small screws that need to be removed. One faces outward, and one that screws upward is located near the edge of the wheelwell.

While you can pull the side markers straight out on the 997, let me show you two better and gentler ways. First, there is a small access hole in the fender lining behind the marker (see Photo 8); inset a screwdriver in and gently push on the back of the clip securing the side marker. It will release, and you can easily pull it out from the bumper. The second way is to just apply a little pressure to the marker, sliding it back and in toward the wheelwell. This pressure will release the marker from its front mount. Once the marker is out, disconnect it and set it aside. There is a T30 screw behind the marker that can be accessed from the same hole that you used to remove the marker. Insert the screwdriver up through the hole and remove it.

On the 996, inside the wheelwell of the driver and passenger side, locate and remove the main three fasteners that are used to attach the inner front wheelwell liner to the front bumper (see the green arrows in Photo 5), which can be removed with either a crowbar or pliers (see the inset of Photo 5).

On the 997, the front wheel liners are two pieces. You do not need to remove them to remove the bumper, but you do need to remove the two lower T30s that attach to the bottom of the bumper. I recommend removing the front liner as it is only held by four Torx screws and makes access to the headlight washer hose and turn signal wiring much easier.

Now, disconnect the temperature sensor that sits in a small hole near the front grille on the right side of the car (see the inset of Photo 1); the temperature sensor is a small device with a wire attached to it that looks a bit like a very short pencil. Finally, remove the screws that attach the bottom of the bumper cover to the car (see Photos 3 and 4).

On the 997, you'll have a few extra steps. Remove a clip located between the bumper and fender on each side (see Photo 9). The clip is accessed from the front trunk. It's best to spray a little lubrication into the clip area first, especially if the clips have never been removed. Insert a hooked tool into the hole on the clip and pull straight out. I have removed several; some slide right out and others you have to pull so hard you think you are doing it wrong. There is nothing else holding the clips in, just take your time and watch that you don't damage your paint. With the clips removed and all of the hardware disconnected, you can pull the bumper cover straight out and forward a few inches.

On the 996s, you can now just remove the bumper. On the 997s, you will need to reach in and disconnect the wiring harness on the right side (see Photo 11) and the hose connection for the headlight washer on the left (see Photo 12). Now you can safely remove the bumper by continuing to pull it forward.

With the 996, removal of the wheelwell liners is not quite as easy as pulling off the front bumper cover. First, remove the two road wheels. The wheelwell liners are attached using plastic rivets, which must be pried out and unscrewed one by one. If you're planning to replace the shocks, now would be a good time to do it.

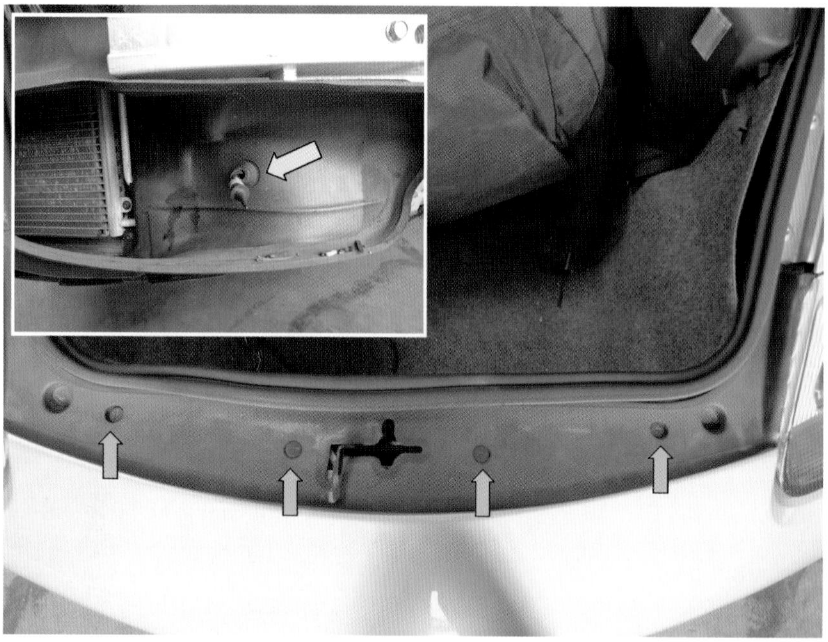

1 Start in the front trunk by removing the black plastic cover piece near the front hood latch. On the 996s, four small fasteners hold this piece in place. Simply rotate them a half turn or so with a flathead screwdriver to loosen them up and remove. The 997 trim piece is held on by Velcro from below and can just be lifted and removed. Lift the trunk latch up to pull the plastic cover piece up and away from the front bumper. The inset photo also shows the temperature sensor clipped on the passenger side of the front bumper that you need to remove from the grille.

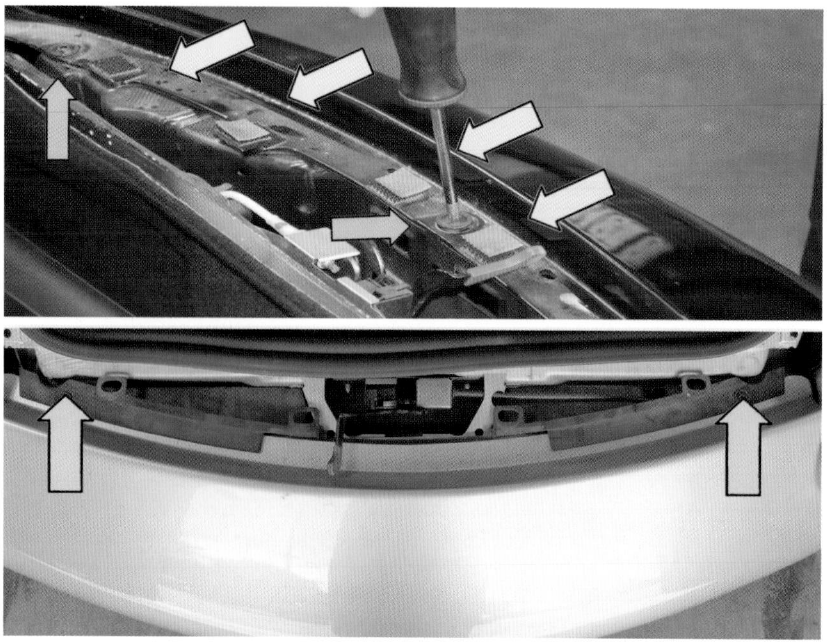

2 With the front black plastic cover piece removed, you can see the two screws that hold the front bumper cover on to the chassis of the 996 (lower image). On the 997 (upper image), three screws hold the bumper on (two shown, green arrows). You can also see the Velcro that holds the trim piece (blue arrows).

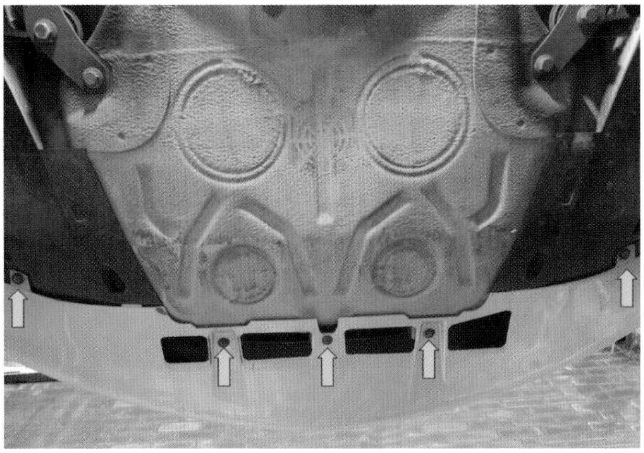

3 Underneath the car are a few more Phillips head (996) and Torx head T30 (997) screws that attach the bumper cover to the chassis. Remove these.

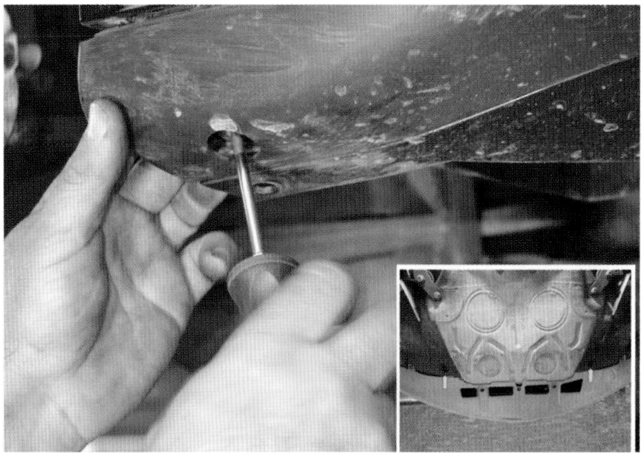

4 At the very corner of the bumper, remove the one Phillips head screw that attaches the wheel fender lining to the each corner of the bumper. The bottom right photo shows the two plastic rivets (996) and Torxs (997) that are used to attach the wheelwell liner to the chassis that must be removed.

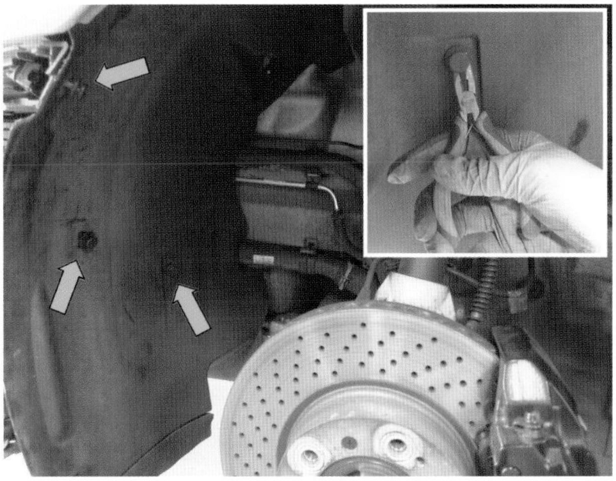

5 From inside the wheelwell of both the driver and passenger side on the Carrera 996, locate and remove the main three fasteners that are used to attach the inner front wheelwell liner to the front bumper (green arrow). These can easily be plucked out with either a small pry bar or pliers (inset photo). A total of seven rivets hold the entire liner onto the car. If you take the liners off you may want to modify them to increase your brake cooling (see Project 82).

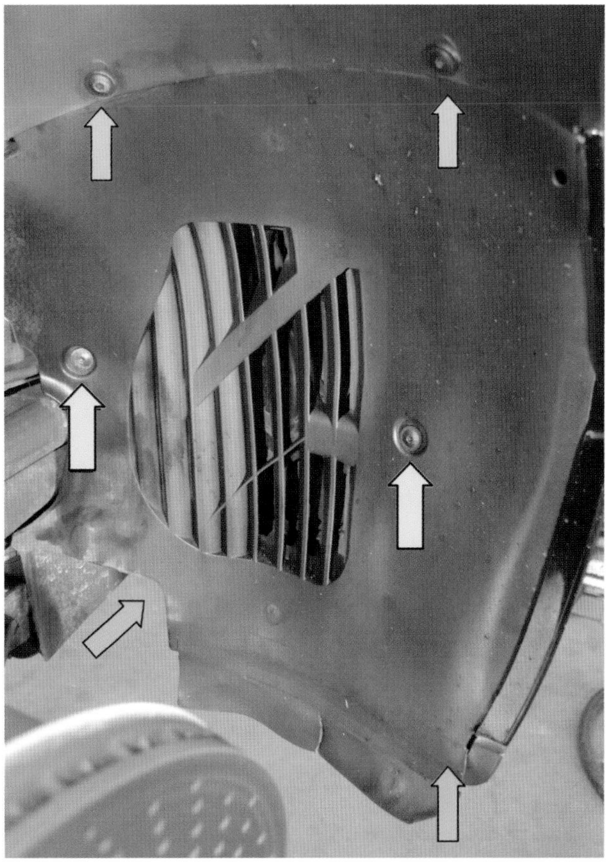

6 On the 997, the front fender lining is secured in place by four Torx screws (T25). Remove the two lower Torx screws (green arrows; screws not visible) and the two Torx screws by the vent (blue arrows). It helps to loosen but not remove the two Torxs that cover the overlap of the liner (yellow arrows).

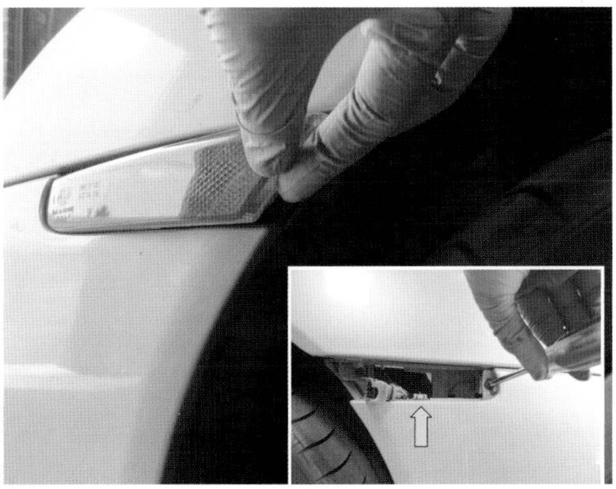

7 Remove the corner turn signals by pulling outward on the corner of the unit. After removing the lamp, remove the Phillips head screw behind it (bottom right inset photo) and the receptacle for the Phillips head screw that must be removed from inside the wheelwell by peeling the liner back (yellow arrow).

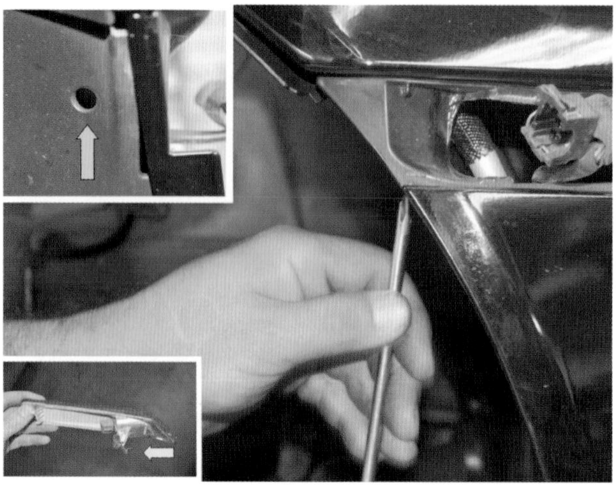

8 While you can pull the side markers straight out on the 997, there are two better and gentler ways. First, there is a small access hole in the fender lining behind the marker (yellow arrow). Inset a screwdriver and gently push on the back of the clip securing the side marker (blue arrow). It will release and you can easily pull it out from the bumper. The other way is to just apply a little pressure to the marker, sliding it back and in toward the wheelwell. This will release the marker from its front mount. Once the marker is out disconnect it and set it aside. There is a screw behind the marker that holds the bumper to the body of the car. It can be accessed from the same hole that you used to remove the marker. Insert the screwdriver up through the hole and remove the screw.

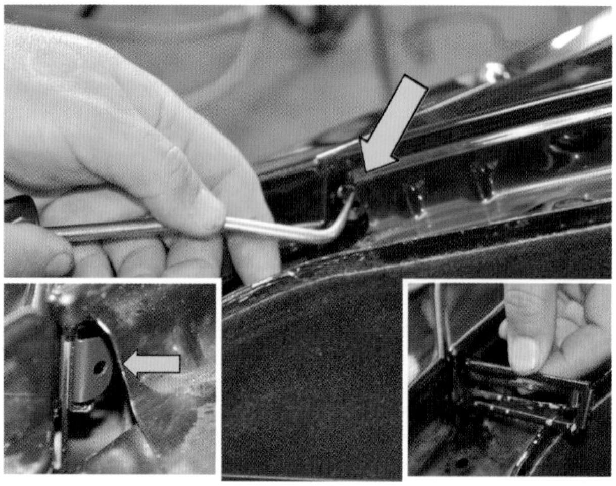

9 On the 997, there is a clip between the bumper and fender on each side that needs to be removed. The clip is accessed from the front trunk. It is best to spray a little lubrication into the clip area first, especially if the clips have never been removed. Insert a hooked tool into the hole on the clip and pull straight out.

10 997-Pull the bumper straight away from the body a few inches. On the driver side, disconnect the headlight washer hose.

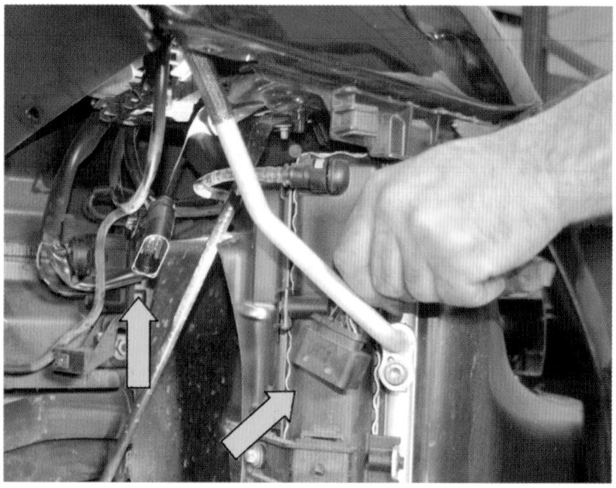

11 997-Next remove the electrical connection located on the passenger side.

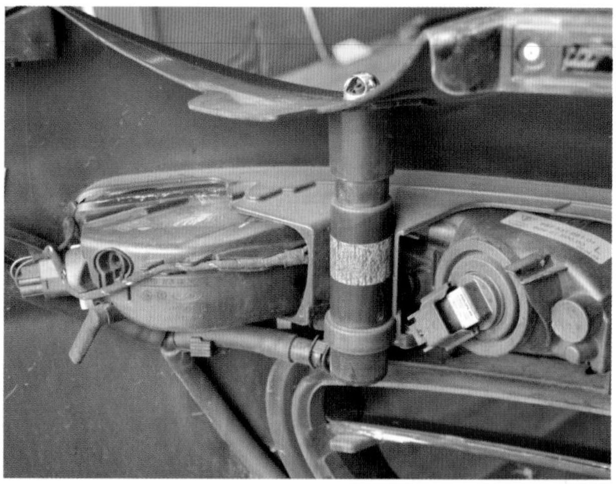

12 997-Here is a picture of the turn signal unit along with the headlight washer. The washer hose connects on the left side of the bumper and feeds both sides, whereas the electrical connector supplies power to both units from the right side.

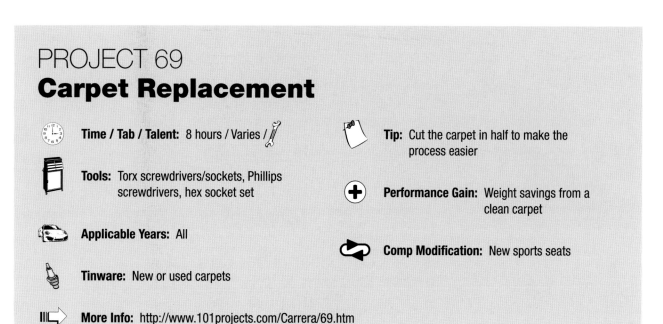

PROJECT 69
Carpet Replacement

Time / Tab / Talent: 8 hours / Varies /

Tools: Torx screwdrivers/sockets, Phillips screwdrivers, hex socket set

Applicable Years: All

Tinware: New or used carpets

More Info: http://www.101projects.com/Carrera/69.htm

Tip: Cut the carpet in half to make the process easier

Performance Gain: Weight savings from a clean carpet

Comp Modification: New sports seats

Over time, general wear and tear on your car's carpets can leave them looking a bit worse for wear. Combine this with a clogged drain hole and you can even have water pool up under the carpets, resulting in a mold infestation. This was the case on our own project car. The good news is that replacing the carpet isn't a difficult job, but it does involve removing a number of items from inside the car. The one-piece carpet is manufactured with a lower foam sponge that is integrated and molded with the carpet. While you may not think so, it is indeed possible to dry out your carpet if it becomes wet. Soak up any excess water from the carpet with paper towels, pushing heavily on the carpet to squeeze the water out. Use some heaters placed carefully in the car to dry it out overnight. Be sure to inspect and clean out your drains in the front trunk near the battery to prevent it from happening again. If caught early, a wet carpet can recover 100 percent.

Follow along with the photos for detailed instructions on how to remove the carpet. Installation is the reverse of removal, just lay the new carpet in and you'll be good to go.

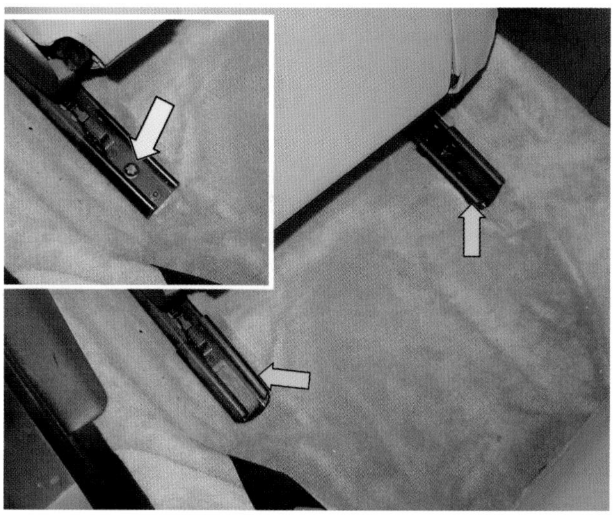

1 Move the seat forward as far as it will go to access the ends of each seat rail on the floor. Slide the plastic covers off the ends of the rails (green arrows). Once removed, remove the two Torx bolts underneath (blue arrow).

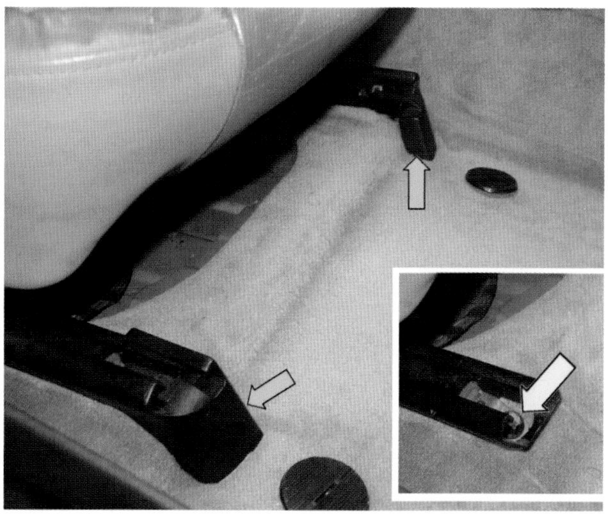

2 Now push the seat all the way back to remove the plastic covers over the front mounting bolts and remove them (green arrows). Just like the rear bolts, remove the two Torx bolts underneath (blue arrow, inset). Don't forget to disconnect the battery right after you have unbolted the seats. You just need the battery connected so that you can move the seats back and forth.

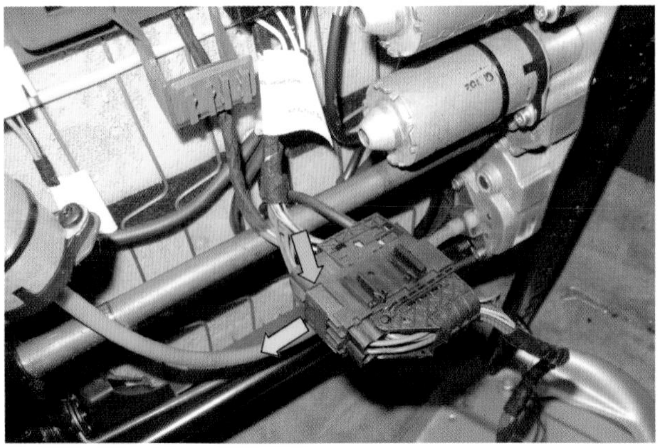

3 On the underside of the seat, you'll see a black plastic connector. Use a small screwdriver to carefully push the cam latch (green arrow) in the direction of the yellow arrow. As you push it, it will separate the connector. Now just lift the seat out and set it aside for the time being. (**Note:** Left side connector is shown; the right side is identical.)

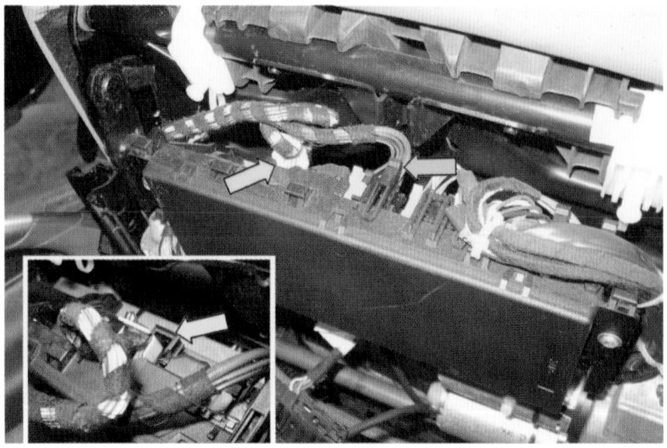

4 The space under the driver side seat contains two additional electrical connections. Under the seat you will see a white plug (yellow arrow) and a combination black/blue plug (green arrow). Squeeze the tabs on the black/blue plug and pull it up and out of the module on the front of the seat. Use a small screwdriver to carefully pry the black plastic locking tab (blue arrow, inset) in the center of the white plug up. This will allow you to pull the plug off the module.

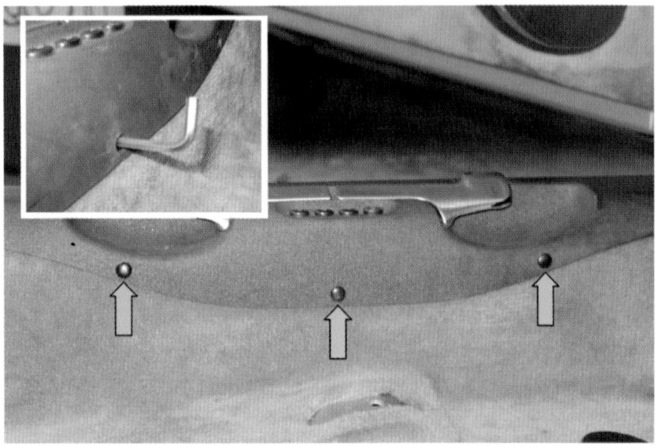

5 Pry out the small plastic plugs shown here (green arrows) to access the screws that hold the hood and engine deck lid panel down to the sill. Use a long 5mm hex socket to reach in and loosen (but do not remove) the screws at the bottom of each hole (inset, upper left). It will take a little fishing around to center the tool in the screw.

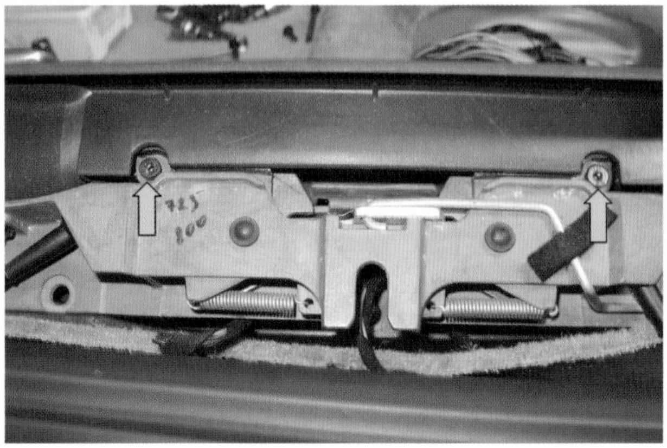

6 Now lift up the panel and turn it over. In this picture, you can see the two 3mm bolts (green arrows) that hold the hood and deck lid cable ends to the release handles. Remove these two screws and carefully pry the cable ends out of the panel.

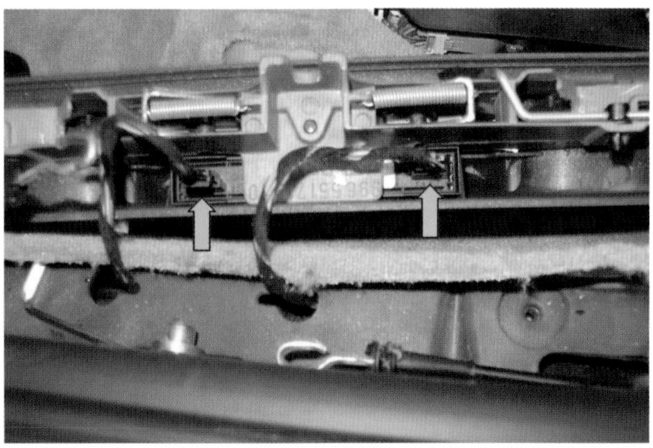

7 Don't forget to also disconnect the two electrical connections on the underside of the panel (green arrows). They simply pull out.

8 On the passenger side, you'll need to remove the trim panel on the door sill. At the bottom of the panel, you'll see a rubber liner. Use a pick or a screwdriver to remove the liner.

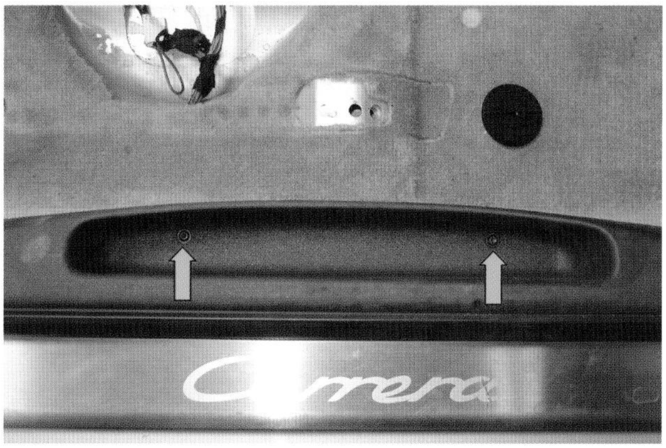

9 Under the rubber liner, you'll see two screws. Remove these to lift the whole panel up and off the door sill.

10 Move to the front of the driver footwell and pry the cover piece off the fusebox (green arrow). Also remove the small Phillips head screw holding the dead pedal to the front of the carpet as shown here (yellow arrow).

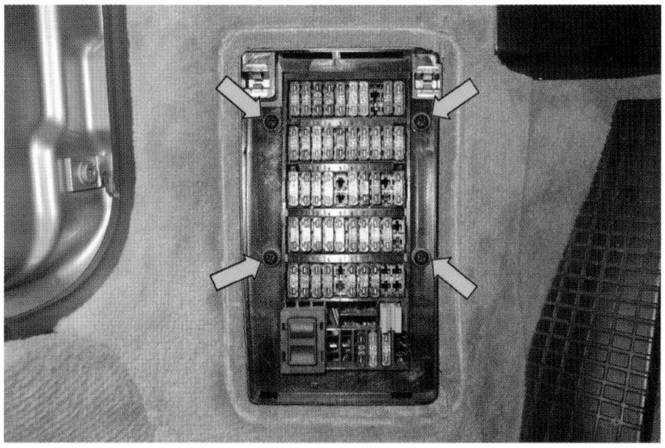

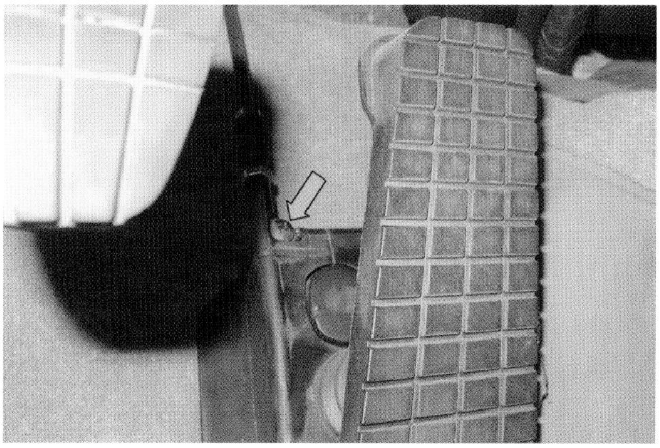

11 Remove the four Phillips head screws on the fusebox cover panel (green arrows). Remove the entire front fuse box cover and also the dead pedal. Double-check that the battery has been disconnected prior to loosening up the fuse box panel.

12 Remove the accelerator pedal assembly from the car by unscrewing the Phillips head screw shown here (green arrow). Removal requires pulling the pedal up about ½" then out toward the rear of the car. Keep in mind that on some cars, this comes off very easily and on some cars, it will barely budge. Just keep at it. You can pull the front of the pedal off the ball joint for a little better access to the mounting screw.

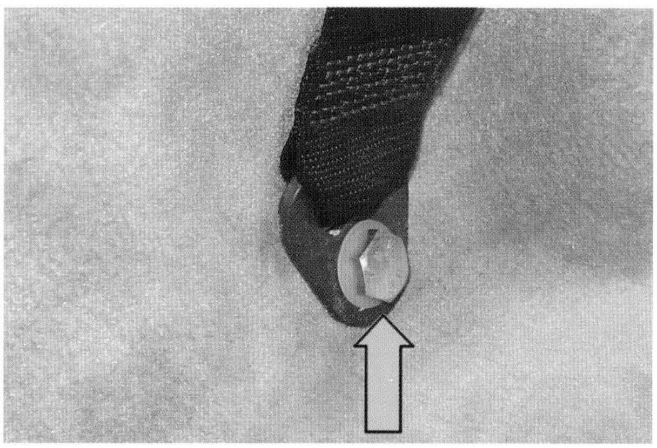

13 You can now begin to remove the carpeting from the left (driver) footwell of the car by pulling it up along the edges (green arrows).

14 Follow both driver and passenger side sills until you locate the lower mounting point on the seat belt. You'll see a plastic cap covering the mounting bolt. Pry this cap off and remove the 16mm bolt under the plastic cap (green arrow). Take note of the order in which the bolt, plastic washer, and spacer are stacked. Store these parts in a safe place for the time being and note the orientation of the seat belt.

15 Begin removing the front center console by removing the two side trim panels on both sides of the storage box: they simply pull off with a bit of force (green arrows). Next, pry out the lower trim panel that holds the switches for the heated seats (blue arrow) and unplug the harness connector going to each switch.

16 Now remove the remaining storage trays from the front center console. Next, pull away the carpet trim that is located on both sides of the front console (green arrow).

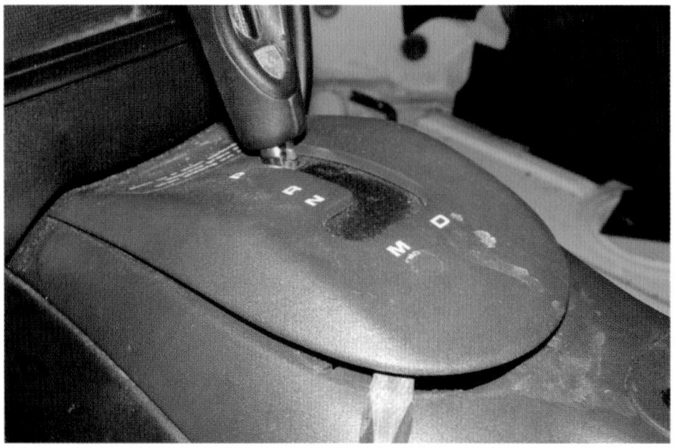

17 With the screws disconnected, pull the front center console up and out of the car. You will have to shift the car into 2nd gear or put it in drive (Tiptronic transmission shown here) in order to gain enough clearance to remove the console. Pry up on the shift lever base plate (Tiptronic shown here) and carefully pop it out of the center console.

18 Some cars with manual transmissions use a set screw, and some require you to twist the lower collar 90 degrees and then lift to remove: be careful not to accidentally smack yourself in the face! On cars with automatic transmissions, you'll need to press the shift button down and insert a small screwdriver in the gap at the bottom of the button. Use the screwdriver to pry the button off the knob but use caution as there is a small spring in there under tension. Once the button and spring are removed, pull the clip off the bottom of the knob (green arrow) and pull the whole knob off.

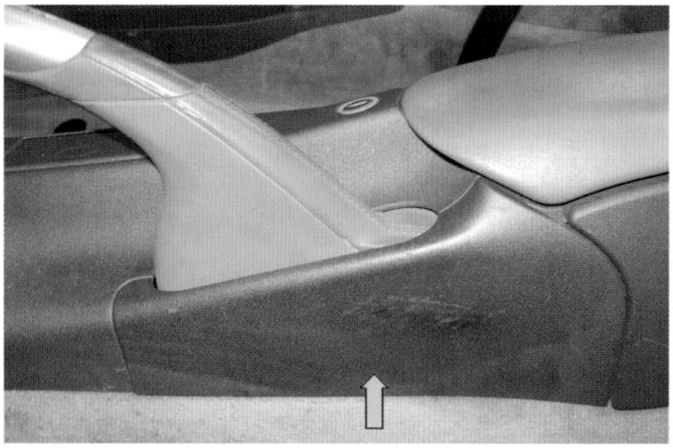

19 Pull the trim panel off the side of the center console that covers the emergency brake handle (green arrow).

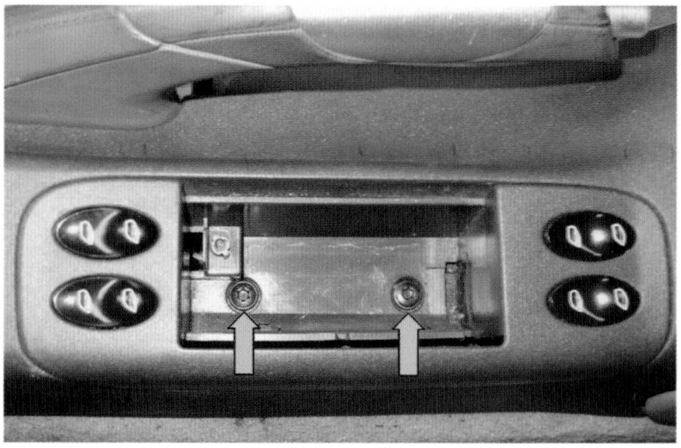

20 Now remove the ashtray and remove the two small plastic Torx screws and expanding sleeves shown here (green arrows). The sleeves can be pulled out once the screws are removed.

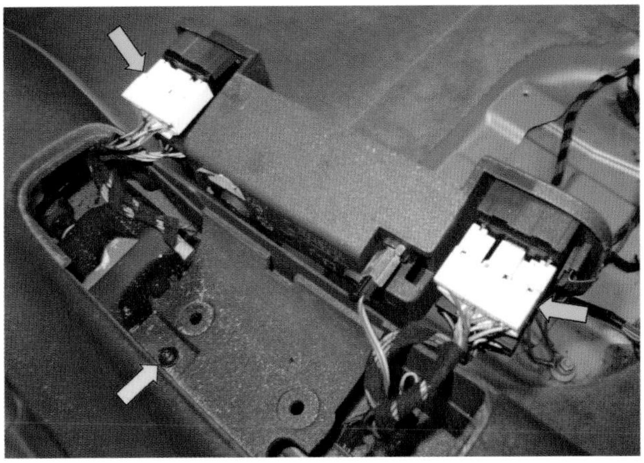

21 Pull the whole window switch panel up and out of the center console. Make a note of which electrical connection goes where and pull the harnesses off the switches (green arrows). Also remove the mounting screw underneath (yellow arrow).

22 Open the rear storage box and remove the rubber liner at the bottom (green arrow). Remove the Torx screw at the bottom of the plate and remove the access plate (under liner; see blue arrow).

23 Remove the coin storage insert (green arrow) by prying it up and off the console. Now remove the Torx screw under the coin storage insert (blue arrows, inset).

24 Remove the remaining center console retaining screw at the front of the console near the shifter. You can now carefully remove the center console from the car.

25 Before you can remove the shifter assembly on automatic cars, you'll need to remove the cable connection for the gear indicator. Squeeze the two clips together at the front of the shifter (green arrows) and remove the cable from the hooks on the gear lever (purple arrow).

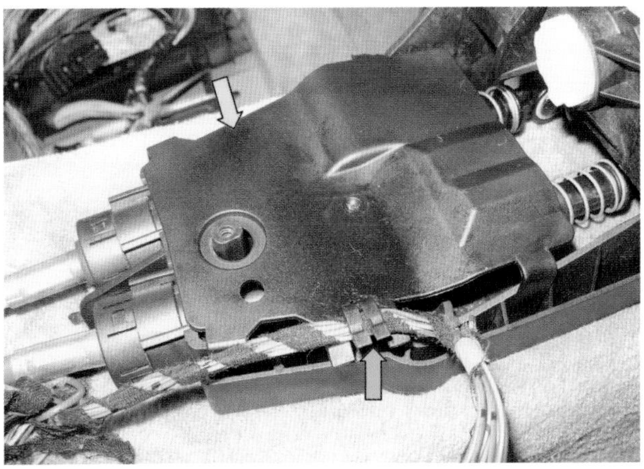

26 Pull the wiring harness for the window switches out of the clip on the shift housing (green arrow) and remove the black plastic cover (yellow arrow).

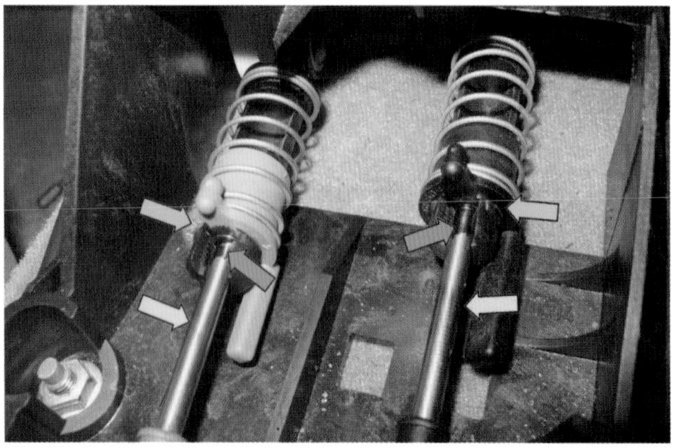

27 Now begin to disconnect the shift cables from the gear shift console. Remove the metal clips on the ends of the cable stays by pushing them in the direction of the yellow arrows. Once removed, squeeze the plastic tabs (green arrows) and pull up on the cables to remove them from the shifter housing. Make sure to mark the length of the rods on the rods themselves with a permanent marker for reassembly later (purple arrow). See Project 43 for more details.

28 At the other end of the shift cables are the grommets that hold them to the gear shift assembly. Use a pair of pliers to squeeze the black plastic tabs (green arrows) on each grommet enough so that you can slide the metal retaining clip off (yellow arrow). Once off, squeeze the tabs again to pull the grommets up and out of the assembly. Now remove the 10mm nuts holding the gear shift assembly to the center tunnel and set it aside.

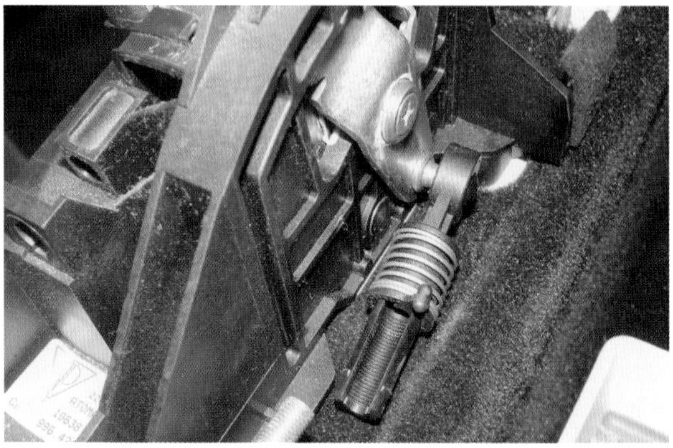

29 Note that on cars with automatic transmissions, there is only one shift cable attachment as shown here.

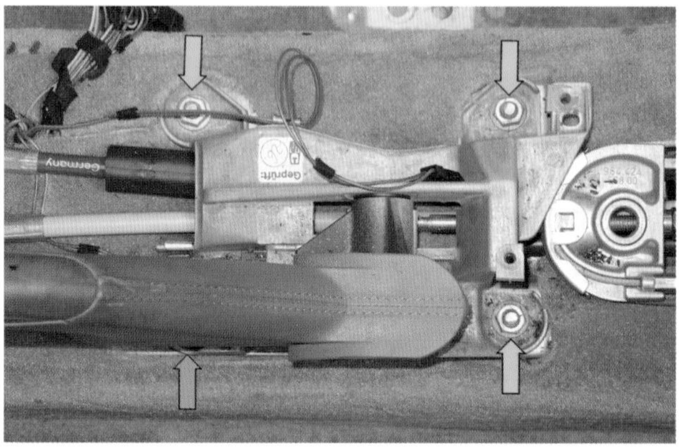

30 Now remove the 13mm nuts holding the parking brake assembly to the center tunnel. Three of the nuts are readily accessible (green arrows); however, one of them (purple arrow) is located directly below the parking brake handle and requires the use of a small wrench to remove it.

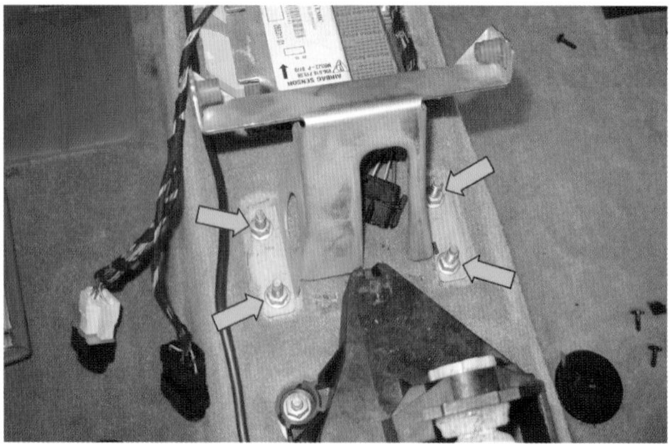

31 Now remove the four 10mm nuts holding the front center console support bracket to the center tunnel (green arrows).

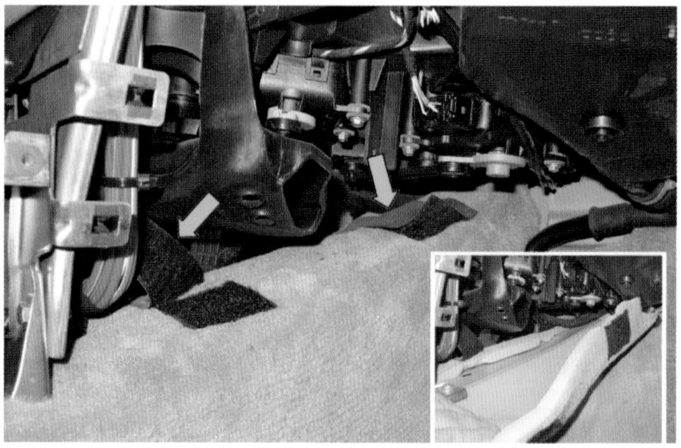

32 Now look at the very front section of the carpeting on the center tunnel in front of the airbag module. You'll see that the carpeting is split down the middle to aid in its installation. It is held together by two Velcro straps (green arrows). Pull the Velcro straps apart and begin pulling the carpeting out from underneath the dashboard (inset).

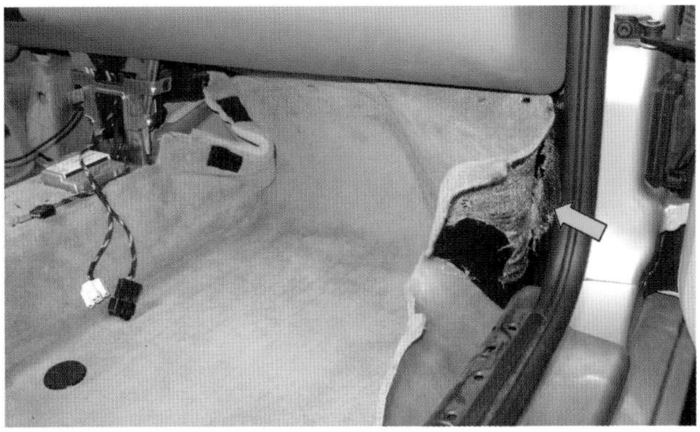

33 Here is another photo showing the carpeting being removed from the center tunnel and also the front passenger side footwell. Note the section pointed to by the green arrow. This section of the carpeting is glued in place. The glue is not terribly strong, and the carpet should be able to be easily peeled off.

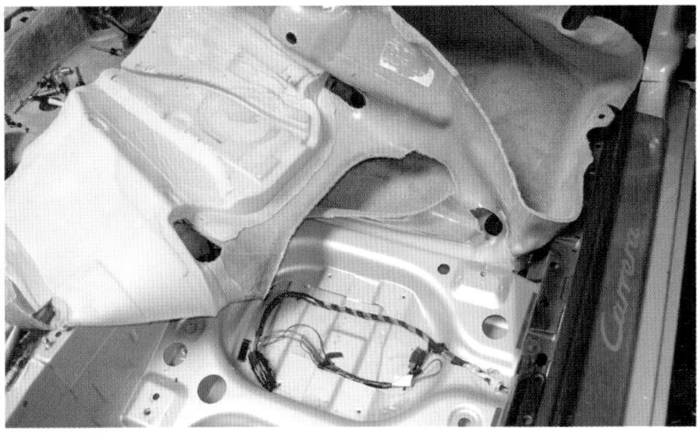

34 Here you can see the carpeting being fully removed from the car. Take care to route the shifter cables through the hole on the center tunnel. When installing the new carpet, don't forget to spray a little contact cement on the section of carpet that is glued to the right front footwell.

35 Replacing the rear carpeting that goes over the "hump" in the center and also the rear seats involves a bit more work. Begin by pulling the seat cushions out of the car (green arrow). They are just held in place with Velcro. Now remove the upper cushion (purple arrow). It is also held in place with Velcro. Also pull the black plastic cover off the bottom of the seat belt receptacle (yellow arrow).

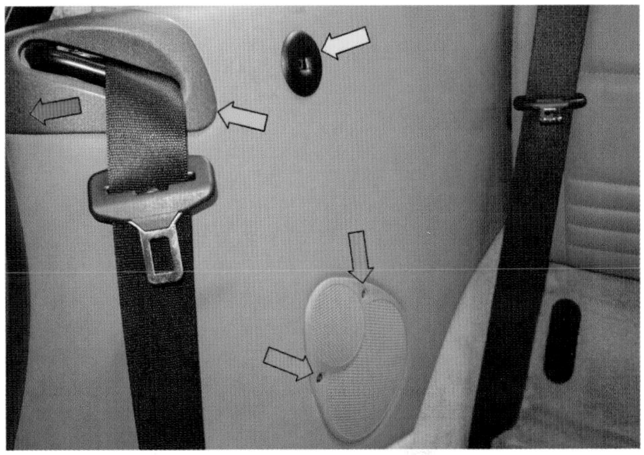

36 The side panels will need to be removed from the car in order to remove the rear carpeting. Begin by first prying the plastic cover off the seat belt opening (green arrow) by pulling it straight off in the direction of the red arrow. Next, pry off the trim ring (yellow arrow) with a small screwdriver. Lastly, remove the two Torx screws holding the speaker into the panel (purple arrows).

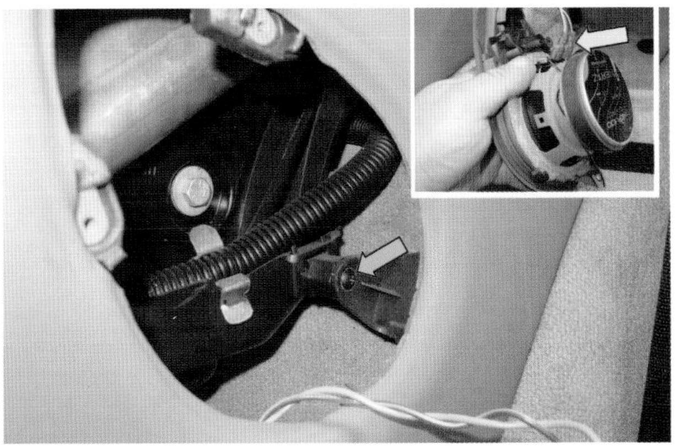

37 Remove the speaker from the side panel and disconnect the electrical connections to the speaker (blue arrow, inset upper right). Note that the picture here shows an aftermarket speaker, however the stock speakers are similar. Inside the side panel, remove the small Phillips head screw that holds part of the panel to the car (green arrow). There is a small compression fitting just forward of this screw that helps hold the panel on. You will have to pull the panel out to get this fitting to release it.

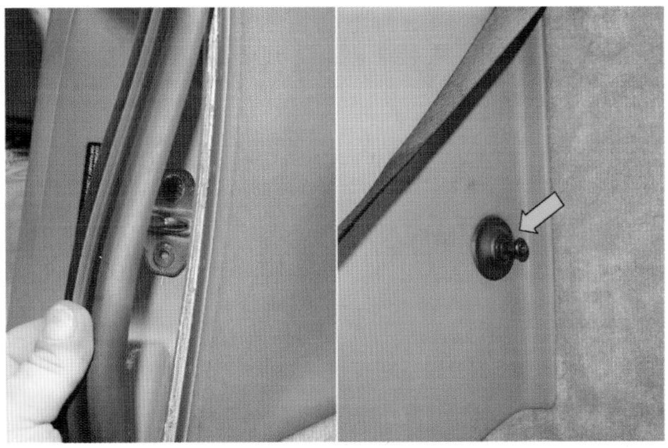

38 Pull the weather stripping off the front of the side panel on each side of the car (left photo). Lower the upper seats and remove the catch pins (green arrow, right photo) on both sides of the car.

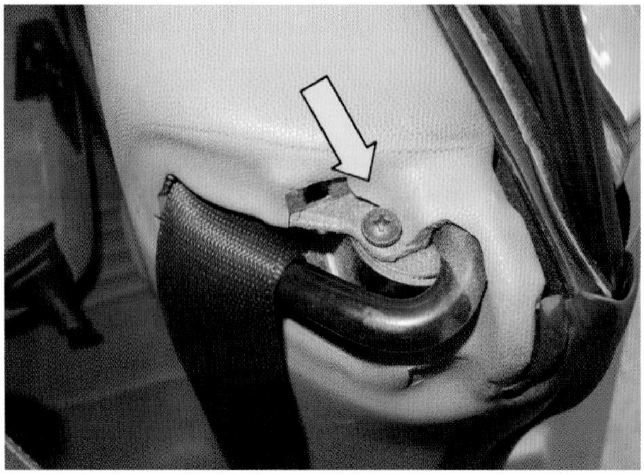

39 Remove the small Phillips head screw at the top of the side panel near the seat belt hole (yellow arrow). You are now ready to remove the side panel. You'll want to pull it up first, then carefully pivot it upward, using the catch pin location as the pivot point. It will take a bit of effort, but you should be able to get it out with little difficulty.

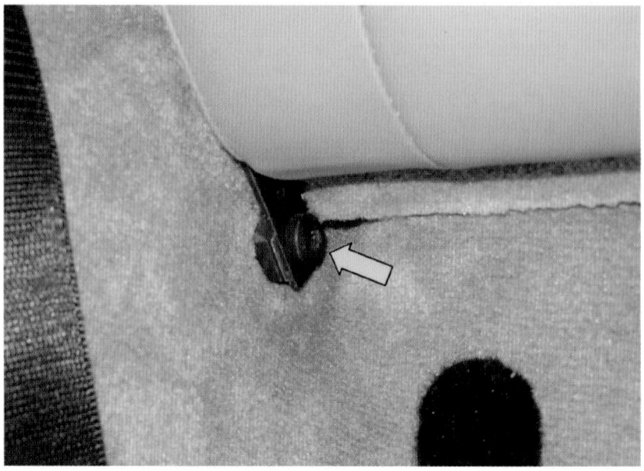

40 The bottom of the upper seats uses a bolt and a slider as the pivot point and also as the attachment point (green arrow). You'll need a tri-square bit in order to remove these on both sides of the car.

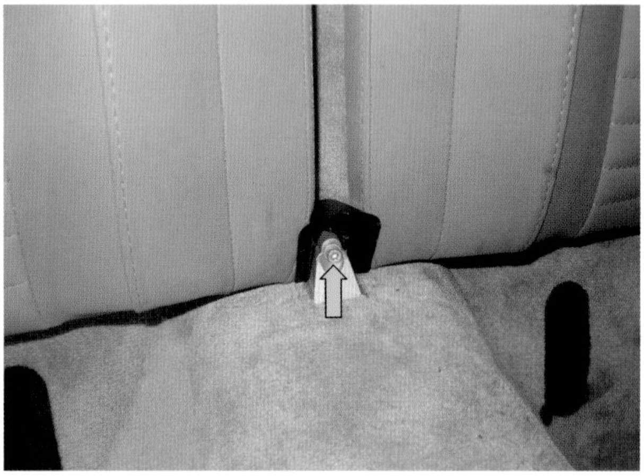

41 There is also one other attachment point for the rear seats in the center of the car. Pry up the black plastic cover and remove the small hex bolt underneath (green arrow). Now lift the seats out of the car.

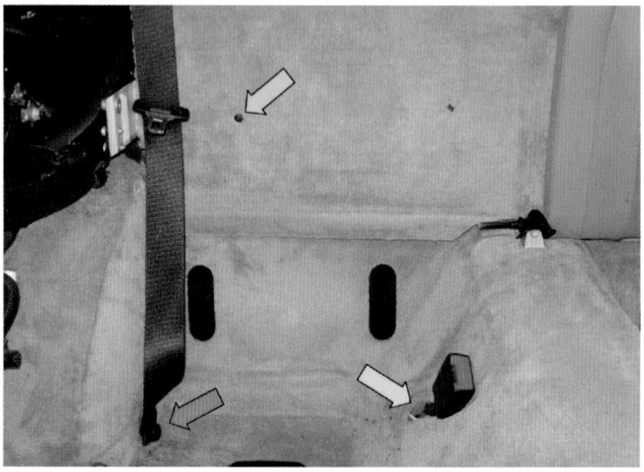

42 Now remove the two Phillips head screws holding the rear panel in place (green arrow). **Note:** Only one screw is shown here; the other side is identical. Remove the 16mm bolts holding the seat belt receptacles to the hump (yellow arrow). Pry the black plastic cover off the lower rear seat belt attachment point and remove the 16mm bolt underneath (red arrow). Be sure to note the orientation of the spacer underneath.

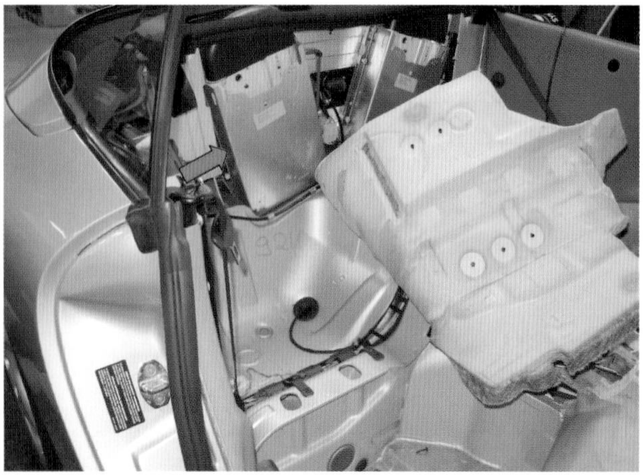

43 Begin removing the rear carpeting by pulling it out of the small pockets and corners underneath the side panels. Shown here is the rear carpeting almost completely removed from the car. The odd-looking devices indicated by the red arrow are activators for the convertible rollover protection system. If the car's sensors detect that it's about to flip over, these will deploy to prevent the occupants from being crushed.

PROJECT 70
Fixing Common Convertible Top Problems

Time / Tab / Talent: 2 hours / $0 /

Tools: Torx screwdrivers/sockets, Phillips screwdrivers, hex socket set

Applicable Years: All convertibles

Tinware: New seals, glue

More Info: http://www.101projects.com/Carrera/70.htm

Tip: Drive around with the radio off to listen of for leaks in the top

Performance Gain: Convertible top leaks no more

Comp Modification: Replace the top

It's a fact, sooner or later, all convertible tops will need a bit of work. As the car ages, the convertible top is asked to withstand a variety of elements, be it heat, cold, dirt, or rain. Couple this with constant stretching and releasing, and you can understand how much wear and tear the overall system goes through. (For problems with the convertible top mechanism, see Project 71.)

This article is not intended to show you how to replace the convertible top fabric; that's a very difficult job that is best left to an upholstery professional. Instead, use it to learn some easy tips that can help to keep water out or fix a sagging headliner. The first step is to observe the convertible top when up and driving. Has it become louder over time? Are there leaks when it rains?

One of the most common problems with the top is the inner soft fabric headliner separating from the outer, heavy fabric top. This is due to age and temperature. Over time, the elements work to break down the glue that holds the two fabrics together. You can easily fix this by carefully scraping away as much of the old glue as possible and then applying some contact cement between the two fabrics. Do not use any heavy industrial cleaners or strippers to clean away the old glue without first checking their effect on an inconspicuous area to make sure they will not mar or damage your top. Depending on the repair area, if you tension the top in the closed position, it should provide enough force to hold the pieces together. Otherwise, the use of a few paint stirrers and a few C-clamps work great.

If your headliner is sagging, check the long plastic clip piece in the center of the headliner. Check to see if the clip has come lose from the metal bow on the convertible top. Exposure to the sun can weaken this clip over time. If it has come loose, it just pops back up into place. If the clip has lost its ability to grip, a nonpermanent glue can help hold it in place.

Another area of concern is the two metal hooks on the front edge of the convertible top. Over time, these can fatigue and even snap off. The good news is that they are easily replaced as they are only held on with two Torx bolts each.

1 In this photo, you can see where the headliner has separated from the convertible top (green arrow). Over an extended period of time, sunlight, heat, and the cold weather work to break down the glue that holds the headliner fabrics together. An easy fix here is to scrape away as much of the old glue as possible, apply some contact cement, and tension the top. In most areas where the headliner is glued to the top, the force exerted by the top in the open position is sufficient hold the two pieces of fabric together while the glue dries. In some areas there is not enough tension to hold the headliner and the top fabric together when the roof is closed. So I recommend that you leave the top down and use a few paint stir sticks and spring clamps to hold the headliner and top fabric together. This will distribute the pressure along the fabric seams while the glue dries. If you are repairing an area that will not be held together under tension you can use a couple of paint stir sticks and a few C-clamps to hold the two pieces together. Do not use any heavy industrial cleaners or strippers without first double checking on an inconspicuous area to make sure they will not mar or damage the top.

If the top is leaking water, you'll need to check the seals on the top as well as the seal that meets the top edge of the windshield. If there are any rips or cracks, replace them as needed. Additionally, check the six seal sections that make up the sides of the convertible top. The areas to check in particular are where the rubber portions overlap. Replacement of these seals is pretty easy as they come off as a separate assembly, held to the convertible top frame with Torx bolts.

A very common area for leaks is the plastic rear window. These older style top windows were originally zipped into place on the inside of the top and then glued along the outside perimeter. Over time, the elements can work to deteriorate these pieces, often separating them along the seams. In a pinch, you can apply a bit of glue to the affected area, but eventually you'll need to cut through the old glue and replace the window. If you have a factory glued-in window that needs to be replaced, I recommend you have it done at an upholstery shop. The top needs to be retensioned, and it's a very difficult task for someone who has never done it before.

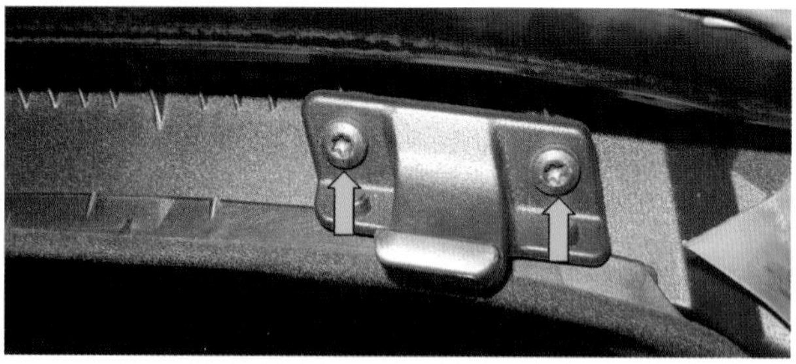

2 Shown here is one of the two hooks on both ends of the front convertible top. Over time, the metal can fatigue and eventually snap, resulting in a top that will not latch. Replacement is easy: simply unbolt the two Torx bolts shown here and swap in a new one (green arrows).

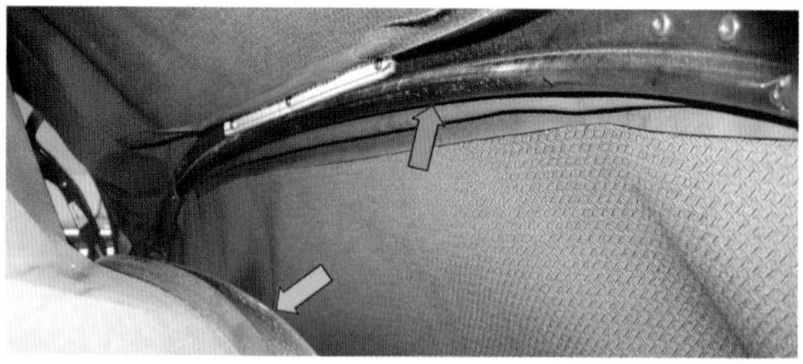

3 If your headliner is sagging inside your convertible with the top up, the fix may be as simple as pushing the plastic headliner clip (green arrow) back up onto the top bow of the convertible (purple arrow).

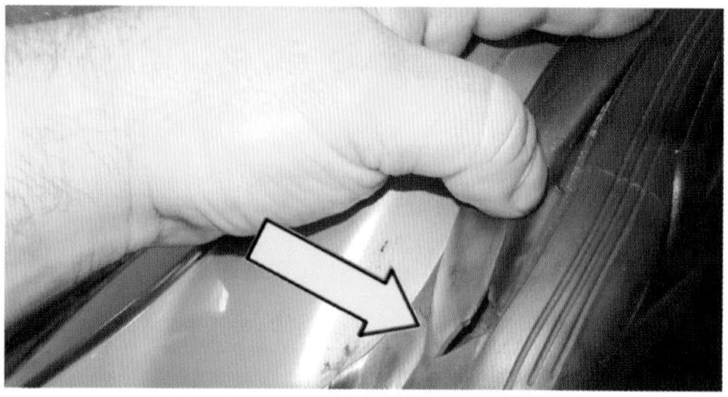

4 Check the front seal on the windshield for any cracks or tears in the rubber (blue arrow). This can lead to water leaking in over time.

5 Also carefully inspect the main side seals on the convertible top for cracks or tears. There are three main sections to check, which overlap each other (green arrows). The overlapping parts are the places you want to inspect in detail. If any are cracked or ripped, they should be replaced (see Photo 6).

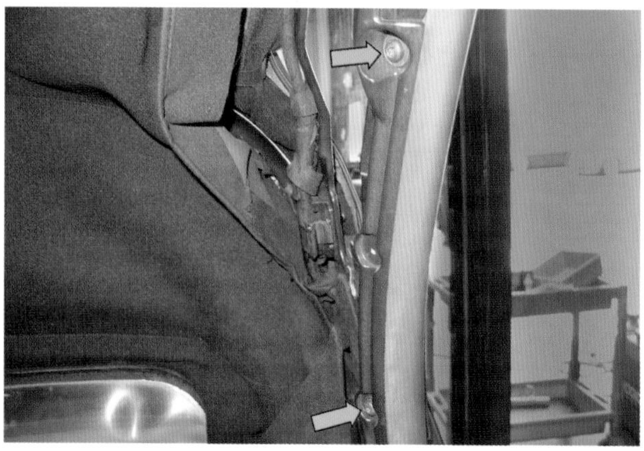

6 Replacing the rubber sealing strips is easy, simply remove the Torx bolts that hold each section of rubber to the convertible frame (green arrows) and swap them out for the new ones.

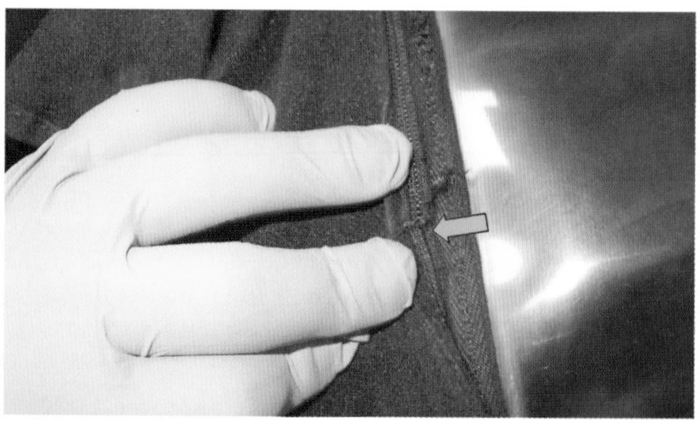

7 The plastic rear window on these cars can also be a source of leaks and wind noise. The older style windows are held in place by a zipper on the inside (green arrow), while the newer style windows are glued in at the factory. If the window is leaking you can try to apply some sealant around the edges, but if it needs to be replaced I recommend you have a professional upholstery shop handle the job.

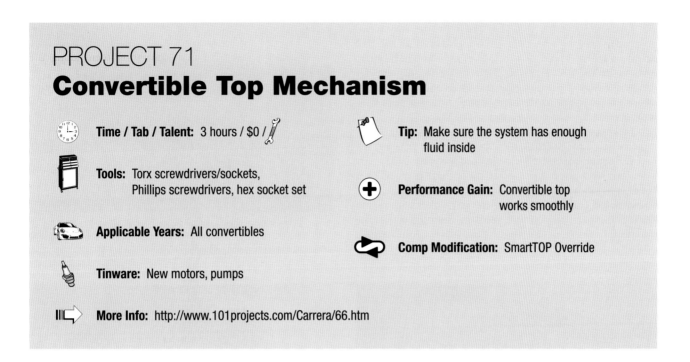

PROJECT 71
Convertible Top Mechanism

Time / Tab / Talent: 3 hours / $0 /

Tools: Torx screwdrivers/sockets, Phillips screwdrivers, hex socket set

Applicable Years: All convertibles

Tinware: New motors, pumps

More Info: http://www.101projects.com/Carrera/66.htm

Tip: Make sure the system has enough fluid inside

Performance Gain: Convertible top works smoothly

Comp Modification: SmartTOP Override

The convertible top on the Porsche Carrera is hydraulically actuated. This means that rather than using the traditional approach of cable and pulleys, the car uses a set of pressurized cylinders to both open and close the top. Over time, the system can leak or fail, causing the convertible top to get stuck in either the up or down position. (For problems with the actual fabric top itself, see Project 70.)

The basic operation of the system boils down to the use of two hydraulic actuators, mounted inside each rear interior panel. Each actuator is fed by the main system pump. If the system is low on fluid, it can operate loudly and cause the top to stop working. If you are having problems with the top, there is a chance you could just be low on hydraulic fluid. Sometimes simply adding fluid to the system can get it working again. Additionally, the fluid in the reservoir can deteriorate, especially if there are leaks or contaminants, causing the system to work harder.

Begin by moving the convertible top to the service position. In this position, the front edge of the convertible top is about 12–15 inches from the top edge of the windshield. From here, you can keep the body flap open and also gain access to the pump. Once the top is in the service position, look under the rear window flap to find the guide cable connections. These are attached to the car with two ball joints (Photo 1). This design keeps the rear window flap down when the top is opening or closing. Pop both cables off the ball joints and fold the rear window flap up over the top (Photo 2).

Directly below, you'll see a carpeted area held in place with four plastic rivets. Pry the rivets out with a small screwdriver and carefully work the carpeting over the two large plastic blocks on either end. Once the carpet is clear of the blocks, pull the carpeting up and out of the car. You'll see the hydraulic pump for the system underneath. You'll also have access to the rear body flap motor as well as the digital motor electronics (DME) computer and the relays. Locate the two hydraulic lines going out from the pump to the actuators. In between the lines on the pump, you'll see a hex plug. This is where you fill the system. Directly under the pump is the fluid reservoir. Shine a flashlight behind it to see the fluid level inside. The fill level line is right below the fill port plug. If you have determined that the fluid level is low, remove the hex plug and use a small syringe along with some plastic tubing to fill up the reservoir.

Another part of the system that can cause issues is the front latch mechanism on the center front of the convertible top. This motor assembly extends a hook out that latches the top against the windshield frame. If the motor inside fails, you can still manually open or close the latch. To access the latch assembly, pry the plastic cover off the latch mechanism from the front. Underneath you'll see the manual override actuator and the mounting points for the latch mechanism. To open or close the latch, insert the 6mm hex key into the override actuator and turn it counterclockwise to close the latch (this is the same tool used to open/close the entire top in an emergency, located behind the rear seat panel). Rotating it clockwise opens the latch. If you need to replace the entire latch mechanism, remove the four Torx bolts holding it to the convertible top and then disconnect the electrical connectors going to it. Installing the new latch mechanism is the reverse of removal.

If the convertible top cannot be opened using the switch, you can open it manually. This procedure is intended to be used only as a last resort as you can lose the reference points for the system to operate correctly, requiring the use of the Porsche factory test computer (PST2 or PIWIS) to reset them. Begin by removing the rear panel behind the seats. This is held in place by two Phillips head screws.

Once the panel is removed, you'll see the two access points for opening and closing the top as well as the tool stored on the bulkhead. In most cases, the top will be stuck open and needs to be closed. Begin by prying the circular covers off the roll bar bulkhead and insert the tool into the hex slot below. Now rotate the tool until both side flaps have been opened.

Now move back to inside the car. Locate the port on the right, which turns the convertible body flap motor. Insert the tool and rotate it counterclockwise until the body flap is fully extended. Now insert the tool into the left side port and turn it counterclockwise one turn. This port is a pressure relief screw for the convertible top. Opening it allows you to grab the top and manually move it yourself. Grab the top in the middle and pull it up and over the car. Now use the manual override on the front latch mechanism to lock the top down.

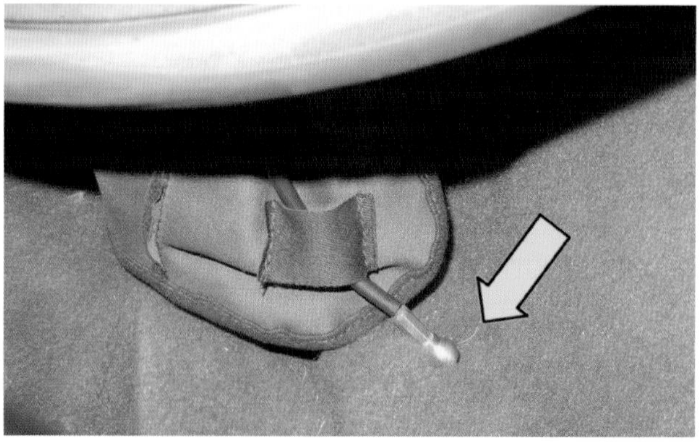

1 Once the top has been extended into service position and the rear body flap is open, access the hydraulic pump by first prying the rear window guide cable ends off the ball joints on either side of the car (blue arrow).

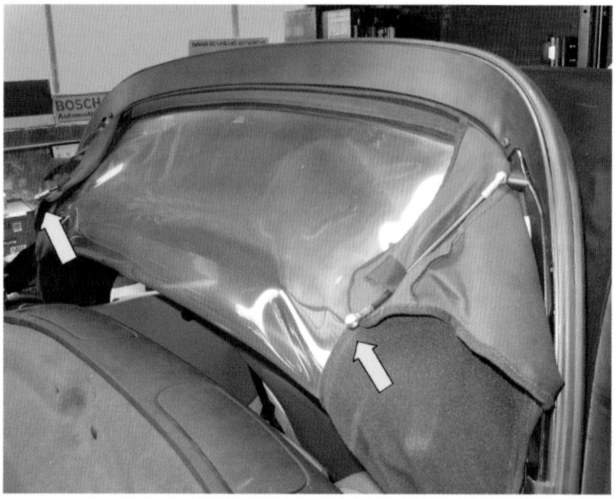

2 Now fold the rear window flap up and over the convertible top to access the area directly below. You can see end of the guide cables that have been disconnected here (blue arrows).

3 Pry out the four black plastic tabs holding the upper part of the carpeting to the roll bar bulkhead (green arrows).

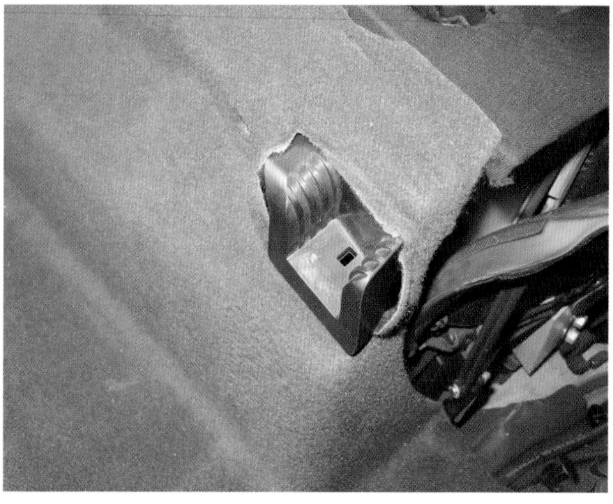

4 Begin removing the carpeting by stretching the carpeting over the black plastic block on both sides of the car. Once free of both blocks, lift the carpet out of the car.

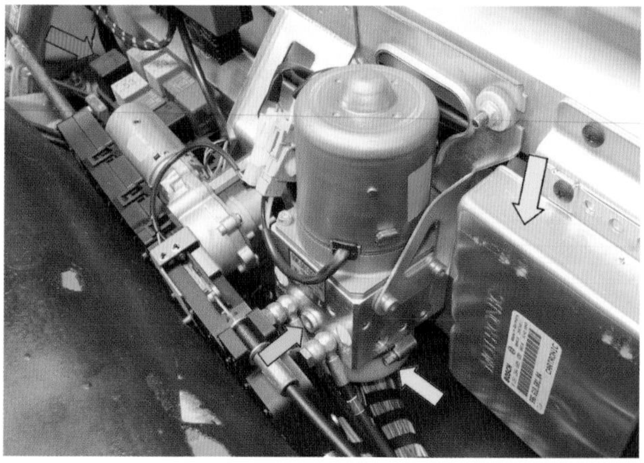

5 Shown here is the hydraulic pump that powers the whole mechanism. Over time, it may be necessary to add fluid to the reservoir below the pump (yellow arrow). To add fluid, remove the fill port plug (green arrow). Add hydraulic fluid until the level in the reservoir reaches the high mark, which is located below the fill plug. Use a syringe with a long tube to both withdraw the old fluid from the reservoir and also add new fluid. Here you can also see the digital motor electronics (DME; blue arrow) and the DME relays (red arrow). The DME is the main brain that controls fuel, ignition, and timing within the engine.

6 Shown here is one of the two hydraulic actuators used to both raise and lower the top (green arrow). They are located behind each rear side panel. The actuators are mechanically linked to the convertible top frame, so that when the actuators expand, the top raises. Here you can see parts of the convertible frame (blue arrows). If your top is having issues, check the linkage for failed parts and/or a leaky actuator. In general, these linkage components are pretty reliable.

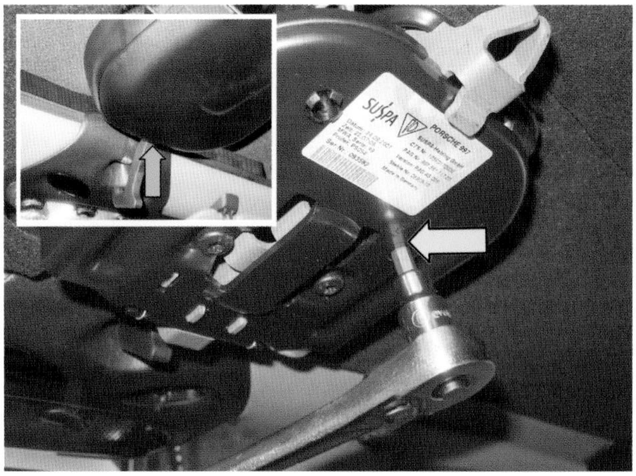

7 The front latch at the windshield can also fail over time. However, you can manually override the electric motor. Pull the cover off the front latch mechanism by pulling down on the plastic cover at the front (inset upper left, green arrow). Shown here is the front latch assembly with the cover removed. In this picture, you can see the manual override port (blue arrow). Turning the inside 6mm screw counterclockwise closes the latch; turning it clockwise opens the latch.

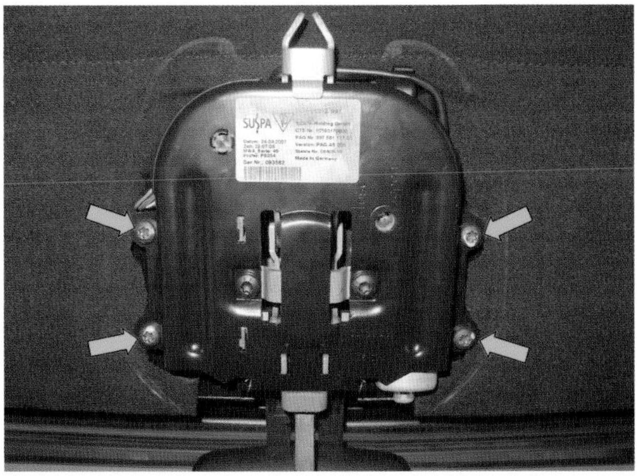

8 To remove the latching mechanism, remove the four Torx bolts holding the latch assembly to the front of the convertible top (green arrows).

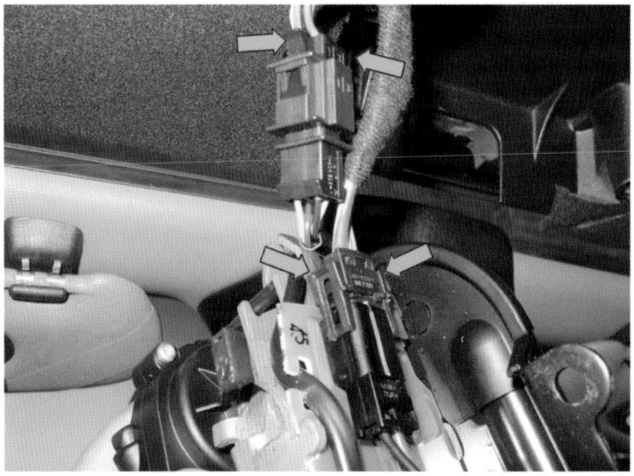

9 Once the front latch assembly has been removed from the top, squeeze the black tabs on both of the electrical connectors (green arrows) to disconnect them. Now you are ready to install the new latch assembly.

10 Access to the manual override for the top requires removal of the panel directly behind the upper rear seats. Fold the rear seats down and remove the two Phillips head screws holding it in place. Now pull the panel out of the car.

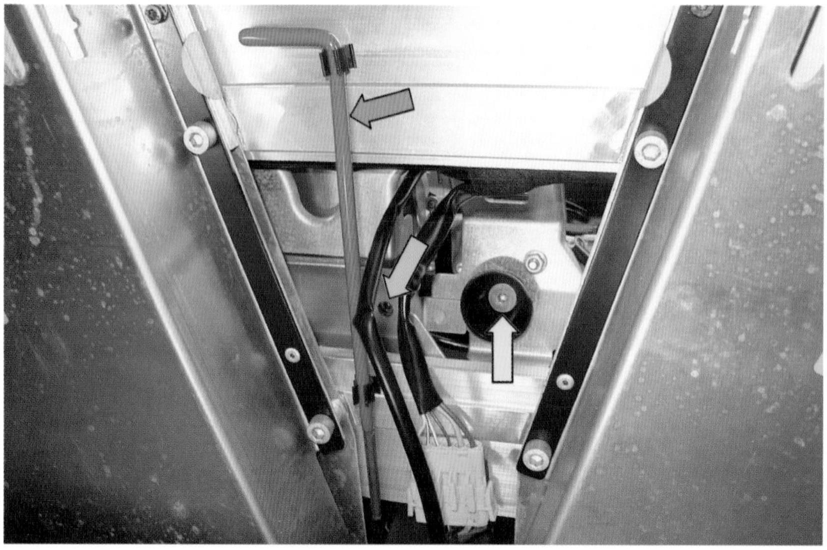

11 Once the rear body flap has been removed, you'll have access to manually lower or raise the top. Shown here is the bleed valve used to actuate the convertible top frame (green arrow), the manual motor override for the rear body flap (yellow arrow), and the actuation tool stored on the bulkhead (purple arrow).

12 To manually open or close the top, you'll first need to use the tool to open the side flaps on the car (green arrow). Rotate the tool counterclockwise until the side flap is fully open (yellow arrow).

13 You'll next need to open the body flap on the rear of the car. Insert the tool into the port on the right (green arrow) and turn the tool counterclockwise until the body flap is fully extended. The left port on the car is simply a pressure relief valve for the convertible top pump (blue arrow). You'll need to open this port to allow the system pressure to bleed off. Turn this valve counterclockwise one revolution. If the top is already closed, simply push the top backward until it folds back into the car by itself. If the top is already open, grab the top in the middle and pull it up and over until it is just nearly closed. Now use the front latch assembly override port to close the top fully (see Photo 7). Once closed, retighten the valve. Keep in mind that using this method of opening and closing the top may require you to reset the reference points in the system using a factory Porsche computer, such as a PST2 or PIWIS.

PROJECT 72
SmartTOP/Rolling Top Override

Time / Tab / Talent: 30 minutes / $250 /

Tools: NA

Applicable Years: 1998–2005

Tinware: SmartTOP control module

Tip: Operate the automatic feature with extreme caution

Performance Gain: Open the top while driving less than 25 miles per hour

Comp Modification: Check your fusebox for blown fuses

More Info: http://www.101projects.com/Carrera/72.htm

The 911 Carrera roof controller is somewhat bothersome in that in the cars up until 2003 you needed to bring the car to a full stop and apply the emergency brake in order to raise or lower the roof. This can be annoying to both you and other drivers if you're trying to raise or lower the roof at a stoplight. This restriction is designed to protect the roof so that you don't damage it while driving and exposing it to large wind forces.

Fortunately, there is a way around this restriction. You can purchase an aftermarket module that plugs into your car. The SmartTOP, designed and manufactured by Mods4cars and available at PelicanParts.com, is one of these replacement relay/controller modules for your convertible 911. This module allows you to raise and lower the roof while the car is cruising at speeds under 25 mph (40 km/h). In addition, the roof can be raised and lowered with one-touch operation; simply press the button once and the roof will completely raise or lower itself without you having to hold down the button. But beware: if the roof catches on something or someone sticks his or her hands in the roof during this one-touch operation, the results can be ugly.

Installation is a snap. The convertible top will need to be moved to the service position and the rear area carpet moved. (Please see Project 71 for the instructions on how to access the convertible top mechanism.)

With access to the rear bulkhead you can see the convertible top control box. Unlock the left connector by pushing in the little black tab under the white bracket while moving the white bracket to the right. Unplug the connector from the control box, insert the SmartTop module into the control unit in its place making sure the SmartTop unit is snug and tight in the unit, and then plug the original connector into the base of the SmartTop. It is a good idea to use the supplied Velcro to wrap the module and plugs to keep everything together.

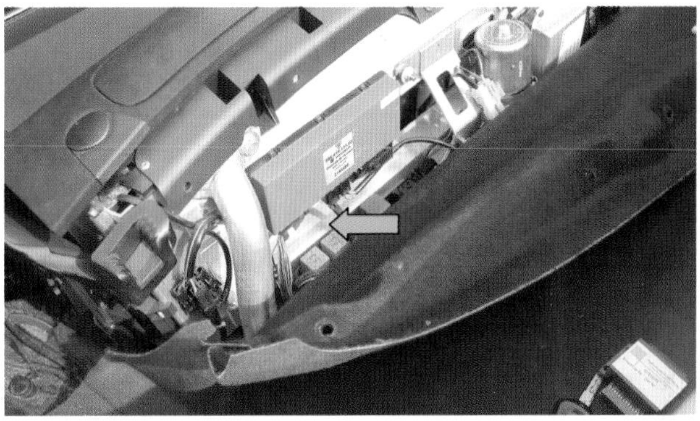

1 With the top in the service position and the rear carpet removed, you can see the convertible top control module and the location where the wiring harness plugs into the unit (green arrow).

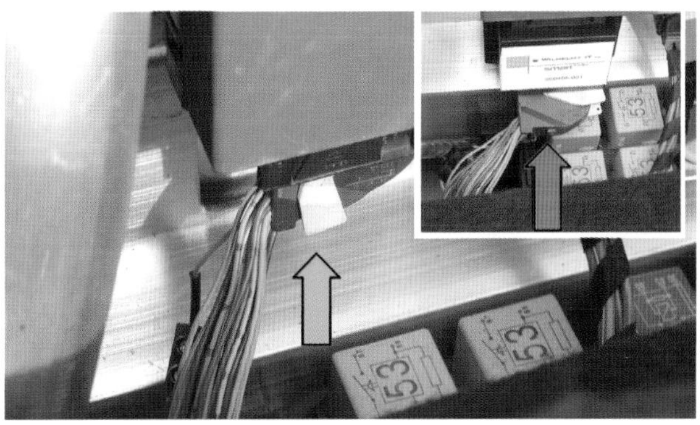

2 Remove the factory wiring harness (green arrow) where it attaches to the module by pushing in the little black tab under the white bracket while moving the white bracket to the right. Unplug the connector from the control box, insert the SmartTop module into the control unit, make sure the SmartTop unit is snug and tight in the unit, and then plug the original connector into the base of the SmartTop (red arrow).

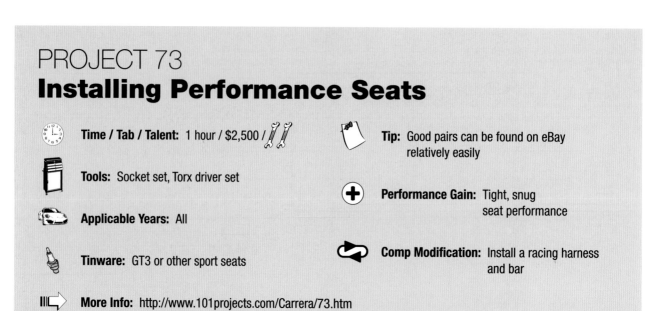

PROJECT 73
Installing Performance Seats

Time / Tab / Talent: 1 hour / $2,500 /

Tools: Socket set, Torx driver set

Applicable Years: All

Tinware: GT3 or other sport seats

Tip: Good pairs can be found on eBay relatively easily

Performance Gain: Tight, snug seat performance

Comp Modification: Install a racing harness and bar

More Info: http://www.101projects.com/Carrera/73.htm

Having the right seats really make a huge difference in any car. The good news is that the seats that are used on the venerable Porsche GT3 or even sport seats from a different Carrera can be easily swapped back and forth. The GT3 seats are sportier, are more supportive, and have the appropriate cutouts in order to accommodate an appropriate multipoint racing harness. The GT3 mounting brackets also have a lower bar to accommodate a subbelt too. Stock seats, particularly the power ones, weigh a ton, and the GT3 seats typically save about 30 pounds of weight or more over the stock seats. At about $3,000 each, genuine Porsche seats (with the Porsche crest embossed on them) are not cheap, but they are definitely the coolest seat around. Aftermarket ones and original equipment manufacturer (OEM) Recaro seats can be had for less—replicas tend to run around $1,500 a pair.

In order to mount the seats to your car, you need a set of seat mount brackets. Brey-Krause manufactures a dizzying array of brackets and adapters for race seats and is the obvious choice when selecting a seat bracket. The parts required for installation depend upon the seat, the year of your Carrera, and whether you plan to mount the seat to the floor or to sliders. In general, I recommend the adapters that allow you to mount the seat to the stock nonpower seat sliders. The GT3 seats also tend to sit lower in the car than stock seats or aftermarket race seats, which is great if you're tall and your helmet tends to stick up too much in the car. The GT3 seats should be a direct swap into the 1998–2008 Carreras with no air bag computer programming required.

If you install an aftermarket seat in your car, you will initially have a problem with the air bag computer giving you errors. You need to reprogram the computer (using the Porsche factory PST2 or PIWIS) to ignore the error signals. Side air bags also need to be disabled in late-model cars. If you use a five-point harness with your seats, then you will need to disable the seat belt sensors. Finally, you need to turn off the Automatic Weight Sensor (AWS) for the passenger seat. If you take your car to the Porsche dealer or an independent with the PIWIS tool, then it should take about 20–30 minutes for them to reprogram the air bag controller for you.

1 Here's what the Genuine Porsche GT3 seats look like installed. These are the ultimate in high performance seats, and they maintain the stock look as well.

2 This photo shows a close-up shot of the GT3 seats mounts. These seats are adapted to a set of manual seat adjusters and maintain the functionality of adjustable seats while offering a super-easy bolt-in solution.

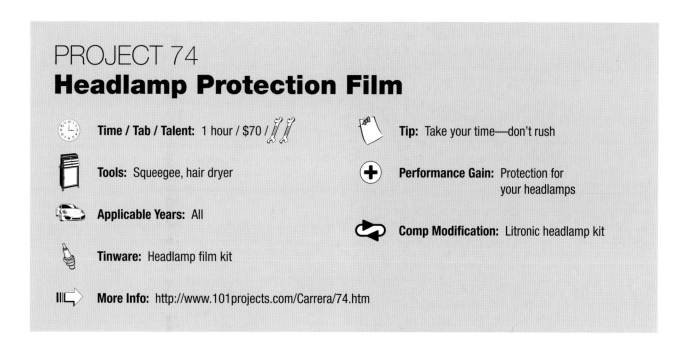

PROJECT 74
Headlamp Protection Film

Time / Tab / Talent: 1 hour / $70 /

Tools: Squeegee, hair dryer

Applicable Years: All

Tinware: Headlamp film kit

Tip: Take your time—don't rush

Performance Gain: Protection for your headlamps

Comp Modification: Litronic headlamp kit

More Info: http://www.101projects.com/Carrera/74.htm

If you install new headlamps on your Carrera, you may be concerned with keeping rock chips and other debris from damaging them. Replacing a broken headlamp assembly can be very expensive, particularly if you have the Litronic headlamps ($1,500 each). One solution that I typically like to deploy on each car I own is the application of headlamp protection film. The film I typically use is manufactured by 3M and is a few millimeters thick. According to the specifications, the film can supposedly protect against 1-inch rocks travelling at 120 miles per hour. Film kits are available for the Carrera headlamps in precut shapes, which makes installation very easy. The film is also available in different colors like yellow, which may be cool for track cars. The kit used for this project was manufactured by Xpel, using 3M film, and is available from PelicanParts.com for about $70.

You can install the film dry or wet. In general, you typically get better results with a wet installation, although I have personally done it both ways with similar results. For a dry installation, carefully clean the surface of the headlamp to remove any grease, tar, dirt, bug residue, and so on. I like to use a glass cleaner to start, then use a degreaser, and then go over it again with the glass cleaner. For a final wipe, I use isopropyl alcohol and some lint-free wipes, but that may be overkill for most applications. Be sure the headlamp is completely dry. Perform the installation of the film with the car at room temperature; you don't want it to be too cold. In colder environments, you can turn on the headlamps to warm them up prior to installation.

Prior to removing the paper backing off the film, test-fit the film to the headlamp; it can sometimes be easy to confuse the left and right sides, as they are cut differently but look the same if they are accidentally flipped upside down. When ready, remove the paper backing from the film, taking care not to touch the adhesive side. As many times as I have done this, I have learned that it's helpful to have an assistant peel the backing while you hold the film. The film is a bit expensive, and you don't want to make any mistakes or drop it while you're pulling off the backing paper.

With the adhesive exposed, simply line up and place the film on the headlamp starting with the lower inside corner, making sure the top part is properly aligned. Press the film down on the headlamp from the inside to the outside. Use the squeegee that comes with the film kit to press it down on the headlamp. If there are any significant bubbles on the film, simply lift it up and reapply it to the lamp. Since the film is clear, small bubbles don't show up unless you look at the lamp very, very carefully. It takes about two days for the adhesive to fully cure, so don't wash your car or let it get wet for about 48 hours after installation.

For wet installation, you need a spray bottle, a hair dryer, 70 percent isopropyl rubbing alcohol, and some ordinary tap water. Thoroughly clean the headlamp as described in the previous section on dry installation. Mix a solution of about 25 percent alcohol and 75 percent water and put it into the spray bottle. For the wet installation, the temperature should be above room temperature. Turn on the high beams and let the lamp housings get warm to the touch. Also warm up the film pieces using a heat gun or hair dryer. Test-fit each piece to the headlamp prior to removing the paper backing. Wet your fingers completely with the water/alcohol solution, and then have your assistant help you by removing the paper backing from the film. With you holding the film, have your assistant spray the adhesive side of the film. Do not touch the film with dry fingers, as this will leave marks that will not go away when the film is installed. Now spray the warmed up headlamp with the water/alcohol solution. Apply the film to the headlamp and use your hand to smooth the piece onto the lamp from the inside out. Using the squeegee supplied in the kit, press down on the film and from the center out squeeze out any of the water/alcohol solution toward the sides of the headlamp. Use firm continuous strokes to achieve the best results.

The Carrera headlamp is slightly contoured, which means that the adhesive may not stick to the lens immediately. If this is the case, then simply use the hair dryer to heat the film and smooth it out. The heat will soften up the film and also help to evaporate some of the solution to allow for a better fit. It's important not to overheat the film; you just need to get it warm and compliant. There may be a hazy appearance in the film after installation, which is caused by excess moisture trapped between the headlamp and the film. This is typical and should disappear within a week or so. The application of heat helps to dissipate the moisture, so I recommend that you drive with your headlamps on at all times for about a week. As with the dry installation, avoid letting the car get wet for about 48 hours after installation.

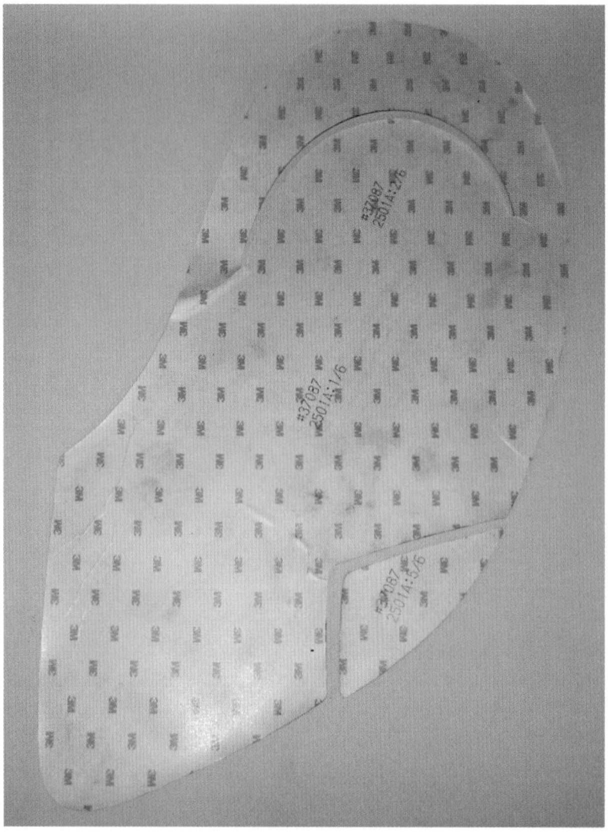

1 This photo shows one side of the Xpel headlight film kit. The kit is specially cut for the earlier Carrera headlamp pattern from 3M film and contains two separate pieces. The film is available in various colors, which allows you to color your headlamp, as is shown in Photo 3.

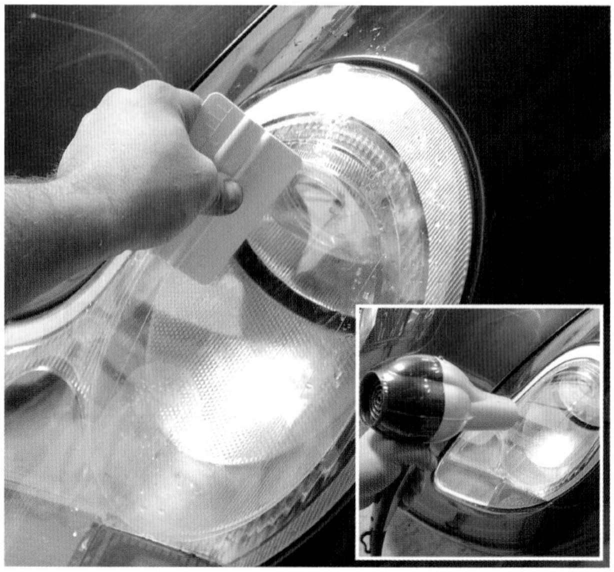

2 For the wet installation, apply firm pressure from the center of the headlamp working your way to the outer edges. Squeeze out as much residual moisture from the water/alcohol solution. If the film isn't adhering completely to the headlamp, then heat the film up with a hairdryer (inset), being careful not to apply too much heat to the film.

3 The installation of the film allows you the freedom to change the color of your headlamps (the headlamp and fog lamp on this late-model Cayman are both tinted yellow). Check with your local vehicle codes to determine if this is legal in your area.

PROJECT 75
GT3 Center Console Delete

Time / Tab / Talent: 2 hours / $175 /

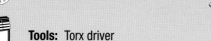

Tools: Torx driver

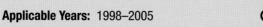

Applicable Years: 1998–2005

Tinware: GT3 console and trim cover

More Info: http://www.101projects.com/Carrera/75.htm

Tip: This is a great upgrade for tall people

Performance Gain: More comfortable driving

Comp Modification: Install short shift kit

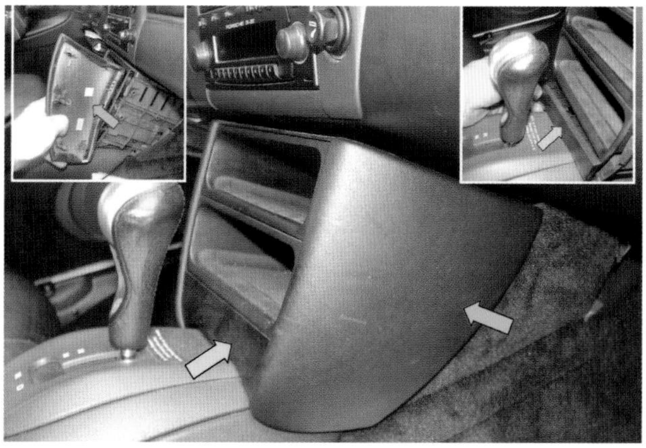

1 The 1998–2005 911 Carrera can be a bit difficult to drive if you're just a bit taller than normal. If your legs are just a little bit too long, you can remove the not-so-useful center console bins and install the GT3 cover in its place. Unfortunately, this option is not available in the 997 Carreras. The two parts that you need are 986-552-113-02-A10 (A10 is black, many other colors are available) and 986-552-241-02-A03 (plastic trim piece, black). At $175 for the pair, they are a bit expensive; but if it makes the car more drivable, then it's probably worth it. Begin the process by removing the two side trim panels. They simply pull off with a bit of force (green arrows). Also, pry out the plastic trim piece located under the center console tray (yellow arrow).

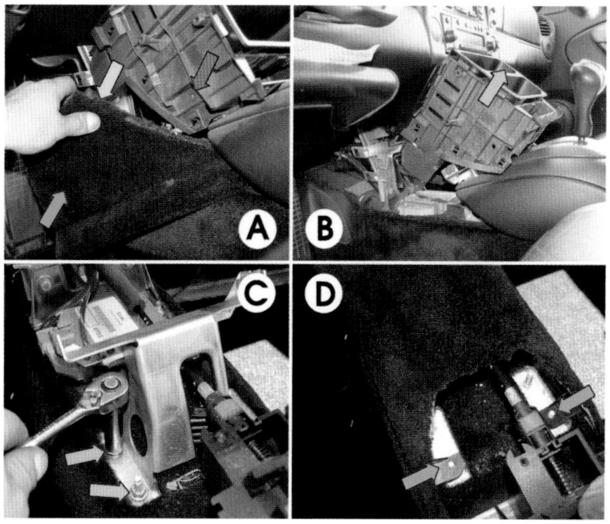

2 **A:** Next, pull away the carpet trim that is located on both sides of the console (green arrow). Remove the screws that hold the center console to the chassis (red arrow and yellow arrow, two screws on each side of the console). **B:** With the screws disconnected, pull the console up and out of the car. You will have to shift the car into 2nd gear or put it in drive (Tiptronic transmission shown here) in order to gain enough clearance to remove the console. **C:** At this point, you need to remove the bracket that holds the center console to the chassis. Remove the shift knob and remove or lift up the entire center console (see Project 42 for instructions on how to accomplish this). You don't need to completely remove the entire center console, simply give yourself enough wiggle room to remove the bracket and install the new GT3 piece. With the console removed, remove the four nuts that hold the bracket to the center tunnel. **D:** Install the GT3 center console cover in place using two of the studs that formerly secured the console bracket. Reinstall the center console when you're done.

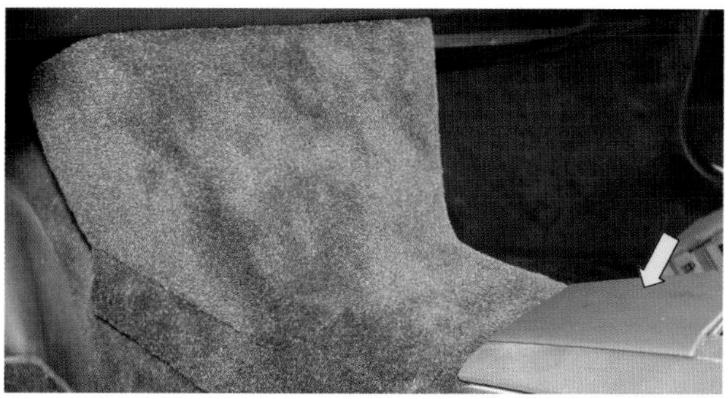

3 Shown here is the completed installation with lots of extra legroom for you. The final step is to snap the plastic trim piece onto the center console (blue arrow).

PROJECT 76

Door Panel Removal

Time / Tab / Talent: 1–5 hours / 0 /

Tools: Torx driver set, trim removal tools

Applicable Years: All

Tinware: Door handle, door stay, mirror switch, speaker

More Info: http://www.101projects.com/Carrera/76.htm

Tip: Don't pull too hard on the foam moisture barrier

Performance Gain: Working door equipment

Comp Modification: Repair your window regulator

If you are not the original owner of your 911, then chances are that quite a few things might be wrong with your car and you wonder how they got broken. There probably isn't a place on the car with more gadgets and devices that break than inside or on the door. Not only do you have window glass and seals that leak, but you have door handles, mirror switches, window regulators, door stays, and door panels—all of which are very susceptible to damage and breakage. Even if you work on your car only moderately, there is a very high chance that you will need to dive into the door to fix something that has broken. This project shows you how to remove the door panel, specifically so that you can get to the door lock assembly and the window regulator (see Projects 77 and 78), but because there are so many moving parts on the door, I'll discuss just about everything else as well.

The first step in working on just about anything on the door is the removal of the door panel. If you are going to be removing the panel, you are going to be working around the air bag. I recommend you disconnect the battery and leave the car for at least 15 minutes to give it a chance to discharge the electrical system.

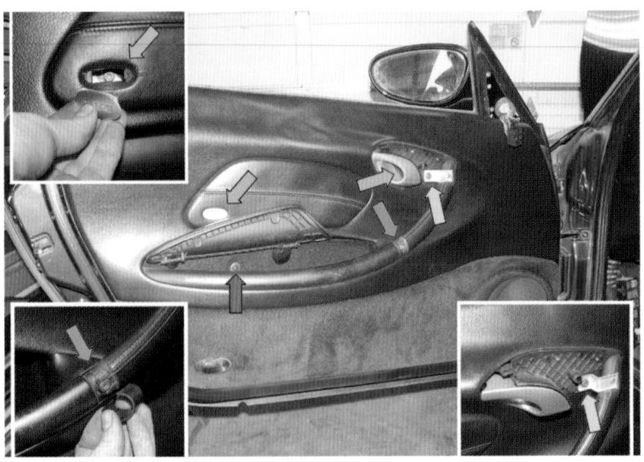

1 Shown here are the fasteners that secure the door panel. Pluck out the small air bag emblem and remove the screw underneath (green arrow). Remove the small screw underneath the trim clip on the pull handle (purple arrow). Under the plastic trim that surrounds the door handle, a screw needs to be removed (yellow arrow). Remove the screw inside the door pocket (red arrow) and the one behind the inside of the door handle pull (orange arrow).

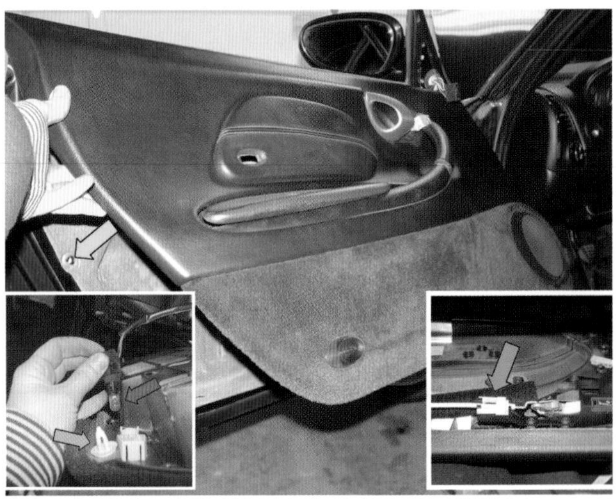

2 The 996 Carrera panel is attached to the door using plastic clips (green arrow). To remove the door panel, simply pull on the panel near where the plastic clips are located, and they should pop right out of the holes in the door (yellow arrow). Use Photo 3 for guidance on where the clips are located around the outer edges of the door panel. With the door panel loose, pull it out from the bottom and release the door lamp bulb from its holder (red arrow). Pull the panel off of the door and then reach around the rear to disconnect the door handle cable (purple arrow). You may have to clip it with a cable tie in order to disconnect the cable.

996 CARRERA (1998–2005)

There isn't really anything you can do to set off the air bag but why take a chance? The door panel is attached with nine plastic clips that can be difficult to snap out of their mounting holes in the frame of the door. When the door panel has been removed, you should see a foam covering that is "glued" onto the backside of the door. A black, sticky goo is what attaches this to the door; it can be removed and reused again if the gooey material is still pliable. Be careful not to tear the foam covering when you remove it.

With the panel removed, you have access to a whole lot of items inside the door. The door stay can be simply unbolted from the door frame and removed. The plastic door handle can easily be swapped out. The window regulator can be removed or repaired (see Project 77). Any door seals or channel guides that need to be renewed are available to you as well. If one of your door-mounted speakers is broken, don't forget to replace it while you have the chance.

Closing up the door panel is straightforward. I always like to use new plastic door panel clips because new ones are cheap and the old ones get brittle and may break in the very near future, causing an annoying rattle. Don't forget to install the foam covering; it's common to accidentally leave this on your workbench, only to discover it later on when you're putting your tools away!

997 CARRERA (2005–2008)

Porsche resigned the door for the 997 and gave it a more modular design. The doors have an inner aluminum panel that houses the speakers, wiring harness, power window controls and motor, and the air bag and its control module. These all reside in what is referred to as "the dry zone." This means they are not subject to leaks or any moisture from the weather. This has also enabled Porsche to do away with the foam covering that had to be placed between the door skin and panel.

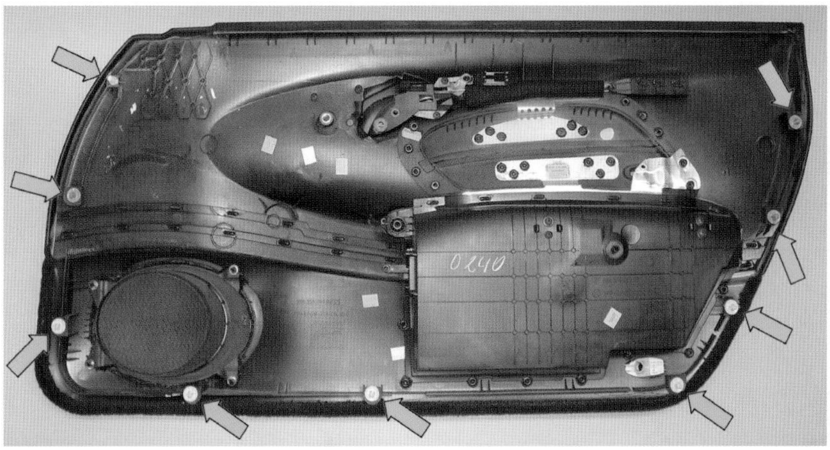

3 Shown here is the back side of the 996 left driver side door panel. There are nine plastic clips that attach the panel to the door. You need to remove each of these clips from the holes in the door prior to removing the door panel. It will feel like you're breaking the door panel, but you will need to apply significant force to pull off each of the plastic clips. Use a stiff plastic spatula to wedge the door panel out without scratching the paint on the door.

4 With the door panel off, disconnect and remove the air bag. Be sure that you disconnect the battery and wait about 15 minutes prior to disconnecting the air bag (see Project 81). The air bag is simply attached to the door using four screws (green arrows). The speaker located in the lower corner is attached to the door with four screws (blue arrow). Remove the screws and then unplug the speaker connection. All that remains is the foam moisture barrier, which is removed in the next photo.

To remove the door panel you begin by prying out the mirror triangle piece (pull out from the bottom then lift straight up), unplugging the harness, and removing the door panel T30 screw behind it. Then remove the T20 screw inside the door handle pull and remove the handle piece. Behind the door handle, there is an oval trim piece: gently pry this off and then remove the T30 screw behind it. Remove the lower speaker trim and the T30 screw behind it. Open the arm rest and gently pry up the trim by the handle. Once the trim is sufficiently lifted to get your T30 driver under it, remove the screw. Remove the end cap on the top inside of the door panel and remove the T30 screw behind it. With all the screws removed, you can begin removing the door panel. There are nine plastic clips holding the door panel to the door frame. The clips need a surprising amount of force to remove; the first time I ever did this I thought for sure I was going to break something. Just make sure to use a good trim removal tool, and once the first one lets go, you can get your hand under the panel and get a little more leverage on the others.

5 The premolded foam moisture barrier is glued onto the door with a gum-like adhesive. You should be able to carefully pull it back without damaging it. Use a plastic spatula and take your time; it's very easy to rip or tear it, and a new one costs about $70. As you can see, with the moisture barrier removed, you can access all of the door components underneath (see Project 78 for the door locks; see Project 77 for the window regulator).

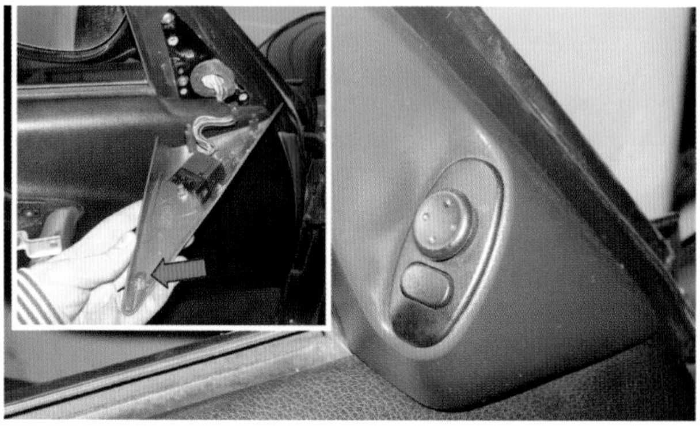

6 The mirror switch simply pops out of the door panel plastic trim piece. If you need to replace this switch, pry it up out of the door and unplug it. Be sure to install it with the left/right switch on the bottom; it's very easy to install it upside down. If you need to pull off the triangular panel, pull on it from the bottom and slide it up. There's a small tab on the top that breaks very easily (red arrow). The good news is that a new piece is only about $10 if/when you break it.

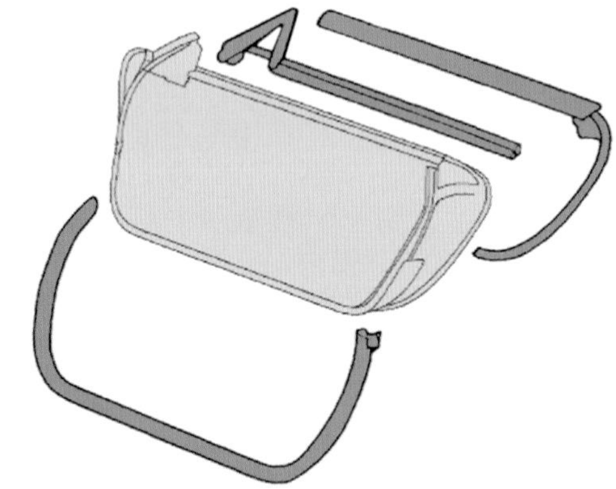

7 With the door apart, it might be a good time to think about replacing the door seals. At the time of this writing, the door seals are super expensive (over $250 each). However, I expect the costs of these to come down as more and more of them start to wear out and the aftermarket manufacturers start making replacement reproduction rubber available.

8 The door stay is another item that you can replace with the door panel removed. Disconnect the stay from the body by removing the pin that holds the stay to the body (red arrow). Then remove the two bolts that attach the stay to the door. Finally, remove the stay from the inside of the door by reaching into the forward access panel in the door.

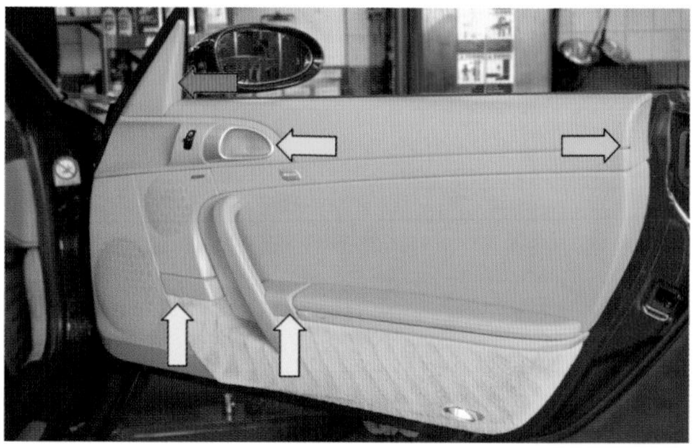

9 On the 997 door panels, there are five trim areas that need to be removed to get access to the screws holding the panel to the door. The mirror triangle (red arrow) pulls away from the door on the lower corner then lifts straight up. The door handle (yellow arrow), speaker trim and pull handle trim (blue arrows), and the end trim (green arrow) all need to come off.

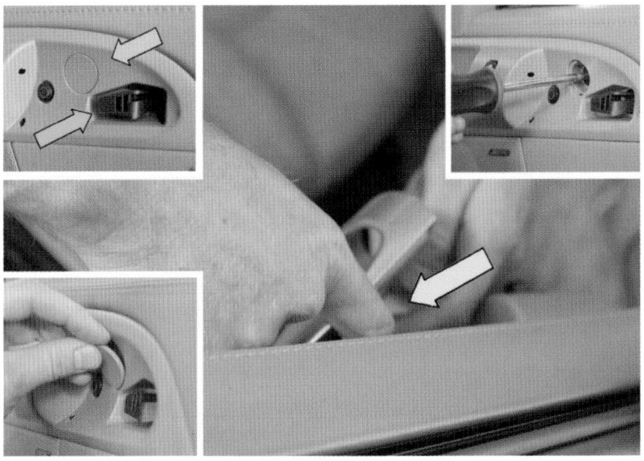

10 The actual interior door handle is attached with a T20 screw to the mechanism. You need to remove this to get access to the cover behind it. To remove the handle, pull it away from the panel and hold it out with your finger (blue arrow) while using your other hand to remove the T20 screw. Once the screw is removed, slide the handle off its mount (inset, green arrow). Next you need to remove the trim cover (yellow arrow). Push this in from the bottom and the top should pop out (inset, lower left). Once the trim piece is out, remove the T30 screw behind it (inset, upper right).

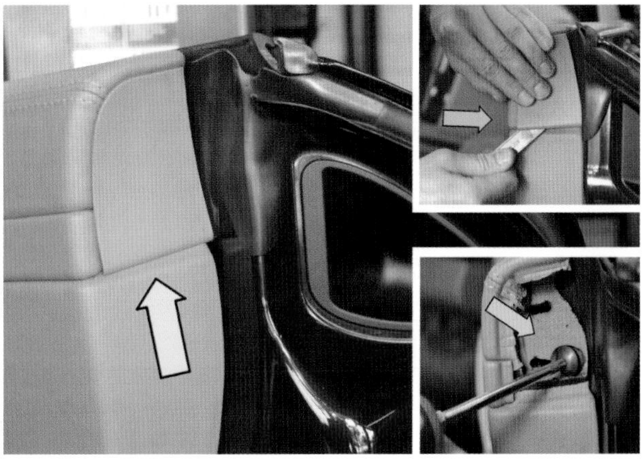

11 To remove the end trim (blue arrow) insert your trim removal tool under the trim piece and gently pull away (inset, green arrow). Once the trim piece is off you can unscrew the T30 fastener (yellow arrow).

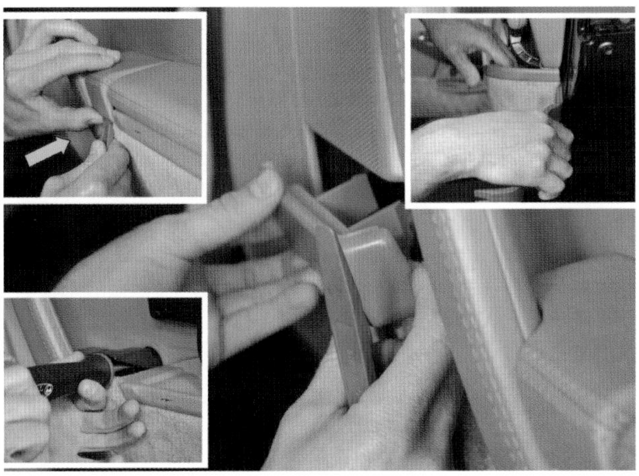

12 Using the trim tool (green arrow), remove the speaker and pull the handle trim pieces and the T30 screws behind them. Once these are removed, use your larger trim removal tool and start to remove the fasteners that hold the panel on (inset, upper right). These fasteners take a fair amount of effort to remove.

13 Here is the door with the interior panel off. The 997 doors are modular in design and contain an aluminum inner door panel. This design allows for the doors' electronics to be located in the "dry zone" of the door, which eliminates the moister barrier between the interior door panel and door. This photo shows the air bag (yellow arrows), the power window motor and control module (green arrow), the audio speaker (blue arrow), and the door handle actuator cable (red arrow).

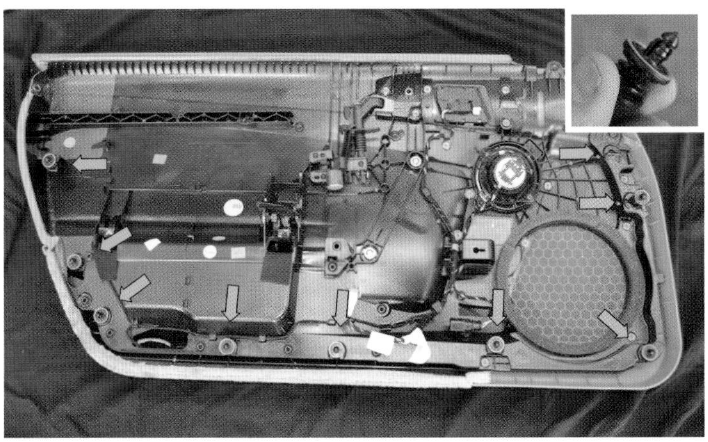

14 The green arrows point to the location of the nine fasteners that hold the door panel to the door frame. The upper right inset photo shows one of the fasteners. Once removed, the fasteners need to be reset to place the panel back in the door. Use your trim removal tool and slide the large base of the clip forward.

PROJECT 77

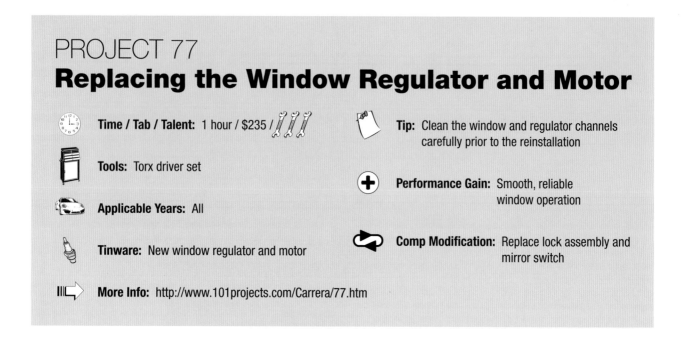

Replacing the Window Regulator and Motor

Time / Tab / Talent: 1 hour / $235 / 3 wrenches

Tools: Torx driver set

Applicable Years: All

Tinware: New window regulator and motor

More Info: http://www.101projects.com/Carrera/77.htm

Tip: Clean the window and regulator channels carefully prior to the reinstallation

Performance Gain: Smooth, reliable window operation

Comp Modification: Replace lock assembly and mirror switch

Have you gotten tired of having to open your door and get out to retrieve your burger at the drive thru window? Is your roof stuck up because the window is broken and the car won't let you open the roof without the window rolling down? Perhaps it's time to replace or clean your window regulator or install a new power window motor. Nothing's better than driving in your 911 Carrera with the windows down on a nice sunny day. Having a broken window regulator can surely put a damper on that.

The first step in replacing either the regulator or the power window motor is to remove the door panel (see Project 76). Make sure that you eliminate the power window switch as a potential problem before you start tearing into your door. Double-check all the fuses that control the power windows, and swap out the relays to make sure that there isn't a problem with them. If one of the windows works and the other doesn't, then chances are that it's the window motor or the window switch. The switches themselves are often faulty, which can sometimes make this an easy fix. On the 996, test the switch by removing it from the center console and swapping it with one that is working. On the 997, the door panel has to come off to test the switch. If there is any noise coming from the door (clicks and whines) and the window isn't moving, then it's quite obvious that the motor is fine, but the regulator needs to be repaired. If your window is not dropping down when you pull open the door handle, then you probably have an issue with the electrical switch that is integrated into the handle itself. (See Project 78 for more details on replacing the handle and that switch.)

For details on removing the door panel, see Project 76. On the 996, when you have the door panel removed, you can view the window regulator. The 997 has an inner panel, so you will have to watch the actual window as you test. With your fingers clearly out of the way, roll down the window until it's about 75 percent down. Observe what is happening; the goal here is to figure out if the motor or the regulator needs to be replaced. If there is no movement, then the motor is suspect. If the motor moves or clicks, then your regulator probably needs to be replaced. Remove the motor and then the regulator.

With the regulator detached from the door frame and the window, you should test the motor. With your hands out of the way of the motor, carefully press lightly on the window switch and see if the motor moves properly. If the motor doesn't move at all, then it probably is worn out, assuming that you've checked the window switch. Check the voltage to the motor when you press the window switch to see if it's getting 12V.

Before you reinstall the window, I recommend that you inspect and replace the front window channel guide if it's worn. This channel guides the front of the window as it is raised and lowered by the regulator. Also worth replacing are the window slot seals if they are worn out. These inner and outer "window scrapers" keep water from dripping down into the recesses of the door. You should also grease all of the moving parts of the regulator: the slides, the motor, the gears, and so on.

Before you close everything up inside your door, it's a wise idea to test the proper operation of the window. With your fingers clearly out of the way, hook up the power connections to the window motor, and try to raise and lower the window. Also verify and adjust the stop positions of the window once you have reinstalled the regulator (see Photo 6). There are screws located on the regulator that control these stop positions. If the power is disconnected from the car, the power windows lose their reference point for the closed position and need to be reinitialized. If you have a convertible, fully close it. To reinitialize the windows, press the up button on each window and then continue pressing down for about five more seconds. On the 997, you need to hold the switch in both the up and down position twice to reinitialize the system.

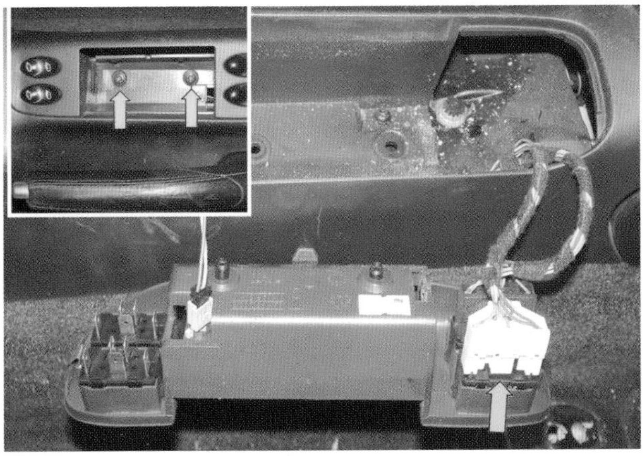

1 For the 996: The first step in checking the proper operation of your window is to verify that the window switches are working. Remove the two screws in the coin tray (inset), and then pull out the assembly. If one window works and the other does not, try swapping the switches with each other. Replacement is easy: they snap out the back (in the direction of the green arrow) after the tab inside is released with a small screwdriver.

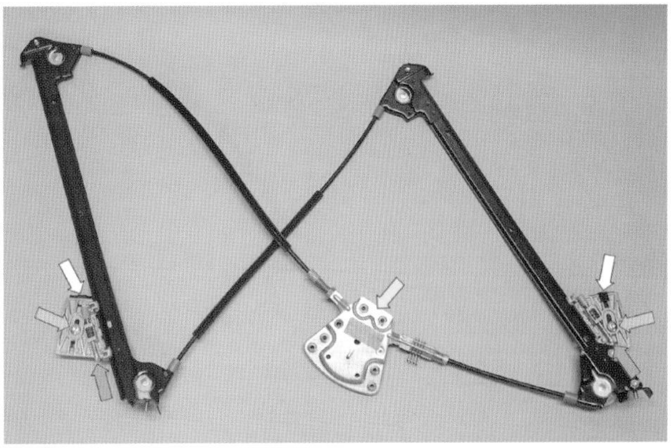

2 Here's a photo of a brand new 996 regulator. Compared to the "old days," modern window regulators are an advanced design, incorporating the cables, gears, and rails into a single assembly. The blue arrow shows where the motor bolts to the regulator. The white arrow points to where the lower edge of the window mounts to the regulator. The orange arrows show the adjustment/tightening screws for the window clamps. The purple arrow shows the height adjustment points for the window (see Photo 6).

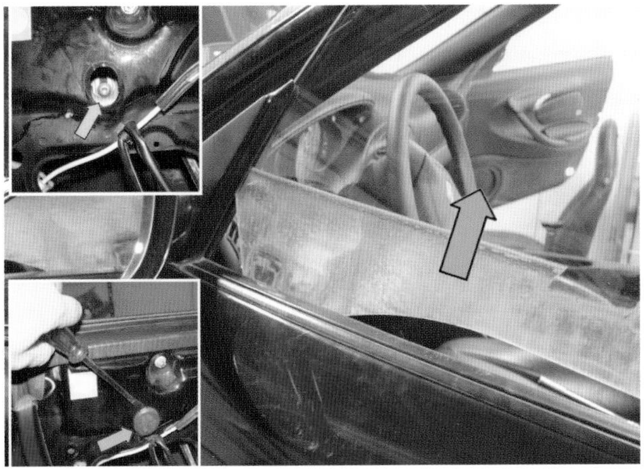

3 Shown here is the procedure for window removal. Raise the window all the way up and stick a screwdriver in the door latch mechanism to trick the car into thinking the door is fully closed. This will keep the window in the top elevated position (see Frame A of Photo 6). Pry off the rubber plugs that cover the access holes (green arrow). Loosen but do not remove the two window clamping screws (yellow arrow). Finally, pull the window up out of the door (purple arrow).

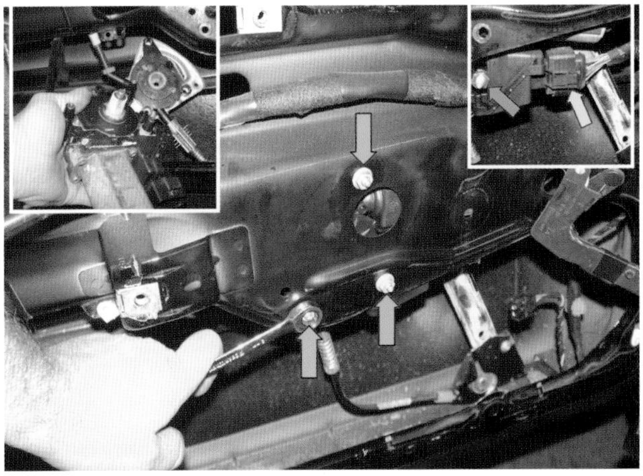

4 Removal of the window motor is fairly easy. Disconnect the electrical harness connection (blue arrow). Then remove the three nuts that hold the motor to the door. Push the motor into the door and pull it down so that you can access the studs that you just took the nuts off of. Remove the three studs (purple arrow). They hold the motor and the regulator together. Finally, pull the motor off of the regulator (inset photo, upper left).

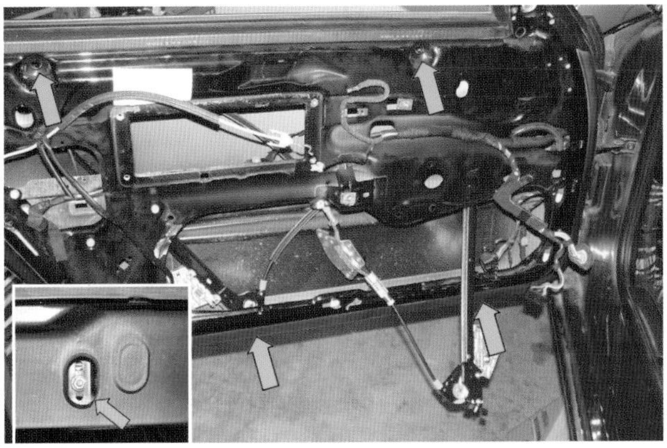

5 With the motor disconnected and detached, removal of the regulator is a snap. Disconnect the four mounting points for the regulator (green arrow) and it should slide out of the lower part of the door. On the very bottom surface of the door, you need to remove the two inner door plugs to reveal the mounting nuts (orange arrow).

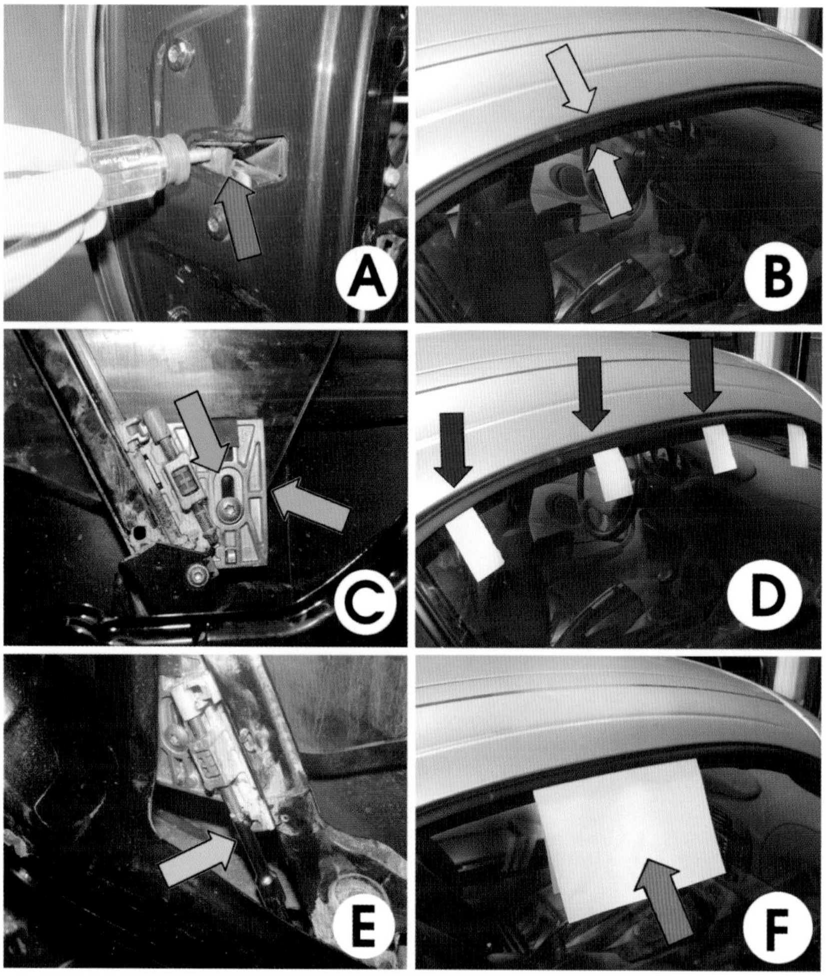

6 Window adjustment can be a bit tricky. **A:** Trick the door into thinking it's closed by putting a short screwdriver into the lock mechanism. The window should rise about 12mm. **B:** With the roof up, push the door near to being closed and measure the distance that the top of the window is located above the bottom edge of the seal. This should be about 2mm or so. **C:** Make sure that the glass is aligned properly left to right in the holding clamps. The edge/corner of the glass should be aligned with the edge of the aluminum clamp (purple arrow). To align the left-right angle of the window, use the slot indicated by the green arrow (only the rear slot is adjustable). **D:** Check the distance that the window sits into the seal by using small pieces of stick-on notes affixed to the window. Open the door and measure the distance from the top of the stick-on notes to the top of the window. This should be about 4mm. **E:** Adjust the window height by removing the outer plugs in the bottom of the door and using an E6 Torx socket to turn the stopper (counterclockwise = higher window). **F:** Check the window rake angle by placing a sheet of paper in the window and rolling it up. You should not be able to remove the paper. Adjust the rake angle by moving the position of the two lower mounting studs for the regulator, which are located in the slots in the door (remove the inner lower door plugs to access these).

7 **For the 997:** To remove or replace the window switches you will need to remove the door panel (see Project 76). Once the panel is off, you can remove the window switch by first disconnecting the wiring. Squeeze the tab (red arrow) and pull straight back. The switch is held in place by a locking tab (green arrow); gently pry it down and slip the switch out.

8 The 997 doors have a modular design that incorporates an inner aluminum panel within the door frame. This panel works as a moister barrier and protects all of the electronics in what is known as "the dry zone" (see Project 76). Once the door panel is off you will see the window motor (red arrow) and door control module (yellow arrow). Unplug the wires leading into the control module and remove the three screws (green arrows) holding the module to the window regulator and inner panel. The motor, gear drive, and control module will come off as a complete unit.

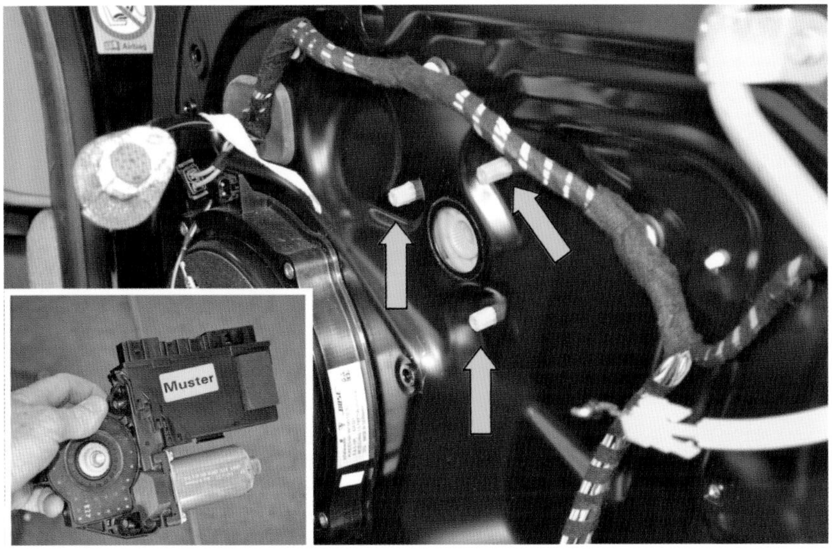

9 997-This photo shows the mounting points (yellow arrows) to the window regulator located behind the dry zone panel. Remove the screws holding the panel on and carefully pass the wiring harness through the panel. The inset photo in the lower left shows the complete control module as well as the motor and gear to the regulator.

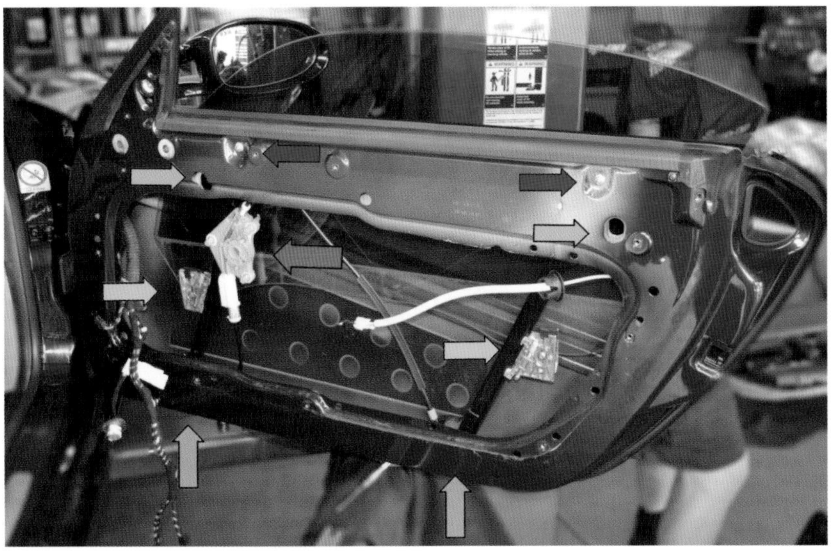

10 997-Here is the door with the panel removed. To replace the window regulator you will need to remove the window. Slide the window all the way to the top and loosen but do not remove the screws holding the window in place, via the access holes in the door (green arrows). Once the window is out, reach in and unclip the harness running along the very top inside of the door between the green arrows. Remove the nuts securing the upper part of the regulator (blue arrows). Next, pull of the rubber plugs on the bottom of the door (purple arrows) and unfasten the nuts holding the lower mount (you will need to remove the access plugs in the lower door frame). Squeeze the regulator together and carefully remove it from the door. Installation is the opposite of removal. When installing the lower limit stop, there are three adjustment holes located in a row in the front rail; make sure the stop is fitted in the bottom hole.

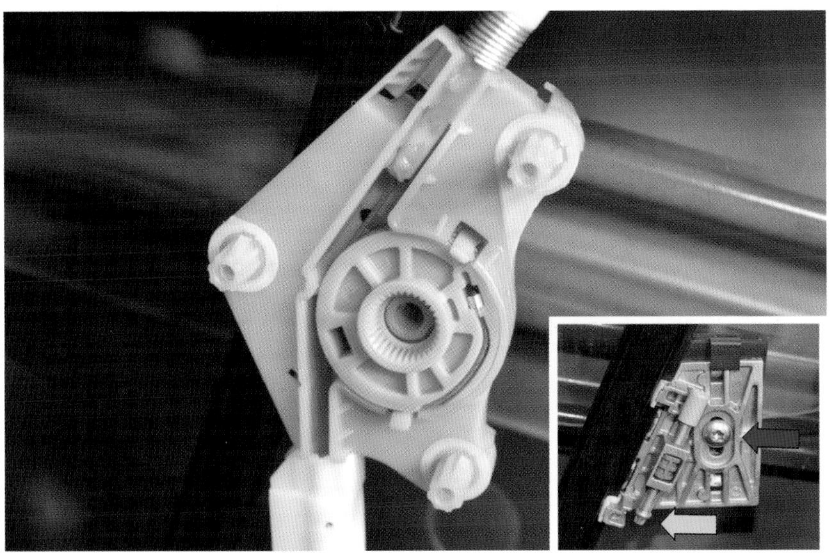

11 Shown here is the mechanism that joins the motor to the regulator. The inner door panel helps hold everything in place. The inset photo shows the adjustments available in the mount. The yellow arrow points to the bottom height adjustment; the blue arrow shows the screw used for fine tuning the up/down and side-to-side location as well as clamping the window to the regulator. Do not over tighten this nor undo it completely (see Photo 6 for instructions on adjusting the window). On the 997s, after installation you must raise the window up until it is fully closed and hold the switch in the closed position for five seconds. Then do the opposite: roll the window down fully and hold it there for five seconds. With all of the electronics now contained in the door module, it's not uncommon to have to have the door systems reprogrammed with the Porsche factory PIWIS tool to achieve perfect alignment. This may be required if the alignment is off once you button everything back up.

PROJECT 78
Door Locks and Handles

Time / Tab / Talent: 1–5 hours / $30–$300 /

Tools: Torx set

Applicable Years: All

Tinware: Door lock mechanism

Tip: There are lots of little plastic pieces that can easily break inside the door

Performance Gain: Able to open and close doors

Comp Modification: Replace the window regulator

More Info: http://www.101projects.com/Carrera/78.htm

The 911 Carrera door handles and door lock mechanism take a lot of use and abuse over the years and can experience many different failures. The first step in fixing any door lock or handle problems is to remove the door panel (see Project 76). Follow along with the photos in this project to work through the steps involved in replacing the door handle parts and also the integrated lock assembly.

One of the big failure points of modern cars are the small switches located inside the power lock assemblies. These switches get a lot of use, and when they wear out, they can cause all sorts of problems. Switches that are stuck open tell the car that the door is ajar all the time. The dashboard chime may ring continuously, or the gauge cluster may experience some erratic behavior. If the switch is stuck closed, then owners may have a heck of time opening and closing their doors because the window won't roll down that quarter inch or so to allow you to pull it away from the car. The integrated lock assembly also contains all of the motors for the power locks, which also tend to fail over time.

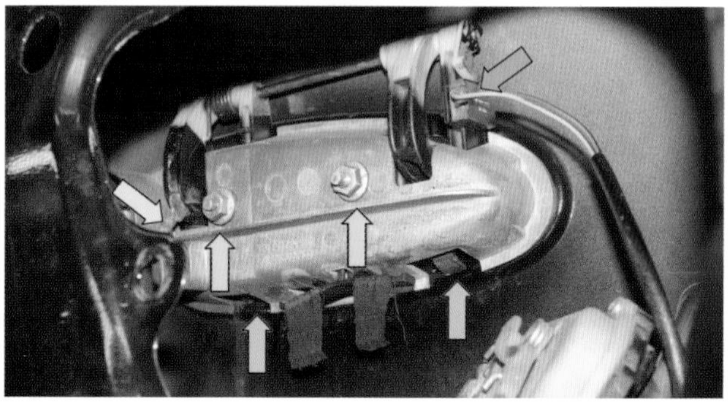

2 This photo shows the back side of the door handle assembly from inside the door. The blue arrow points to the connection where the handle itself connects to the door lock mechanism. Disconnect this in order to remove the door lock mechanism (see inset of Photo 5). The purple arrow points to the electrical switch, which tells the car to lower the window in preparation for opening the car door. The two yellow arrows point to the nuts that fasten the door handle to the rear assembly, and the green arrows show the two clips that hold the assembly inside the door.

1 **For the 996 Carrera (1998–2005):** With the door panel removed, you can easily access the door lock mechanism. Begin by removing the inner metal door trim panel by removing the three screws (red arrow). Pull the small clip that holds the door handle cable from its hole (green arrow). Then, disconnect the door lock mechanism from the side of the door (yellow arrows).

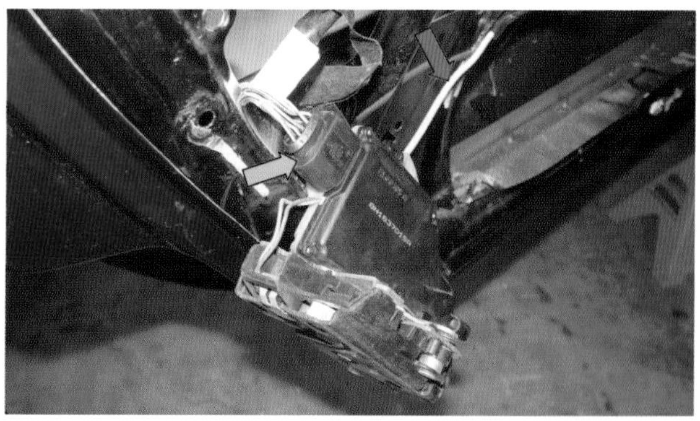

3 With the door lock mechanism disconnected, you should be able to pull it out of the door. The red arrow shows the cable that was previously connected to the door handle. Disconnect the electrical harness from the lock mechanism to remove it from the door.

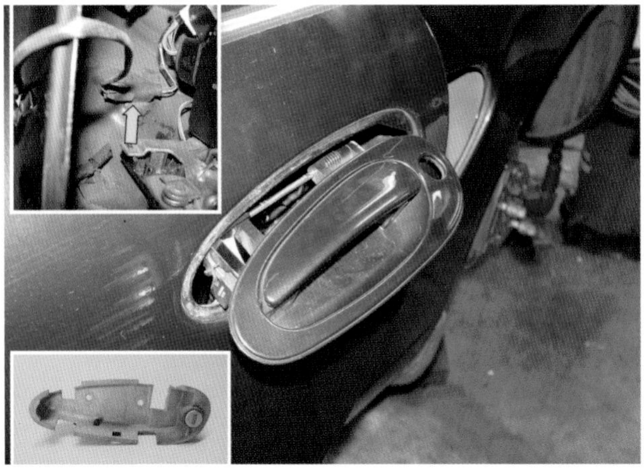

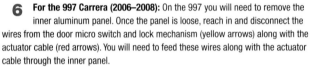

4 Shown here is the removal of the door handle assembly. After removing the two nuts shown in Photo 2, press outward on the clips to unsnap the door handle (Photo 2, yellow and green arrows). The door handle switch is plugged in to a connector located near the door lock mechanism (yellow arrow). The inner door handle housing, which contains the lock cylinder, is shown in the lower left inset photo.

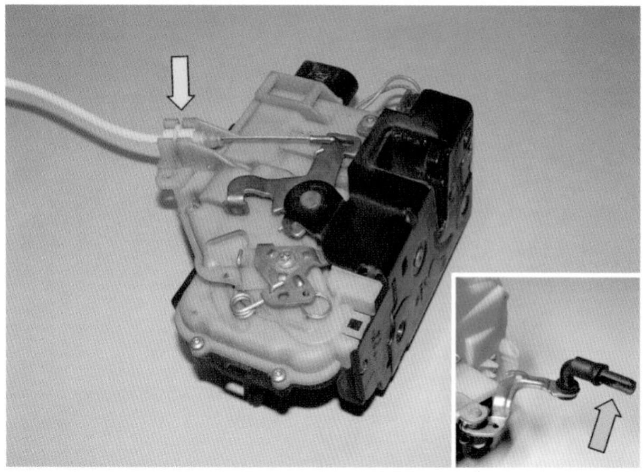

5 Here's the original door lock mechanism removed from the car. The yellow arrow shows the inside door handle cable attachment point. One plastic piece that may break is the connector for the outside door handle (green arrow). If you're taking the time to refurbish the inside of your door, I recommend replacing this piece.

6 **For the 997 Carrera (2006–2008):** On the 997 you will need to remove the inner aluminum panel. Once the panel is loose, reach in and disconnect the wires from the door micro switch and lock mechanism (yellow arrows) along with the actuator cable (red arrows). You will need to feed these wires along with the actuator cable through the inner panel.

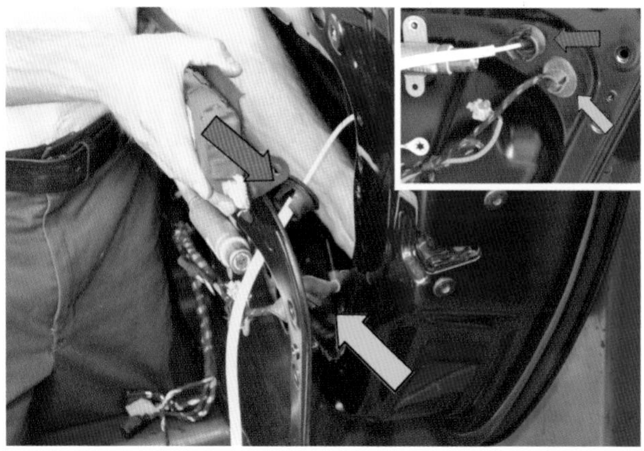

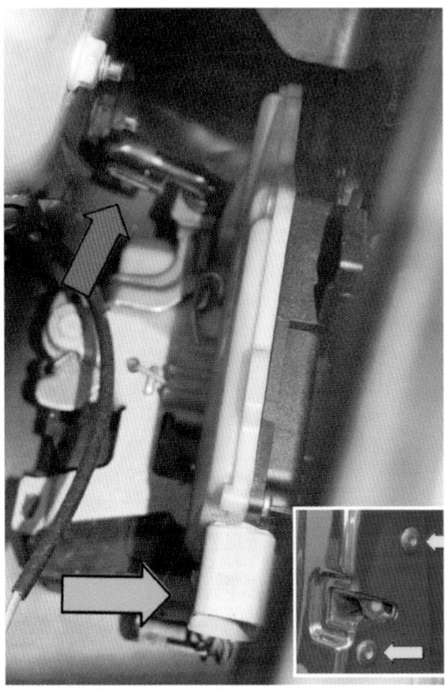

7 Shown here in the inset photo is the door lock mechanism. In order to disconnect the exterior door handle from the mechanism squeeze in the tab (red arrow), slide it away from the door handle, and unclip the piece from the shaft. Next remove the two screws from the outside of the door skin (yellow arrows, inset) that hold the locking mechanism to the door. The green arrow shows where the wiring for the assembly connects with the harness running through the inner door panel. Remove the unit from the door after the screws have been removed.

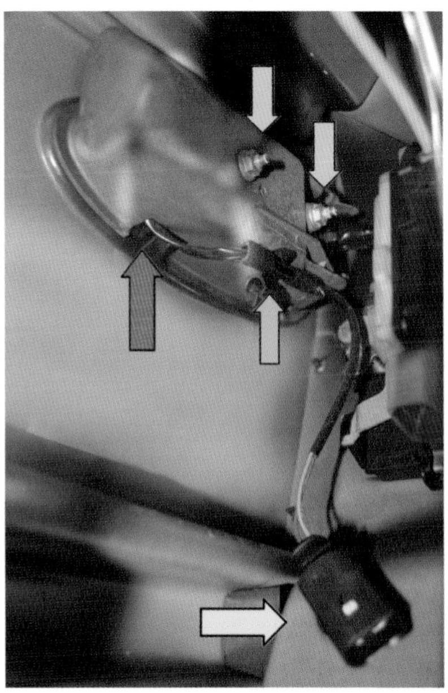

8 This photo shows the door handle as viewed from the inside of the door. You can see where the micro switch harness connects to the wiring going through the inner door panel (blue arrow) as well as where it enters the handle mechanism (red arrow). To replace the micro switch on the exterior door handle, first unclip the wiring harness (green arrow), then remove the two nuts (yellow arrows) and pull the inner casing away from the handle. To remove the switch, gently loosen the locking tab and pull the switch straight back. The exterior door handle can now be removed by pulling downward and out. Installation is the reversal of removal. After installing the door handle do not close the vehicle door. Use a screwdriver to engage the locking mechanism fully in the second notch. Using the remote control, lock and unlock the door; then, press the door handle while the door is still open.

PROJECT 79

Replacing Hood Shocks

Time / Tab / Talent: 30 minutes / $40 /

Tools: Needle-nose pliers, small screwdriver

Applicable Years: All

Tinware: Hood shocks, two for each lid

More Info: http://www.101projects.com/Carrera/79.htm

Tip: Be careful not to drop the small clips

Performance Gain: No more bumping your head on the hood

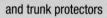

Comp Modification: Install the Das Schild hood and trunk protectors

Are you getting tired of having your front or rear trunk lids fall on your head? It's probably time to replace your hood shocks. These items are among the most disposable of parts on the 911 Carrera. They will fail; it's just a matter of when. Replacing them is an easy task, but one that is made easier with small hands that can manipulate tiny pieces. With a little bit of patience, you can replace the hood and trunk lid shocks in about 30 minutes. Total cost is about $40 or so for good quality hood shocks from PelicanParts.com.

The front hood uses two gas-pressurized shocks that hold up its weight. Start by lifting up the front hood and securing it using a long stick or a baseball bat. Make sure that this support is securely affixed, as the hood will hurt you if it falls on your head. Starting with the right side, use a small screwdriver to pry out the hood retainer clip. Then use a screwdriver to pop the hood shock off of the pivot ball that is attached to the chassis. Remove the other half of the shock in the same manner.

Replace the old shock with the new shock in the same place and orientation as the old one. Snap the new shock into place. If you can't get it around the pivot ball, then remove the retainer clip, push the shock over the ball, and then resnap the clip into place. It is relatively easy to drop the clip down into the recesses of the trunk, so work carefully and don't rush.

The rear engine lid shocks are very similar in their replacement process. Don't forget to put the plastic sheath that holds the wiring harness for the wing back in place when you're done. The whole process should take you less than 30 minutes or so.

1 Each shock has two sockets on either end. To remove the shock, carefully pry out the retaining clip with a small screwdriver (inset). With the clip loosened, you can then pry off the hood shock from the car. Wrap the screwdriver in duct tape if you don't want to scratch your paint during the replacement process. The new shocks should last you several years, until they begin to wear out again.

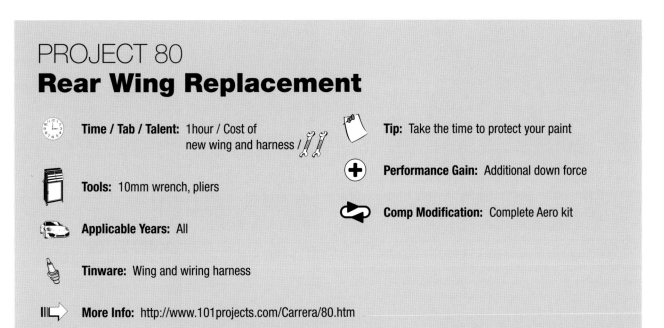

PROJECT 80
Rear Wing Replacement

Time / Tab / Talent: 1hour / Cost of new wing and harness /

Tools: 10mm wrench, pliers

Applicable Years: All

Tinware: Wing and wiring harness

More Info: http://www.101projects.com/Carrera/80.htm

Tip: Take the time to protect your paint

Performance Gain: Additional down force

Comp Modification: Complete Aero kit

Replacing the rear decklid on your Carrera with a wing is probably one of the most image enhancing changes you can make to your car. It only takes about 60 minutes to install a rear wing, provided you have the correct parts, a prepainted wing, and also the correct wiring harness.

Begin the procedure by first disconnecting the battery. This prevents the spoiler on the stock decklid from activating accidentally. While this job can be done by yourself, it is a lot easier if you can get someone to help. Prepare for the task by protecting the painted area around the rear of the car. A couple of layers of painters tape can go a long way in saving your paint job if you slip with the wing. Place a few towels or some moving blankets over the painted surfaces as well.

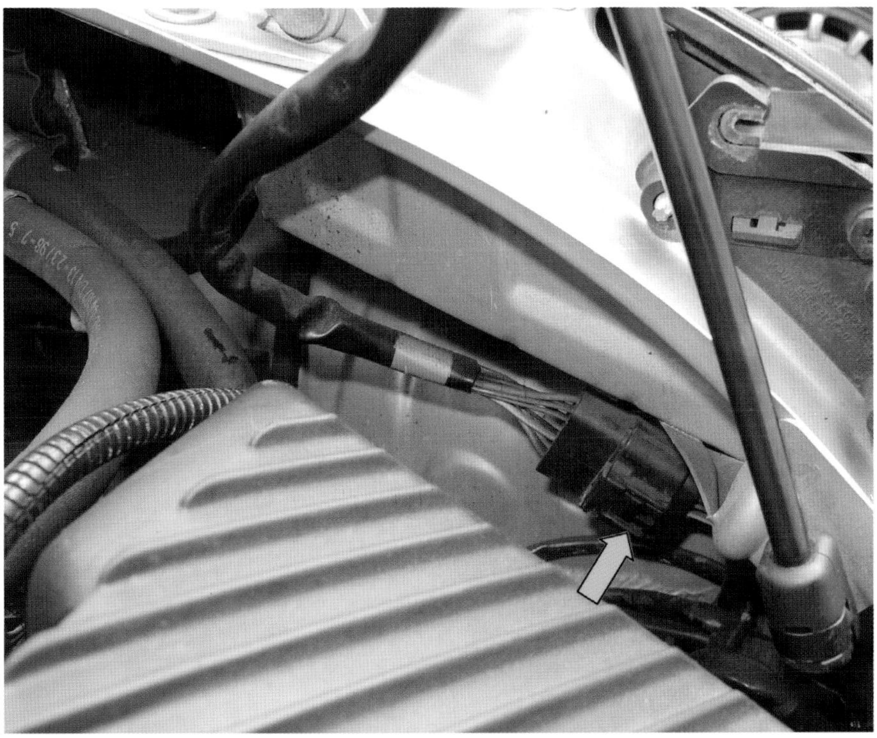

1 Look inside the engine compartment on the right side. You'll want to trace the wiring harness from the stock decklid down to the connector as shown here. Press the tab on the connector (green arrow) to release the part of the harness connecting to the stock decklid. If you are going from a stock decklid with a movable wing to a fixed wing, the easiest way to keep the dashboard spoiler warning light from illuminating is to replace the wiring harness with a fixed wing harness available from Pelican Parts.

2 First, securely support the decklid in the open position. If you don't have a friend helping you with this part of the job, make sure you use something that will hold the wing up and locked in place while you are working on it. Remove the plastic cover on the decklid shock that holds the wiring harness (green arrow).

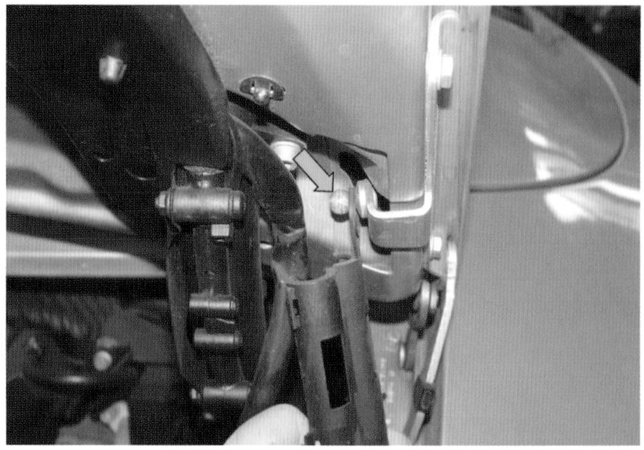

3 Next, pry the upper decklid shock connection off the ball mount (green arrow).

4 Now loosen and remove the four 10mm bolts that fasten the hinges to the rear decklid (green arrows). Shown here is the right side; the left side is identical. Once unbolted, have someone help you lift off the stock decklid.

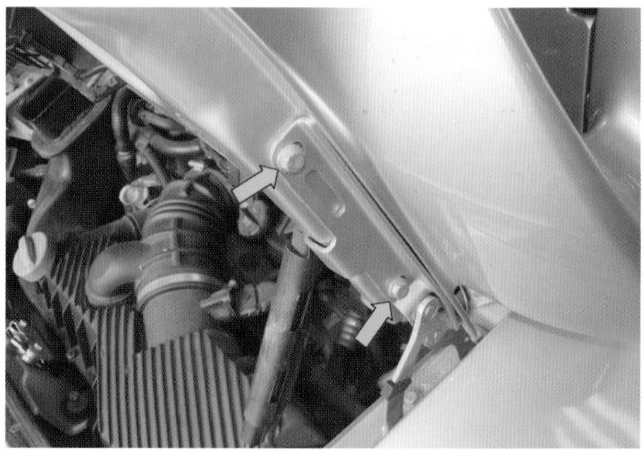

5 Now have someone help you mount and align the new rear wing/decklid assembly up with the hinges on the car. Once lined up correctly, thread the 10mm bolts back in and tighten them by hand, leaving them somewhat loose; you may have to make several adjustments to get the new deck lid to fit correctly. You can see in this photo that there is a fair amount of room for adjustments. Remember to reattach the plastic cover holding the wiring harness to the decklid shock.

6 Don't forget to plug the new wiring harness from the new rear wing (purple arrow) into the connector in the engine bay (green arrow).

7 Here's a shot of my 996 with the factory GT-3 wing installed. I think this is pretty much the craziest and coolest rear wing that I've ever seen on a 996.

PROJECT 81
Sunroof Adjustment and Repair

Time / Tab / Talent: 2 hours / $500 /

Tools: Torx bits

Applicable Years: All

Tinware: New seals, sunroof motor

More Info: http://www.101projects.com/Carrera/81.htm

Tip: Work slowly. There are lots of little plastic bits to damage

Performance Gain: Sunroof works again

Comp Modification: Replace the door seals

The sunroof on the Carrera is one of those items that can either work great or be a colossal pain. In this project, I'll go over some of the basics of the system and what you can do to fix some issues. A common failure item is the sunroof actuation switch on the front panel. Before you actually replace the switch, you may want to try resetting it. Do this by fully closing the sunroof and holding the button down for 10 seconds after the roof has closed. Many times, this can resolve a faulty system.

To replace the switch, begin by prying out the two small trim pieces at the bottom edge with a small screwdriver. Underneath the trim pieces are two Phillips head screws that hold the entire panel to the roof. Once removed, pull the whole panel off the roof. You'll now see the emergency retraction tool as well as the electrical connection to the sunroof switch. Squeeze the tabs on the connector and pull it off. Now just pry the sunroof switch out from the panel. The new one simply pops in.

If you can't get the sunroof panel to close, you may have to use the emergency retraction tool stored on the inside of the sunroof panel. Pull it off and stick it in the port on the sunroof motor. Keep turning it clockwise until the entire panel is closed.

If you have determined that the motor needs to be replaced, remove the two Torx bolts that hold it in place on the roof and then carefully maneuver the motor out of the sunroof transmission. Also remove the electrical connection going to the motor.

One other adjustment you may need to make is to the height of the sunroof panel. Do this by first removing the inner roof panel that rides on the underside of the sunroof. This is one part that is very delicate; use caution.

Begin by opening the sunroof slightly and pulling the carpeted panel back about 30 millimeters. Work very slowly and cautiously. Close the sunroof and raise it all the way up so that it tilts forward. Now pull the carpeted panel all the way back, very slowly. This will give you access to the adjustment screws on both sides of the panel. Unfortunately, adjustment is achieved mostly by trial and error, requiring that you mark the starting location with a permanent marker and then make small changes until you can get the sunroof panel to sit flush with the roof.

Two small side curtains on the sunroof attach to the roof and are designed to block the sun from the side as well as provide a sound and wind barrier when the sunroof is tilted upward. Sometimes these flimsy curtains become loose and can jam the sunroof when you're trying to close it. They should be replaced if this happens, and in a pinch they can be pulled out of the roof and removed.

1 Looking at the sunroof switch panel on the front headliner of the car, you will need to pry out the two trim pieces shown here with a small screwdriver (green arrows).

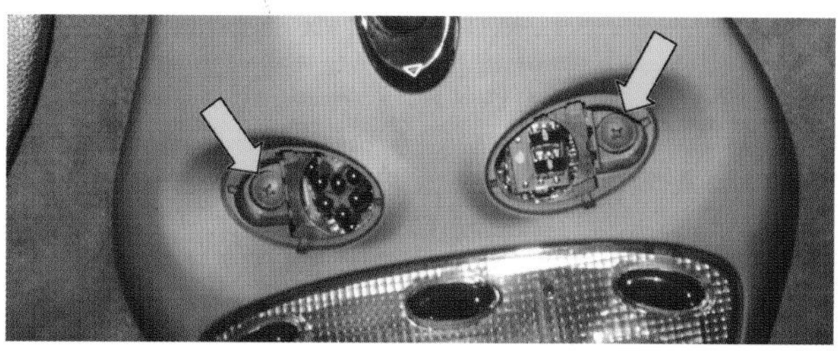

2 Remove the two Phillips head screws from underneath (green arrows).

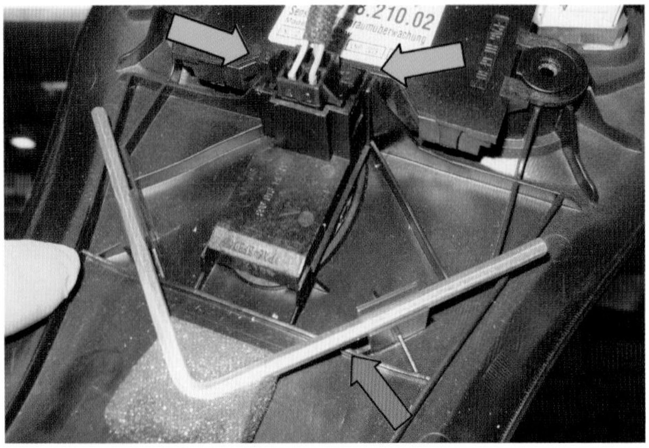

3 Pull the whole panel off the headliner from the top. Inside the panel, you'll see the emergency sunroof closing tool (purple arrow) as well as the electrical connection to the sunroof switch (green arrow). Squeeze the tabs (green arrows) to remove the electrical connection to the sunroof switch and then pop the switch back through the panel to remove it.

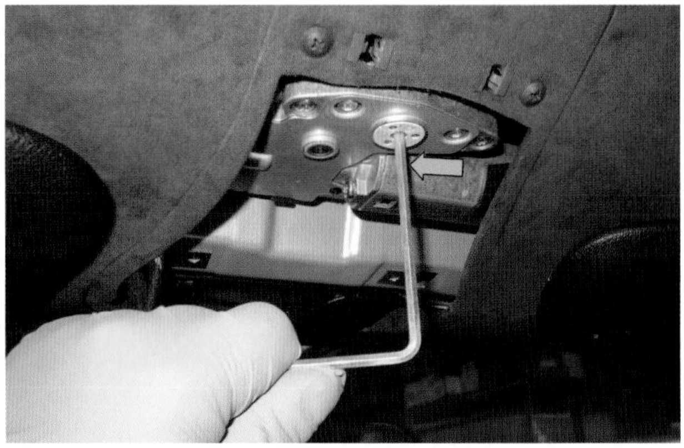

4 If the motor for the sunroof malfunctions, you can use the emergency tool in the slot as shown to manually close the sunroof panel (green arrow). Turn the tool clockwise to close the sunroof.

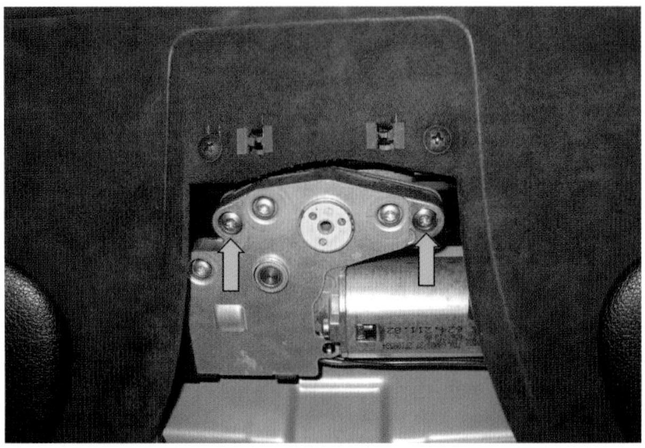

5 To replace the sunroof motor, remove the two Torx bolts shown here. Once loose, carefully maneuver the motor off the sunroof transmission piece and disconnect the electrical connector going to the motor.

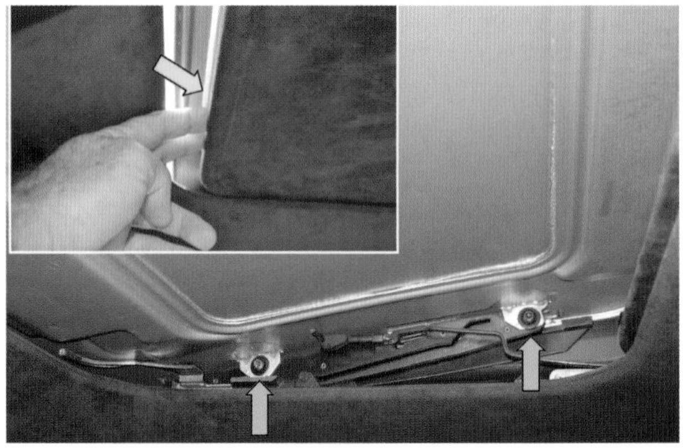

6 Now open the sunroof slightly and pull back the covering panel about 30mm. Close the sunroof and tilt it up. Once up, pull the covering panel all the way back very slowly. Once the panel has been retracted (yellow arrow), you will see the four Torx bolts that allow you to adjust the height of the sunroof panel (green arrows). **Note:** Only the passenger side is shown here. The driver side is similar.

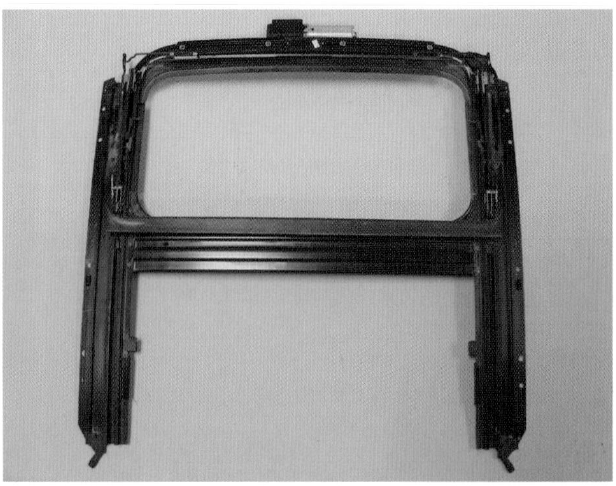

7 This picture shows the sunroof assembly that can only be purchased as a complete unit. **Note:** The sunroof motor does not come with the sunroof assembly. This must be purchased separately.

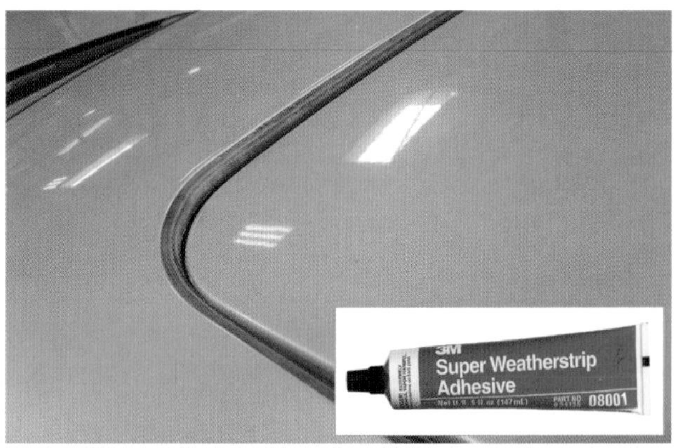

8 This photo shows the felt roof lining gasket (part number: 997-564-211-00) that surrounds the sunroof panel. To replace this seal, first retract the sunroof back and peel the existing lining off. Then clean the contact surface with a clear-coat safe liquid solvent (always test any cleaning solvent on an inconspicuous section of paint before applying to your vehicle). Next, apply a thin coat of 3M Super Weatherstrip Adhesive (Pelican Parts part number: TOL-3M-8001) and set the new lining in place. Once the gasket is set, close the sunroof and allow the adhesive to dry for about 36 hours.

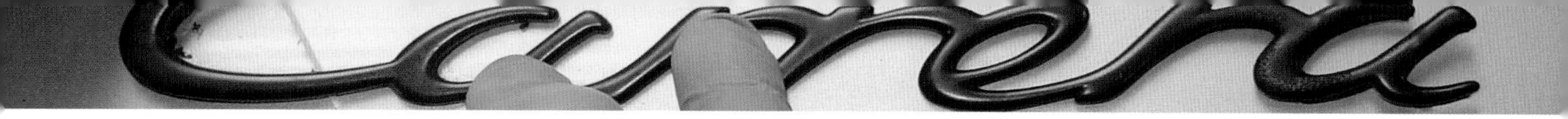

PROJECT 82
Modifying Your Wheelwell Liners

Time / Tab / Talent: 8 hrs / $0 / 3 wrenches

Tools: 10mm and 13mm sockets and socket wrench, Phillips screwdriver, flathead screwdriver, T-25 Torx driver, pliers or a crowbar, Dremel, file, 2 cable ties

Applicable Years: 1998–2005

Tinware: N/A

More Info: http://www.101projects.com/Carrera/82.htm

Tip: Wear goggles, remove both front tires, and use jack stands

Performance Gain: Improved brake cooling

Comp Modification: Service the front brakes, radiators, or radiator fans

The 2005 and later (997) use a newer style wheelwell liner that reduces lift and drag while diverting more air to the brake cooling system. While these new liners cannot be installed in a 1998–2005 996 Carrera, the older ones can be modified to resemble the later-style ones. These later-style liners route the air that passes through the radiators to cool your front brakes. The modification also has the added bonus of reducing drag and lift. So if you're handy with a Dremel rotary tool, you can easily create your own set of 997-style brake ducts by following this guide.

Start off by jacking up the car (see Project 1) and removing both front wheels. Next, remove your front bumper and both front wheelwell liners (see Project 68). Now, remove the front radiator air ducts, which are held in place by five T-25 Torx screws (see green arrows in Photo 1). Remove the ambient temperature sensor on the passenger side air duct by simply pushing it out with a flathead screwdriver (see inset of Photo 1).

Next, using a cable tie, affix the upper end of each radiator to the plastic bracket above it. This way you can hold the radiator while you remove the rear metal frame. Once the ties are in place, remove the two side clamps of each radiator by lifting the metal tab with a flathead screwdriver and pushing it out.

Now, remove the metal bracket holding the radiator to the chassis by removing the T-25 Torx screw behind the plastic radiator fan duct, the 13mm nut on the side and the two 13mm bolts underneath. Also, unclip the two blue clamps attached to each radiator bracket with a flathead screwdriver and the air sensor located on the inside corner of the metal radiator bracket. Once all has been completed, remove both the metal bracket and radiator fan duct for modification (see Photo 3).

On a flat surface, align the metal brackets with the plastic fan ducts to give you an idea of where to make your cut. I found it useful to utilize the existing Torx screws for more accurate markings. Now take a permanent marker and draw vertical lines and a lower horizontal base on the fan duct to represent the brake cooling slits in the 997 fender liner (see inset of Photo 4). Next, using a Dremel (wear safety goggles), carefully cutout the highlighted areas. You can also use a file to clean up the edges.

Next, draw vertical lines and highlight a lower horizontal base on the fender liner. Again, I found it useful to align the metal bracket, fan duct, and fender lining for more accurate markings. Once that's done, carefully make the cuts with a Dremel.

Clean up the edges and don't worry if your cuts are too large, too small, awkward-looking, or whatever, since it will not be easily visible to the naked eye and will only help cool those brake rotors. Enjoy!

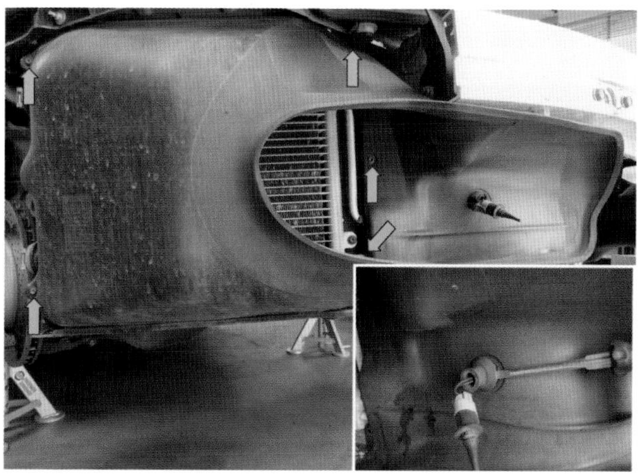

1 Remove the five T-25 Torx screws (green arrows) and push the ambient temperature sensor through the opening to remove each air duct.

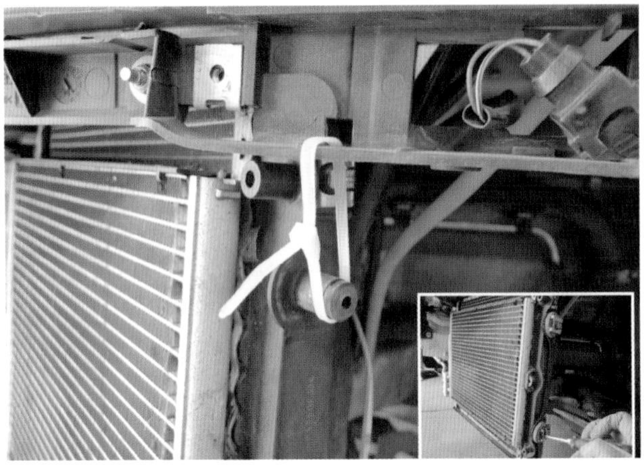

2 Tie the upper end of each radiator to the plastic bracket above it as a way to hold the radiator while removing the rear metal frame. Once the ties are in place, remove the two side clamps of each radiator by lifting the metal tab with a flathead screwdriver and pushing it out (inset photo).

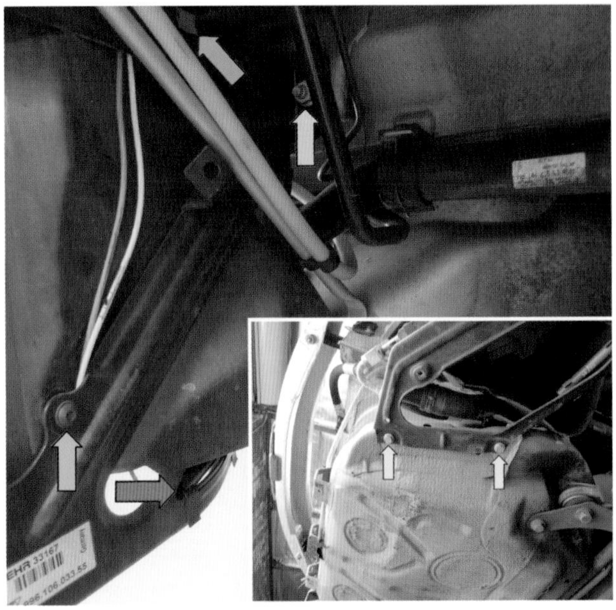

3 Now, remove the metal bracket holding the radiator to the chassis by removing the T-25 Torx screw behind the plastic radiator fan duct (green arrow), the 13mm nut on the side (yellow arrow), and the two 13mm bolts underneath (inset photo). Also, unclip the two blue clamps attached to each radiator bracket with a flathead screwdriver (purple arrow) and the air sensor located on the inside corner of the metal radiator bracket (red arrow). Remove both the metal bracket and the radiator fan duct for modification.

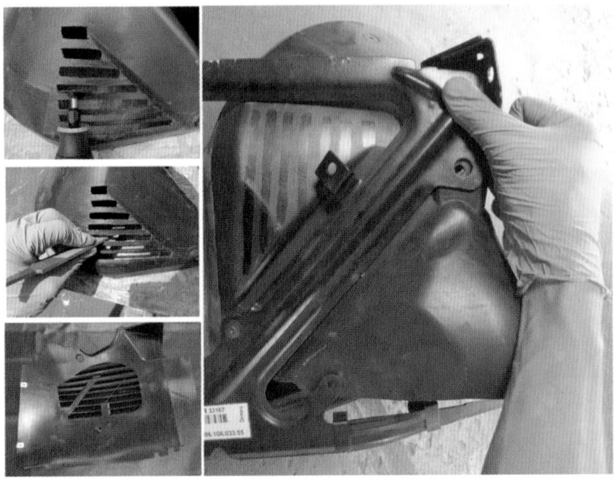

4 Align the bracket and fan duct to make your cut. With a marker, draw vertical lines and a lower horizontal base on the fan duct to represent the brake cooling slits in the 997 fender liner. Use a Dremel (wear safety goggles) to carefully cutout the highlighted areas and then file the edges down for a cleaner look. The top two inserts on the left show the modifying of the inner wheelwell liner, and the bottom shows the newer style liner from the 997.

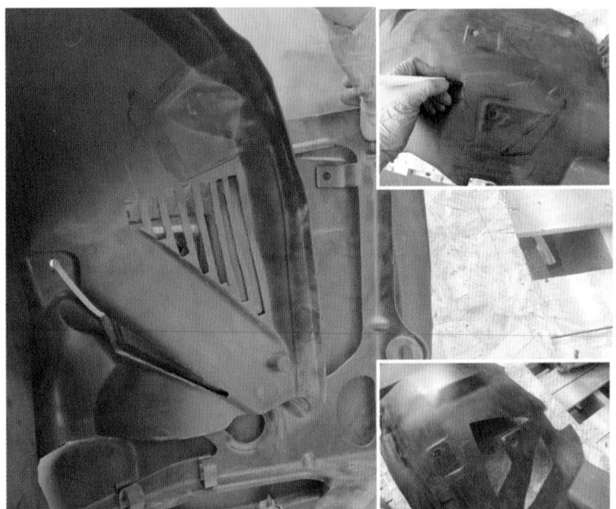

5 Next, take your fender liner and, similarly, draw vertical lines and highlight a lower horizontal base. Again, I found it useful to align the metal bracket, fan duct, and fender lining for more accurate markings. Once that's done, take the Dremel and carefully make your cut.

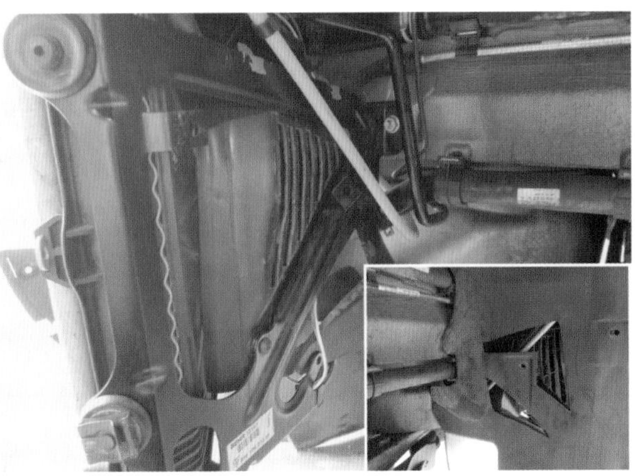

6 This photo shows the modified fan duct installed on the on the left side prior to installing the wheelwell liner. The inset photo shows the wheelwell liner modified and reinstalled on the right side with the duct behind it. Enjoy your new 996 brake cooling ducts!

SECTION 10
GAUGES AND ELECTRICAL SYSTEMS

This section covers a wide variety of projects aimed at reducing the amount of electrical problems and gauge-related problems in the car. In addition, I've also tossed in several projects that focus on upgrades and improvements to your Carrera. Whether your car has a faulty headlamp switch or has trouble turning over the starter, the projects in this section will help you troubleshoot and repair these nagging problems.

PROJECT 83
Battery Replacement/ Trickle Charger Installation

Time / Tab / Talent: 1 hour / $150 /

Tools: NA

Applicable Years: All

Tinware: New battery, trickle charger

More Info: http://www.101projects.com/Carrera/83.htm

Tip: Check your battery before it leaves you stranded

Performance Gain: Reliable starting

Comp Modification: Install a trickle charger

Sooner or later, everyone will have problems starting his or her 911. The first place to look for trouble in the starting system is the battery. The battery is perhaps the most important electrical component on the car, and due to its design and nature, it is perhaps one of the most troublesome. Before doing anything drastic like replacing your starter or looking at your fuel injection computer (more commonly the ECU—electronic control unit), you should make sure that your battery is in good condition.

Begin by checking the voltage on the battery posts using a voltmeter. Place the meter's probes on the posts of the battery, not the clamps. This placement will give the most accurate indication of the voltage in the battery. A normal battery should read a voltage slightly above 12 volts with the car sitting still and no electrical devices on. (The small trunk light in the front trunk shouldn't make a difference in the voltage reading.) A typical reading would be in the 12.6-volt range when the battery is fully charged. If the reading is 12 volts or less, then the battery needs to be charged or replaced with a new one. To be certain, you can take your battery to your local auto parts store for testing.

While older batteries often exhibited deteriorating performance prior to their failure, I recently had an original equipment manufacturer (OEM) BMW battery fail on me in my BMW 5-Series. The car was running perfectly fine—I had just driven about 350 miles the previous day, so it should have been well charged. The next morning, I got in the car, and it started fine. I drove about three miles and stopped off to pick something up. I shut off the car and was inside three minutes at the most. When I got to the parking lot, the battery was completely dead. There was not even enough power left to open the power door locks. It did turn out to be a complete battery failure. I was surprised because I'd never had a battery fail like this before—it always seemed to give out slowly. Some of the informal research I've done since then seems to indicate that the newer technology used in these batteries tends to lead to this type of occasional failure.

When the car is running, the alternator should be outputting anywhere from about 12.5 volts to about 14.5 volts. If you don't see any significant change in the voltage after you start up the car, then your alternator could be faulty. If the voltage is high at the battery (around 17 volts or higher), then the alternator's regulator is most likely faulty and needs to be replaced. Overcharging the battery at these higher levels may cause it to overflow and leak acid all over the inside of your car. (See Project 84 for instructions on how to replace the alternator.)

Do not ever disconnect the battery ground strap from the battery while the car is running. The battery acts as an electrical capacitor and filter on the entire electrical system, and the car's electrical components expect it to be there, even if it doesn't hold a charge. Disconnecting the battery terminals while the engine is running can seriously damage the computers and systems of the car.

Sometimes it may be necessary to reset the computers of the car, for example, to clear error codes. Some books recommend disconnecting both terminals of the battery and touching the unconnected terminals together to empty all of the capacitors and stored electricity in the system. While this works, it can possibly create a quick electrical shock to the system. A trick I learned from Tony Callas of Callas Rennsport is instead to place a resistor across the two terminals or simply use a diagnostic lamp that will act like a resistor. This approach will slowly dissipate the electricity over a few seconds instead of all at once.

Once you have determined that your battery is fine, you should make sure that your engine ground strap is properly installed. The engine and transmission are mounted to the chassis using rubber mounts. While great for the suspension, the rubber mounts make lousy electrical conductors. To compensate, an engine ground strap electrically connects the transmission and engine assembly to the chassis. It's located on the right side behind the rear wheel (see Photo 1). Check the strap to make sure it's not corroded or damaged. Make sure that you clean both ends of the strap and the areas that it mounts to on the chassis. With all electrical connections, it's a good idea to clean the area that you are mounting to with rubbing alcohol and also to sand the area lightly with some fine-grit sandpaper or a wire brush. Doing so will remove any dirt, grime, surface rust, or other corrosion that may interfere with creating a good electrical connection. While you're at it, clean up the battery terminals as well in a similar manner.

If you have discovered that your battery is weak and needs to be replaced, then you need to replace it. Follow the steps in the photos of this project. When purchasing a new battery, I recommend the newer style sealed, or "maintenance free," types. Sealed batteries may be more prone to damage when you deep cycle them (let them run all the way down) but require less preventative maintenance. Be sure to purchase a battery that has the same group number and CCA (Cold Cranking Amps) rating. Check the freshness date on the battery that you are purchasing and avoid any batteries that are more than six months old.

You disconnect the battery by disconnecting the negative or ground lead from the battery. Always disconnect the negative or ground lead first—if you disconnect the positive/hot lead, there is a chance that your tool may touch the metal chassis, which will result in a short circuit and would be quite dangerous. The worst case scenario would probably be where your wrench hit the chassis and was instantly welded there by the current, and then the battery overheated and exploded because you couldn't break the connection. In other words, be sure to disconnect the ground first.

If your car has the original radio in it, be aware that you will need the radio code if you disconnect the battery. This code is typically included with the documentation/owner's manual that came with the car. The Porsche dealer can look this code up for you if you don't have it, but that can be a huge pain, and most dealers will charge you for the service.

Leaving your lights on in your car can seriously damage the battery. Automotive batteries are not typically deep-cycle batteries, which means they do not like to be fully discharged. If you leave your lights on and drain your battery several times, then you will weaken it each time and have to replace it sooner rather than later. If you need to jump start your battery, you should refer to the section in your owner's manual. The procedure is very straightforward and very similar to other cars.

The Carrera has a few power-saving standby modes that it will enter after certain periods of time. If the ignition key is removed, accessories such as the trunk lamp, interior lamp, radio, and so on will be switched off automatically after approximately two hours. If the car is locked, then these will switch off after 10 minutes. If the car is not started or unlocked for more than five days (seven days on the 2005 and later models), the remote control standby function is switched off, and you will need to unlock the car using the key.

After you disconnect your battery, the digital motor electronics (DME) computer will lose some of its history memory used for adapting the fuel injection system. As a result, the idle may fluctuate, and the fuel injection mixture may be slightly off as the car relearns its settings.

Probably the best way to protect your battery from drain and damage is to install a trickle-charger/battery maintainer on it. This charger plugs into the wall when you are not using the car and constantly monitors the battery, charging it as needed when the voltage runs down. Every car battery has internal electrical leakage that will cause it to become fully discharged over time if not properly maintained. A trickle charger can keep your battery fresh year-round, even if you don't drive the car for months at a time. Beware of cheap chargers though, as they can accidentally overcharge your battery, causing more harm than good. The trickle charger I like to use in all of my Porsches is the Battery Tender, available for $40–$60 at PelicanParts.com.

1 The infamous drivetrain ground strap is one of the easiest parts on the car to overlook, yet it can cause so many electrical troubles. Since the transmission and engine are insulated by rubber mounts, the ground strap is the only significant ground to the engine. If the ground strap is disconnected or missing, then the current that turns the starter must travel through the engine harness or other small points of contact. When I was working on my project Boxster for one of my other books, I forgot to install the ground strap. When I went to start the car, it wouldn't start, and instead, the current ran through the right side stainless steel brake lines and completely cooked the line. That was a new experience for me—don't forget your ground strap!

2 The battery is located in the front trunk compartment on the Carrera. Turn the plastic tie-downs to remove the black plastic cover (yellow arrows).

3 Always disconnect the black-colored negative or ground connection first from the battery post (green arrow). If you are not planning on removing the battery, then this connection is all you need to disconnect; there is no need to disconnect the positive/hot lead to the battery. When you disconnect the ground from the battery, make sure that you place or tape the ground lead aside because you don't want it accidentally falling on the terminal of the battery while you're working and effectively connecting the battery again. If you are replacing the battery, be sure to properly hook up the vent hose once you have installed it in place (blue arrow). The yellow arrow shows the wire for the Battery Tender harness. You can route it through the fire wall (see Photo 3 of Project 87), or you can simply use a cable tie to secure it to the plastic mesh located on the right side.

4 If you are removing the battery, then simply loosen and remove the hold-down clamp that attaches the battery to the chassis (yellow arrow). Stand inside the trunk and lift the battery out of the car from there (they are quite heavy). The inset in the upper left-hand corner shows the permanent attachment of the Battery Tender cable to the negative lead. A handy device I like to install on all my cars is a battery cutoff switch (lower inset). Installation of this switch on the battery ground allows you to remove the green knob and shut off all power to the car. An added tip: Connect a small inline fuse from one end to the other, and a small amount of current will continue to flow, keeping your radio and digital motor electronics from being cleared out when the battery is disconnected.

5 Whenever I pick up a new car, I almost always install one of these within the first few weeks. The Battery Tender is a necessary tool if you're not planning on driving your car every day. It plugs into the wall and trickle-charges the battery so that it won't run down. Although the kit comes with alligator clips for temporary installations, I prefer to hard-wire the charger into the battery and simply leave the charging unit in the bottom of the front trunk.

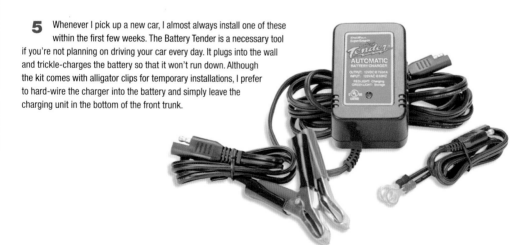

PROJECT 84
Alternator Troubleshooting and Replacement

Time / Tab / Talent: 4 hours / $400 /

Tools: Socket set

Applicable Years: All

Tinware: New alternator, new drive belt

More Info: http://www.101projects.com/Carrera/84.htm

Tip: Tap the inside bushing to release it from the bracket

Performance Gain: Consistent charging output

Comp Modification: Replace the drive belts

One of the nice things about the configuration of the Carrera engine is the relative ease with which you can replace the alternator. The alternator is nestled neatly on the left side of the engine compartment and is fairly easy to reach. The replacement and repair process is straightforward and should take you about an afternoon to complete.

The first thing that you need to do is to make sure that the alternator is indeed the cause of the problems with your charging system. Sometimes bizarre electrical problems can be caused by a number of faults other than the alternator. It's important to troubleshoot the system prior to replacing your alternator.

If the alternator seems to be the culprit, check the belt that drives the alternator. Is it tight and amply turning the alternator pulley? If it's worn or close to breaking, then replace it and recheck the alternator (see Project 5). Modern belts seldom break, but they get brittle and glazed with age and can slip on their pulleys.

The next item to check is the voltage at the battery. This should read a little more than 12 volts with the engine off. With the engine running at 2,000 rpm, the voltage should read at in the range of 13 to 14.5 volts. If your battery appears to be leaking, then your alternator's voltage regulator has probably failed. The battery will usually only leak acid if it has been overcharged at a much higher voltage. If the voltage measured at the battery is more than 16 or 17 volts when the engine is running, then the regulator is probably bad. If your battery has boiled over and has acid overflowing out the top, make sure that you clean up any spilled acid immediately. Dousing the area with a water and baking soda solution should help considerably to neutralize the acid and prevent it from eating away at the metal. Be sure to wear gloves and eye protection.

An important item to check on your car is the engine ground strap. The engine is electrically isolated from the chassis by rubber motor mounts. If the engine ground strap is missing or disconnected, then you might have a whole bunch of problems, including electrical system malfunctions and difficultly turning over the starter. See Project 83 for the exact location of this ground strap.

Before starting any work, make sure that you disconnect the battery. The positive battery terminal is directly connected to the alternator, and it can be dangerous to work on if it is live (see Project 83).

The first step in removing the alternator is to remove the airbox from the car (see Project 3). Once the air filter is removed, you will need to remove the serpentine belt that drives the alternator (see Project 5). You may also need to remove the vacuum connection for the brake booster directly above the alternator for additional space. This is held in place with two 8mm screws. Remove the screws and carefully set the check valve off to the side.

Now, loosen but do not remove the lower alternator bolt, then loosen the idler pulley that is located next to the alternator. Loosen the bolt and back it out about three to four full turns. Then, using a drift and a hammer, tap on the bolt. The tapping will loosen up the metal bushing that is located inside the rear flange of the alternator. With the bushing loose, lift up on the idler pulley, and the alternator assembly should rotate counterclockwise. Remove the lower bolt, and you should be able to lift the alternator up and out of the engine.

On this particular car, the bushing was a tight fit and required quite a bit of tapping and wiggling to remove. Specifically, I had to use a very long drift to tap directly on the rear bushing to get the assembly loose. Other mechanics seem to indicate that this is a common problem, so you might have to work at it a bit to get your alternator out.

With the alternator unbolted, disconnect the electrical connections from the rear. Reminder: Don't touch these connections while the battery is still hooked up (see Project 83).

If you are replacing the alternator completely, then the installation of the new alternator is simply the reverse of the removal process. Make sure that you reconnect all of the wires to their proper terminals when you are done. If you're still not sure if your alternator is bad, you can take it to any good auto parts store, and they should be able to test it for you for a modest fee.

1 Shown here is a brand new rebuilt alternator. Unlike older-style Porsche alternators, this one is pretty much plug-and-play. The regulator is internal, and the alternator should come with the proper pulley installed on the front. The green arrow in the inset photo shows the metal bushing that may give you trouble when you try to remove the alternator. This bushing is the one that needs to be tapped on in order to loosen the assembly for removal.

2 Shown here are the two 15mm mounting bolts for the alternator on a Carrera engine. You'll need to first loosen and remove the upper bolt (green arrow), and back it out about three or four full turns. Then, using a drift and a hammer, tap on the bolt. The purpose for doing this is to loosen up the metal bushing that is located inside the rear flange of the alternator. With the bushing loose, lift up on the idler pulley, and the alternator assembly should rotate counterclockwise. Now remove the lower bolt (purple arrow).

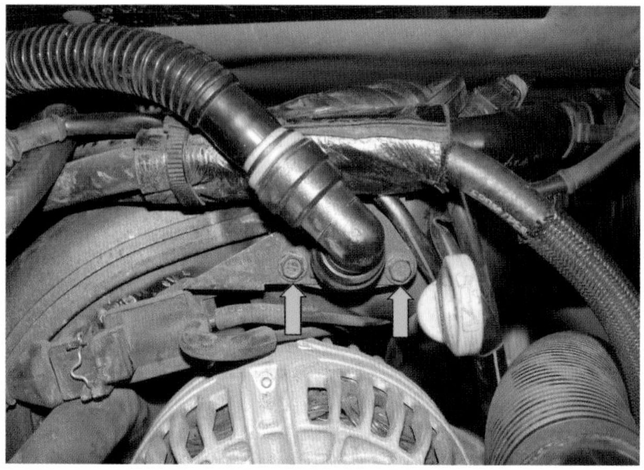

3 On the 996 engines, remove the two 8mm screws (green arrows) holding the brake booster vacuum connection to the left (driver) side intake. This will allow a little more wiggle room to remove the alternator from the engine compartment.

4 Rotate the alternator to remove it from the engine. It may take a bit of maneuvering to remove, but it is possible. The inset photo shows the brake vacuum line on the 997 engines (green arrow). You can disconnect it from the crossmember to give you addition room.

5 With the alternator unbolted, disconnect the electrical connections from the rear. Reminder: Don't touch these connections while the battery is still hooked up.

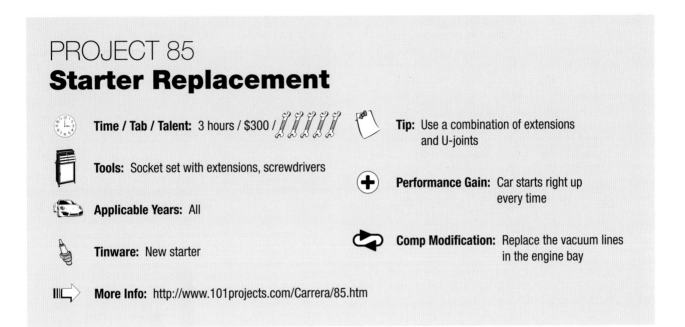

PROJECT 85
Starter Replacement

Time / Tab / Talent: 3 hours / $300 /

Tools: Socket set with extensions, screwdrivers

Applicable Years: All

Tinware: New starter

More Info: http://www.101projects.com/Carrera/85.htm

Tip: Use a combination of extensions and U-joints

Performance Gain: Car starts right up every time

Comp Modification: Replace the vacuum lines in the engine bay

Starter motors fail over time: it's just a fact of life. It may be that a starter motor is working fine one day and then all of a sudden dies the next day. Or, sometimes the motor gets weaker and weaker and turns the car over slower and slower. This is a possible sign that you should replace your starter motor. However, before replacing the starter, check the condition of the battery and make sure the ground strap is properly installed (see Project 83). Also check the clutch pedal switch (see Project 93) and the proper operation of the electronic immobilizer system. Try a different ignition key: the key has a built in RFID (radio frequency identification) chip that may have somehow become damaged. If possible, have the system checked using the Porsche factory scan tools (PST2 or PIWIS).

Once you are certain that the starter is the problem, begin by first disconnecting the battery. You'll be working around the starter, and there is always a 12-volt load going to the starter. If you accidentally touch it, you can injure yourself or cause a variety of problems with the car's electrical system. Be safe; take the extra time to disconnect it. Another good tip here is to get a bunch of zipper-top plastic bags to hold all of the various nuts and bolts you will be removing from the engine.

Open the engine lid and begin by removing the airbox (see Project 3). Loosen and remove the 13mm bolt at the very back of the airbox (996 only) and the hose clamp holding the boot to the throttle body. You'll also have to unplug the connector to the mass airflow sensor (MAF) by squeezing the connector. Now pull the boot off the throttle body and remove the airbox from the engine bay. If you have a 3.8-liter engine make sure you disconnect the wire for the resonance valve.

Now remove the throttle body (see Project 29). The throttle body is held in place on the intake plenum by four 10mm bolts and a 10mm nut attached to an eccentric bracket at the bottom. Remove all four bolts, taking care not to drop the bolts into the engine bay. You'll now need to disconnect either the throttle cable (on early cars) or the electrical connector for the throttle (on later cars). The throttle cable ferrule runs along a plastic cam on the side of the throttle body. If you manually open the throttle, the cable tension will go slack, allowing you to unhook the ferrule from the shoulder in the plastic cam. On cars with electronic throttle bodies, simply unhook the electrical connector.

On the early cars, rotate the throttle body over to access the hose connection on the back side. Use a pair of pliers to loosen and remove the hose clamp holding the hose onto the throttle body. Don't forget to pull the O-ring out of the intake plenum that seals the throttle body. Now set the throttle body aside in a safe place.

Once the throttle body is removed, you'll need to remove the front intake plenum. Begin by removing the air hose connection to the oil separator. Squeeze the black plastic connector to disconnect the hose from the plenum. Once free, set the hose connection aside. Now loosen the hose clamps securing the plenum to each manifold. A good idea here is to loosen the inner hose clamps first and then rotate the plenum to help break the seal that may have formed between the rubber; then, tighten the inner and loosen the outer clamps and do the same to break the connection between the rubber seals and the intake manifolds. Sometimes they can stick together making removal a bit difficult and this treatment will help free them up. As you will note, there is not much room to work and anything that makes it easier will help. Slide the rubber seals onto the plenum and wiggle the plenum out.

Once the plenum is removed, you should be able to see the starter directly under the rear intake plenum. One of the electrical connections will have a rubber boot over it. Behind the boot is the 13mm nut that holds the 12-volt lead going

from the battery to the starter. You'll need to remove this nut and pull the 12-volt line off. Now, before you touch this nut, double-check that you have disconnected the battery. If you didn't, you'll probably get a huge shock the second you touch the nut with a wrench. Be safe; double-check. Now remove the nut and also the 10mm nut directly to the right. This is the electrical connection that triggers the solenoid on the starter motor.

Once both electrical connections are removed, you'll need to remove the two 15mm bolts that hold the starter to the engine. As with the electrical connections, you'll need to use a combination of extensions and U-joints to reach the bolts. The bolt on the right of the starter is fairly easily removed. However, the one on the left isn't even visible; this one will give you the most grief. You'll have to find just the right combination of U-joints and extensions to get it off. Just have patience and you should be okay.

Once the bolts are removed, carefully remove the starter from under the plenum and up and out of the engine bay. Installation is indeed the reverse of removal.

1 Open the engine decklid and remove the airbox. Begin by loosening the hose clamp holding the boot to the throttle body (green arrow), then squeeze the tabs on the mass airflow sensor connector to release it (yellow arrow). Now open the two harness holder clips (purple arrows). Finally, unbolt the 13mm bolt (996 only) holding the airbox inside the engine compartment (red arrow) and carefully lift the airbox out of the car. If you have a 3.8 liter, make sure you disconnect the wire for the resonance valve.

2 Remove the four 10mm bolts (green arrows) and also the 10mm nut (purple arrow) holding the throttle body to the engine. At the same time, also remove the electrical connector going to the throttle position sensor (yellow arrow). Cable-throttle shown here (1998-99).

3 If you have an early car with a throttle cable, rotate the throttle back enough to relieve tension on the throttle cable and slip it out of the plastic cable cam as shown here (purple arrow).

4 On the earlier cars, you will need to rotate the throttle body over to access the hose connection on the back side. Use a pair of pliers to loosen and remove the hose clamp holding the hose onto the throttle body. Don't forget to pull the O-ring out of the intake plenum that seals the throttle body to it.

5 Follow the hose connection coming off the throttle body back to the control solenoid and press the wire piece in to release the electrical connector. Now place the hose/solenoid assembly off to the side.

6 Once the throttle body is removed, you'll need to remove the first intake plenum. Begin by removing the air hose connection to the air-oil separator. Squeeze the black plastic connector (purple arrow) to disconnect the hose from the plenum. Once free, set the hose connection aside. Now loosen the hose clamps securing the plenum to each manifold. A good idea here is to loosen the inner hose clamps first (red arrows) and then rotate the plenum to help break the seal that may have formed between the rubber and the plenum. Then tighten the inner clamps and loosen the outer clamps (green arrows) and do the same to break the connection between the rubber seals and the intake manifolds.

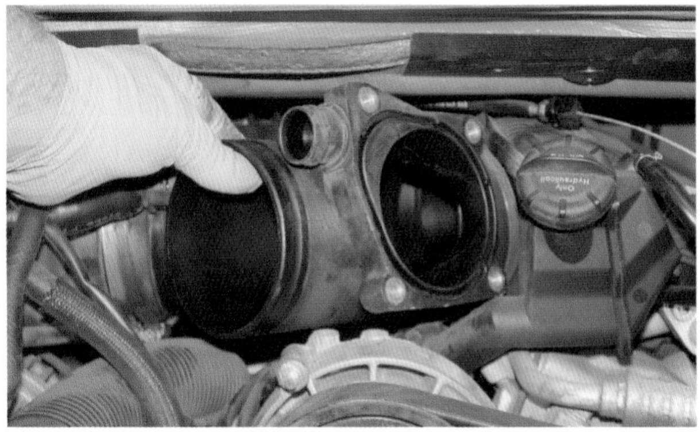

7 Once the hose clamps are loose, you should be able to push the intake plenum over to one side and pull it free of the manifold, as shown here.

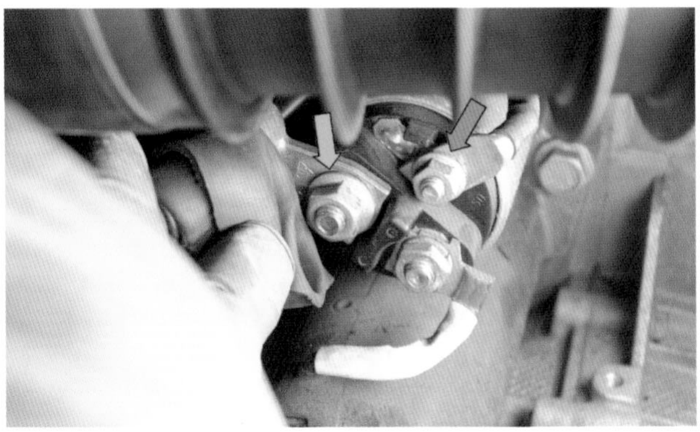

8 Shown here are the two electrical connections you'll need to remove from the starter. The green arrow points to the main power connection coming directly from the battery of the car to the 13mm nut on the starter motor. The purple arrow points to the 10mm nut securing the electrical connection to the solenoid.

9 You'll need to use a combination of extensions and U-joints to remove the nuts holding the electrical connections to the starter, as shown here.

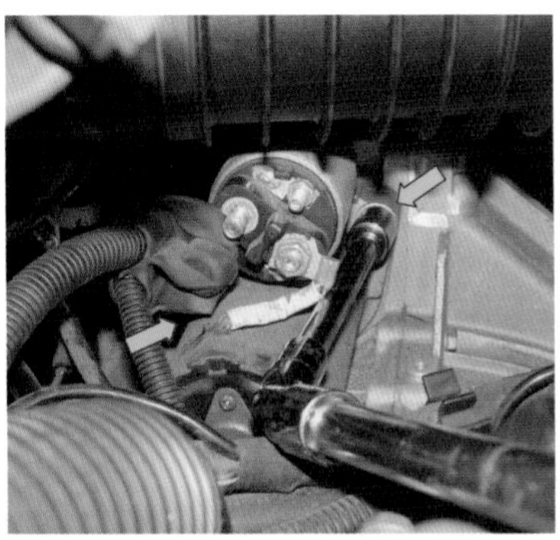

10 As with the electrical connections, you'll need to find the correct combination of U-joints and extensions to reach the two 15mm bolts on both sides of the starter motor (green arrows). In this picture you can see the right-side bolt being removed.

11 Once both bolts are removed, carefully remove the starter from under the intake plenum and pull it out from the engine compartment.

12 Shown here is a shot of the engine with the starter removed. You can see the teeth of the flywheel through the hole in the case. At this point, installation is the opposite of removal.

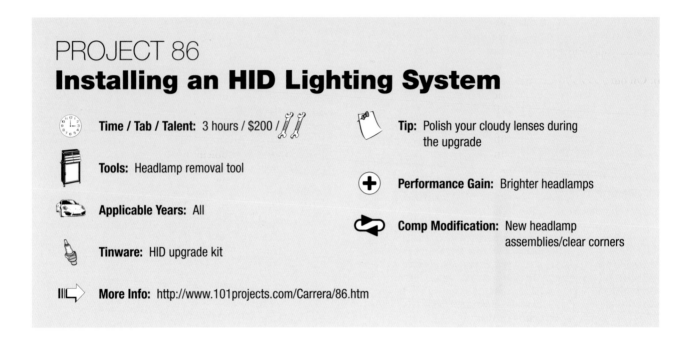

PROJECT 86
Installing an HID Lighting System

Time / Tab / Talent: 3 hours / $200 /

Tools: Headlamp removal tool

Applicable Years: All

Tinware: HID upgrade kit

More Info: http://www.101projects.com/Carrera/86.htm

Tip: Polish your cloudy lenses during the upgrade

Performance Gain: Brighter headlamps

Comp Modification: New headlamp assemblies/clear corners

One of the more exciting upgrades you can perform on your Carrera is the installation and upgrade of your lamps to a high-intensity discharge (HID) system. This type of lighting system is sometimes also referred to as xenon lighting or under the Bosch brand name of Litronic. The lamps use electric current that runs through a xenon gas mixture to create light—not unlike the operation of an ordinary fluorescent light bulb. In order to get the lamps working, the gas mixture must be subjected to an initial voltage of about 28,000 volts. Two small ballast units create this high voltage when starting the lamps and then taper it down to about 40 volts to keep the light on.

There are two paths that you can take to perform this upgrade. The most expensive xenon upgrade is the installation of the factory Bosch Litronic kit (see Project 87). The "poor man's" solution is to use a retrofit kit that simply replaces the stock H7 bulbs used in the standard Carrera lamp housing.

I prefer to use genuine Hella units as they have a built-in safety circuit to prevent the 28,000 volts from being discharged if there are any disruptions or anomalies in the circuit.

Replacement bulbs tend to be very expensive, at about $100 each. I expect this cost to decrease though in the near future as more and more cars come equipped with this technology as stock equipment. The good news is that unlike traditional halogen bulbs, the HID bulbs do not often burn out—they have no internal mechanical components and actually run very cool (like a normal fluorescent light bulb).

The lamp kits typically use 35-watt bulbs, which means that they draw about 2–3 amps of current after the initial startup. It's not uncommon for the ballast units to draw about 15 amps for less than a second as they are starting up the bulbs. The actual startup phase is typically less than a second—barely a noticeable difference from the stock configuration. With a conventional halogen lamp system, a large portion of the energy spent in the system goes toward excess heat given off by the bulb. The HID systems are much more efficient—a typical HID 35-watt bulb is about three times as bright as a 100-watt halogen bulb.

The installation is not difficult—it simply requires that you mount the ballast, integrate the bulbs into your housing, and wire up the system. The headlamps have large plastic covers on the rear that need to be slightly modified. Most of the HID kits available have a wire harness that has a large grommet on it. You need to take a small hole saw or Dremel tool and cut a hole in the rear of your plastic housing for the grommet to fit (see Photo 1). Two wires are connected to the HID bulb; the other two tap into the connections for the old halogen bulb. The harness that is included with the kit powers the HID lamps off of the power that formerly powered the original bulb inside the headlamp housing.

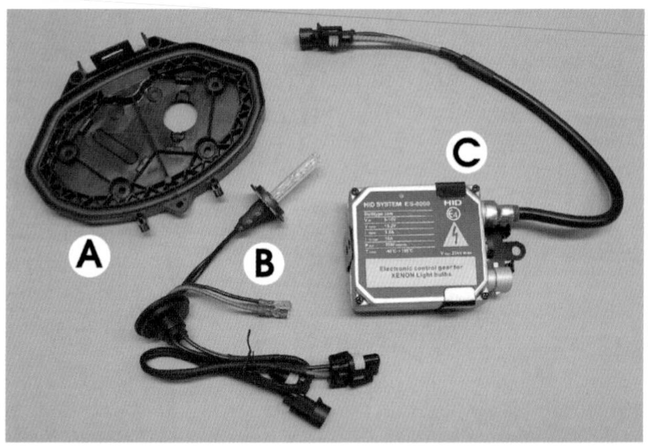

1 This photo shows the basic high intensity discharge (HID) upgrade kit for the standard USA sealed-beam headlamps. **A:** Modified rear cover for the sealed headlamps. **B:** Bulb assembly and wire harness. **C:** HID ballast/controller for the HID bulbs.

Mounting of the ballast is pretty easy. Component locations changed quite a bit over the years; find a safe, secure spot near your headlamps and use the double-sided sticky tape or mounting brackets that come with the HID kits (see Photo 3). On our 1999 996 Carrera, I found a good place to mount it on a flat surface just to the outside of the headlamp retainer.

You can install an HID kit for low beams, high beams, and even fog lamps. I have seen cars with three kits installed and their fog lamp switch modified so that all three are on at the same time. When you're finished with the installation, be sure to align your headlamps so that you're not pointing the beam into oncoming traffic. In most states, the use of nonfactory HID kits are designated for off-road use only. Keep in mind that if you don't have a street-legal headlamp system, you may invite tickets from law enforcement.

The only downside I found from installing this type of system was that it created a lot of static on my AM radio. However, the fix for this is rather simple: install a 12-volt RF (radio frequency) car noise filter on the power lines going to the ballasts and the problem should go away.

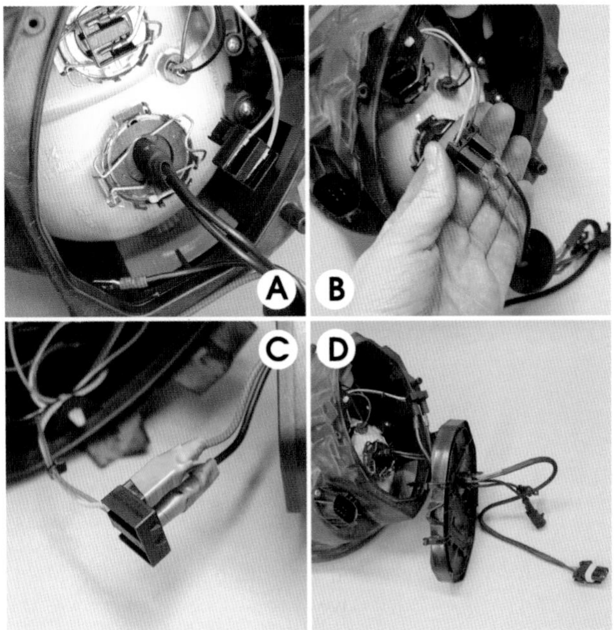

2 Here you can see the various steps of assembly into the rear of the headlamp. **A:** The lower bulb is the standard low-beam headlamp that is on most of the time. Remove the existing bulb and insert the newer HID bulb. You may have to remove the wire retaining ring completely in order to fit the new bulb. **B:** Connect the HID wires to the existing bulb connector. Brown is the ground and typically connects to the black wire on the harness. **C:** Wrap the connectors carefully with electrical tape to prevent a short from within the headlamp in case the connector bounces around. **D:** Thread the wires through the hold in the rear cover of the headlamp.

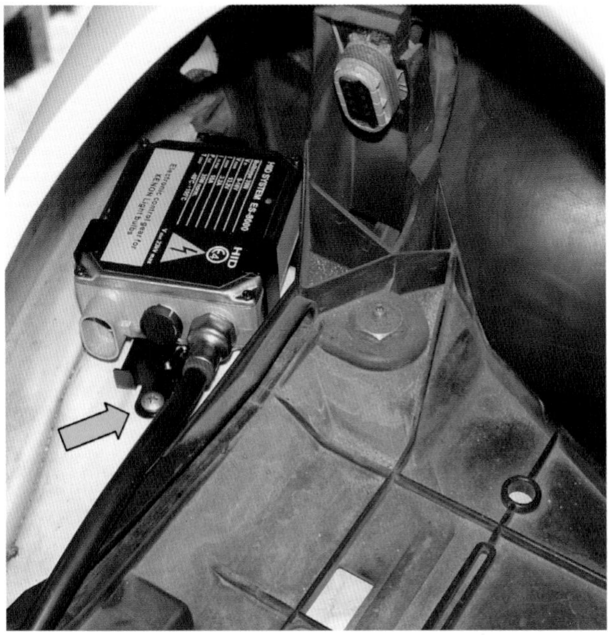

3 I found that a good mounting place for the ballast was on the side, right next to the headlamp tray. There is a flat spot there that is perfect for mounting the HID ballast unit. Clean the area carefully using isopropyl alcohol or glass cleaner and use double-sided sticky tape to secure the unit to the sheet metal. Reinforce the assembly by drilling a hole in the sheet metal and securing the bracket with a sheet metal screw (green arrow).

4 The finished product looks great and is very cost-effective when you compare the lamps to the stock Litronic ones available as a new or upgrade option on the Carrera (see Project 87).

PROJECT 87
Installing Litronic Headlamps

Time / Tab / Talent: 4 hours / $3,000 /

Tools: ¾-inch hole saw and drill

Applicable Years: 1998–2005

Tinware: Litronic headlamp upgrade kit with wiring harness

Tip: This is a good way to upgrade your lamps to clear corners

Performance Gain: Brighter lamps

Comp Modification: Install clear side lamps and headlamp protector film

More Info: http://www.101projects.com/Carrera/87.htm

While the "poor man's" version of upgrading your lamps to a high intensity discharge (HID) system is detailed in Project 86, this project shows what's involved in installing the factory Bosch Litronic HID upgrade kit. The name of the system was changed to Bi-Xenon when Porsche redesigned the headlights for the 997, but the principles remain the same. There are quite a few compelling reasons why you would want to install the factory Litronic over a retrofit kit like the one detailed in Project 86. First, the factory upgrade kit replaces your entire lamp assemblies. If your existing lamps are getting old, the lenses might begin to appear cloudy. Installing new headlamps with new lenses creates a dramatic facelift for your car. In addition, the Litronic upgrade kit uses the updated "clear corners" instead of the standard U.S.-spec orange ones.

It is important to note that the Porsche Litronic upgrade kit is different than the one installed at the factory when the car was new. The factory-installed Litronic option is tightly integrated with the rest of the car's subsystems and as a result has additional features not found on the upgrade kit. The factory-installed kit will adjust the lamps up and down when the car is accelerating or braking to keep the light pattern aimed at the same level in the road at all times. In addition, the system is integrated with the central computer bus to pass fault codes if there is a problem. These are neat features, but they are not important enough to discourage you from installing the upgrade kit.

The procedure for installation is as simple as replacing the actual headlamp (see Project 65). However, there is an add-on controller module that you can install that will automatically rotate the orientation of the lamps up 1.5 degrees when the high beams are turned on. This change in the beam creates an improved light-filled pattern when the high beams are activated. Installation of this controller module is the primary focus of this project and is relatively easy if you're somewhat familiar with basic electrical wiring. (The Porsche factory installation instructions can be found in Tech Bulletin 9415 for the Boxster/Carrera.)

The first step is to remove the battery cover and disconnect the battery (see Project 83). Then, remove your old headlamps (see Project 65). Unplug and remove the CD changer and/or amplifier from the front trunk, if you have one. Remove the spare tire. Now, remove the front trunk liner. It's held on with plastic rivets that are almost guaranteed to break. I suggest ordering new ones before you begin, part numbers 999-703-456-40 (qty 1), 999-703-432-40 (qty 8), and 999-703-455-40 (qty 2).

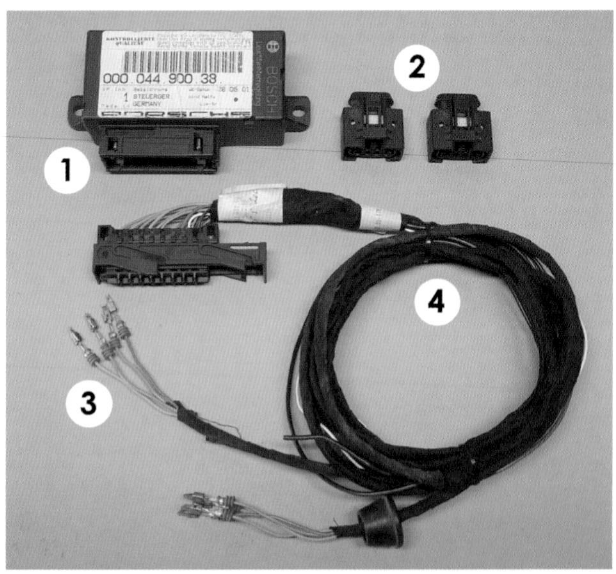

1 This photo shows the complete wiring kit that is required in order to install the factory Litronic headlamps. **1:** Electronic control unit. **2:** Harness connectors; **3:** Wire harness end-pins. **4:** Complete wiring harness.

Next, remove the covers on the brake booster (see Photo 1 of Project 57) and the right side panel that covers the cabin filter (see Photo 4 of Project 3). Drill the wire harness holes as per Photos 3 and 4, and run the wire harness through these holes to the inside of the left and right fender. The left-side fender uses the longer portion of the wire harness. Insert the harness through the holes using the supplied grommets to seal around each hole. Next, install the pins into the connectors as detailed in Photo 5. Plug these connectors into the back of the headlamp assemblies and install them back into each fender.

Mount the control unit to the side of the front trunk compartment. Photo 3 shows an ideal spot for it where it will mount well and be hidden under the front trunk carpet. Install the three wires that power and control the module. Attach the brown wire to ground. The white wire is tapped into the existing white wire in the connector assembly (see Photo 3); this will signal the module that the high beams are on. The red wire is installed near the battery area where it gets constant power (see Photo 4).

After you install the Litronic kit, you should check the fuses in your fuse panel; they may need to be upgraded. Fuses A9 and A10 should be 15-amp fuses. If they are less than that, then swap them out. If you leave the stock 7.5-amp fuses in place, then they will probably blow under the increased current flow (see Photo 1 of Project 92 for the fuse box location).

Also important to note is that the small corner lenses do not come with the kit—you need to purchase them separately. The corner lenses are different depending upon whether you have a headlamp washer system or not. I recommend purchasing the clear corners instead of the standard unattractive U.S.-spec amber ones.

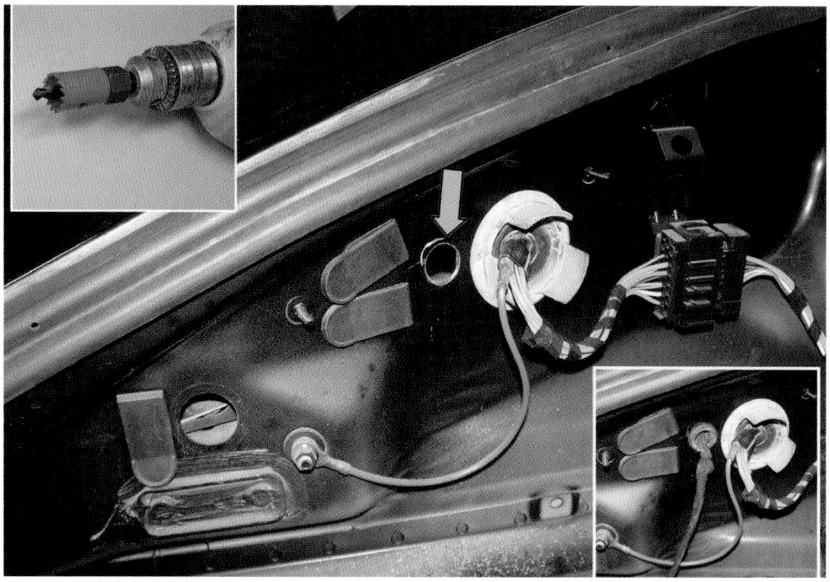

2 Begin the process by drilling a 3/4-inch hole in the inside of the trunk on both the left and right sides. Use a standard hole saw available at your local hardware store. The wires for the headlamp will run through this hole. Affix the grommet in place (lower right).

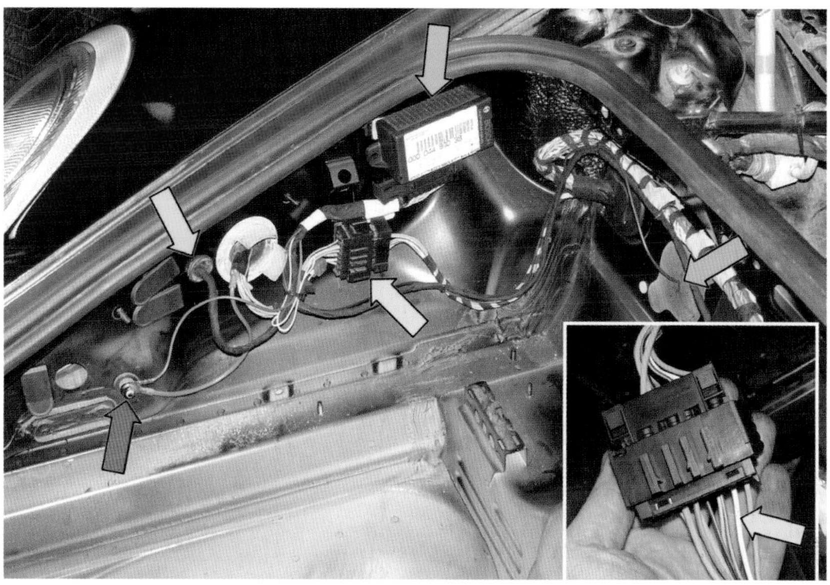

3 Install the control unit in the front trunk on the left side. Use Velcro or double-sided tape to affix the unit to the side of the trunk in the flat spot shown (green arrow). Thread the shorter of the two headlamp harnesses through the hole you drilled in the sheet metal and affix the grommet in place (yellow arrow). Attach the brown wire from the harness to the ground point (red arrow). Using a standard wire tap connector, tap the white wire from the new Litronic wire harness into the front side of the white wire exiting out of the connector (blue arrows). Finally, route the red wire up the existing wire harness and poke a small hole through the rubber plug in the firewall bulkhead (orange wire).

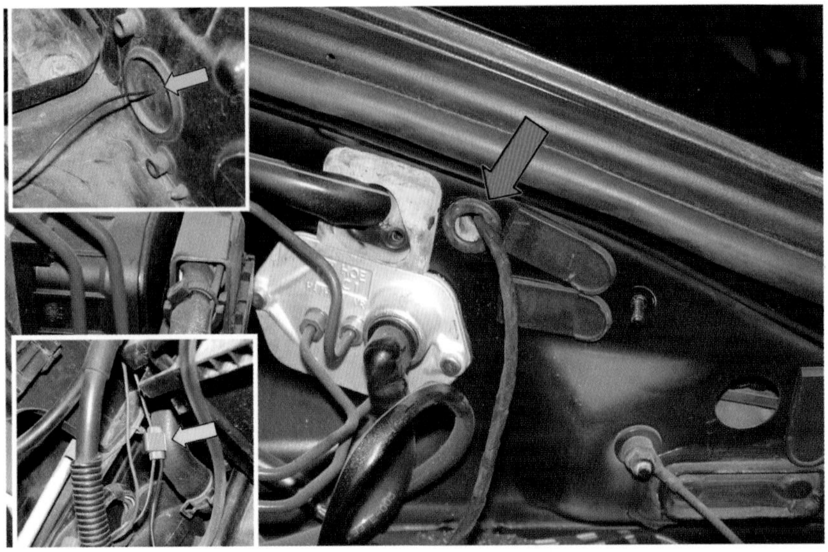

4 The red arrow shows the location of where the ¾-inch hole should go on the left side of the car. The upper left shows a rubber plug located on the firewall, as shown from the side of the bulkhead right next to the battery (green arrow). The red/black wire needs to be tapped into the black/yellow wire that is connected to the plug for the right windshield washer nozzle (yellow arrow).

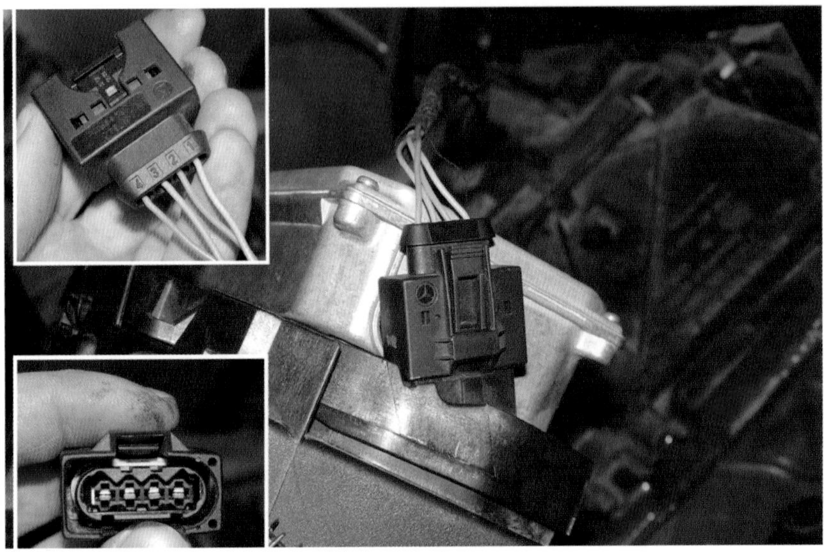

5 After threading the wire harness through the ¾-inch hole that you drilled in the sides of the front truck, place each of the pins into the wire connectors. **1:** Pink. **2:** Green. **3:** Grey. **4:** Purple (upper left). Make sure that they are well seated in the connector housing (lower left). Finally, plug them into the back of the Litronic headlamp unit.

6 Not only do the Litronic xenon lamps look great at night, but you also get the clear corner look that vastly improves the appearance of your 911. Gone are the unsightly U.S.-spec orange turn signal lenses. The Litronic lamps use clear corners and orange-colored bulbs.

PROJECT 88
Replacing the Ignition Switch/Steering Lock

Time / Tab / Talent: 4 hours / $175 /

Tools: Torx driver set, mini screwdriver

Applicable Years: All

Tinware: Updated steering lock assembly

Tip: Porsche redesigned this part; use the latest version

Performance Gain: Reliable starting

Comp Modification: Replace the headlamp switch and replace the gauge bulbs

More Info: http://www.101projects.com/Carrera/88.htm

One of the most common electrical items to fail on some of the older Porsches is the ignition switch. This failure can show up in any number of ways. The car can refuse to start some of the time, the key may not turn too easily in the ignition, or strange electrical problems may appear. In any case, the correct solution is to replace all or part of the ignition switch.

1998-2005 996 Carrera. The switch itself is comprised of two separate sections: one that holds the key and the lock mechanism and another that contains a somewhat complicated electrical switch that controls the starter and the other electrical systems of the car. The good news is that the electrical portion of the ignition switch can easily be replaced. Typical cost of this part ranges from $15–$40 depending upon which brand part you choose. If your key doesn't turn too well in the ignition, then chances are you have a worn out tumbler. You can attempt to rekey and refurbish the tumbler yourself, but the process can be quite difficult. It requires that you drill out a pin that has been pressed into the housing. If you make a mistake, you can damage the entire assembly. In other words, the ignition switch assembly wasn't really designed to be taken apart.

Early Carreras had some problems with the ignition switch/steering lock assembly, and Porsche subsequently redesigned the part. If you're having problems with your ignition switch (as many 911s do), I recommend that you replace the whole mechanism. The electrical portion of the switch is different for this upgraded assembly, so be sure that you purchase the correct electrical switch to match what you have in your car. You may need to take some photos and compare what you have to the photos online in order to determine if your switch assembly has been upgraded or not. If you purchase an entirely new assembly, it should come complete with the electrical portion attached.

If you are replacing only the electrical portion of one of the early steering locks (part numbers 996-347-017-05 through 996-347-017-06), then use part number 4A0-905-849B). For the later steering lock, which was first used on 2004 cars (996-347-017-07), use part number 4B0-905-849 for the electrical portion replacement. If you're unsure of which one you have in your car, remove it first—the part number should be printed on it.

If you are only replacing the electrical portion of the switch (1999–2005 996), the project is quite easy. Simply remove the heater ductwork described in Photo 1 (it should pull out from underneath the dash with a few tugs). Disconnect the electrical plug by pulling it out of the back of the switch. Then, simply unscrew the set screws that hold the electrical portion to the back of the switch and replace it with a new one. The switch has a locating pin cast into the housing, so there is only one way that it can be put back together.

Replacing the electrical portion could most certainly solve some ignition and starting problems. Electrical systems flickering on and off as you turn the key are a good clue that your switch is worn. Also, a bad switch sometimes causes unexplainable starting problems where the starter solenoid doesn't even click. I even had an experience with one car (not a 911) that wouldn't shut off the starter after the engine kicked over. Both the engine and the starter kept running together—even after I had removed the key!

If you are planning on replacing/upgrading your ignition lock assembly, then follow the steps laid out in Photos 2, 3, and 4. You will need to remove the headlamp switch (see Project 89) and also the gauge cluster (see Photo 3) in order to gain access to the steering lock assembly.

For 2005 and later 997 models, the entire ignition switch/steering lock assembly was removed from the car and replaced with an electro-mechanical solenoid that locks the steering rack instead. You can only remove the locking

mechanism after dismantling the entire steering system. In addition, removal of the locking device is only possible in the unlocked state. As of November 2013, I haven't heard of any reported problems with these solenoids needing to be replaced, but these cars are only seven years old right now. In addition, the electrical switch is an entirely different and simpler design and is easy to remove. Simply pull off the rubber surround (see Photo 6) and then unscrew the large nut underneath. Unplug the switch from underneath the dash and then remove it.

FOR THE 996

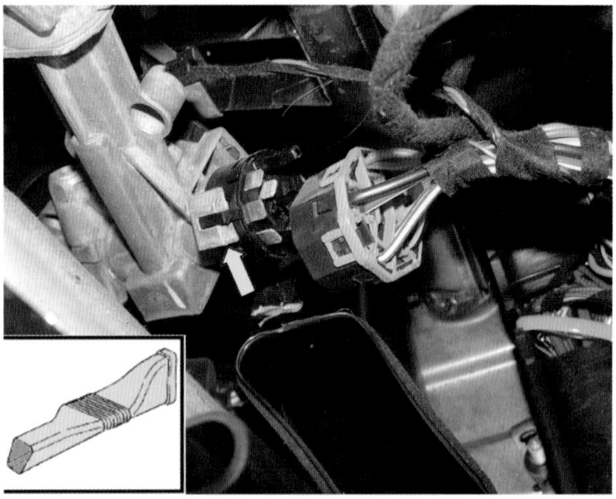

1 First disconnect your battery (Project 83). The electrical portion of the ignition switch can be accessed from underneath the dashboard. First, you need to remove the heater air duct (inset), which blocks your access to the switch. Pull out the connector and then loosen up the set screws that are located behind the red marking paint (blue arrow). Use a miniature flat-head screwdriver; access is tight, but the screws can be removed.

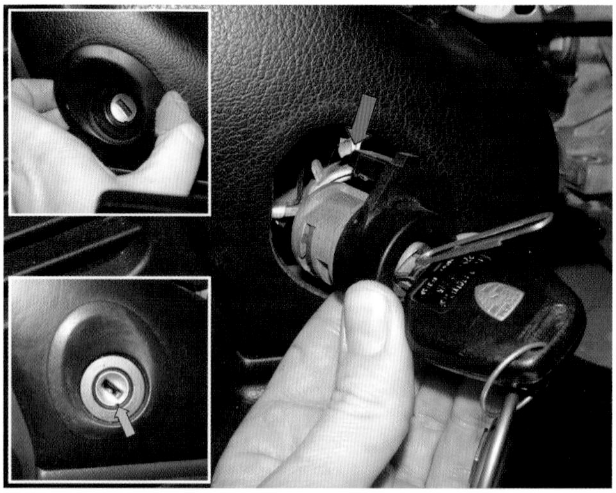

2 To remove the ignition key cylinder, first begin by pulling out the rubber ignition switch surround (upper left). Then, turn the ignition switch to position 1 (ignition on), and insert a large paper clip into the release hole in the key cylinder (orange arrow). Push the paper clip in as far as possible and insert the key, which should release the mechanism and allow you to pull out the assembly. Finally, disconnect the small connector that attaches to the immobilizer induction coil (red arrow).

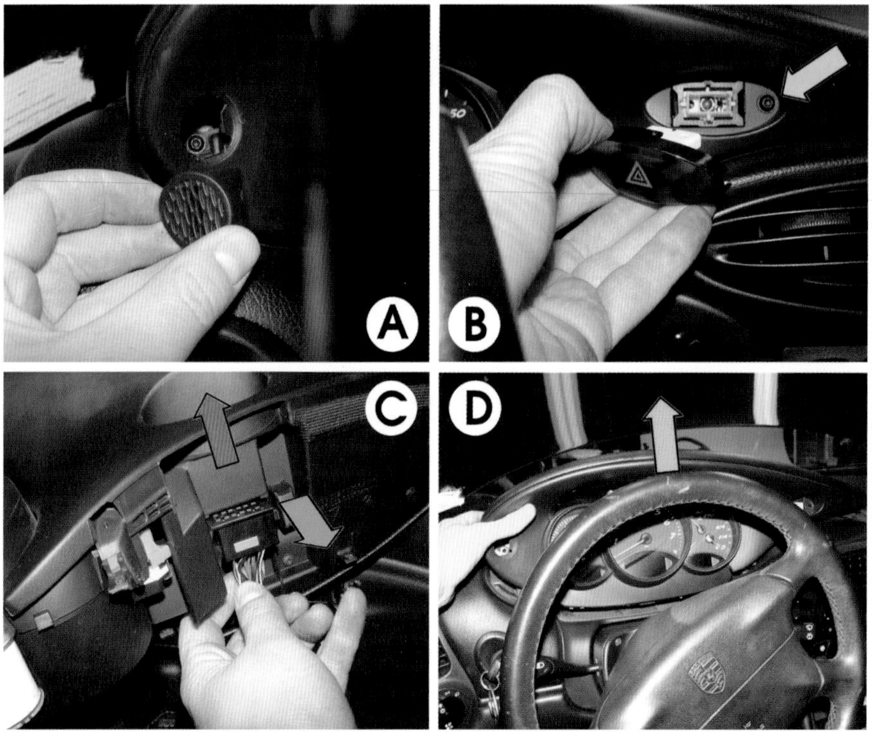

3 Here are the steps for removing the gauge cluster. **A:** Pull out the microphone cover and remove the Torx screw underneath. **B:** Pull out the hazard switch button and remove the Torx screw underneath. **C:** Using some long pliers, grab the white plastic part of the hazard switch (shown in B) and pull it out of its plug (press on the two black tabs on either side of the white plastic switch and pull in the direction of the red arrow). Then, slide the black connector in the direction of the green arrow. **D:** Lift up the gauge cluster so that you can disconnect the wire harnesses on the back.

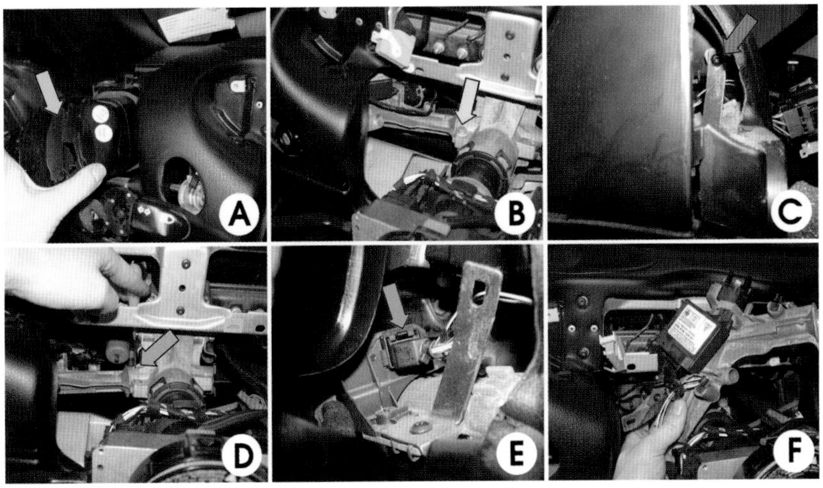

4 This photo details the steps required to remove the ignition cylinder/steering lock assembly. **A:** With the headlamp switch and side dashboard piece removed (Project 89), pull out the heater duct (blue arrow). **B:** Remove the nut that fastens the lock assembly to the steering column (yellow arrow). **C:** From the left side of the dash, remove the Torx screw that holds the small bracket to the dash. **D:** Using a small screwdriver, push down on the push lock pin to release the lock assembly from the steering column (purple arrow). **E:** Unplug the immobilizer harness (green arrow). **F:** Pull out the entire lock assembly from behind the steering column.

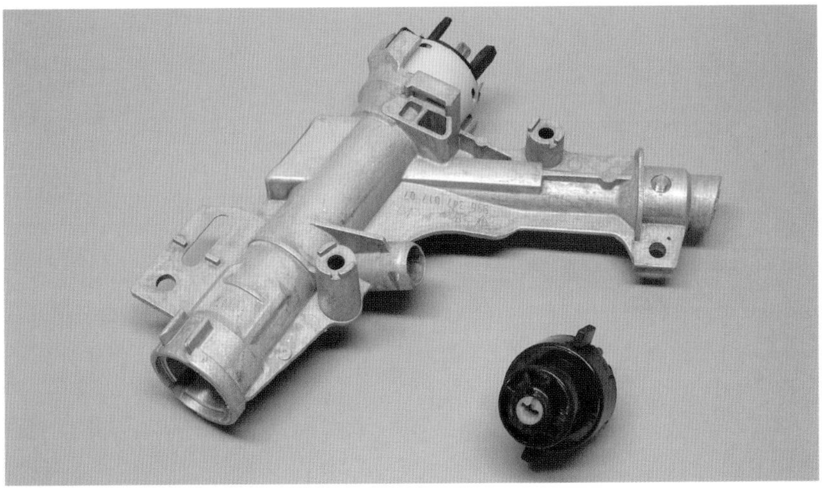

5 Shown here is the updated ignition cylinder/steering lock assembly. The assembly typically includes an electrical ignition switch (shown attached at the rear of the assembly and separately in the lower right).

FOR THE 997

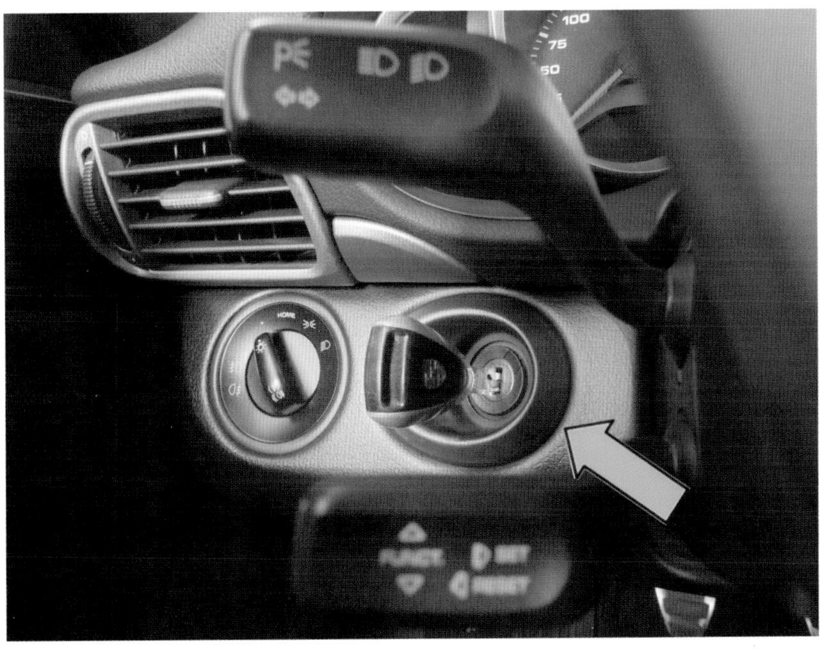

6 This photo shows the ignition switch for the 997. To remove the assembly, insert a trim removal tool under the plastic ring around the switch. Remove the ring and unscrew the nut underneath. Press the switch inward and remove from below the dash. Unplug the switch and replace.

PROJECT 89
Headlamp Switch Replacement

Time / Tab / Talent: 1 hour / $35 /

Tools: Torx socket set, 24mm deep socket

Applicable Years: All

Tinware: New headlamp switch

More Info: http://www.101projects.com/Carrera/89.htm

Tip: Replace mini bulbs inside switch housing as well

Performance Gain: Ability to drive at night again

Comp Modification: Replace the bulbs in the gauges

It's not uncommon to experience a failure of your headlamp switch. Years of repeated use and abuse have a tendency to take their toll on the switch. Some symptoms of a faulty switch include headlamps that won't turn on or perhaps inoperable fog lamps, just to name a few. In addition, there's a few small light bulbs contained within the switch housing that can burn out.

Replacement is fairly easy and only requires about an hour of your time. See the photos in this project for the breakdown of the replacement procedure. The only tricky part, may be the removal of the large nut that fastens the switch to the vent housing. If you have a 24mm deep socket, then you can simply place this socket on the nut and turn it by hand. If you don't have access to a deep socket of this size, then you may have to resort to a pair of needle-nose pliers to remove the nut.

For the 2005 and later 997 cars, the procedure is super simple. Press in the rotary knob on the light switch (but not to the limit), and turn the switch to the right. Then pull the entire switch assembly out.

The part number for the replacement switch is 996-613-535-00 (through 2004) or 997-613-535-01 (2005 and later), and it costs about $150 from the online catalog of PelicanParts.com.

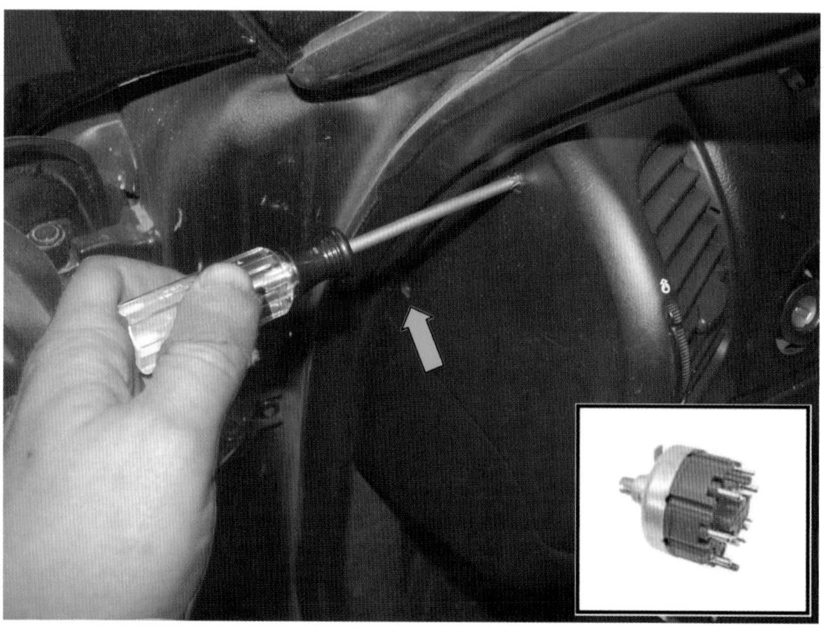

1 Begin by removing the two screws on the leftmost side of the dash with a Torx driver. In the lower right is shown a brand new headlamp switch assembly.

2 Remove the headlamp knob by pressing on the release tab and then pulling off the knob (upper left, red arrow). With the knob removed, you can access the hidden Torx screw inside the inner bezel (yellow arrow).

3 Pull off the side vent and headlamp switch together (lower right). Disconnect the large circular plug and then the smaller four-wire harness as well (yellow arrow). To remove the switch, simply unscrew the large nut on the face of the bezel (24mm deep socket).

4 On the 997, press in the rotary knob on the light switch (but not to the limit), and turn the switch to the right (green arrow). Then pull the entire switch assembly out.

PROJECT 90
Radio Head Unit Installation

Time / Tab / Talent: 3 hours / $300 /

Tools: Radio removal tools

Applicable Years: 1998–2005

Tinware: Radio, antenna adapter, wire harness adapter

More Info: http://www.101projects.com/Carrera/90.htm

Tip: Get the correct adapters for your car, so you don't have to cut any wires

Performance Gain: Great-sounding tunes!

Comp Modification: Upgrade your speakers

One of the first projects many new 911 owners perform on their car is to remove and replace their stereo head unit. I know that if I buy a car that has a weak stereo, it's one of the first things to go. The factory Porsche head units (manufactured by Becker) are best described as barely adequate—the technology is at least 10 years old in most cases, and the controls on the units are beyond terrible. This chapter specifically contains only wiring information for the 1999–2004 Carreras, but is also somewhat applicable to the 2005 and later cars, although they use a new digital CAN BUS system that is worthy of several chapters in itself.

The good news is that the replacement process is relatively easy, providing you have the right information and the right parts. First, disconnect the battery (see Project 83). The radio harness has constant voltage supplied to it, and you don't want to accidentally blow any fuses or damage any electrical components. Using the set of factory radio removal tools (available from Becker, part number BNA-1184-989), pull out the radio as detailed in Photo 2. On the back of the unit, there may be a few wire connectors and a smaller antenna connector. Remove the antenna connector by simply tugging on it.

In order to install a new radio, you will need some cable adapters for the Carrera's wiring harness. The adapters plug into the factory connectors and have leads on them that you can then connect to the leads or connector on your new radio. You can cut the original equipment manufacturer (OEM) connector off and tap directly into the factory harness, but I strongly caution against this—it's best to use the adapter cables (cost about $20). I put some spade connectors on the ends of the harness adapter and the connector that plugged into my new radio. The kits I used for my 2000 Porsche were Metra brand (PN: 70-1787; VW/Bose AMP Integration) and the Euro antenna adapter kit from Scosche (PN: VWA-KB; Volkswagen Antenna Adapter Kit). This antenna adapter kit contains two adapters so that you can use an aftermarket stereo and/or install an in-line FM modulator iPod interface (see below). These kit part numbers should be good for all of the Carreras through 2004. For 2005 and up models, check the radio you have in your car before you order the adapters.

In general, the most difficult part of installing a new radio is figuring out how to wire it. I've done all of the legwork for you here by putting together this handy wiring chart (1998–2004). The green connector and blue connector on the back of the radio are for the operation of the CD changer, if your car has one (mounted in the front trunk, see 101Projects.com website for pinouts on those connectors).

If your car does not have an external amplifier, then the speakers for the Carrera will plug directly into the brown Connector B on the back of the radio. If your Carrera has an external amplifier, then there will be a smaller yellow connector that outputs the signals from the head unit to the amplifier. If you have a factory amplifier installed, then you can simply adapt the signal from your new stereo into the leads on the yellow plug, as I have done with this stereo installation. If not, then you simply hook up the speaker leads from the new stereo to the adapter that plugs into the brown connector.

Wire the harness adapter together according to the wiring chart and the instructions included with the new radio. Plug the harness adapter into the factory connector, and then plug the harness into the back of the head unit and connect all of the spade connectors. On this particular head unit, I found that the antenna jack on the back of the unit was not compatible with the one in the factory harness, so I needed the antenna adapter mentioned previously. Plug the adapter into the back of the unit, and then you should be able to plug the antenna cable into the unit. With the new head unit wired up, reconnect the battery, and turn it on to test it. If all of the speakers, radio, and lights work, then install the

Color	Purpose	Connector and Pin
Grey/Pink	Speed dependent volume control	Black Connector A – Pin 1
	Unused	Black Connector A – Pin 2
Yellow/Black	Mute for telecom interface	Black Connector A – Pin 3
Red/Black (thick)	Constant power 12 V (Fuse D8)	Black Connector A – Pin 4
White	Power antenna control	Black Connector A – Pin 5
Grey/Blue	Illumination (headlamps on)	Black Connector A – Pin 6
Orange	12-volt switched power (Fuse E1)	Black Connector A – Pin 7
Brown (thick)	Chassis ground	Black Connector A – Pin 8
Blue	Right rear speaker positive	Brown Connector B – Pin 1
Brown/Blue	Right rear speaker negative	Brown Connector B – Pin 2
Red	Right front speaker positive	Brown Connector B – Pin 3
Red/Brown	Right front speaker negative	Brown Connector B – Pin 4
Yellow	Left front speaker positive	Brown Connector B – Pin 5
Yellow/Brown	Left front speaker negative	Brown Connector B – Pin 6
White	Left rear speaker positive	Brown Connector B – Pin 7
Brown/White	Left rear speaker negative	Brown Connector B – Pin 8
Yellow/Red	Left rear line output positive	Yellow Connector C – Pin 1
Red/Blue	Right rear line output positive	Yellow Connector C – Pin 2
Brown/Blue	Common audio ground	Yellow Connector C – Pin 3
Green/Red	Left front line output positive	Yellow Connector C – Pin 4
Violet/Red	Right front line output positive	Yellow Connector C – Pin 5
Black/Red	12-volt switched power	Yellow Connector C – Pin 6
Blue	CD changer – BUS On	Green Connector C – Pin 7
Red	CD changer – battery	Green Connector C – Pin 8
Black	CD changer – ground	Green Connector C – Pin 9
Green	CD changer – data	Green Connector C – Pin 10
Yellow	CD changer – clock	Green Connector C – Pin 11
Violet	CD changer – reset	Green Connector C – Pin 12
Blue/Green	Telephone audio	Blue Connector C – Pin 13
Blue/Yellow	Telephone audio common	Blue Connector C – Pin 14
	unused	Blue Connector C – Pin 15
	unused	Blue Connector C – Pin 16
	unused	Blue Connector C – Pin 17
Brown	CD changer – common audio ground	Blue Connector C – Pin 18
Yellow	CD changer – left	Blue Connector C – Pin 19
Red	CD changer – right	Blue Connector C – Pin 20

radio bracket into the center dashboard. This is the bracket that comes with the new unit and typically has tabs that you bend into place once you position the bracket. When the bracket is secure, simply slide the radio into its spot on the center dashboard. Be careful: most of these units are designed to be easy to install but very difficult to remove, so make sure that everything works before inserting it into the dashboard.

The radio I chose to use for this project was a Pioneer head unit with a built-in CD player and iPod support. These types of head units allow you to plug your iPod into the stereo and then choose and select songs to play from the stereo itself. In addition, the stereo charges the iPod while it's playing. This arrangement is very cool, but I don't recommend it if you happen to have an iPhone. One of the coolest features of the iPhone is its ability to stream music from alternative sources like Pandora. For iPhone users, I recommend the installation of an FM modulator interface that allows you to play music from the iPhone onto the stereo by emulating a radio station. Using this setup, you can listen to any music on the iPhone and/or any music that may be provided by a music service that streams music over the cell phone network. For example, using the DICE Electronics FM adapter installation detailed in Photo 3, I am able to listen to music streamed off of my home computer, through the cell phone network, and to the car, as I am driving. Even better is to purchase a head unit with built-in Bluetooth connectivity for your phone or iPod. That way, you can wirelessly stream audio and track information from your phone to your stereo without any cables (you lose the ability to charge though).

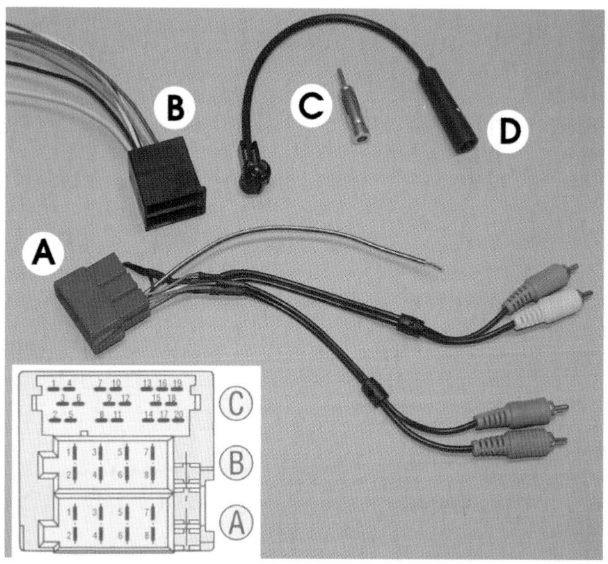

1 Shown here are the adapter harnesses I used for this installation. **A:** This harness emulates plug C on the radio and breaks the signal up into RCA jacks that you can plug into the back of your new head unit. Be sure to properly connect the blue wire as well, which sends the signal to power up the amplifier. **B:** This plug is the main plug that supplies power to the radio. **C:** This is the antenna adapter for the back of the new radio. It converts the long tube-style plug into the smaller, European-style connector. **D:** This reverse antenna adapter is required along with the other one if you are using the iPod FM modulator interface. When connecting the harness adapters, I recommend using simple spade connectors to link the two together. In general, I do not recommend cutting wires in your car; it becomes very difficult to fix and/or restore the electrical system back to stock if anything goes wrong.

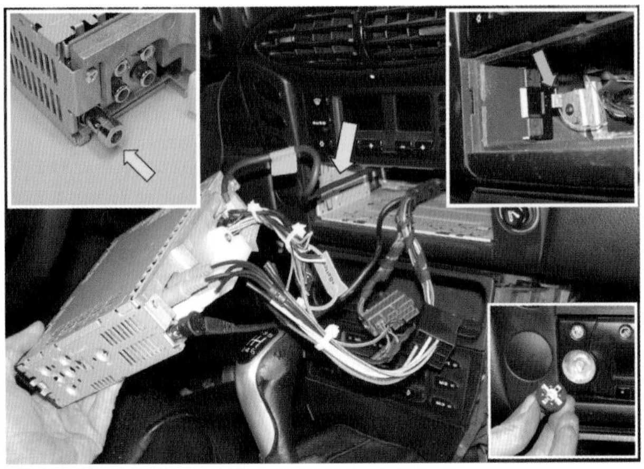

3 Shown here is the new radio ready for installation into the car. The yellow arrow shows the antenna adapter installed. The bracket is installed into the center dashboard (blue arrow), ready for the radio. The factory harness is connected to the adapter, and the connector for the radio is plugged into the back of the new head unit. It's normal to have one or two wires that are not used. In this photo, I plugged in all of the connections and then turned on the ignition to test the proper operation of the radio. I recommend testing prior to the final installation, as these radios are designed to be difficult to remove. New buttons for your stock radio are easy to install; simply pull them off and push on the new ones (inset, lower right, PN: 996-645-901-00). The green arrow shows the alarm radio detection switch, which must be grounded when installing a new unit (brown/blue wire).

2 Use the radio removal keys (available direct from Becker and also supplied with the factory kit; green arrow) to pull out the radio by inserting them into the head unit and pulling on the two keys using two screwdrivers. The unit should slide right out. The keys release the spring-loaded locking mechanism on the side of the radio (yellow arrow). Another way of playing through the stock radio with virtually no cost at all is by using the auxilliary (AUX) input. The factory radio CDR-220 has the ability to take input from an external source. You can purchase a blue connector plug from Becker (PN: 1319.116-276) that will fit into the back of the radio and interface with an external source, or you can tap into the blue plug that is provided as part of the CD changer interface. Tap into and wire up your input source (iPod, etc.) using the three wires that exit out of the blue connector (pins 18, 19, 20). Then turn the radio on, and then hold down the TP button until the message BECKER 1 is displayed. Then turn the tuning knob until the message AUX OFF is displayed. Press the down arrow and change the message to AUX ON. Turn the radio off, and now you have auxiliary input enabled.

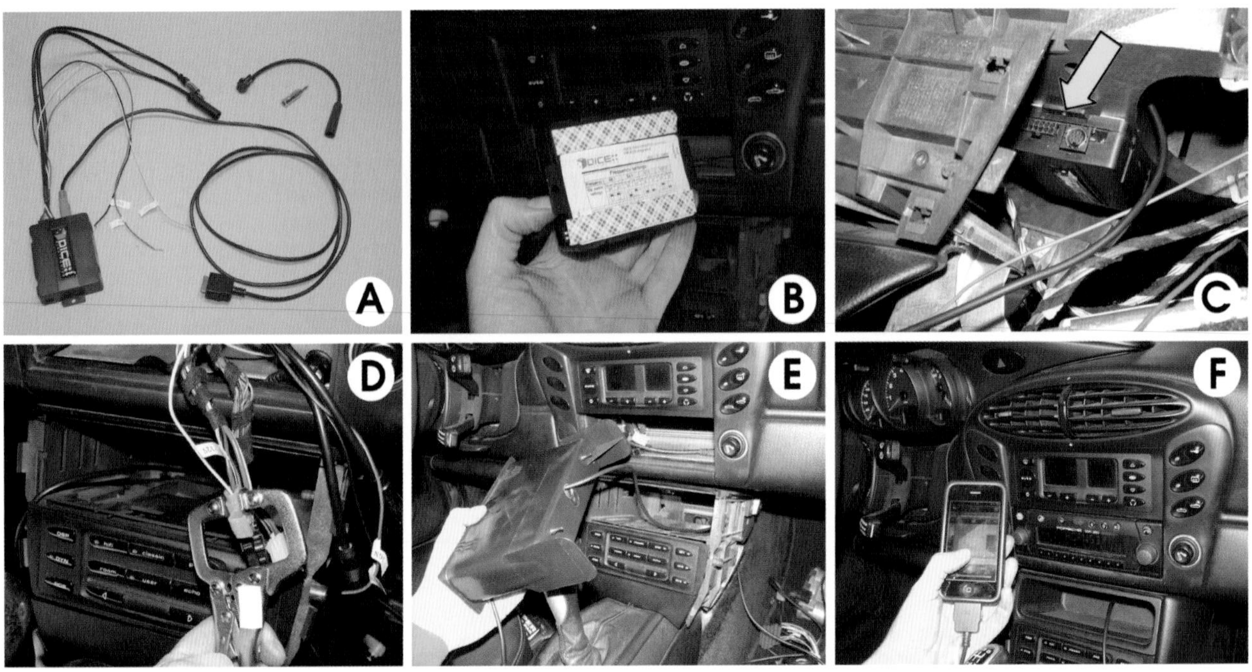

4 This photo array shows the installation of the DICE universal iPod adapter. **A:** Here is the FM modulator kit as it comes out of the box. You also need the Scosche VWAKB antenna adapter set (upper right) to work with the factory radio and its European connectors. **B:** Mount the DICE unit with double-sided sticky tape. **C:** Mount it on the underside of the center console and give yourself enough room to access the connectors (yellow arrow). **D:** Use three tap-in connectors to connect the unit to the 12-volt supply, the ignition 12-volt switched supply, and the ground. Plug in the antenna adapters and the inline antenna cable. **E:** Drill a hole in the back of the storage compartment and route the cable through. **F:** Test the system and then reinstall the stereo. Although there are many different iPod adapter units available on the market, this particular one has the ability to display the iPod song and artist on the radio through the FM-RDS protocol. I tested the unit and compared the sound quality to the CD input—it was indistinguishable. The only small drawback appears to be that the volume level of the iPod interface is a bit lower than simply playing CDs.

PROJECT 91
On-Board Computer/Turn Signal Installation

Time / Tab / Talent: 4 hours / $300 /

Tools: Torx driver set

Applicable Years: 1999–2004

Tinware: Turn signal switch and parts

More Info: http://www.101projects.com/Carrera/91.htm

Tip: Buy the cruise control switch; it's cheaper

Performance Gain: Activate on-board computer, cruise control

Comp Modification: Cruise control installation

One of the neat options available on the 911 Carrera was the on-board computer (OBC). This computer adds additional functionality to your gauge cluster: range on remaining fuel, outside temperature, speed alert/gong, average fuel consumption, and average speed calculations. Many cars were not equipped with this option, but fortunately the programming and circuits are built into the gauge clusters. To activate the OBC, all you need to do is install the turn signal switch with the control stalk and have the OBC functionality enabled by the Porsche factory programming tool (PST2 or PIWIS).

The following table shows the list of parts that are required for the OBC upgrade. All of these hard-to-find parts are easily available for purchase at the 101Projects.com website or PelicanParts.com.

Even if your car doesn't have cruise control and you're not planning on adding it, you might want to consider using this switch instead, as the cost is much cheaper than the one without the cruise control. You can simply purchase the new stalk, remove the new OBC stalk portion, and then transfer it to your old stalk. The two connector wires are Volkswagen parts that appear to be available only from the dealer. These are probably pretty common repair items though, as my dealer had them in stock on the shelf when I arrived there.

Qty	Part Number	Description
1	999-650-056-40	Connector
1	999-650-057-40	Connector cover
3	000-979-009	Connector wire and pins for stalk (Volkswagen part)
2	000-979-010	Connector wire and pins for cluster (Volkswagen part)
1	996-613-219-10-EWC	Turn signal stalk with cruise control
1	996-613-215-10-EWC	Turn signal stalk without cruise control
1	996-613-509-10-A05	Turn signal cap
1	996-613-507-10-A05	Wiper cap
1	996-613-503-10-A05	On-board computer cap
1	996-613-508-10-A05	Cruise control cap

The four-stalk version part number is 996-613-219-10-EWC and is only currently available in the black matte/satin black finish. The early-style steering wheel switches were a glossy black. The small tabs on each of the stalks can be transferred over to the new stalk, but if they are glossy black, they will not match terribly well. The best option is to order four new tabs in the matte black/satin black finish, as per the part numbers in the table above.

The first step is to assemble the mini wire harness with the connectors and pins that you purchased. Take two of the three connector wires (000-979-009) and cut the two of them in half. Then insert the four wires with pins attached into Slots 2 through 5 on the five-pin connector 999-650-056-40. Take the remaining connector wire (000-979-009) and cut one of the pins off very close to the pin. Attach a ground eyelet on the end of this wire and then place it into Slot 1 of the five-pin connector. Then snap on the connector cover. Now, cut in half the other two connector wires (000-979-010) and attach each one to the wires that exit from 2 through 5 on the connector. Label each wire with the proper pin number and then tie them together with some small zip ties (see Photo 5). Be sure not to confuse the five connector wires; they look almost exactly the same to the naked eye but fit into the different connectors.

Now, disconnect the battery and wait for at least 15 minutes (see Project 83); then, pull out the steering wheel as far as possible using the lever at the bottom of the steering

column and remove the steering wheel (Project 62). Disconnect and remove the gauge cluster (see Project 88). Remove the steering wheel covers (see Photo 1). Tape the air bag spring so that it doesn't rotate and remove it (see Photo 2). Pull the left and right rear connectors off the turn signal stalk, mark its position on the steering shaft with a permanent marker, loosen the retaining clamp, and remove it from the steering column (Photo 3). Route the new black harness connector alongside the other wires near to the large connector on the left side of the steering column.

Now it's time to plug the wires into one of the connectors that plugs into the back of the instrument cluster (see Photo 6 for instructions). Attach the eyelet to one of the ground screws on the chassis (see inset of Photo 3). Follow the table at the right for your year Carrera:

911 Carrera 1999–2000

Connector Pin 2	Gauge Cluster Pin 20	Select Mode Down
Connector Pin 3	Gauge Cluster Pin 21	Speed Alert/Gong
Connector Pin 4	Gauge Cluster Pin 22	Select Mode Forward
Connector Pin 5	Gauge Cluster Pin 25	Select Mode Backward

911 Carrera 2001–2004

Connector Pin 2	Gauge Cluster Pin 23	Select Mode Down
Connector Pin 3	Gauge Cluster Pin 22	Speed Alert/Gong
Connector Pin 4	Gauge Cluster Pin 21	Select Mode Forward
Connector Pin 5	Gauge Cluster Pin 24	Select Mode Backward

If you happen to break the electrical connector plugs on the back of the cluster, then you can replace them with connector pieces from Porsche. For the 2001–2004 clusters, the kit comes with the three connectors and all three black insert plugs as well. The part number for this is PNA-721-043-00-202-OEM and costs about $32. For the early-style clusters (1998–2000), these connectors are available in a generic repair kit from Porsche for about $5. This Porsche Electrical Connector Repair Kit has a part number of OEM-PNA-721-043-600-QR.

With the new pins installed into the gauge connectors, reinstall the gauge cluster. Reinstall the new turn signal switch, and tighten down the clamp that holds it to the steering column. When you install the switch, the top metal surface should be positioned approximately 55mm from the end of the steering shaft. Don't slide it in all the way on the shaft, as this will give you trouble with the proper operation of the turn signal canceling function. Line up the metal clamp with the knurled section of the steering column when you tighten it. If need be, you can adjust this later on as well.

Reinstall the air bag contact spring and the side covers for the steering column. Install the steering wheel back on the car and reconnect the battery. If your car didn't have the cruise control and OBC enabled, then you need to make a trip to the Porsche dealer to have them turn on this functionality with the Porsche PST2 or PIWIS tool (see Photo 7). Once the main computer is reprogrammed, you should have a working OBC.

Poor man's version. Some people who have not wanted to go through the trouble or expense of purchasing the new turn signal stalk have instead installed extra rocker switches

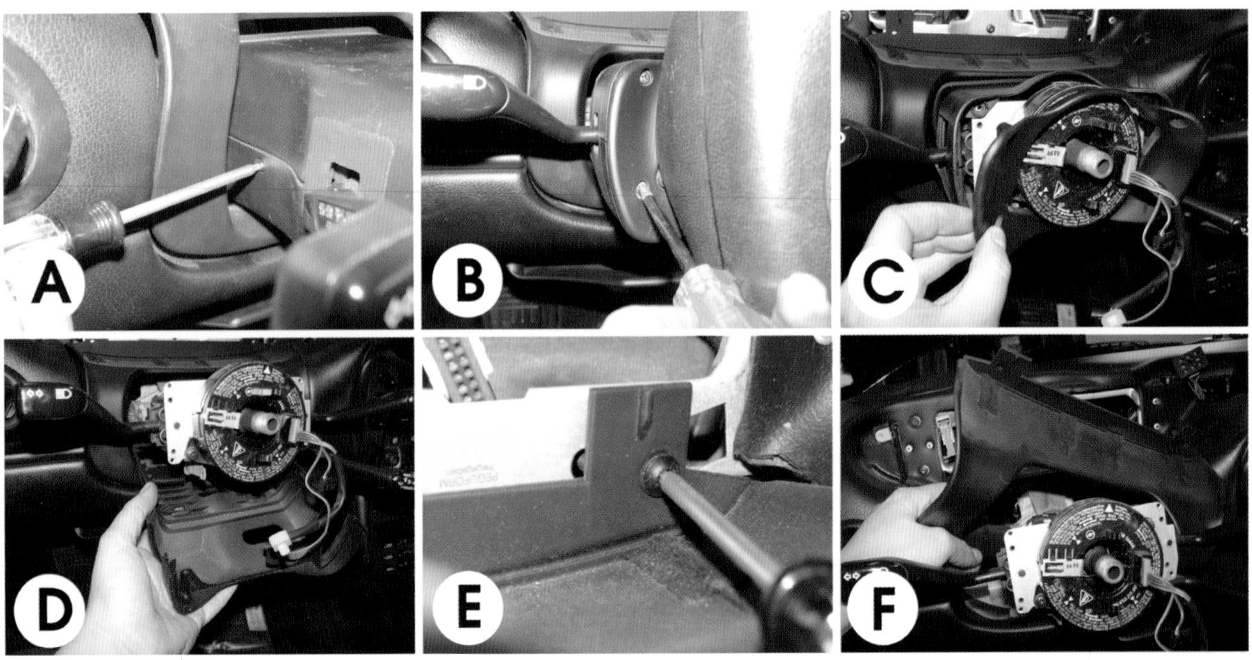

1 After you have removed the steering wheel, you can then remove the equipment that covers the stalk. **A:** The side surrounds are held on with two small screws. **B:** The front surround is held on with four screws. If the steering wheel is still attached, then rotate it until you can access the screws. **C:** Pull off the front cover. **D:** Remove both the top and bottom steering column covers. **E:** A few screws hold the upper fascia to the metal part of the dashboard. **F:** Remove the fascia to expose the steering column.

into the dash and wired them up to the gauge cluster to gain functionality of the computer without the installation of the expensive stalk. You can use the same wires as above, but instead use two rocker switches (PN: 996-613-980-00) that fit into the spare places in the center dash, to the left of the vents (see Photo 8).

Really poor man's version. If you don't want to go through the process of installing any of the switches and have a 1998–2000 Carrera, you can simply have the dealer turn on the OBC function in the computer. This will bring up the temperature display, although you cannot cycle through any of the other options. Starting in 2001, this no longer works.

2 This photo shows the details involved in removing the air bag contact ring. Be very careful of the fragile plastic tabs on the contact ring; they are very easy to break off, and this piece is about $200 to replace. The red arrow indicates the plastic piece (shown broken here) that is very easy to snap off if you are not careful. The blue arrows show the air bag and horn connectors that need to be disconnected, and the orange arrow shows the turn signal switch connectors. Although you can simply loosen the air bag contact ring and leave it installed on the steering column, I recommend removing it completely and putting it aside, as it's way too easy to damage it while you're working in that area.

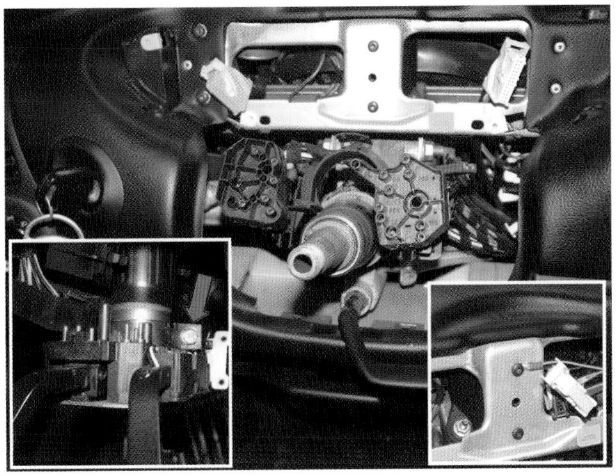

3 Here's what the steering wheel column looks like with the switch removed. When attaching the new one, you need to clamp it down by tightening the pinch bolt (red arrow). The inset photo in the lower right shows where you need to attach the grounding harness for the new stalk switch.

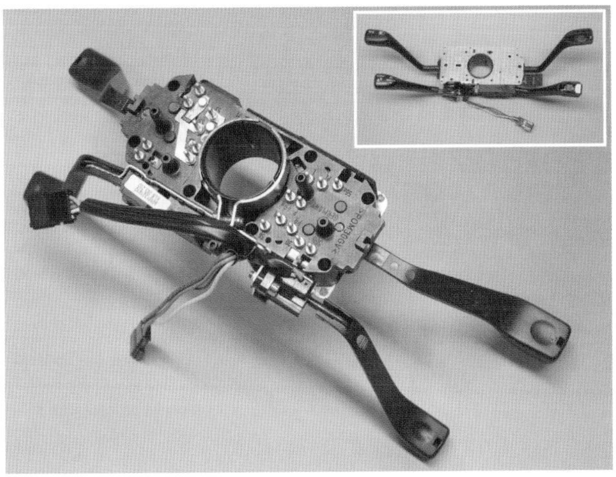

4 Shown here is the upgraded turn signal that contains all of the switches and stalks required for both the on-board computer and cruise control. If your 2000 and later Carrera didn't originally come with cruise control and you wish to add it, then you should install this turn signal switch. Shown here is the matte black version of the four-stalk switch (part number 996-613-219-10). The small tabs on each of the stalks can be transferred over to the new stalk.

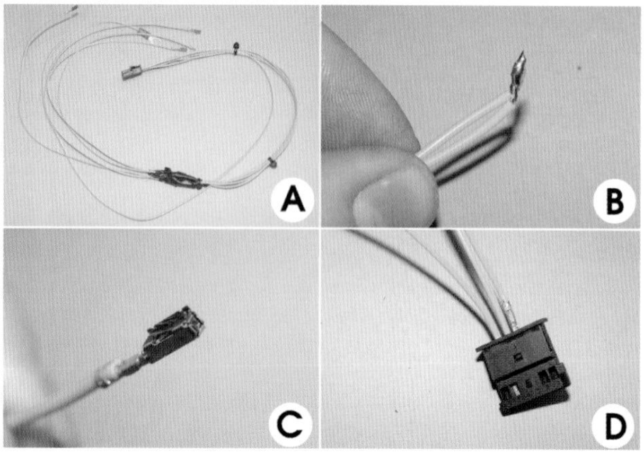

5 This photo shows the process of creating the small wire harness that connects the on-board computer switch stalk to the gauge cluster. **A:** Shown here is the completed harness, with the ground lead and three pins that must be mated into the connector that plugs into the gauge cluster. Use small cable ties to join the whole harness together. It's also smart to label each wire (not shown here). **B:** I prefer to solder all my connections when possible to avoid any of them coming loose in the near future. Wrap each connection with electrical tape, of course. **C:** Here's a close-up of the tiny pin that needs to be inserted into the black connector. Keep in mind that there are two different types of pins, and they both look the same. **D:** The pins should easily snap into the connector. If they don't, you are probably using the wrong pin and need to grab the other one. I suggest inserting the wires and pins into the connector prior to soldering the connections, just so that you don't have to take the whole harness apart if you find you have made a mistake.

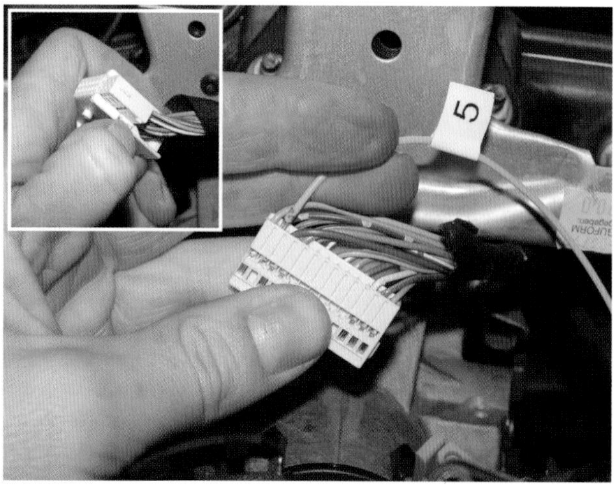

6 You can open up the connectors and remove the inner portion by squeezing the base of the plug. The inner portion, which contains all of the wires and pins, will slide out of the side of the connector. Insert your new pin into the appropriate slot. Be aware that there are two different pins used on these wires: a small one and a larger one. The small one will very easily snap into place, and the larger one will only snap into place with a lot of force. Make sure that you create the wire harness using the proper pins for this connector. As shown in the photo, I found it useful to label the wires since they were all yellow colored.

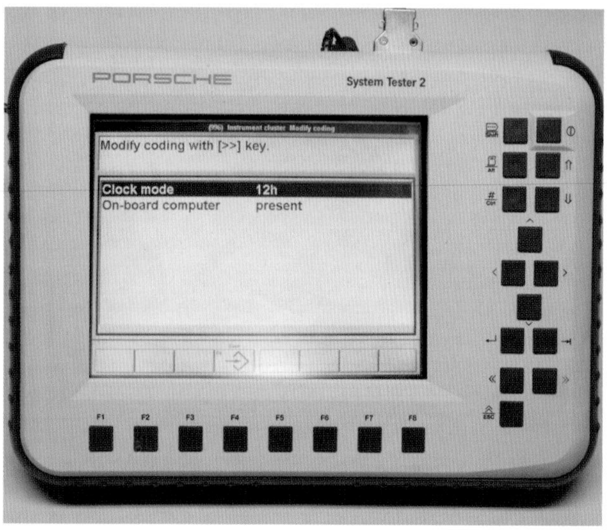

7 When the installation is complete, the computer will not work, unfortunately, until the coding is modified in the instrument cluster using the Porsche factory PST2 or PIWIS programming tool. This tool is only found at Porsche dealers and the occasional independent shop, such as Callas Rennsport in Torrance, California. Under Instrument Cluster, change the coding to show on-board computer to be "present" and save the changes. After this change is made, the on-board computer should function normally. Be sure that your car is not missing the Option Code spec, as this will generate errors when you try to update the car with the tool.

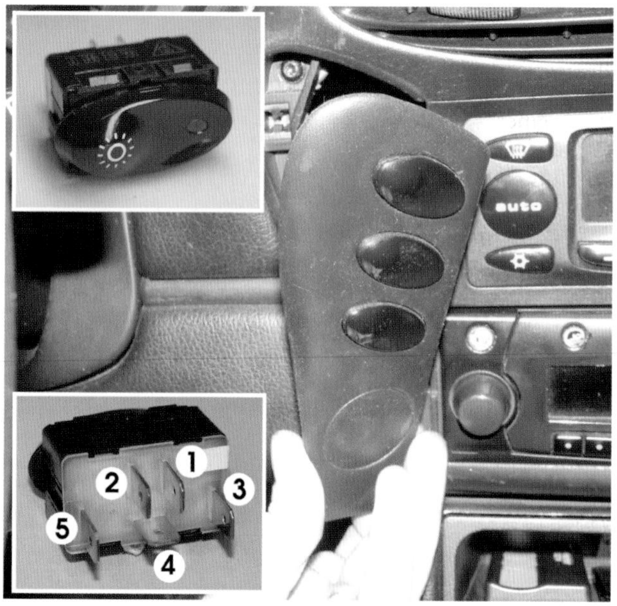

8 The poor man's version is a great way to get the functionality of the computer without having to install the stalk. Simply install two rocker switches into the blanks on the left side of the dash, and wire them up to the pins on the back of the cluster. Wire one of the two switches to the pins that control "mode forwards" and "mode backwards," and the other switch to "select mode down" and "speed gong/alert" (see table in the text). The rocker switches that are available are pretty neat and useful. This one (for footwell lighting, PN: 996-613-980-00) contains two switches (left and right), an internal LED, and an internal light bulb for nighttime illumination. **1:** Switch left. **2:** Switch right. **3:** Nighttime illumination. **4:** Common. **5:** LED lamp. To use this switch with the on-board computer, wire Pins 2, 3, 4, and 5 from the table above to Pins 1 and 2 of two different switches, and then connect the green ground wire to Pin 4 of both switches.

PROJECT 92
Cruise Control Installation

Time / Tab / Talent: 6 hours / $300 /

Tools: Torx driver set

Applicable Years: 2000–2008 (1999 C4)

Tinware: Cruise control switch, connectors, and wire

More Info: http://www.101projects.com/Carrera/92.htm

Tip: Easy to install with the on-board computer

Performance Gain: No more sleepy feet

Comp Modification: On-board computer installation

In 2000, the Carrera 2's engine management system was upgraded with a new system that used an electronic throttle body (E-gas). The Carrera 4 had seen this introduced the previous year (1999). This upgrade eliminated throttle cables, and instead the gas pedal had a sensor on it that controlled an electronic stepper motor located on the throttle body in the engine compartment. Because this entire arrangement is completely electronic, the car no longer needed to have a separate, complicated cruise control system. As a result, if you have a 2000 and later Carrera (or 1999 C4) that didn't come with cruise control installed from the factory, then you can install the turn signal switch with the cruise control stalk, run some wires, and turn it on electronically in the computer.

This project is very similar in principle to the on board computer (OBC) installation (Project 91). Similar to that one, you need to remove the gauge cluster, the steering wheel, and the turn signal switch in order to upgrade your car. (Please refer to Project 91 for specific instructions on how to replace the turn signal switch.) This project will focus mostly on the additional steps that are required to wire up and activate the cruise control feature.

There are a few parts that you will need. First, you will need a Four Lever Stalk unit (996-613-219-10-EWC-M100). You will also need a connector that plugs into the stalk (PN: 999-652-972-40), a VW wire connector (000-979-010, see Project 91), and eight female pins in order to install inside the two connectors (PN: 999-652-901-22, get some extras). You will also need enough 22-gauge wire to run four separate wires from the dashboard of the car to the Motronic computer located behind the rear seats. I suggest using four different-colored wires for this task.

Crimp the pins on to the five wires (four from the Motronic unit in the rear and one from the cruise control connector to the fuse panel) and run them through the car according to the following table and also using the guidance provided in the accompanying photos. Use the pins from the VW wire 000-979-010 to plug into the back of your instrument cluster (see Project 91). Also make sure that you have a good working bulb (for non-LED lit clusters) in the cruise control indicator socket of the gauge cluster.

Cruise Control Connector Carrera 2000–2002 (C4 1999–2002)

Cruise Control Connector Pin 1	Motronic Connector IV – Pin 27 (black)
Cruise Control Connector Pin 2	Fuse B7 (black)
Cruise Control Connector Pin 3	Motronic Connector IV – Pin 25 (yellow)
Cruise Control Connector Pin 4	Motronic Connector IV – Pin 19 (brown/yellow)
2000-02 Gauge Cluster with a Blue Connector I Pin 16, or if you have a Black Connector III Pin 17	Motronic Connector IV – Pin 18 (orange/red)

For 2003–2005 996 cars, it's much easier. The cruise control functions are integrated into the instrument cluster, and all you need to do is wire the cruise control stalk switch to the appropriate pins in the instrument cluster. This arrangement is nearly identical to how the OBC is wired up (see Project 91). Connect the cruise control connector to the gauge cluster using the following table.

Cruise Control Connector – 996 Carrera 2003–2005

Cruise Control Connector Pin 1	Plug C on the Gauge Cluster (Grey) – Pin 17 (blue/white)
Cruise Control Connector Pin 2	Fuse B7 (black)
Cruise Control Connector Pin 3	Plug C on the Gauge Cluster (Grey) – Pin 4 (blue/red)
Cruise Control Connector Pin 4	Plug C on the Gauge Cluster (Grey) – Pin 1 (blue/black)

For all 996 Carreras, 2000–2005 (and 1999 C4) cars, once you have all of the wiring done, you will need to have the dealer activate the cruise control function using the PST2 or PIWIS programming unit. The section for programming this information in the tool is located in the digital motor electronics (DME) module, under the Coding section. You also need to activate the instrument cluster for cruise control as well. This is found in the Instrument Cluster coding section within the Porsche programming tool. Make sure your car has the "order code" properly set; otherwise you may have trouble properly programming the instrument cluster.

Carrera C2s in 1999 didn't have an electronically controlled throttle—instead they have a special servo motor that's attached to the gas pedal and controlled by a separate cruise control module. It is possible to retrofit these components to a car that did not have cruise control from the factory, but it's quite a bit more complicated. You need to purchase the cruise control pedal assembly and the control module/servo motor (see Photo 4) and then wire the assembly to the car.

For the 997 Carreras from 2005–2008, the installation is much easier. You need to purchase a cruise control switch (PN: 997-613-261-00), a small wiring harness (PN: 997-622-674-00), a new lower steering column cover (PN: 997-552-475-03), and two Torx screws to secure the new switch (PN: N-909-068-01). A factory retro-fit kit includes all of these parts and instructions (PN: 997-044-903-00), but you can save money by simply buying the parts separately. Simply remove the bottom cover, install the new switch and harness, plug the harness into the connector on the switch above it, and then install the new lower cover. The cruise control function then needs to be turned on by a Porsche dealer or independent shop with a PIWIS programming tool. The whole process should take about 30 minutes—very simple.

Cruise control troubleshooting. If your new cruise control installation doesn't work, check your wiring. Also double-check to make sure that the technician who programmed your Carreras computer properly set the cruise control function in both the DME and in the Instrument Cluster section. If you are still having difficulty or if you have cruise control installed from the factory and it's not working properly, you might want to try the following troubleshooting steps:

- Check the stalk switches. Unplug the connector and use a multimeter to test the proper functioning of the switches.
- Check the brake pedal and clutch switches (see Project 93). Both of these deactivate the cruise control, and if the switches are faulty, they will prevent the computer from activating the system. Not only can they fail, but they can also slip out of their bracket, which causes them to not work either.
- Check to make sure the bulb in the cluster is not burned out and that it turns on for a second or so when you turn the ignition on.
- Check the B7 slot in the fusebox to make sure the fuse powering the system is not blown.

1 The wire from Pin 2 of the cruise control connector needs to be wired to the black wire running to fuse B7 at the rear of the fuse panel. Remove the passenger side footwell covers and you should be able to see the fuse panel. Remove the panel (be sure to disconnect the battery first) by removing the four Phillips-head screws and then squeezing the tabs on the side (yellow arrow). Attach the wire to the black fuse B7 as shown using a tap-in connector (green arrow). The fuses should be labeled on the plastic box itself. This will provide the cruise control circuit with the brake pedal signal to turn off the cruise control function.

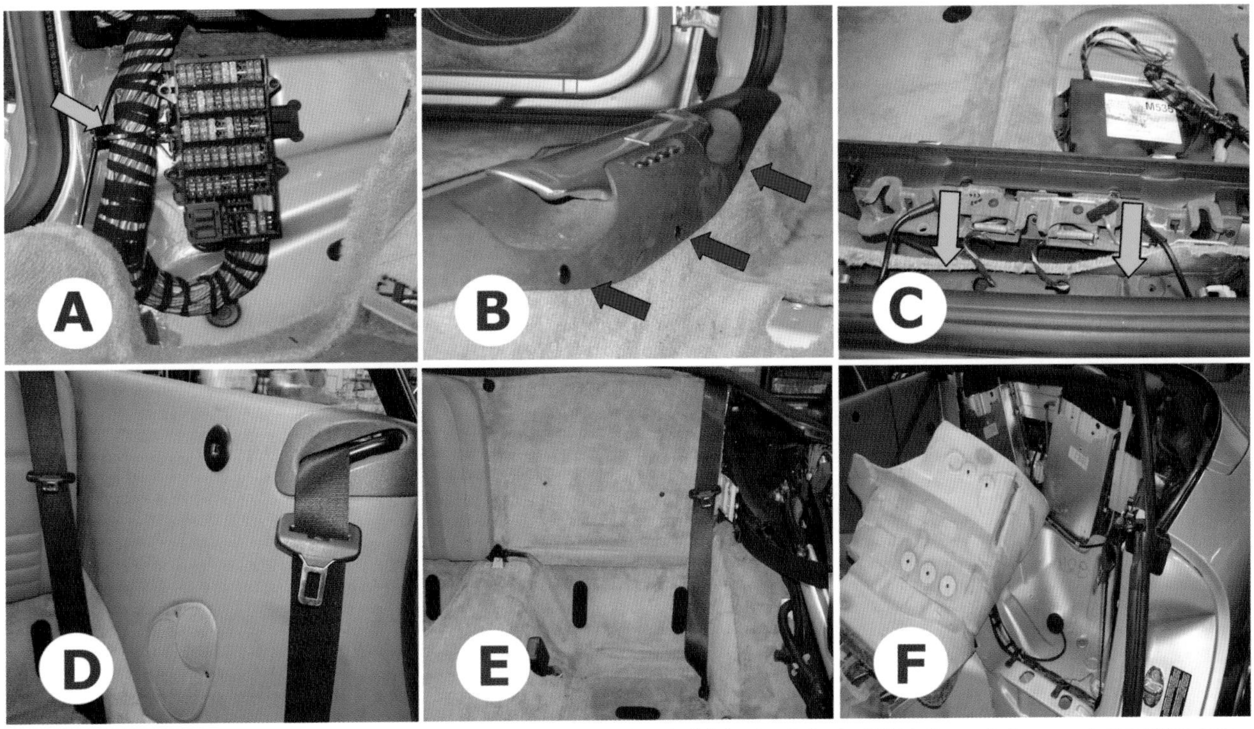

2 On cars up to and including 2002, in order to get the control signals from the Motronic digital motor electronics (DME) in the rear to the gauge cluster and the cruise control stalk, you need to run four wires down the left side of the car and into the rear area. In the coupe, the DME is behind the rear seats under the shelf. In the convertible, the DME is located behind the roll bar bulk head and under the carpeted body flap. Begin by taping the four wires together to make them easier to fish through the chassis. **A:** Run the new wires attached to the cruise control connector alongside the left-side harness down to the fuse panel (green arrow). **B:** Pop off the three plastic rivets that hold on the covers for the hood and trunk release mechanism (blue arrows). Loosen the bolts that hold the mechanism in place, but do not remove them. Having the right tool really works here, and a fold-up Torx set works perfectly in this tight space (some cars may use a hex head screw instead). **C:** Pull upward on the plastic trim, and the assembly unit will snap up and out of the way. Do not disconnect the cables. Run the new wires next to the existing wire harness underneath (green arrows). **D:** Remove the side panel in the rear seat area that covers the seat belt and sun roof mechanism (see Project 69). **E:** Now remove the rear seat on the left side along with the rear panel (see Project 69). **F:** Lift the rear carpet up and run the wires alongside the existing wire harness. The wires never need the leave the "dry" area of the car, so you can just safely route them back to the DME. It is a good idea to secure them to the existing wiring harness with cable ties. Do not route them anywhere near moving or sharp areas of the car.

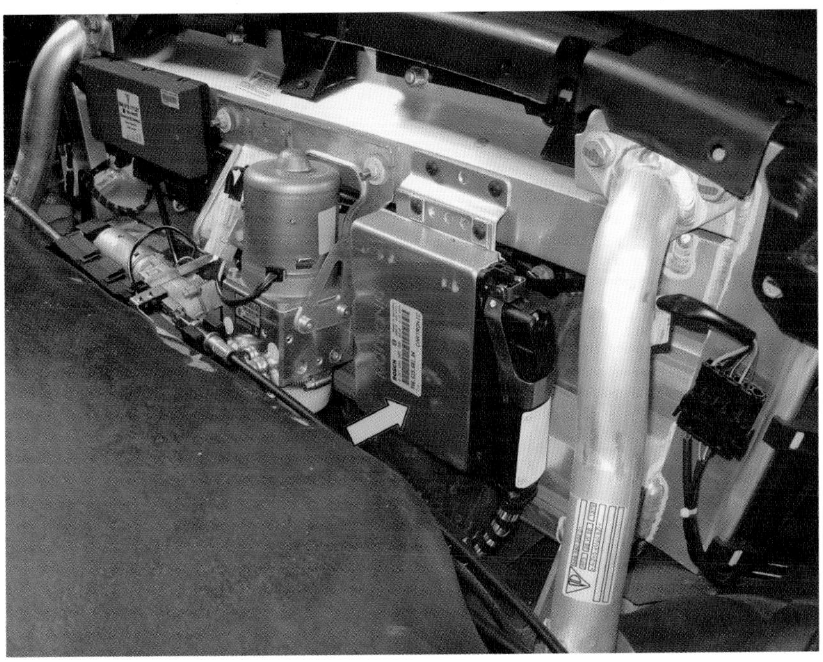

3 Shown here is the location of the Motronic DME in the rear bulkhead of a 996 Cabriolet (green arrow). Remove the connector from the back of the unit and then add the pins into the empty slots according to the table in the text of this project.

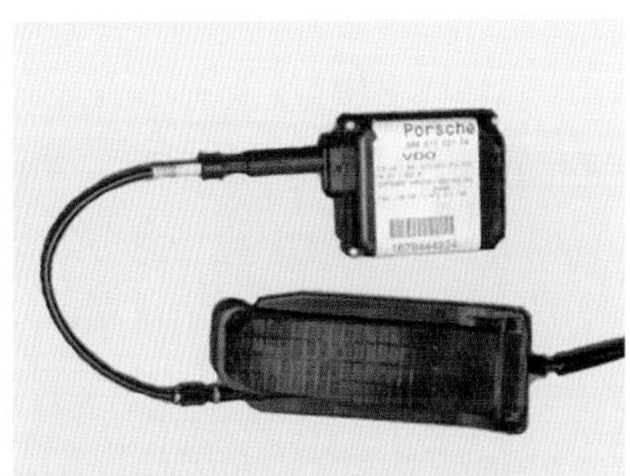

4 Shown here is the cruise control servo module and gas pedal for the 1999 Carrera (2-wheel drive version) with the cable driven accelerator. The E-gas cars do not have the accelerator cable, and the 2005 (997) and newer pedals have the servos built into the pedal unit.

PROJECT 93
Brake, Clutch, and Cruise Control Switch Replacement

Time / Tab / Talent: 30 minutes / $20–$50 /

Tools: Screwdriver

Applicable Years: All

Tinware: New pedal switches

More Info: http://www.101projects.com/Carrera/93.htm

Tip: Twist the old switch to remove it

Performance Gain: Working brake lamps, cruise control

Comp Modification: Install aftermarket pedals

There are three pedal switches on the 911 Carrera: two on the clutch pedal and one on the brakes. They get a lot of use, and they all have a tendency to fail once in a while. Replacement is really easy and should take only about 30 minutes.

For the brake switch, the first step is to verify that your brake lamps are not working. If you're by yourself, then wait until nighttime and back up against a wall. You should see the reflection off of the wall when you step on the brakes. If you don't, then your switch is probably shot. It's important to note that the switch has redundancy built in, and the warning system should tell you when your switch is failing, but this doesn't always work.

The clutch pedal has two switches: one switch controls the cruise control (turns it off when you push in the clutch) and the other won't let you start the car without the clutch pedal pushed in. The microswitch only activates when the clutch is fully depressed whereas the cruise control switch disengages the cruise control as soon as you begin to activate the clutch. If you're having intermittent starting problems with your car, I would look at the microswitch first.

Curious, but the cruise control switch is identical to the brake pedal switch, except that the cruise control switch is red and the brake pedal switch is a translucent brown. Both switches have three of the same part numbers printed on them.

The switches are relatively easy to access, as they are located right above the pedals. You will have to open the passenger door and then stick your head into the footwell to see them. You may find removing the knee panel gives you more room. Replacement is easy: simply unplug the harness from the end and then twist to remove the switch. If you need to manhandle and/or break the switch to remove it, that's perfectly okay, since you will be replacing it with a new one anyways. The clutch pedal switch that prevents the car from starting is a standard microswitch mounted with screws.

To finish the job, simply install the new switch into place and reconnect the wire harness. Test the brake lights to make sure that they are working properly, and then reinstall the knee panel.

1 Here are the two clutch pedal switches. The yellow arrow points to the micro-switch that prevents the car from starting if you don't have the pedal pushed in. The red switch is the one that deactivates the cruise control when you push the clutch in.

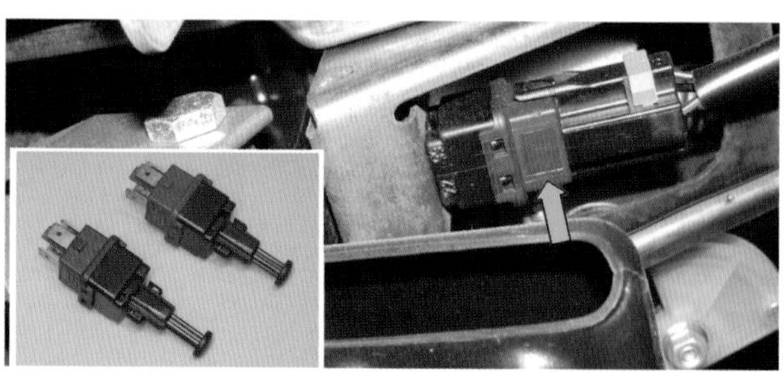

2 Here's a photo of the brake pedal switch (green arrow). Simply unplug the harness, twist the switch, and then remove it from the chassis. The lower left inset photo shows the brake and cruise control switches together. The only difference between these two is the color of the housing.

PROJECT 94
Installing the Sprint Accelerator Booster

Time / Tab / Talent: 30 minutes / $330 /

Tools:

Applicable Years: 2000–2008

Tinware: Sprint Booster module

Tip: The company has a risk-free money-back guarantee policy for the unit

Performance Gain: Quicker throttle response

Comp Modification: Replace the pedal switches

More Info: http://www.101projects.com/Carrera/94.htm

The Sprint Booster is one of those products that is a bit difficult to explain in words. In 2000, Porsche did away with the traditional cable that connects the gas pedal to the throttle body and replaced it with what is known as drive-by-wire. Basically, an electronic sensor on the gas pedal tells the main computer (DME) how much the driver is pressing down the pedal, and then the computer opens the throttle body on the engine by the correct amount. Some people claim that the electronic throttle (also known as E-gas) is less responsive than a normal cable throttle. I have both types of Carreras (pre-2000 and post-2000), and I haven't been able to detect a difference between the two.

The pedal has a variable sensor on it that senses the exact position of the pedal as your foot presses on it. This position is read by the computer and then used to open the throttle body. A fully depressed gas pedal makes the computer throw the throttle body fully open. Likewise, with the gas pedal at resting position, the throttle body is almost completely closed (open about 6 percent to allow the engine to idle). As you press the gas pedal toward the floor, the computer opens the throttle body somewhat proportionately to how much "gas" you're giving the car—pushing down the gas pedal halfway means that the computer opens the throttle body enough to allow air into the engine at half its maximum capacity. It's interesting to note that the relationship between the pedal and the throttle body is not linear—for example, when the pedal is pushed down 50 percent, the throttle body is only open about 27 percent. When the pedal is pushed down 85 percent, the throttle body is open 74 percent, and when the pedal is pushed 100 percent down to the floor, the throttle body is open 100 percent.

So, how does this Sprint Booster device work? Basically, I like to call it a "short shift kit for your gas pedal." It takes the signals from your gas pedal and changes them so that the computer is tricked into thinking that you've stomped down on your gas pedal when you really haven't. Basically, you reach about full throttle when the pedal is roughly halfway to the floor. The device does not increase horsepower or overall performance of the car, however the car "feels quicker." The resulting effect is real, even if the horsepower gains are not.

It's very difficult to explain the effect to someone who hasn't actually driven the car with the unit installed. It does actually feel a lot quicker. For my last book, I had an old BMW 318is project car that had about 50 or so less horsepower than my 325is. But the car was high-revving, and because of other mind tricks, it just "felt quicker" and was generally more fun to drive. I liken the effect of the Sprint Booster to that experience. It takes a little bit of getting used when you first install it, but after a few days it will feel like second nature.

There are a few potential downsides to the Sprint Booster, however. The first one is the price. At $330 from PelicanParts.com, it's definitely not cheap. The relatively high price combined with the fact that it's very difficult to explain what exactly this unit does is probably one of the reasons why the manufacturer offers a 30-day money back guarantee on it. So, if you don't like it, the risk is about 30 minutes of your time. Another potential drawback is the fact that you may experience a decrease in gas mileage. Common sense seems to indicate that if you're an "electronic lead foot" more of the time, your gas mileage will decrease. However, an informal search on the Internet seems to indicate that most people have not experienced any decrease in gas mileage. I installed mine in spring of 2013 and have not yet had enough personal drive time with the device to determine what its impact on gas consumption might be.

One more thing to note—since this is purely an electronic modification—if you are having your DME remapped (see Project 24), then you can also have the software reprogrammed to offer the same effect as the Sprint Booster.

If this is something you're interested in, you might want to discuss it with the provider of your software map before you complete your purchase.

Installation is really a snap. All you do is disconnect the connector to the gas pedal and plug in the Sprint Booster so it's now in-line with the harness. The toughest part is squeezing your body underneath the dashboard so that you can reach the connections (see Photo 1). I was able to do it and take photos without disconnecting any of the duct work under the dash, but it takes some patience and dexterity.

1 Here's a shot under the dash of the Sprint Booster installation. The plug for the accelerator is up under the dashboard; simply unplug it and insert the Sprint Booster device in its place. Then, reconnect the plug that connects to the chassis. The Sprint Booster is sandwiched between these two connectors. On the 2005 and later Carreras, the gas pedal has been redesigned. In a similar but easier manner, installation of the Sprint Booster attaches directly onto the rear of the accelerator pedal between the pedal and the cable that comes plugged into it.

SECTION 11
MISCELLANEOUS

This section contains all the projects that didn't quite fit into any of the other predefined categories. Take a look at the Personal Touches project for my pick of the most interesting and unique additions that various owners have made to their Carreras. Air conditioning recharging, track prep, wheel/tire selection, and dyno testing are also detailed in the projects within this section.

PROJECT 95
HVAC Fan Replacement

Time / Tab / Talent: 1 hours / $320 /

Tools: 6mm socket with ratchet, screwdriver

Applicable Years: All

Tinware: New blower fan assembly

More Info: http://www.101projects.com/Carrera/95.htm

Tip: Take your time removing the plastic air duct

Performance Gain: Working heater and A/C

Comp Modification: Clean out the inside of the blower housing, if needed

Over time, the blower fan that provides both heated and cooled air to the inside of the car can wear out and eventually fail. The good news is that this is an easily replaced part. Sometimes you'll get some signs that the fan is failing, usually a high pitched squeal when the fan spins, indicating a worn fan bearing. Sometimes the fan just won't spin at all.

To replace the fan, begin by disconnecting the negative terminal on the battery. This is the most important part of the job. You don't want to risk accidentally turning the fan on while removing it (see Project 83).

Follow along with the photos for instructions on the removal process.

Now it's a simple matter of taking the new fan, plugging the wiring harness connector in, and sliding the new fan up into place. You'll see that there is a groove in the fan housing that the fan slides into. Once the fan is in place, slide the wiring harness up and over the retaining hook, then refit the access cover on the bottom of the fan and housing.

Now refit the air duct between the center and passenger side vents. As before, this can be a bit tricky. You'll want to make sure that both ends of the duct slide into place on each end. This process will probably take a bit of work, but it can be done—just take your time. After the duct is in place, fit the foam cover piece back into place.

1 The heating/ventilation/air cooling fan on the Carrera is one of those items that tend to fail as the cars reach over 10 years old. The good news is that replacement is very easy and can be done in about a half hour. As always, you can easily find the replacement fan on PelicanParts.com. The cost is about $300.

2 Begin by disconnecting the battery and looking under the passenger side dash. You'll see a foam plastic cover secured with two plastic retaining screws. Remove the two screws and pull the foam cover from underneath.

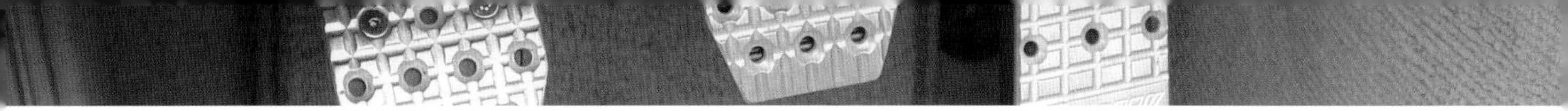

3 With the foam cover removed, you'll see the two 6mm screws securing the bottom cover of the fan housing on (green arrows). Remove the two screws and set the bottom cover aside.

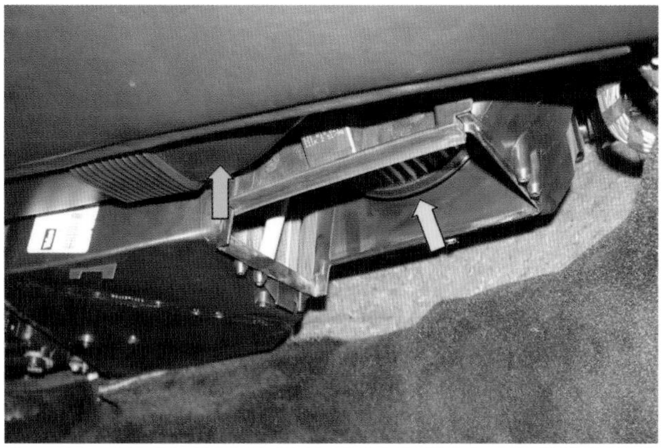

4 This is what you should see with the fan cover removed. You can just see the blades of the fan up inside the fan housing (yellow arrow). Take note of the air duct directly in front of the fan housing (green arrow). You'll need to remove this to have room to lower the fan out.

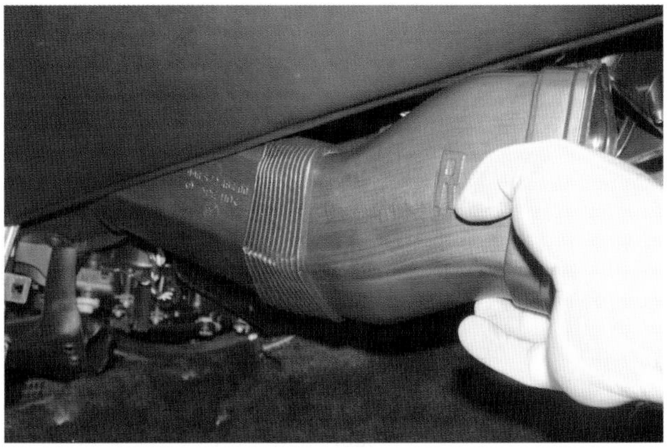

5 If you look up under the dash, you'll see the duct that connects to the center blower vents on the left and to the passenger side vents on the right. At first, it may seem as though you have no room to remove the duct from in front of the fan housing, but the bellows that are molded into the center of the duct allow you enough flexibility to remove it from one side, and then carefully maneuver it out. Take your time, and it should come out with just a little bit of effort.

6 With the duct and the lower cover removed, the fan should simply drop out of the housing, only being held in place at this point by the wiring harness shown here (green arrow). Push the fan back up inside the housing enough to slide the harness over the hook. The fan assembly should now drop completely out of the housing.

7 After you slip the harness out of the hook on the side of the fan, lower the fan down and squeeze the two tabs on the harness connector to release it from the fan (green arrow).

8 Shown here is a clearer shot of the wiring harness connector that plugs into the back of the fan (green arrow). It's a bit difficult to get a picture of this connector when it's installed on the fan. Here you can see the two tabs on the top of the plug. Just squeeze them toward each other and pull the plug off.

PROJECT 96
Child Seat Air Bag Deactivation

Time / Tab / Talent: 1 hour / $250 /

Tools: Torx socket set

Applicable Years: All

Tinware: Air bag deactivation bar or Porsche Latch System

More Info: http://www.101projects.com/Carrera/96.htm

Tip: If you're planning on installing the on-board computer, have the dealer activate that at the same time

Performance Gain: Ability to take your driver-in-training along

Comp Modification: Add on-board computer

One of the first projects I performed on my Carrera was the installation of the Porsche factory air bag deactivation bar, so that I could take my 3-year-old son along for rides. If you're not familiar with the process of preparing the car so that you can disable the air bag, it can be very confusing. In reality, it's very easy to do, as I explain here for both versions of the system.

The 1998–2005 (996) Carreras use a deactivation bar. The deactivation bar is nothing more than a metal bar that holds a buckle attached to the bottom of the passenger seat (PN: 996-803-083-02). The kit from Porsche comes complete with the bar/buckle assembly and two longer bolts that replace the existing bolts that fasten the passenger seat to the chassis. This new buckle contains an electrical switch that connects to a plug under the passenger seat. All of the Porsche factory child seats have a seat belt receptacle that plugs into this buckle. When this belt is plugged in, the electrical switch is activated and it tells the air bag computer to shut off the air bag in the car.

Installation is a snap. Simply remove the two Torx bolts that hold the seat to the chassis, slide in the bar, and then install the new bolts to reattach the bar and seat assembly. Refer to Photo 2 for the proper orientation of the buckle (it is possible to install it upside down). Plug in the connector to the empty connection under the seat. The last step is to have the "Child Seat Occupancy" turned on by using the factory Porsche System Tester 2 (PST2), which you can typically only find at the Porsche dealers. Some dealers will charge for performing this task; others will do it for free. It takes about five minutes total to set.

The problem with this air bag deactivation system is that it only works with Porsche factory child seats, as they come with the special buckle attached. For my own application, I did not use a Porsche factory seat but instead used a different seat and attached the buckle from a factory seat to the bottom of my seat. I got this buckle from an old factory seat that a friend of mine had that was too big for my 3-year-old child. In the same manner as the factory seat, I attached and plugged in the buckle when I installed the child seat into the car. I then confirm that the air bag was disabled by checking the light on the dash (see Photo 1). I have not been able to locate this buckle or receptacle separately, but the TRW part numbers are 33000311 35 06/99680328302 for the buckle and 56030A (part number on metal)/7670842 (part number on plastic).

Air bags are lifesaving devices; however, they can be deadly to small children. Regardless of how you install your child seat into the car, exercise extreme caution and always check that the air bag is disabled (via the blinking lamp on the dash—see Photo 1—996 only) prior to driving the car. For more information, see also Technical Service Bulletin (TSB) 15/98 6923 Porsche Child Restraint System – Installation (dated 3-7-2000).

For 2005 and later cars, Porsche used a similar but slightly more complicated system. Dubbed the Latch (Lower Anchorage and Tether for Children) System, the kit includes fastening loops and lower anchorage points for mounting between the seat surface and backrest, as well as a key switch for deactivation of the passenger side air bag (PN: 997-044-800-15). Starting with 2006, the 911 Carrera seats have a "weight sensing" system that turns off the air bag if there isn't an adult sitting in the seat. Although, these can be less than reliable when the weight of a car seat is added into the equation, I recommend installing the air bag deactivation key switch.

Installation of the switch involves removing the center console to install the passenger air bag off (PAO) lamp and the removal of the side dash panel and a few under dash

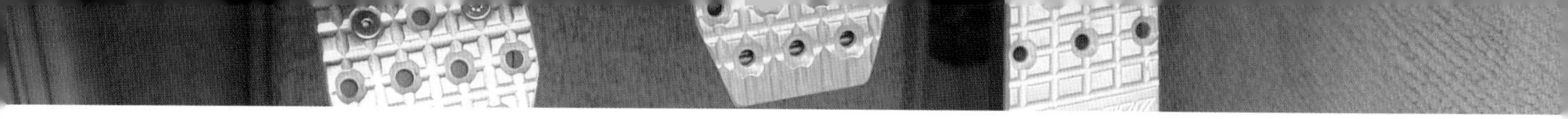

panels to plug in the switch (see Project 69 for removal of the center console for photos and tips). Once it's installed, you simply turn off the passenger side air bag with your key, check that you hear the auditory warning and that the PAO is illuminated, and you are good to go. For more information, see Technical Service Bulletin (TSB) 3/06 6929 Child Seat Preparation For Passenger Seat (dated 4-16-2007). While this is a little more work, I feel it is worth it for the peace of mind.

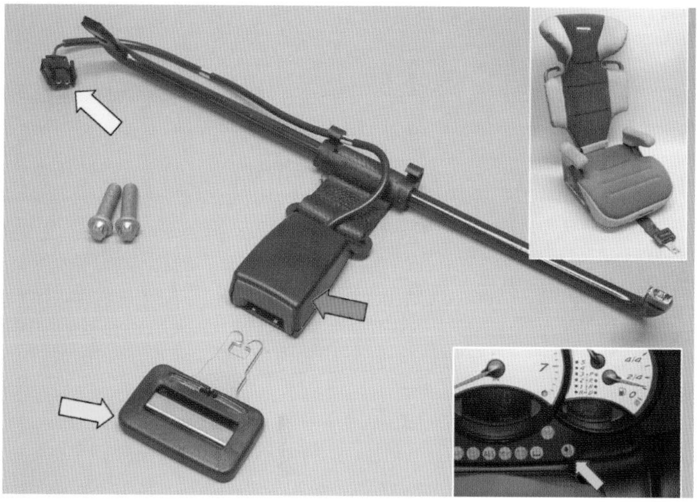

1 This photo shows the Porsche air bag deactivation bar. This part is simply a metal bar with a seat belt receptacle attached. Porsche branded child seats come with a buckle attached to the front of the seat (upper right inset). This buckle piece (yellow arrow) mates with the receptacle attached to the bar (red arrow) and activates an electrical switch that turns off the air bag. The electrical connector (blue arrow) needs to be mated with an open connector that is located beneath the passenger seat. When the buckle is plugged in, the air bag lamp on the dashboard will blink repeatedly for 10 seconds (or 60 seconds in cars manufactured after 03/31/1999) to inform you that the passenger side air bag is properly disabled. On the 2005 and later Carreras (997), the air bag is turned off or deactivated by inserting the key into the passenger side air bag switch located on the side of the dashboard trim. You will need to open the door to perform this. Once off, the system acknowledges you have deactivated the passenger side air bag with an acoustic signal and a continuously lit "Passenger Airbag Off" warning light on the center console by the handbrake. This system is not installed at the factory and, if you do not want to install it yourself, can be retrofitted by a Porsche dealer.

2 This photo shows the air bag deactivation bar installed in the passenger seat. Note the direction of the plastic clips on the buckle (green arrow). New, longer mounting screws for the seats come with the bar kit, as the bar is attached to the top of the seat mount (blue arrows). The electrical connection for the air bag is located under the seat (lower right, inset).

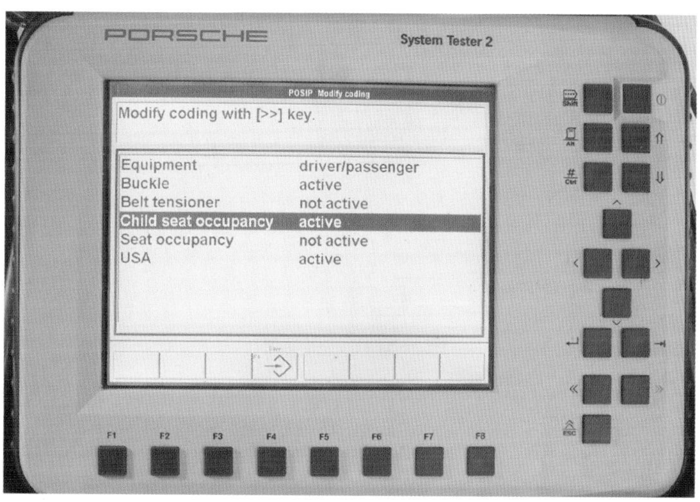

3 Shown here is the Porsche System Tester 2 (PST2). This computer needs to be plugged into your car to turn on the "Child Seat Occupancy" setting in the air bag computer of the 1998–2005 (996) Carreras. I'm not sure why this wasn't turned on by default, but most dealers will perform this five-minute task for free or for a nominal charge.

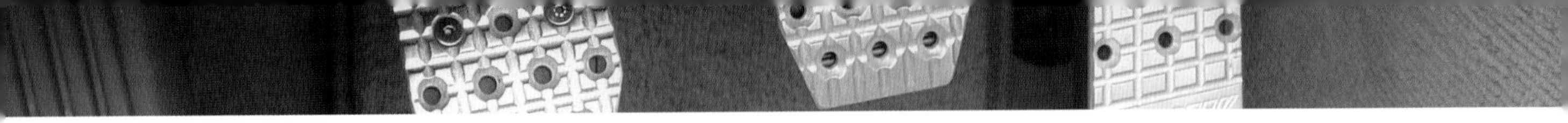

PROJECT 97
Air Conditioning Maintenance/Recharge

Time / Tab / Talent: 1 hour / $25–$750 /

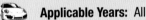

Tools: Air conditioning pressure gauge, specialized AC equipment

Applicable Years: All

Tinware: R134a recharge kit

More Info: http://www.101projects.com/Carrera/97.htm

Tip: Don't use non-134a replacement refrigerant

Performance Gain: Better cooling during the summer months

Comp Modification: Replace the main accessory belt

On any car, the AC system is a complicated beast. This project is not intended to be a repair manual for your AC system but to serve more as a guide on how the system works and the maintenance involved with its upkeep.

Almost all AC systems work on the theories of thermodynamics, whereby heat flows from a warmer surface to a colder one. Heat from inside the car is transferred to the cold metal fins of the evaporator. The refrigerant in the system picks up the heat from the evaporator and takes it to the compressor. The gas is then pressurized, which concentrates the heat by raising the temperature of the refrigerant gas. The gas is then sent to the condenser. The condenser cools the refrigerant and turns it back into a liquid from a gas. The liquid is then sent to the receiver-dryer, where any water vapor that may have formed in the system is removed. The receiver-dryer also acts as a storage container for unused fluid. From the receiver-dryer, the liquid flows into the expansion valve, which meters it into the evaporator located inside the car. Here the liquid absorbs heat and becomes a low-pressure gas. This evaporation, or boiling of the refrigerant, absorbs heat just like a boiling pot of water absorbs heat from the stove. As heat is absorbed, the evaporator is cooled. A fan blows air through the evaporator and into the cockpit of the car, providing the cooling effect.

The compressor pumps the refrigerant through the entire system. An electromagnetic clutch on the compressor turns the AC system on and off. In addition to cooling the car, the system also removes water vapor from the ambient air via the cooling process. It is not uncommon to find a small puddle of water underneath your car from the condensation of the AC system. A thermostat control on the evaporator keeps the condensation in the evaporator from freezing and damaging the unit.

So what can be done to maintain and protect the system from deterioration? First and foremost, the air conditioning system should be operated at least once a week if the outside temperature is above 50 degrees Fahrenheit. This will circulate the refrigerant in the system and helps keep all the seals in the system from drying out. Most failures are caused by refrigerant leaking out of the system and can be prevented by making sure that the system is run frequently.

The belt that runs off of the main crankshaft operates the AC compressor. If you think that you might be having problems with your compressor, check the condition of the belt first. Turn on the system, and check to make sure that the electromagnetic clutch is engaging. If not, then you may need to replace it. Check the power connection to make sure it is live before replacing it. The system also has a pressure switch located right next to the high-pressure port in the front cowl area, which will shut it off if the pressure inside the system is too high or too low. Check the pressures in the system and/or the operation of this switch if you're having AC problems.

REFILLING AC SYSTEMS

The biggest problem with AC systems is a loss of refrigerant. Luckily, the replacement and top-off of refrigerant is a relatively easy task. All 911 Carreras use R134 refrigerant, which can be purchased inexpensively at your local auto parts stores. The Carrera AC system capacity is 850 grams (30 ounces) of R134. In addition, the compressor needs a synthetic lubricant for proper operation. If you're filling a completely empty system, add 195 ml (6.6 ounces) of ND 8 refrigerant oil.

The kit I used to refill the car in this project is manufactured by Interdynamics (see Photo 1). Start the car outside of your garage, turn on the AC system and fan to full blast, and let the car run with the system on for about three

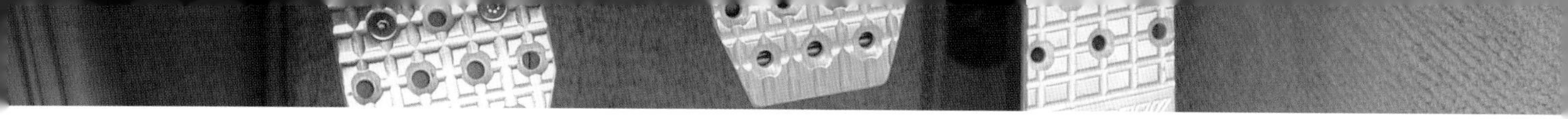

minutes. Following the instructions included with the kit, connect a new can of refrigerant to the hose/gauge assembly. Connect the gauge assembly to the low-side port on your AC system (see Photo 2). Be sure to wear eye protection and heavy leather gloves when handling the coolant and gauge assembly. If coolant leaks out at any time, it can freeze a small patch of skin on your hands quite easily and give you frostbite.

With the car running and the AC system turned on full blast, take a reading on the pressure gauge. If your system is properly charged, it should read between 25 and 45 psi. If the pressure is low, then turn the valve on the can to release more refrigerant into the system. Be sure that you shake the can for about 30 seconds and turn it upside down when you connect it to the gauge assembly. Also be aware that the pressure gauge reading will automatically elevate as you are adding more coolant—periodically close the valve on the can to check if the pressure is rising in the system. If the pressure doesn't increase after adding one complete can, then you most likely have a major leak in your system and you should seek the help of an AC system professional mechanic.

With the system properly filled and measured with your gauge, you should head to the passenger compartment and check the temperature of the air exiting the vents. On a system that is operating well, the temperature will be in the mid-30 degrees Fahrenheit. For systems that are older and weaker, the temperature readings will mostly like be higher. Also keep in mind that if your system is cooling air in the 30-degree-Fahrenheit range, the compressor on the car will tend to turn itself on and off, and the temperature will climb up and down slightly. This is not a defect of the system: the compressor turns itself off as the temperature in the evaporator nears the freezing temperature of water. This prevents the evaporator from becoming frozen and clogged with icy buildup.

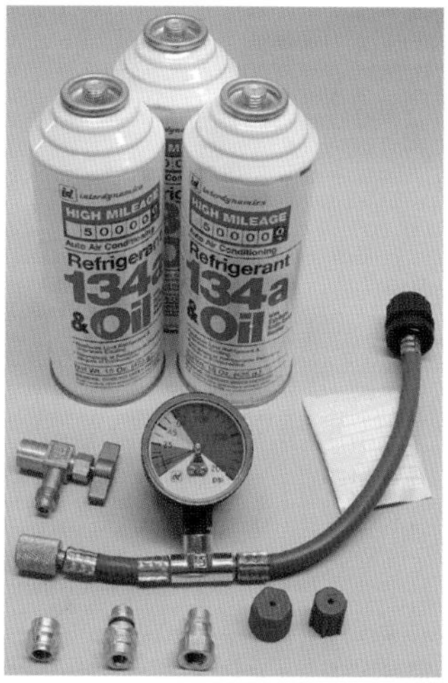

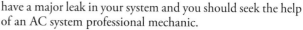

1 Shown here is a great starter air conditioning (AC) kit from Interdynamics. This kit contains three cans of R134a refrigerant and oil and is specifically designed to replenish older cars that may have a few small leaks in the O-rings of the AC system. Included with the kit are a can adapter valve, an in-line pressure gauge, and several adapters that are not required for use with the Carrera. The kit is available for about $35 at most general automotive stores and contains everything that you need to recharge your R134a AC system.

2 This photo shows the location and orientation of the AC ports on the 911 Carrera. The AC ports are normally covered with plastic covers that simply screw off (inset). The low side—to which you attach the gauge and refrigerant,—has the smaller port adapter and is attached to the larger pipe (yellow arrow). The high side—used primarily for checking the compressor during diagnostic testing—has the larger adapter (green arrow) and has a smaller diameter pipe.

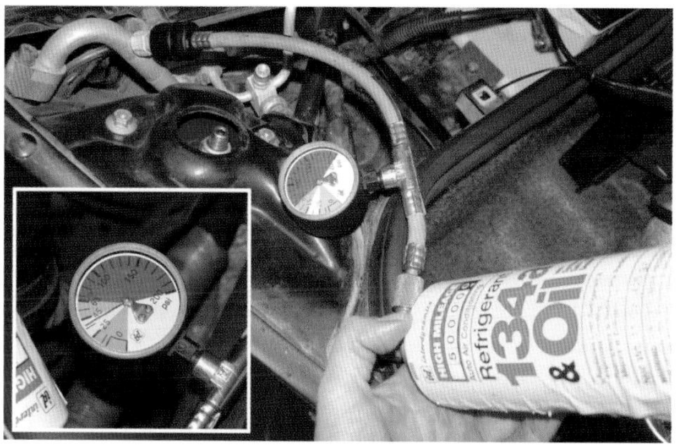

3 With the engine running and the system engaged, connect the gauge to the low-pressure port on the AC system. The high side has a larger adapter, so that you can't accidentally attach the gauge to the wrong port. With the gauge attached, you can now turn the valve to add more refrigerant to the system. In the photo inset, you can see that the pressure for this AC system is exactly where it should be—in the middle of the white range. Remember to use heavy-duty leather gloves and eye protection when working around AC components; it's possible that a fitting or a valve may break or leak refrigerant on your hands.

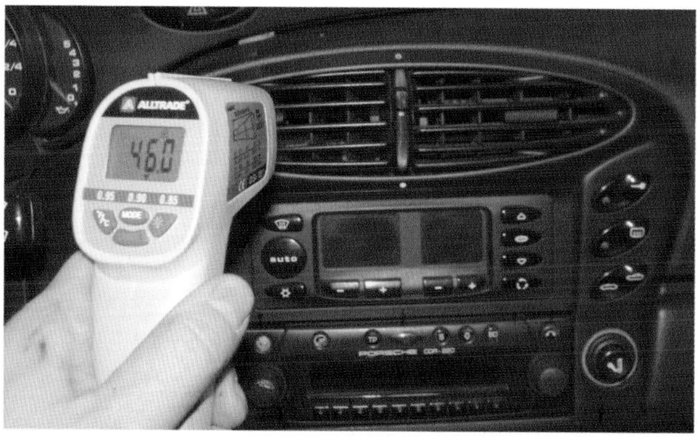

4 Your hand is a pretty poor indicator of relative temperature. In order to get an accurate reading, I recommend that you use a digital thermometer, like the one shown in this photo. Final temperature performance of your AC system will vary based upon a number of factors: age, quantity of refrigerant in the system, and the condition of the compressor and associated components. This car is a 1999 Porsche with 80,000 miles on the odometer. The vent reading is 46 degrees Fahrenheit (8 degrees Celsius) with the AC at full blast. Outside temperature when this reading was taken was probably around 70 degrees Fahrenheit. You should expect at least about a 20-degree drop from the outside ambient air.

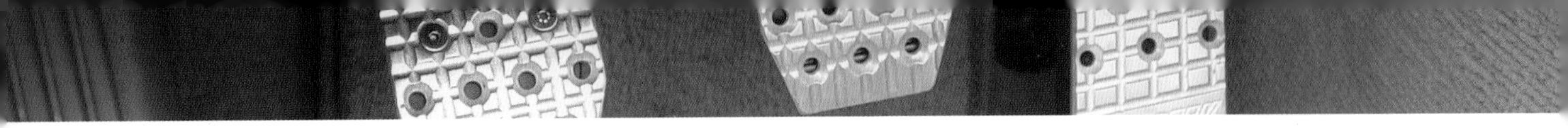

PROJECT 98
Track Preparation and Weight Removal

Time / Tab / Talent: Unlimited / Unlimited / Unlimited

Tip: Buy someone else's project.

Tools: All of them

Performance Gain: Faster lap times

Applicable Years: All

Comp Modification: Home equity line of credit

Tinware: Everything your money can buy

More Info: http://www.101projects.com/Carrera/98.htm

Any *101 Projects* book worth a grain of salt needs to have a section on preparing your car for the track. The 911 Carrera has always been a popular weapon of choice as a dedicated track car. Its relatively lightweight construction, combined with its rear-engine placement, creates an excellent starting point for building the ultimate track car. I could probably write an entire book on the subject of creating the ultimate Carrera track car, but for now I'll just give a brief overview of some of the changes I would make if I were to turn a stock Carrera into a dedicated track car:

- Install a permanent roll cage (Photo 1)
- Upgrade braking system (Project 53)
- Upgrade shocks to an adjustable system (Project 61)
- Install the GT3 adjustable control arms (Photo 9 of Project 59)
- Have a full racetrack alignment and corner balance performed on the car
- Install adjustable sway bars (Project 61)
- Replace the doors and hood panels with fiberglass units
- Use lightweight race wheels with slicks
- Install a fully certified fuel cell
- Install a fire suppression system
- Upgrade the transmission to include a limited slip (Project 40)
- Install a real-time data logger and/or electronic dash computer
- Install racing seats and a five or six-point harness
- Install an Accusump and/or the deep-sump kit
- Install an aftermarket MOMO wheel
- Remove as much weight as possible (see next section)

WEIGHT REDUCTION

A project on track preparation would not be complete without discussing the option of placing your car on a diet. The benefits from weight reductions to rotational components in the engine are twofold: they not only reduce the rotational mass that the engine needs to spin up, but they also reduce the total weight of the car. These rotational components exist all over the car—not just in the engine. All of the rotational drivetrain components (wheels, transmission gears, axles, brake discs, etc.) have a significant effect on your car's overall performance. Using lighter-weight wheels, for example, will have a similar effect to reducing the weight of your flywheel: the drivetrain will accelerate faster, and the total mass of the car will be reduced as well. Again, the gain is twofold. It is for this reason that most racers try to remove as much mass as possible from drivetrain components when lightening their chassis.

While reducing the mass of drivetrain components can produce the most efficient gains, you can go only so far. This limit exists because the drivetrain is responsible for delivering power to the wheels and accelerating the car. You can remove only so much weight; you don't want to weaken the drivetrain to the point that it is going to fail. The second-best thing to do is to remove weight from the chassis of the car. Theoretically, a 10 percent reduction in weight is equivalent to a 10 percent increase in equivalent horsepower. On a 200-horsepower, 3,000-pound car, it may be far more practical to remove 300 pounds than it would be to produce 20 more horsepower from your engine.

So what can you do to reduce weight? There are a couple of rules of thumb. The first place you should remove weight is from "unsprung" components. These are the parts of the car that are not supported by the suspension. Examples include trailing arms, A-arms, brake discs, wheels, and so on. The next-best place to remove weight is from the highest points on the car (sunroofs, windscreens, etc.). Removing weight here helps lower the car's center of gravity. Next, you want to target the mid/rear of the car because the Carrera is already very tail-heavy due to the rearward mounting bias of the engine and transmission.

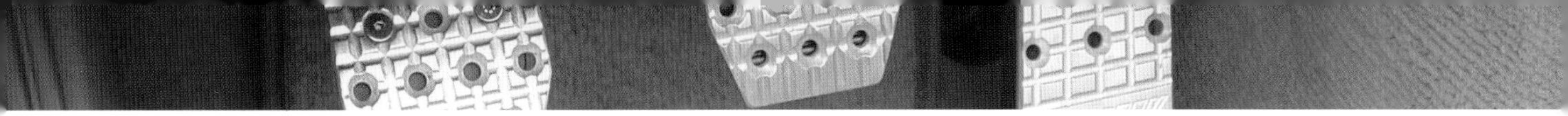

If your goal is pure performance, you can lighten your car significantly simply by removing or replacing the following on the car:

- Remove the entire heating and air conditioning system
- Remove window regulators/support braces in doors
- Replace glass with Lexan
- Replace decklids and doors with fiberglass
- Remove most interior components (carpet, door panels, interior trim)
- Remove undercoating on the chassis
- Replace the drivers/passenger seat with a lightweight one
- Move or replace the battery with a lighter one (Porsche has a brand new Lithium-ion battery that just came out for the GT3)
- Remove any unnecessary components from the front trunk (spare, jack, etc.)
- Remove the stock DOT bumpers and replace them with fiberglass
- Remove the stereo system, amplifier, and speakers
- Remove the convertible top and replace it with a fiberglass hardtop
- Install cross-drilled brake rotors
- Remove power mirrors

Most of this weight removal can also be done to a street car, but any weight removal must be balanced with the practicalities of daily driving. While many live by the motto, "If it doesn't make the car go or stop, it's just extra weight," there are exceptions. If you enjoy air conditioning and a good stereo, then you probably won't want to sacrifice these amenities for the improved performance. However, if your mission is to maximize performance, you might be surprised at how much of a difference weight removal can make.

1 Any dedicated track car requires a welded-in roll cage. Be sure to have someone install it who has previously fabricated one for a 996 or 997 Carrera. Shown here is a roll cage installed in a Boxster so you can see the cross bracing, door protection, and shoulder bar for the five- or six-point system (you don't see a lot of Carrera Cabriolets as purely dedicated track cars). If you are planning on tracking your car, make sure you check with the sanctioning body where you are going to be competing, as different organizations have different rules.

2 Shown here is a Kinesis K28 wheel, one of the best choices available in high-performance wheels. This wheel has a reputation for being one of the lightest and strongest you can buy for your track car. The wheel centers are forged from 6061-T6 aluminum and are mated to rim sections that are spun by computer-controlled machines assuring trueness and consistency throughout the wheel. These wheels not only look cool, but their performance and reliability has been proven time and again at various races like the 24 Hours of Daytona.

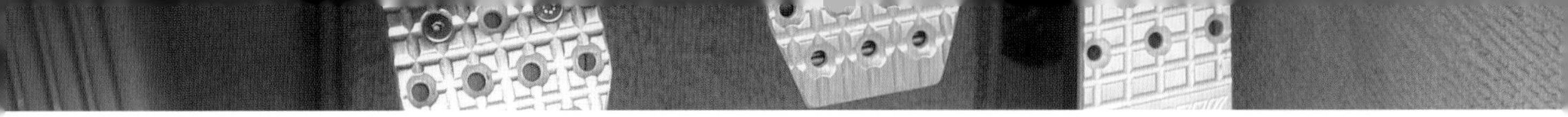

3 Here's a shot of two Porsche interiors that have been gutted and prepped for the track. The car on the left has had a replacement dash computer installed in front of the normal gauge display. This programmable dashboard allows you to monitor all of the systems of the car, while also logging data such as lap times and engine performance. It also has a quick release steering wheel. This upgrade is very common in track cars, as it helps getting in and out of a vehicle that has a full roll cage. On the car on the right, you can see that a custom box has been fabricated to raise the gearshift lever off of the floor. This allows for less movement from the driver's hand to the lever, resulting in quicker shifts and more time with your hands on the wheel. In addition, both these cars have had most of the interior gutted and removed, as well as lightweight seats, full cages, and five-point racing harnesses.

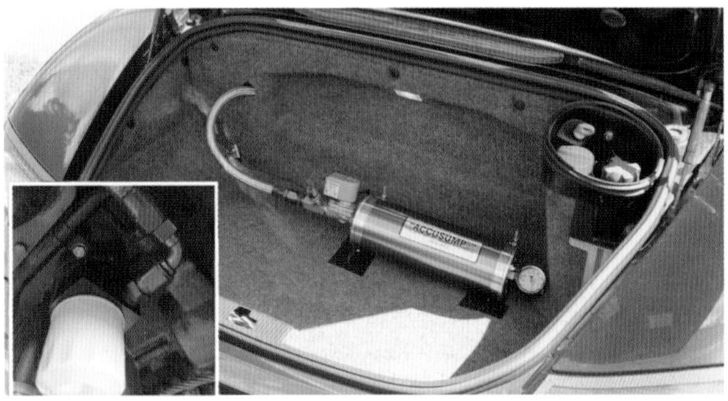

4 Here's a photo of an Accusump installed in LN Engineering's Boxster test car (it is easier to see the system mounted in a Boxster than a Carrera). The Accusump is a cylinder-shaped aluminum storage container that acts as a reservoir of pressurized oil to be released when there is a drop in the oil pressure. The Accusump is connected to the pressure side of a Carreras oiling system (typically through an adapter on the oil filter; inset photo) and is charged by the engines own oil pump. Its simple, efficient design revolves around a hydraulic piston separating an air precharge side and an oil reservoir side. The oil side of the Accusump has an outlet controlled by a valve that goes into the engine's oiling system. On the air side, it's equipped with a pressure gauge and a schrader air valve, which allows you to add a precharge of air pressure to the Accusump. Installing one of these on a dedicated track 911 helps compensate for the fact that the 911 engine does not have a dry-sump oiling system.

5 Nothing says fun quite like driving your Carrera on the track. The car shown here is being driven at California Speedway, but there are usually tracks within easy driving distance of most major cities. While the Carrera is a wonderful car to drive on the street, there is nothing like testing the limits of you and your car in a safe environment like a race track. Be careful though—it can be a very slippery and expensive slope.

6 Big rear wings are a staple of track cars, and no matter how many events you go to, you'll always be able to find a wing that you haven't seen before. I took a whole bunch of fluid and aerodynamics classes when I was at MIT, but even armed with that knowledge, I think it would be difficult to find the optimum wing design and settings without the use of a wind tunnel. It's tough to tell whether the use of a rear wing adds enough benefit to counter the added weight and wind resistance. That being said, one of the added benefits of owning a Carrera as a track car is the involvement of Porsche in racing. You will be able to easily find a wide variety of Porsche and aftermarket wings that will work with your Carrera.

PROJECT 99
Personal Touches

Time / Tab / Talent: Infinite / $1-$10,000 /

Tools: Unlimited

Applicable Years: All

Tinware: Just about everything in the catalog

More Info: http://www.101projects.com/Carrera/99.htm

Tip: Keep an eye out at local swap meets and shows for cool additions that can add to your Carrera

Performance Gain: The sky is the limit

Comp Modification: Wash your car

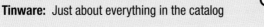

As principle photographer and owner of the Internet-based company PelicanParts.com that sells parts for Porsches, I've had the opportunity to photograph a lot of different modifications that people have done to their 911 Carreras over the years. While not all of them improve the looks of the car in my own opinion, it can certainly be said that Porsche 911 Carrera owners like to modify their cars more than most other car owners do. Whether it's the addition of new wheels or a custom spoiler, if you can think of it, it's likely that some passionate Carrera owner has spent hundreds of hours and thousands of dollars to do it. This project is designed to give you some ideas for your 911. Many of these items are currently available in the online catalog at PelicanParts.com.

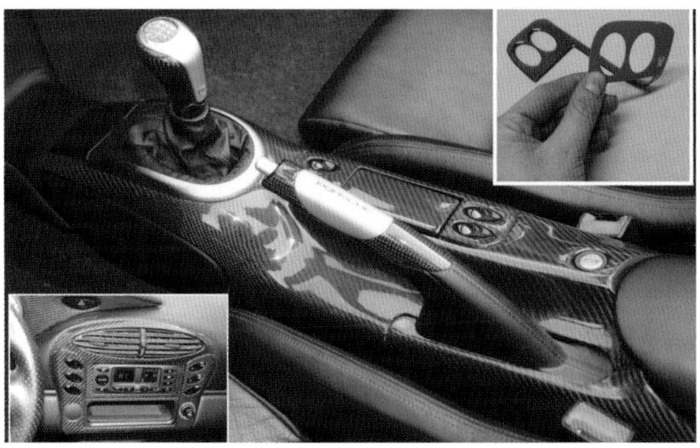

1 Dressing up your interior makes sense, as it's the one thing that you look at the most. Porsche and some aftermarket companies offer almost all of the interior trim pieces in the car in genuine carbon fiber (shown in this photo). However, the real deal can cost you up to $6,000 to outfit the entire interior of your Porsche with the genuine stuff. The poor man's option is carbon fiber–look overlays that give the appearance of real carbon fiber for 1/100th of the cost. While not my particular cup of tea, some people may find this approach appealing.

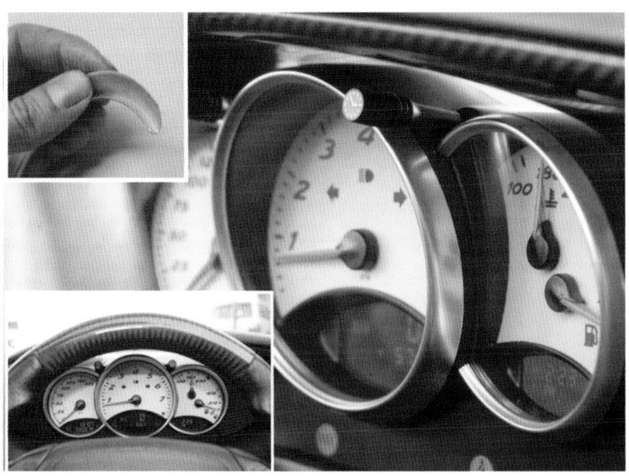

2 Chrome trim rings are a popular interior dress-up item for the Carrera gauges. They are typically manufactured out of extruded aluminum and contain extra-sticky adhesive that you simply peel and stick to the outer edges of the gauges. The gauges are the one thing that you look at the most inside the car, so they should at least be appealing to your eye. **Note:** The three-gauge Boxster cluster is shown here.

3 This photo shows the interior of my 996 Carrera, which was ordered new from the factory in this configuration. Some uncommon yet interesting things to point out are the red seat belts ($580 option), the inlaid Porsche crest in the headrest, and the painted silver seat backs and center console (it cost $700 for each panel for this option). Although I really like the look of the silver-painted center console, in reality it doesn't hold up very well to wear and tear and tends to look a bit worn as it scratches very easily.

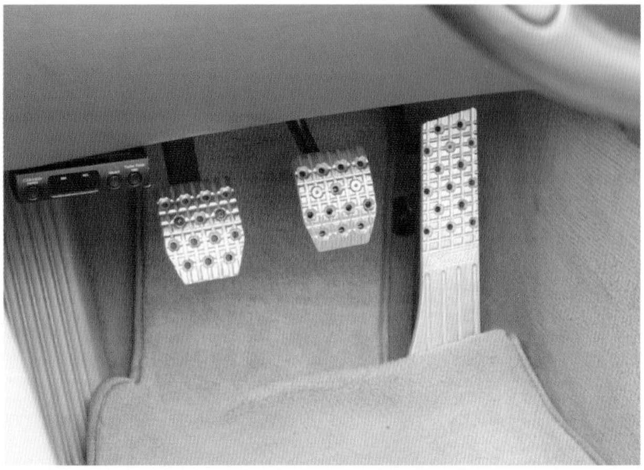

4 Pedal upgrades are another common accessory for Carrera owners. Beware though: You want to make sure that you get a set that isn't slippery. These pedals are great looking, but they might be a little too slippery for my tastes—particularly if I'm wearing leather-soled shoes. I recommend sets that have integrated anti-slip rubber inserts in them.

5 I've included this press-release photo of the 2011 Carrera Speedster because it incorporates so many neat design elements that can be applied to earlier cars as well. For starters, the 19-inch Fuchs-style wheels with yellow painted calipers look great on this car. Also noteworthy are the flared wheelwells and raked windscreen, similar to the Speedster predecessor from 1989. Finally, the Speedster-style humps, which were an original option last seen on Boxster Spyder, have made a return with the Speedster.

6 Spoilers can be big on Carreras (see Project 80). This one perched on the back of this GT3 looks purposefully built. I've never been a huge fan of the Carrera motorized "popup" spoiler from day one—I've always thought it was a bit inelegant. Adding the right spoiler to the rear of the Carrera gives it a more muscular look in my opinion.

7 One of the smallest detail touches you can place on your car are Porsche crest valve stem caps for your wheels. These are really neat, factory OEM valve caps, and typically run about $20 at PelicanParts.com (PN: PNA-705-001-99 silver crest, PN: PNA-705-002-00 colored crest).

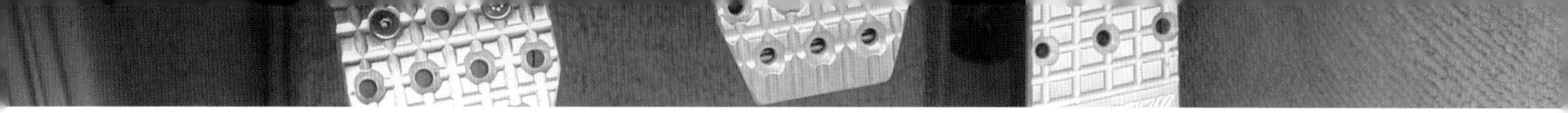

8 Some creativity and a few dollars spent at a good vinyl sign shop can really add some personalization to your car. This particular design is clean, simple, and really makes the car stand out from the others.

9 One nice thing about Porsches is that you can typically swap parts from one model to another quite easily. This is true in particular for the front bumper of the car. There are a ton of options out there for replacing your front bumper, from the GT2 or GT3 look to a whole host of custom-designed solutions from aftermarket vendors. Shown here is a GT3-style front bumper and valance.

10 Here are two more options for spoilers: the one on the left is the rear end of a rare GT2. The one on the right is a speed-yellow 996 GT3. The clean lines of these rear wings really make the car stand out from the rest in my opinion.

11 If you're tired of the way your Carrera is looking, then you might want to update it with a body kit. Here's an interesting modification to what appears to have started out as a typical 996 Turbo. 911 Design built this car into a horsepower monster that ended up with 1083 horsepower. There are quite a lot of neat touches here—so many that the car was featured on the cover of *Excellence* magazine in May 2013.

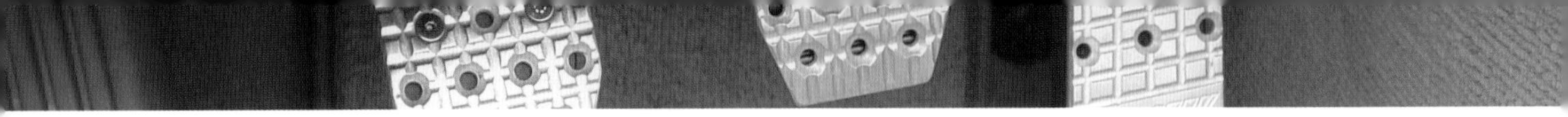

PROJECT 100
Tire and Wheel Sizing

Time / Tab / Talent: 4 hours / $300–$1,000 /

Tools: Soft socket

Applicable Years: All

Tinware: New tires, valve stems

More Info: http://www.101projects.com/Carrera/100.htm

Tip: Find a tire shop that will allow you to try fitting certain sizes and types of tires on your car, or find a friend who has a tire/wheel combination you like and borrow it

Performance Gain: Good tires can increase your handling and braking significantly

Comp Modification: Upgrade to larger or lighter wheels

For this project, I polled a number of people on a few Internet chat boards in an attempt to figure out what the best and most popular combinations of tire and wheel sizes were for the 911 Carrera. I confirmed what is inherently true about almost all hardcore Porsche owners—they love to modify and tweak their cars. Out of all the responses, no two were exactly alike. I've compiled and summarized the feedback here so that you can make an educated decision when equipping your ride.

Let's talk for a few moments on tires in general. Although you can write volumes on tire sizing and design, we'll try to cover the basics here. Tires are sized using a system that takes into effect the tire's aspect ratio. This aspect ratio is a function of the tire's height with respect to its width. An example of a common European tire size is 195/65R15. The number 195 refers to the width of the tire in millimeters. The second number, 65, refers to the height of the tire as a percentage of the width. Therefore 65 percent of 195 would give a tire height of about 127mm. The letter following the width and length is the tire's maximum speed safety ratings. The last number in the tire size is the wheel diameter in inches. In this case, "15" refers to a 15-inch-diameter wheel.

Needless to say, a good Z-rated tire should be more than adequate for standard drivers.

Tread is another important consideration in selecting a tire. You should select your tire based upon what type of driving you are planning on doing. With the 911, sometimes it's a bit more complicated because some people don't drive their cars in all types of weather. With a family sedan located in a snowy environment, an all-weather tire is a natural choice. However, many Porsche owners do not drive their cars in the snow or the rain.

In an ideal setting, such as on the racetrack, flat-surfaced tires called racing slicks are best because a maximum amount of tire rubber is laid down on the road surface. However, slicks have almost no traction in wet weather. The water has a tendency to get underneath the tire and help hydroplane the car by elevating the wheel onto a wedge of water as it is moving forward.

The array of choices for tire tread is way beyond the scope of this project; however, one rule of thumb is to make sure that you purchase a tire that is appropriate for your climate. Using a snow tire or all-weather tire on a 911 Carrera that is rarely driven in the snow will significantly reduce the tires contact patch area and reduce cornering performance on dry roads. However, not equipping your car for bad weather can result in disastrous effects if you are ill-equipped during an unforeseen storm. If you drive your car only during the dry summer months, then look for a conventional performance tire with a maximum contact patch area.

Another important consideration is the tread wear and traction. The tread wear refers to the average number of miles that can be put on the tires before they will need to be replaced. A tread wear indicator of 100 means that the tires should last about 30,000 miles. An indicator mark of 80 means that the tires will last 20 percent less, or 24,000 miles. Wear will be different for each car and each driver's personal driving habits, but the various ratings are good for comparisons among different brands and different types of tires. Traction is related to the type of materials used in the tire. The more hard rubber is used in the tire, the longer the tires will last. However, the hard rubber provides much less traction. A rating of A for traction is best. These tires will grip the road well, but will generally wear out faster than the B or C traction rated tires.

Maximum Speed Safety Ratings for Tires

R = 106 mph, 170km/h	V = 149 mph, 240km/h
S = 112 mph, 180km/h	W = 168 mph, 270km/h
T = 118 mph, 190km/h	Y = 186 mph, 300km/h
U = 124 mph, 200km/h	Z = 149 mph, 240km/h and over
H = 130 mph, 210km/h	

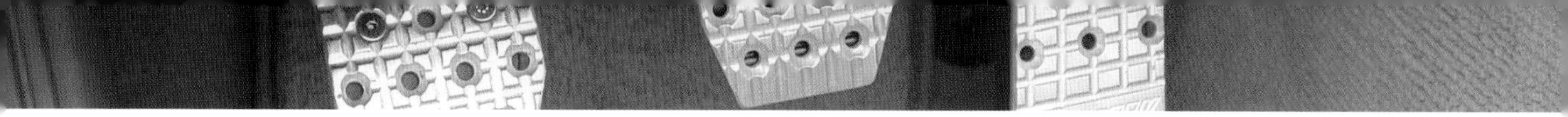

It is important to consider another factor in addition to tread wear when selecting a tire. Most tires have a shelf life based on the rubber's natural process of breaking down and becoming brittle. It doesn't pay to purchase a 30,000-mile tire if you are only going to be putting 3,000 miles a year on your car. After 10 years, the rubber may be cracked and deteriorated beyond safe use, even if there is plenty of tread left on the wheel. This is also an important consideration if you are purchasing a car that has been in storage or sparsely driven for many years. Although the tires may have plenty of tread on them, they may actually be dried out and ready to fail. If the tires develop cracks in the sidewalls from aging, they can blow out when heated up from driving. A blowout is a very bad situation and can cause you to lose control of your car very quickly.

So, what tires and wheels can you fit on your 911? It all depends upon the wheel design and offset and which tires you prefer to run on your car. With so many different combinations out there, it's impossible to fully document them in a mere few pages. I made a wheel collage that you can use for ideas on which wheels to mount on your car. This array was assembled from photos of Boxsters and 996/997 Carreras I took at various meets and club events over a period of three years.

Expanding the pool of options, you can also use spacers to accommodate different wheels that weren't originally designed for your car. I recommend the use of hub-centric spacers, which are located on the hub by a machined center hole as opposed to the lug-centric spacers that are located by the position of the lug nuts alone (see Photo 6 of Project 52).

With some older cars, the tire sizes that you can fit on the car may depend upon the condition of the car. Sometimes the chassis are perfectly balanced from left to right, and sometimes they are slightly off from being in an accident or simply from body sag. It's best to find a tire shop that will allow you to try out several tires on your car in order to find the best fit. Go in the afternoon on a slow day and talk with your tire salesman to see if he will let you size the tires on your car. If he won't, then go to a different shop; there are plenty of them out there willing to cater to you, especially if you are going to shell out some money for high-performance tires.

Different tires will look and perform differently with various wheels, so the best option is to consult with a good tire shop for their recommendations. You can fit 20-inch wheels to a 911 Carrera, but at that point, the tire thickness is so small that the ride and handling suffers quite a bit. I don't recommend installing anything greater than 19-inch wheels. I currently run Genuine Porsche 18-inch Sport Design wheels manufactured for Porsche by BBS on the project 911 Carrera for this book.

With the wider wheels, the options for the installation of tires grow exponentially. The type of offset used on the wheel and the tire size will affect whether it will fit or not. The offset of a wheel is the distance of the center of the wheel from the edge of the mounting flange on the hub. Different wheels with varying offsets will affect tire sizing considerably, so make sure that you know which types of wheels and offsets you have before you attempt to mount tires to them. It's also important to keep in mind that Porsche made very similar-looking wheels for the Boxster and the 996 Carrera, with the only major difference being the offset of the wheel. If you're buying used wheels, be sure that you purchase ones with the correct offset for the Carrera and not the Boxster.

So after reading this project, are you still confused? You should be—and rightly so. The Carreras came from Porsche with everything from a 7J × 17 on the front to the huge 12J × 19 on the mighty GT3. It would appear that there is a never-ending amount of options for tire sizing. The best way to figure out what type of tires to place on your car is to inquire around. Check on the Internet at the various technical bulletin boards, like the one at PelicanParts.com. I'm also fond of the TireRack.com website—they have useful tools there for determining the right wheel/tire combinations that will fit on your car. Porsche also runs tests on aftermarket tires and puts out a recommendation for the Carreras. They offer this free from the dealerships, and when I asked for one, I received over 50 pages of Porsche approved rims and tires. Regardless, you will find that everyone will have an opinion to share and a wheel/tire option that they have tried on their car.

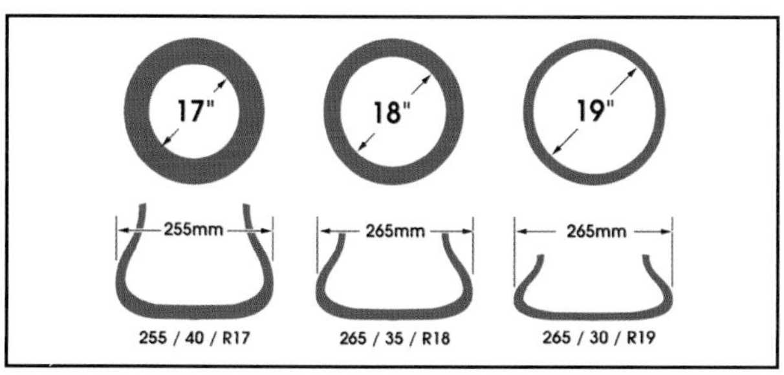

1 This photo shows how the aspect ratio of the tire changes with the change in wheel size. In general, you do not want the outer circumference of the wheel to change because this will affect handling and also change your speedometer readings. So, when you go with a larger wheel, you must go with a lower-profile tire. The lower-profile tire results in less of an air pocket under the car, and this typically reduces the ride comfort. This photo shows some examples of three rear-wheel options for the 911 Carrera. It is generally my recommendation to run 18-inch wheels for the best combination of looks, performance, and ride.

2 The upgraded, polished lug nuts really look great on the 911 Carrera. If you use them, be sure to use what is known as a "soft socket" (also available from PelicanParts.com). This special socket has a softer inner liner that will allow you to install lugs without damaging them. If your center caps are looking aged, then you can try removing them and sanding them with some fine-grit sandpaper. The outer plastic covering on the crests gets old and cloudy after many years, and a few minutes of sanding can improve the overall appearance tremendously.

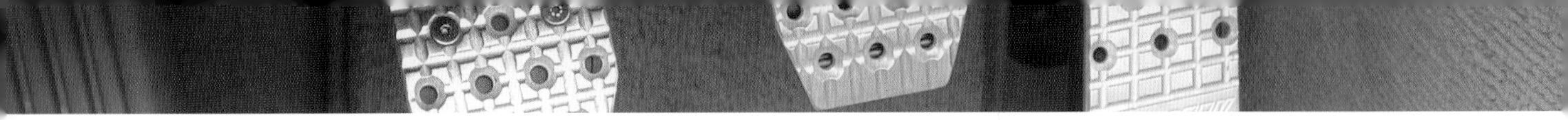

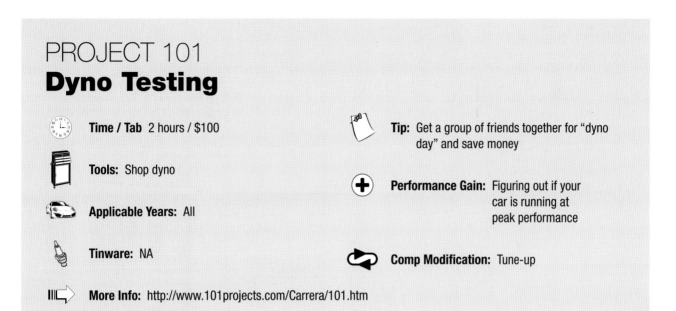

PROJECT 101
Dyno Testing

Time / Tab 2 hours / $100

Tools: Shop dyno

Applicable Years: All

Tinware: NA

More Info: http://www.101projects.com/Carrera/101.htm

Tip: Get a group of friends together for "dyno day" and save money

Performance Gain: Figuring out if your car is running at peak performance

Comp Modification: Tune-up

What project book would be complete without a section on dynamometer testing? One of the neatest trips you can make is to your local dyno shop. For about $100 or so, you can make a few runs on the dyno and actually measure the horsepower that is generated by your engine. The whole process is somewhat complicated, with varying degrees of detail and accuracy, but for the sake of this section, we'll just cover the basics.

What is a dyno? Short for dynamometer, the dyno measures the horsepower output by your engine. There are two basic types of dynos: one that you bolt the engine up to and run and one that measures horsepower at the rear wheels of your car, which is also called RWHP (rear wheel horsepower). Most modern dyno testing is performed on a rolling dyno that measures the power output at the wheels. You drive your car onto big rollers and accelerate at full throttle until you reach your rev limit. Then, you let the clutch out and let the rollers spin down freely. Large fans and environmental controls aim to keep the test environment at a steady state so that you can compare dyno runs. The dyno works by placing a load on the car, similar to how you would experience air friction as you were driving down the road at high speeds. By measuring this load, combined with the total rpm of the vehicle, a graph of the power output by the car can be derived.

Torque/horsepower. The dyno actually measures the torque output by your rear wheels. Torque is a measurement of rotational force and is related to the overall power output by your engine. The horsepower output by your engine is equivalent to the following formula, which is derived from an early English standard:

Horsepower = Torque × rpm / 5252

This translates into a power relation that horsepower is defined as 33,000 ft-lb (force) per minute. This is also referred to as the horsepower definition as defined by the Society of Automotive Engineers (SAE horsepower).

You may have also seen other definitions for horsepower and wondered what they meant. European documentation often gives horsepower numbers in kilowatts. For reference, one horsepower equals 0.746 kilowatts. Porsche's ratings are often listed in the European standard of DIN HP or kilowatts (kW). One DIN HP is rated as the power required to raise 450,000 kilograms one centimeter in one minute (or about .73 kW). The values of SAE and DIN HP are very similar, with 1 SAE HP being equal to .98629 DIN HP. For all practical purposes, you can think of them as relatively the same.

You may have also heard the term brake horsepower (BHP). The BHP is measured at the flywheel of the engine with no load from the chassis, without any electrical or mechanical accessories attached, under ideal fuel and timing conditions. In modern terms, the BHP figure would be mostly associated with what is now called gross horsepower.

Air/fuel measurement. In addition to measuring output torque and rpm, some dynos can also monitor your air/fuel mixture. This will allow you to adjust the mixture tables on a custom engine map to correctly match the power output (see Project 24). In other words, if you find that your engine is running lean at 4,500 rpm, you can adjust the fuel injection mixture to richen it up and produce more ideal combustion. This translates to more horsepower output from the engine.

Dyno results. The dyno will generate a graph of horsepower versus rpm for the engine being tested. With this graph, you will be able to determine the engine's peak horsepower and peak torque. The graph will also show you the peak horsepower output from the engine. On a six-cylinder 911 Carrera engine, this will typically be at the higher end of the rpm range, near 6,000 rpm. The engine will peak in horsepower and then fall off dramatically as the rev-limiter kicks in and the engine cuts off the ignition system.

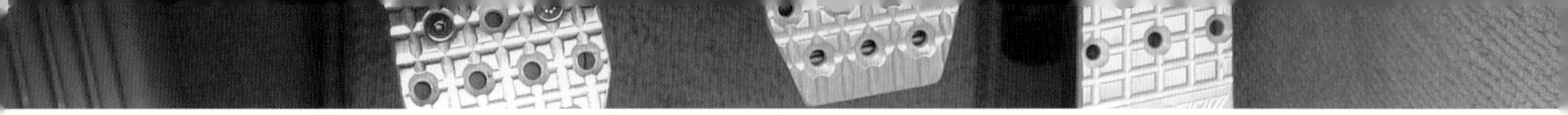

Comparing results. An unfortunate downside to dyno tests is that they often cannot be accurately compared to one another. Environmental conditions play a large part in these variances, as well as the fact that the large dynos cannot be easily calibrated. As a result, tests from the same dyno with the same car on different days may produce different results. Even the manufacturers of some dynamometers admit that their dyno at one location may test 5–10 percent differently than the same model at another location. When you consider that the figure may become bigger when you include dynos from different manufacturers, the ability to accurately compare results becomes significantly less useful.

An important issue to mention with respect to dyno figures is that the test is influenced heavily by environmental conditions. This includes temperature, humidity, and altitude, to name a few. Since conditions may change from day to day, dyno runs that span multiple days may produce different results.

Engine optimization. As previously mentioned, dyno testing can be very subjective. Other than bragging rights, pure dyno numbers are not very useful. The true benefit of the dyno test comes when you are able to use it to optimize your engine. Particularly with software ECU flashes (Project 24), you really need extensive dyno testing in order to determine what your optimum operating parameters should be on the fuel ratio and ignition timing maps. The factory used the same type of procedure to optimize and program the Bosch Motronic factory maps used in the stock engine management system.

In order to gain the most horsepower out of your engine, you need to perform several dyno runs while varying many different engine parameters (timing, mixture, advance curve, etc.). Only after carefully analyzing the data can you determine what the best values are for your engine management system map. Measuring the power output of the engine will allow you to optimize your engine and get the peace of mind knowing that you are extracting the maximum horsepower that you possibly can.

Driveline losses. Since the dyno testing is performed using rollers on your car, there are going to be forces that are going to slow down and reduce the power in between the flywheel and the rear wheels. These driveline losses include friction from the transmission, losses from brake discs dragging slightly, and friction in the wheel bearings. On the Carrera, typical driveline losses are often estimated at about 15 percent, although modifications to the chassis can raise or lower that value. Through a complicated process of calculations that are computed by the dynamometer, you can calculate your driveline losses by counting the time it takes the dyno rollers to stop when you let out the clutch. Using these calculations, you can then estimate what your horsepower output is at the flywheel.

Transmission gearing. One of the benefits of dyno testing is the ability to design your transmission ratios to meet the exact power characteristics of your engine. Depending upon where you want optimum performance, you can install taller or shorter gears into any of the five or six speeds on your transmission. The results of the dyno test will give you specific horsepower numbers for each rpm range and allow you to tailor your transmission gearing to suit your desires.

Software dynos. This is what I call the poor man's dyno. It is software that plugs into your Carrera's on-board diagnostics (OBD) II port and estimates power and torque based upon a variety of factors. The AutoEnginuity software that you can use to monitor OBD-II functions also has a very good dyno emulator built in. With preprogrammed profiles for the Carrera, it has proven itself to be extremely accurate in predicting engine performance (see Project 20).

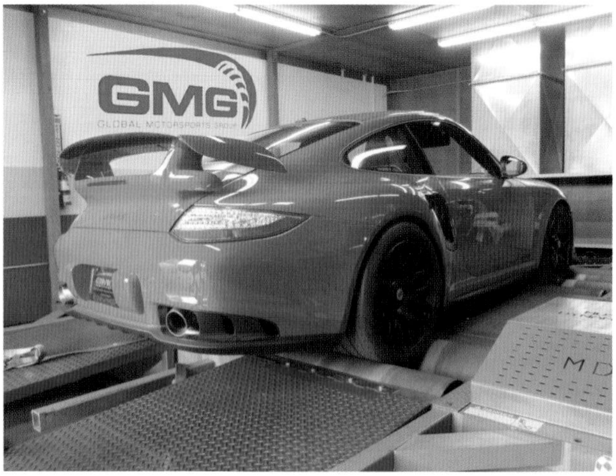

1 This photo shows a Porsche GT2RS on the dyno that has been modified by Global Motorsports Group. The GMG upgrades on the car include suspension, wheels, intercoolers, a full exhaust system and software upgrades. Even though the GT2RS is two-wheel drive, top of the line Dyno shops like Global Motorsports Group also have four-wheel drive dynamometers (as shown here), which can really come in handy if you are running a four-wheel drive car like the 996 Turbo.

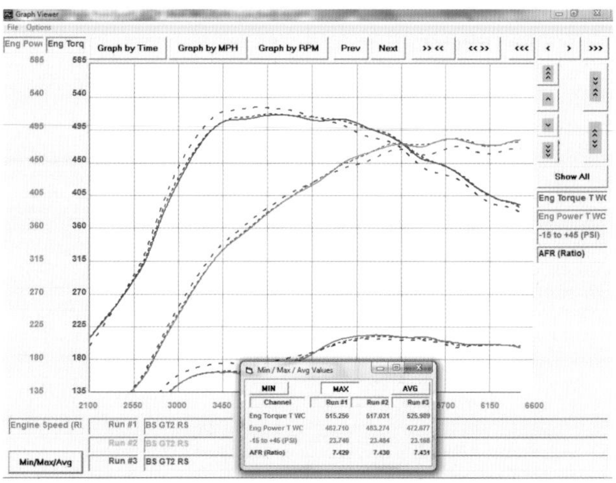

2 Shown here is a dyno graph for three separate runs of the GT2RS from Photo 1. The graph shows rear wheel peak horsepower of 483 and a peak torque of 525. Conditions are tightly controlled using fans and air temp/humidity measurement devices to ensure that the environment remains constant between dyno runs. Even with the tightest environmental controls there will be slight deviations in the results as shown by the graphs.

Index